Online Terrorist Propaganda, Recruitment, and Radicalization

Online Terrorist Propaganda, Recruitment, and Radicalization

Edited by
John R. Vacca

CRC Press
Taylor & Francis Group
Boca Raton London New York

CRC Press is an imprint of the
Taylor & Francis Group, an **informa** business

CRC Press
Taylor & Francis Group
6000 Broken Sound Parkway NW, Suite 300
Boca Raton, FL 33487-2742

First issued in paperback 2021

ISBN 13: 978-0-367-77823-1 (pbk)
ISBN 13: 978-1-138-04826-3 (hbk)

Library of Congress Cataloging-in-Publication Data

Names: Vacca, John R., editor.
Title: Online terrorist propaganda, recruitment and radicalization / edited by John R. Vacca.
Description: Boca Raton, FL : CRC Press, Taylor & Francis Group, [2020] | Includes bibliographical references and index. | Summary: "Online Terrorist Propaganda, Recruitment, and Radicalization is most complete treatment of the rapidly growing phenomenon of how terrorists' online presence is utilized for terrorism funding, communication, and recruitment purposes. The book offers an in-depth coverage of the history of how terrorist groups developed an online presence and capability, emergence of various groups; the advancement of terrorist groups' online presences; their utilization of video, chat room, and social media; and the capability for propaganda, training, and recruitment"-- Provided by publisher.
Identifiers: LCCN 2019011110 | ISBN 9781138048263 (hardback) | ISBN 9781315170251 (ebook)
Subjects: LCSH: Internet and terrorism. | Terrorists--Recruiting. | Terrorists--Recruiting--Technological innovations. | Terrorism--Computer network resources. | Radicalization--Computer network resources. | Social media--Political aspects. | Internet--Political aspects.
Classification: LCC HV6431 .O559 2020 | DDC 363.325--dc23
LC record available at https://lccn.loc.gov/2019011110

Visit the Taylor & Francis Web site at
http://www.taylorandfrancis.com

and the CRC Press Web site at
http://www.crcpress.com

This book is dedicated to my wife, Bee.

Contents

SECTION I Introduction

SECTION II A Transnational Recruitment Problem of Violent Online Extremist Terrorists

SECTION VI   ISIS and the Dark Web

SECTION VII   International Cooperation
with Online Terrorism

SECTION VIII   Private Sector Cooperation and Responsibility for Countering the Use of the Internet for Terrorist Purposes

SECTION IX   Appendices

Foreword

The Islamic State of Iraq and the Levant or ISIL, sometimes referred to as Islamic State of Iraq and Syria or ISIS, mounted an online recruitment and radicalization campaign that had previously not been accomplished or even imagined by much of the world. ISIL constructed a narrative that encompassed all aspects of life. The campaign was professionally managed and staffed by a variety of very skilled propagandists that created the ISIL master narrative, as well as a range of sub-narratives tailored to appeal to men and women of different age groups who lived in dozens of countries around the world. This campaign was launched through social media, online magazines, and websites.

Now the ISIL stronghold has been all but destroyed, and the fighting force has been shattered and dispersed. Many people feel that ISIL has been defeated, but others feel it will rise again in a different form in another place. What is not gone is the proven ability for an extremist organization to launch an online campaign to recruit, indoctrinate, and radicalize malleable individuals into violent extremism. The world is now aware that it can be done. ISIL may be considered defeated, but others like it will take its place.

In the quest for global security, future internet and social media platforms like those that ISIL used must be monitored and analyzed. When appropriate their online activities must also be countered and neutralized. This will require a global coalition with technical, language and cultural skills, and an understanding of how the internet can be used to recruit and radicalize. This book provides the knowledge to help do that. It is an essential tool for intelligence gathering, counter intelligence, national and global security professionals, and students of the continuing fight against violent extremism and terrorism activities on the internet.

Michael Erbschloe, information security consultant, teaches information security courses at Webster University in St. Louis, Missouri, and is the author of *Extremist Propaganda in Social Media: A Threat to Homeland Security and Social Media Warfare: Equal Weapons for All.*

Preface

SCOPE OF COVERAGE

This comprehensive handbook serves as a professional reference as well as a practitioner's guide to today's most complete and concise view of the rapidly growing phenomenon of how an online presence is utilized for terrorist purposes. It offers in-depth coverage of the history of how the online presences of terrorist groups occurs; emergence of various groups; the development of online presences; training; videos; chat rooms; other propaganda/recruitment machines; and Islamic State of Iraq and Syria's (ISIS) or Islamic State of Iraq and the Levant (ISIL), as the ultimate lone wolf/self-radicalizing entities at this juncture. A functional approach will be adopted regarding the classification of the means by which an online presence is often utilized to promote and support acts of terrorism. This approach explores practical solutions in identifying the following somewhat overlapping categories: propaganda (including recruitment, self-radicalization, and incitement to terrorism); financing; training; planning (including through secret communication and open-source information); execution; and cyber-attacks. This book examines the threat posed by terrorist propaganda and the U.S. government's efforts to counter it, with a particular focus on ISIS and the Dark Web. It also examines other terrorist networks' uses of online communications to self-radicalize and recruit within the United States. Finally, this handbook will answer the ultimate question: how do terrorists at home and abroad go about radicalizing and recruiting individuals to violence within the United States?

The primary audience for this handbook is:

- International policy-makers and legislators that are interested in monitoring and analyzing specific measurable effective criminal justice responses to threats presented by the use of an online presence by terrorists that requires governments to develop clear national policies and laws dealing with the criminalization of unlawful acts carried out by terrorists over the internet or related services; the provision of investigative powers for law enforcement agencies engaged in terrorism-related investigations; the regulation of online related services (ISPs) and content control; the facilitation of international cooperation; the development of specialized judicial or evidential procedures; and the maintenance of international human rights standards.
- International investigators and intelligence-gathering services that are charged with conducting effective investigations relating to online activity that rely on a combination of traditional investigative methods; knowledge of the tools available to conduct illicit activity via the internet; the development of practices that identify, apprehend, and prosecute the perpetrators of such acts; and a proactive approach to investigative strategies and supporting specialist tools that capitalize on evolving online resources

promoting the efficient identification of data and services likely to yield the maximum benefit to an investigation.

- International law enforcement professionals and criminal justice practitioners that develop and implement legal frameworks to effectively disrupt terrorists' activities online so that they will make a valuable contribution to making our communities—both real and virtual—safer places.
- Security and counterterrorism practitioners, including senior prosecutors, law enforcement officers, and academics that are developing increasingly sophisticated tools to proactively prevent, detect, and deter terrorist activity involving the use of the internet and social media.
- Other individuals with an interest in effectively investigating online terrorism cases that are broadly similar, regardless of the particular jurisdiction involved, with differences in national policies and legislation reflecting the diversity in legal systems, constitutional arrangements, and other factors (cultures).
- Undergraduate, graduate, academia, government, and industry.
- Anyone seeking to exploit the development and enforcement of laws criminalizing the incitement of acts of online terrorism, while fully protecting human rights such as the rights to freedom of expression and association.
- Anyone involved in the security aspects of the investigation of terrorism cases involving the use of online or other related services by suspected self-radicalized terrorists that will often necessitate some type of intrusive or coercive search and surveillance or monitoring activity by intelligence or law enforcement agencies.

ORGANIZATION OF THIS BOOK

The book is organized into nine sections composed of 27 contributed chapters by leading experts in their fields as well as three appendices, including an extensive glossary of online terrorist propaganda, recruitment, and radicalization terms and acronyms.

SECTION I: INTRODUCTION

Section I discusses self-radicalization and how it occurs online. This section also covers contested terms and conceptual clarity; the relationship between social media and radicalization; and the rule-of-law and respect for human rights considerations. The section includes the following chapters.

Chapter 1, Online Utilization for Terrorist Self-Radicalization Purposes, sets the stage for the rest of the book, by presenting insight into the main ideas of the Deep and Dark Web. This chapter also covers encrypted communications; online recruitment techniques and methodology; online radicalization and self-radicalization methodology; planning; incitement to action; execution; cyber-attacks; cyber-jihad; and the cyber-caliphate.

Chapter 2, Online Radicalization: Contested Terms and Conceptual Clarity, provides a detailed description of the importance of conceptual clarity. This chapter also covers radicalization; self-radicalization; online radicalization; and the echo chamber.

Chapter 3, The Relationship between Social Media and Radicalization, presents a description of the radicalization process. This chapter also covers what social media is; the role of social media in the radicalization process; and a description of the radicalization process.

Chapter 4, Rule-of-Law and Respect for Human Rights Considerations, introduces the liberty versus security debate. This chapter also covers collective security; individual liberties; infringement on human rights; and finding the balance between security and liberty.

SECTION II: A TRANSNATIONAL RECRUITMENT PROBLEM OF VIOLENT ONLINE EXTREMIST TERRORISTS

Section II discusses how homegrown violent extremism will likely continue to evolve as a significant threat. This section also covers counterterrorism strategies from an extended global online level and tools to study complexity in the virtual world of counterterrorism lessons learned from the Stuxnet and Shamoon viruses. The section includes the following chapters.

Chapter 5, How Homegrown Violent Extremism Will Likely Continue to Evolve as a Significant Threat, looks at the relationship between communication technology, extremism, and terrorism, and the historical patterns and examples of their relationship. Then the chapter focuses on the impacts of the developments of digital technologies and the way these technologies initially functioned synergistically—what is called "the Iraq effect," and then how these technologies, as they continued to evolve, created completely new opportunities for terrorist groups. Finally, the chapter concludes with a discussion of extremely disturbing directions for the future—not a future that is ten years off—but one that may only be months or weeks away. Of course, that refers to events that have already occurred—the linking of violent acts and live stream functionalities of social media platform.

Chapter 6, Counterterrorism Strategy from an Extended Global Online Level, explores the United Nations' global counterterrorism strategy. This chapter also covers the G20 and its counterterrorism strategy; G8 recommendations for counterterrorism; the counterterrorism action group (CTAG); public–private partnerships to counter terrorism; NATO's policy guidelines on counterterrorism; the Council of Europe; and the Organization for Security and Cooperation in Europe (OSCE).

Chapter 7, Tools to Study Complexity in the Virtual World of Counterterrorism: Lessons Learned from the Stuxnet and Shamoon Viruses, discusses the nature of complex systems and why the development of visionarios or stories about those systems helps to explore complex systems to better understand their idiosyncrasies and characteristics. This chapter also describes complex systems such as terrorist cells and proposes a method through the use of system maps and stories, called visionaries, to learn about and explore them. In addition, cyber-weapons, potential tools of terrorists, are also discussed.

SECTION III: POLICY AND LEGISLATIVE FRAMEWORKS RESPONSES TO THREATS PRESENTED BY ONLINE TERRORISTS

Section III discusses legislation that specifically targets the use of the internet to recruit terrorists. This section also covers legal restrictions and challenges for police and law enforcement authorities and web vulnerability-based spear phishing: a modern combination of tools in cyberterrorism. The section includes the following chapters.

Chapter 8, Legislation Specifically Targeting the Use of the Internet to Recruit Terrorists, examines the general state of legislation in Western nations as it affects the ways that radical organizations use the internet as a tactical and strategic tool. The authors first consider the ways that extremists and terrorists use the internet for recruitment and information sharing. Next, they discuss the differences in legislation with a specific focus on the United States, the UK, and the European Union. They also review the actions taken by social media companies and internet service providers to respond to the threat of terrorism. The authors conclude with a discussion of the implications of these laws for individual free speech and privacy protections.

Chapter 9, Legal Restrictions and Challenges for Police and Law Enforcement Authorities, identifies the restrictions and challenges that have an influence on the outcomes for police and law enforcement strategies. The chapter also discusses how legal restrictions are varied—with two of the more prominent issues that include jurisdictional boundaries and the protection of constitutional rights. In addition to these legal restrictions, the chapter explores the understanding of non-Western communities and how practicing cultural sensitivity poses a challenge, as does the need to acquire the cooperation and participation of the private sector—a lack of these factors can influence the success of a counterterrorism campaign. This chapter finally focuses on the preceding particular considerations within the context of the strategies and measures employed by law enforcement to counter escalating extremism.

Chapter 10, Web Vulnerability-Based Spear Phishing: A Modern Combination Of Tools in Cyber terrorism, details a number of different techniques that modern attackers use to enhance phishing attacks and bring the success rate of such attacks to a significantly higher level by using advanced methods of crafting phishing pages—including pages created by using vulnerabilities of legitimate web applications. After a brief review of existing classic methods used by phishing attacks, the chapter reviews the methods of developing phishing pages with attempts to make them look like genuine ones by using inherent vulnerabilities of different natures and levels, such as the IDN name display method of browsers, web certificate issuance process imperfections, and classic cross-site scripting vulnerabilities of web applications.

SECTION IV: INVESTIGATIONS AND INTELLIGENCE-GATHERING OF TERRORISM-RELATED ONLINE ACTIVITIES

Section IV discusses investigations of terrorist cases involving the internet. This section also covers terrorism recruitment and radicalization into the twenty-first century as well as domestic terrorism and digital media—describing how planning occurs in cyberspace. The section includes the following chapters.

Chapter 11, Investigations of Terrorist Cases Involving the Internet, provides an in-depth analysis of terrorist cases on the internet. The chapter is divided into four sections. Section I provides an introduction to the topic. Section II provides a conceptualization of how terrorists use the internet. The third section introduces the concept of e-jihad, explaining its evolution and how different terrorist organizations have embodied this over time. Finally, the fourth section offers concluding remarks regarding terrorism and the internet. Woven throughout the chapter is a discussion of online radicalization and social media.

Chapter 12, Terrorism Recruitment and Radicalization into the Twenty-First Century, provides a brief summary of the historical and conceptual development of terrorism recruitment trends and radicalization models as they have developed over the twentieth and into the twenty-first centuries. Then the chapter shifts into contemporary adaptations, specifically to messages, audiences, and media built upon the past to represent the range of recruitment and radicalization that we see today. Specific examples are used where applicable to provide concrete applications.

Chapter 13, Domestic Terrorism and Digital Media: Planning in Cyberspace, explores the prevalence, frequency, and types of digital media use among the three most prominent terrorist movements operating in the United States since the early 1990s. In addition to exploring how and why terrorist groups use digital media, the authors examine the individual characteristics of terrorist movement adherents in relation to those who reportedly used (and did not use) digital media within the pre-incident planning process, providing important insights into understanding the nature of technology use within terrorist movements. Also in this chapter, the authors focus on the prevalence of specific types of digital media use among environmental, far-right, and Islamic extremist movements, and they discuss how the characteristics of such movements and their adherents adopt and use technologies during the incident planning process. Finally, in this chapter, the authors examination of digital media is three-fold: first, they examine prevalence, types, and purposes of digital media use among terrorist movements; second, they examine the demographic differences of terrorists who used (and did not use) digital media during the pre-incident planning process; third, they conclude by discussing the implications of their findings for understanding the role of digital media in homegrown radicalization as well as for counterterrorism policy and practice.

SECTION V: ONLINE TERRORIST PROPAGANDA

Section V discusses metaphors of radicalization: a computational and qualitative analysis of jihadi propaganda. This section also covers information, motivation, and behavioral skills perspectives of terrorist propaganda and the relationship between personal data protection and use of information in order to fight online terrorist propaganda; strategic messaging employed by Al Qaeda and ISIS; Daesh's multimodal strategies of online propaganda; and supporting the authentication of digital evidence. The section includes the following chapters.

Chapter 14, Metaphors of Radicalization: A Computational and Qualitative Analysis of Jihadi Propaganda, presents a background on online radicalization. This chapter also covers the linguistic and psychological models of radicalization; what is the information–motivation–behavioral (IMB) model and how does it relate to radicalization; how does conceptual metaphor function in relation to radicalization; technical literature on NLP; metaphor identification and classification; where and how the Islamic State writes; operationalization of IMB; and patterns of metaphor in jihadi propaganda.

Chapter 15, An Information, Motivation, and Behavioral Skills Perspective on Terrorist Propaganda, situates violent extremist behavior in an empirically validated and extensively researched framework of health behavior change: the information–motivation–behavioral (IMB) skills model of behavior change. The authors first describe the origins of the IMB model and the constructs and relationships it proposes. Next, they review empirical support for the IMB model in the context of intervention research in the area of HIV prevention. The authors then discuss current approaches to countering violent extremism as well as procedures for translating the IMB approach into conceptually based, empirically targeted, and rigorously evaluated CVE prevention efforts. They conclude with reviewing applications of the IMB model in the prediction and understanding of health behaviors like HIV prevention, compared to current conceptualizations and understanding of violent extremist behaviors.

Chapter 16, The Relationship between Personal Data Protection and Use of Information in Order To Fight Online Terrorist Propaganda, Recruitment, and Radicalization, explores the relationship between personal data protection and the use of information by law enforcement authorities and Europol, when countering online terrorist propaganda, recruitment, and radicalization. This chapter also questions what information and under which circumstances law enforcement officials should gather together to remove terrorist propaganda from social media platforms and other websites and consequentially further disrupt terrorist activities, and when this activity should fall under the EU legal framework of personal data protection. The authors then outline the applicable EU data protection legal framework by focusing on the provisions of the two most relevant legislative instruments, in particular the newly enacted Directive 2016/680 and Regulation 2016/794 (Europol Regulation). They then look into the main pieces of information that the national law enforcement authorities and Europol (in particular its EU internet referral unit (EU IRU)), potentially need to collect, in order to counter terrorist propaganda, recruitment, and radicalization, and consider whether and when this information can qualify as personal data. Finally, the authors examine the main obligations stemming from the two applicable legal frameworks for law enforcement authorities and Europol.

Chapter 17, Online Terrorist Propaganda: Strategic Messaging Employed by Al Qaeda and ISIS, examines the content of AQAP's *Inspire* magazine and ISIS's *Dabiq* and *Rumiyah*. This chapter first discusses the theoretical and methodological conceptualization of the project. It then turns to a discussion of the findings pertaining to each individual magazine. Finally, the chapter finishes with cross-case comparisons between *Inspire*, *Dabiq*, and *Rumiyah* and offers policy recommendations.

Chapter 18, Daesh's Multimodal Strategies of Online Propaganda, begins by reviewing previous scholarly work that examines how music and visual messaging can impact viewing audiences in a variety of contexts. The chapter then explains the authors' method for analyzing the sonic and visual elements of propaganda and identifies the casualty-related themes where Daesh employed sonic/visual reinforcement. Finally, it concludes by discussing the findings and identifying fruitful areas of future study.

Chapter 19, Supporting the Authentication of Digital Evidence, explores the types of online mechanisms that can be used to further the cause of the terrorist groups, the digital evidence that is created and left behind in the process, and the methods that can be used to determine and protect the authenticity of the evidence.

SECTION VI: ISIS AND THE DARK WEB

Section VI discusses how ISIS virtual planners on the Dark Web recruit, indoctrinate, and inspire attacks in Europe and North America. The section also covers monitoring and tracking ISIS on the Dark Web and how ISIS and Russia use threats of influence spreading and ISIS's future. The section includes the following chapters.

Chapter 20, How IS Virtual Planners Use the Dark Web to Recruit, Indoctrinate, and Inspire Attacks in Europe And North America, examines the ISIS's Dark Web use for recruitment purposes and for directing and inspiring attacks. This chapter is composed of three parts: first, it discusses the role that the late IS spokesman Abu Mohammad al-Adnani played in crafting ISIS's terror-media strategy; second, it examines the caliphate's use of encrypted technology to direct, virtually guide, and inspire attacks; and, third, it assesses Western efforts to disrupt, degrade and destroy the jihadist movement's virtual network including countering violent extremism (CVE) approaches.

Chapter 21, Monitoring and Tracking ISIS on the Dark Web, covers the internet—Surface Web, Deep Web, and Dark Web. The chapter also covers how big the Surface, Deep, and Dark Webs are. Next, it takes a quick look at a few web technologies: encryption, virtual private networks, and cracking. Then, the chapter covers financing and the technologies for traversing the Dark Web: Tor browser, Tor browser that uses onion routing, email, and other sites and services. In addition, the chapter discusses ISIS's use of technology and how tracking ISIS requires understanding and exploiting human and technological vulnerabilities: Mac addresses, IP addresses, browsers, and meta-data. Finally, the chapter concludes with a discussion about the government's response in regard to big data, operation onymous, beebone botnet, NSA's xkeyscore and prism, the Defense Advanced Projects Research Agency's (DARPA) memex, and human behavior.

Chapter 22, ISIS and Russia: The Use of Threat for Spreading of Influence and ISIS's Future, describes the "weakest link" that is to the margins of jihad and to Moscow's benefit. This chapter also covers the emergence of the emirate and the disintegration of resistance, splitting and jihadization of the movement, outsourcing fighters, outsourcing of Chechen fighters, supporters of the Chechen Republic, the reasons for joining ISIS, supporters of ISIS, critics of ISIS, Moscow and ISIS, fear of ISIS in the West and the appeal to the West, and Russia's common cause, no cooperation with United States, the Iranian equation, Central Asian equation, and the European equation.

SECTION VII: INTERNATIONAL COOPERATION WITH ONLINE TERRORISM

Section VII focuses on how virtual planners in the Dark Web recruit, indoctrinate, and inspire attacks in Europe and North America. This section also covers monitoring and tracking ISIS on the Dark Web and how ISIS and Russia use threat to spread their influence. The section includes the following chapters.

Chapter 23, Instruments and Arrangements against Online Terrorism Relating to International Cooperation, analyzes some of the key policy areas such as strategies, action plans, and cases against online terrorism—understood here as incitement to violent radicalization. The authors' discussion on instruments and arrangements, focuses on non-legislative measures of cooperation between the United States and Canada. As background, they offer broader international counter-online radicalization frameworks such as Five Eyes (FVEY) and G7 actions plans, of which the United States and Canada are long-standing founding members.

Chapter 24, Intelligence Sharing Among Agencies and Internationally, briefly reviews information sharing. This chapter also covers the United States' approach to intelligence sharing, department of homeland security, U.S.A. Patriot Act, international approaches to intelligence sharing, and whether to cooperate or not in intelligence sharing.

Chapter 25, Role of Prosecutors in Online Terrorism Cases, discusses the rule-of-law approach to criminal prosecution of online terrorism cases. This chapter also covers the role of the prosecutor in online terrorism cases: the investigative phase, the charging phase, the trial phase (evidential issues), and the first online terrorism case ever prosecuted, as well as jurisdictional issues.

SECTION VIII: PRIVATE SECTOR COOPERATION AND RESPONSIBILITY FOR COUNTERING THE USE OF THE INTERNET FOR TERRORIST PURPOSES

Section VIII focuses on a typology of public–private partnerships: how do you create a new email and its implications for counterterrorism and cyber-security? This section also covers public–private partnerships and the private sector's role in countering the use of the internet for terrorist purposes. The section includes the following chapters.

Chapter 26, A Typology of Public–Private Partnerships and Its Implications for Counterterrorism and Cyber-security, examines the security benefits of public–private partnerships within the context of the exponential growth of intensive globalization since the end of the Cold War made possible by technological innovation. The framework of discussion involves traditional and contemporary notions of national security; examples of threat in the physical and virtual worlds; a typology of public–private partnership types with a brief description of certain public–private partnership types operatives in the larger world of action; and applications potential for security-driven, public–private partnerships in the context of "smart cities." Finally, since this chapter provides only rudimentary and brief coverage of existing programs, salient issues, and challenges, the policy prescriptive message is clear: to craft network alliances and gradually work to thicken networks of protection through coordinated and collaborative efforts to create or enhance a web of partnerships to confront traditional physical assaults and cyberspace attacks.

Chapter 27, Public–Private Partnerships and the Private Sector's Role in Countering the Use of the Internet for Terrorist Purposes, analyzes the relationship between public and private partnerships; addresses both the positive and negatives sides of it; and highlights areas where it could be improved. This chapter begins with a discussion on what is terrorism on the internet; defines both the public and private sectors; and provides an analysis of the relationship between the two sectors. Finally, the chapter concludes with suggestions for improvements, and addresses policy implications.

John R. Vacca
Managing and Consulting Editor
TechWrite
Pomeroy, Ohio

Acknowledgments

There are many people whose efforts on this book have contributed to its successful completion. I owe each a debt of gratitude and want to take this opportunity to offer my sincere thanks.

A very special thanks to my Senior Editor, Mark Listewnik, without whose continued interest and support would not have made this book possible. And, to Editorial Assistant, Katie Horsfall, who provided staunch support and encouragement when it was most needed. Thanks to my Production Editor, Jay Margolis; Project Manager, Rachel Cook; and Copyeditor, Kristin Susser, whose fine editorial work has been invaluable. Thanks also to my marketing manager, Amy Vanderzee, whose efforts on this book have been greatly appreciated. Finally, thanks to all of the other people at CRC Press (Taylor & Francis Group), whose many talents and skills are essential to a finished book.

Thanks to my wife, Bee Vacca, for her love, her help, and her understanding of my long work hours. Also, a very, very special thanks to Michael Erbschloe for writing the Foreword. Finally, I wish to thank all the following authors who contributed chapters that were necessary for the completion of this book: Richard A. Anderson, Stuart Macdonald, Joe Whittaker, Cori E. Dauber, Kemal Ilter, Omi Hodwitz, Mark D. Robinson, José de Arimatéia da Cruz, Sheila R. Ronis, Tom Holt, Steven Chermak, Joshua D. Freilich, Emin Huseynov, Yannis A. Stivachtis, Allison Miller, James M. Smith, Maeghin Alarid, Kevin M. Fitzpatrick, David Woodring, Jeff Gruenewald, Brent Smith, Ben Miller, Weeda Mehran, Yassin Kosay Alsahlani, Haroon Qahtan, Anthony F. Lemieux, Rebecca Wilson, Paolo Balboni, Milda Macenaite, Elena Pokalova, Carol K. Winkler, Jonathan Pieslak, Sarbari Gupta, Anthony Celso, William F. Gross, Dmitry Shlapentokh, Christian Leuprecht, Ali Dizboni, Becky K. da Cruz, and Richard J. Chasdi.

Editor

John R. Vacca is an information technology consultant, professional writer, editor, reviewer, researcher, and internationally known, bestselling author based in Pomeroy, Ohio. Since 1982, John has authored and edited 80 books, and some of his most recent books include:

- *Computer and Information Security Handbook*, 3rd edn, Morgan Kaufmann, (an imprint of Elsevier Inc.), 2017.
- *Security in the Private Cloud*, CRC Press, (an imprint of Taylor & Francis), 2016.
- *Cloud Computing Security: Foundations and Challenges*, CRC Press (an imprint of Taylor & Francis), 2016.
- *Handbook of Sensor Networking: Advanced Technologies and Applications*, CRC Press (an imprint of Taylor & Francis), 2015.
- *Network and System Security, Second Edition*, 2nd edn, Syngress (an imprint of Elsevier), 2013.
- *Cyber Security and IT Infrastructure Protection*, Syngress (an imprint of Elsevier), 2013.
- *Managing Information Security, Second Edition*, 2nd edn, Syngress (an imprint of Elsevier), 2013.
- *Computer and Information Security Handbook*, 2nd edn, Morgan Kaufmann (an imprint), 2013.
- *Identity Theft (Cybersafety)*, Chelsea House Pub, 2012.
- *System Forensics, Investigation, And Response*, Jones & Bartlett Learning, 2014.
- *Managing Information Security*, Syngress (an imprint of Elsevier), 2010.
- *Network and Systems Security*, Syngress (an imprint of Elsevier), 2010.
- *Computer and Information Security Handbook*, Morgan Kaufmann (an imprint of Elsevier), 2009.
- *Biometric Technologies and Verification Systems*, Elsevier Science & Technology Books, 2007.

He has authored 600 articles in the areas of advanced storage, computer security, and aerospace technology (copies of articles and books are available upon request).

John was also a configuration management specialist, computer specialist, and the computer security official (CSO) for NASA's space station program, Freedom, and the International Space Station Program from 1988 until his retirement from NASA in 1995.

In addition, John is also an independent online book reviewer. Finally, John was one of the security consultants for the MGM movie, *AntiTrust* (2001). A detailed copy of his author biography can be viewed at www.johnvacca.com. John can be reached at john2164@windstream.net.

Contributors

Maeghin Alarid
U.S. Air Force Academy
USAF Institute for National Security Studies
Colorado Springs, CO

Yassin Kosay Alsahlani
Georgia Institute of Technology
Atlanta, GA

R. Allen Anderson
Trident University International
Cypress, California

Paolo Balboni
ICT Legal Consulting Balboni, Bolognini &
    Partners Law Firm, Milan, Italy
European Centre on Privacy and
    Cybersecurity (ECPC)
Maastricht University Faculty of Law
    Maastricht, the Netherlands

Anthony Celso
Department of Security Studies and Criminal
    Justice
Angelo State University
San Angelo, TX

Richard J. Chasdi
Department of Political Science
The George Washington University
Washington, DC

Steven M. Chermak
Michigan State University
School of Criminal Justice
East Lansing, MI

Becky K. da Cruz
Valdosta State University
Professor of Criminal Justice
Department of Sociology, Anthropology, &
    Criminal Justice
Valdosta, GA

José de Arimatéia da Cruz
Georgia Southern University
Comparative Politics and International
    Studies
U.S. Army War College Strategic Studies
    Institute
Brazil Research Unit at the Council
    on Hemispheric Affairs (COHA) in
    Washington, DC
Savannah, GA

Cori E. Dauber
Department of Communication
University of North Carolina at Chapel Hill
Chapel Hill, NC

Ali Dizboni
Department of Political Science and
    Economics
Royal Military College of Canada
Kingston, Ontario

Kevin M. Fitzpatrick
Department of Sociology & Criminal Justice
Community & Family Institute
University of Arkansas
Fayetteville, AR

Joshua D. Freilich
Department of Criminal Justice; &
    Program in Doctoral Studies in Criminal
    Justice
John Jay College
New York, NY

William F. Gross, Jr.
Gross Security, LLC
Spencer, WV

Jeff Gruenewald
Indiana University
Indianapolis, IN

Sarbari Gupta
Electrosoft Services, Inc.
Reston, VA

Omi Hodwitz
Department of Sociology and
    Anthropology
University of Idaho
Moscow, ID

Thomas J. Holt
School of Criminal Justice
Michigan State University
East Lansing, MI

Emin Huseynov
University of Geneva, Switzerland
Centre Universitaire d'Informatique
Carouge, Switzerland

Kemal Ilter
Department of Communication
University of North Carolina at Chapel Hill
Chapel Hill, NC

Anthony F. Lemieux
Georgia State University
Transcultural Conflict & Violence Program
    (2CI)
Atlanta, GA

Christian Leuprecht
Department of Political Science and War
    Studies Graduate Program
Département de science politique et le
    programme d'Études supérieures sur la
    guerre
Faculty of Arts
National Defence
Kingston, Ontario

Stuart Macdonald
College of Law and Criminology
Swansea University
Swansea, Wales

Milda Macenaite
ICT Legal Consulting
Balboni, Bolognini & Partners Law Firm
Milan, Italy

Weeda Mehran
Georgia State University
Atlanta, GA

Allison Miller
School of Public and International Affairs
Virginia Tech
Blacksburg, VA

Ben Miller
Department of English
Affiliate Faculty, Institute for Quantitative
    Theory and Methods
Emory University
Atlanta, GA

Jonathan Pieslak
The City College of New York, CUNY
Princeville, HI

Elena Pokalova
College of International Security Affairs
National Defense University
Washington, DC

Haroon Qahtan
Georgia State University
Atlanta, GA

Mark D. Robinson
Department of Communication
University of North Carolina at Chapel Hill
Chapel Hill, NC

Sheila Ronis
Department of Management and
    Communications
Walsh College
Troy, Michigan

Dmitry Shlapentokh
Indiana University South Bend
Department of History
South Bend, IN

Brent Smith
Department of Sociology & Criminal Justice
Community & Family Institute
University of Arkansas
Fayetteville, AR

James M. Smith
U.S. Air Force Academy
USAF Institute for National Security Studies
Colorado Springs, CO

Yannis A. Stivachtis
Virginia Tech
Department of Political Science
International Studies Program
Blacksburg, VA

Joe Whittaker
College of Law and Criminology
Singleton Park
Swansea University
Swansea, Wales

Rebecca A. Wilson
Georgia State University
School of Medicine & Rollins School of Public
    Health
Emory University
Atlanta, GA

Carol K. Winkler
Georgia State University
Atlanta, GA

David Woodring
University of Georgia
Athens, GA

Introduction

Chapter 1

Online Utilization for Terrorist Self-Radicalization Purposes

R. Allen Anderson

CONTENTS

1.1 INTRODUCTION

We live in an internet-connected world where we are increasingly connected through social media, email, and many other forms of communications that allow us to text, talk, even video conference with friends, family, and those in our professional networks anywhere on the planet with a simple internet connection. The internet has opened the door to instant communications from large metropolitan cities to the countryside, from a vacation cruise ship to the office, even from a remote jungle (through a satellite connection) to literally anywhere in the world.

This book focuses on terrorism in general by examining the threat posed by terrorist propaganda and U.S. government efforts to counter it, with a particular emphasis on ISIS and the Dark Web. It will examine how Islamic and other terrorist groups use online communications to self-radicalize and recruit within the U.S. This book will serve as a comprehensive handbook and professional reference, as well as a practitioners' guide to today's most complete and concise view of the rapidly growing phenomenon of how online presences are utilized for terrorist purposes.

This book offers in-depth coverage of the history of how online presences of terrorist groups come about, the emergence of various groups, the development of their online presences, training, and communications. The authors will examine terrorist videos, training materials, propaganda and recruitment machines, and the interaction between terrorists and recruits from an initial candidate interest through recruit development, training, and execution of a terrorist attack.

ISIS/ISIL's ultimate goal is to provide the means for lone wolf self-radicalization in the West, particularly the U.S., and to recruit small numbers of dedicated followers to carry out their objectives. A functional approach will be adopted regarding the classification of the means by which an online presence is often utilized to promote and support acts of terrorism. This approach explores practical solutions in identifying the following somewhat overlapping categories: propaganda (including recruitment, self-radicalization and incitement to terrorism), financing, training, planning (including through secret communication and open-source information), execution, and cyber-attacks. Finally, this handbook will answer the ultimate question: how do terrorists at home and abroad go about radicalizing and recruiting individuals to violence within the U.S.?

For example, this chapter covers the availability and use of publicly available information and how terrorists use that information to select their targets and plan attacks. Next, it will familiarize the reader with the surface and hidden internet and provide insight as to the differences between the surface internet, and those areas in the hidden internet called the Deep Web and Dark Web and explain why one cannot simply use a regular browser and common search engine to explore those regions.

This chapter will go on to discuss online recruitment techniques and methodologies and examine common tactics used by recruiters, and what sort of recruits these organizations are seeking. Next, it will examine the processes, similarities, and contrasts of the online radicalization and self-radicalization methodology. Following these, the author will take the reader through some of the main resources available for the lone wolf terrorist to train, plan an attack in accordance with the objectives of the organization to the point which the attack is ready for execution.

This chapter will also discuss a wide range of the types of cyber-attacks both common in the current age, and what cyber-attack methodology is preferred by what type of actor (criminal, hacktivist, state actor, terrorist, etc.). Finally, this chapter will introduce the reader to the concept of cyber jihad and group known as the cyber caliphate, including a discussion regarding their objectives and capabilities.

1.2 PUBLICLY AVAILABLE INFORMATION

Publicly available information is any information which is available to the public through any means. There is a vast array of information available on the internet through a variety of sources which include social media, public records, brochures, newspapers, books, and pay-for data services just to name a few. As other sections in this chapter discuss information available which enable radicalization and self-radicalization through the internet, the focus of this section will include publicly available information which enable or empower an individual to:

- Train to conduct a terrorist attack
- Gather intelligence
- Select their targets
- Plan an attack
- Execute an attack

Publicly available information is easily accessible, and in this globally connected, sophisticated, technological age in which we live, most of it is available now in one form or another through the internet. Most private businesses, government and non-government organizations have made considerable advances in a push toward a paperless society, thus, have put their resources and other information on the internet, most of which is accessible easily, not requiring authentication in many cases.

In this chapter, the author will discuss the surface and hidden internet, thus, what is available through common search engines, and the masses of information hidden on the Deep Web, and further into the Dark Web. These resources, the surface internet, the Deep Web, and the Dark Web can all be considered information which is publicly available. The only obstacle to availability for the most part is one's understanding of the internet, the Deep, and Dark Web, and the ability to pay for the information in some cases.

Publicly available information that enables a potential terrorist to train to conduct a terrorist attack is also discussed in other sections of this chapter, however, it is necessary to include additional resources other than ones mentioned in other sections. For example, training is available in many forms. Again, focusing on the individual, not a group of terrorists, there is a vast library of knowledge available with only a few keystrokes.

Useful training information may include technical specifications and how-to videos and manuals regarding firearms skills, tactics, ammunition, and combat mindset are readily available through any search engine or on social media. There are also several law enforcement and military training manuals and videos which can further enhance the trainees' knowledge and reveal strategies and tactics used by law enforcement and the military which the terrorist may attempt to counter.

News articles related to current or past terrorist events and the after-action reports conducted by government agencies in the aftermath of terrorist events are often published online. Furthermore, some building and complex layouts and other structural detail can be found online in many cases if the target is a school, university, hospital, or public building. Maps and satellite photos are commonplace on the internet; these and the other resources mentioned are particularly valuable in each of the training, intelligence gathering, target selection, planning, and execution phases of a terrorist operation.

If a specific human or soft target is selected for kidnapping or assassination, the amount of information which can be obtained either free or for a small fee on a person in a single online report is enough to plan a mission against the person or any number of their family members. In the case of pay-for databases that charge anywhere from around US$30 to $50 for a comprehensive report, these databases derive information from credit bureau headers and reports, medical and other collections agencies, tax records, motor vehicle and driver license records, employment verification services, social media platforms, census reports, magazine and online subscription services, criminal records and accident reports, civil court, vital statistics data-bases, news and social media postings, and much more.

The amount of information contained in a single-source comprehensive data report on an individual can portray a current and historical account of a persons' life: addresses, phone numbers (listed or unlisted, including cellular phone numbers), age, date of birth, even a partial social security number. They also include information on family members, neighbors, relatives, and associates, vehicles driven, driver license number, history, and current status, and a plethora of other information.

Anytime there is a major data breach such as the Equifax or Office of Personnel Management breaches for example, there is a heightened awareness of the vulnerability of our personal and other sensitive data. Regardless of data breaches, the fact remains that the majority of information relating to any given member of our society is publicly available through the internet and public records. It is important to note that a simple follow-up search of an individual who has been to civil or family court may easily reveal the full dates of birth and social security numbers of the person and their family members in the hard copy court file to which access is easily granted by visiting the local courthouse.

If the target is a business, especially a larger corporation or non-profit organization, a single-source comprehensive report can be purchased, again for a small fee, which compiles public records related to the target business into one report. These reports include a list of corporate officers, in some cases tax filings, financial data and credit ratings, and more. Additionally, most corporations, government, and non-government organizations publish a great deal of information regarding their organization, structure, leadership and other personnel, data systems, even details about cyber-security measures they have taken in an effort toward customer assurance to build customer confidence in their organization.

Every person who has ever obtained a social security number, a driver license, been employed, filed a tax return, gone to college, registered for the selective service system, applied for a credit card, opened a bank account, been named in a trust, been a party to a criminal or civil action, or legally (and sometimes illegally) entered the U.S. has a data trail. Every small or large business from independent contractors to Fortune 500 companies and non-governmental organizations leave a detailed data trail readily available to anyone who wants it.

Publicly available information often includes much of the information people hold most sacred—details about our identifying information, credit, personal lives and associations, the places we do business, and most importantly, our family members. Whether a terrorist wishes to conduct a physical or cyber-attack against an individual or their family, business, organization, or government entity or specific personnel within an organization, it does not take more than US$100 and a few follow-up online searches, or a simple trip to a courthouse to obtain all the data needed to start planning a physical or cyber-attack. Whether the objective is assassination, espionage, hostage taking, public or personal destruction of a reputation, or other disruption, the only thing lacking might include real-time surveillance *unless* the target is within view of any one of thousands of publicly published online video cameras throughout the U.S.

1.3 INTRODUCTION TO THE DEEP AND DARK WEBS

When most people think of the internet, some of the first things that come to mind are e-commerce, Google, Facebook, or YouTube for example. This book would not be complete without an introduction to the Deep and Dark Webs, those places which cannot be accessed by ordinary web browsers and common search engines. It is important to develop a basic understanding of the internet from a roadmap or access perspective.

The browsers and search engines most commonly used can only access the Surface Web. Consider this, of all the content on the Web, popular browsers and search engines can only access around 4 percent. Thus, 96 percent of all content on the internet is hidden within the chambers of the Deep Web. In other words, the Deep Web is hidden to Google, Yahoo, and other popular search engines. The Deep Web is actually estimated to contain around 500 times the data as the surface web and consist of around 7500 terabytes.

The Deep Web and Dark Web, for starters, are not the same thing. The Deep Web generally contains data which is not listed in popular search engines. Some examples may include databases, web forums which require registration, webmail sites, and pages located behind paywalls. The Dark Web is an area in which one can operate in total anonymity without being tracked. The Dark Web is considerably smaller than the Deep Web, and this is where most of criminal activity takes place.

Common misconceptions regarding the Deep and Dark Webs are that *nothing good exists there*; it is where one can buy or sell illegal drugs, guns, illegal pornography, or even hire a hitman. As for the Dark Web, many of these things are true, one can make illegal transactions, and it is a haven for criminals. However, much more exists in this dark region of the internet which is lawful and can be especially useful for the intelligence community, particularly relating to cyber threats and activities of criminal or terrorist organizations.

First, lawful use of the Deep Web simply includes the fact that people want privacy, thus, they do not want to be tracked and spied on. If you are tired of tracking cookies which analyze your search and shopping habits, and of course obtain even more personal information about you in many cases, then using the Deep Web may be right for you. Many legitimate businesses are now using the Deep Web and appealing to the privacy of their customers. The most popular browser for accessing the Deep Web is the Tor browser, and a popular search engine for this is Duckduckgo.

To go further into the Dark Web using the Tor browser, one can find a variety of search engines which sport the .onion domain suffix. The .onion suffix at the end of a domain indicates that it is a hidden site on the Dark Web. This is where much of the criminal activity takes place among a host of forums, chatrooms, and there is other material that is prohibited in other areas of the internet.

There is both good and bad on the internet; some of the most serious crimes which take place on the internet, however, take place on the Dark Web. The legality of whether one can search on the Deep or Dark Web primarily would depend on what one views or purchases.

Fact is though, the Dark Web is not a place one wants to visit without a solid understanding of what it is and why you are going there. Criminal activity and other malicious enterprises exist there, and it is only accessible using special software as discussed above such as the Tor browser. Tor, and other similar browsers, conceal one's IP address and identity therefore providing anonymity. Additionally, monetary transactions that take place on the Dark Web are commonly paid for through the trading of cryptocurrency such as bitcoin or others through escrow services which are also found on the Dark Web.

A vast amount of criminal activity takes place on the Dark Web in addition to that already mentioned, such as the buying and selling of stolen financial account and credit card numbers, child pornography, prepaid debit cards, user names and passwords to a wide array of types of accounts, and even stolen lifetime subscriptions to products and services for pennies. The Dark Web was even used to crowdfund the assassination plot of President Donald Trump and Vice President Mike Pence.

Just as there is an array of products and services available, causes to contribute to, and for the criminal enterprise, much money to be made, there are also plenty of scams. Most notoriously known as the place where criminals (and many terrorists) go to do business, the Dark Web has a bright side as well. The Dark Web also has its own social media—chat rooms, and messaging. Even Facebook has tried to venture into the Dark Web by providing its users with a ".onion" address, which is a type of hidden address aside from normal DNS addresses, and can only be visited by going through the Tor network.

Much because of its anonymity, the Dark Web has also become a forum for those exercising free speech, such as many who may reside in a country where they experience oppression or persecution for speaking out against their government, or for a religious cause. As well, some people from countries with strict censorship laws go to the Dark Web to search for what in many free nations would be considered legitimate content. Even some legitimate businesses are flocking to the Dark Web to do legal, legitimate business in order to block companies like Facebook and Google from tracking their customers and internet searches to avoid targeted and other unsolicited advertisements.

What is the value of the Dark Web to cyber-security and counterterrorism professionals? As you may have guessed it by now—intelligence!

As terrorist organizations and other radical groups seek the same anonymity other criminals do to carry out their nefarious agendas and missions, many utilize the Dark Web much in the same manner as cyber-criminals to communicate, raise funds through crowdfunding, recruit, train, and indoctrinate new members. Make no mistake, these organizations use the regular internet for some of the same reasons, however, particularly when distributing videos of beheadings, torture, and other barbaric activities that quickly get taken down or banned from mainstream social media such as YouTube and Facebook, their distribution is much easier on the Dark Web.

Other sensitive information such as bomb making and training videos including instructions on how to carry out a terrorist attack along with an abundance of additional terrorist and radical group videos, materials, and communications networks are easily accessed.

On the cyber side of the equation, the cyber-security (cyber-warfare) professional can gain an abundance of cyber-threat information on the Dark Web which can be analyzed to produce cyber-threat intelligence (CTI). This CTI is extremely valuable in determining where the next cyber threats and attacks are coming from in the ever-changing and morphing technological environment known as cyberspace [12, 34, 35].

1.4 ENCRYPTED COMMUNICATIONS

In the twenty-first century, encrypted communications are not something from the future but a part of our everyday lives. For instance, cellular phone calls are encrypted to prevent interception over a common radio receiver. Other, more advanced encryption can be used by anyone, including terrorists, government agencies, and law-abiding citizens alike for email communications and SMS text messaging applications. This section will discuss some of the popular types of encryption, their associated applications, and other techniques preferred by terrorists.

Terrorists are well-known for their use of SMS text messaging applications which use end-to-end encryption and cannot be decrypted simply by intercepting the message, but would be intercepted at one end, likely on a server. Some older messaging apps used SSL encryption, which could be intercepted on an end server and presented vulnerabilities, however, newer types of encryption have emerged which have mitigated many of those concerns such as PGP (Pretty Good Privacy) encryption [11, 31].

PGP is encryption that converts a message at the sender's end into encrypted text which can only be decoded and read at the other end by the receiver using the same technology. PGP can not only convert a message but can encrypt entire files using what is called public-key cryptology. This technology creates two mathematical keys, called private-keys, which are related. Encrypted messages can be safely copied and pasted into unsecured media such as emails and publicly viewable social media posts because they cannot be decrypted except by another user, the other private-key. Extremist publications, such as *Inspire* magazine, discussed throughout this chapter, publish their private-key so those with PGP can access and view their encrypted messages [11].

TrueCrypt is a volume file encryption technique which encrypts the entire drive and can be used to replace end-to-end encryption. This can also be considered a form of full-device encryption. Using this technology, the system would create text files inside a virtual disk drive in the physical system. Once a file is created, it can be uploaded to file-sharing websites and other forums, often found on the Dark Web. Since the file is created in a virtual drive, there is no trace of it on the physical hard drive of the system [11, 31].

Considering operational security, the use of a self-destructing message feature in combination with end-to-end encrypted messaging is most effective. There are several SMS text messaging applications which offer both features: end-to-end encryption and a message self-destruct feature that destroys messages sent or received based on the user's preferences and settings (such as within one minute, five minutes, or longer time periods after the message is sent or read) [11, 31].

It is common knowledge that terrorists were some of the earliest users of new SMS text messaging applications, even before authorities and intelligence agencies had a chance to research new applications' vulnerabilities. This makes it especially difficult for counterterrorism professionals, as in the case of communications, terrorists are often at least one step ahead.

Popular video and/or SMS text messaging apps which utilize end-to-end encryption include Telegram, Signal, Wire, WhatsApp, Dust, Viber, Facebook Messenger, iMessenger, Voxer, Silent Phone, Wickr, Threema, and Chatsecure. Some of these apps include the self-destruct feature mentioned above. Some of the most popular messaging apps with terrorists include Telegram, Signal, Wickr, and WhatsApp. These popular phone apps are free to use and most can be accessed through any smartphone operating system [31].

In spite of encryption, which is available to everyone through open-source code and its free use, some of the most popular traditional means of e-communications utilized by terrorists include email platforms such as Gmail and social media to include Facebook, Twitter, and others. To credit the companies who provide these services, several thousand accounts linked to terrorists and terrorist propaganda have been shut down. Now that these companies have shut down thousands of terrorist-linked accounts, which on one hand slows down the spread of their propaganda and temporarily inconvenienced these groups who used those platforms, the real question is how we will be able to monitor and track them now. Does action taken by the companies who own these platforms aid or hinder counterterrorism efforts?

Since the source code for end-to-end encryption is open-source, anyone, including terrorists, can create their own applications, thus making them extremely difficult to discover. Therefore, terrorists can improve their communications security by developing their own apps for use within a small segment of an organization. The use of these custom developed apps in small groups often provides little indication to intelligence officials, except that a previous communications platform has gone dark, unless a phone or computer with the app installed falls into the hands of counterterrorism intelligence [31].

The Dark Web, through the use of the Tor browser, which is a modified version of the Firefox browser, is a dungeon of sites, file drops, and chat forums where open and PGP encrypted communications can be exchanged between terrorists, their handlers or control agents, and others who would like to communicate during various levels of the radicalization process. The Tor browser uses a distributed network of relays worldwide which prevents surveillance on an internet connection. Data requests sent through Tor pass through three proxy servers, each with separate layers of encryption, before reaching its destination, thus concealing the IP address and location of the user.

PlayStation 4 (PS4) has its own online network which is used for online gaming and messaging. Users can send messages directly to other users in the PS4 network or through online games. The PS4 game *World of Warcraft* is a free online game available to PS4 users which has become very popular with terrorists for online communications [21].

Terrorists have often used satellite phones to communicate as they are encrypted. However, this encryption has been unmasked and is not an effective means of secure communications. In some remote areas though, satellite phones are the only means of communications available other than face-to-face or contact through a human courier.

Small, compact, and encrypted USB drives are a popular means to exchange communications and other data, particularly via human courier. Large amounts of data which can include photos, maps, schematics, and a vast amount of additional intelligence information can be placed on a USB drive and delivered to its intended recipient who will use a private-key to decrypt the data as discussed above.

Encrypted messages can be placed inside JPG and GIF photos using a process referred to as steganography. This is where a message is hidden within another message. These pictures can then be publicly posted, emailed, or sent to their destinations through other messaging platforms without encryption.

1.5 ONLINE RECRUITMENT TECHNIQUES AND METHODOLOGY

Before examining recruitment techniques of terrorists and their online methodologies, it is important to understand who many of the younger, fighting age terrorists are, and where they come from. There are many terrorist groups worldwide guided by a variety of political, religious, racial, or ideological principles; the most common to the U.S. in the early twenty-first century include the Islamic jihadist organizations such as Al Qaeda and ISIS. Many young terrorist recruits do come from third world countries with little to no technology, often guided by indoctrination into extreme religious ideology, and experience frustration, despair, and hatred of the West. However, there have been increasing numbers of young Muslims and converts recruited into Islamic jihad from Western countries including Europe, Canada, and the U.S. Other extremist groups have also used violence on the domestic front; a few of these groups include Antifa, Black Lives Matter, the Ku Klux Klan, and the American Indian Movement. Some of the violence exhibited by these groups can be considered terrorism or domestic terrorism.

Not all terrorists are under-educated extremists. Many come from the ranks of the educated, such as doctors, engineers, and those well versed in information technology. Many come from traditional Western middle-class backgrounds with no criminal or other violent history who convert to Islam and take up the cause of jihad. Many are raised and educated in the West, or in Europe, Asia, and the Middle East with technologies such as cell phones and the internet at their disposal. Many of these young jihadists are well versed in the use of the internet for communications, marketing, e-commerce, and education.

As the author focuses primarily on Islamic terrorism, or jihad, the reader should consider all the techniques and methodologies jihad terrorists use, can be used by any radical or terrorist group. No one group has a proprietary claim to their use, and many of the strategies and tactics employed by one group can be replicated by others. In fact, many of the techniques and methodologies terrorists and other radicals use for recruiting, radicalizing, training, and communications are the same technologies and methodologies used by other criminal organizations, including some legal businesses. Terrorists are often the earliest users of new encrypted communications apps too, making it hard for authorities to monitor and track their activities.

With the fifth dimension, cyber, at their disposal, online terrorist radicalization and recruiting and other activities have proliferated. Much like a structured criminal organization, a good example being the Mexican drug cartels, terrorist organizations are run much like a business or non-governmental organization (NGO). They need resources to operate; they need money. Some non-profit organizations have also been known to support terrorism, but so have some companies, governments, religious groups, and private donors.

Online recruiting techniques and methodology by radical and terrorist groups range from using their websites and social media pages containing favorable and enticing propaganda and Twitter, Instagram, and Tumblr postings to recruitment videos which encompass either a softer and compassionate narrative and show the organization in a favorable light versus a negative light shed upon them by governments, the media, and society or to display their success stories. In the case of ISIS (Islamic State of Iraq and Syria), for example, this organization has been particularly effective in its ability to recruit sympathizers, fighters, converts, and other Muslims from around the world including the U.S., using a well-oiled, online social media and propaganda campaign. ISIS selective narratives have been found to be particularly appealing to youth in America from all classes and walks of life.

To understand the Islamic State, it is important to understand what Islamism is. Islamism is not Islam the religion but the ideology which justifies the establishment of an Islamic State governed by Sharia Law, and an ideology which must be *sold* to many Muslims throughout the world. Thus, it is promoted as a calling to young Muslims to their duty and destiny as Muslims to join the cause.

Pro-ISIS propaganda also appeals to several psychological and ideological factors in potential recruits through their well-oiled al-Hayat multimedia project. At one time, the al-Hayat project had an active presence on Twitter and has used unrelated hashtags to obtain wider coverage of its propaganda messages and videos. Many of al-Hayat's publications included online magazines and videos of interviews with ISIS fighters and of the brutal beheadings that they are well known for. Twitter has since removed al-Hayat from their platform, however, thousands of individual accounts have been deemed as pro-Islamic State.

Given al-Hayat's and ISIS high-tech, proficient, 24-7 online recruiting efforts, where the organization is displayed in a kinder, gentler, victim-like defender-of-the-oppressed light, where ISIS fighters even appear in videos handing out ice cream to children, they can be especially effective at manipulating would-be sympathizers, supporters, and recruits. ISIS recruiters are very skilled in psychological techniques appealing to loners, those with anger issues, or who *want to belong* to something. When a potential recruit reaches out and contacts an ISIS recruiter, they are often greeted very kindly and with welcoming phrases such as "blessings to you brother" or "greetings to you in the name of Allah." From the initial contact, ISIS is warm and welcoming to their new candidate.

ISIS does not attempt to appeal to the masses but to small numbers by showing a romanticized life as a jihadist fighter, showing the camaraderie of fellow brothers having fun and images of eating pizza together. YouTube is still a popular platform for pro-ISIS propaganda and even contains channels such as Mujatweets which contains several videos similar to the al-Hayat publications, such as status of ISIS operations and interviews with fighters.

Another infamous online recruiting tool originally created by Al Qaeda is *Inspire* magazine, from Al-Malahem Media. Created by Shaykh Anwar Al-'Awlaki, *Inspire* magazine is a professionally produced, well-articulated publication that contains appealing and inspiring articles promoting the cause of jihad, letters from the editor, history, stories from the front lines, messages to the West, attack methods, and how-to instructions and much more that allow would-be jihadists to train at home without the need to travel to a terrorist training camp often located in another country, thus these are open-source jihad and "America's worst nightmare."[14] *Inspire* is the one-stop resource for self-radicalization which will be discussed later in this chapter.

Online recruiting, much like the personal, face-to-face recruiting techniques outlined in the *Al Qaeda Training Manual,* involves the recruiter grooming the candidate through a series of contacts (online in this case), getting to know the recruit, then giving them small assignments, testing the candidate for trustworthiness and reliability. Some examples of this radicalization process will be discussed later in this chapter.

As ISIS makes no attempt to appeal to the masses but instead to smaller numbers as mentioned above, their philosophy is they do not need large numbers of new soldiers to carry out their missions, but smaller numbers of individuals and small groups, particularly in the West, willing to commit to their cause and carry out missions that foreign nationalities would have more difficulty carrying out within the U.S. New recruits who have been mesmerized by the allure of the romanticized approach come from all walks of life from the angry, bullied, loner wanting revenge, to upper middle class, educated, young people who are willing to throw it all away to commit jihad for the Islamic State.

As governments and the media have portrayed ISIS as a blood-thirsty, brutal group of extremists that have nothing to do with Islam, it behooves strategists and decision-makers to consider that ISIS thinks of itself as being all about Islam. Therefore, to counter the efficiency of ISIS recruiting of young Muslims, there needs to be change and education within the Muslim community among elder and younger Muslims to counter the old ideology which promotes an Islamic State, and which offers young Muslims options other than to become fighters for Allah.

Another radical group which has utilized the internet for recruitment and promotion of its cause is Antifa (Anti-Fascist Action). Antifa has promoted involvement and membership through several local chapter websites, Facebook pages, Twitter postings, protest videos, and an array of other popular social media postings. Antifa does not attempt to display a compassionate or softer side to their narrative, rather this organization attracts those who oppose fascism, capitalism, racism, and authoritarian government and who are willing to take often violent and destructive action during organized protests and harass, intimidate, and threaten those who they see as the enemy, including their families.

Antifa is a Left Wing, cross-party, socialist and communist alliance organization whose origins stem from fighting fascist Nazi's during the pre-World War II 1930s era. After the war, those who survived either hunted down Nazi's who had escaped prosecution after the war or sought socialist policies and power in the post-war German government (Balhorn, 2017).

Though of international origin, Antifa in the U.S. has protested several groups they deem fascist or racist such as the Ku Klux Klan, and allied itself with race-based groups such as Black Lives Matter. Antifa of today differs greatly from its early days fighting true Fascists in Nazi Germany, as their actions and modus operandi consist of promoting a radical socialist/communist agenda and anarchy. Antifa of today has been instrumental in the organization of and carrying out of numerous protests in the U.S., many which have become violent and resulted in physical attacks on opposing groups, disruption of public services and private business, destruction to private property, and attacks on public servants and their families. Antifa has also condoned and encouraged acts of violence including train derailments, and at one time, posted how-to instructions on one of their northwestern U.S. local chapter websites which eerily mimic those instructions contained in *Inspire* magazines' volume 17 in 2017 which features detailed instructions on how to derail a train. This posting has since been removed after the April 2017 incident where perpetrators poured cement on railroad tracks in Washington which resulted in a train derailment.[15]

Online recruiting methodology employed by Antifa is geared toward local membership. Thus, local chapter websites contain information on how to support Antifa, including membership. When a candidate is interested in becoming more involved with Antifa, they would be invited to attend some of Antifa's local open meetings. Once the candidate has attended usually several local open meetings, and other members have had a chance to get to know the candidate, the candidate would ask to become a member. Antifa does not publicly advertise their vetting processes, however, several of their local chapter websites indicate the candidate would be given instructions on the next step toward membership by local leadership.

Unlike ISIS recruitment of smaller numbers to carry out discreet assignments and eventual violent acts of Jihad, Antifa's philosophy involves strength in numbers, evidenced by often violent mass protests. Though Antifa utilizes several online platforms for organizing events, recruiting, and obtaining funding, this group primarily concentrate their online recruiting efforts toward drawing in masses of supporters to their organized, staged protests.

1.6 ONLINE RADICALIZATION AND SELF-RADICALIZATION METHODOLOGY

Online radicalization and self-radicalization are areas which are under researched and where the conduct of valid science-based research is, in many instances, not possible due to the inability to maintain accurate control groups and other factors. Many questions arise regarding the internet and its influence in the radicalization process. It is also difficult to conduct a proper study due to the inability to access extremists who have not been arrested.

Several studies have been conducted regarding online radicalization and self-radicalization and the various methodology utilized by various radical groups with varying results, in part because of the problems and issues mentioned above, and there is little accurate data available regarding the radicalization process. Each study conducted, therefore, presents different theories regarding stages or pathways toward radicalization.

For this section, the author will not focus on any one or combination of theories based on the studies conducted on this topic, but rather the author's observations made while researching actual online terrorist and radical group recruiting propaganda. As much of this chapter focuses on Islamic jihadi organizations and their activities and methodology, it is important to expand this discussion to include other radical groups and ideologies to explore the concept of online radicalization or self-radicalization.

In this chapter, the author discusses the early publications of Al Qaeda including *Inspire* magazine, the cyber caliphate, and Antifa particularly regarding online recruitment. Observations of each of these organizations' propaganda and methodology have an underlying component— human contact.

To be clear, recruitment and radicalization are not one and the same, although they are closely related. Radicalization itself stems from the new candidate's or recruit's studious immersion in the ideological propaganda provided through various online sources and personal acceptance of their teachings, followed by action. Direct contact with a recruiter or agent of the radical group may or may not be facilitated before said recruit acts out based on the group's ideology or instructions provided through various online sources.

There are a variety of online propaganda resources, not only regarding radical Islam, but relating to racist groups such as far right-wing white supremacy and other race-based ideologies like Antifa and other radical groups available on the internet, particularly on the Deep and Dark Webs. The cyber caliphate, which is a relatively new group, has become known for its recruiting and radicalizing propaganda, and *Inspire* magazine, Al Qaeda's online extremist publication, which serves to recruit, radicalize, and train prospective followers. Radical far-right white supremists have dominated the Dark Web for far longer than Islamic jihadism, and other radical organizations with their ideological propaganda, apparently stemming back to the 1990s.

Online radicalization, which includes the element of human contact with a recruiter, includes traditional elements such as getting to know the recruit, their motivations, and a series of tests the recruiter may employ. The online process is usually initiated by the candidate, who is interested in the organization or its cause or ideology through the Internet via chatrooms, forums, or email. In many instances, the relationship between the recruiter and the recruit will be online and involve no direct, face-to-face contact.

The recruiter will assess the candidate or recruit for reliability and trustworthiness through the completion of smaller challenges or missions; this is where, in some schools of thought, the radicalization process starts to take form. The new recruit will be given relatively small assignments at first, such as taking pictures or other intelligence-gathering operations for example, before being given assignments which will prove or disprove the recruit's loyalty to the cause.

As evidenced particularly in Islamic jihadist recruitment and radicalization propaganda (particularly *Inspire* magazine), the recruit is constantly exposed to psychological elements which emphasize the recruits' *importance to the cause, how much the organization needs them,* and *how valuable they are.* Furthermore, there is great emphasis on *unity* and *belonging; unity* toward the cause or struggle, ideology and the *allure or enticement* which attract the recruit to *belong* and *be a part of something bigger than they are.*

As the new recruit is conditioned, tested, and groomed through a gradual immersion into the group's ideology, and after passing a series of low-level tests to determine whether they will be useful to the cause, the new recruit is given bigger, more important missions, again, to test their loyalty. At some point, such a mission could include killing someone or carrying out a terrorist attack.

Self-radicalization is possible solely via the internet in a similar fashion as online radicalization. The key difference between online radicalization and self-radicalization is that there is no need for contact with a recruiter or other agent for the self-radicalized person to carry out an operation. Between information readily available online, which includes the entire series of *Inspire* magazine and numerous other informational sources, videos, and radical websites state a group's objectives and, in some cases, even a list of suggested missions. Solely online, the self-radicalized person can go through the entire process from candidate to operational terrorist.

As mentioned earlier, there are several studies that have been undertaken thus far which have achieved mixed results and propose a variety of theories. Since some of the most common issues experienced in many of these studies include inaccessibility to actual persons at various steps in the radicalization process, these studies lack the ability to create and evaluate control groups. As there are several theories which have been derived, it is recommended the reader conduct further research into the various studies to examine and compare theories and results.

1.7 PLANNING

When it comes to the planning of terrorist attacks by radical organizations, the most comprehensive strategies this author assessed include those employed by Al Qaeda and other elements of Islamic jihad. Al Qaeda emphasizes the lone wolf attacker develop a thorough understanding of the organizational strategies in their planning and carrying out of subsequent attacks. To Al Qaeda and other Islamic jihadist groups, it is important to carry out attacks in the heart of a nation they are at war with, which serves to demoralize the enemy and deprive it of its security. Attacks within the homeland cause the U.S. to re-evaluate its security procedures, implement stricter regulations, and conduct invasive searches, mass spying, and increased infringement on the privacy of its citizens, build new infrastructure and improve existing ones. In the eyes of Al Qaeda (and other like groups and organizations), each attack within the U.S. homeland is a defeat for the U.S. and causes it to have to prove itself again to its people and on the world stage.

As it is important to Islamic jihad that this strategy be existent in the planning of all attacks, it is particularly emphasized to the lone wolf attacker. Next, it is vital that secrecy be maintained; thus, any compromise could jeopardize a potential attacker and any planned operations. Like any para-military operation, operational security is of an extremely high priority.

It is common practice, with some exception, among Al Qaeda, ISIS, and other Islamic jihadists, to employ the use of inexpensive military tactics and methodology that do not require complex, thus vulnerable, operational and logistical support. Another characteristic of Al Qaeda, specifically the lone wolf planning model is the emphasis on tremendous flexibility in the planning process, which Al Qaeda sees as contributing to greater chances of success when the plan becomes operational.

Keeping with the organizational strategy, any plan for lone wolf jihad should be carried out with an objective to cause as much turmoil and chaos as possible and result in the attack being more chaotic and more effective than the one preceding it. Therefore, their strategy stresses careful selection of targets to maximize the psychological and social impacts on the nation being targeted.

Al Qaeda has placed a strong emphasis on jihadists learning the methodology and processes, thus, the art of assassination. Assassinations of select targets such as public figures, officials, soldiers, and their family members within the interior of their home nation is believed to inflict more fear into the target nation than bombings and other mass killings because of the direct, personal nature of assassinations of targeted individuals and their family members.

Al Qaeda's planning model is clear, concise, and encourages attention to strict detail coupled with tremendous flexibility in the planning and target selection process. Other Islamic jihadist groups have similarly followed suit in accordance with the Al Qaeda model when it comes to preparing radicalized or self-radicalized lone wolves for terrorist attacks. Though there is a lot of material available regarding the planning of terrorist attacks for lone wolf terrorists on the internet (in the form of videos, literature and other publications, websites, and chat forums), particularly on the Dark Web, the single most comprehensive resource would include the entire series of Al Qaeda's *Inspire* magazine. The Al Qaeda planning model can be easily adapted for use by any terrorist group or lone wolf terrorist, domestic or international.

1.8 INCITEMENT TO ACTION

To examine incitement to action, the author will discuss particular online elements involved in the incitement process. The majority of elements come from static, online resources, however, one element, the human element, may or may not be present in individual cases. Next, incitement can be derived from religious text (such as the Quran) either literally or via interpretation and the decision to act on a violent religion-based ideology.

Incitement to action will be a part of or follow the online or self-radicalization process. When we think of incitement to action, what often comes to mind are the end-game terrorist attacks carried out by extremists. However, this author's research of various online jihadi and other extremist propaganda and review of terrorism cases that involve an online form of radicalization has found that there are, in some instances, multiple actions carried out during the radicalization process.

During the new recruit's testing and evaluation phases, which include the human element and online contact with a recruiter or control agent, incitement may come from the recruiter or control agent testing the recruit with low-level assignments, such as taking pictures, setting off a fire alarm, calling in a bomb threat, or other smaller missions that present an opportunity to evaluate the recruits' ability to follow orders, commitment to the cause, any security risks involving the newbie, and their response upon completion of each mission to assess their readiness for the next. In many cases, a recruit's early missions will be assigned to test the recruit by comparing results to those already known from previous missions. As this chapter has a great deal of emphasis on Islamic jihad extremism, other groups and ideologies often follow a similar path in testing new recruits, whether online or in person.

Solely online incitement to action can come in several forms such as video or written messages from an organization's leadership or through online chat forums, email, social media posts, or encrypted online applications. An example could include a call to jihad against Western targets in retaliation for actions or policies of the West, or to otherwise advance the cause of the organization in the form of a video message, social media postings, or messages to followers in an online forum.

Religious text, such as the Quran, are readily available online and contain several passages which dehumanize unbelievers and call for violent action against them. Religious texts can be taken in a literal context or interpreted by the reader. These texts can be elements which incite action based on the fundamental or interpreted religious calling.

Whether a religious, political, ideological, or racial motive, other factors which this author assesses as contributing to incitement include anger, frustration, and despair. As the radicalized extremist lives in a world which may not conform to their belief system of ideology and experiences, what can be considered as common human emotions such as frustration and anger, along with emotional factors or the belief that there is no other alternative, can strongly influence the individual to act out. As mentioned elsewhere in this chapter, certain radical ideologies rely heavily on psychological factors to influence and incite their followers to a call to action.

In this author's research, the surface and hidden internet include a plethora of extremist and ideological propaganda to influence, recruit, train, and inspire followers, ultimately to prepare for and respond to a call to action to carry out the agendas they promote. Incitement to action is the final step toward carrying out or executing the mission. The conditioned and trained extremist is theoretically considered ready to carry out the intended mission and called into action to do so.

1.9 EXECUTION

This section will not focus on a particular terrorist group or ideology but will include commonalities between both physical and cyber-attacks. In this context, whether a physical (non-cyber) attack is executed by a political, religious, racial, or ideological group, the principles and elements of an organized, planned attack are for the most part universal according to the type of attack to be carried out. Thus, the execution of physical lone wolf terrorist attacks has commonalities with organized attacks, as do the execution of cyber-attacks.

The physical attack: once the radicalized individual has been trained, planned, and prepared for activation of a terrorist mission, there are several considerations, most of which have been addressed in the planning phase. Once the target has been identified and assigned by a control agent or self-chosen, and the common elements including who, what, when, where, why, and how are identified, then up-to-date pre-launch intelligence is verified (such as real-time presence of, capabilities of, and vulnerabilities of the target, counter-surveillance, weather, and other environmental and geographic conditions), the terrorist would make last minute preparations for their attack.

The timing of the physical attack or order to execute can come from a control agent, online video, message, or other communication. The timing of the attack can also correlate with anniversaries, holidays, or specific events that provide the best opportunities to maximize effectiveness, such as how to inflict as many casualties as possible. Often the most difficult to detect in advance would be an attack to be carried out by a terrorist who was radicalized and trained completely online, and whose chosen methods of attack may include the use of a vehicle or legally obtained firearm. This self-radicalized terrorist could conceivably carry out their attack without anyone noticing in advance, especially if the individual had no prior criminal history or has not come to the attention of law enforcement.

Physical terrorist attacks come in a variety of forms, some of which include bombings, shootings, stabbings, mass killings, attacks on critical infrastructure, nuclear attacks, or biological attacks to name a few. As this chapter focuses primarily on the individual who has been radicalized through the internet, the types and methodology of how these attacks are carried out will ultimately depend on the capabilities of the individual and their available resources and can vary greatly.

The timing of the execution of a cyber-attack can be carried out in the same way as a physical attack, however, the pre-attack methodologies of the cyber-attack. It may have some similarities to a physical attack, however, some variables do not apply. In this chapter, the author discussed cyber-attacks, cyber-jihad, and the cyber-caliphate. The cyber-caliphate is an online army which supports the ISIS ideology to advance the cause of Islamic jihad via the internet. An actor prepared to commit a terrorist cyber-attack can literally represent any extremist political, religious, racial, or ideological cause, thus cyber-terrorist attacks are not limited to any specific group, ideology, or cause. A radicalized individual may therefore be operating alone or as part of a coordinated group.

Once the radicalized individual has been trained, planned, and prepared for a cyber-attack by acquiring the logistical support to carry it out (see cyber-attacks section and the various types of attacks which can be carried out and what they encompass), then up-to-date pre-launch intelligence is verified (such as the continued existence of predetermined target vulnerabilities), and the attack is launched through a chosen means, such as a phishing email, denial-of-service (DoS) or distributed denial-of-service (DDoS) attack or other means.

1.10 CYBER-ATTACKS

We live in a world connected via the internet through the many devices we use and carry with us. As people can communicate via text, voice, or video from anywhere on the planet with an internet connection, geographical separation is meaningless. With the advances, benefits, and conveniences of the very technology which has brought families closer, enabled businesses to operate internationally, and increased the efficiency of industrial systems, also comes great risk.

U.S. critical infrastructure is composed of sixteen sectors; each sector relies on computer systems and networks for day-to-day functionality. These sixteen critical infrastructure sectors include:

- Chemical
- Commercial Facilities
- Communications
- Critical Manufacturing
- Dams
- Defense Industrial Base
- Emergency Services
- Energy
- Financial Services
- Food and Agriculture
- Government Facilities
- Healthcare and Public Health
- Information Technology
- Nuclear Reactors, Materials, and Waste
- Transportation Systems
- Water and Wastewater Systems

The computer networks and the systems connected to these infrastructures include information and command and control systems which are necessary for day-to-day functionality. These systems control our power grid, pumps for water and wastewater systems and oil, gas, and chemical pipelines, railroad switching, traffic lighting, and cellular and Internet communications systems for starters. They also control chemical and food processing systems, fuel refinery, and nuclear power plant cooling systems. The list goes on.

The majority of our critical infrastructure networks and computer systems that keep them operational are composed of often decades-old computer hardware, software, and outdated operating systems such as Windows 98 and New Technology (NT). These aged hardware, software, and operating systems are highly susceptible to cyber-attack through known vulnerabilities; many of these vulnerabilities cannot be mitigated because of age and should be upgraded, or preferably custom re-designed from the ground up for each critical infrastructure.

These systems have been the target of hackers, criminal organizations, state-sponsored actors, hacktivists, and others for various reasons and motives. Criminal, activist, terrorist organizations, and state actors alike would benefit from successful cyber-attacks against U.S. targets, particularly against critical infrastructure. In this section, the author will begin by addressing some of the methods of cyber-attack and potential motives and preferred targets by a variety of actors. The importance of increased vigilance and preparedness in cyber-security cannot be understated. Common types and methods of cyber-attack may include:

- Advanced persistent threats (APT)
- Brute force attack
- Social engineering/cyber fraud
- Distributed denial-of-service attack (DDoS)
- Phishing attacks
- Malware, spyware, ransomware, including cross-platform malware (CPM), and metamorphic and polymorphic malware, and phishing

Advanced persistent threat (APT) is a type of sophisticated cyber-attack that involves a coordinated group of attackers concentrating on a single target. Objectives of this type of attack include gaining undetected access to sensitive information within the targeted system and leaving few traces of its presence and accomplishments. The APT attack is optimal in cases involving espionage [25].

The APT attack is not detectable or thwarted via conventional cyber-security methods. and there is no one technology or method to stop such an attack. The reality is that most organizations have not given cyber-security the high priority it deserves and have under-invested, leaving themselves even more vulnerable. It is necessary to consider new approaches in dealing with APT attacks—continuous persistent monitoring—and increased vigilance is a must [25].

In a brute force attack, automated software attacks a system by any means. It searches for any vulnerabilities it can detect and often attacks password-protected mechanisms. This type of attack uses dictionaries and other resources to formulate hundreds of thousands of words, combination of words, and numbers to crack the system and obtain data.

Insider threat issues come to the forefront considering social engineering and cyber fraud attacks. These attacks are dependent upon the victims' interaction and authorization. These cyber-attacks usually come in the form of an email which links to an authorization link that the recipient would click on, which would initiate the attack. The predatory email usually comes from what appears to be a familiar source, possibly from someone on ones' email list or another familiar source. This type of cyber-attack is very common not only against businesses and government agencies, but against individuals also, especially the elderly and others unfamiliar with internet-related scams. Often cyber fraudsters will design scams tailored to a particular audience, such as the elderly [18]. Some examples of elderly targeting include spam and phishing email which focus on elderly issues or concerns such as medicare and health insurance, counterfeit prescription drugs, funeral and cemetery benefits, anti-aging products, investment schemes, reverse mortgage, sweepstakes, lottery, and grandparent scams. Grandparent scams are when the fraudster impersonates a friend of the grandchild and requests money for an emergency or bail

The distributed denial-of-service attack (DDoS) is a disruptive cyber-attack directed at overloading servers with high concentrations of requests. Common targets for these attacks include governmental and non-governmental organizations. The objective is to overload the targeted system and prevent the organization from doing business. It is common that during a DDoS attack, once the attacker has gained access to the target system, the attacker uses the opportunity to steal or destroy sensitive data or implant malware as a prelude to future attacks.

Phishing attacks are likely the most common type of cyber-attack. Attackers are constantly creating new methods that make it difficult for cyber-security professionals to keep up. Most commonly, these attacks come in a mass email sent to hundreds of thousands of recipients with an attachment or link in the email. When the attachment is opened, or the link is clicked, the hacker gains access to the victims' computer system, and it enables the attacker to conduct internal attacks on the victim's system and software, bypassing any passwords, firewalls, or security software which may have been installed on the system.

Malware, spyware, and ransomware attacks each have their own objectives and methodology. These are malicious software-based attacks meant to gain unauthorized access. These attacks could contain malicious viruses, spyware, or ransomware, particularly in the case of ransomware attacks where a system is locked and held hostage by the attacker who typically demands a ransom to be paid, often in cryptocurrency, in exchange for access. It is also common for an attacker to inject spyware into a system to spy electronically, monitor keystrokes, and thus gain access to passwords and sensitive data.

Worms are similar to viruses, however, they spread differently within a computer system or network. Worms affect your files by eating their way into a system and running autonomously. Some worms can replicate themselves and spread to other systems, such as in the case of the Stuxnet virus which remained undetected for a considerable length of time, collected system and mapping data of the Iranian nuclear facility, then ultimately caused the meltdown if its reactors.

Cross-platform malware (CPM) was at one time exclusive to the Windows operating systems, however, that is no longer the case. cyber-attackers' incentives to build CPM increase as there are increasing numbers of systems which use a variety of different operating systems [25]. For example, OSX, Windows, and Linux operating systems can be affected by CPM malwares such as Koobface and McRAT. Even when patches are made to mitigate CPM, it is common that the malwares reemerge, even years after the initial attack when it identifies new vulnerabilities [30].

Metamorphic and polymorphic malware change their own code, thus, each new version is different than the last. These metamorphic and polymorphic malwares can easily evade detection and are considered to be the single biggest threat to organizations worldwide, Polymorphic malware is much more complicated and difficult to write, involving techniques such as register renaming, code expansion, code shrinking, code permutation, and insertion of garbage code, however, larger organizations with well-supported and experienced hackers can utilize these methods. Some organizations that may employ this method may include adversarial governments or terrorist organizations [30].

There are two primary types of internet-related crime, as viewed by law enforcement, advanced cyber-crime (considered high-tech crime), which includes sophisticated attacks carried out against software and system and connected hardware, and cyber-enabled crime. Cyber-enabled crimes are traditional crimes that have taken new pathways to their commission. Some of these crimes include financial crimes, terrorism, crimes against children, and the like.

Many attackers, such as state-sponsored actors and global terrorist or radical organizations, share similar goals. The differences lie in their agendas, goals may be based upon ideological, religious, or political grounds rather than on economic and military dominance. In some cases, though, aspirations of terrorist extremists may also include governmental and military dominance, such as the case with the Islamic caliphate. The cyber caliphate will be discussed below in Section 1.11.

Who are the potential targets for a cyber-attack, particularly by an adversarial state, terrorist group or other extremist organization? Depending on the specific goals and objectives of the attacker and their cyber-capabilities, the list of targets could include any of the nation's critical infrastructure or defense systems and even include private industry.

Critical infrastructure (CI) is a major target for cyber-attack, especially by an adversarial state or terror organization, again, depending on their cyber-capabilities. The golden egg of prizes for such an attacker would be a successful attack to disable, even destroy elements in our energy sector, namely the power grid, oil, and gas pipelines, refineries, and storage facilities. In particular, the power grid is the one element in our critical infrastructure that every other infrastructure depends on, including power generating infrastructures such as nuclear energy facilities and hydro-electric dams.

Now that the types and methods of attack have been discussed, the author will identify the various types of cyber-attackers and indicate which methods are most common or most preferred by each type. Some types of cyber-attackers include:

- Criminal
- Hacker
- Hacktivist
- Spy
- Recruiter

These categories may appear on the surface to be broad, however, there will be subcategories included such as terrorists, radical political groups, state actors, etc., which will provide clarity. A description of the most common methods of attack will be included for each category. Some examples include spearfishing, denial-of-service, brute force attack, etc.

1.10.1 Criminal Cyber-Attacks

Some of the common methods used in criminal cyber-attacks include the use of spyware, botnets, and cookies. Spyware, for example, can be used to obtain usernames and passwords, financial accounts, corporate systems account access, and personal identity information. This sort of information can be exploited by the criminal(s) to steal money from bank accounts and credit cards, obtain credit for merchandise and services using the victim's identity and credit, and access corporate user accounts for other nefarious purposes. Criminals may carry out these purposes or see the information to other criminals.

Cyber-criminals use bots and botnets to launch denial-of-service (DoS) and distributed denial-of-service (DDoS) attacks to access servers and websites. DoS and DDoS attacks are when a network or system is flooded with requests that flood its bandwidth and resources, thus denying the owner access to its own system. These attacks are commonly used to disrupt services provided by the target or deny access to the target's system while cyber-criminals perform other actions in the background such as accessing, stealing, or destroying data, or injecting trojans, worms, and other forms of malware onto the targeted system or computer to further their criminal objectives (specifics on motives will be discussed to below) [30].

One of the most common methods used today is phishing and spear phishing through social engineering and email. These attacks are initiated by the cyber-criminal sending an email that appears to be from a familiar source, such as someone on your email address list with a malicious attachment or link included in the message. When the malicious attachment or link is clicked on, one thing that may appear is a login box requesting you to log back into your account. However, the box is not a legitimate login box and will collect and transmit your username and password back to the cyber-criminal [30].

The criminal cyber-attacker may have a variety of motives, the majority of which are centered around money. The cyber-criminal seeks financial gain and power; however, other illegal cyber-activity such as cyber-terrorism and the topics discussed below, overlap in the cyber-criminal activity category. To narrow this discussion, the cyber-criminal will not include the other types of criminal activity but instead focus on those motivated by financial and power gain [2].

Some objectives include, as mentioned above, obtaining the target's usernames and passwords, financial account information, usernames and passwords of the target's workplace accounts (corporate systems), or the target's personal identity information. By obtaining these and other account information and the user's personal identity information, the cyber-criminal can use this gold mine of data to access private and corporate accounts. They can also use this data to impersonate real people on the internet and other venues to obtain merchandise, services, or money or to communicate with other people to perpetrate crimes such as spying, medical and other forms of fraud, and theft and monetization of sensitive corporate, government, and healthcare data [2, 30].

The ultimate targets of the criminal cyber-attacker may include, but are not limited to, a variety of data repositories such as banks, retail companies, healthcare organizations, government agencies, and cryptocurrency wallets, which can all be monetized [2]. To gain access to their ultimate targets, they commonly use the methods described above such as social engineering and phishing emails to obtain user credentials, account, and identity information [2, 30].

1.10.2 Hacker Cyber-Attacks

1.10.2.1 State Actors, Terrorists, and Radical Groups

Methods used by the cyber-hackers include some of the same ones mentioned above, however, to be more specific, the author will include ten of the most common methods cyber-hackers use to gain access to their targeted systems.

The keylogger is software that records keystrokes from a keyboard. Keyloggers can also be installed as physical hardware on the target's system. Log files collected by a keylogger could include work and personal email addresses, logins, and passwords, and those of social media and other accounts. Keyloggers are the main reason why online financial institutions provide users with an option to use their virtual keyboards, particularly when users are on a public computer such as in a library or hotel [35].

Denial-of-service (DoS) attacks, which are also mentioned above, overload a website or system with a plethora of internet traffic beyond its capacity to process, thus, taking down the target website or network. The DoS and distributed denial-of-service (DDoS) attack is a prevalent technique used by a variety of criminal actors discussed in this report [35].

Waterhole attacks are relatively unique in nature. They are called waterhole attacks because they operate much like something you might see on the Discovery or National Geographic channels, where poison is placed at the most accessible point to the intended victim. An example of this would be when a water source, such as the source of a river, is contaminated (poisoned), the poison naturally flows downstream and affects animals or people drinking further down. In the same way, hackers target a popular or highly used access point such as an internet café, coffee shop, or hotel to attack their victim [35].

As hackers become aware of their victims' internet habits and timings, they can employ this technique. One way hackers can trap their victim is by creating a phony WiFi access point, then modify the victims' most visited websites to redirect them to obtain their personal information. This type of attack collects information on users from a specific place, and detecting and identifying the attacker is very difficult.

Fake wireless access points (WAP) are effortless to create, and a hacker can create one in the vicinity of a public hotspot, such as open WiFi at a coffee shop, mall, hospital, or airport. When the victim attempts to access the fake WAP, the hacker can access their system information, credentials, and data [35].

Eavesdropping (or passive attacks) are where the hacker monitors victims' computer systems and networks to gain some desired information. Motives behind such attacks may not be to harm the victims but gain information from computer systems and networks [35].

Phishing is a hacking technique that traps its victims by creating a spoofed (fake) website link to the victims' most-accessed sites via email. When the victims enter their information, such as their login credentials, to the phony login screen, the hacker obtains their information. Phishing is a byproduct of social engineering and is the most commonly used method of cyber-attack. It is also the most detrimental to and costly for the victim [35].

Viruses or trojans are malicious software programs. These programs collect target victims' data and send it to the hacker. They can also provide false advertisements with spoofed links, sniff data, lock files (common in ransomware attacks), and spread throughout the computer and its network. Additional dangerous programs include worms, malware, and spyware [35].

Clickjacking, also known as User Interface (UI) redress, is where the hacker hides the real UI and takes the victim to advertising sites. This is most commonly done in apps, movie streaming, and torrent websites. Mostly, this is done to get money from advertising click sites, but the victim's information can also be stolen [35].

Cookie theft is where a hacker gains access to cookies stored in ones' browser history and obtains information such as personal data, usernames, passwords, and browsing history; the hacker then steals that information and can use it to compile information the victims' identity obtain unauthorized access to the victims' online accounts [35].

Bait and switch is where a hacker purchases advertising spaces on websites, then later when someone clicks on the ad, they are directed to another page infected with malware. Once the victim's computer is infected with malware or adware, the hacker can run malicious programs that appear authentic, granting the hacker unauthorized access to the victim's computer [35].

Cryptocurrencies (like bitcoin) are frequent targets for hackers, as are the internet of Things (IoT) as part of washers, dryers, other household appliances, and vehicles; cloud storage, healthcare; and nations' critical infrastructure (CI), such as power grids, oil and gas pipelines, nuclear power plants, communications, and transportation [2] Other targets include sports teams, banks, celebrities, corporations (for the purpose of theft, espionage, or disruption by DoS and DDoS attacks etc.,), social media, and global trading markets [2].

Often the motive of the hacker can be determined by the target. Once the attacker's actions can be evaluated, motives can usually be assessed. For example, if the attacker can make money as a direct or indirect result of their attack, the motive would likely be financial. It could also be a competitor's attack on the company to destabilize competition [2].

The hacker may be ideologically motivated if their attack is directed to bring harm to the victim's reputation, deny services to customers, or sabotage systems to further propagandize or eliminate what the attacker perceives as threats to the environment for example. (See the "hacktivist" attacker below.) This type of hacker could also be a disgruntled employee.

Political motivations are when the attacker benefits from gaining intimate knowledge of or secrets and strategies of an organization, or even a political candidate. Hackers are also motivated by prestige and curiosity; hackers may be attracted by something interesting about the target or may desire to breach the mark for something as simple as bragging rights to say that they did.

One thing to remember when considering hackers, there are what we would consider the good guys and the bad guys: white hat hackers are considered the good guys and black hat hackers are the bad guys. White hatters are experts who specialize in penetration testing to ensure a computer system is secure. Black hatters, or just hatters, are those criminal hackers who break into computer systems and inject viruses and malware, and they, for the most part, do it for financial gain [22].

Other motivations of the various kinds of hackers can include any mentioned in this chapter. Some may be part of criminal or terrorist organizations, solo actors, or even state sponsored who serve a state's military or spying objectives against another state, or even against private sector corporations in another state [22].

1.10.3 Hacktivist Cyber-Attacks

1.10.3.1 Terrorists, Radical Groups, and Disgruntled Employees

The cyber-hacktivist is an internet-based activist, otherwise known as an e-activist or hacktivist. These are a type of cyber-criminal who has a cause, opinion, or point they want to force on others and who will use any cyber means available to get it across. Some of the recent trends of hacktivists include their use of email, blogs, and social media networks and hacking popular, corporate, religious, or government websites to inject their rhetoric and propaganda [2, 22, 32].

Hacktivists motives can be political, economic, social, or to exercise free speech. Hence, the hacktivist is motivated by an ideology. They will also gather sensitive information on their target, who in many cases may be an individual such as a CEO, politician, or public servant such as a police officer or their family, then leak the information to the public and in some cases, call for violence against their targets [2].

1.10.4 Spying Cyber-Attacks

1.10.4.1 State Actors, Corporations, and Disgruntled Employees

Spying and espionage can take place at many levels by a variety of attackers. It is common that corporations hire hackers to access a competitor's computer systems and steal trade secrets, and this can lead to devastating financial losses, which can, in some cases be irrecoverable by the targeted business. Governments use espionage all the time to spy on adversaries, even allied governments.

In concert with the methodology of this and other malware type attacks, the attacker seeks out vulnerabilities in software, otherwise known as errors, flaws, mistakes, and failures in development and implementation. As well, attackers seek out hardware vulnerabilities in the computer or network that they can also capitalize on. Mainly, government operatives and agents tend to target publicly known vulnerabilities and others discovered through their internal research efforts in adversarial software and systems. This is a common practice to gain access to enemy plans and other intelligence.

It is worthwhile to discuss social engineering in the context of cyber-spying and espionage. Social engineering involves users willingly giving out their usernames and passwords (and other information) to the attacker. Now, the attacker may be disguised as a known or friendly contact or may appear on the user's screen as a legitimate login box for example, or the user might give their information directly to a coworker or contractor they believe has authorized access, but who may misuse, give away, or sell the information. In the above scenario, social engineering exploits the person providing their information.

However, a much darker side of social engineering exists that involves the full knowledge, willingness, and intention of the person providing their information. Their motives could range from the most common, financial gain, to ideological or political reasons.

There are five technologies which the author discovered are not disabled by merely going offline or disconnecting from the internet, or even the computer network. Just like gadgets from the old James Bond and Star Trek movies and television programs, these technologies are becoming more commonplace in today, and some technologies initially developed for governmental use are becoming more available for commercial and criminal use. These technologies include electromagnetic attack, laser attack, radio signals, heat emission, and ultrasound spying.

Electromagnetic attack can be initiated through any operational device that generates electromagnetic radiation and is connected to an electrical line. There are technologies that can intercept electromagnetic radiation and retrieve data. The U.S. and U.S.S.R. (the Union of Soviet Socialist Republics, or the old Soviet Union before its fall in 1989), were concerned with electromagnetic leaks, as it was discovered information can be obtained this way. Some of the most vulnerable links found between electromagnetic waves and devices include monitors, keyboards, wireless devices, and unshielded VGA cables. Keyboards have become a favorite target for this type of attack because keystrokes can be intercepted with great accuracy from as far away as 20 meters using a simple homemade device that analyzes the radio spectrum emitted from the device.

As all devices work on the same principle and generate electromagnetic noise, the only real difference between them is signal power. As we know, wireless devices emit a signal with a range from several feet to several meters; signals emitted by wired devices depend on the length of the wire (VGA or other cables) and can even be transmitted over power lines. If the target computer is connected to the power line (the power grid), data can be easily intercepted by measuring power fluctuations and noise generated by keystrokes in the ground line.

Laser attack is accomplished by aiming an inconspicuous laser beam at the target and measuring keystroke vibrations. Each key on the keyboard has its own distinct vibration, thus, patterns of vibrations are measured and assessed. This technique is accurate enough to produce meaningful text, however, usually not exact enough to generate strong passwords.

Radio signal attack was developed by Israel and deploys malware which can infect a target system via external media. The malware modulates electromagnetic radiation in the target computer's hardware. The radio signal can then be picked up on any standard FM receiver, even on an FM receiver phone. This method spies on the target by siphoning off information through a type of physical medium.

Heat: The Israeli's also demonstrated an exotic scenario to steal data through heat emissions. This method of attack is performed like this: two desktop computers sit close to each, typically around a foot to fifteen inches apart; one computer is connected to the internet, the other is not and presumed to be secure. The internal motherboard temperature sensors of one computer tracks and measures temperature changes of the other computer. The malware installed in the internet-connected computer system's load level (within the amount of work, or load, the computer performs over a period of time—thus, the malware embeds itself within the systems workload) and produces a modulated heat signal. The internet-connected computer reads the data from the non-internet-connected computer in its proximity then decodes it and sends it to the attacker via the internet.

Ultrasound spying overcomes shielding used by governments and other institutions to protect against electromagnetic noise leakage. For ultrasound to work, it requires two hardware elements: one placed inside the shielded room and another outside of it. Data transfers utilizing the ultrasound technique can transmit up to a rate of 12 Mbps (megabits per second), and no power supply is required for the receiving unit because the energy needed is transmitted along with the stolen data.

Motives for cyber-spying include financial gain, the ultimate disruption of a competitor, political opponent or other person or entity, critical infrastructure or government service through the later use of the information gained by the spying activity. Cyber-spying is also conducted by government agencies during the course of government investigations of terrorism or criminal activity and is often referred to as intelligence gathering or conducted on the authority of a warrant.

1.10.5 Recruitment Cyber-Attacks

1.10.5.1 Terrorists and Radical Groups

The recruitment cyber-attack is common among conventional terrorist and activist organizations and cyber-terrorists and hacktivists alike. This type of attack is conducted primarily to gain support for the attacker's cause with methods used such as spewing propaganda over a targeted, highly trafficked website or destroying or disrupting a target's systems including critical infrastructure, carrying with it the attacker's ideology. This sort of attack, in addition to trying to gain support for a cause, agenda, or ideology, can also have the intent to deter opposition to a cause and can very well be cross-classified in some cases as cyber-terrorism as well as recruitment [2].

Methods used in recruitment cyber-attacks include other methodologies such as social engineering, spear phishing, denial-of-service (and distributed denial-of-service), all mentioned previously in this chapter. Motives include stealing login and other access information that they will need to access the target network or website and carry out future objectives, some of which are mentioned above, like the targeting of a website or disruption or destruction of critical infrastructure. The ultimate goal of the recruitment attack, even when it involves other forms of attacks and crosses over with the hacktivist and the terrorist organization's recruitment efforts (often aligned with the cyber-terrorist), is to generate support for and deter opposition of the attacker's cause or ideology [2].

Now that we have examined the types and methods of cyber-attacks, types of attackers, and the methods most commonly preferred by each type of attacker, one can observe that there are a variety of cyber-attack types and methods; however, no single group or type of attacker has a proprietary claim to any type or method of attack. Therefore, whether the attacker's intent is financial gain, espionage, propaganda, or to disrupt or destroy services and infrastructure, what defines the attacker is their motives. This stated, as technology advances and new vulnerabilities are discovered, cyber-attackers will continually devise new ways to capitalize on those vulnerabilities. Cyber-security should be at the forefront of our agenda going forward.

1.11 CYBER JIHAD AND THE CYBER CALIPHATE

We are familiar with Islamic jihad, hence, *the struggle*, the struggle as being acted out, from a Western perception, in the form of terrorist attacks, torture, beheadings, and the like—pure brutality. Not to delve deeply into jihad here, except to answer the question: what is *cyber jihad*?

There are many definitions of cyber jihad, defined by as many sources as there are definitions. Here is a simple explanation: cyber jihad simply put means to use all possible cyber-tools toward the expansion of modern Islamic jihad, which is guided by the ancient texts of the Quran and modern (nineteenth through twenty-first centuries) Islamism (which is also referred to in some communities as political Islam).

In the early days of Al Qaeda, Osama bin Ladin called for an electronic jihad. When we think of an electronic jihad in practice, we see this in the internet and all its forms of communications. azzam.com, which was aimed at younger Muslims, came online in 1994 and was the earliest website to promote Islamic extremism and serve as a point of communications and recruitment for the Al Qaeda terrorist organization [3]. In a short time, several sister websites to azzam.com appeared on the internet promoting Islamic extremism and jihad.

The Al Qaeda online magazine, *Inspire*, which is discussed in other sections of this chapter, published its first issue in 2010 and is considered by many to be the single most dangerous resource for violent extremists on earth [26]. Upon review of *Inspire* magazine volumes, from the beginning, they rival other professional publications in their organization, quality, articulation, and visual appeal. Though its articles can be upsetting and concerning to the non-jihadist reader, they are full of insight and inspiration to the jihadist or new recruit alike. One commonality which appeared to be on almost every page was the emphasis on the importance of the reader to the cause. The authors of this publication over the years have consistently used a psychological approach to attract young Muslims or new converts who are either desperate to belong to something bigger than themselves, or who are frustrated and see no other option.

The internet is a viable venue for any group to get its message out to the world. Among many other things, it is a place for inspiring, communicating, recruiting, training, and sharing news of success, failure, and calls to action. Cyber jihad has mastered the art of using all these and continues to recruit educated people with technological skills through the internet, thus expanding their abilities to use the internet for their cause.

Cyber jihad can be credited for its role in numerous terrorist attacks to date, just some of which include or are suspected to include:

- Corey Johnson, who was 17 in 2018 when he stabbed three people in Florida
- The Boston Marathon bombings, 2013
- The London Bridge terrorist attack in 2017 and the radicalization of other several individuals which include:
  - Sayfullo Saipov, who killed eight people in 2017 with a truck in New York City
  - Joshua Cummings from Texas who shot and killed a transit guard in Colorado in 2017
  - Omar Mateen, who killed forty-nine people in the Orlando Pulse nightclub attack in 2016
  - Syed Rizwan Farook and Tashfeen Malik who killed fourteen in San Bernardino, California, in 2015
  - Mohammad Youssef Abdulazeez who killed five people in Tennessee in 2015
  - Alton Nolen, who in 2014, beheaded a coworker in Oklahoma
  - Ali Muhammad Brown, who killed four people in 2014 between Washington state and New Jersey
  - Emerson Begolly, whose 2010 attack was foiled but was arrested by the FBI

Cyber jihad has proven to be a very effective means to spread Islamism and jihad worldwide, particularly to the West. As Islamic terrorist groups continue to gain support of educated, tech-savvy persons who join their ranks, it stands to reason they will continue to become more sophisticated and proliferate their use of cyber jihad and enhance the cyber caliphate.

What is the *cyber caliphate*? We are familiar with the Islamic caliphate, and in recent years, the Islamic States' (ISIS) objective to conquer territories and either convert or kill non-believers. Now the cyber caliphate is this effort being taken into the fifth dimension, cyberspace. The cyber caliphate, also known as the United Cyber Caliphate (UCC), is the hacking division of the Islamic State. It can also be described as a group of hacktivists (cyber-soldiers) who use their computers and the internet (cyber-weapons) on behalf of the Islamic State. This group was founded by a British National named Junaid Hussain who was killed later during a U.S. airstrike in Iraq. Many of its members are young Muslims and sympathizers who grew up in Western countries and are very familiar with internet technologies.

Some of the exploits of the cyber caliphate include publishing violent, graphic videos of hostages being murdered, publishing a hit list including the names of almost nine thousand people that it wanted killed on the Dark Web, and videos threatening U.S. President Donald Trump and several other people [28]. The cyber caliphate uses its computer hacking skills to deface websites and post ISIS extremist propaganda. One of the earliest cyber-attacks conducted by the cyber caliphate was the hacking of the U.S. Central Command's Twitter and YouTube pages in January 2015, timing this attack with President Obama's speech on cyber-security. Their hacks have also included nearly 20,000 French websites, the attack on the Charlie Hebdo magazine, Twitter handles of prominent news publications, and hacks of U.S. news stations, and non-profit organizations. In addition to the plethora of ISIS propaganda, hacks, defacing of websites, publishing kill lists, and other threats, the cyber caliphate has also directly threatened the family of U.S. President Donald Trump.

Are all attacks which appear to be the cyber caliphate legitimate or are there imposters? As Twitter and other social media have taken a stance against a large segment of ISIS-related accounts on their forums and suspended or revoked many of these accounts, it has become more difficult to identify and track members of ISIS and the cyber caliphate who use these forums to spread propaganda and communicate objectives and calls for action. This was one tool the intelligence community could utilize to help identify and track a large number of jihadists. Since the cyber caliphate is a spread out community of like-minded ideologists with technical savvy, it is often difficult to identify the actors in these hacks and other attacks. Tracking and identifying those actors in the cyber caliphate who conduct cyber-attacks is essentially the same as other cyber-criminals.

The cyber caliphate utilizes the same methods of attack and tactics as other criminal cyber-attackers, like hacktivists, those engaged in injecting malware, denial-of-service (DoS and DDoS) attacks, and others mentioned in the cyber-attacks section of this chapter. Considering this, the cyber caliphate does not possess any new techniques or more sophisticated skills than others. As well, the cyber caliphate, surprisingly, has not accomplished more considering its time in operation and access to educated, tech-savvy supporters and members.

There is evidence that some attacks that were claimed to be conducted by the cyber caliphate, were in fact, not from the cyber caliphate at all, but from a Russian hacking group named APT28, posing as the cyber caliphate, hence, these were false-flag operations. APT28 is known for conducting cyber-attacks which benefit the Russian government. Considering how easy it is in cyberspace to pose as someone else and conceal locations and identities, each attack should be evaluated on the evidence, and evidence should be carefully scrutinized to make the distinction between actual and false-flag operations.

The cyber caliphate has demonstrated that its hacking abilities have been able to penetrate thousands of websites, including the U.S. government and social media accounts using a variety of cyber-attack methodology. At the time of this writing, there is no unclassified evidence discovered which demonstrated the cyber caliphate has the capability to launch a successful major attack on U.S. critical infrastructure, however, it can be presumed this group will continue to develop skills and resources toward that goal.

One striking similarity between the cyber caliphate in the present day and Al Qaeda in the days before the 9/11 attacks in 2001 is that our intelligence community is limited in its intelligence collection capabilities within the organization. This being said, there is a historical tendency to underestimate would-be attackers whether for political or other reasons, and governments can be complacent. Therefore, it is this author's contention that the cyber caliphate should not be underestimated, nor should it be underestimated that the cyber caliphate receives support.

There are a number of adversarial actors who would like to launch a series of major cyber-attacks against the U.S., including state and state-sponsored actors. It is foreseeable that those adversaries with a common cause could align themselves for a single purpose, to launch crippling cyber-attacks. This possibility in particular could cause an alliance between such actors as Russia, Iran, the cyber caliphate, and possibly North Korea, even China given the right circumstances. In such an alliance, it is foreseeable that the cyber caliphate would receive assistance to advance their cyber-capabilities rapidly prior to a combined-force series of cyber-attacks.

Whether operating in conjunction with other actors or by itself, the cyber caliphate, in this author's assessment, will increase its attack capabilities and attempt to launch a major, disruptive cyber-attack against the U.S. It is imperative to further develop intelligence regarding the cyber caliphate, its members and operatives, advances in technologies and capabilities, and the methods and platforms in which they may utilize and increase corroboration and cooperation between cyber-threat intelligence, cyber-security, and other members of the intelligence community and to make continual efforts toward identification, detection, and mitigation of future threats.

1.12 SUMMARY

The definitions of terrorism are as many as there are agencies that define it. There is no universally accepted definition of terrorism, as of the time of this writing, upon which international consortiums and federal agencies can agree. Thus, in this chapter the author has made little distinction between terrorism and domestic terrorism, thus, focusing the discussion on the elements that are common in the recruitment, radicalization, and development of an operational lone wolf terrorist.

Publicly available information is a broad term, but in this internet age, it encompasses a wide variety of resources which enable a terrorist candidate to self-radicalize through the internet and train at home rather than risk travel to attend a terrorist training camp. Al Qaeda and other jihadist organizations provide detailed instructions on how to conduct military-style operations which could result in mass casualties, and all very accessible and free on the internet.

Furthermore, the author showed how easy and inexpensive it is for a terrorist to use the internet to obtain what many would consider private or sensitive information that they can use as intelligence to select their target, plan and carry out any number of physical attacks. This chapter also examined several types of internet-based encrypted communications technologies which are both readily accessible, and often taken for granted, but that terrorists can use to communicate, with little the NSA and other intelligence agencies can do to intercept it.

The cyber-attack methodologies examined in this chapter are the current gamut of tools available to cyber-hackers, criminals, terrorists, and state actors which, depending on one's resources, can be employed against an adversary. There are no new cyber-threats which have emerged (yet) that enable attacks outside this technology. As technology increases at an exponential rate, it can be expected there will be new vulnerabilities in new and upcoming technologies and those seeking to do so will exploit those vulnerabilities. Thus, the cyber-threats imposed by terrorists are the same cyber- threats imposed by other actors.

Finally, the author provided an introduction to cyber jihad and the cyber caliphate, a cyber-army of hackers who support the Islamic State. These hackers have demonstrated capabilities to hack into U.S. government websites and thousands of others worldwide. Though they have not yet been successful in launching a devastating cyber-attack against the U.S. and its critical infrastructure, it can be presumed that the cyber caliphate intends to increase their cyber-capabilities and could launch such an attack at some point in time. Theoretically, it can also be presumed that the cyber caliphate may, like other adversaries, if given an opportunity, ally with other enemies of the U.S. in a joint, multi-state, and organization cyber-operation against the U.S.

REFERENCES

1. A Group Calling. (2018). 'Cyber Caliphate' hacks Malaysia Airlines website. Retrieved December 06, 2018, from https://www.usatoday.com/story/tech/2015/01/25/malaysia-airlines-hack/22332867/
2. Ablon, L. (2018). Data thieves: The motivations of cyber threat actors and their use and monetization of stolen data. *Rand.org*. Retrieved October 10, 2018, from https://www.rand.org/content/dam/rand/pubs/testimonies/CT400/CT490/RAND_CT490.pdf
3. BBC News UK. (2002). Pro-Jihad Website Draws Readers. *news.bbc.co.uk*. Accessed December 15, 2018. http://news.bbc.co.uk/2/hi/uk_news/1823045.stm
4. British Isis Fighter. (2018). ISIS 'cyber caliphate' takes over 54k Twitter accounts to spread propaganda. *Daily Mail Online*. Retrieved December 06, 2018, from https://www.dailymail.co.uk/news/article-3308734/ISIS-cyber-caliphate-takes-54-000-Twitter-accounts-Terrorists-hack-social-media-site-spread-vile-propaganda.html
5. Caballero, A., Gévaudan, C., Hirschmann, T., Huang, S., Lamont, I., Lowth, M., Mahabhaleshwar, M., Rounsavall, R., Shvartz, A., and Souza, J. (2014). *Open Data Center Alliance Usage Model: Provider Assurance Rev. 3.0*. Open Data Center Alliance, Inc., Beaverton, OR, pp. 6–15. http://www.opendatacenterallliance.org/accelerating-adoption/usage-models
6. Chris Smith. (2018). ISIS is assembling a cyber army. *BGR*. Retrieved December 06, 2018, from https://bgr.com/2016/04/28/isis-united-cyber-caliphate-hackers/
7. Deep Web Sites. (2016). How Big Is the Deep Web? A Complete Guide about the Deep Web. Available from https://www.deepweb-sites.com/how-big-is-the-deep-web/2/. December 6, 2018.
8. Department of Defense. (2018). Terrorism definition. Retrieved from http://www.dtic.mil/doctrine/dod_dictionary
9. Digital Strategy Consulting. (2018). The internet's secret: Does the 'Dark Net' have any benefits? - Digital Intelligence daily digital marketing research. Retrieved December 06, 2018, from http://www.digitalstrategyconsulting.com/intelligence/2016/03/the_internets_secret_does_the_dark_net_have_any_benefits.php
10. Force. (2018). British jihadist orchestrated cyber attacks on the US government for & # 39; revenge & # 39; on Western society. Retrieved December 6, 2018, from https://whatsnew2day.com/british-jihadist-orchestrated-cyber-attacks-on-the-us-government-for-39-revenge-39-on-western-society/
11. Gardner, F. (2018). How do terrorists communicate? *BBC News*. Retrieved December 15, 2018, from https://www.bbc.com/news/world-24784756
12. Happiest Minds. (2018). *Cyber Threat Intelligence*. Happiest Minds. Retrieved 13 August 2018, from https://www.happiestminds.com/Insights/cyber-threat-intelligence/
13. Deepwebadmin. (2016). How Big Is the Deep Web? A Complete Guide about the Deep Web. December 06, 2018. Web. December 06, 2018. https://www.deepweb-sites.com/how-big-is-the-deep-web/2/

14. Al Qaeda. (2010). *Inspire*, Vol. 1. Azelin.Files.Wordpress.Com. Accessed December 11, 2018. https://az elin.files.wordpress.com/2010/06/aqap-inspire-magazine-volume-1-uncorrupted.pdf

15. Miguel, L. (2017). "Antifa deletes posts about sabotaging train tracks—after Washington train derailment." *Conservative News Today*. Retrieved May 10, 2019, from https://www.bizpacreview.com/2017/1 2/19/antifa-deletes-posts-sabotaging-train-tracks-washington-train-derailment-577612.

16. Intel® Cloud Builders Guide. (2013). Integrating Intel® IPT with OPT and Symantec* VIP for Dynamically Assigning Permissions to Cloud Resources, pp. 4–21. http://trapezoid.com/images/pd f/Intel_Cloud_Builders_Intel_IPT_2013.pdf

17. Joint Publication 3-12. (2018). Cyberspace Operations. *Jcs.mil*. Retrieved October 8, 2018, from http:// www.jcs.mil/Portals/36/Documents/Doctrine/pubs/jp3_12.pdf?ver=2018-07-16-134954-150

18. Kaplan, E. (2009). *Terrorists and the Internet*. Council on Foreign Relations. Retrieved December 15, 2018, from https://www.cfr.org/backgrounder/terrorists-and-internet

19. Lister, T. (2015). ISIS: What does it really want? *CNN*. Retrieved November 10, 2017, from http://edi tion.cnn.com/2015/12/11/middleeast/isis-syria-iraq-caliphate/index.html

20. Loeffler, B. (Publisher) and Dial, J. (Last Revision). (2013). *Private Cloud Security Operations Principles*. MicrosoftTechnet Article, Microsoft Corp. http://social.technet.microsoft.com/wiki/contents/artic les/6658.private-cloud-security-operations-principles.aspx

21. Lohrmann, D. (2015). Cyber Terrorism: How dangerous is the ISIS cyber Caliphate threat? *Government Technology*. Retrieved from http://www.govtech.com/blogs/lohrmann-on-cybersecurity/Cyber-Terr orism-How-Dangerous-is-the-ISIS-Cyber-Caliphate-Threat.html

22. Mastroianni, B. (2015). How terrorists could use video games to communicate undetected. *CBS News*. Retrieved December 15, 2018, from https://www.cbsnews.com/news/how-terrorists-could-use-v ideo-games-to-communicate-undetected/

23. McAfee. (2011). 7 Types of Hacker Motivations. *McAfee Blogs*. Retrieved October 14, 2018, from https ://securingtomorrow.mcafee.com/consumer/family-safety/7-types-of-hacker-motivations/

24. McDonald, L. (2018). British Jihadist orchestrated cyber attacks on US Government for 'revenge' on Western Society. *Daily Mail Online*. Retrieved December 06, 2018, from https://www.dailymail.co. uk/news/article-6416047/British-Jihadist-orchestrated-cyber-attacks-Government-revenge-Wes tern-Society.html

25. Morgan Chalfant. (2018). GOP chairman warns of ISIS's "cyber caliphate." *The Hill*. Retrieved December 06, 2018, from https://thehill.com/policy/cybersecurity/363554-gop-chair-warns-of-islamic-states-cyber-caliphate

26. Mukaram, A. (2014). *Cyber Threat Landscape: Basic Overview and Attack Methods*. Recorded Future. Retrieved November 9, 2017, from https://www.recordedfuture.com/cyber-threat-landscape-basics

27. Nast, C. (2013). Inspire, Al Qaeda's Magazine For Terrorists. GQ. Accessed December 15, 2018. https:// www.gq.com/story/inspire-magazine-al-qaeda-boston-bombing?verso=true

28. Open Data Center Alliance, Inc. (2011–2012). *Open Data Center Alliance Usage Model: Security Monitoring Rev. 1.1*. Open Data Center Alliance, Inc., Beaverton, OR, pp. 1–8. http://www.opendatac enteralliance.org/docs/Security_Monitoring_Rev%201.1_b.pdf

29. Paganini, P. (2017). 10 Biggest Cyber Espionage Cases. *Security Affairs*. Retrieved October 14, 2018, from https://securityaffairs.co/wordpress/66617/hacking/cyber-espionage-cases.html

30. Pescatore, J. (2013). *Ask the Expert Webcast: The Critical Security Controls*. SANS, Bethesda, MD, slide 7. http://www.slideshare.net/Lancope/lancope-webcast-022014-cs-cs-lancope

31. Rapid 7. (2018). Common Types of Cybersecurity Attacks and Hacking Techniques. Rapid7. *Rapid7. com*. Retrieved October 10, 2018, from https://www.rapid7.com/fundamentals/types-of-attacks/

32. Recorded Future Solutions. (2014). *Observing the Ebb and Flow of Cross-Platform Malware*. Recorded Future. Retrieved November 10, 2017, from https://www.recordedfuture.com/ebb-and-flow-of-cro ss-platform-malware/

33. Rossi, B. (2015). Understanding cybercriminals: motives and tactics of the modern day attacker. *Information Age*. Retrieved October 10, 2018, from https://www.information-age.com/understanding -cybercriminals-motives-and-tactics-modern-day-attacker-123459402/

34. Schindler, J.R. (2018). False Flags: The Kremlin's Hidden Cyber Hand. *Observer*. Retrieved December 06, 2018, from https://observer.com/2016/06/false-flags-the-kremlins-hidden-cyber-hand/

35. Search Engines Such. (2018). How Terrorists Communicate – Dark Web. *Retirely.* Retrieved December 15, 2018, from https://www.retire.ly/how-terrorists-communicate-dark-web/

36. Shekhar, A. (2017). Top 10 Common Hacking Techniques You Should Know About. *Fossbytes.* Retrieved October 11, 2018, from https://fossbytes.com/hacking-techniques/

37. The National Science Foundation. (2018). Scientists Use the "Dark Web" to Snag Extremists and Terrorists Online. NSF - National Science Foundation. Retrieved December 06, 2018, from https://www.nsf.gov/news/news_summ.jsp?cntn_id=110040

38. Trend Micro. (2015). Understanding Targeted Attacks: Goals and Motives - Security News - Trend Micro USA. *Trendmicro.com.* Retrieved October 14, 2018, from https://www.trendmicro.com/vinfo/us/security/news/cyber-attacks/understanding-targeted-attacks-goals-and-motives

Chapter 2

Online Radicalization
Contested Terms and Conceptual Clarity

Stuart Macdonald and Joe Whittaker

CONTENTS

2.1 INTRODUCTION

Online radicalization is widely regarded as one of today's most pressing security challenges. Its importance has been emphasized by core European institutions including the Council of Europe [1], the European Commission [2], EUROPOL [3], and the Organization for Security and Co-Operation in Europe [4]. These warnings have been echoed by other international governmental organizations—UN's *Plan of Action to Prevent Violent Extremism*, for example, states that the "manipulative messages of violent extremists on social media have achieved considerable success in luring people, especially young women and men, into their ranks" [5]—and by national governments. The UK's Home Affairs Committee has described the use of the internet to promote radicalization and terrorism as "one of the greatest threats that countries including the UK face" [6], while the 2015 White House Summit underscored the need to intensify efforts to counter recruitment and radicalization to terrorist violence.

Against this backdrop, it is unsurprising that there is a burgeoning literature on online radicalization. Within this literature, use of the terms "radicalization," "self-radicalization," "online radicalization," and "echo chamber" is common. Also common is the tendency for those who use these terms to assume that their meanings are self-evident. In this chapter we seek to show that this is not in fact the case. The terms can be, and indeed are, understood in different ways. The tendency to assume that there is a shared understanding of what these contested terms mean, we argue, results in a lack of conceptual clarity.

The chapter begins by explaining why conceptual clarity is important. It then examines in turn the terms "radicalization," "self-radicalization," "online radicalization," and "echo chamber," detailing the different ways in which they are used and explaining the problems to which this definitional uncertainty gives rise. Drawing on this discussion, the chapter concludes by suggesting some directions for future research that will advance understanding of the role the internet plays in contemporary violent extremism.

2.2 THE IMPORTANCE OF CONCEPTUAL CLARITY

In our opinion, there are at least three reasons why conceptual clarity is important. The first reason is the robustness of the research. Suppose that a concept is capable of being understood in three ways: X, Y, and Z. If the researcher fails to consider these different understandings and select the one that will be deployed, this could result in internal inconsistency and incoherence. An example would be a policy analysis that analyses the problem situation through the lens of understanding X, articulates analysis criteria that are premised on understanding Y, and generates alternative strategies that speak to understanding Z. The same point would apply to empirical research. Many concepts are not readily measurable: "Some are complex, not definable in a simple way, mean different things to different people and do not have definite boundaries" [7]. Abstract concepts must therefore be operationalized by the construction of observable and measurable variables. It is essential that the variables validly represent the abstract concept. Flitting between different understandings of the abstract concept could result in some variables representing understanding X, other representing understanding Y, and still others representing understanding Z. The result will be a flawed measurement of the abstract concept. More generally, a failure to articulate which understanding is being deployed will mean that it is impossible for others to assess whether the variables validly represent the abstract concept or not. Similarly, before sampling a researcher must first define the population to be sampled specifically and unambiguously. If the ambit of the population is unclear, then it will not be possible to determine whether the sample the researcher took was representative and whether the findings are generalizable [8].

The second reason is that a lack of conceptual clarity impedes research reviews and meta-analyses. The former provide "a synthesis of existing knowledge on a specific question, based on an assessment of all relevant empirical research that can be found" [9], while the latter provide "an *integrated* and *quantified* summary of research results on a specific question with particular reference to statistical significance and effect size" [10]. In both cases, the basic premise "is that a series of studies address an identical conceptual hypothesis" [11]. If it is not clear whether the studies on a certain topic adopted understanding X, understanding Y, or understanding Z, synthesizing the results from the different studies may not be possible.

Leading on from this, the third reason is that conceptual clarity aids the effective and accurate communication of research to others, including other researchers, policy-makers, the media, and interested publics. A failure to articulate the sense in which one is using a contested term can result in a discussion in which participants are speaking at cross-purposes. For example, the researcher's message to policy-makers that there is an urgent need for reform might be premised on understanding X, but if this is not made clear then what the policy-maker takes from the research might be that there is an urgent need to deal with the problem in the sense of understanding Z.

2.3 RADICALIZATION

Definitions of terrorism commonly include a requirement that the actor had a political or ideological motive [12]. As a result, it is often assumed that terrorist actors first develop "radical" beliefs, which subsequently drive their violent behavior. The word radicalization is used to describe this process. However, there are a number of difficulties with the term [13–18], two of which are particularly relevant for present purposes.

The first difficulty is that if radicalization denotes a process, it is unclear exactly what is (or should be) regarded as the end result of this process. Three answers are possible. Semantically, the first most obvious answer is that the radicalization process results in the person becoming a "radical." But, while this is how some construe the term [18–21], the second and third understandings are more common. The second of these is that the radicalization process results in the person possessing "extremist" beliefs [22, 23], while the third most popular understanding is that the culmination of the radicalization process is engaging in acts of terrorism or other terrorism-related activity (picking up extremist beliefs along the way) [24–29].

While the terms "radical," "extremist," and "terrorist" are each contested, the essence of the terms differ. A radical is one who rejects the status quo and believes that there should be sweeping change [18, 19], while an extremist holds views that are not only on the margins of society but also foster hate toward an out-group or out-groups [18, 22, 30]. Meanwhile, a terrorist engages in acts of violence, for political or ideological reasons, with the intention to intimidate or coerce civilians and/or national governments or international governmental organizations [31, 32]. In spite of these differences, the word radicalization is frequently used without any answer being offered to the "radicalization to what?" question. This leads to the terms "radical," "extremist," and "terrorist" being conflated: a tendency that is no doubt encouraged by the lack of an appropriate "ization" suffix for the words extremism and terrorism (there is no "extremization" and "terrorization" does not denote the process of becoming a terrorist).

The second difficulty inherent in the term relates to the understanding of radicalization that takes terrorism to be the end result of the process. Explicitly or implicitly, this understanding of the term often assumes both the adoption of extremist beliefs and the causative role of these beliefs in the actor's decision to engage in terrorist activity. While it is clear that not all extremists are terrorists—this, after all, is a premise on which much countering violent extremism work is based—what is less understood is the fact that not all terrorists can be described as extremists [16]. As Schuurman and Taylor explain, "terrorism is a tactic; a particular way of using deadly force that can stem from extremist beliefs just as much as it can be adopted for reasons of expediency" [33]. Admittedly, beliefs will often be important, but the notion that an extremist ideology is a *necessary* precondition for terrorist activity does not withstand empirical scrutiny [33–35]. As such, an understanding of "radicalization" that paints extremist beliefs as playing a causative role in every choice to engage in terrorist activity is inherently problematic. A more promising approach is to instead study *how* beliefs affect actors' decisions to take part in terrorist activity, in order to understand the "nature and dynamics of extremist belief systems and their relationship with other factors and influences" [36].

2.4 SELF-RADICALIZATION

In this section and the one that follows we turn our attention to two descendants of the term radicalization: self-radicalization and online radicalization. In addition to the problems they inherit from their parent term, these concepts suffer from additional difficulties of their own. These difficulties are compounded by the fact that most of the (academic) literature that uses these terms treats their meanings as self-evident. In the process of writing this chapter, we conducted a targeted literature search. The results of this search were reviewed, and a snowballing methodology was employed to identify further items of relevance. After compiling all of the items discovered into a database, we then filtered out those that did not contain any of the terms: "online radicalization," "online radicalisation," "self-radicalization," or "self-radicalisation." The remaining items were reviewed and filtered out if neither online radicalization nor self-radicalization was a principal focus of the piece. PhD theses were retained if they met our criteria, but Master's level theses were not. We were left with 43 items that mentioned and had as their principal focus online radicalization, and 13 for self-radicalization.[1] We then examined these pieces to determine how many explicitly provided a definition of the relevant term. We found that just nine (21 percent) contained an explicit definition of online radicalization, while the total for self-radicalization was four (31 percent). In this section we focus on the latter term, before turning to the former in the section that follows.

In spite of the lack of an explicit definition in most pieces, it was nonetheless possible to make some inferences about commentators' understandings of the relevant concept. This revealed some significant differences. For example, the term self-radicalization was understood by many to mean that there had been no interaction with or involvement of others during the individual's radicalization. This conception was made explicit by von Behr et al., who stated that the term self-radicalization "implies a process whereby no contact is made with other terrorists or extremists, whether in person or virtually" [37]. Yet others seemed to adopt a looser conception which allows for some interaction with others.

The Institute for Strategic Dialogue (ISD), for example, stated that "the Internet allows individuals to 'self-radicalize' without input or encouragement from individuals in an off-line setting (so-called 'lone wolves')" [38]. On its face, this definition only excludes offline interactions with others and so appears to envisage online interactions as being consistent with an individual self-radicalizing. Similarly, Picart speaks of a "lone wolf" terrorist self-radicalizing through some "sympathetic connection with an organized terrorist network," adding that "interaction through the internet allows a self-radicalizing terrorist to move into the stage of radical violent action" [39].

These different understandings of how self-radicalization should be construed can result in significant classificatory differences. Take the case of Shannon Maureen Conley as an example. Conley was aged 19 and living in Colorado when she planned to travel to Syria, via Turkey, and there marry a fighter from the so-called Islamic State (IS) whom she had met online [40]. Conley was a trained nurse and planned to provide medical services and training within an IS camp. She aroused suspicion when she went to a church with a notepad and asked strange questions. When questioned by the FBI she displayed a number of worrying indicators, including referring to military bases as "targets" and seeking to justify "defensive jihad" when Islam is under attack. According to the definition offered by von Behr et al., Conley's case would not be an instance of self-radicalization because of her online interactions (including Skype conversations) with her suitor. But according to the ISD and Picart, Conley was self-radicalized because there was no input or encouragement from individuals in an offline setting; her only interactions were via the internet.

The previous extracts from the ISD and Picart both describe those who self-radicalize as lone wolves. This is also problematic, both conceptually and empirically. A lone wolf is "a person who acts on his or her own without orders from—or even connections to—an organization" [41]. So, while the term self-radicalization is commonly used to refer to the process by which someone forms extremist beliefs and/or reaches the point of willingness to engage in terrorist activity, the term lone wolf refers to those who have engaged in some terrorist activity. Conceptually, there is no necessary connection between an individual self-radicalizing and an individual engaging in terrorist activity as a lone wolf. A self-radicalized individual may well choose, post-radicalization, to join a group or network of like-minded individuals. Here the internet offers opportunities for individuals to seek out like-minded others and experience a sense of community, thereby solidifying their extremist views [41]. Conversely, individuals that were not self-radicalized, i.e. those who were radicalized through interaction with others, may choose to act as lone wolves and engage in terrorist activity alone [42]. Indeed, one study found that 62 percent of the lone actors examined had had prior contact with clearly radical, extremist or terrorist individuals [43]. Empirically, the vast majority of commentators agree that radicalization rarely occurs without interaction with other people [44–46]. Radicalization is a "social process" [47]. Yet, the proportion of terrorist attacks that are perpetrated by lone wolves is not similarly low [48]. The assumed connection between self-radicalization and acting as a lone wolf is thus not only conceptually unsustainable, it also obscures the former's relative infrequency.

2.5 ONLINE RADICALIZATION

According to the von Behr et al. understanding of self-radicalization—in which there is no interaction with, or involvement of, others during the individual's radicalization—there is nothing inherent in the term that is specific to the online domain. In other words, in theory at least, an individual might self-radicalize through the consumption of online materials, offline materials or a combination of the two. In this sense, the possibility of an individual self-radicalizing is at least as old as the printing press [20]. In contrast, the term online radicalization is domain specific. It is limited to radicalization through online activities only.

A striking feature of the term online radicalization is the variety of behaviors to which it is used to refer:

> A wide-range of virtual behaviors is subsumed into the category of online radicalization. A simple search of news articles from March 2015 shows that a range of behaviors from accessing information on overseas events via the Internet, to accessing extremist content and propaganda, to detailing attack plans in a blog post, have all been considered as online radicalization [49].

To a large extent, this reflects one of the difficulties outlined above pertaining to the term radicalization: it is used to denote both a cognitive process (the formation of extremist beliefs) and a cognitive plus behavioral process (the formation of extremist beliefs that manifest themselves in the individual engaging in terrorist activity). While the detailing of attack plans might be consistent with the latter use of the term, it is difficult to reconcile with an understanding of radicalization as solely a cognitive process: the fact that the person has created an attack plan suggests that they had already formed extremist beliefs.

There are several studies that focus on the online milieu which construe the radicalization process as an exclusively cognitive process, i.e. as culminating in the formation of extremist beliefs. For example, in their study of a YouTube group Bermingham et al. define online radicalization as the process by which someone comes to view violence as a legitimate method of solving social and political conflicts [44]. In Torok's conceptual framework for online radicalization, she too understands the term to mean the development of extreme beliefs which can lead to terrorism [50], while Huey's research into online "memes" does not define the term online radicalization specifically but does implicitly suggest that it means the development of support for a terrorist group (in this case, IS) [51]. Similarly, Neumann describes online radicalization as the learning and normalization of beliefs in virtual communities which allows mobilization to violence to become possible [17]. All four of these studies thus refer to the possibility of, or support for, violence, but none regards engaging in terrorist activity as a necessary condition for an individual to have been radicalized.

The study by von Behr et al. does not explicitly address the question of whether radicalization is an exclusively cognitive process or a cognitive and behavioral process [46]. The findings of the study are drawn from a total of 15 in-depth case studies: ten of these focused on individuals that had engaged in terrorist activity, while the other five focused on participants from the Channel Programme (a part of the UK's Prevent Strategy, which aims to dissuade those who have developed, or are in the process of developing, extreme beliefs). By not differentiating between these two groups of case studies the researchers assumed that all 15 individuals had radicalized, even though only ten had engaged in terrorist activity. They therefore implicitly affirmed the solely cognitive understanding of radicalization. Meanwhile Holt et al.'s research into victim and jihad videos does distinguish carefully between radicalization of opinion and radicalization to action, and focuses on the latter. However, their statement that they chose to "focus on extremist content related to radicalization to violent action" [52] strongly suggests that they assumed a causal relationship in which radicalization of opinion is a prerequisite for radicalization to action. Other studies have adopted a more nuanced approach, seeking to assess how those who have been cognitively "radicalized" go on to develop violent behaviors. For example, Koehler's interview-based research with neo-Nazis sought to analyse the significance of the internet in transmitting extremist beliefs into political activism (including violence) [53]. Similarly, Saifudeen's conceptual model describes how the formation of extremist beliefs online can lead to violent conduct offline [54]. The value of these studies lies in their interrogation of the role that extremist beliefs play in an individual's decision to engage in terrorist activity, without assuming that such beliefs are a necessary prerequisite for, or play a causative role in, an individual's decision to engage in such conduct.

Beyond the divergent views as to the end result of the radicalization process, perhaps the most problematic feature of the term online radicalization is its sharp division between the online and offline realms. A number of commentators contrast online interactions with ones in the "real world" (see, e.g. [41, 45, 51, 54]). As Conway explains, this privileging of real-world activity understates the social aspect of social media:

> Today's Internet does not simply allow for the dissemination and consumption of "extremist material" in a one-way broadcast from producer to consumer, but also high levels of online social interaction around this material. It is precisely the functionalities of the social Web that causes many scholars, policymakers, and others to believe that the Internet is playing a significant role in contemporary radicalization processes [55].

The case of Zacharia Yusuf Abdurahman provides a useful example [56]. He was a member of an offline network of Somalis from the metropolitan area of Minneapolis who was charged (along with five of his peers) with attempting to travel to Syria in April 2015. The group members were alleged to have radicalized at informal gatherings, such as playing basketball together. However, their inspiration was Abdinur Mohamed Mohamud—one of the first to travel from the U.S. to Syria in May 2014—who relayed propaganda, encouragement and operational advice back to the group via

Twitter, Ask.FM and other sites. So, whilst the case involved a strong, offline social network, at the same time the group's activities were facilitated by—and, arguably, dependent upon—the internet.

Whilst it is important not to underestimate the influence of the online realm, it is also important not to commit the opposite error and overstate the significance of the role that the internet plays in the radicalization process. To date, there have been very few empirically grounded studies. What studies there are have found that whilst the internet creates more opportunities to become radicalized, is a key source of information, communication and propaganda and facilitates the process of radicalization, it is not a substitute for offline communication and networks, but rather facilitates in-person communication, creating more opportunities to become radicalized [46, 57, 58]. So, the process of radicalization commonly straddles the offline and online realms. Interactions in both domains frequently go hand-in-hand and there is no stark offline-online dichotomy. Gill et al. accordingly argue that instead of disaggregating the radicalization process into discrete groups (online radicalization, prison radicalization etc.), it may instead be more useful to disaggregate the concept of a "terrorist" into discrete groups (e.g. group actors versus lone actors) [58]. This would shift the focus to why the offender chose the particular environment, rather than purely looking at the affordances the environment produced.

2.6 ECHO CHAMBER

The term "echo chamber" refers to a setting in which an individual engages with like-minded others and where opinions are amplified and reinforced, thus increasing polarization. In the current context, the term's use has three difficulties. The first of these stems from the fact that the term can be used to describe two different phenomena. The first is the manifestation of confirmation bias, which when aggregated in a group of people may take the form of "group think" [59] or "group polarization" [60]. It is well established that people tend to seek viewpoints that agree, rather than conflict, with their own, and many scholars have argued that this can result in a number of undesirable effects, such as poor judgement or the normalization of the most extreme views within communities. In terms of radicalization, this can lead to the demonization of the "other" to the point where violence is regarded as acceptable, or even obligatory [61].

The second phenomenon is more contemporary and refers to the personalization of internet technologies, described by Eli Pariser as the "filter bubble" [62]. Rather than the long-established self-sorting of confirmation bias, which can occur both online or offline, the filter bubble has only existed since around 2009 when Google and Facebook began to utilize users' internet "cookies" for a more personal experience. This works by sorting posts via algorithms that factor in a number of different values, including friend relationships, explicit user interests and prior user engagement [63]. Although this topic is rarely empirically analyzed within terrorism studies literature, an argument could be made that if a user views violent extremist content online, the filter bubble could be responsible for artificially putting a greater amount of such content in users' feeds.[2] This would exacerbate the effect of the first phenomenon, creating a vicious cycle in which dissenting voices are minimized and extreme ones normalized.

In spite of the differences between these two phenomena, the term "echo chamber" is frequently used without any definition being offered, leaving it unclear which of the two phenomena is being referred to [64–69]. Even when a definition is provided, which of the two phenomena is being considered may still remain unclear [38, 41, 46].

The second difficulty with the term echo chamber is that there has been a tendency to simply assume, in the absence of supporting empirical data, that the echo chamber phenomena contribute to online radicalization [67–69]. For example, in his book *Understanding Terror Networks* Sageman argued that "the interactivity between a 'bunch of guys' acted as an echo chamber, which progressively radicalized them collectively to the point where they were ready to join a terrorist organization" [70]. In his later book *Leaderless Jihad*, Sageman suggested that this effect also occurs online, with online fora displacing radical mosques as the breeding grounds for terrorists, claiming that their interactivity is key to radicalization [71]. In particular, he argued first, that on the internet success is celebrated and copied, while failure is more easily forgotten, giving the impression that the movement is more effective than it really is, and second, that moderate members of the movement have an easier exit route if they are dissatisfied (by simply not logging on), leaving the more radical members to rule the roost [72]. Despite these seemingly intuitive arguments, Sageman offered no empirical evidence of these effects in action.

The previously mentioned study by von Behr et al.—which was empirically grounded—also discussed the role of echo chambers. The evidence from their case studies supported the hypothesis that the internet acts as an echo chamber: the actors in their sample did tend to engage online to confirm, rather than challenge, their existing beliefs. However, this was subject to an important caveat: "this finding may be due to the fact that the information recovered related to a late stage of the individual's radicalization" [73]. In other words, it was likely that the actors already held extreme beliefs prior to the data being collected. This leads to a problem of underdetermination; it is not clear whether the online "echo chamber" actually contributed to the process of radicalization, or, rather, if being radicalized caused the actors to engage in echo chambers.

The study by Wojcieszak surveyed a number of online actors that held extreme beliefs on two online fora (one environmentalist and one neo-Nazi) to assess whether participants demonstrated false consensus, i.e. they believed that their cause was more popular than was actually the case. She found evidence of false consensus on both fora and, importantly, that for the neo-Nazi forum time spent online was significantly correlated with false consensus, even after controlling for a number of factors: "engagement in ideologically homogeneous online groups substantially exacerbates the tendency among the analysed neo-Nazis to project their attitudes onto others" [74]. This study thus offers some empirical support for Sageman's claim that online a group may appear to be more successful than it actually is. However, on the environmentalist forum, online participation did not account for the false consensus, therefore this effect cannot simply be assumed to always exist.

The lack of empirically grounded research into the echo chamber phenomena has been highlighted by O'Hara and Stevens. They point out that what empirical data does exist is methodologically limited, relying on surveys or other kinds of self-reporting (e.g. the Wojcieszak study) on often small or otherwise unsatisfactory samples (e.g. the von Behr et al. study) [75]. These methodological concerns lead us to the final of the three problems with the term echo chamber, which is a combination of the previous two: empirical studies have failed to (at least attempt to) disaggregate the impact of the two discrete "echo chamber" phenomena. This failing is not unique to terrorism research. Outside the field of terrorism studies there is a sizable amount of research that focuses on how users tend to group together [76], how this affects their sentiment [77, 78] and whether some users are more susceptible to this than others [79]. However, none of this research managed to ascertain the roles of individual users as opposed to the personalization effects of the platform they were using and, as a result, conclusions could not be drawn as to which was primarily responsible for any echo chamber effect.

There are, however, two promising pieces of empirical research that do isolate these variables, one within the field of terrorism studies and one outside. The first, conducted by O'Callaghan et al. analyzed extreme right-wing videos on YouTube and the "recommendations" that are offered to users (based on their cookies). It found that the recommendations "can result in users being excluded from information that is not aligned with their existing perspective, potentially leading to immersion within an extremist ideological bubble" [80]. It should be pointed out, however, that the study focused on what potentially radicalizing users *could* view online, rather than how users actually *do* interact with personalized suggestions. It is therefore no more than a promising start for research into the filter bubble effect in the context of radicalization. The second piece of research, commissioned by Facebook, separated and compared the two phenomena in a different context. Its findings suggested that users' own choices play a larger role than personalization technology [81]. Whether this same finding would emerge in the context of extremist content remains to be seen. In the meantime, researchers should be careful to pass this epistemological uncertainty along when discussing echo chambers in their work, so as not to ascribe to the echo chamber phenomena a causal role in the radicalization process that has not yet been established.

2.7 SUMMARY

Radicalization, self-radicalization, online radicalization, and echo chambers are contested terms. In this chapter we have shown that each is capable of being understood, and is in fact used, in different ways. Radicalization may refer to either a solely cognitive process —resulting in the formation of either radical or extremist beliefs—or a cognitive and behavioral process. These different understandings of the term radicalization result in different understandings of the behaviors that fall within the ambit of the term online radicalization. Meanwhile, self-radicalization is used by some to denote that there was no interaction with others in an offline setting, while others use it to denote that there was no interaction with others at all. And, finally, the term echo chamber can be used to refer to either the self-sorting of individual users or the personalization effects of the platform they are using.

In spite of the different possible understandings of each of these terms, more often than not researchers fail to state the sense in which they are using them. This is illustrated by the fact that, in our literature search, only one in five of the research items with a principal focus on online radicalization provided an explicit definition of the term. This lack of conceptual clarity has a number of detrimental consequences. First, it can detract from the robustness of the research. For example, previous empirical studies of the echo chamber effect have failed to distinguish between the role of individual users (confirmation bias) and the personalization effects of the platform they were using (filter bubble), meaning that conclusions could not be drawn as to which of these phenomena was primarily responsible for any echo chamber effect. Second, it can hamper the construction of research reviews and meta-analyses. Synthesizing the findings of different research items within a field requires that the understanding of key concepts is made clear. This is especially important when the different understandings of a term like self-radicalization can lead to widely diverging classifications of individual cases, such as that of Shannon Maureen Conley. Third, it has an obfuscatory effect on communication of the research to others. For example, use of the term online radicalization perpetuates a sharp distinction between the offline and online realms even though this distinction is problematic and appears to be unsustainable. Similarly, we saw above that using the term radicalization in a way that paints extremist beliefs as playing a causative role in every choice to engage in terrorist activity is at odds with the findings of empirical research. Using the term in this way thus not only exaggerates the role of ideology, it also downplays the role of other factors that in some cases may have had a more significant influence.

At this point, one might wonder exactly what can be done to resolve the issues we have raised in this chapter. To seek to impose on researchers homogenized language is, of course, unrealistic and undesirable, while a call to researchers to define the terms they use more clearly and explicitly may sound somewhat trite. Instead, we conclude by highlighting the beginnings of a promising research agenda that has emerged in the course of our discussion. This agenda seeks to: understand how ideological beliefs affect actors' decisions to engage in terrorist activity, alongside other factors and influences; disaggregate the concept of a "terrorist" (as opposed to the concept of "radicalization"), in order to shift the focus to the actors' reasons for choosing a particular environment for specific behaviors and empirically assess the relative influence of confirmation bias and filter bubbles within violent extremist echo chambers. Importantly, this agenda not only moves away from the befuddling batch of buzzwords we have discussed in this chapter, it also promises a deeper understanding of the role that the internet plays in contemporary violent extremism.

NOTES

1. Some items were deemed to have both online radicalization and self-radicalization as a principal focus.
2. Recently, it has been suggested that Facebook's "Suggested Friends" algorithm is responsible for introducing contact between extremists online [82]. Also, it was reported in 2013 that Twitter's account suggestion algorithm was having the effect of connecting individuals at risk of radicalization with extremist propagandists [83].

REFERENCES

1. Council of Europe. Revised EU Strategy for Combating Radicalisation and Recruitment to Terrorism. 9956/14. 2014. http://data.consilium.europa.eu/doc/document/ST-9956-2014-INIT/en/pdf.
2. European Commission. The European Agenda on Security. Com. 185. 2015. https://ec.europa.eu/anti-trafficking/sites/antitrafficking/files/eu_agenda_on_security_en.pdf.
3. EUROPOL. European Union Terrorism Situation and Trend Report 2016. 2016. https://www.europol.europa.eu/activities-services/main-reports/european-union-terrorism-situation-and-trend-report-te-sat-2016.
4. Organization for Security and Co-operation in Europe. *Preventing Terrorism and Countering Violent Extremism and Radicalization that Lead to Terrorism: A Community Policing Approach*. Organization for Security and Co-operation in Europe. 2013. https://www.osce.org/atu/111438
5. United Nations. Plan of Action to Prevent Violent Extremism: Report of the Secretary General. A/70/674. 24 December 2015. p. 19.
6. Home Affairs Select Committee. Radicalisation: The Counter Narrative and Identifying the Tipping Point (8th Report of 2016-17). HC 135. 2017. p. 2.
7. Gary D. Bouma. *The Research Process*. 4th Edition. Melbourne: Oxford University Press. 2000. p. 39.
8. Robert B. Burns. *Introduction to Research Methods*. 4th Edition. London: Sage. 2000.
9. Catherine Hakim. *Research Design: Strategies and Choices in the Design of Social Research*. London: Unwin Hyman. 1987. p. 17.
10. Catherine Hakim. *Research Design: Strategies and Choices in the Design of Social Research*. London: Unwin Hyman. 1987. p. 19. Emphasis original.
11. Harris Cooper. *Research Sythesis and Meta-Analysis*. 4th Edition. Thousand Oaks, CA: Sage. 2010. p. 150.
12. Lord Alex Carlile. *The Definition of Terrorism*. Cm 7052. London: The Stationery Office. 2007.

13. Jonathan Githens-Mazer. The Rhetoric and Reality: Radicalization and Political Discourse. *International Policial Science Review* Vol. 33. 2012. pp. 556–567.

14. Charlotte Heath-Kelly, Christopher Baker-Beall and Lee Jarvis. Introduction. In: *Counter Radicalisation: Critical Perspectives*. Editors: Christopher Baker-Beall, Charlotte Heath-Kelly and Lee Jarvis. Abingdon: Routledge. 2015. pp. 1–12.

15. Arun Kundnani. Radicalisation: The Journey of a Concept. In: *Counter Radicalisation: Critical Perspectives*. Editors: Christopher Baker-Beall, Charlotte Heath-Kelly and Lee Jarvis. Abingdon: Routledge. 2015. pp. 14–35.

16. Randy Borum. Rethinking Radicalization. *Journal of Strategic Security* Vol. 4(4). 2011. pp. 1–6.

17. Peter Neumann. Options and Strategies for Countering Online Radicalization in the United States. *Studies in Conflict and Terrorism* Vol. 36(6). 2013. pp. 431–459.

18. Alex P. Schmid. *Radicalisation, De-Radicalisation, Counter-Radicalisation: A Conceptual Discussion and Literature Review*. The Hague: ICCT. 2013.

19. Jamie Bartlett and Carl Miller. The Edge of Violence: Towards Telling the Difference Between Violent and Non-Violent Radicalization. *Terrorism and Political Violence* Vol. 24(1). 2012. pp. 1–21.

20. Randy Borum. Radicalization into Violent Extremism I: A Review of Social Science Theories. *Journal of Strategic Security* Vol. 4(4). 2011. pp. 7–36.

21. David Snow and Remy Cross. Radicalism within the Context of Social Movements: Processes and Types. *Journal of Strategic Security* Vol. 4(4). 2011. pp. 115–130.

22. J.M. Berger. *Extremist Construction of Identity: How Escalating Demands for Legitimacy Shape and Define In-Group and Out-Group Dynamics*. The Hauge: ICCT. 2017.

23. Shawn Matthew Powers. Conceptualizing Radicalization in a Market for Loyalties. *Media, War & Conflict* Vol. 7(2). 2014. pp. 233–349.

24. Bertjan Doosje, Fathali M. Moghaddam, Arie W. Kruglanski, Arjan De Wolf, Liesbeth Mann and Allard R. Feddes. Terrorism, Radicalization and De-Radicalization. *Current Opinion in Psychology* Vol. 11. 2016. pp. 79–84.

25. Jytte Klausen, Selene Campion, Nathan Needle, Giang Nguyen and Rosanne Libretti. Towards A Behavioural Model of "Homegrown" Radicalization Trajectories. *Studies in Conflict and Terrorism* Vol. 39(1). 2015. pp. 67–83.

26. Fathali M. Moghaddam. The Staircase to Terrorism: A Psychological Exploration. *American Psychologist* Vol. 60(2). 2005. pp. 161–169.

27. Mitchell D. Silber and Arvin Bhatt. *Radicalization in the West: The Homegrown Threat*. New York, NY: NYPD Intelligence Department. 2007.

28. Lorenzo Vidino, Francesco Marone and Eva Entenmann. *Fear Thy Neighbour: Radicalization and Jihadist Attacks in the West*. Milan: Ledizoni. 2017.

29. David Webber and Arie W. Kruglanski. Psychological Factors in Radicalization: A "3N" Approach. In: *The Handbook of the Criminology of Terrorism*. Editors: Gary LaFree and Joshua D. Frelich. Chichester: John Wiley & Sons. 2017. pp. 33–46.

30. HM Home Office. *Revised Prevent Duty Guidance For England and Wales*. London: HM Home Office. 2015.

31. HM Home Office. *Proscribed Terrorist Organisations*. London: HM Home Office. 2017.

32. Alex P. Schmid. Terrorism – The Definitional Problem. *Case Western Reserve Journal of International Law* Vol. 36(2). 2004. pp. 375–419.

33. Bart Schuurman and Max Taylor. Reconsidering Radicalisation: Fanaticism and the Link Between Ideas and Violence. *Perspectives on Terrorism* Vol. 12(1). 2018. p. 7.

34. Hamed El-Said and Richard Barrett. *Enhancing the Understanding of the Foreign Terrorist Fighters Phenomenon in Syria*. UNOCT. 2017.

35. John M. Venhaus. Why Youth Join Al-Qaeda. United States Institute of Peace. Special Report. 2010.

36. Peter Neumann. The Trouble With Radicalization. *International Affairs* Vol. 89(4). 2013. p. 881.

37. Ines von Behr, Anais Redding, Charlie Edwards and Luke Gribbon. *Radicalisation in the Digital Era: The Use of the Internet in 15 Cases of Terrorism and Extremism*. London: RAND. 2013.

38. Institute for Strategic Dialogue. *Radicalisation: The Role of The Internet*. London: Institute for Strategic Dialogue. 2011. p. 2.

39. Caroline J.S. Picart. "Jihad Cool/Jihad Chic": The Roles of the Internet and Imagined Relations in the Self-Radicalization of Colleen LaRose (Jihad Jane). *Societies* Vol. 5. 2015. pp. 354–383.

40. USA Vs. Shannon Maureen Conley. 2014. The criminal complaint can be viewed here: https://extremism.gwu.edu/sites/g/files/zaxdzs2191/f/Conley%20Criminal%20Complaint.pdf.

41. Ghaffar Hussain and Erin Saltman. *Jihad Trending: A Comprehensive Analysis of Online Extremism and How to Counter It*. London: Quilliam Foundation. 2014. p. 9.

42. Lasse Lindekilde, Frances O'Connor and Bart Schuurman. Radicalization Patterns and Modes of Attack Planning and Preparation Among Lone-Actor Terrorists: An Exploratory Analysis. *Behavioral Sciences of Terrorism and Political Aggression* Vol. 11(2). 2017. pp. 113–133.

43. Bart Schuurman, Edwin Bakker, Paul Gill and Noemie Bouhana. Lone Actor Terrorist Attack Planning and Preparation: A Data-driven Analysis. *Journal of Forensic Sciences* Vol. 63(4). 2017. pp. 1191–1200.

44. Adam Bermingham, Maura Conway, Lisa McInerney, Neil O'Hare and Alan F. Smeaton. Combining Social Network Analysis and Sentiment Analysis to Explore the Potential for Online Radicalisation. Proceedings of the 2009 International Conference on Advances in Social Network Analysis and Mining. 2009. pp. 231–236.

45. Tim Stevens and Peter Neumann. *Countering Online Radicalisation: A Strategy for Action*. London: International Centre for the Study of Radicalisation and Political Violence. 2009.

46. Ines von Behr, Anais Redding, Charlie Edwards and Luke Gribbon. *Radicalisation in the Digital Era: The Use of the Internet in 15 Cases of Terrorism and Extremism*. London: RAND. 2013.

47. Home Affairs Committee. *Counter-Terrorism. Seventeenth Report of Session 2013-14*. London: The Stationery Office. 2014. p. 7.

48. Paul Gill. *Lone Actor Terrorists: A Behavioral Analysis*. Abingdon: Routledge. 2015.

49. Paul Gill, Emily Corner, Amy Thornton and Maura Conway. *What are the Roles of the Internet in Terrorism? Measuring Online Behaviors of Convicted UK Terrorists*. Dublin: VOX-POL Network of Excellence. 2015. p. 5.

50. Robyn Torok. Developing an Explanatory Model for the Process of Online Radicalisation and Terrorism. *Security Informatics* Vol. 2(6). 2013. pp. 1–10.

51. Laura Huey. This is Not Your Mother's Terrorism: Social Media, Online Radicalization and the Practice of Political Jamming. *Journal of Terrorism Research* Vol. 6(2). 2015. pp. 1–16.

52. Tom Holt, Joshua D. Freilich, Steven Chermak and Clark McCauley. Political Radicalization on the Internet: Extremist Content, Government Control, and the Power of Victim and Jihad Videos. *Dynamics of Asymmetric Conflict* Vol. 8(2). 2015. pp. 107–120.

53. Daniel Koehler. The Radical Online: Individual Radicalization Processes and the Role of the Internet. *Journal for Deradicalization* Vol. 1. 2014. pp. 116–134.

54. Omar A. Saifudeen. The Cyber Extremism Orbital Pathways Model. RSIS Working Paper (283). 2014.

55. Maura Conway. Determining the role of the Internet in Violent Extremism and Terrorism: Six Suggestions for Progressing Research. *Studies in Conflict in Terrorism* Vol. 40. 2017. p. 80.

56. USA Vs. Mohamed Abdihamid Farah, Adnan Abdihamid Farah, Abdurahman Yasin Duad, Zacharia Yusuf Abdurahman, Hanad Mustafe Musse and Guled Ali Omar. 2015. The criminal complaint can be viewed here: https://extremism.gwu.edu/sites/g/files/zaxdzs2191/f/Abdurahman,%20Z.%20Complaint.pdf.

57. Paul Gill and Emily Corner. Lone-Actor Terrorist Use of the Internet and Behavioral Correlates. In: *Terrorism Online: Politics, Law and Technology*. Editors: Thomas M. Chen, Lee Jarvis and Stuart Macdonald. Abingdon: Routledge. 2015. pp. 35–53.

58. Paul Gill, Emily Corner, Maura Conway, Amy Thornton, Mia Bloom and John Horgan. Terrorist Use of the Internet by the Numbers. *Criminology and Public Policy* Vol. 16(1). 2017. pp. 1–19.

59. Irving Janis, Groupthink. *Psychology Today* Vol. 5(6). 1971. pp. 84–90.

60. Cass R. Sunstein. The Law of Group Polarisation. *The Journal of Political Philosophy* Vol. 10(2). pp. 175–195.

61. Nuria Lorenzo Dus and Stuart Macdonald. Othering The West in the Online Jihadist Propaganda Magazines *Inspire* and *Dabiq*. *Journal of Language, Aggression and Conflict* Vol. 6. 2018. pp. 79–106.

62. Eli Pariser. *The Filter Bubble: What the Internet is Hiding from You*. London: Penguin. 2011.

63. Michael A. DeVito. From Editors to Algorithms. *Digital Journalism*. Vol. 5(6). 2016. pp. 753–773.
64. Audrey Alexander. *Digital Decay? Tracing Change Over Time Among English-Language Islamic State Sympathizers on Twitter*. Washington, D.C.: Program on Extremism. 2017.
65. Jytte Klausen, Elaine T. Barbieri, Aaron Reichlin-Melnick and Aaron Y. Zelin. The YouTube Jihadists: A Social Network Analysis of Al-Muhajiroun's Propaganda Campaign. *Perspectives on Terrorism* Vol. 6(1). 2012. pp. 36–53.
66. Mubaraz Ahmed and Fred L. George. *A War of Keywords: How Extremists Are Exploiting the Internet and What to Do About It*. Centre on Religion & Geopolitics. 2016.
67. Jytte Klausen. Tweeting the Jihad: Social Media Networks of Western Foreign Fighters in Syria and Iraq. *Studies in Conflict and Terrorism* Vol. 38(1). 2015. pp. 1–22.
68. Jerold Post, Cody McGinnis and Kristen Moody. The Changing Face of Terrorism in the 21st Century: The Communications Revolution and the Virtual Community of Hatred. *Behavioral Sciences & The Law* Vol. 32(2). 2014. pp. 306–336.
69. Lorenzo Vidino and Seamus Hughes. *ISIS in America: From Retweets to Raqqa*. Washington, D.C.: Program on Extremism. 2015.
70. Paraphrased in: Marc Sageman. *Leaderless Jihad: Terror Networks in the Twenty-First Century*. Philadelphia, PA: University of Pennsylvania Press. 2008. p. 116.
71. Marc Sageman. *Leaderless Jihad: Terror Networks in the Twenty-First Century*. Philadelphia, PA: University of Pennsylvania Press. 2008. p. 115.
72. Marc Sageman. *Leaderless Jihad: Terror Networks in the Twenty-First Century*. Philadelphia, PA: University of Pennsylvania Press. 2008. p. 122.
73. Ines von Behr, Anais Redding, Charlie Edwards and Luke Gribbon. *Radicalisation in the Digital Era: The Use of the Internet in 15 Cases of Terrorism and Extremism*. London: RAND. 2013. p. 27.
74. Magdalena Wojcieszak. False Consensus Goes Online: Impact of Ideologically Homogeneous Groups on False Consensus. *Public Opinion Quarterly* Vol. 72(4). 2008. p. 788.
75. Kieron O'Hara and David Stevens. Echo Chambers and Online Radicalism: Assessing the Internet's Complicity in Violent Extremism. *Policy and Internet* Vol. 7(4). 2015. pp. 401–422.
76. Alex Krasodomski-Jones. *Talking To Ourselves? Political Debate in Online and the Echo Chamber Effect*. London: Demos. 2017.
77. Michela Del Vicario, Gianna Vivaldo, Alessandro Bessi, Fabiana Zollo, Antonio Scala, Guido Caldarelli and Walter Quattrociocchi. *Echo Chambers: Emotional Contagion and Group Polarization on Facebook*. Nature Publishing Group. 2016. pp. 1–14.
78. Michela Del Vicario, Alessandro Bessi, Fabiana Zollo, Antonio Scala, Guido Caldarelli, Eugene Stanley and Walter Quattrociocchi. The Spreading of Misinformation Online. *Proceedings of the National Academy of Sciences* Vol. 113(3). 2016. pp. 554–559.
79. Alessandro Bessi. Personality Traits and Echo Chambers on Facebook. *Computers in Human Behavior* Vol. 65. 2016. pp. 319–324.
80. Derek O'Callaghan, Derek Greene, Maura Conway, Joe Carthy and Padraig Cunningham. Down the (White) Rabbit Hole: The Extreme Right and Online Recommender Systems. *Social Science Computer Review* Vol. 33(4). p. 473.
81. Eytan Bakshy, Solomon Messing and Lada Adamic. Exposure to Ideologically Diverse News and Opinion on Facebook. *Science Express*. May 2015. pp. 1–5.
82. Gregory Waters and Robert Postings. Spiders of the Caliphate: Mapping the Islamic State's Global Support Network on Facebook. Counter Extremism Project. 2018.
83. J.M. Berger. Zero Degrees of Al Qaeda: How Twitter is Supercharging Jihadist Recruitment. *Foreign Policy*, 14 August 2013.

Chapter 3

The Relationship between Social Media and Radicalization

Cori E. Dauber and Kemal Ilter

CONTENTS

3.1 INTRODUCTION

This chapter will examine the integral relationship between radicalization and social media in general—how and why people get radicalized via social media and how the information age is "turbo-charging" the radicalization process. Additionally, this chapter aims to give a basic understanding of the causes conducive to radicalization, a complex psychological process that prompts individuals to accept violence as an acceptable means—depending on their individual motivations—for attaining political goals, channeling their individual or group frustration, regaining self-esteem by becoming a member of a tight-knit community or for self-sacrifice in the name of a supposedly divine mission.

3.2 DESCRIPTION OF THE RADICALIZATION PROCESS

The purpose of this chapter is to discuss the relationship between radicalization and social media. Before discussing the research on this topic, we want to address the argument made by a number of analysts that there really is no relationship, because the idea that anyone is truly "self-radicalized" simply by exposure to materials on the internet is not borne out by the evidence. We agree that this phenomenon is extremely rare, although it does happen. (And, by the same token, it is hardly the case that simply being exposed to propaganda materials on the web is enough to automatically radicalize someone. After all, if that were the case, pretty much all of the people conducting research in this area would have joined extremist groups long ago given how much of the content they're exposed to.) But first, the phenomenon being rare hardly makes it unworthy of study. And second, the fact that people are not being radicalized by the materials they find on the web *only* does not make their experiences online or the content they are looking at unimportant. To the contrary.

The process of radicalization is complicated and not completely understood, but it seems clear that it is very often a result of a combination of online and offline interactions. For example Lorenzo Vidino and Seamus Hughes discuss the centrality of social media to the Islamic State's (IS) recruiting efforts in the United States, but are also very clear that many of these recruiting "clusters" are initiated by offline contact.[1] Recent research, in fact, suggests that it is a mistake to think of the radicalization process in terms of sharp dichotomies such as "offline" and "online"— it is far more likely that people are brought into extremist groups through a blend of interactions.[2] (The same is true for attack planning.[3])

Further, while it is rarely the case that individuals are "self-radicalizing," that is to say radicalized as a result of materials they are finding on the web all by themselves, exploring by themselves, and then deciding to become violent based on those materials with no interaction with another human being, we believe it is more often the case that they are being radicalized as a result of interactions taking place over the web, that is to say they are interacting with other individuals, but those interactions do not include an offline, in-person component. This was, for example, the case with the Ft. Hood shooter, who exchanged dozens of emails with Anwar al-Awlaki. Awlaki, the American born cleric who was a leader of Al Qaeda's affiliate in the Arabian Peninsula, radicalized a long list of Westerners via not only direct contact, but his YouTube videos. Indeed, some of these individuals were radicalized after his death. YouTube was heavily criticized for a long time because not only were the cleric's videos easily available on the site, *it was the design features of YouTube itself*, the built-in features, that were guiding users who were searching for relatively innocuous material such as news reports, straight to his videos.[4] (Those videos have now been taken down, but, of course, they have been taken down before.[5])

As John P. Carlin wrote:

> there simply weren't regular people who woke up one morning, read a Twitter thread and decided then and there to kill Americans. There's not one track to radicalization, and the web doesn't provide some magical radicalization potion. Radicalization is a process, a journey, but online propaganda and dialogue drastically lower the barriers and complications of recruiting would-be terrorists from far away. Terrorists overseas can communicate directly, intimately and in real time with kids in our basements, here.[6]

As unlikely as it may seem that people are radicalized only by exposure to online materials, it also seems enormously unlikely that materials encountered via social media play *no* role given the enormous amount of resources these groups plough into developing them, filming, editing, and posting increasingly high-end images and video materials,[7] in some cases developing software programs that allow for these materials to be spread automatically, and then interacting with people online about these materials. No one has more prolonged or more direct access to these recruits than the groups going to all this effort. It just seems unlikely that if all this effort was failing they would continue to work so hard at it, year after year, one group after another, across the ideological spectrum.

Then of course there are the pronouncements from the leaders of some of these groups on the respect that is to be paid to those of their members who are engaged in "media-jihad" or "e-jihad" relative to those engaged in actual physical combat:

> bin Laden's successor, Ayman al-Zawahiri … spoke of the "jihad of the spear" and the "jihad of the *bayan*" (message, declaration). He considered the latter more important and praised the "knights of the media jihad."[8]

Something to keep in mind when looking at radicalization is that someone might be radicalized to the point where they consider themselves a member of a movement, and they are willing to engage in low-level behaviors, posting supportive statements online, providing funds, attending rallies, perhaps recruiting others themselves. Once an individual takes that final step and is willing to engage in violence, they may take that step on their own, even if they are motivated or inspired by a specific group. They may take that step under the direction of a group, but act alone. They may act under the direction of a larger group with others. Or they may leave their home to travel to a distant country to fight in a foreign battlefield. It is hard to believe that the process of radicalization does not have at least something in common in each of those cases.

One difficulty in doing research in this area is that it can be almost impossible to directly interact with the relevant populations. That is obviously most true regarding those who have left Western countries to fight in foreign battlefields (though not only true in that case.) How would a researcher gain access to Islamic State fighters in order to survey or interview them? And if you could gain such access, how could you trust the truthfulness of their responses? Gaining access to so-called "returnees," the foreign fighters who have come back to their countries of origin can be safer, but no less complicated, since these individuals often are in hiding, in fear of arrest and prosecution. (Some researchers have managed to obtain access to returnees who are in prison for this reason.) Members of white supremacist groups are not much more likely to be forthcoming, assuming they can be tracked down. So just conducting this type of research is a delicate, time consuming, and possibly dangerous process. One possible answer to these problems is to conduct "proxy" research, to find populations who have direct knowledge of those who have been radicalized, but are themselves one step removed, and thus are more accessible and likely more open. This is the value of the study conducted by Amarnath Amarsingam and Lorne L. Dawson, because while they were able to conduct interviews with a small number of foreign fighters, either over Skype or a text messaging application, the real insights come from extensive face-to-face interviews with the family and friends of individuals who left to join IS. Some of these interviews lasted as long as four hours.[9]

Their study determined much of the stereotype is simply wrong: most of these men did not come from dysfunctional homes, most were not coming from poverty, and most had a high school diploma or, indeed, some college credits. However, critically, it was also the case that their families and even their close friends, while they did see changes, in attitudes, behavior, even in dress, did not register those changes with the degree of radicalization that might mean that their loved ones were at risk for leaving for Syria. (It should be noted that other researchers believe that some of these behavioral changes are predictable on the part of those radicalized by the Salafist-jihadist movement, and therefore might be detectable prior to an overt act.[10])

Another way around this dilemma is to conduct research with subjects who have left extremist groups. An advantage of this approach is that it permits the researcher to explore not only processes of radicalization, but also to consider successful routes to deradicalization. Christer Mattsson and Thomas Johansson conducted interviews with a group of former neo-Nazis, but made the interesting choice to interview them when they had been out of the movement for several years, looking to see if time had given them perspective on their participation in the movement and the way they had left it. It is worrisome that a number of their subjects report wanting to get out, but really having no idea how to accomplish that: it was coincidental, almost random, events that pointed a way forward for them.[11]

Paul Gill, John Horgan, and Paige Deckert undertook a major study of the demographic characteristics and networking behaviors of 119 "lone actor" terrorists falling across the spectrum of ideological motivations, across several decades.[12] In 63 percent of the study group, someone had been told of their specific plans before they acted, but there were a wide range of other behaviors that many in this group had in common: many had joined a religion (whether their act was religiously motivated or not), half had recently moved, many had recently lost their jobs—although a substantial minority were chronically unemployed—and, unsurprisingly, therefore, a substantial minority were under great financial stress. Stress in general was a theme in the months leading up to an attack: a death in the family, losing a place in university. A number felt they were the specific target of an act of discrimination, or even of an assault, whether verbal or physical. More than half felt they were acting on behalf of a wider movement. There were noticeable differences in age, in military status, in criminal history, and in how they prepared for their attack, depending on whether the terrorist was motivated by jihadism, by a right-wing ideology of some variant, or by a "single issue" ideology.

This theme, that the "lone actor" may have been socially isolated but was strictly speaking not alone is supported by preliminary research conducted by David Hofman.[13] While his work is based on more of an analysis of case studies than a robust data set, his work reinforces the idea that there is a good chance lone actors will have told someone at some point of their plans. Other scholars have focused closely on the case of Anders Behring Brevik.[14]

A 2013 study of 98 lone actor terrorists, stretching from 1940 to 2013, reinforced these findings. Their model suggests that the path to the act of lone wolf terrorist begins with

> a combination of personal and political grievances which form the basis for an affinity with online sympathizers. This is followed by the identification of an enabler, followed by the broadcasting of terrorist intent. The final commonality is a triggering event, or the catalyst for terrorism.[15]

These individuals may well have been socially isolated, but they flagged their actions in some way, whether via email, social media post, or a threat. This type of research, and ongoing studies like it, is incredibly important for law enforcement, because at the end of the day, one of the most important (and difficult) challenges is always going to be distinguishing not between those who are radicalized and those who are not, but the real challenge will be telling the difference between those have been radicalized to the point of extremism and those who have been radicalized to the point where they are prepared to act in some way. Some may simply hold extremist views, and never act on them. But some may move from extremist views to a willingness to engage in violence, and it is those actions that pose a danger to the larger society. The time between the assimilation of extremist views and the decision to act is called by some the "flash to bang," and that time period may be shortening.[16]

The confluence of factors that will move someone to act are often so specific to the individual that the chances of catching them in advance are daunting. However, so long as the individual believes that he or she is acting on behalf of a cause, the chances are at least reasonable that they will tell someone in advance of undertaking their plan. They have to: otherwise they would be engaging in "messageless resistance," which has to be the worst possible outcome for a terrorist.[17]

One thinks of the Las Vegas shooter. Whatever his purpose was (assuming he did indeed have one) died with him. If we assume hypothetically that he was in fact a terrorist, then he was actually an enormous failure, because no one has the first idea what message he was trying to send, what cause he (and all his victims) died for—and no one will ever know.

What about the jihadist threat specifically? Riyadh Hosain Rahimullah, Stephen Larmar, and Mohamad Abdalla walk the reader step-by-step through the risk factors that may prime a young person for radicalization, and explain the differing models and theories available to explain how radicalization happens in those cases specifically.[18]

3.3 WHAT IS SOCIAL MEDIA?

We should first step back and, for those not familiar, discuss social media platforms themselves. Social media platforms today are nearly ubiquitous, enough so that if one is not familiar it can be difficult to get a handle on just what these things actually are, what they do, and why it is that they are so popular. Facebook, the first social media platform to pass one billion active users (back in 2012) currently has almost three billion a month. Instagram has one billion and WhatsApp one and a half billion. Twitter has 336 million. Snapchat has 186 million. Other sites, such as Tumblr, are considerably smaller.[19] There is considerable overlap, of course, with most people who have an account on one site probably having an account on at least one other platform.

But what are these "platforms?" And what makes these media "social" relative to traditional (sometimes called "legacy") media?

When the internet first reached the point where it was in wide use in the late 1990s, email was one of the first methods of social connection. For adults of that time it was nothing short of revolutionary to be able to reach out and immediately communicate with anyone in the world who also had a computer connected to the web. The world became an increasingly smaller place. Indeed, for a long time the line between who was considered a "digital native" and who was a "digital immigrant" was demarcated by whether someone remembered receiving their first email or not.[20] (Today's "digital natives" of course actually almost never email unless it's the only way they can communicate with someone: they much prefer to text, or use one of the social media platforms.)

Today, social media is commonplace; children grow up with it in their homes, and on their cellphones. The internet was one thing, but the development of social media required high enough bandwidths that audio and video files could be easily uploaded and downloaded, software that made it possible for individuals with little to no training in computer science to be able to do exactly that, and portable devices with the capacities to use those programs at maximum potential. In other words, for social media to become the phenomena it is today requires more than just the internet, it requires the internet, cellphones that are relatively affordable and that link to the internet—smartphones in other words—and particularly smartphones with the capability to take and to share images.[21]

Social media, therefore, are platforms where anyone can post comments about almost anything (assuming they obey the terms of service for the particular platform) and have the chance to interact with others about what they have posted. Representatives of the "legacy" media use these platforms to report the news, as do ordinary citizens who happen to witness events they deem "newsworthy" (whether that is a terrorist attack, a new baby in the family, or a Kardashian sighting) and anyone on the platform has the ability to respond in an interactive fashion. People can indicate that they agree (by "liking" or "retweeting," it will be different depending on the platform) and receiving those small gestures of validation can become literally addictive. That is in no small part because the companies have knowingly designed the platforms to *be* addictive: if you aren't looking at their sites, they aren't making money.[22] This has been called "brain hacking."[23]

3.4 ROLE OF SOCIAL MEDIA IN THE RADICALIZATION PROCESS

We will discuss the role of social media both as a communication platform used by extremist groups for recruiting and radicalizing in general and as an effective tool playing a key role in the self-radicalization process.

Social media platforms are easy to use with little to no training, and substantially decrease the costs of finding and communicating with others. Again, if they don't work that way, there's no way for the companies to increase the number of users on their sites and thus make money. These platforms can, therefore, significantly increase the audience size for messages created by extremist groups. So the likelihood that their messages will resonate with *someone* in that audience also increases. In other words, with these platforms, terrorists can tailor their message to a narrow audience, and that will still mean that through enlisting the help of the virtual world they will have been able to enter the homes of thousands of people with no actual travel required. Thus from the point of view of the extremist group, the cost is minimal, no logistics or transportation support is needed, and the odds of detection are low. At least as important from their point of view, for the first time ever, terrorists are able to cut out the middleman—they are reliant on no one else to get their message out. They don't have to hope that journalists will represent their message as they themselves would have wanted it represented, the groups can send out the message they want sent out, the way they want it sent out, because it will be seen unedited. (Only recently have the platforms become proactive in seeking out materials on their sites that do not meet their terms of service and removing those materials, an act called "take downs," which we will discuss below.)

Social media is therefore a gateway to extremist content. On YouTube, the site's own architecture leads people to increasingly extremist material, whether they begin with an interest in such content or not. This is true no matter the topic: whatever an individual is looking at, because the site is designed to keep you looking, it will provide you with more and more extreme material. This is a function of engineering designed to make the site "sticky"—that is, to keep you from turning away.[24]

Radicalization is a complex psychological process that prompts individuals to reach the point where they believe violence is acceptable, indeed appropriate. Terrorist and extremist groups have good reason to use social media, whose popularity suits them in many ways. Social media platforms present themselves as just another means of obtaining information, on par with, and equivalent to, mainstream news. After all, legacy news outlets all have a presence on social media, though that presence might be more or less aggressive. That may give the impression to the naïve user that there is an equivalence between what the Associated Press or BBC or *New York Times* posts and what your friend posts. What's the difference? Actually, people may be more likely to believe items posted by people they know—and they don't actually know the reporters for the *Times*.[25]

Most social media platforms are easy to use and cost little (or more likely nothing) to join. This has fundamentally changed the game for recruiters for international groups, who no longer need to worry about gaining direct physical access to recruits, either by finding a way to come to them, or convincing them to travel to the recruiter's location, which could be literally on the other side of the earth.[26]

A candidate for recruitment may come to the group's attention by making a financial donation, downloading extremist propaganda, or visiting extremist content and leaving a comment (or, indeed, visiting less-than-extremist content and leaving a comment.) Social media's entire purpose is to enable loose, decentralized networks of people to come together, where no one person is in charge, and there is no formal structure.

And it has allowed these groups to get their content out to people who were not looking for it at all, for example through the "hijacking" of benign Twitter hashtags.[27] (A hashtag, signified by the number symbol, #, is a way of organizing content. On Twitter, tweets that include the same hashtag in the body of the tweet will be organized together to facilitate users finding them, for example, #GoGermany14 as was used during the 2014 World Cup by fans of the German team.) Islamic State initially did this in the context of military campaigns.[28] But soon they did it with completely benign hashtags, first with those associated with the World Cup in 2014,[29] and later using hashtags for the singer Justin Bieber, particularly disturbing since so many of his fans are so young.[30] Much of the mainstream press coverage of this tactic suggested that the goal was to "recruit" by exposing a new audience to the material, but it's just as likely that their purpose was to horrify and terrify an audience not expecting to see materials including graphic images of beheadings. That does not mean they were not anticipating some benefit in terms of radicalization and recruitment, but it was just as likely to come from those audiences they were already recruiting than from new populations randomly exposed to this material. For their recruits, their ability to reach the unsuspecting, at any time, and terrify them wherever they were and whatever they were doing, would be a demonstration of their power that could easily contribute to the narrative they were building up for the recruits' benefit, one of power and invulnerability. It would be extremely rare for any message to be intended for a single audience, and where a message is meant for more than one audience—in this case, for both a mainstream audience with no connection to the group and their own recruits—it is likely it is intended to be interpreted in different ways by those different audiences. So here the message to the first is, you should be very afraid of us: not only are we capable of doing awful things, we can reach you anywhere when you least expect us. To the second: did you see what we just did? How cool is that? Don't you want to be a part of a group with that kind of power?

Facebook requires that individuals use their own names for their accounts (supposedly) but many other platforms, for example, Twitter, allow individuals to post under any "handle" they choose. When individuals communicate online and they are anonymous, their communicative behavior can become more aggressive, and the attitudes they express can be more extreme. With the help of anonymity during online communication, there is no need to think about the immediate consequences of conversations and it is easier to communicate more aggressively or take "riskier" positions on issues.[31]

Extremist groups take further advantage of this and magnify its impact by using "bots" (accounts that are not actually human and that are typically networked.) Other accounts are run by actual humans but are not intended to reflect their own opinions but those they are told to voice, and indeed may be paid a salary to voice. These "sock puppet" accounts are more often a tool of state actors than of extremist groups, but they clearly have the potential to move opinion within social media audiences.[32]

Extremist and terrorist groups have also taken advantage of software programs that have allowed their followers to, for example, retweet their materials in numbers that made it possible for them to make it appear that their influence was much greater than it actually was. That is not an inconsequential thing. Aside from the fact that early on it made the Islamic State of Iraq and Syria (ISIS) appear far larger than it actually was, making them appear far more powerful in the offline world than they truly were, as power for a group on Twitter is determined by the number of accounts it can move, and they had software that allowed them to control large numbers of accounts with no human attached (bots), as well as having the accounts of their followers retweeting their material automatically (for all intents and purposes acting as if they were bots).[33] Thus they could influence which topics were "trending," and had the "muscle" within the platform to hijack hashtags—you can't do that without substantial numbers.

The other advantage Islamic State had on social media (before aggressive take downs became common) is that its members and sympathizers were relatively unified in their messaging. Those who opposed first ISIS and now IS opposed it for any number of reasons, from any number of perspectives, and therefore it was essentially impossible to get them to follow a united message. An important RAND study of multiple millions of tweets from Arabic twitter found that anti-IS voices outnumbered the pro-IS voices by anywhere from six to one to ten to one on any given day, but they come from four different perspectives, or "meta-communities." Additionally, the pro-IS voices were utterly dominant on Twitter, at least during the time period of the study, July 2014 to July 2015, producing 50 percent more tweets a day. When you take into account that the anti-IS voices are divided, their messages were simply being drowned out.[34]

All of this happens in a context of "interactivity" that makes social media completely different from any form of media that has come before: that interactivity blurs the lines between readership and authorship that previous generations of extremists, terrorists, sympathizers, and audiences dealt with when engaging with pamphlets, newspapers, and newsletters. This blurring can encourage people who interact in such forums to more easily see themselves as part of broader religious or racist extremist movements, and not just as casual readers or online spectators. They may eventually engage in more substantive activity -- actually propagandizing others themselves, providing financial support, or even joining an extremist or terrorist network. The internet allows for vital dialogue between extremist ideas and inquisitive minds to take place in a virtual setting. For this new generation especially, social media are now supplementing and replacing prayer rooms, community centers, and coffee shops as venues for radicalization.

Legacy media outlets have become increasingly partisan over the last few years, which has made it more and more possible for people to create and live in their own echo chambers or bubbles, gradually ignoring or removing opposing voices from their information sources.[35] But the internet, and specifically social media, makes it much easier for this to happen. Empirical research suggests that social media echo chambers in and of themselves function not to radicalize, but to "sort," to isolate people into groups with other people on the same political side.[36] After all, these platforms were designed from the ground up to connect like-minded individuals, to allow individuals to connect with people who share similar ideologies, to connect them globally, and to allow them to connect with others who are increasingly extreme in their attitudes and beliefs

But this structure can be used in the same way to create the social isolation that is a key aspect of recruiting strategies: groups create mini-communities around potential recruits, gradually encouraging them to cut ties to anyone not a member of the group and "love-bombing" them, making sure that they are constantly receiving messages from their new online community.[37] It is for this reason some argue that there is a parallel between recruiting into extremist or terrorist groups and the "grooming" that pedophiles engage in.[38] Previous generations of extremist groups did this offline, to be sure, but to do that they had to be physically in close proximity to the person they were trying to recruit, now they can be on another continent altogether.[39]

The chances of breaking through to any audience, but certainly a wider one, are much higher when appealing to emotions. Social media helps groups to show and magnify emotions. On social media, emotion—positive or negative—is among the most important factors that drives the sharing of content. We are not suggesting that this is a new phenomenon. British far-right groups in the inter-war period (and they were hardly the only ones) tried to use highly emotional images to "other" the enemy, in their case the anti-Fascist left, which they portrayed as violent and anti-Christian, and therefore a threat to Britain.[40] There are entire college courses devoted to the history of political propaganda, most particularly during wartime, and most of it is highly emotional. Our argument is that the medium and technology of social media makes the process easier. Revenge seekers need an outlet for their frustration, status seekers need recognition, identity seekers need a group to join, and thrill seekers need adventure. None of that is new. What is new is that these people can now find what they're looking for—or, at least, people who are offering them what seems to be what they are looking for—without ever leaving their bedroom. A study of Germans who left Germany to fight for the Islamic State (Germans were one of the largest nationalities represented in Syria) showed that they had very mixed motives, but clearly a number of them were seeking status and adventure. (It is also of interest that the Germans tended to travel to Syria in small groups, clearly indicating that they were not being radicalized as individuals.[41]) A study of 49 foreign fighters who had gone to join the Islamic State, some from the West and some from Arab countries, found them motivated by a search for "identity" or "status," seeking "revenge," or "thrill seeking." These are not ideological motivations linked to a religious call, but they are extremely emotional.[42] The speed that social media makes available is key here, with responses to offline events being immediate and immersive.

Interaction with others through these platforms fuels a sense of belonging and common cause that can also amplify the radicalization process. Videos on YouTube can emphasize romantic notions of superiority or brotherhood, revolution and sacrifice in pursuit of an Islamist or far-right utopia. Extremist groups found that these individuals were often confused young people searching to define themselves and gain a sense of purpose. Within these spaces, they provide consumers access to, among other things, rap videos and online magazines with messages aimed directly at disaffected youth.

3.4.1 Micro-Targeting

Producing recruiting materials and posting them to social media is one thing, but at some point if an individual is actually going to take the final steps and become fully radicalized, as opposed to being merely a sympathetic consumer of a group's propaganda, it is likely that there will need to be some direct contact between that individual and members of the group. This is where the parallel to pedophiles comes in. Social media facilitates direct contacts between a target and members of the group. It makes those contacts simple and easy, no matter the geographic distance between them. In fact it makes it easy for members of the group to create a "micro-community," making it seem for the individual as if he or she already has a large number of genuine and caring friends within that community, who seem to know them and want the best for them.

According to the work of J.M. Berger, this process follows a clear sequence of steps in the case of the Islamic State, or at least a menu from which recruiters can choose to tailor an approach that seems to best meet the individual subject who is being recruited.[43] First contact is made, either at the initiative of the recruit or the recruiter. Second, the micro-community is constructed, at which point constant contact with the recruit is maintained by the group working on behalf of IS—and they urge the recruit to isolate themselves from outside influences, by cutting off any contacts who are not members of the group. They shift to private means of communication (for example the direct message function on Twitter.) And they begin to identify and encourage pro-IS activities that might be appropriate for the individual, whether that is travel to IS territories, pro-IS activity on social media, or terrorist activity. (Berger has also written that these steps do offer possibilities for intervention, given the use of appropriate analytical tools at each step.[44])

There was extensive news coverage of a young girl from the U.K. who, convinced to travel to the Islamic State, was put to work recruiting other young girls, fairly effectively, by posting online about her new life.[45]

Estimates vary, but at its peak, the Islamic State attracted 40,000 foreign fighters to come and join its ranks, an astonishing number relative to the history of any other such group in history.[46] It is sometimes simply asserted that people join extremist or terrorist groups for economic reasons, but there is little evidence to support that claim, and in the case of the Islamic State there is good reason to believe that for most recruits (certainly for those coming from the West) economics did not play a part in their reason to leave for IS-controlled territory.[47] If the rationale is not economic, then it is something less based on strictly rational cost-benefit calculations, at least in numeric terms, and instead is something more personal, more *emotional*—something that can be driven by propaganda and by individual contacts and connections.

The other thing that needs to be kept in mind, given all the attention that has been paid of late to the foreign fighter problem, is that many have been recruited, not to leave home and join the Islamic State physically, but to stay in place and engage in violent actions where they are. They have had particular success appealing to young people, getting them to engage in attacks at an alarming rate. These are not necessarily complex plots; often this is just a case of a teenager grabbing a knife and trying to stab as many people as possible before being killed by police, but that does not make the phenomena any less tragic.[48]

3.4.2 Take Downs

Under increasing pressure to act, the social media companies increasingly found themselves with no choice but to begin to aggressively shut down accounts associated with extremist and terrorist content and to remove the content itself. They did this slowly, unevenly, and only after an enormous amount of this material had been on their sites for a great deal of time.

To be clear, these are private companies, and to the extent they are headquartered in the United States—as most of them are—they can, with a very narrow number of exceptions such as child pornography, host whatever material on their sites they choose to allow, and forbid whatever material they choose to forbid. How they police content in entirely up to them. Because they are not government entities, if they decide particular content is not acceptable to them, there is *no* First Amendment issue involved, because that is simply not a matter of the government controlling speech in any way. But while these companies can make choices regarding what content to allow on their sites without triggering a First Amendment complaint from users (*you* do not have an absolute right to tweet whatever you want) because of the First Amendment, many constitutional scholars believe that the companies are immune from many forms of government regulation in the United States. The government may come after them for anti-trust violations, but it is not likely that the government would win in court if they tried to force the companies, for example, to ban "hateful" speech, especially since that is not a legally recognized category in American law.[49]

However, what the companies can be legally forced to do, and what they can be forced to do because of political realities are two different things. Tech company CEOs were forced to testify before Congress recently thanks to scandals regarding disinformation on their sites spread during the 2016 presidential campaign and over user data being shared without consent, particularly a problem for Facebook.[50] But legislators have also been concerned over the presence of hateful propaganda. They were not left with any helpful responses, particularly from Facebook.[51] This is especially distressing given that platform's apparent role in an ongoing genocide in Myanmar—a role it has taken responsibility for, though it doesn't seem to be doing anything to make useful changes.[52]

The other problem for these companies is that while they may be based in the United States, they have subscribers all over the world, and the First Amendment is a uniquely American legal instrument. Even the liberal democracies that make up America's oldest and most reliable allies have nothing like it: they *do* regulate hate speech, and in the wake of recent scandals several appear to be moving closer to regulating the companies in their territories.[53] That would be problematic for the companies to say the least, especially since it would no doubt set a precedent for less free parts of the world.[54]

A great deal of problematic material can still be found on all of these platforms, but the companies have gotten better about taking it down much more quickly. Indeed, some IS-related accounts may now survive only moments on Twitter specifically, which makes it almost impossible for their followers to find them. The result is that the median number of followers for pro-IS accounts on Twitter has fallen over the past few years, according to recent research, by as much as 92 percent.[55] Though, again at least on Twitter, there was a certain amount of "street cred" earned by those whose accounts had been shut down. (Based on extensive interviews with a large number of IS supporters, one study found, interestingly, that when accounts got shut down, many were not just constantly creating new accounts, as had been assumed. Instead they were hacking into accounts left inactive from countries all over the world—but especially in those countries where phone numbers were not necessary for logins.[56])

This does not mean that the problem has been solved, certainly not that it has been solved on all platforms. YouTube, for example, is still hosting clearly dangerous material.[57]

In part the companies' credibility problems stem from the fact that they keep making promises they clearly are not keeping. In part their problems stem from issues such as Facebook's security error which exposed a number of their personnel hired to review extremist content, having their personal data exposed to the very people whose material they were reviewing. These employees of Facebook, who are apparently receiving low pay and virtually no support for a job that can involve spending hours a day looking at material that may include child pornography or beheading videos, depending on their specialty, were exposed to the potentially very dangerous individuals they were supposed to be helping Facebook keep off the platform. They essentially had to go into hiding—with no assistance from the company at all.[58]

3.4.3 Telegram and the Move to Encrypted Platforms

As social media has become increasingly inhospitable to these groups, they needed somewhere to go that would serve the same purposes for them that social media sites had been for years. Often, the answer has been a platform known as Telegram. Telegram has public channels but it also has private "chats" where users can communicate with a number of other individuals simultaneously in a forum that offers end-to-end encryption. Prior to the Paris attacks of 2015, the site had been reluctant to police any content at all, but after evidence emerged that the attack had been planned in part on their platform they have tightened up on content on the public channels somewhat—but they refuse to touch the private chats at all.[59] To be sure, Telegram is not an ideal solution for these groups. While end-to-end encryption may be ideal for planning purposes, that presumes they have selected a target to attack and, crucially, already recruited someone (or someones) to launch the attack. For recruitment and radicalization they need digital spaces that are open and public facing. To invite someone into a private chat, you first have to meet them and convince them to at least go so far as to be interested in further engagement.

3.5 DESCRIPTION OF THE RADICALIZATION PROCESS

This of course begs the question—what is the actual radicalization *process*? How does it occur?

Explaining how radicalization happens, of course, itself begs the question: what *is* radicalization? To date, there has been no agreement in the literature with regard to a single or consensus definition of the radicalization process. Terrorism expert John Horgan defined radicalization as "the social and psychological process of incrementally experienced commitment to extremist political or religious ideology."[60] Yet, Louis Porter and Mark Kebbell offered a definition that is broader yet still manages to provide a more on point perspective, defining radicalization as "the process by which individuals (or groups) change their beliefs, adopt an extremist viewpoint, and advocate (or practice) violence to achieve their goals."[61]

The pathway to radicalization varies considerably from person to person and is a matter of individual choice. Increasingly, therefore, researchers of terrorism no longer view radicalization as a condition isolated in one person, but more as a dynamic and gradual process influenced by a multitude of factors along the way.[62] Samuel J. Leistedt has noted that radicalization, changes in "beliefs, feelings, and attitudes" but in the directions that make violence easier to justify, is often associated

> with a syndrome of beliefs about the current situation and its history: We are a special or chosen group (superiority) who have been unfairly treated and betrayed (injustice), no one else cares about us or will help us (distrust), and the situation is dire.[63]

Again, it is not our position that all radicalization takes place online: it is quite clear that is not the case.[64]

Part of the problem is that, unsurprisingly given that there is no consensus even on what radicalization is, there is no consensus on how it happens. There are different theories,[65] different bodies of research, and different models underlying the research. Fathali Moghaddam, for example, describes radicalization as a winding spiral staircase, which narrows as it goes up, with correspondingly fewer off-ramps as one climbs, until the top—violent behavior—is reached. And once the individual has actually participated in acts of violence, it is extremely difficult to leave the group, relative to what it would be like to get someone away from the group at lower levels (say, watching propaganda videos or exchanging tweets with group members).[66]

3.6 SUMMARY AND CONCLUSIONS

We don't believe there is any question that there is a link between social media and radicalization, even if it is impossible to quantify that link, and even if radicalization without a doubt has occurred in the past without any involvement of social media. These platforms make it easier for people to become radicalized, they make it easier for that process to happen more quickly than it otherwise would, and they make it more likely that people radicalized to extremist points of view may make that final leap, becoming radicalized to believe that violence is appropriate.

Given that, what are possible options? As mentioned, take downs of both accounts and content is one possibility, and where companies have been aggressive, that seems to have had an impact. But it seems highly unlikely, given the enormous amounts of material we are talking about—literally thousands of accounts and tens of thousands of postings—that all of it will be permanently taken down, especially given that there are still individuals trying to put these materials back up. Some of this content will slip through.

J.M. Berger, co-author of the *ISIS Twitter Census*, actually believes this is the right balance. Without the large numbers that the group once had they cannot, as mentioned above, take the kind of actions they once did that involved mobilizing thousands of accounts acting in unison, such as moving trends or hashtags. It's much more difficult for them to radicalize random individuals. But there is enough material on the sites to function as material for open-source intelligence.[67]

The other possibility is CVE or counter-violent extremism (sometimes AVE or anti-violent extremism or PVE preventing violent extremism). This covers a wide variety of programs, some of which are online, some of which are not, and some of which attempt to include both online and offline components. Some CVE programs have been government-run, but these have been almost universally viewed as failures. Over the last few years, most governments, including the United States and U.K., began transitioning to government sponsorship, although federal funding of such programs is on life support in the United States.[68]

In Europe and the U.K. (where, admittedly, the problem of radicalization has been more urgent than in the United States) there has been a more robust network of non-profits working in this field. And there have been "networks of networks," some receiving government funding and some not, helping them to coordinate efforts, resources, conferences and so forth, organizations such as the European Commission's RAN (Radicalisation Awareness Network) or the private FATE (Families Against Terrorism and Extremism).

One glaring problem is that there is almost no research in this area that offers well designed, reliable, social science metrics on the outcomes of any of these programs. Metrics are desperately needed.[69] This need is especially urgent given the number of countries confronting the issue of fighters returning from the so-called Islamic State, or about to be released from prison having completed sentences on terrorism charges. These men and women (and in many cases children) need to be reintegrated into their communities. But how? What programs have the most reliable and proven track record?

We wish we had an answer. All we are certain of is that real data and appropriate study design have to be built in from the beginning, when programs are starting, or at the very least when individuals are starting their experiences in individual programs.

NOTES

1. Lorenzo Vidino and Seamus Hughes, "San Bernardino and the Islamic State Footprint in America," *CTC Sentinel* 8, no. 11 (November/December 2015) https://ctc.usma.edu/san-bernardino-and-the-islamic-state-%E2%80%A8footprint-in-america/.

2. For an excellent review of the recent literature on both sides, see Alexander Meleagrou-Hitchens, Audrey Alexander, and Nick Kaderbhai, "The impact of digital communications technology on radicalization and recruitment," *International Affairs* 93, no. 5 (September 2017): 1233–1249, and note that this article covers the research into both the jihadist and white supremacist sides https://academic.oup.com/ia/article/93/5/1233/4098292.

3. Paul Gill et al., "Terrorist use of the internet by the numbers," *Criminology and Public Policy* 16, no. 1 (2017). https://onlinelibrary.wiley.com/doi/pdf/10.1111/1745-9133.12249.

4. The Counter-Extremism Project, *Anwar Al-Awlaki: Part III: Anwar Al-Awlaki Online* (Washington, DC: Counter-Extremism Project, June, 2017) https://www.counterextremism.com/sites/default/themes/bricktheme/pdfs/Anwar_Online060617.pdf.

5. Scott Shane, "In 'Watershed Moment', YouTube Blocks Extremist Clerics' Message," *New York Times* (November 12, 2017) https://www.nytimes.com/2017/11/12/us/politics/youtube-terrorism-anwar-al-awlaki.html.

6. John P. Carlin with Garrett M. Graff, *Dawn of the Code War: America's Battle Against Russia, China, and the Rising Global Cyber Threat* (New York: Public Affairs Books, October 2018), p. 17.

7. Cori E. Dauber and Mark D. Robinson, "Guest Post: ISIS and the Hollywood Visual Style," *Jihadology.net* (July 6, 2015) http://jihadology.net/2015/07/06/guest-post-isis-and-the-hollywood-visual-style/.

8. Maeghin Alarid, "Chapter13: Recruitment and Radicalization: The Role of Social Media and New Technology," *The Journal of Complex Operations, National Defense University* (May 24, 2016), p. 315 https://cco.ndu.edu/News/Article/780274/chapter-13-recruitment-and-radicalization-the-role-of-social-media-and-new-tech/.

9. Amarnath Amarsingam and Lorne L. Dawson, *"I Left To Be Closer to Allah": Learning about Foreign Fighters from Family and Friends* (Washington, DC: ISD, 2018) http://www.isdglobal.org/wp-content/uploads/2018/05/Families_Report.pdf.

10. Jytte Klausen, *A Behavioral Study of the Radicalization Trajectories of American "Homegrown" Al-Qaeda Inspired Terrorist Offenders* (US Department of Justice, National Institute of Justice, 2013-ZA-BX-0005, August 2016).

11. Christer Mattsson and Thomas Johansson, "Becoming, belonging, and leaving – Exit processes among young neo-Nazis in Sweden," *Journal of Deradicalization*, 16 (Fall 2018) http://journals.sfu.ca/jd/index.php/jd/article/view/161/125.

12. Paul Gill, John Horgan, and Paige Deckert, "Bombing alone: Tracing the motivations and antecedent behaviors of lone-actor terrorists," *Journal of Forensic Science* 59, no. 2 (March 2014): 425–435 https://www.ncbi.nlm.nih.gov/pmc/articles/PMC4217375/pdf/jfo0059-0425.pdf.

13. David Hofman, *How "Alone" Are Lone Actors? Exploring the Ideological, Signaling, and Support Networks of Lone-Actor Terrorists TSAS Working Paper Series* No. 18-02 (Winter 2018) https://www.tsas.ca/wp-content/uploads/2018/02/TSAS-Working-Paper-Hofmann-Lone-Actors-Final.pdf.

14. Raffaelo Pantucci, "What have we learned about lone wolves from anders behring breivik?," *Perspectives on Terrorism* 5, no. 5–6 (2011) http://www.terrorismanalysts.com/pt/index.php/pot/article/view/what-we-have-learned/332.

15. Mark S. Hamm and Ramon Spaaj, *Lone Wolf Terrorism in America: Using Knowledge of Radicalization Pathways to Forge Prevention Strategies* (Washington, DC: US Department of Justice #2012-ZA-BX-0001, 2012), 2 https://www.ncjrs.gov/pdffiles1/nij/grants/248691.pdf.

16. Evan Dyer, "Anti-terrorism experts still grappling with what it means to be 'radicalised,'" *CBCNews.com* (August 20, 2016) https://www.cbc.ca/news/politics/radicalized-experts-tools-1.3728049

17. Paul Gill, "What can we learn from the life histories of lone wolves?" *Radicalisation Research* July 6, 2015 https://www.radicalisationresearch.org/debate/gill-lone-wolves.

18. Riyadh Hosain Rahimullah, Stephen Larmar, and Mohamad Abdalla, "Understanding violent radicalization amongst muslims: A review of the literature," *Journal of Psychology and Behavioral Science* 1, no. 1 (December 2013): 19–35 https://core.ac.uk/download/pdf/143865434.pdf.

19. All numbers from *Statista*.

20. Mark Prensky, "Digital Natives, Digital Immigrants," *On the Horizon*, 9, no. 5 (October 2001) https://www.marcprensky.com/writing/Prensky%20-%20Digital%20Natives,%20Digital%20Immigrants%20-%20Part1.pdf.

21. For a highly readable history of the move from the origins of the internet to social media, see P. W. Singer and Emerson T. Brooking, *LikeWar: The Weaponization of Social Media* (Boston, MA.: Eamon Dolan Books of Houghton Mifflin Harcourt, 2018), particularly the first two chapters.

22. See Catherine Tremble, "Wild Westworld: Section 230 of the CDA and social networks' use of machine-learning algorithms," *Fordham Law Review* 86, no. 2 (2017) https://ir.lawnet.fordham.edu/cgi/viewcontent.cgi?referer=https://www.google.com/&httpsredir=1&article=5450&context=flr.

23. Roger McNamee, "I invested early in Google and Facebook. Now they terrify me." *USA Today* (August 8, 2017) https://www.usatoday.com/story/opinion/2017/08/08/my-google-and-facebook-investments-made-fortune-but-now-they-menace/543755001/.

24. Jack Nicas, "How YouTube drives people to the internet's darkest corners," *Wall Street Journal* (February 7, 2018) https://www.wsj.com/articles/how-youtube-drives-viewers-to-the-internets-darkest-corners-1518020478.

25. This drives the echo chamber problem, and has been a driver behind fake news and conspiracy theories. See the section on "homophily" in Singer and Brooking, *LikeWar* starting on p. 123.

26. Alarid, "Chapter13,"

27. Katerina Girginova, "Hijacking Heads and Hashtags," *Global-E*, 10, no. 56 (August 24, 2017) http://www.21global.ucsb.edu/global-e/august-2017/hijacking-heads-hashtags.

28. P.W. Singer and Emerson Brooking, "Terror on Twitter," *Popular Science* (December 15, 2015) https://www.popsci.com/terror-on-twitter-how-isis-is-taking-war-to-social-media.

29. Warwick Ashford, "Jihadists in Iraq hijack World Cup hashtags," *ComputerWeekly.com* (June 23, 2014) https://www.computerweekly.com/news/2240223131/Jihadists-in-Iraq-hijack-World-Cup-hashtags.

30. "Islamic State hijack Justin Bieber hashtag to try and spread graphic video about the terror group," *News Corps Australia* (January 22, 2016) https://www.news.com.au/technology/online/hacking/islamic-state-hack-justin-bieber-hashtag-to-try-and-spread-graphic-video-about-the-terror-group/news-story/fdccc50b8a87f09aa14f77c0fc7d4816. As near as we can tell, weirdly, this was primarily a news story in Australia and New Zealand.

31. It is true that the evidence is not all one-sided regarding anonymity. There is some potential for individuals to be more helpful when they are anonymous, for example. Joe Dawson, "Who is that? The study of anonymity and behavior," *Association for Psychological Science* (April 2018) https://www.psychologicalscience.org/observer/who-is-that-the-study-of-anonymity-and-behavior.

32. See the discussions of this phenomena scattered throughout Singer and Emerson, *LikeWar*.

33. It's a bit dated, because it does not account for the fairly large waves of accounts Twitter has shut down, but the classic study of this is J.M. Berger and Jonathon Morgan, *The ISIS Twitter Census: Defining and describing the population of ISIS supporters on Twitter* (The Brookings Project on Relations with the Islamic World, Analysis Paper No. 20, March 2015) https://www.brookings.edu/wp-content/uploads/2016/06/isis_twitter_census_berger_morgan.pdf.

34. Elizabeth Bodine Baron, *Examining ISIS Support and Opposition Networks on Twitter* (Santa Monica, CA.: RAND Corporation, 2016) https://www.rand.org/content/dam/rand/pubs/research_reports/RR1300/RR1328/RAND_RR1328.pdf.

35. Amy Mitchell et al., "Political polarization and media habits," *Pew Research Center on Journalism and Media* (October 21, 2014) http://www.journalism.org/2014/10/21/political-polarization-media-habits/.

36. Laura Jakli and Paul Gill, "Follow the echo chamber: measuring political attitude change and media effects on twitter," *Vox-Pol* (October 10, 2018) https://www.voxpol.eu/follow-the-echo-chamber-measuring-political-attitude-change-and-media-effects-on-twitter/.

37. See, for example, Bertjan Doosje et al., "Terrorism, radicalization, and de-radicalization," *Current Opinion in Psychology* 11 (2016): 79–84 https://nvvb.nl/media/cms_page_media/694/Terrorism%2C%20radicalization%20and%20de-radicalization.pdf.

38. Jamie Dettmer, "What ISIS learned from pedophiles," *Daily Beast* (April 9, 2015) https://www.thedailybeast.com/what-isis-learned-from-pedophiles.

39. As an example of how a terrorist group can reach out to someone (who had evinced no interest in extremism) over social media see Rukmini Callimachi, "ISIS and the lonely young American," *New York Times* (June 27, 2015) http://www.nytimes.com/2015/06/28/world/americas/isis-online-recruiting-american.html?hp&action=click&pgtype=Homepage&module=second-column-region&region=top-news&WT.nav=top-news&_r=0.

40. Paul Jackson, "The British extreme right, reciprocal radicalisation and constructions of the other," *Radicalisation Research* (September 3, 2018) https://www.radicalisationresearch.org/debate/jackson-british-extreme-right-reciprocal-radicalisation/.

41. Dorie Hellmuth, "Of alienation, association, and adventure: Why German fighters join ISIL," *Journal of Deradicalization* 16, no. 6 (Fall 2018) http://journals.sfu.ca/jd/index.php/jd/article/view/42.

42. Quantum Communications, "Understanding Jihadists in their own words," *Quantum Communications: The White Papers* no. 2 (March 2015), link via Patrick Tucker and Defense One, "Why join ISIS? How fighters respond when you ask them," *The Atlantic* (December 9, 2015) https://www.theatlantic.com/international/archive/2015/12/why-people-join-isis/419685/.

43. J.M. Berger, "Tailored online interventions: The Islamic state's recruitment strategy," *CTC Sentinel* 8, no. 10 (October 2015) https://ctc.usma.edu/tailored-online-interventions-the-islamic-states-recruitment-strategy/.

44. J.M. Berger, "How terrorists recruit online (and how to stop it,)" *Markaz*, November 9, 2015 https://www.brookings.edu/blog/markaz/2015/11/09/how-terrorists-recruit-online-and-how-to-stop-it/.

45. Kimiko De Freytas-Tamura, "Popular teen now a 'poster girl' for Islamic State recruitment," *The Seattle Times* (February 24, 2015) https://www.seattletimes.com/news/popular-teen-now-a-poster-girl-for-islamic-state-recruitment/.

46. "ISIS after the Caliphate," *The Wilson Center* (January 8, 2018) https://www.wilsoncenter.org/article/isis-after-the-caliphate-0.

47. Efraim Benmelech and Esteban F. Klor, "What Explains the Flow of Foreign Fighters to ISIS?" Kellogg School of Management Northwestern University, April 2016, unpublished ms. https://www.kellogg.northwestern.edu/faculty/benmelech/html/BenmelechPapers/ISIS_April_13_2016_Effi_final.pdf.

48. Robin Simcox, "The Islamic State's Western Teenage Plotters," *CTC Sentinel*, 10, no. 2 (February 2017) https://ctc.usma.edu/the-islamic-states-western-teenage-plotters/.

49. Lata Nott, "Free Expression on Social Media," *Freedom Forum Institute*, 2018 https://www.freedomforuminstitute.org/first-amendment-center/primers/free-expression-on-social-media/.

50. See Ryan Mac, "Literally Just A Big List of Facebook's 2018 Scandals," *Buzzfeed*, December 20, 2018 https://www.buzzfeednews.com/article/ryanmac/literally-just-a-big-list-of-facebooks-2018-scandals.

51. Evelyn Douek, "Zuckerberg's New Hate Speech Plan: Out With the Court and In With the Code," *Lawfare*, April 14, 2018 https://www.lawfareblog.com/zuckerbergs-new-hate-speech-plan-out-court-and-code.

52. Euan McKirdy, "Facebook: We didn't do enough to prevent Myanmar violence," *CNN.com* (November 6, 2018) https://www.cnn.com/2018/11/06/tech/facebook-myanmar-report/index.html.

53. Daniel Boffey, "EU threatens to crackdown on Facebook over hate speech," *The Guardian* (April 11, 2018) https://www.theguardian.com/technology/2018/apr/11/eu-heavy-sanctions-online-hate-speech-facebook-scandal.

54. We could not find a breakout of Facebook users specific to EU membership, but in Europe there are 376 million active users as of the last quarter of 2018. *Statistiva* https://www.statista.com/statistics/745400/facebook-europe-mau-by-quarter/.

55. Maura Conway, "Islamic State's social media moment has passed," *Demos Quarterly* (November 2017) https://quarterly.demos.co.uk/article/issue-12/islamic-states-social-media-moment/

56. Amarnath Amarasingam, "What Twitter really means for Islamic state supporters," *War on the Rocks* (December 30, 2015) https://warontherocks.com/2015/12/what-twitter-really-means-for-islamic-state-supporters/.

57. Joshua Fisher-Birch, "Continuing availability of ISIS bomb-making videos on Google platforms," *CEP:Tech and Terrorism* (January 11, 2018) https://www.counterextremism.com/blog/continuing-availability-isis-bomb-making-videos-google-platforms-0.

58. Olivia Solon, "Revealed: Facebook exposed the identities of moderators to suspected terrorists," *The Guardian* (June 16, 2017) https://www.theguardian.com/technology/2017/jun/16/facebook-moderators-identity-exposed-terrorist-groups.

59. Counter-Extremism Project, *Terrorists on Telegram* (Washington, DC: Counter-Extremism Project, May, 2017) https://www.counterextremism.com/sites/default/files/Terrorists%20on%20Telegram_052417.pdf particularly pp. 3–5, "How Terrorists Use Telegram."

60. John Horgan, *Walking Away from Terrorism: Accounts of Disengagement from Radical and Extremist Movements* (New York: Routledge, 2009).

61. Louis E. Porter and Mark R. Kebbell, "Radicalization in Australia: Examining Australia's convicted terrorists," *Psychiatry, Psychology and Law* 18, no. 2 (2011): 213.

62. See Randy Borum, "Radicalization into violent extremism I: A review of social science theories," *Journal of Strategic Security* Vol. 4, no. 4 (Winter 2011): 7–36 https://scholarcommons.usf.edu/cgi/viewcontent.cgi?referer=https://www.google.com/&httpsredir=1&article=1139&context=jss for a discussion of the literature.

63. Samuel J. Leistedt, "Psychiatry and behavioral sciences on the radicalization process," *Journal of Forensic Sciences* Vol. 61 (2016): 4.

64. Clark McCauley and Sophia Moskalenko, "Mechanisms of political radicalization: Pathways toward terrorism," *Terrorism and Political Violence* Vol. 20, no. 3 (2008): 425.

65. For an excellent review of much of the literature see Borum, "A Review."

66. Fathali M. Moghaddam, "The staircase to terrorism: A psychological explanation," *American Psychologist* Vol. 60, no. 2 (February–March 2005): 161–169 http://fathalimoghaddam.com/wp-content/uploads/2013/10/1256627851.pdf.

67. J.M. Berger, Testimony before the House Committee on Foreign Affairs, "The evolution of terrorist propaganda: The Paris attack and social media," *Brookings* (January 27, 2015) https://www.brookings.edu/testimonies/the-evolution-of-terrorist-propaganda-the-paris-attack-and-social-media/.

68. Peter Beinart, "Trump shut programs to counter violent extremism," *The Atlantic* (October 29, 2018) https://www.theatlantic.com/ideas/archive/2018/10/trump-shut-countering-violent-extremism-program/574237/.

69. National Consortium for the Study of Terrorism and the Responses to Terrorism, *Surveying CVE Metrics in Prevention, Disengagement and Deradicalization Programs* (Report to the Office of University Programs, Science and Technology Directorate, US Department of Homeland Security, March 2016) https://www.start.umd.edu/pubs/START_SurveyingCVEMetrics_March2016.pdf.

Chapter 4

Rule-of-Law and Respect for Human Rights Considerations

Omi Hodwitz

CONTENTS

4.1 INTRODUCTION

Terrorists have become increasingly sophisticated in their recruitment and radicalization strategies. As social media and other online forums become popular, extremist groups adopt these tools as the primary means by which to distribute their message and solicit allegiance for their causes. Evidence suggests that their tactics have been successful. More often than not, investigations carried out in Western nations following high-profile terrorist attacks indicate that assailants went through a process of online radicalization. In short, many of the more prominent attacks in Western democracies have been carried out by single individuals or couples that found inspiration and instructions on the internet.

In response to the increasing online presence of radical elements, intelligence and enforcement agencies have engaged in a variety of cyber activities. The purpose of these activities is multifold: to identify potential extremists, to isolate and remove pro-terrorist content, and to undermine the organizational capacities of militant groups. Ranging from mass public surveillance to cyber offensives designed to disrupt network communications, these state-led tactics have produced positive outcomes. However, they have also raised a number of concerns.

Nations are required by international law to ensure the security of their citizens. Carrying out targeted surveillance, gathering data with the intent of locating potential terrorists, removing pro-terrorist online content, and disrupting communication networks are all measures intended to ensure the security of the general public. In addition, states are required to protect citizens' liberties, such as the right to privacy and non-discrimination. Mass surveillance and targeted profiling, while promoting security, may infringe these liberties and, therefore, violate international law.

The tension between securities and liberties is not a new tension, but it has been pushed to the forefront in light of terrorist cyber presence and state response to the threats posed by these radical elements. The following chapter elaborates on the current iteration of the tension between ensuring security and upholding liberties. Beginning with three case studies designed to illustrate the different perspectives key to the conversation, this chapter provides a brief introduction to the security versus liberty debate. In addition, the reader is introduced to the liberties protected under international, European, and United States law. Potential infringements of these laws are discussed, with a focus on oversurveillance and profiling, censorship, the increasing invisibility of police activities and the chain of evidence, and the risk of the identification of false positives. The purpose of this chapter is to provide an overview of the legal considerations inherent in security responses to terrorists' cyber presence; it is beyond the parameters of this chapter to offer a solution to the security versus liberty debate. Nevertheless, the chapter concludes with some considerations regarding how to best respect liberties while still working to ensure security.

4.2 CASE STUDIES

On December 2, 2015, Syed Rizwan Farook and Tashfeen Malik opened fire on employees of the Department of Public Health attending a holiday party at the Inland Regional Center in San Bernardino, California. The couple fled, leaving behind a backpack containing explosive devices that failed to detonate; they were later killed by police in a shootout. In addition to the perpetrators, another 14 people were killed and 22 people were injured in the attack. In the aftermath, authorities scoured Farook and Malik's online profile, uncovering a number of exchanges that would have raised serious concerns of radicalization if identified before the attack. In 2012 and 2014, for example, Malik had sent private messages to Pakistani friends pledging her support for Islamic jihad while Farook maintained contact with overseas terrorist organizations, including Al-Nusra Front and Al-Shabaab [1].

On June 19, 2017, Makram Ali collapsed at a bus stop near Finsbury Park in London. Passers-by, including a group of Muslims, stopped to offer aid to Ali. As they were providing assistance, Darren Osborne drove a rental van into the crowd, injuring at least nine people and killing Ali. As Osborne was taken into custody, witnesses reported hearing him say that he "wanted to kill more Muslims" [2]. Following Osborne's arrest, authorities scanned his computer and found evidence of online radicalization; Osborne had spent a considerable amount of time searching extreme-right figures and consuming hate-based propaganda. He had also received Twitter and email messages from leaders of well-known far-right groups, such as Britain First. Osborne's rapid radicalization went unnoticed by law enforcement until he carried out his attack.

In June, 2013, the Western world was stunned to learn the details of a global surveillance program implemented in the aftermath of the 2001 terrorist attacks in the United States (9/11). Edward Snowden, a contractor for the National Security Agency (NSA), in a move of impressive clandestine proportions and armed with caches of classified documents, met with reporters in Hong Kong after fleeing the United States. Throughout the course of a 14-hour interview, Snowden described in detail the process by which legal authorities in the United States had empowered the NSA to engage in mass surveillance of the internet, telephone, and location records of entire populations. Shortly after the Hong Kong meeting, Snowden was charged with violations of the espionage act and theft of government property. Snowden claimed that, in revealing classified secrets, he was complying with his oath of allegiance which, he argued, is an oath to the Constitution, not to secrecy [3].

These case studies illustrate two points that will be a theme of this chapter. First, collective security is threatened by the use of online mediums by extremist elements and, second, while governments are beholden to address these threats to security, they are also required to consider liberties protected under the rule of law when crafting responses to these threats.

4.3 LIBERTY VERSUS SECURITY DEBATE

Benjamin Franklin once stated that "Those who would give up essential liberty, to purchase a little temporary safety, deserve neither liberty nor safety." This statement is often inserted into debates concerning individual rights and collective safety or what has been popularized as the security versus liberty debate. Conflicting viewpoints stem from the central question of how a country should balance the two necessary conditions of ensuring the safety of its citizens while also respecting their individual liberties. States are required to protect their citizens but place limited compromises on individual freedoms; the sacrosanct and often conflicting nature of each of these obligations leads to a great deal of tension. The case studies cited previously illustrate this. The attacks in San Bernardino and London likely elicit a negative response from the reader; perhaps you are wondering why law enforcement failed to identify these assailants before they had an opportunity to cause harm. Likewise, the knowledge that the United States may have been spying on you and your community in an aggressive and potentially unconstitutional manner may also solicit anger. However, in order to identify and waylay threats such as those posed by extremists like Osborne, Farook, and Malik, it may be necessary to infringe on some constitutionally protected freedoms, such as a right to privacy. Snowden claimed that by releasing classified documents, he was protecting citizen rights to liberty, while his opponents claim that he was compromising individual security. Therein lies the catch-22: how do we gain security without losing freedoms? Where is the balance in these perspectives?

4.4 COLLECTIVE SECURITY

Western democracies have an obligation to provide security to their citizens and to do all that can be reasonably expected in order to protect their populations from harm. This obligation includes both domestic and international threats posed by state and non-state actors alike. Following the

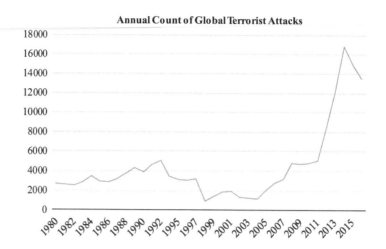

Figure 4.1   Annual Count of Global Terrorist Attacks, 1980–2016 [4].

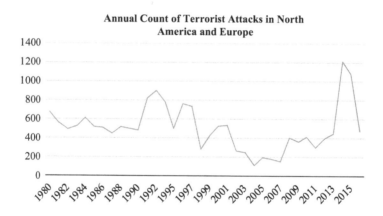

Figure 4.2   Annual Count of Terrorist Attacks in North America and Europe, 1980–2016 [4].

attacks in the United States in 2001 (9/11), the need for a coordinated and effective counterterrorism agenda has become a prominent part of that obligation. This need is even more pressing in light of increasing trends in terrorism. As illustrated in Figure 4.1, global terrorist attacks have risen dramatically since 2011. Although violence declined modestly starting in 2014, the last half decade has witnessed an unprecedented number of politically motivated attacks. Much of this increase has occurred in states plagued by civil conflict and political instability, such as Afghanistan and Iraq; however, the Western world has been subject to similar trends in terrorism on a smaller scale. Figure 4.2 reports annual numbers of attacks in North America and Europe between 1980 and 2016 illustrating recent patterns that are similar to global trends.

As terrorism increases so too has the use of information and communication technologies (ICTs) and terrorists' use of such technologies. ICTs offer an accessible, cheap, less risky, and more effective method of planning and conducting terrorist operations, spreading propaganda, and recruiting, fundraising, and pursuing other criminal activities. Terrorists can reach a wider audience, sow fear through the distribution of execution videos, facilitate radicalization, and inspire support, all at the click of a button. As the San Bernardino and London cases demonstrate, ICTs can be quite effective at inspiring terrorism.

Faced with record high numbers of terrorist attacks and an obligation to protect citizens from harm, states have turned their attention toward monitoring and regulating cyberspace in an effort to hinder terrorists' use of ICTs. One primary method used by law enforcement agencies involves the use of data mining. Data mining is the process of extracting patterns and trends from large amounts of data using a variety of techniques such as machine learning and pattern recognition. Data mining has the potential to uncover a great deal of information given the sheer volume of data available for analysis. For example, IBM has estimated that global society produces approximately 2.5 quintillion bytes of data every day [5]. To put this into perspective, if each byte were a penny, laying them side-by-side would cover the world five times over. These data include both stored and temporary information, including phone call content and records, financial records, social media posts, photos, videos, emails, and the like. Data can be analyzed in order to locate someone in time and space, establish links between individuals, and search for signs of nefarious activities.

Governments have accessed private and public sector databases in order to monitor data trails left by individuals in cyberspace. Combining the information from these databases creates a detailed picture of an individual's life, activities, affiliates, and beliefs. States are exploring the use of software that would not only identify suspicious behavior but also hostile intent, directing state attention to those activities. Once threats have been determined, authorities can install spyware on personal computers or use other forms of tapping and tracing technology to monitor the behavior and activities of suspects and their affiliates [6].

States have solicited cooperation from the corporate sector to aid in the monitoring and control of online activity. Under the direction of governments, social media platforms have adopted a number of policies that facilitate the removal of terrorism-related content. In many cases, this entails strengthening company terms of service in order to remove content more easily. Twitter, for example, reported removing more than 375,000 accounts in the latter half of 2016 for content violations related to the promotion of terrorism [7]. A second development is the creation of a database that records "hashes" of terrorist content that companies have identified and removed from their sites; this allows other companies to follow suit more easily [8]. A third development is the formation of the Global Internet Forum to Counter Terrorism, a collective of technology companies that have banded together in order to curtail terrorist content on their consumer sites.

Whether it is through the use of data mining, other forms of "dataveillance," or soliciting corporate participation, Western democracies have been actively engaged in the monitoring of cyberspace in order to curtail terrorist use of ICTs for recruitment, propaganda, and fundraising. These activities, while in line with the obligation to ensure collective security, have been criticized for violating collective liberties guaranteed under the rule of law.

4.5 INDIVIDUAL LIBERTIES

Individual liberties are codified and protected in a number of ways, including international, national, and state law (see Figure 4.3). On an international level, human rights are enshrined in the Universal Declaration of Human Rights, presented by the United Nations General Assembly in 1948. And, although there are a number of Western democracies that have similar legislation, the debate about surveillance and human rights has focused on the European Union and United States laws and regulations, so this chapter will follow suit. The European Union protects

Figure 4.3 International and Federal Law Protecting Individual Liberties.

human rights in the Charter of Fundamental Rights, which was adopted in 2000 and made binding in 2009. Meanwhile, the United States Constitution, adopted in 1789, provides similar protections. Critics of cyber surveillance, interception, and targeting have argued that these practices and procedures infringe on a variety of human rights protected under these international and national laws. Specifically, critics claim that intelligence and enforcement agencies are violating rights to privacy, data protection, expression, and non-discrimination.

4.5.1 The Right to Privacy

On an international level, the right to privacy is protected by Article 12 of the Universal Declaration of Human Rights, which decrees that "no one shall be subjected to arbitrary or unlawful interference with his (or her) privacy, family, home or correspondence, nor to unlawful attacks on his (or her) honor and reputation" [9] (see Figure 4.4). This right is also protected by Article 17 of the International Covenant on Civil and Political Rights. The right to privacy is not absolute; any interference with this right must be necessary, legitimate, and proportionate.

The right to privacy is also protected at the state level, although these liberties differ between states. In older constitutions, case law and constitutional courts have recognized the right to privacy [10]. In the United States, for example, the Supreme Court determined that the right to privacy was enshrined in the Fourth Amendment: the prohibition of unreasonable search and seizure. In other states, the right to privacy is a new adoption, such as in the European Union, where the right to privacy was enshrined in 2000 in Article 7 of the Charter of Fundamental Rights.

4.5.2 The Right to Protection of Personal Data

In addition to the right to privacy, there are a number of additional human rights that are relevant when discussing the monitoring and regulation of cyberspace. Although not explicitly protected by overarching federal legislation, the protection of personal data in the United States is addressed through a series of overlapping and sometimes contradictory laws and regulations at the state and federal level. These include laws providing broad consumer protection, safeguarding activities that use personal information, and protecting particular categories of information. Unlike the United States, the European Union has binding data protection laws enshrined in the Charter of Fundamental Rights. As stated in Article 8, "everyone has the right to the protection of personal data concerning him or her" [11]. Similar protections are not afforded at the international level.

4.5.3 The Right to Freedom of Expression

Dataveillance also brings up concerns regarding freedom of expression. This is a recognized human right under Article 19 of the Universal Declaration of Human Rights. It is stated that, "everyone shall have the right to hold opinions without interference ... everyone shall have the right to freedom of expression; this right shall include freedom to seek, receive and impart information and ideas of all kinds, regardless of frontiers, either orally, in writing or in print, in the form of art, or through any other media of his (or her) choice." Similar to the right to privacy, this international human right is not absolute but can only be interfered with in extreme circumstances. The United States provides protections for free expression in the First Amendment of the Constitution, while the European Union protects it in Article 10 of the European Convention on Human Rights.

4.5.4 The Right to Non-Discrimination

Freedom from discrimination is also of concern when surveilling for security purposes. Article 1 and 2 of the Universal Declaration of Human Rights declares that all persons are "born free and equal in dignity and rights" and "everyone is entitled to the rights and freedoms without distinction of any kind, such as race, color, sex, language, political or other opinion, national or social origin, property, birth or other status. Furthermore, no distinction shall be made on the basis of the political, jurisdictional or international status of the country or territory to which a person belongs" [12]. The United States provides for equal protection of the laws under the Fourteenth Amendment, rather than protection against discrimination. The European Union provides protection for non-discrimination under Article 21 of the Charter.

In 2013, the United Nations General Assembly adopted Resolution 68/167 in response to concerns about authorities' surveillance and interception practices of ICTs and potential violations of human rights. The General Assembly requested that all states review their legislation and practices around communications surveillance and the collection of personal data. The resolution served as a reminder that the states needed to ensure compliance with international human rights law and formally validated concerns regarding enforcement procedures in these areas.

4.6 INFRINGEMENTS ON HUMAN RIGHTS

Following 9/11, counterterrorism policy began to focus on the incitement of terrorism through radicalization and recruitment campaigns. In May, 2005, for example, the Council of Europe implemented a requirement that states criminalize the provocation to commit terrorist acts and, in September of the same year, the Security Council introduced Resolution 1624, a request

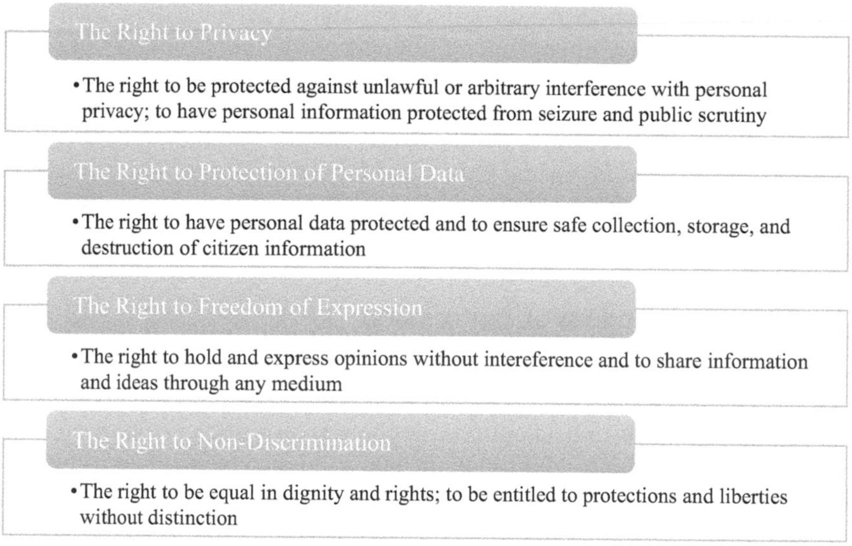

The Right to Privacy

- The right to be protected against unlawful or arbitrary interference with personal privacy; to have personal information protected from seizure and public scrutiny

The Right to Protection of Personal Data

- The right to have personal data protected and to ensure safe collection, storage, and destruction of citizen information

The Right to Freedom of Expression

- The right to hold and express opinions without intereference and to share information and ideas through any medium

The Right to Non-Discrimination

- The right to be equal in dignity and rights; to be entitled to protections and liberties without distinction

Figure 4.4   Description of Individual Liberties.

of United Nations member states to prohibit and prevent incitement. Human rights advocates expressed concern that measures of this kind would lead to violations of civilian rights. Opponents of these broad policies and regulations pointed to a number of areas where they believed security would infringe on liberties, including the excessive and unjustified monitoring and censorship of the public, blurring of the lines between police and intelligence officials, the expectations and demands being placed on private companies and subsequent jurisdictional issues, unintended consequences of a cyber counteroffensive, and the likelihood and impacts of false positives. Each of these are addressed in the following sections.

4.6.1 Excessive and Unjustified Surveillance

Surveillance technologies have increased dramatically in recent years and include a number of methods to monitor, analyze, and screen human activity. As mentioned previously, states now have the capacity and tools to capture phone and email communications, to turn computers and cell phones into listening devices, to install and use spyware on personal devices, to access passwords, observe online activity and, through the use of algorithms, to detect and draw state attention to perceived threats. However, the rules that guide surveillance can be ambiguous and opaque, allowing intelligence agencies to circumvent expectations of privacy. In the United States, for example, there is no judicial consensus on the legalities of dataveillance (the process of monitoring data trails left behind by individuals). In regards to the Snowden case described at the beginning of this chapter, some judges determined that the NSA surveillance program was likely unconstitutional, some ruled that it was legal, while others have questioned the legitimacy of either ruling [13]. Without boundaries that legally define and limit state surveillance of private citizens, there is a great deal of potential that individual rights to privacy and data protection will be violated.

An exacerbating factor of the limited oversight on surveillance is that often individuals with no connection to terrorism or any other form of security threat will be caught up in the process of surveillance; their data are gathered and held by state authorities despite their innocence. In the name of countering terrorism, a number of states have adopted the practice of gathering large amounts of personal information from registers of students, residents, and travelers, as well as commercial databases. Linking these registers and databases produces a very detailed picture of each individual's life, interests, beliefs, and activities. The goals of such collection efforts are to assess individuals on physical, behavioral, and psychological characteristics to determine if they match profiles believed to have a high probability of being involved in terrorist activities [14]. Intelligence agencies will cast the net wide, trawling these databases indiscriminately with the intent of flagging individuals that match key characteristics. These data mining and profiling practices pose a continued threat to rights to privacy and non-discrimination. Agencies using these methods inevitably target a large population of people and employ profiles that are, at least partially, constructed from characteristics such as race, religion, and gender, which are legally protected from distinction. In addition, the very act of trawling these databases is an exercise in futility, also known as base rate fallacy; if the goal is to find a needle, it makes no sense to throw a bunch of hay on top of it.

The war on terror has also facilitated a great deal of transnational cooperation and information sharing on terrorist online activities. Although there may be much to gain from transnational collaboration, these activities can run counter to the rule of law. Specifically, governments now have the ability to bypass constitutional protections of privacy by eliciting the support of foreign governments to monitor their own citizens [10]. Along the same lines, repressive states can use these arrangements to justify unreasonable censorship of local residents.

Lastly, mass surveillance can affect the right to freedom of expression. Users of social media and other methods of communication may censor their own opinions and perspectives for fear that they are being scrutinized and are thus subject to sanctions. Private individuals may also limit their communication with others for similar reasons; a fear that they or other parties are being monitored and that communication puts them at risk.

4.6.2 The Relationship between Police and Intelligence Officials

As police and intelligence agencies attempt to combat terrorist activity in cyberspace, they have developed relationships that rely on police collecting information and passing it on to intelligence agents. In order to increase efficiency in this relationship, many police departments are using the tools and techniques of intelligence agencies. As a consequence of interagency collaboration and technology sharing, police transparency and accountability is decreasing [6]. In addition, those who are subject to police scrutiny may not have access to the reasons underlying this scrutiny and, therefore, are not able to challenge the unwelcome attention. This can affect the fairness of trials, given that persons accused of activities related to terrorism may not have access to evidence gathered through such channels.

4.6.3 The Role of Private Companies

Social media exploded in the years following 9/11. In 2006, both Twitter and Facebook became readily available to the public, and similar social media platforms followed shortly thereafter. Social media platforms became a significant way to build community, share information, and publicize personal and political agendas. These platforms gained popularity among members of the general public and, recognizing the value of these mediums, extremists began to use them for the purposes of radicalizing and recruiting target populations. Governments identified and responded to these trends by putting pressure on private social media companies, placing these companies in the middle of a difficult dynamic: balancing the rights of privacy and free expression promised to their customers and the demands of enforcement agencies.

Many states demanded that social media companies strengthen their terms of service in order to remove content that advocated for or promoted terrorism or political violence. Industry responded by adopting new policies and practices, many of which were focused on private censorship. YouTube, for example, uses an automated video removal system, while Facebook recently announced its intention to automatically scan users' posts and contact law enforcement if the content is flagged [15]. Although private censorship of this kind is a protected right (in the United States, for example, it is protected under the First Amendment), critics have suggested that some policies have gone too far. Concerned parties point out that social media companies tend to engage in excessive content takedown or account deactivation, often removing content or blocking users simply because a user included a picture of a well-known terrorist in their online communication [8]. They posit that automated censoring algorithms are imprecise and result in a large number of false positives, or the inaccurate identification of potential terrorist content. Critics also note that it is not clear what constitutes pro-terrorism speech; there are no explicit definitional boundaries. Lastly, they note that this is not an evidence-based practice; the intelligence and/or the research community has not determined that private censorship has an impact on the promotion of terrorism and may even be counterproductive. The Streisand Effect suggests that attempting to hide a piece of information can only result in its wide distribution, further exacerbating the issue.

Government demands on private companies raise a number of broader issues regarding the scope and breadth of state interference. First, each state applies a unique definition of terrorism which can result in inconsistencies across nations regarding acts that may or may not be illegal and, thus, subject to counterterrorist responses. Online mediums are not defined by national boundaries and, as such, states that demand that private companies remove content that complies with their definition of terrorism may be violating jurisdictional and legal boundaries if those companies are headquartered in other countries, if the content originates from somewhere else, and if the content does not meet the definition of terrorism in its origin country. In addition, critics have suggested that governments that feel legally restricted in their ability to censor may be outsourcing censorship by requesting that companies remove content [16]. In the United States, for example, pro-terrorism content is protected by the First Amendment and, therefore, the state's control over this kind of content is very limited. Lastly, by pressuring companies to strengthen their terms of service, states are seeking enforcement of terms relating to graphic content, malicious speech, and other characteristics that tend to far exceed what the government is permitted to censor.

4.6.4 Unintended Consequences

The United States Department of Defense (DOD) now officially recognizes cyberspace as the fifth domain of warfare, alongside land, air, sea, and space [17]. As such, United States Cyber Command (CYBERCOM) has waged war on terrorist groups, using cyber-attacks, for example, to degrade the Islamic State's presence online in order to interrupt their abilities to recruit and communicate. The success of these military offences is relatively unknown; however, there are a number of unintended consequences or collateral damages that have been sources of concern for the state and civil society alike. One tactic involves targeting cellular networks that are known to be used by extremists. While this may interrupt their ability to communicate and organize, these networks are often shared by other parties, including residents and key institutions, such as hospitals and schools. Weighing the costs of cutting hospital communications with the gains of cutting terrorist communications is a difficult zero-sum task and one that could facilitate violations of human security, regardless of the choice made. In addition, military officials have launched cyber counteroffensives in areas like Syria where networks are shared by both terrorists and humanitarian organizations. In these regions, attempts to disable extremists can actually prolong civil conflicts by hindering the ability of aid workers and service providers from effectively carrying out operations intended to benefit communities hard hit by terrorism.

4.6.5 False Positives

The last concern levied at the security versus liberty debate relates to the simple futility of many security measures. As mentioned previously, one response to terrorist online activities involves the dataveillance of large portions of the population. Data mining can produce trillions of pieces of information that are sifted through for potential targets. The sheer volume of the material leads to errors. False positives, or the false identification of a positive result, can lead to tens of thousands of misidentifications. Each of these leads needs to be investigated, draining state resources and encroaching on the lives of the innocent. In addition, false negatives, or a failure to identify a legitimate threat, can be just as likely. As such, the exchange between security and liberty is far from equitable with these practices; instead, a great deal of liberty is sacrificed for very little security.

4.7 FINDING THE BALANCE BETWEEN SECURITY AND LIBERTY

The goals of counterterrorism should not be given priority over maintaining the rule of law and respecting human rights except in the most extreme of circumstances and, even then, with great caution. Events such as 9/11 may warrant such an imbalance, but only after a careful assessment of the circumstances and consideration of the short- and long-term consequences, the communities most likely to be affected, and after diligent examinations of alternative courses of action. If liberties and rights are to be compromised in the name of security, measures such as surveillance, profiling, and the retention of personal data should be subject to a number of principled restrictions, as illustrated in Figure 4.5.

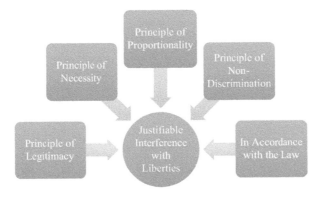

Figure 4.5   Principles of Justifiable Interference.

The European Convention on Human Rights states that interference with fundamental human rights must be justified as legitimate, necessary, proportionate, non-discriminatory, and in accordance with the law [18]. In other words, state actions and laws that interfere with liberty must meet these requirements. These principles extend beyond the European Union and underlie jurisprudence in democracies all over the world (Figure 4.6). The principle of legitimacy is perhaps the most complex; it has three components: the general public who are being asked to comply with authority must have an active voice and the ability to be heard, the law must be predictable, and the authority must be reasonable and fair. The principle of proportionality refers to the legal requirement of a balance between competing values. In order to ensure this principle is met, judges need to have the ability to assess whether measures have exceeded what is expected in order to achieve specific goals and determine that the costs of those measures do not exceed the benefits. The principle of necessity is more commonly applied to military acts (only using military force in defense against an armed attack), but can be extended beyond overt violent action. Specifically, complying with this principle means that state action can only be lawfully taken when it is strictly necessary; the state action must be in response to an established social need. The principle of non-discrimination is a principle of equality. This principle stipulates that all people should be treated equally and without discrimination before the law. Lastly, the principle of acting in accordance with the law refers to the requirement that any limitations placed on the exercise of human rights must be defined by the law and done in conformity with the law.

Governments that engage in a cyber counteroffensive should ensure that their policies meet these principled requirements. Practices must be legitimate, proportionate, and necessary. They must be in accordance with the law and be applied equally and without discrimination. Whenever possible, state actions and policies must minimize interference with liberties, such as the rights of privacy, non-discrimination, data protection, and expression. The best security practices are the ones that follow basic standards of integrity, are as transparent as is possible, that minimize harms and abuses, and are subject to some form of oversight and accountability. Policies and practices that do not comply with the principles should be eliminated and discontinued. For example, data collection on individuals due to their race, religion, political beliefs, and similar characteristics will likely not meet these standards. Nor, for that matter, will accusing individuals of engaging in terrorism-related activities through cyber surveillance and

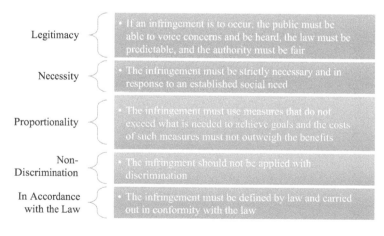

Figure 4.6 Assessing the Principles of Interference.

then restricting their access to the evidence, thus limiting their abilities to present an informed defense. In the current context within which security has been given priority, the principles of legitimacy, necessity, proportionality, non-discrimination, and operating in accordance with the law provide a framework within which to ensure that concerns regarding liberty do not go unanswered.

4.8 SUMMARY

States are required to ensure the safety and security of their citizens, but they are also required to ensure that citizen liberties are not compromised. As terrorists increase their use of cyberspace, citizen safety is potentially compromised. As such, governments must take steps to counter these threats and minimize the potential harms levied at the citizenry. State actions may include the implementation of policies and practices that infringe on citizen liberty, such as invading privacy through mass surveillance, violating rights of data protection through invasive data gathering, infringing on freedom of expression through censorship and punitive responses to open expression, and engaging in discriminative profiling practices. In addition to these direct intrusions on human rights and liberties, state responses to terrorist activities can also have unintended and indirect consequences. Many state responses to online terrorist presence and content may also be counterproductive given that their findings are subject to a high quantity of false positives and false negatives, thus resulting in the needless expenditure of time and resources.

Concerns regarding state responses to the online activities of terrorists need to be balanced against any potential gains from such policies and practices. Cyber counteroffensives, censorship, surveillance, and data collection also need to be assessed with an eye toward the legitimacy, the necessity, and the proportionality of the act. State action needs to proceed in accordance with the law and be applied equally and without discrimination. It is only when the gains of prioritizing security outweigh the costs to liberties and the state's response to terrorism complies with these principles that such actions are just and fair in a democratic society.

REFERENCES

1. The Los Angeles Times. Everything We Should Know About the San Bernardino Terror Attack Investigation So Far. December 4, 2015. http://www.latimes.com/local/california/la-me-san-bernardino-shooting-terror-investigation-htmlstory.html
2. Michael Holden. Man Radicalized by TV Drama Rammed Van into Muslims near London Mosque. *The Japan Times*. February 1, 2018. https://uk.reuters.com/article/uk-britain-security-finsbury/man-radicalised-by-tv-drama-rammed-van-into-muslims-near-london-mosque-idUKKBN1FL5SC
3. Barton Gellman. Edward Snowden, After Months of NSA Revelations, Says His Mission's Accomplished. *The Washington Post*. December 23, 2013. https://www.washingtonpost.com/world/national-security/edward-snowden-after-months-of-nsa-revelations-says-his-missions-accomplished/2013/12/23/49fc36de-6c1c-11e3-a523-fe73f0ff6b8d_story.html?utm_term=.ab60dab926db
4. Global Terrorism Database. 2018. http://start.umd.edu/gtd/
5. Joe Pappalardo. NSA Data Mining: How It Works. *Popular Mechanics*. September 10, 2013. https://www.popularmechanics.com/military/a9465/nsa-data-mining-how-it-works-15910146/
6. Commissioner for Human Rights. Protecting the Right to Privacy in the Fight Against Terrorism. December 4, 2008. https://insanhaklarimerkezi.bilgi.edu.tr/media/uploads/2015/07/31/Ozel_Hayat.pdf
7. Charles Riley. Theresa May: Internet Must Be Regulated to Prevent Terrorism. June 4, 2017. http://money.cnn.com/2017/06/04/technology/social-media-terrorism-extremism-london/index.html

8. Sophia Cope, Jillian C. York, Jeremy Gillula. *Industry Efforts to Censor Pro-Terrorism Online Content Pose Risks to Free Speech.* July 12, 2017. Electronic Frontier Foundation. https://www.eff.org/deepl inks/2017/07/industry-efforts-censor-pro-terrorism-online-content-pose-risks-free-speech

9. United Nations. International Human Rights Conventions and Other Legal Instruments. http://www .un.org/esa/socdev/enable/rights/ahcstata22refinthr.htm

10. Federico Fabbrini. Privacy and National Security in the Digital Age. *Tilburg Law Review.* 2015. Volume 20, pp. 5–13. http://heinonline.org/HOL/LandingPage?handle=hein.journals/tiflr20&div=6& amp;id=&page=

11. European Union Agency for Fundamental Rights. EU Charter of Fundamental Rights. http://fra.euro pa.eu/en/charterpedia/article/8-protection-personal-data

12. United Nations. Universal Declaration of Human Rights. http://www.un.org/en/universal-declarati on-human-rights/

13. Mahmood Monshipouri. Human Rights in the Digital Age: Opportunities and Constraints. *Public Integrity Journal.* 2017. Volume 19, Issue 2, pp. 123–135. https://www.tandfonline.com/doi/abs/10.1 080/10999922.2016.1230690?journalCode=mpin20

14. Ian Brown, Douwe Korff. Terrorism and the Proportionality of Internet Surveillance. *European Journal of Criminology.* 2009. http://journals.sagepub.com/doi/abs/10.1177/1477370808100541

15. Rishi Lyengar. Google is Hiring 10,000 people to Clean Up YouTube. *CNN.* December 6, 2017. http://mon ey.cnn.com/2017/12/05/technology/google-youtube-hiring-reviewers-offensive-videos/index.html

16. David P. Fidler. Cyberspace, Terrorism, and International Law. *Journal of Conflict and Security Law.* 2016. Volume 21, Issue 3, pp. 475–493. https://academic.oup.com/jcsl/article-abstract/21/3/475/2525 373?redirectedFrom=fulltext

17. NPR. Rules for Cyberwarfare Still Unclear, Even As U.S. Engages in It. April 20, 2016. https://www.npr .org/sections/parallels/2016/04/20/475005923/rules-for-cyber-warfare-still-unclear-even-as-u-s-engages-in-it

18. Council of Europe. European Convention on Human Rights. https://www.echr.coe.int/Documents/ Convention_ENG.pdf

A Transnational Recruitment Problem of Violent Online Extremist Terrorists

Chapter 5

How Homegrown Violent Extremism Will Likely Continue to Evolve as a Significant Threat

Cori E. Dauber and Mark D. Robinson

CONTENTS

5.1 INTRODUCTION

The threat posed by violent extremism has substantially evolved over the years and particularly rapidly recently. These changes are only partly driven by the nature of the terrorist groups. They are also driven by changes in technologies available to such groups and so we can predict one thing with certainty: the threat will continue to evolve. Predicting *how* it will evolve is a somewhat more difficult challenge. To do that, we must go back in time in order to chart the trajectories of both violent extremist groups and the technologies on which they have been, and are, dependent. We must start by looking both historically and internationally. Doing so, however, is well worth the effort. After all

> [T]he defeat of IS in Iraq was loudly proclaimed by US President Donald Trump and his Iraqi counterpart …. Their declaration came far too early …. IS remains a potent insurgent and terrorist movement. If anything, the global threat might have increased….[1]

Keep in mind that the threat posed by extremist groups is, and from the beginning has been, linked to questions of media, persuasion, and propaganda. After all, without the ability to spread their extremist messages and recruit, they cannot sustain themselves. Without the ability to spread their messages, not to mention the ability to take credit for any attacks, any violence they engage in registers as simply random, inexplicable violence, unjustifiable and unjustified, as likely to turn people against the cause as win them over. Propaganda (and media that enables sharing of the propagandistic message) is absolutely central to the very nature of violent extremism.

Often using terrorism as a tactic is equally central to the nature of "violent extremism." As opposed to other kinds of violence, the violence in which extremists engage is political by design, a uniquely communicative form of violence. Unlike other violent acts (for example, robbery or murder) it must be witnessed to be effective. Thus violent extremist groups are concerned with persuasion on two tracks: first getting their message out in traditional forms (posters, newsletters, speeches, leaflets—*saying* something) and second in a form unique to terrorist acts, their violence is meant to be "read" as a form of messaging, so they need to ensure somehow that people find out about those acts, and preferably that they *see* some type of evidence of what was done.

And, indeed, from the very beginning of this phenomenon, these groups understood that and focused on questions regarding messaging and propaganda. Some of the earliest terrorists of the modern era, the anarchists, are remembered today in part because they contributed the idea of "propaganda of the deed," the idea that acts of violence themselves can "speak" in a sense. According to this idea, a group's methods and particularly their choice of target, can send a message more loudly, and perhaps more clearly, than any theoretical treatise.[2]

Mao, inspiration for many national guerrilla movements, wrote of the way such movements needed to begin in rural areas with the people (meaning the peasants). But he was thinking of insurgencies. Terrorism is a tactic that some insurgencies use and some do not, but it is a tactic of the cities.[3]

This was recognized by the Brazilian Carlos Marighella in the late 1960s, when he wrote the *Mini-Manual of the Urban Guerrilla*. In it he theorized that for the "urban guerrilla" (really, for him meaning the terrorist) actions required two phases: first the act itself, and second the acts of a second team of specialists, prepared to step in and maximize and spread the impact of the violent act, to make sure through every available means of persuasion that the violence was framed and interpreted through the lens the group intended.[4]

This follows on the trajectory laid out earlier by the Algerian insurgents fighting for independence from France, using terrorism as a tactic, who laid out for their fighters "Directive Nine" phrased as a rhetorical question: "Is it preferable for our cause to kill ten enemies in an oued [dry river bed] of Telergma when no one will talk of it . . . or a single man in Algiers which will be noted the next day by the American press?"[5]

It is impossible to understand the way these theories actually worked without understanding the way these earlier insurgent and terrorist groups of the 1950s and 1960s utilized available technologies. In particular, digital media became a kind of force multiplier for them.

Ironically, it was the jihadists, the groups looking to turn back the clock, who put all other categories of groups to shame, using the tools of the twenty-first century to spread their message that the world needs to go back to the seventh century. How did that progression to digital media take place?

No matter the specific ideology for which these groups have been fighting, one thing all of them have had in common is that they have been particularly skilled at adopting cutting edge media technologies to their ends, whatever was "cutting edge" at the time that they were operating. At the turn of the last century, for example, hand crank printers (and then mimeograph machines) were the highest of high-end technology, despite the fact that generations raised in the digital age might not recognize, much less know how to use these machines. Still, their introduction made possible the production of relatively inexpensive posters and handbills, small leaflets and even newsletters that were beyond the government's ability to control. The technological shift was a huge boon for anarchists and other groups seeking to attract members in the urban environment of the day.[6]

Skipping ahead several decades, in pre-revolution Iran in the 20th century, although clearly this is not entirely parallel to a terrorist organization, personal audiocassettes were used by the Ayatollah's supporters. They recorded him in exile in Paris, dubbing copies, which was easy and inexpensive to do (two machines were kept running at all times), and then successfully smuggled the cassettes back into Iran past the Shah's censors, at which point the recordings could be listened to and then passed hand to hand, supporter to supporter. Music stores slipped in copies with regular purchases.[7] Alternative technologies such as these were critically important at a time when governments employed complete control over the media within their borders, prior to the advent of the internet and satellite television. If a government wanted to keep its population from hearing and seeing a particular message, it was not that difficult for them to do so.

But it was always the visual image that was most important to these extremist groups and most closely tied to their power. It's one thing to hear about a terrorist attack, or read about it, but for an attack to have real power the violence must be seen. There is no requirement that it be seen in person: mediated images will do. The power of these images explains why terrorism really began to take off once television became more widespread in more and more markets and households.[8]

This makes sense given what we know of the power of the image from studies regarding the power of the visual specifically. This body of work comes from psychology, communication, journalism and mass communication, film and cinema studies, as well as from advertising and public relations: essentially all the academic disciplines that would be concerned with the overarching question of whether (and how) the image has power over the audience. And the findings of these studies seem to be consistent across fields and across time. Unlike words, whether in written or audio form, images are processed in a non-linear way, thus our brains process them much more rapidly than words are processed. That, of course, has to do with the way our brains and eyes work together, which is not a cultural but a biological phenomenon, so it is of course cross-cultural. Because the brain processes images more rapidly, images can pack a much greater emotional "punch." We are not comparing image versus sound, but image versus the way language works, where word plus word plus word builds until you have a sentence, sentence plus sentence builds until you have a paragraph, and so forth and that's the case for how meaning is constructed in any language. Images are remembered for a greater length of time than words and with greater accuracy. Importantly, this impact on recall translates to words linked with images, for example news articles that appear with images.[9] Further, negative images, for instance images of the bodies of those killed in terrorist attacks, stand out more and thus have an even greater impact.[10]

The rapidity, immediacy, and high impact of images are a large part of the reason terrorist and insurgent movements in the post-war era were not guerrilla movements, (something we think of as linked to rural areas, as Mao envisioned), but instead were urban phenomena. Insurgencies, and particularly terrorists, moved into the cities where the international press, with their cameras, were following the lead of such groups as the National Liberation Front (FLN) in Algeria.

The Palestinian attack on the Israeli athletes during the Munich Olympics was a critical inflection point that may reasonably be called the first "terrorist spectacular." This, in other words, was the first "made for TV" terrorist event on a global scale, not only made for TV, but made specifically for international television, and equally importantly, it was made for *live* international television, thus creating a live, international, television spectacle. The Olympics of 1972 were smaller than those of today: there were fewer countries competing,121 in Munich to 207 in Rio, simply because prior to the end of the Cold War there were fewer countries, there were fewer sports,191 in Munich to 307 in Rio,[11] prior to the addition of any number of sports added in an attempt to attract younger viewers, and prior to internet streaming and cable and satellite channels there were literally thousands of hours less television coverage scheduled.[12] Nevertheless, the Olympics in 1972 were *culturally* of greater importance. Before the end of the Cold War, the Olympics were a symbolic, proxy way to fight out the ever-present battle between the two political systems of the bifurcated world of that era that could never be allowed to move to an actual battlefield: who had the better system, the Capitalists or the Communists could be determined, the subtext ran, through medal counts.[13] And before the decision to stagger the summer and winter games, the Olympics themselves, far more spaced out, a much more rare event, just seemed a bigger deal, emphasized by their rarity.

In short, hundreds of millions of people around the world turned on their televisions to watch the games in 1972—people who were not sports fans, who would not have tuned in to watch any other sporting event and who might not have turned on their televisions had they known there was a tense stand-off underway between German officials and a group of terrorists playing out instead of the Games.[14] But the very nature of that tension, of its suspense, of the terrorist spectacular, meant that once the audience tuned in, they were unlikely to look away. This is the advantage of the live broadcast. Once the audience was fixated on the events unfolding in another country, with technology closing the gap and providing an immediacy through the knowledge of simultaneity, that the events onscreen were happening at the same time as they were being witnessed, it became almost impossible to look away before the events played out in full. Without a doubt the Israeli athletes were held hostage in Munich. But in a very real sense, the international viewing audience was held hostage, too.

In an age when live broadcasts, particularly international ones, required a great deal of equipment and preparation, going to the Olympics meant going where the press was already pre-positioned with all their equipment and with satellite time pre-arranged. All the television crews had to do, literally, was point their cameras in a slightly different direction. There were 6,000 journalists accredited to cover Munich and of those 2,000 were from television networks (including both reporters and crew).[15]

Munich was the ultimate example of the "old school" attack—go where the cameras are.

The importance of the coverage of Munich, and specifically the fact that it was live, becomes clear when Munich is compared to another attack that took place only two years earlier. Palestinians were behind this attack as well and simultaneously hijacked four civilian international flights, an amazing feat even with the significantly lower airport security of the time.[16] British security re-established control over one of the planes, which left the hijackers in control of three commercial flights –planes, crews, and passengers. The pilots were ordered to fly to Dawson's Field, a remote airfield in Jordan. They waited for the international press to arrive (waiting for the cameras to come to them in this instance), and when the television crews were there, the terrorists deplaned all the hostages and blew up the planes. (Getting the passengers off first was a nice touch, and it makes clear the distinction between a secular, nationalist terrorist movement and the radical religious ideologies more prevalent today.)

Almost everyone today has some knowledge of what happened at Munich in 1972, and those old enough all remember it. The Dawson's Field hijacking, however, is a historical footnote at best, remembered only by experts. What is the difference? The group was Palestinian, the demands similar, the targets international. But *the coverage was not live.*

Why would such a suspenseful moment not be covered live? The answer is very simple: television networks lacked the technological capability to do so. The two years between 1970, the date of the Dawson's Field hijackings, and 1972, when Munich occurred, made all the difference. In 1968 the first television satellite was launched by the U.S. But that alone was not enough. It did not permit live coverage of events outside a studio. That required the addition of the "mini-cam," a video camera light weight enough to be portable and battery powered, freeing operators from the confines of a studio, and also a time-base corrector, the piece of equipment that converted the footage into a signal that could actually be transmitted.[17]

What has changed today is that any examination of violent extremist or terrorist groups' propaganda and persuasive efforts requires that we divide our analysis so that we are taking into consideration *both* the means by which messages are being produced *and* the means by which they are being disseminated.

5.2 ADAPTATION: VIOLENT EXTREMISM MOVES FROM AN ANALOG TO A DIGITAL PHENOMENON

How did that shift happen?

Again, it was driven by technology, or, in this case, *technologies*. Several new technologies reached relative maturity at approximately the same time at the turn of this century, which meant that they could be used in ways that were symbiotic. This of course begs the question: when discussing information and communication technologies, what do we mean by "relative maturity?" To the authors it means a specific piece of technology meets three criteria.

First, it must be cheap enough to be widely affordable. When considering technology and electronics, in general prices typically fall when the technology has been in the market for a while. Cellphones, HD and then 4K televisions, and digital cameras are all examples where price has fallen, but this is true of almost every category of technology. What starts as being priced far out of reach of most consumers, sometimes at prices so high that their acquisition in itself offers a way of demonstrating or signaling great personal wealth, becomes more or less rapidly something that the average consumer can afford. What starts as a luxury item becomes a consumer item or even an item seen as a basic utility in the case of cellphones. The first cellphone, after all, was sold in 1984 for $3,995.00, weighed 28 ounces, was 13 inches long—and when fully charged provided all of thirty minutes battery time. Given the easy availability of pay phones (charging only a dime) it's not hard to understand why this Motorola was considered "a gimmick, a 'look what I got!' rich man's toy with dubious utility."[18]

Second, it must be globally or close to globally available. Technology spreads far more rapidly than was once the case, but to consider an individual item relatively mature it must be widely available in areas outside North America, Europe, and the "Asian tigers," in other words outside what used to be called the "developed world."

Third, it ought to be portable. Computers were available for offices for years, but they were so large individual computers could take up an entire room. Desktop models revolutionized the market since they made computers viable for home use, but they were still far too heavy (and bulky) to be truly portable.

These criteria suggest a specific list of technologies that are important in the context of understanding extremist content. First, of course, are laptop computers, widely available, many models are certainly affordable and small and lightweight enough to be carried in a backpack. Second, were digital cameras. Today, of course, almost all cameras are digital, but initially digital cameras were a distinct, somewhat more expensive category. And the final piece is the software used to edit and manipulate images. Such software had been available for some time for professional use. A major change took place when there was software cheap enough for the consumer market and, importantly, that could be used with no more training than the included instructions.

These three pieces taken together made it possible for violent extremist groups to essentially weaponize the internet.[19] They could now film, edit, and upload material on their own, with no need to rely on the professional press. It was this technological moment, these innovations taken together, that made possible the leap to what we can consider New School terrorism: rather than launch attacks in the vicinity of the press' cameras, groups could instead attack wherever was most convenient for them, and simply take their own cameras along.

"New School terrorism" can also be considered the "Iraq innovation," because the war in Iraq is what brings all these pieces together for the first time along with a situation where there are regular chances, not to put too fine a point on things, to blow stuff up. The result was the opportunity for many groups to experiment with these new technologies as well as the way these technologies interacted, the opportunities they presented, and how the images and materials being produced could be used for maximum impact. For the first time, groups experimented with uploading very short clips that could be made modular, so the clips could be downloaded in areas where better computers and software were married with personnel with the training to take advantage of those resources. This allowed the groups to use the clips as the building blocks for longer, more heavily produced videos.[20]

What was being produced on behalf of the Iraqi groups was very different from anything the original Al Qaeda organization had been putting on the web, in part because the technology being used signaled a generational change. The original Al Qaeda organization exploited the fax machine as their "cutting edge" technology.[21] The web, and certainly posting videos to the web, was new to them, not something that came naturally. Those fighting in Iraq were much more familiar and much more comfortable with all these technologies.

And this generational change in part centered on differences in the way they thought about the use of images:

> Al Qaeda specifically shied away from covering the more violent side of its global jihad. It saw the global battle for "hearts and minds" as best won with ideas, not searing images .... That difference in approach represented a sign of a coming generational divide, between the older leaders of al Qaeda, such as bin Laden and Zawahiri, and a new, more tech-savvy generation who understood the power of images online. It mirrored a generational divide that we're seeing play out in every sector of the world. Companies and institutions around the globe are living this divide, between those who remember an age before computers and those for whom using an iPhone is as natural as breathing.[22]

It's worth noting that years before, in the Chechen's war against Russia, the Chechens had tried to do something very similar, filming their attacks on Russian soldiers for purposes of intimidation and terror. But their conceptual innovation was too far ahead of the technology available, as they were limited to large, bulky, heavy video cameras that used VHS cassettes. They had to fill a tape with 45 (or 90) minutes of material, depending on the quality they chose to record in, and they then had no real way to disseminate that which they had made in that pre-internet world other than getting the tape itself physically to Moscow. They had a digital strategy in a still analog world.[23]

5.3 EVOLUTION: WEB AND "NEW NEW SCHOOL" TERRORISM

The real match to the flame in terms of the "Iraq innovation" came with the advancement of the internet itself—the capacity to disseminate and share material to a target audience with immediacy.

When bandwidths, or the speed at which large amounts of information can be uploaded and downloaded, began to increase it suddenly becomes feasible for consumers to begin to download (and share) video and audio files, even relatively large ones, relatively easily. There follows a concomitant reduction in the cost of technology and in infrastructure, all while message potential increases.

These developments happen at approximately the same time as the change from "web 1.0" to "web 2.0,"[24] the change from basically static websites to sites where people can easily interact. Soon, therefore, an expectation grew both that content would be updated regularly and that readers would be allowed their own "voice" on sites. The new web, now a dynamic one, provides a space where people expect an ability to communicate directly with one another as well as with the website's administrators.

Web 2.0 was driven in part by the widespread appearance of "blogs." There had been "web logs" in the 1990s, but back then keeping one of these sites required a minimum degree of competence in HTML coding language, a threshold that kept most people from participating.[25] It wasn't until the turn of the century when several companies began offering software—for free— that made it possible for anyone to create and maintain their own blog, on any topic, that the medium exploded. Admittedly, numbers were inflated at first with blogs that really were just personal diaries or, in some cases, so-called "kick the tire" blogs, blogs created by people who read about the phenomena, thought it was interesting, started one, posted once or twice, and then left their blog inactive.[26]

It isn't long before social media platforms as we know them today began to replace chat rooms. Social media permitted a degree of interactivity (and public facing) that attracted users, and which made these sites, ultimately, irresistible. General interest social media platforms had enough other content that the groups could simply hide theirs in plain sight. As an example of the kind of response that simply made it impossible for extremist groups to ignore the new platforms and continue simply keeping to themselves on their own isolated chat rooms: on May 22, 2007, a father in the UK posted a short video of his two young sons for friends living abroad. He had no idea that "Charlie bit my finger" would one day become a meme (the video today boasts more than 864 *million* views) but that one posting served to demonstrate the concept of "going viral" and the possibilities of the then brand-new site, YouTube.[27]

The second change that, if possible, fans the fires even more, is the shift from laptops, computers generally, to the combination of platforms and *devices* – most particularly the smartphone— and apps, or applications. It is during this period, for example, that people stop self-identifying as a "Mac" or "PC" person, and begin self-identifying as an "Apple" or "Android" person, as the specific handset becomes less important to explaining one's affiliation than the operating system one uses.[28] Today the smartphone alone contains all of the technologies that had combined in the 2000s to make the weaponization of the web possible. In one piece of technology that the consumer can hold in their hand or carry in their pocket, is a digital video camera of decent quality, editing software, and the ability to upload what they have created to the web. Needless to say, the implications are profoundly disturbing.

We were, as a country and a society, providing technology to our adversaries—technology developed with our creativity and through our national investments in education; technology that allowed them to communicate securely and instantly among themselves and potential recruits; technology that was specially designed to allow them to keep their conversations private and prohibit law enforcement from listening even with a valid court order; technology that allowed them to reach into our schools, our shopping malls and our basements to spread poison to our children, tutor them and provide them operational directions and supervision to kill fellow Americans. And we'd given it all to them for free — available for an easy download in the app store, just a few clicks away. It was as if we developed game-changing military command-and-control technology at the height of World War II and just handed it over to Tokyo Rose and Axis Sally.[29]

There is no question that these developments also have enormous implications for ordinary people's ability to circumvent governments' control of information which, with the extreme exceptions of China and North Korea, seems to have been completely shattered wherever there are cell towers. The fact that the handsets themselves may be expensive and the people poor has not been a barrier: in very poor parts of the world, people have worked around that problem by simply sharing phones.[30] Today, if a webpage isn't built on the assumption that people will be viewing it on a phone or a tablet, its design simply will not work.

Technology had now developed to the point that it was possible for terrorists to bring their own cameras, making the professional press essentially irrelevant, at least in terms of the needs of extremist and terrorist groups. They can film, edit, and upload all themselves, using social media platforms to disseminate the footage—from that point the mainstream media can find the material and distribute it further. Even during the war in Iraq, what insurgents were doing was essentially using materials they filmed and uploaded as basic building blocks, as early on they themselves lacked the software (and training) to put together sophisticated propaganda videos.[31] But by uploading short clips, they allowed others with greater skills and resources to take that footage and build longer, more complete propaganda videos. They realized that the only pieces that actually had to come from the conflict theaters were the parts where things blew up.

The *new* new school of terrorism took this one step further: terrorists did not need to bring cameras with them, but instead depended on their victims to have cameras with *them,* in other words, simply assumed that the victims of an attack would have cameras with them *when they were attacked.* For that to be true, terrorists had to be able to assume that victims would have cameras with them at any given time or place. Today, that assumption hardly seems to be extraordinary, but for the first hundred years of photography, that would be nothing short of an insane thing to assume. No one would "just" happen to have a camera with them who wasn't a professional photographer, because cameras were heavy, bulky, and often cumbersome. It was only when cellphone ownership became a completely ordinary and expected thing, as did the idea that those cellphones would have cameras on them, and that the cameras were not an expensive single-use technology but something ordinary people were likely to have (a "mature" technology) only then could terrorists reasonably anticipate that ordinary victims of terrorist attacks might photograph the aftermath of such an attack themselves.

The inflection point demarcating this shift in cell and camera technology occurs with the London subway attacks. (Though even there, the technology wasn't quite mature because the people who took these images were dependent on newspapers—traditional media—to disseminate the images for them.)[32]

Consider that the iconic images for 9/11 all come from either television or the print press, but either way from professional photojournalists. The iconic image for the "Miracle on the Hudson" by contrast, was taken by an ordinary citizen, who pushed the image out over Twitter. There it was found by traditional media outlets and used by (and made famous by) those outlets.[33] The media outlets had little choice since, by the time professional journalists had arrived on the scene, the plane had long since sunk.

Today, two things are happening simultaneously. First, terrorist groups continue to use available technology to produce materials, some of which includes footage from attacks and some of which do not, using social media platforms to push them out in order to recruit and radicalize, to rally the already committed, to fundraise, to terrorize their enemies (and those populations who may live in areas they control). Some groups are only capable of extremely primitive materials that, frankly, most American middle school students could improve upon. Some groups are putting out extremely sophisticated, near professional quality materials, and often in shocking quantities.[34]

Second, no longer dependent upon their own cameras at attacks, today they know they can rely on victims to have cameras with them and that victims themselves will post to their own social media accounts after attacks. There is no longer any need at all to plan ways to ensure propaganda can be created effectively in the aftermath of an attack: this is the significance of the Boston Marathon bombing. P.W. Singer and Emerson T. Brooking report that it took 30 seconds for Boston's emergency coordination center to find out about the attack, but by then the news was already on Twitter. It was only a few seconds after the first tweet that the first image was uploaded to Twitter. It was a full three minutes before a professional news outlet reported the attack, and an hour before the Boston police confirmed it.[35] Eventually, the images of the explosions were on a loop on cable news. Meanwhile, as the citizens of Boston were told to "shelter in place" during the hunt for the bombers, the street scenes were utterly bizarre and eerie, not only to Bostonians, but to anyone who had ever visited the city. It was those images being passed around on Twitter, which made the scene appear as if two individuals had managed something shockingly akin to the Zombie apocalypse.[36]

These developments are not accidental. The groups are just capitalizing on trends in larger society. A gap between people and media product correlates to a corresponding gap between people and technology of production. Prior to the democratization of media and technology, a certain number of people were identified as professionals, those who were deemed competent by a larger professional culture to shoot and produce advertisements, persuasive media products because only a certain number of people could afford the necessary technology for creating those products, and only a small number of people had access to the training necessary to learn the stringent rules that had to be followed for a product to be authorized and licensed, in other words, "blessed" as having followed stringent industry standards. There was a large gap between those who consumed and those who produced media products. But over time processors decreased in size—and simultaneously increased in speed—we saw the birth of the internet, followed by the mass availability of first cellphones and then smart phones. The result was that the gap between consumers of media and producers of media began to rapidly close. Today some will accept the video their kid brother shot as acceptable working material for an ad. Standards, rather than being stringently enforced by a professional class, are now diffused out over the population.

This transformation directly impacts extremist and terrorist groups because while much of what is available on YouTube may not be considered "professional," the videos posted there still train young people how to make work (in part because watching videos on YouTube trains them as to what is defined as "acceptable"), especially if they do not have access to any other kind of professional training. When analysts say, "ISIS production quality is high," that can mean either that their people were trained or that they have simply been working at it for long enough that their standards have risen.

As Al Qaeda's dominance in propaganda faded, the global audience saw first ISIS then IS break with old standards. Those old standards of Al Qaeda were dominated by talking heads or field (battle) footage characterized by poorly composed images, shaky handheld cameras, and naïve action shots filmed from a great distance, from so far in fact that often the noise and monochromatic display of sand merged to disguise the subject of an IED exploding in the distance, so far off that the viewer could hardly discern what, if anything was happening as the scene progressed. Both the propaganda and the dissemination were focused around the already converted, the already radicalized, professing academic, religious citations as to the meaning of the group and its version of jihad. Whereas ISIS moves toward control of the message, how it appears is critical to that message, to radicalization, to attracting fighters and therefore to its future, not what they already had but instead that which they could have: the caliphate, more fighters, engineers, doctors, etc. ISIS was capitalizing on the convergence of media to make certain their message was seen, heard, witnessed, shared, and consumed. The convergence of technology was such that quality equipment became affordable, and thus quality creation became possible, the idea that footage was free or nearly so. Production costs were extremely low such that they could shoot as they pleased at high-end quality, giving them more raw material from which to work, and open social media where video found viral homes meant that the gap to market closed to become almost instantaneous transmission with the use of cell phones and the internet. This was happening along with the simultaneous development of mass quantities of media that provided textbooks, digital manuals and tutorials, which provided insights such that the knowledge gap regarding how to tell a story narrowed. The evolution of ISIS propaganda incorporates all forms of media, typography, animation, video editing, special FX, music, voice, and perhaps above all images that are dramatic, reflecting the spectacle which was their vision.

Separating their vision and propaganda from previous jihadist propaganda (and perhaps the most impactful element) was intent. The videos demonstrated purposeful repetition, rhythm, carefully composed scenes, and voice-overs. They demonstrated the three stages of media production and communication: (1) pre-production, where the idea is developed and plans are made on how best to execute the intent; (2) production, where the footage is acquired along the lines of that plan, as well as development of branding logos, careful execution of compositions, story elements, special FX, animations, drone shots etc.; and (3) post production, where the pieces are assembled in order to efficiently tell the story, all set forth with clear intention. This demonstration of intent accelerated the creation of product because it organized ideas and permitted the rapid sharing of those ideas disseminated to a broad audience of the potentially radicalized, rather than only the already radicalized. The overall quality of the production itself was evolving, becoming more convincing in argument, more carefully constructed, more accurate for the audience, and more globally influential to other groups hoping to radicalize similar audiences to their flavor of jihad. All these evolutions, all the gaps closing, tether ISIS propaganda to the technology more so than the tether that anchored Al Qaeda to its propaganda.

The democratization of technology has contributed to the threat posed. Having so far discussed the means by which materials are disseminated, we need to stop for a moment and consider the *product*, what it is that is being disseminated. Increasingly, as has been the pattern for all electronic technology, equipment that just a few years ago would have been found in a professional media lab, or in a television studio, and cost thousands upon thousands of dollars, is now available in the consumer market for anywhere from just several hundred dollars on the low end to just a few thousand dollars on the high end. The perfect example of this kind of technology is the GoPro, a cheap, durable, action camera capable of producing a seemingly endless variety of creative and compelling immersive shots. GoPro footage has shown up in advertisements, in countless YouTube videos,[37] and in one terrorist propaganda video after another. This phenomenon is also the reason why more and more terrorist groups are integrating drone footage into their propaganda, which, again, gives them a capability to shoot extremely compelling shots they never could have made before.[38]

Part of what matters here is that when this equipment becomes affordable and available it couples moving images with sound—therefore allowing groups to supplement text and still images in extremely powerful ways. Beyond any images of attacks, here we are speaking of the finished, polished product with which they have taken time and care. These videos may or may not include images of attacks, but where attack imagery is included, the footage often drops some time after the attack itself, edited into a longer video. An example of this might be the video "celebrating" the attack on Brussels, which integrates Western news footage of the attack (itself in large part taken from social media posts from the phones of passers-by, that is, they depended on the cameras of the victims).[39]

One of the things that makes the Brussels video so striking, of course, is the quality of the computer-generated animations, that is, the graphics, for example the map of Europe on which the outline of Belgium bounces and shakes, thus shaking the entire map. (At 3:40.) This also is an outcome of the democratization of technology: graphics software is now widely available and increasingly easy to use with little or no training; that was not the case even a few years ago. Today groups that are not capable of producing high-quality videos by any measure, still possess the capability to begin their videos with relatively decent graphics.

Some of the first uses of these graphics were sophisticated emulations of those seen in legitimate news sources. The visuals, therefore, without ever explicitly making the argument, clearly suggested that the propaganda videos put out by these groups were at least as reliable as anything from legacy news sources.[40] All of them serve a branding function and thus demonstrate authenticity, as one of the primary purposes of these graphics is to display group logos: this video was made by group X, it represents group X, and it is fully sanctioned by group X. In that regard the logos (and these graphics packages) function in much the same way as the Nike "swoosh."[41]

And like the "swoosh" these logos also promote brand recognition, denoting property and ownership and in turn implying longevity, stability, and reliability. Through a centralized presence, the viewer can depend upon the logo as a promise that the product will indeed deliver an expected aesthetic. A particular animated graphic need only be rendered once, a parent of sorts, and then when it is spliced onto any video, that child carries forth the same codes and meaning inherited from the parent. This analogy holds true for all the copies, and all the subsequent instances of the same animation, and as the logo and graphic are repeated, so does "truth" become an associated value. The graphics in the propaganda videos reflect a foothold in traditional values, while maintaining an aggressive and radicalized character of youth. This is part of the importance of still images giving way to videos.

The viewer continuously attempts to reconcile what is seen and heard, and part of that reconciliation is tied to believability, the suspension of one's reality in order to be able to immerse oneself completely into the world of the film (or in this case, video). Audio quality significantly influences how information is perceived.[42] If the audio is of low quality, then the maker runs the risk of the images and sound being reconciled as fake, due to a lack of believability, which further diminishes the rhetorical weight of the entirety of that which was contaminated. But what about cellphone news clips where good quality sound is not a paramount or conscious goal, if anything those grainy cellphones shots convey *authenticity* one might say? The significance of the dismissal due to poor audio quality is tied to the quality of the image and audio being in a relationship that is proportionate. The dismissal occurs when time is perceived to be advancing, not perceived to be frozen (that would be a still image), so there needs to be a relationship between the audio and the image that makes sense, *but* in this instance the comparative difference between the image and the sound are irreconcilable. This can occur when the image is of relatively high quality and sound is not, or when both are of poor quality and the progression of time is therefore meaningless or irreconcilable. In effect, if time is passing then the marks of difference should become clearer, like any explanation, and if they don't, then the conclusion of meaning is reduced to a relegation to fake, or not of temporal importance.

The cellphone news report presents authenticity due to the immediacy of the image and sound, conveying a historical reference of time rather than a meaning – it is documentary. The meaning is left to the audience to reconcile after the instance is consumed. (*Hoax* is a unique condition of fake, where the believability is accepted as truth even though fake: think about the famous Big Foot video, treated as real and as evidence until admitted as a hoax by the maker.) The low quality of audio and image, inherent to this type of news clip, are inextricably tied together in the moment being captured. The bad audio reconciles the bad video and vice versa. The same is true of early Al Qaeda videos, where the image and sound of field recordings were of poor quality; that's why their propaganda was often talking heads because it is easier to control quality. It is not that the field or battle footage of Al Qaeda was not viewed as real, it is the case that the meaning was lost in a shroud of confusing and indiscernible information or noise, and because the signal to noise ratio was very low, only the most sophisticated viewer could filter to find the signal, whereas most viewers simply merged the two and few had the patience or the ability to apply the correct reconciliation filter.

5.4 HOMEGROWN EXTREMISM

What do we mean by "homegrown" groups? The term itself is problematic: there is no consensus on its meaning. Some authors use "homegrown" to refer to those extremist groups for which there is no international connection whatsoever, meaning their ideology has no link to any overseas group, thus they use the term to refer to white supremacist, sovereign citizen, white nationalist, and alt-right groups. (Although this too is a bit of a misconception, as increasingly American and European white nationalist and alt-right groups are beginning to communicate and share strategies and so forth.)[43]

While others simply mean not *directed* internationally—essentially lone actors, or what is known colloquially as the "lone wolf." Daveed Gartenstein-Ross and Madeleine Blackman have written about the difference between Al-Qaeda's model of the "lone wolf" where they "inspired" individuals they had never met to commit acts of violence in their name, compared to the Islamic State's model, where individuals they have never met are actually "directed" to act. They discuss the role of the "virtual planner," made possible today in large part because of the ubiquity of social media and technological advances in end-to-end encryption.[44] It can be extremely difficult to figure out, given this, who actually is a "lone wolf" and who isn't, particularly since anytime anyone swears loyalty to the jihadist cause, the Islamic State is likely to take credit for their actions (sometimes taking credit even if they have not sworn loyalty, and even when there is no evidence anywhere of any link at all).[45] Assuming, of course, that they have had some degree of success. (The so-called "Chelsea bomber" managed to set off bombs that didn't do much damage, managed to get himself arrested, and couldn't even get himself killed in a shootout with police. The Islamic State never claimed him as a "soldier of the Islamic State," their typical wording when they claim the actions of someone inspired by them.)

Recruiting these actors is one half the equation; the other half is the act itself.

Another consequence of today's technology, exploited globally by terrorist groups, is that the very nature of "the spectacular" has shifted. Munich in 1972 was the very first terrorist attack televised to a live, international audience, and because it was first, and because the target was in part the Olympic games themselves, the number of hostages required to hold the world's attention was not very large. Over time, though, in order to be sure they would capture the audiences' full attention, terrorist groups needed to constantly ratchet up the scale of their attacks, until of course, we ended up at 9/11, with almost 3,000 dead in a single morning. But that was at a time when the internet was still in its infancy compared to today. It's difficult to remember now, but news websites were not able to handle the traffic and crashed almost immediately,[46] and there was no social media as we know it today—Facebook itself did not launch until 2004, YouTube until 2005, the iPod wasn't released until nearly a month after the attack, much less the iPhone. Cellphones barely had texting capacity as we know it today.[47] The idea that you might be able to "watch" the news in real time, complete with visuals, on your phone was a fantasy in 2001.

With social media, far fewer need to die to freeze a society in its tracks. The Mumbai attacks of 2008 held the commercial center of India paralyzed, and much of the world transfixed, for nearly three days. 164 died but only 10 terrorists were involved. What made those attacks important was their pattern, their structure. They were low tech and had high media impact: the terrorists went for targets that were of high symbolic value, where people were likely to be densely packed, but all they themselves had were guns, a few hand grenades and an IED or two per person.[48] But the real key to those attacks was that each terrorist carried with him a Blackberry that allowed him to communicate with his handler back in Pakistan, who of course was watching the news coverage. It was the 21st-century version of those long-ago Munich terrorists watching themselves on televisions in the athletes' apartments. Those Blackberries also had Google Earth on them, a fact that so angered the Indian government that they tried to sue Google.[49] Google won because the Indian government's position—that Google had put "sensitive" sites on their maps—didn't really hold up, as the sites that are "sensitive" in this context are the most public sites imaginable. Declaring the largest tourist attractions in the city "sensitive" points to the challenges intrinsic to the terrorist threat, but it's also a bit of a non sequiter.

Multiple attacks of the same structure followed in rapid succession. A series of small attacks also gained a great deal of attention, even if for only short periods of time. They may not be "sticky" in the way larger attacks are, but they do achieve *virality*, and as long as they can achieve that, they are worth doing from the perspective of the terrorists.

The attack on the Westwood mall in Kenya represents another key inflection point. This attack is notable because it was the first ever live tweeted (in English) by the terrorist group responsible, as it was happening. Kept back from the mall for obvious reasons, the press had no way to verify anything Shabaab was tweeting, and they had nothing they could actually report on their own—except for what the group was tweeting. Twitter, meanwhile, was suspending the accounts used by the group, and as each account was suspended, the group popped back up with another, having obviously anticipated the company's response.[50]

The Islamic State again changed the nature of the spectacular entirely when it posted video to social media of the execution of James Foley.[51] In this instance, only one individual died, but it was the *means* of his death, and equally important, the fact that his death was filmed (and then the video widely distributed) that turned his death into a new kind of spectacular.[52] It was as much about the video and its dissemination as it was the plain fact of the execution. It is the case, of course, that IS's precursor organization, Al Qaeda in Iraq, had previously posted videos of the decapitations of Western hostages.[53] But that was before social media was nearly as developed as today. (The video of Nick Berg's beheading was posted to the website of an insurgent group with ties to Al Queda in Iraq, a precursor group to Islamic State. That was the common method then; groups had their own websites and they posted material directly onto those sites.) More to the point, it was long before these groups had the technical capacity to film video of such high quality. The Nick Berg video is blurred, fuzzy, poorly edited, with shots that are not well framed. That doesn't mean it was not shocking or impactful, but the Foley video, despite the fact that it does not actually show the beheading itself, is in a completely different category.

The Foley video was followed by a series of other beheadings, and these videos without a doubt received as much attention as they did in part because that first set of victims were Westerners—British and American.[54] But the Islamic State, having redefined the spectacular as being about the method by which a victim died rather than the number of people to die, proceeded to experiment with an entire sequence of video releases, one more gruesome than the next. A group of Egyptian Copts was beheaded in a synchronized fashion.[55] Underwater photography was used to film men being drowned.[56] A captured Jordanian pilot was burned alive.[57] Other groups may have killed people, killed people in large numbers, or killed people in comparably grotesque fashion, but they had not worked to utilize the latest in technology, on both the production and distribution end, to ensure that the world had no choice but to marvel at their achievements.

In terms of terrorist attacks, lower and lower body counts were getting more and more attention. It is true that these relatively small attacks (as opposed to the executions) were not "sticky," that is they were not memorable. People not directly impacted do not speak today about the attack on the Canadian Parliament where one soldier was killed,[58] or the free speech gathering in a coffee shop in Copenhagen where two died,[59] or the hostage taking in the chocolate shop in Sydney where three died (though this maybe an example of IS claiming events opportunistically—it seems as if a genuine IS operative would not have needed to ask the police for an IS flag).[60] We could list a dozen other attacks. But they dominated both social media and traditional media when they happened, even though body counts were low or in some cases non-existent. They had learned their lesson. After all, pre-Islamic State, the *failed* bombing attempts of Times Square in New York in 2010 and of a London nightclub in 2007 completely dominated cable news for hours.

> [They] achieved this by simply changing the definition of "spectacular," applying it to the reaction instead of the attack itself. The focus has shifted from a high casualty count to a high response count. These attacks involve planning but relatively little skill, and are never judged to be failures.[61]

This is not to say, obviously, that groups were intentionally trying to keep body counts low, as the Manchester bombing, Orlando nightclub, and Paris attacks demonstrate. The point is that fairly small attacks were able to capture attention almost comparable to larger ones, (if for a shorter period of time) which matters a great deal given that it is attention that is the metric most important to these groups.

The mold was well and truly broken with a particular attack in 2016.

The truck attack in Nice, France, was particularly disturbing: it takes no special training to use a vehicle as a weapon.[62] The attack in Nice was fairly carefully planned, which is why the body count was so high.[63] But multiple vehicle attacks followed[64] because they worked, and they worked because at least at first municipalities had frankly given little thought to how to prevent them—though that does not mean that there are no possible options.[65]

It is not clear the vehicle attack in Charlottesville, Virginia, in 2017, was planned at all (though it seems fairly clear it was premeditated, a different thing) yet it was still deadly.[66] And, dangerously, it still received a great deal of media attention that, after all, is what terrorists care about. The coverage is not proportional to the number killed, which makes this kind of attack extremely attractive.

On the white supremacist side of the house, groups who were barely hanging on, mailing cheap newsletters, found new life because they could find one another on the internet, even though they are far behind the jihadis in terms of the quality of their product. They have nothing like the high-end, high-def video, for example. And yet, first the internet in general, and then social media has been invaluable to these groups. We do not mean this to be an overly glib example: consider the flat-earthers. People who believe the earth is really flat have been around for a very long time, but they needed YouTube to be able to recruit.[67]

By the same token, the various splinter groups we might collectively think of as white supremacist never went away, but they were isolated. Their material often consisted of cheap, badly made small newsletters. The internet gave groups the ability to post material, to recruit, and—vitally— to realize that they were not alone, even if they were isolated in their own locales. Stormfront, for example, one of the very first "hate" websites, because of recent publicity, has only suddenly found it difficult to be hosted, despite that it had been up and running for a very long time prior to the publicity.[68]

Most only became aware of the presence of many of these accounts in the aftermath of the shooting at the Pittsburgh synagogue, when it was suddenly an open issue of discussion that many accounts pushed off Twitter had migrated to an alternative platform called Gab. But those following the issue were well aware of both the problem posed by hateful accounts on social media that, while clearly in violation of Twitter's terms of service, were still protected political speech, and of the issues raised by Gab.[69]

For both jihadist and white supremacist sides, the material remains, if in a smaller amount. And the quality will continue to improve as times go by, technology becomes more affordable, and it is easier to use with less and less training and experience.

This problem is not going away anytime soon, indeed, things may be about to get far, far darker.

5.5 THE FUTURE: WHERE ARE WE HEADED?

The technology is taking us to a place where we will soon watch terrorists kill their victims live, not on television, but on social media. That is not a prediction, it is a knowable fact, because it has already happened. In Chicago, a group of teenagers kidnapped a youngster who was mentally disabled, and tortured him over Facebook Live.[70] Because of the auto-play feature, especially via Twitter, there is no way to know how many people saw the footage of a local television news crew murdered during an on-air live shot: viewers did not choose to watch that disturbing footage, it simply played when they opened the platform.[71]

Given the attention these events received and the shock and horror of the people who viewed the material, it was a sure bet that terrorist groups would begin searching for ways to integrate Facebook's live stream functionality and Twitter's equivalent, Periscope, into their tactics and planning. It's surprising that this hasn't happened so far, actually, although several instances have come extremely close. In France, a terrorist killed two police officers in their home. The killings themselves were not live streamed, however the killer's rants afterwards were, as the officers' toddler cowered in the corner.[72]

Also in France, and also Islamic State inspired, an elderly priest was murdered while celebrating mass. The terrorists ordered a parishioner to film the murder, and it is inconceivable that this would have been for any purpose but for posting, but the police arrived and shot the pair before they could do so.[73] There is no reason to believe that in the future an attack will not involve three terrorists: two to do the killing and a third to film it and post it live.

So long as live-streaming services are available on social media platforms, this possibility remains real; it is technologically driven, and it is completely separate from ideological motivation or geographic limitation. The only way to avoid the terrorist event aired live, it seems, is to end live-streaming services.[74]

So where does this leave us? Some platforms have begun to aggressively remove extremist-affiliated accounts and extremist content. Others continually promise to do so, but their performance to date has been uneven at best. The wisest course, it seems, is to continue to press the platforms to behave responsibly, while planning for them to fall short. It is also critical to remember that much of the extremist content that will appear on social media in the months and years to come *will not be from extremist-associated accounts*. We live in an age when people's automatic response to what they see happening around them, particularly if it is in any way out of the ordinary, is to take out their phones, film it, and then post that footage. This isn't done with malice; it isn't clear that this is done with much thought at all. It's only afterwards that people may realize that they have posted material that may be extremely inappropriate. (One Ohio man who filmed a fatal car crash while others were trying to help the victims did end up getting arrested—the police admitted they were looking for any reason they could find to arrest him.)[75]

Our point is this: if you could overnight get every account affiliated with a white supremacist or jihadist group off of social media, if you could get rid of every account that even vaguely sympathized, you still have an entire population that is now trained to do these groups' work for them. As soon as there is an act of violence committed by one of these groups, everyone in the area will immediately begin filming—and then post that footage to *their* accounts. Every time there is an attack, there are multiple calls on Twitter to please not "retweet" images that are particularly graphic, and those calls are inevitably ignored. And once a group issues a claim of responsibility, their work is done.

All they need to do is then download the footage provided to them without their even asking, incorporate it into their own videos, and disseminate it on sites such as Telegram, and at least some people will find a way to watch it, particularly as the professional press will dutifully report on the existence of the video. After all, it is "newsworthy."

5.6 SUMMARY

We believe that by their very nature extremist and terrorist groups are inextricably entwined with persuasion and propaganda: to understand the one, you must understand the other. Furthermore, to understand how these groups have attempted to persuade and propagandize, it is useful to understand how they have made use of communications technology. In order to think through the way the threat of homegrown groups will likely evolve, it is helpful to look back and consider how we have come to this point, both historically and internationally.

To do that it is useful to keep in mind that technologies that today are most likely to be found in a museum were, at one point, the most cutting edge available. And the types of groups we are interested in have historically been enormously adept at finding creative uses for this category of technology.

Thus in this chapter we looked at the relationship between communication technology, extremism, and terrorism, and then we looked at historical patterns and examples of this relationship. We then focused particularly closely on the impacts of the developments of digital technologies, the way these technologies initially functioned synergistically, what we call "the Iraq effect," and then how these technologies, as they continued to evolve, created completely new opportunities for terrorist groups.

We concluded by discussing extremely disturbing directions for the future, not a future that is ten years off, but that may only be months or weeks off, given events that have already occurred linking violent acts and the live stream functionalities of different social media platform.

NOTES

1. Liesbeth van der Heide, Charlie Winter, and Shiraz Maher, *The Cost of Crying Victory: Policy Implication's of the Islamic State's Territorial Collapse* (ICCT, The Hague, ICCT Report November 2018), p. 4 https://icct.nl/wp-content/uploads/2018/11/ICCT-VanDerHeide-Winter-Shiraz-The-Cost-of-Crying-Victory-November-2018.pdf.
2. Marie Fleming, "Propaganda by the Deed: Terrorism and Anarchist Theory in Late Nineteenth Century Europe," *Studies in Conflict and Terrorism* 4, no. 1 (1980): 1–23.
3. It is well beyond the scope of this piece, but there was an enormous debate, particularly at the height of the United States' participation in the Iraq war, regarding the use of counter-insurgency (COIN) strategies to combat the enemy in that conflict. It is very important to keep distinct the question of insurgencies and terrorism, despite that fact that the insurgents the US fought in Iraq – and are fighting in Afghanistan – often use the tactic of terrorism.
4. It's interesting that today in the West there is a certain romanticism associated with Che (and ironically a certain commercialism as a result) but scholars discuss Marighella as an attempt to deal with the fact that Mao's and Che's theories had failed, a sort of course correction. Pablo Brum, "Revisiting Urban Guerrillas: Armed Propaganda and the Insurgency of Uruguay's MLN Tupamaro's, 1969-1970," *Studies in Conflict and Terrorism* 37, no. 5 (2014): 387–404 https://www.tandfonline.com/doi/abs/10.1080/1057610X.2014.893403 or Anita Peresin, "Mass Media and Terrorism," *IZVORNI ZNANSTVENI RAD UDK* (2007): 7 ftp.iza.org/dp10708.pd.
5. Bruce Hoffman, *Inside Terrorism* (New York: Columbia University Press, 1st ed., 1998), p. 61.
6. Kathy E. Ferguson, "Anarchist Printers and Presses: Material Circuits and Processes," *Political Theory* 42, no. 4 (August 2014): 391–414.
7. John Rahaghi, "New Tools, Old Goals: Comparing the Role of Technology in the 1979 Iranian Revolution and the 2009 Green Movement," *Journal of Information Policy* 14, no. 2 (2012): 160–161. The Ayatollah had been sending tapes into Iran for years along the Iran-Iraq border and via Pilgrims to the annual Haj to Mecca, but when he was sent to Paris, (with the government's permission), he was given access to direct phone lines into Iran, and that greatly facilitated his people's efforts. See also Gladys D. Ganley, "Power to the People via Personal Electronic Media," *The Washington Quarterly* (Spring 1991): 9.
8. See Peresin, "Mass Media."
9. For a review of a great deal of this research, see Cori E. Dauber and Carol K. Winkler, "Radical Visual Propaganda in the Online Environment: An Introduction," in Winkler and Dauber, eds., *Visual Propaganda and Extremism in the Online Environment* (Carlisle, PA: US Army War College Press, 2014): 1–30. http://publications.armywarcollege.edu/pubs/2285.pdf.
10. Michael Pfau, Michael Haigh, Andreelynn Fifrick, Douglas Holl, Allison Tedesco, Jay Cope, David Nunnally, Amy Schiess, Donald Preston, Paul Roszkowski, and Marlon Martin, "The Effects of Print News Photographs on the Casualties of War," *Journalism and Mass Communication Quarterly* 83, no. 1 (Spring 2006): 150–168.
11. For all statistics Olympic see the site www.Olympics.org.
12. If you take into account both broadcast and cable channels, the web, and apps, the Rio Olympics set a record (for American television) with a total of 6,755 hours of coverage, more than 260 of them on the traditional broadcast network, NBC. See, "NBC Universal To Present Unprecedented 6,755 Hours of Rio Olympic Programming," *Comcast News Release* (June 28, 2016) https://corporate.comcast.com/news-information/news-feed/nbcuniversal-to-present-unprecedented-6755-hours-of-rio-olympic-programming. Its difficult to get an accurate fix on the hours planned for Munich because the coverage of the hostage taking so distorted the programming, but in Mexico City, the Olympics

immediately prior, ABC provided 44 hours of coverage – 10 in prime time. It is the case though that a number of innovations in the way things are filmed stemmed from those earlier Olympics. See Edith Noriega, "From Slow-Motion to Live TV: '68 Olympics Impacted How We Watch Today," *globalsportsmatters* (October 29, 2018) https://globalsportmatters.com/mexico/2018/10/29/from-slow-motion-to-live-tv-68-olympics-impacted-how-we-watch-today/.

13. See Allen Guttmann, "The Cold War and the Olympics," *International Journal: Canada's Journal of Global Political Analysis* 43, no. 4 (December 1988): 554–568 https://journals.sagepub.com/doi/10.1177/002070208804300402.

14. Simon Reeve claims the audience was 900 million, although we have seen figures as high as one billion. "Olympics Massacre: Munich – The Real Story," *The Independent* (January 22, 2006) https://www.independent.co.uk/news/world/europe/olympics-massacre-munich-the-real-story-5336955.html.

15. Hoffman, *Inside Terrorism*, p. 74.

16. They actually seized five total, as the last one was meant to be traded for the surviving hijacker in custody after control of one of the planes in the first waive was taken back by the British. See Pierre Tristam, "The 1970 Hijackings of Three Jets to Jordan," *ThoughtCo* (May 8, 2017) https://www.thoughtco.com/palestinian-hijackings-of-jets-to-jordan-2353581

17. Hoffman, *Inside Terrorism*, p. 137. Please note, while later editions are still superb, this material is only in the first edition, it was unfortunately (in our opinion) cut from later ones.

18. Stewart Wolpin, "The First Cellphone Went on Sale Thirty Years Ago for $4,000," *Mashable* (March 13, 2004) https://mashable.com/2014/03/13/first-cellphone-on-sale/#.3egNhCM3sqg. By 2018, in contrast, 95% of Americans owned a cellphone of some variety, and 77% of those were a smartphone. "Mobile Fact Sheet," *Pew Research Center: Internet and Technology* (February 5, 2018) http://www.pewinternet.org/fact-sheet/mobile/. It was not that long ago that some wondered whether HDTVs, now standard, were potentially the next "Edsel." David J. Atkin et al., "Predictors of Audience Interest in Adopting Digital Television," *The Journal of Media Economics* 16, no. 3 (2003): 159. https://academic.csuohio.edu/kneuendorf/SkalskiVitae/Atkin.etal.2003.pdf.

19. For a more detailed version of this argument, see Cori E. Dauber, *You Tube War: Fighting in a World of Cameras in Every Cellphone and Photoshop on Every Computer* (Carlisle, PA: US Army War College Press, 2010), pp. 5–8. Notice that at the time of publication the idea of cameras on cellphones was new enough to be worthy of mention in the title.

20. Dauber, *You Tube Wars*, 13–14.

21. When bin Laden wanted to issue a statement regarding American forces initially fighting in Afghanistan, he did so by sending a fax to Al Jazeera. "Bin Laden's Fax: Statement released to Arabic news network al-Jazeera calling on Pakistanis to resist an American attack on Afghanistan," *The Guardian* (September 24, 2001) https://www.theguardian.com/world/2001/sep/24/afghanistan.terrorism22.

22. John P. Carlin with Garrett M. Graff, *Dawn of the Code War: America's Battle Against Russia, China, and the Rising Global Cyber Threat* (New York: Public Affairs Books, October 2018), p. 6.

23. Dauber, *You Tube Wars*, 9. For a more detailed discussion of the early history of jihadist film and video, see Anne Stenersen, "A History of Jihadi Cinematography," in Thomas Hegghammer, ed., *Jihadi Culture: The Art and Social Practices of Militant Islamists* (New York: Cambridge University Press, 2017): 108–127.

24. For a detailed example of the way the Web 2.0 discussions were first applied to the issues of insurgency and terrorism, see Thomas Rid and Marc Hecker, *War 2.0: Irregular Warfare in the Information Age* (Westport, CT: Praeger Security International, 2009).

25. WDD Staff, "A Brief History of Blogging," *Webdesignerdepot* (March 14, 2011) https://www.webdesignerdepot.com/2011/03/a-brief-history-of-blogging/.

26. At one point it was estimated, for any number of reasons, 95% of blogs ended up abandoned. Douglas Quenqua, "Blogs Falling in an Empty Forest," *New York Times* (June 5, 2009) https://www.nytimes.com/2009/06/07/fashion/07blogs.html.

27. https://www.youtube.com/watch?v=_OBlgSz8sSM

28. An early discussion of the implications of apps is Brian X. Chen, *Always On: How the iPhone Unlocked the Anything-Anytime-Anywhere Future – and Locked Us in* (Cambridge, MA: DeCapo Books, 2011). As of that writing there were a mere 400,000 apps available for Apple users, (and that seemed worthy of a book) as of this writing there are 2 million, but Android has surpassed that slightly, with 2.1 million. "Number of Apps Available in Leading App Stores as of 3rd Quarter 2018," *Statista* (n.d.) https://www.statista.com/statistics/276623/number-of-apps-available-in-leading-app-stores/.

29. Carlin, *Dawn of Code War*, 18–19.

30. See Garrett Jones, "The Revolution Will Be Brought to You By Text Messaging," *FPRI e-notes* (March 3, 2008) https://www.fpri.org/article/2008/03/the-revolution-will-be-brought-to-you-by-text-messaging/ – and note that this article is a full 10 years old.

31. Daniel Kimmage and Kathleen Ridolfo, *Iraqi Insurgent Media: The War of Images and Ideas: How Sunni Insurgents in Iraq and Their Supporters Worldwide Are Using the Media* (Washington, DC: RFE/RL Special Report, 2007): 34 https://docs.rferl.org/archive/online/OLPDFfiles/insurgent.pdf.

32. James Owen, "London Bombing Pictures Mark New Role for Camera Phones," *National Geographic News* (July 11, 2005) access August 20, 2017 http://news.nationalgeographic.com/news/2005/07/0711_050711_londoncell.html.

33. David Shedden, "Today in Media History: 2009 Hudson River crash-landing photo sent with Twitter," *Poynter.org* (January 15, 2015) https://www.poynter.org/news/today-media-history-2009-hudson-river-crash-landing-photo-sent-twitter.

34. For the discussion of quality, see Cori E. Dauber and Mark D. Robinson, "Guest Post: ISIS and the Hollywood Visual Style," *Jihadology.net* (July 6, 2015) http://jihadology.net/2015/07/06/guest-post-isis-and-the-hollywood-visual-style/. For the discussion of numbers, see Daniel Milton, *Down But Not Out: An Updated Examination of the Islamic State's Visual Propaganda* (United States Military Academy at West Point: Combating Terrorism Center, July 2014) https://ctc.usma.edu/app/uploads/2018/07/Down-But-Not-Out.pdf.

35. P. W. Singer and Emerson T. Brooking, *LikeWar: The Weaponization of Social Media* (Boston, MA: Eamon Dolan Books of Houghton Mifflin Harcourt, 2018), p. 66.

36. Meghan Colloton, "Eerie Photos of Boston on Lockdown During the Marathon Bombing Suspect Manhunt," *Boston.com* (April 14, 2014) https://www.boston.com/news/local-news/2014/04/18/eerie-photos-of-boston-on-lockdown-during-the-marathon-bombing-suspect-manhunt.

37. See FREEDOM, "Dubai World Record Eagle Flight" (March 14, 2015) https://www.youtube.com/watch?v=6g95F4VSfj0 where a GoPro is strapped to the back of a trained bird who flies from the top of a skyscraper for five minutes (currently at almost 9 million views) or any number of videos posted by fighter pilots from the cockpit during training exercises, carrier landings and so forth.

38. Jason Burke, "The Age of Selfie-Jihad: How Evolving Media Technology is Changing Terrorism," *CTC Sentinel* 9, no. 11 (November/December 2016) https://ctc.usma.edu/the-age-of-selfie-jihad-how-evolving-media-technology-is-changing-terrorism/

39. "New Video Message from the Islamic State: 'An Appropriate Recompense – Wilayat Ninawa,'" *Jihadology.net* (March 25, 2016) Posted by Aaron Y. Zelin https://jihadology.net/2016/03/25/new-video-message-from-the-islamic-state-an-appropriate-recompense-wilayat-ninawa/. (Warning: some very graphic images.)

40. We are thinking here of the introductory graphics of the Al-Kataib News Network, circa 2010, which purported to be the "voice" of the Al-Shabaab group, the AQ affiliate in Somalia. When lined up against the graphics of the BBC it was obvious that the design aesthetic was a straight rip: the similarities were too great to be accidental. But none of these videos are available on YouTube any longer.

41. Dauber, "The Branding of Violent Jihadism," 137–164.

42. Eryn J. Newman and Norman Schwartz, "Good Sound, Good Research: How Audio Quality Influences Perceptions of the Research and Researcher," *Science Communication* 40, no. 2 (2018): 246-257 https://journals.sagepub.com/doi/full/10.1177/1075547018759345.

43. Jacqueline Thompson, "Richard Spencer Stopped by Authorities While Traveling in Europe: Report," *The Hill*, July 5, 2018 https://thehill.com/blogs/blog-briefing-room/news/395745-richard-spencer-confirms-ban-on-traveling-to-european-countries.

44. Daveed Gartenstein-Ross and Madeleine Blackman, "ISIL's Virtual Planner's: A Critical Terrorist Innovation," *War on the Rocks* (January 4, 2007) https://warontherocks.com/2017/01/isils-virtual-pl anners-a-critical-terrorist-innovation/.

45. Samy Magdy, "Without Evidence, Islamic State Claims Las Vegas Shooting," *Bloomberg* (October 2, 2017) https://www.bloomberg.com/news/articles/2017-10-02/urgent-islamic-state-claims-las-ve gas-mass-shooting.

46. Key news sites reported traffic doubling roughly every seven minutes from the point the first plane hit the first Tower. They were struggling to keep up with three to ten times normal load, and that is completely aside from any stresses from physical damage. See Committee on the Internet Under Crisis Conditions: Learning From September 11, Computer Science and Telecommunications Board, *The Internet Under Crisis Conditions: Learning From September 11* (Washington, DC: National Research Council of the National Academies; The National Academies Press, 2003), p. 22 https://www.nap.edu/ read/10569/chapter/1#ii.

47. In the year 2000, right before the attacks, Americans sent an average of 35 texts a month. Christine Erikson, "A Brief History of Texting," *Mashable* (September 21, 2012) https://mashable.com/2012/09/2 1/text-messaging-history/#oCLDta3HJZqm. By 2015, they were sending that many texts per day, far outpacing the number of phone calls they were making. "No Time To Talk: Americans Sending/ Receiving Five Times as Many Texts Compared to Phone Calls Each Day, According to New Report," *PRNewswire* (March 25, 2015) https://www.prnewswire.com/news-releases/no-time-to-talk-ame ricans-sendingreceiving-five-times-as-many-texts-compared-to-phone-calls-each-day-accordin g-to-new-report-300056023.html. The report indicates the US is not isolated in this.

48. CNN, "Mumbai Terror Attacks: Fast Facts," *CNN Library* (November 12, 2018) https://www.cnn.com/ 2013/09/18/world/asia/mumbai-terror-attacks/index.html.

49. Rahul Bedi, "Mumbai Attacks: Indian Suit Against Google Earth Over Image Use by Terrorists," *The Telegraph* (December 9, 2008) https://www.telegraph.co.uk/news/worldnews/asia/india/3691723/ Mumbai-attacks-Indian-suit-against-Google-Earth-over-image-use-by-terrorists.html.

50. Peter Bergen, "Are Mass Murderers Using Twitter as a tool?" *CNN.com* (September 27, 2013) https:// www.cnn.com/2013/09/26/opinion/bergen-twitter-terrorism/index.html.

51. Chelsea J. Carter, "Video shows ISIS beheading US journalist James Foley," *CNN.com* (August 20, 2014) https://www.cnn.com/2014/08/19/world/meast/isis-james-foley/index.html.

52. See Simone Molin Friis, "'Beyond Anything We Have Ever Seen:' Beheading Videos and the Visibility of Violence in the War Against ISIS," *International Affairs* 91, no. 4 (July 2015) https://www.chathamh ouse.org/publication/ia/beyond-anything-we-have-ever-seen-beheading-videos-and-visibility-viole nce-war.

53. Sewell Chan and Ariana Eunjung Cha, "American Beheaded on Web Video," *Washington Post* (May 12, 2004), p. A01 http://www.washingtonpost.com/wp-dyn/articles/A19048-2004May11.html.

54. The first five victims also received as much attention as they did in part because the executioner, who was eventually identified and killed in a drone strike, was himself British. Victoria Ward, "Jihadi John's Victims: Who Were They?" *The Telegraph* (November 13, 2015) https://www.telegraph.co.uk/ne ws/worldnews/islamic-state/11992798/Jihadi-Johns-victims-who-were-they.html.

55. "Bodies of 20 Egyptian Christians Beheaded in Libya Arrive in Egypt," *Reuters* (May 14, 2018) https ://www.reuters.com/article/us-libya-egypt/bodies-of-20-egyptian-christians-beheaded-in-libya-ar rive-in-egypt-idUSKCN1IF0J4.

56. "ISIS Used Underwater Cameras to Film Last Desperate Breaths of Five Men Drowning in Cage," *Al-Nahar* (June 24, 2015) https://en.annahar.com/article/247387-isis-used-underwater-cameras-to- film-last-desperate-breaths-of-five-men-drowning.

57. Martin Chulov and Shiv Malik, "Isis Video Shows Jordanian Hostage Being Burned to Death," *The Guardian* (February 3, 2015) https://www.theguardian.com/world/2015/feb/03/isis-video-jordania n-hostage-burdning-death-muadh-al-kasabeh.

58. "Canada Sergeant-At-Arms Kevin Vickers Hailed Hero Over Gun Attack," *NBC News* (October 23, 2014) https://www.nbcnews.com/storyline/canadian-parliament-shooting/canada-sergeant-at-arm s-kevin-vickers-hailed-hero-over-gun-n232176.

59. Sabina Zawadski and Ole Mikkelsen, "Danish Police Kill 22-Year Old Suspected of Copenhagen Shootings," *Reuters* (February 14, 2015) https://www.reuters.com/article/us-denmark-shooting/dan ish-police-kill-22-year-old-suspected-of-copenhagen-shootings-idUSKBN0LI0N720150215.

60. Raf Sanchez et al., "Gunman and Two Hostages Killed in Sydney Siege: As It Happened," *The Telegraph* (December 16, 2014) https://www.telegraph.co.uk/news/worldnews/australiaandthepacific/aust ralia/11293694/Islamists-take-hostages-in-Sydney-cafe-siege-live.html.

61. The Soufan Group, "The New Spectacular Terrorist Attack," *TSG Intel Brief* (January 12, 2015) http:// www.soufangroup.com/tsg-intelbrief-the-new-spectacular-terror-attack/.

62. We actually believe the first vehicle attack was on the UNC campus in 2006. It had been all but for-gotten until people began researching "vehicle attacks" after Nice because for whatever reason the attacker did not fully commit, he drove into the crowd fairly slowly, so that only a small number were injured, none so seriously as to need overnight hospitalization.

63. France24, "Nice Truck Killer Had Support, Accomplices for Carefully Planned Attack," *France24* (July 21, 2016) https://www.france24.com/en/20160721-nice-truck-attack-killer-support-accomplices-pre meditated-attack.

64. Counter-Extremism Project, "Executive Summary," *Vehicles as Weapons of Terror* (New York: CEP, 2018) https://www.counterextremism.com/vehicles-as-weapons-of-terror.

65. Colin P. Clarke, "The Continuing Plague of Vehicle Attacks: What Can Be Done?" *The RAND Blog* (April 26, 2018) https://www.rand.org/blog/2018/04/the-continuing-plague-of-vehicle-attacks-what-can-b e.html.

66. Dakin Andone and Laura Dolan, "Charlottesville Suspect Shared Posts Showing Car Driving into Protesters before Attack," *CNN.com* (November 30, 2018) https://www.cnn.com/2018/11/30/us/c harlottesville-james-fields-trial/index.html.

67. See Alan Burdick, "Looking for Life on a Flat Earth," *The New Yorker* (May 30, 2018) https://www.new yorker.com/science/elements/looking-for-life-on-a-flat-earth.

68. Joseph A. Schafer, "Spinning the Web of Hate: Web-Based Propagation of Hate by Extremist Organizations," *Journal of Criminal Justice and Popular Culture* 9, no. 2 (2002): 69–88 https://www.alb any.edu/scj/jcjpc/vol9is2/vol9is2.pdf#page=39.

69. Emma Grey Ellis, "Gab, The Alt-Right's Very Own Twitter, Is the Ultimate Filter Bubble," *Wired* (September 14, 2016) https://www.wired.com/2016/09/gab-alt-rights-twitter-ultimate-filter-bubble/.

70. Megan Crepeau, "Ringleader Given 8 Years in Prison for Beating Teen with Disability in Attack Live Streamed on Facebook," *Chicago Tribune* (July 5, 2018) https://www.chicagotribune.com/news/loca l/breaking/ct-met-facebook-live-hate-crime-20180705-story.html. It's ironic, though, that the *Trib* story includes an embedded clip from the Facebook attack itself. So it's awful, awful enough to merit jail time, but not so awful that it can't be used as click bait.

71. Jordan Valinsky, "News Crew Shooting Shows Perils of Auto-Play Videos on Twitter, Facebook," *Digiday* (August 26, 2015) https://digiday.com/media/news-crew-shooting-shows-perils-auto-pl ay-videos-twitter-facebook/. The article notes that one of the most popular tweets that morning sent instructions for disabling autoplay.

72. James McAuley, "ISIS-Inspired Attacker Kills French Police Officer and Streams It on Facebook," *Washington Post* (June 14, 2016) https://www.washingtonpost.com/world/french-president-killin g-of-police-officials-undeniably-a-terrorist-attack/2016/06/14/db71760f-68be-48d3-96e9-df35dc5d 7e5b_story.html?utm_term=.23d999d03382. It's interesting that a good amount of the press cover-age elides the fact that the Facebook post was a live stream.

73. Kim Willsher, "Teenagers Who Killed French Priest Made Film Declaring Allegiance to Isis," *The Guardian* (July 28, 2016) https://www.theguardian.com/world/2016/jul/27/french-authorities-under -pressure-to-explain-release-of-priests-killer. See also Burke, "Selfie-Jihad," according to whom one of the pair seemed to be promising such a live stream to his followers on social media prior to the attack.

74. Terrorism is not the only concern here. It should surprise no one that teenagers have chosen to com-mit suicide on social media, live, and if there were fears of "suicide contagion" from simple reports of suicides in old media print newspapers, its hard to imagine the impact watching an actual event in

real time is having. Erica Euse, "Teens Are Live-Streaming Their Suicides at an Alarming Rate," *i-D Vice*, July 12, 2017 https://i-d.vice.com/en_us/article/59ggek/teens-are-live-streaming-their-suicides-at-an-alarming-rate.

75. Sarah Larimer, "This Man Filmed a Fatal Car Crash Instead of Helping. Then, Ohio Police Arrested Him," *Washington Post* (July 16, 2015) https://www.washingtonpost.com/news/morning-mix/wp/2015/07/16/this-ohio-man-filmed-a-fatal-car-crash-instead-of-helping-then-police-arrested-him/?utm_term=.9e6030a150c8.

Chapter 6

Counterterrorism Strategy from an Extended Global Online Level

José de Arimatéia da Cruz*

CONTENTS

6.1 INTRODUCTION

Richard Haass, President of the Council on Foreign Relations and author of *A World in Disarray: American Foreign Policy and the Crisis of the Old Order* (2017) asserts that the world today is not Las Vegas. The implication of this statement is that what happens around the world has a direct impact on our nation just as what happens domestically has a direct impact internationally. The globalization of the world in terms of faster communication speed, the birth of the internet, travel, and governments around the world dependence on the expansion of the means of communication, means that the world of the twenty-first century will be not only more interconnected but also more complicated. The proliferation of cyber-attacks and the increase of cyber-criminal activities online necessitates a whole-of-government approach. In this new "brave world," nations cannot go it alone. This chapter discusses the regional as well as the international associational approaches to address counterterrorism from an extended global online level.

---

* The views expressed in this essay are those of the author and do not necessarily reflect the official policy or position of the Department of the Army, the Department of Defense, or the U.S. Government.

6.2 UNITED NATIONS GLOBAL COUNTERTERRORISM

The United Nations Office of Counter Terrorism was established through the adoption of General Assembly Resolution 71/291 on 15 June 2017. Russian diplomat Vladimir Ivanovich Voronkov was appointed Under-Secretary-General of the Office on 21 June 2017. According to the UN Global Counter-Terrorism Strategy, their office has five main functions to implement counterterrorism internationally:

- Provide leadership on the General Assembly counterterrorism mandates entrusted to the Secretary-General from across the United Nations system.
- Enhance coordination and coherence across the 38 Counter-Terrorism Implementation Task Force entities to ensure the balanced implementation of the four pillars of the UN Global Counter-Terrorism Strategy.
- Strengthen the delivery of United Nations counterterrorism capacity-building assistance to member states.
- Improve visibility, advocacy, and resource mobilization for United Nations counterterrorism efforts.
- Ensure that due priority is given to counterterrorism across the United Nations system and that the important work on preventing violent extremism is firmly rooted in the strategy [1].

The United Nations Office of Counter Terrorism premises its efforts to combat counterterrorism based on four pillars. As stated on their website, the United Nations Office of Counter Terrorism adopts those four pillars as a unique global instrument to enhance national, regional, and international efforts to counterterrorism [2]. The General Assembly reviews the United Nations Office of Counter Terrorism strategies every two years. The strategy is comprised of documents which must be adapted and adopted to the new environment of the twenty-first century in which terrorist organizations or transnational organized criminal organizations are always one step ahead of law enforcement agencies. The United Nations Office of Counter Terrorism's Pillar I addresses the conditions conducive to the spread of terrorism. The strategy, which was adopted by consensus in 2006, argues that within Pillar I, the United Nations along with its member states are resolved to undertake the following measures aimed at addressing the conditions conducive to the spread of terrorism such as prolonged unresolved conflicts, dehumanization of victims of terrorism in all its forms and manifestations, lack of rule of law and violations of human rights, ethnic, national, and religious discrimination, political exclusion, socioeconomic marginalization, and lack of good governance [3].

Pillar II, preventing and combating terrorism, is particularly concerned with preventing and combating terrorism so that those organizations will not have access or the ability to purchase the means to carry out their attacks. In order to do so, the United National Office of Counter Terrorism encourages its member nations to cooperate fully in the fight against terrorism, ensure the apprehension and prosecution or extradition of perpetrators of terrorist acts, intensify cooperation in a timely fashion, especially when it comes to information sharing, and finally strengthen coordination and cooperation among states in combating crimes that might be connected to terrorism [4]. Given the advancement of technology and reliability on the internet to conduct business, pleasure, or simply to browse, criminal organizations are becoming savvier in their schemes to steal individual personal information (IPI), social security numbers, etc. Prosecution of those individuals is extremely difficult given their deniability and the fact that many of those individuals operate under the protection of some sovereign power. Attribution is also a major concern when a computer is used in the commission of a crime. How do we know if the individual using the computer is responsible or if his computer has been taken over by a botnet? Pillar II encourages member states to stop asserting their national sovereignty as a justification for flaunting international norms and allowing criminal organizations to use their territory as a safe haven.

Under Pillar III, building states' capacities and strengthening the role of the United Nations, the United Nations Office of Counter Terrorism recognizes that a failed state or a rogue state does not have the capacity or autonomy to carry out its obligations to protect its citizens as well as the international community. Their geographic boundaries become a safe haven for terrorist organizations looking for a location to set up headquarters and carry out malfeasance. This type of situation is very similar to what has happened in Afghanistan in the aftermath of the rise of the Taliban and its support of Osama bin Laden and the terrorist organization Al Qaeda. Due to Afghanistan's weak state capacity, Osama bin Laden and Al Qaeda were able to organize, plan, and carry out the 9/11 attacks against the United States. In order to strengthen Pillar III, the United Nations encourages its participating members to consider making voluntary contributions to the United Nations counterterrorism cooperation and technical assistance projects in addition to encouraging the United Nations to work with member states and relevant international, regional, and sub-regional organizations to identify and share best practices to prevent terrorist attacks on particularly vulnerable targets [5].

Pillar IV encourages member states to take every necessary measure to ensure respect for human rights for all and the rule of law as the fundamental basis of the fight against terrorism. One important recommendation under Pillar IV is for member states to ensure that whatever steps they take in order to combat terrorism, respect for international law, human rights law, and international humanitarian law must be observed at all times.

6.3 THE G20 AND ITS COUNTERTERRORISM STRATEGY

The G20 is a special group of nations. Some are extremely wealthy nations that rely solely on an extraction industry such as Saudi Arabia and its petroleum. Other nations, such as Argentina and Brazil, are developing nations still very reliant on agro-business, and they are still primary exporters of agricultural products and importers of manufactured goods. The members of the G20 are Argentina, Australia, Brazil, Canada, China, France, Germany, India, Indonesia, Italy, Japan, Republic of Korea, Mexico, Russia, Saudi Arabia, South Africa, Turkey, the United Kingdom, the United States, and the European Union.

While the United States and Europe recognize the threat of cyber-terrorism, in Latin America, the focus is more on cybercrime due to higher rates of real and perceived insecurity and a rapidly growing number of internet users. The Inter-American Committee Against Terrorism, composed of members from the Organization of American States (OAS), works to advance counter-cyber strategies and techniques. The Symantec Corporation, SecDev Foundation, and Igarapé Institute are examples of independent organizations, like the Inter-American Committee and OAS, that conduct studies of state efforts to collect information and provide advice to boost current cybercrime counter-measures [6]. Countries in Latin America are becoming more aware of the national security implications of cyber (in)security in their region. The Argentine government substantially improved cyber-security during the past few years in response to growing domestic and international concerns. Argentina, one of the first Latin American countries to implement a national cyber-response team, the National Office of Information Technology National Program for Critical Information Infrastructure and Cyber Security, created the Argentine Computer Emergency Response Team in 1994, which became the National Program for Critical Information Infrastructure and Cyber Security [7]. The Snowden leaks prompted many Latin

American nations to build multilateral partnerships, such as the cooperative agreement between Argentina and Brazil, to improve cyber defense capabilities announced in September 2013. Approximately 22 million Brazilians were victims of cybercrimes in 2012, and that number continues to grow.

The Brazilian Information and Communication Technology Management Committee established their Cyber Security Incident Response Team in 1997, which was renamed CERT.br in 2005. CERT.br establishes and maintains supportive partnerships, conducts cybercrime trend analyses and training, builds awareness, and monitors networks to respond to cyber incidents. Private-public cooperation in Brazil embodies an ideal cyber defense situation because the public sector voluntarily shares cyber incident information, thereby enabling CERT.br to plan prevention strategies and responses appropriate to the most prominent types of cyber-attacks and high-value targets in the absence of legal direction [8]. Atypical among Latin American states, Brazil invests in military-based cyber defense capabilities to curb cybercrime. Created and operational in 2010, the Cyberdefence Center of the Brazilian Army currently coordinates the army's cyber-security actions. Eventually, the center will also oversee the Brazilian Navy and Air Force to ensure federal and military network protection from foreign and domestic attacks. Several other Latin American countries have established computer security incident response teams (CSIRTs) throughout Latin America to counterterrorism within the region [9].***

At the Hamburg G20 meeting held in Hamburg, Germany on 7–8 July 2017, members of the G20 released a statement on countering terrorism. According to the members present, terrorism is a global scourge that must be fought and terrorist safe havens eliminated in every part of the world [10]. Member states set the following priorities at the 2017 G20 summit: building resilience, improvising sustainability, and assuming responsibility. Under the assuming responsibility umbrella, member states pledged to combat terrorism and money laundering in addition to fighting corruption. Member states also pledged to exchange information between intelligence and law enforcement and judicial authorities on operational information sharing, preventive measures, and criminal justice response. Furthermore, member states pledged that there should be no safe spaces for terrorist financing anywhere in the world. In order to implement this principle, member states agreed to a comprehensive implementation of the recommendations of the Financial Action Task Force (FATF). Member states also agreed to countering radicalization conducive to terrorism and the use of internet for terrorist purposes. To accomplish this ambitious goal, member states promised to exchange best practices on preventing and countering terrorism and violent extremism conducive to terrorism, national strategies and de-radicalization and disengagement programs, and the promotion of strategic communications as well as robust and positive narratives to counterterrorist propaganda [11].

6.4 G8 RECOMMENDATIONS FOR COUNTERTERRORISM

The G8 are the world most industrialized and wealthy nations in the world. The G8 is now the G7 since Russia was expelled from this elite group when it invaded the Republic of Georgia. The G8/G7 attaches great importance to combating and counterterrorism. The G8/G7 has defined a series of steps it will take to counter terrorism. Those steps were outlined in the G8 Counter-Terrorism Experts Group also known as the Roma Group. The recommendations update the

---

* English designations differing from literal translation reflect currently accepted agency titles.
** The Mexican CSIRT is located at a university and addresses incidents nationally.

Counter-Terrorism Experts Group 25 Measures to address new terrorist threats as well as to complement the 40 Recommendations of the G8 crime group, known as the Lyon Group (1996). The Lyon Recommendations have also been modified in order to address more effectively the challenge of transnational crime threats. The revised Lyon Group Recommendations, now entitled the G8 Recommendations on Transnational Crime, were endorsed by G8 Ministers of Justice and the Interior (Mont-Tremblant, May 13-14, 2002) [12]. There are 10 sections or recommendations from the G8 to combat terrorism. For the purpose of this article, Sections 5, 8, and 9 are most relevant. Section 5 [Financing of Terrorism] recommends the implementation of several mechanisms such as the United Nations Security Council Resolution 1373, the International Convention for the Suppression of the Financing of Terrorism and the Financial Action Task Force's (FATF) Special Recommendations on Terrorism Financing. Section 8 [International Cooperation] urges member states to take all possible measures to deny safe havens to those who finance, plan, support, or commit terrorist acts and to take strong measures with other member states to prevent terrorist acts, the international movements of terrorists, and to ensure that claims of political motivation are not recognized as grounds for refusing requests for the extradition of alleged terrorists [13].

The G8/G7 is guided by the following principles:

1. All terrorist acts are criminal and unjustifiable, and must be unequivocally condemned, especially when they indiscriminately target or injure civilians.
2. Suicide bombings are a particularly despicable tactic, and recruiting the young or disadvantaged to carry out such acts must be uniformly condemned.
3. Abductions and the taking of hostages are repugnant practices to be strongly condemned.
4. Conflict, oppression, and poverty do not excuse or justify terrorism.
5. Terrorist abuse of freedoms inherent to democratic societies to spread hatred and incite violence, such as through abuse of modern technologies and open borders, will not be tolerated [14].

6.4.1 The Counter-terrorism Action Group (CTAG)

The Counter-Terrorism Action Group (CTAG) was established in July 2003 by G8 nations (France, Japan, Canada, Germany, the USA, the UK, Italy, and Russia). The function of the CTAG is to provide technical, legal, and training help for third world countries in the combat against terrorism. Furthermore, CTAG aims to support the UN Security Council Counter-Terrorism Committee, primarily through coordination and outreach efforts. Among the goals in creating the CTAG was to offer the CTC a donor forum in which to share information regarding priority assistance needs related to the implementation of Security Council Resolution 1373, with a view to identifying the appropriate donors to address each identified need [15]. According to Eric Rosand, the CTAG should take several steps in order to be relevant in the fight against terrorism including but not limited to the following recommendations:

1. Practice of convening local CTAG meetings should be reinvigorated.
2. CTAG member countries with the strongest interest in particular countries or regions should organize local or regional CTAG meetings on a permanent basis to ensure more continuity and sustained CTAG interest in the field, rather than the current approach, which gives the CTAG presidency responsibility for organizing such meetings around the globe during its year-long term.

3. CTAG members should show a greater willingness to share relevant information about pertinent ongoing or planned activities with their CTAG colleagues.
4. Other active counterterrorism donors should be invited to join the group to make it more representative and ensure all the major donors are around the table.
5. The Japan-led efforts to strengthen the CTAG relationship with the CTC and its group of experts, the Counter-Terrorism Executive Director (CTED), should continue; and the CTED should continue to provide CTAG members with timely and sound analysis of country or regional needs and priorities, well enough in advance of CTAG meetings to allow the group to focus on particular countries, regions, or themes.
6. An expanded CTAG should be delinked from the G8's Lyon-Roma Anti-Crime and Counter Terrorism Group meetings (for organized crime/counterterrorism practitioners) to help ensure that the CTAG meeting attracts more interest and CTAG still offers the best opportunity currently available for enhanced coordination of donor counterterrorism assistance [16].

6.4.2 Public–Private Partnership to Counter Terrorism

Roughly 90 percent, if not more, of the United States' critical infrastructure is in private hands; therefore, cooperation between governments and the private sector is more important than ever in the twenty-first century. The importance of this partnership was highlighted at the G8 summit in St. Petersburg, Russia, in July 2006. At the summit, Russia along with other world leaders emphasized their commitment to promote better collaboration nationally and globally between governments and the private sector in the fight against terrorism. Member states endorsed the following declaration which was approved unanimously in the form of the St. Petersburg Summit Declaration on Counter Terrorism issued on July 16, 2006.

The Declaration includes the following statement:

> We emphasize the importance in a globalized world of working closely with our private sector partners in our efforts to counterterrorism and bolster capacity to protect our citizens and businesses as they pursue their work and leisure. We commend the "Global Forum for Partnerships between Government and Businesses to Counter-Terrorism", to be held in Moscow in November 2006 and commit to close cooperation within the G8, with other States and with business partners to make this initiative a sustained and successful process [17].

Member states at the G8 summit in St. Petersburg identified a number of measures that will have to be undertaken by governments worldwide in their efforts to truly combat and counter terrorism in the age of the democratization of technology and the death of distance. The following actions were recommended by the member states and were adopted by unanimous consent:

1. Implementing and improving the international legal framework on counterterrorism
2. Ensuring that national legislation is modified to address new terrorist challenges
3. Suppressing attempts by terrorists to gain access to weapons and other means of mass destruction
4. Enhancing efforts to counter the financing of terrorism based on agreed standards
5. Effectively countering attempts to misuse cyberspace for terrorist purposes, including incitement to commit terrorist acts, to communicate and plan terrorist acts, as well as recruitment and training of terrorists
6. Promoting supply chain security, based on existing international standards and best practices [18]

In addition to the above recommended measures, the member states at St. Petersburg also recognized the need for greater cooperation between the private and public sectors, especially in regard to national workforce and education. One of the challenges member states will encounter in the future regarding the workforce necessary to counterterrorism is the fact that few universities are graduating the workforce necessary to respond to demands in the field of cyber-security. Therefore, there is a necessity to promote public–private partnerships to address this shortcoming in the number of graduates with the necessary degrees, certifications, and credentials. The member states also identified three key areas of improving private sector cooperation:

1. Sharing information on private sector "targets"
2. Improving internal security measures
3. Creating resilient and robust systems [19]

6.5 NATO'S POLICY GUIDELINES ON COUNTERTERRORISM

The North Atlantic Treaty Organization (NATO) is an international alliance that consists of 29 member states from North America and Europe. It was established at the signing of the North Atlantic Treaty on 4 April 1949. Terrorist attacks on the European continent are nothing new. However, given the increase in recent years in the number of attacks due to ideology and religious motivations, terrorism is once again a major national security concern among European leaders, especially in light of the recent attacks in London (2018) and Barcelona (2018).

As member states have stated in their Policy Guideline on Counter Terrorism, terrorism poses a direct threat to the security of the citizens of NATO countries, and to international stability and prosperity more broadly and will remain a threat for the foreseeable future [20]. NATO's response to terrorism and counterterrorism has been a response to the terrorist attacks of 9/11 in the United States homeland when three airplanes piloted by international terrorists hit the twin towers in New York City, the Pentagon in Washington, D.C., and the third plane, United Airlines Flight 93, crashed in the Pennsylvania countryside (Shanksville, PA).

NATO's Policy Guideline on Counter Terrorism goals are the following:

- Provide strategic and risk-informed direction to the counterterrorism activities ongoing across the Alliance as part of NATO's core tasks of collective defense, crisis management, and cooperative security.
- Identify the principles to which the Alliance adheres.
- Identify key areas in which the Alliance will undertake initiatives to enhance the prevention of and resilience to acts of terrorism with a focus on improved *awareness* of the threat, adequate *capabilities* to address it and *engagement* with partner countries and other international actors [21].

In order to support those three policy guidelines, NATO and its member states are guided by the following principles to combat terrorism: compliance with international law, NATO's support to allies, and non-duplication and complementarity [22]. NATO and its members as well as allies agreed to coordinate and consolidate its counterterrorism efforts by focusing on three key areas of concern: awareness, capabilities, and engagement [23]. According to NATO's Policy Guideline on Counter Terrorism, NATO will ensure shared awareness of the terrorist threat and vulnerabilities among Allies through consultations, enhanced sharing of intelligence, continuous strategic analysis, and assessments in support of national authorities (awareness).

NATO has acquired much valuable expertise in countering asymmetric threats and in responding to terrorism. NATO's work on airspace security, air defense, maritime security, response to CBRN, non-proliferation of weapons of mass destruction, and protection of critical infrastructure is well established (capabilities), and the challenge of terrorism requires a holistic approach by the international community, involving a wide range of instruments (engagement) [24].

6.6 THE COUNCIL OF EUROPE

The Council of Europe's response to terrorism and counterterrorism is also driven by the recent attacks in London and Barcelona. In July 2018, the Council of Europe adopted a new counterterrorism strategy for 2018–2020. According to the Council of Europe Secretary General Thorbjørn Jagland, the Council of Europe must improve the ability of member states to prevent and combat terrorism in full compliance with human rights and the rule of law. This strategy takes account of the growing terrorist threat and should provide European governments with additional, effective means of response [25]. The Council of Europe priorities are prevention, prosecution, and protection. The Council of Europe will pursue the following in order to counter terrorism before it becomes an issue: policy guidelines on preventing and countering terrorist public provocation, propaganda, radicalization, recruitment, and training including on the internet (prevention); will work with prosecutors and police officers on the gathering of evidence from conflict zones and the internet, in order to improve international cooperation in criminal matters and enable the prosecution of foreign terrorist fighters (prosecution); will collect and disseminate best practices on de-radicalization, disengagement, and social reintegration (protection) [26].

6.7 ORGANIZATION FOR SECURITY AND CO-OPERATION IN EUROPE (OSCE)

The Organization for Security and Co-Operation in Europe (OSCE) is a forum for political dialogue on a wide range of security issues and a platform for joint action to improve the lives of individuals and communities. The organization uses a comprehensive approach to security that encompasses the politico-military, economic and environmental, and human dimensions [27]. The OSCE contributes to the efforts against terrorism led by the United Nations, addressing the manifestations of terrorism, as well as the various social, economic, political, and other factors that might engender conditions in which terrorist organizations could engage in recruitment and win support [28]. According to the OSCE's announcement of its counterterrorism strategy to the media, it states that terrorism is one of the most significant threat to peace, security, and stability. Terrorism has become the new pandemic of the twenty-first century. One important observation regarding the release of the OSCE's strategy is that it makes clear that terrorism is not to be associated with any race, nationality, or religion.

The OSCE's strategy to combat terrorism and counterterrorism adopted these strategies:

1. Promoting the implementation of the international legal framework against terrorism and enhancing international legal cooperation in criminal matters related to terrorism
2. Countering violent extremism and radicalization that lead to terrorism, following a multidimensional approach

3. Preventing and suppressing the financing of terrorism
4. Countering the use of the internet for terrorist purposes
5. Promoting dialogue and cooperation on counterterrorism issues, in particular, through public–private partnerships between State authorities and the private sector (business community, industry), as well as civil society and the media
6. Strengthening national efforts to implement United Nations Security Council resolution 1540 (2004) on non-proliferation of weapons of mass destruction
7. Strengthening travel document security
8. Promoting and protecting human rights and fundamental freedoms in the context of counterterrorism measures [29]

6.8 SUMMARY

At the beginning of this article, I quoted Richard Haass who has asserted in his book *A World in Disarray: American Foreign Policy and the Crisis of the Old Order* (2017) that the world today is not Las Vegas. More than ever the international community cannot on its own solve issues that have truly become more globalized and require international collaboration and commitment. One truly globalized issue is terrorism and how to combat it in the age of globalization, development of the internet, and the death of distance as the world becomes more globalized and interconnected. Terrorism does not recognize geographic boundaries. Thus, more than ever, governments around the world must be one step ahead of potential perpetrators. To combat and counter terrorism will require a whole-of-government approach. International collaboration will be essential: intelligence sharing, extraditions agreements, and sharing of information will be important as well. Indeed, the world of the twenty-first century is no longer Las Vegas. What happens abroad has a direct impact domestically just like what happens domestically has an impact globally. Issues in the globalized world are more than ever "intermestic," that is, both domestic and international.

REFERENCES

1. United Nations Office of Counter-Terrorism available at http://www.un.org/en/counterterrorism. Accessed December 8, 2018.
2. United Nations Office of Counter-Terrorism available at https://www.un.org/counterterrorism/ctitf/un-global-counter-terrorism-strategy. Accessed December 8, 2018.
3. Jose de Arimateia da Cruz and Taylor Alvarez, "Cybersecurity Initiatives in the Americas: Implications for U.S. National Security," *Marine Corps University Journal* Vol. 6, No. 2 (Fall 2015): 45–68.
4. Gustavo Diniz and Robert Muggah, *A Fine Balance: Mapping Cyber (In)Security in Latin America*, Strategic Paper 2 (Rio de Janeiro: Igarapé Institute, 2012), 15.
5. The Hamburg G20 Leaders' Statement on Countering Terrorism available at http://www.g20.utoronto.ca/2017/2017-g20-statement-antiterror-en.pdf. Accessed December 9, 2018.
6. G8 Recommendations on Counter-Terrorism available at https://www.mofa.go.jp/policy/economy/summit/2002/g8terro.html. Accessed December 14, 2018.
7. G8 Leaders Statement on Counter-Terrorism available at file:///C:/Users/jdacruz/Downloads/Counter-Terrorism%20(1).pdf. Accessed December 14, 2018.
8. Eric Rosand, "The G8's Counterterrorism Action Group," Policy Brief May 2009 Center on Global Terrorism Cooperation available at https://www.files.ethz.ch/isn/100976/rosand_policybrief_092.pdf. Accessed December 14, 2018.

9. "G8 Initiative For Public-Private Partnerships To Counter Terrorism," Private Sector Action Beyond 2006 EWI's Discussion Paper, November 2006 available at https://www.files.ethz.ch/isn/90482/2006-11-28_G8-Initiative-for-PPPs.pdf. Accessed December 14, 2018.

10. "NATO's policy guidelines on counter-terrorism: Aware, Capable and Engaged for a Safer Future," May 24, 2012 available at https://www.nato.int/cps/en/natohq/official_texts_87905.htm. Accessed December 14, 2018.

11. "The Council of Europe adopts a new counter-terrorism strategy for 2018-2022," available at https://www.coe.int/en/web/portal/-/the-council-of-europe-adopts-a-new-counter-terrorism-strategy-for-2018-2022. Accessed December 14, 2018.

12. "Who Are We," available at https://www.osce.org/who-we-are. Accessed December 14, 2018.

13. "Terrorism," available at https://www.osce.org/countering-terrorism. Accessed December 14, 2018.

Chapter 7

Tools to Study Complexity in the Virtual World of Counterrorism

Lessons Learned from the Stuxnet and Shamoon Viruses

Sheila Ronis and Richard J. Chasdi

CONTENTS

7.1 INTRODUCTION

In a world of complexity, there are many lessons to be learned from the development and use of viruses such as Stuxnet and Shamoon. Probably the most important of these lessons is there are ways to enable a decision and policy-maker to ask better questions and learn enough about threat development to improve analysis outcomes. This chapter will discuss the nature of complex systems and why the development of visionarios—system maps and stories—helps to explore those systems for better understanding of their idiosyncrasies and characteristics. Since nation states and "insurgent" terrorists can use cyber-weapons, understanding the complex systems that can lead to the use of these weaponized versions of code can be useful. In addition, cyber-weapons, that are potential tools of terrorists, are also discussed.

7.2 WHO IS A TERRORIST? WHAT KINDS OF THREATS CAN THEY POSE?

Broadly speaking, a terrorist can be defined as an individual who disrupts society in a surprising or unusual manner or both through the threat, use or promotion of force to produce fear and abject terror in a civilian population with change in political dispositions or policy as the primary objective [1]. This "disruption" can occur using kinetics, such as a suicide bomber, or in the case of cybercrime or cyber-terrorism, more subtle tools such as ransomware to blackmail victims. But with the world learning about the Stuxnet and Shamoon viruses, much about threat perception has changed because these cyber-weapons were able to use code to effect changes in the real world and produce substantive kinetic effects.

The Stuxnet virus was a covert operation carried out by a nation state against another nation state, though no country has ever claimed responsibility for it. By using the virus as part of a cyber-attack or operation in a classified, secret way, the nation can remain anonymous. The United States' NSA, CIA, and U.S. Cyber Command and Israel's Unit 8200 have been identified by journalists as the likely perpetrators. This "worm" was released into Iran's German-built centrifuges and physically destroyed part of its uranium enrichment program that most analysts believe was designed to develop a nuclear bomb. It was not successful in destroying the program—only in slowing it down briefly. In response, the Iranians sent a "worm" called Shamoon to wipe out the code on 30,000 computers in Saudi Arabia's Aramco to send a stern warning to the United States. Saudi Aramco, the Saudi Arabian Oil Company is considered one of the largest companies in the world. That not very subtle warning was that the United States needed to stop attacking Iran using cyber-weapons, since Iran had cyber-weapons too and could do a lot of damage. Many decision-makers in the United States want U.S. Cyber Command to, in a defensive way, shut down foreign governments' abilities to use the internet for malicious purposes. Although U.S. cyber-capability is extensive, any intrusion or interference undertaken is perceived as offensive—not defensive—and an excuse for other nation states to respond in kind or to attack the United States and its critical infrastructure and processes. Those dynamics are exemplified by the national and certain state elections compromised by Russian interference in 2016, probably for several reasons: to respond to what were perceived as aggressive U.S.-led sanctions against Russia over Crimea's annexation, to promote the Donald J. Trump campaign because of Secretary of State Hillary R. Clinton's tough stance against the Russians and in the broader sense, to weaken Western style liberal democracy and its processes through support of reactionary politics in the United States.

The emergent reality is that cyberterrorists can use cyber-weapons far more easily in ways that circumvent the hard work and resources needed to gain traditional weapons of mass destruction but with the same potential for massive disruptive capability.

7.3 COMPLEX SOCIAL SYSTEM BEHAVIOR

The world is a complex system. It obeys the natural rules or "laws" of complex system behavior. Complex systems:

- Cannot be controlled
- Have loosely coupled cause-effect relationships
- Cannot be predictable
- Exhibit "emergent" and proactive self-organizational behavior

- Have elements that interact with one another
- Have elements that are usually interdependent with one another
- Have an open or permeable boundary where forces inside the system can influence the outside and vice versa.

The social, religious, political, economic, technological, and environmental forces in the world affected by the actions of human beings influence complex social systems' behavior. Within these systems, there are few linear relationships and cause-effect relationships are unclear and may not follow sequential theory or logic. Because humans are part of social systems, these social systems almost always become complex, since human beings can make decisions based on emotion—what Jervis calls "perception and misperception" [2]—other group decision dynamics, or myths that taint more accurate appraisals of fact and logic processes, therefore making prediction of the behavior of a complex system virtually impossible.

Another human-based characteristic of a complex system is that it can exhibit "self-organization" as an emergent property. This means that human beings can organize themselves to further an objective. It is this behavior that possibly created civilization in early human society. A community of practice or interest or networks of individuals who come together naturally to accomplish a mission, is an example of self-organization. Such networks can be thought of as a "nation of shared interests" to use a less traditional notion of the term "nation."

Terrorist networks are complex social systems. It is for that reason that the tools described in this paper could be of assistance to researchers who are thinking about how to better understand the complex systems under consideration and associated decision-making processes.

7.4 THE SYSTEM MAP

System maps are very useful tools to begin to understand the complexity of a system's operational environment. Although there are many software tools that can be used to construct a system map, it is almost as effective to simply conduct a paper and pencil exercise with knowledgeable individuals and subject matter experts in systems dynamics. What is essential is that a team of these individuals identifies elements of the system internal and external to the system, specifically considering forces on the system from the external environment known as stressors. In addition, stakeholders or actors within and outside the system must be identified. In the United States, the War Colleges of the Department of Defense teach their students to function in a world of VUCA [3]—volatility, uncertainty, complexity, and ambiguity. This makes the use of linear thinking of little value for complex systems analysis since much of the world and human behavior in it is non-linear and does not follow sequential logic.

How can a policy-maker create guidelines or policies in a world where nothing is steady and is constantly changing? From the start, one of the most important methods is to develop a "system map." System maps can be representative of organizational process and design, such as what is found in an agency or department in the public, private, or non-profit sectors. Alternately, they can be subject based, such as an inventory of devices and an account of their interactive effects in the Internet of Things. System maps can also be representative of the economy where, for example, decisions by the U.S. Federal Reserve are scoped out with pathways of effect that capture monetary policy and consumer spending with their links to inflationary pressures. In many cases, the system map depiction reflects a particular institution's manufacturing plant and associated operations. In contrast, a system map could reflect geography-based, physical systems such as the Ohio Valley. As major factors or elements are defined, they are also drawn with relationships to other elements, flows of information, influence, or other activities that exert influence; they can be vectored, that is, identified as to the size of the relationship or influence and the direction. Those dynamics are illustrated in Figure 7.1.

What follows is a system map developed by Sheila Ronis to account for factors and factor effects associated with the breakdown of U.S. industrial capacity. This system map was developed while she was conducting a study for the U.S. House of Representatives Committee on Small Business in 2005 [4]. Don Manzullo was from Rockford in Illinois's 16th congressional district and was the chairman of the committee. The city of Rockford, Illinois had a thriving infrastructure that supported industrial manufacturing throughout the Midwest. The kinds of industry Rockford hosted were hundreds of companies that represented the tool and die industry; these companies were disappearing at an alarming rate and the Small Business Committee Chairman wanted to understand why.

Using a team of experts, the "system map" that is described in Figure 7.1 identified major elements of the manufacturing system in the United States, and in specific terms focused on the erosion of the U.S. industrial base. Elements that contributed to the U.S. industrial base decline included forces such as: the growth of political and economic influence of China, wage rate differentials in various places in part due to increasing rates of globalization, worker safety standards in different international locales, dependence on corresponding industrial capabilities in foreign countries, U.S. capability to go to war, vanishing engineering jobs and capabilities, DoD procurement, and so on.

This system map describes what is fundamentally a complex social system that consists of dozens of issues, stakeholders and forces—all of which interact and are interdependent with one another and are difficult or even impossible to quantify and define with specificity. Figure 7.1 only represents a high-level set of relationships characterized by a birds-eye view of connections by contrast to a low-level set of relationships that are granular. Most complex system maps resemble this, but they can be far messier and look more like a bowl of spaghetti!

Lone wolf, terrorist group, and counterterrorist schematic maps can also be drawn and can be instructive in helping to define the complex environment and set of forces that could impact an individual terrorist, a network, or cell. Once a map is developed and elements are identified, critical pathways can be identified and explored [5]. Then, stories are written based on the system map that make the linkages between elements of the system, their interactions, and interdependencies. The complex system is further explored and defined through the story telling that serves as the basis of a visionario. The difference between a traditional scenario and a visionario is that the latter explores the systemic characteristics unique to the system being studied.

7.5 A FRAMEWORK: THE CYNEFIN FRAMEWORK

As a first step, a framework useful to consider before system maps are drawn is the Cynefin framework developed by Snowden (2010) [6]. According to Snowden, "The Cynefin Framework ... allows executives to see things from new viewpoints, assimilate complex concepts, and address real-world problems and opportunities. Using the Cynefin framework can help executives sense which context they are in so that they can not only make better decisions but also avoid the problems that arise when their preferred management style causes them to make mistakes." In the four "decision-making contexts or domains," Snowden describes four types of systems and the characteristics of those systems. The "string" boundaries of the Cynefin

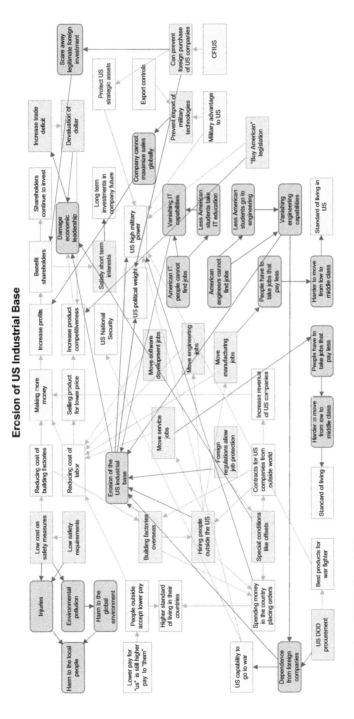

Figure 7.1 Erosion of US Industrial Base.

framework, that separate the four elements are not matrix boundaries, but levels of order that reflect degrees of complexity. Solution sets that are developed for problems in one type of system do not necessarily work for a different type of system. It is important, therefore, to understand the system context inclusive of system characteristics and both the physical and conceptual parameters of the system being studied. It is critical to make certain that the potential policies being developed and adopted are useful for the problems within the type of system under study.

The four domains of the framework are increasing levels of order from "chaos" with no order to "simple" with stability and order. The ability to make decisions improves or derives from the ability to move from chaotic situations to complex to complicated to simple providing more orderly conditions and that requires energy, resources, and an intimate understanding of the system.

7.5.1 The Obvious, or Simple Domain

In the obvious, or simple quadrant, linear decision-making can occur and the level of "order" is high. Cause-effect relationships are definable and best practice is a useful construct. Prediction is possible as well. Many industrial processes fall into this category. They can be statistically controlled within control limits [7]. Many executives and managers assume that most systems—and decisions—fall into this category. If processes are understood, they can be controlled. Measurement is possible and a level of certainty is also possible. Unfortunately, not all systems fall into the simple category like industrial processes. Nevertheless, because simple systems are easy in comparison to other systems, individuals tend to want to use solution sets that work in simple systems for all systems. Nothing could be more useless or wasteful. Solution sets that work in simple systems do not work in the complicated, complex, or chaotic domains. And, most of the challenges facing humanity, including the scourge of terrorism, do not fall into this domain. So, the simple solution sets available are inappropriate, and different approaches are needed for the other domains. Within the context of a terrorist group's rewards and sanctions for activists, a reward or sanction is oftentimes results-based, based on activities that either further or impede the goals of the group and simultaneously or after lag time, enhance or diminish its stature. In addition, aside from those drivers of action, there are in many cases, personal jealousies, disagreements over policies and practice, and personal connections and grievances that are also contributing factors. As a result, promotions or demotions can fall within comparatively high-order simple set domains (i.e. "simple" or "obvious" domains), where reasons for actions are relatively straightforward.

7.5.2 The Complicated Domain

In the complicated domain, there is less "order" than in the simple domain, but a sufficient amount of order so that cause-effect relationships are still definable. An example of a complicated system is a vehicle or a weapon system. There are "10 million lines of code in a Chevy Volt and 1.7 million lines of code in an F-22 Raptor" [8]. Although these systems of systems are incredibly complicated, they are still predictable, at least within statistical controls, though only with great knowledge and expertise.

Once a human being enters a complicated system, e.g. a driver in a vehicle or a pilot in an aircraft, the system becomes complex because a person brings non-rational and in some cases impulsive behavior to bear on machines. Autonomous vehicles, for example, will probably become the norm in the next few decades because functionality and solving problems in a complex system are far more difficult with drivers behind the wheel than in a complicated system where autonomous vehicles are exempt from road rage and similar sentiments. And, as a human being in the system makes it complex, removing them will increase safety and security when the machine does the driving and/or flying, pushing the disorder domain down a level to a simpler one whenever possible. Using drones for counterterrorism purposes could be an example of movement from a "complex" condition to a "complicated" solution set, as human error in targeting and other combat-related stresses such as life-threatening anti-aircraft fire are reduced as analysts can observe and make decisions in more dispassionate ways from remote locations.

7.5.3 The Complex Domain

In the complex domain, cause-effect relationships are decoupled. Prediction is impossible and there is a high level of disorder. Although patterns can emerge, such as self- organization of individuals into working groups, control is impossible, though influence is possible, if the system is well understood. As such, all systems populated and influenced by humans are complex systems. Systems can be thought of as existing on a continuum of decreasing order from simple to complicated to complex and, ultimately, chaotic. By adding order and resources to a chaotic system, eventually, you would find yourself working in a complex system. But, complicated and simple systems are human-less. No amount of energy or resources will make a human system complicated or simple, since the human dimension is unpredictable and uncontrollable and cause-effect relationships are not clear.

As previously mentioned, in complex human systems, problem solving can improve by moving a situation from the complex domain to the complicated domain through efforts (i.e. energy) to add technology or other organizational protocols or resources to a system to order to increase system order. Weather systems may be the best example of a natural complex system, and the global economy may be a good example of a human complex system. In terms of counterterrorism, use of technology, new and/or standardized organizational protocols, and policy to reduce the effects of "chaotic" environmental factors represent extensive efforts to move a situation from the complex to the complicated domain, and these might include the use of influence over constituent group support with positive inducements supplied by governments. Government responses such as the condition of using suicide bombers might be an example of efforts to move from a "chaotic" to a "complex" system in Snowdon's Cynefin framework where in this example, the use of new types of incentives such as little or no jail time if a suicide bomber defects to authorities prior to the commission are representative of such efforts.

7.5.4 The Chaos Domain

In a chaotic system, the level of disorder is as high as it can be and there is no order. The best thing decision or policy-makers can do in a chaotic environment is to increase the level of order in the situation by infusing energy and/or resources to move the situation into the complex domain where cause-effect relationships are loosely coupled and the situation can be, at least, influenced. An example of a chaotic situation or system could be 9/11 and its aftermath. Once the towers came down, think of the international effort that it took to understand what had occurred, what it would take to address the situation in Afghanistan, and to understand the international footprint of the terrorists, their execution of the plan to fly commercial jets into

Figure 7.2   Dave Snowden's 'Cynefin Model'.

buildings to create weapons of mass destruction, and the process and resources to get both New York City and the Pentagon in Washington, D.C., back to a state of normality and functionality. For example, in Snowdon's Cynefin framework, movement into the realm of the "complicated" from the "chaotic" condition might involve political, diplomatic, and military responses or high-lighted alert conditions. For example, the political and diplomatic actions to invoke Article 5 of NATO's Washington Treaty to trigger collective self-defense arrangements, and United Nations actions in the aftermath of 9/11 are examples of efforts to move from the "chaotic" to "complex" domains to create more "orderly" action through process. In Figure 7.2 Snowden's Cynefin framework is presented with movement from the "obvious" cell, counterclockwise, through the "chaotic" cell.

7.6 A BRIEF 2020 VISIONARIO

Things are getting worse. It has only been a few days, but so much damage has already been done. Russia and Iran thought they could contain the worm, but it didn't work. A few months ago, tensions were soaring between Russia and the United States. In 2016, Vladimir Putin had interfered in the U.S. election to promote chaos and weaken faith in the democratic process and institutions in the United States. He had succeeded and he hoped to repeat his efforts in 2020. Iran wanted vengeance for the betrayal it felt at the United States walking away from the nuclear agreement they and several other countries had negotiated and the U.S. president decided to end. Iran, with its enormous cyber-army assured Russia that they could disrupt the U.S. election but also wreak havoc on America by creating a "terrorist incident" that they hoped would be perceived as coming from ISIS. A subtle cyber-attack was planned and aimed at a narrowly focused facility to shut it down and cause confusion to prevent the United States from success-fully completing its election.

What was not foreseen was the unintended spread of the code with its "zero day" exploits that spread without additional interference using artificial intelligence algorithms. The coders thought they would be so subtle, no one would know where the worm came from and what it was intended to do. But, the use of "zero day" exploits made the worm "visible." The problem was the coders were not as sophisticated and competent as they thought. The software infected networks around the world, including Russia, the United States, and Iran. Everyone became infected. What was meant to shut down a part of the U.S. power grid, shut down the entire nation's grid and disrupted life in over 100 countries when the cyber-attack went terribly wrong, was not focused, and spread to infect critical infrastructure computers all over the world.

The global internet was disrupted. Many national power grids around the world also went down. Unfortunately, in the process of taking down the grids, physical damage to those grids also occurred, making it very difficult to bring the grids back up. With no power, with no water systems, with no fuel systems, no communications systems, the very fabric of society is breaking down as governments and their ability to safeguard the basics of civil society, are disintegrating. The world is becoming increasingly chaotic. Things are spiraling out of control and there is no method to stop it.

7.7 CONCLUSION: LESSONS FROM STUXNET AND SHAMOON

Reading a story that deliberately investigates the interdependencies, open boundaries, and interactions within a complex system enable policy-makers to explore and learn about the complexity of a situation including one that could involve terrorists—even state-sponsored terrorists.

The realities of complex systems include an inability to control a situation. The story examines second, third, and fourth order effects of phenomena. Systemically looking at and exploring the byproduct effects of a situation can examine unintended situations:

- Cyber-attacks must use "stealth code" to ensure anonymity.
- What one side can do to others, the other side can do as well.
- In complex systems, control is impossible and second, third, and fourth order effects can be disastrous.
- Unintended consequences will occur and cannot be predicted.
- Cyberspace is insecure and the future will unfold in ways that can produce catastrophic results—especially if policy-makers are not thinking clearly about complexity.

7.8 SUMMARY

In a world of complexity, there are many lessons learned from the development and use of viruses such as Stuxnet and Shamoon. The most important is there are ways to enable the decision and policy-maker to ask better questions and learn enough about threat development to improve analysis outcomes. This chapter discusses the nature of complex systems and why the development of stories about those systems helps to better understand their idiosyncrasies and characteristics. Since nation states and "insurgent" terrorists can use cyber-weapons, understanding the complex systems that can lead to the use of these weaponized versions of code can be useful. This chapter describes complex systems such as terrorist cells and proposes a method through the use of system maps and stories, called visionarios, to learn about and explore them. Cyber-weapons, that are potential tools of terrorists, are discussed.

REFERENCES

1. Chasdi, Richard J. 1999. *Serenade of Suffering: A Portrait of Middle East Terrorism, 1968-1993.* Lanham, MD: Lexington Books, 24.
2. Jervis, Robert. 1976. *Perception and Misperception in International Politics.* Princeton. NJ: Princeton University Press.
3. Jacobs, T.O. 2002. *Strategic Leadership: The Competitive Edge.* Washington, D.C.: Industrial College of the Armed Forces, National Defense University, Revised, 2005.
4. Ronis, Sheila R. March 2006. *2006 Industrial Base Study.* Committee on Small Business, U.S. House of Representatives, Prepared for: The Honorable Donald A. Manzullo, Chairman.
5. Chasdi, Richard J. 2018. *Corporate Security Crossroads: Responding to Terrorism, Cyberthreats and Other Hazards in the Global Business Environment.* Santa Barbara, CA: Praeger Publishers.
6. Snowden, David. 2010. Cognitive Edge, The Origins of Cynefin, Part 3. http://cognitive-edge.com/articles/summary-article-on-cynefin-origins/.
7. Deming, W. Edwards. 1982, 1986. *Out of the Crisis.* Cambridge: W. Edwards Deming Institute, MIT.
8. https://insideevs.com/infographic-chevy-volt-has-10-million-lines-of-code-f-22-raptor-only-has-1-7-million/

Policy and Legislative Frameworks Responses to Threats Presented by Online Terrorists

Legislation Specifically Targeting the Use of the Internet to Recruit Terrorists

Thomas J. Holt, Joshua D. Freilich, and Steven M. Chermak

CONTENTS

8.1 INTRODUCTION

The development of the internet has radically transformed modern life, shifting communications and personal finance from physical encounters and telephony to computer-mediated communications (CMC) platforms such as websites and social media [4, 46, 52]. Individuals now depend on sites like Facebook, email, and texting applications for personal communications with close friends and the world at large [17, 35].

The benefits of CMC platforms are manifold, enabling individuals to share their experiences and ideas on events from across the globe in real time. Users can provide an up-close view of their life and be informed of events occurring anywhere in the world as though they were there [17]. Individuals also exert direct control over the content of the messages they produce, meaning there may be no attempt to filter the content through a mainstream lens as happens in traditional media such as television or radio [8, 27, 41]. The connected nature of social media platforms also encourages individuals to find others who share their point of view, creating echo chambers that reinforce one's world view. Finally, the unique features of different social media platforms enable users to craft messages that will entice others to view their posts, whether through images on Instagram and Snapchat, the use of hashtags on Twitter, or provocative video and text on Facebook.

Extremists and terrorist organizations have seized upon these platforms as a valuable tool to spread their ideology directly to interested audiences, regardless of their physical location [6,20,27].

Additionally, the demographic composition of certain media platforms, like Twitter, enable organizations to target and recruit younger people to their cause [13, 49]. The growth of the internet as a tool for radicalization and terror has raised substantive concerns among governments and privacy advocates as to how to legislate against these activities. This is partially because online content transcends national boundaries, making it difficult to efficiently regulate user behavior. Additionally, the perceived freedom to say and do whatever a person feels in online spaces adds to the difficulty in criminalizing certain forms of speech or action [4, 45].

This chapter will consider these issues and examine the general state of legislation enacted in Western nations to affect the ways that radical organizations use the internet as a tactical and strategic tool. We first consider the ways that extremists and terrorists use the internet for recruitment and information sharing. Next, we discuss the differences in legislation with a specific focus on the United States, the United Kingdom, and the European Union. We also review the actions taken by social media companies and internet service providers to respond to the threat of terrorism. We conclude with a discussion of the implications of these laws for individual free speech and privacy protections.

8.2 TERROR, SOCIAL MEDIA, AND THE INTERNET

It is necessary to situate acts of terror within the spectrum of political behaviors on and offline, ranging from non-violent expression to serious physical violence [23, 33, 34]. There are myriad forms of non-violent resistance that individuals engage in daily. Prior to the emergence of the web, individuals could express their dissent with political positions through letter-writing campaigns, via print media outlets, and by contacting their legislative representatives. Freedom of speech throughout the industrialized world also enables individuals to express their opinion in public settings, regardless of how negative it may be. The web has extended this capability, as individuals regularly post messages about their views on politics and social issues on Facebook, Twitter, and other social media [27, 33, 34]. In fact, individuals now contact politicians and representatives through the internet at the same volume as postal mail and telephone [3].

Due to the prospective variations in the behavior and motives of actors, it is necessary to consider how technology may be used and to what ends. First and foremost, the internet has tremendous value as a communications vehicle for extremists, terror entities, and nation-state actors. The easy and immediate access to technology, coupled with the anonymity and scale afforded by computers and the internet, make email, forums, instant messaging, and virtually all other forms of CMC ideal for interpersonal communications. Almost every nation on earth now has some form of internet connectivity, whether through cellular service providers, high-speed fiber optic connectivity, or even dial-up internet access. Groups can maintain contact and reach out to others, no matter the location, through text messages, email, or forums.

The ability to regularly communicate with others from diverse backgrounds ensures that individuals can be slowly, but steadily, introduced to a movement's core principles [15, 18, 48]. Constant exposure and reinforcement of an ideology allow individuals to become accepting of an otherwise unusual perspective, and it may eventually enable the acceptance of an extremist ideology or identity [15]. There are myriad web forums operating to support various white nationalist and neo-Nazi ideologies, including The Daily Stormer, National Socialist Movement (NSM), and even portions of the relatively broad Reddit community [20]. One of the oldest of these forums is stormfront.org, which is extremely popular among neo-Nazis for discussion of all facets of their movement and even day-to-day activities seen from a white-power perspective

[7, 15, 48]. The site serves as a venue for individuals to engage in conversations and connect with others virtually and through the real world via localized sub-forums by nation, state, and city. There are also multiple sections devoted to politics, technology, philosophy, and entertainment.

In addition to direct communications, the internet allows groups to directly communicate their beliefs and ideologies to the world without the need for mass-media marketing or news media coverage. Any terror or extremist group can post messages on blogs or websites to directly control the delivery of their message to the media and the public at large [13]. For instance, members of the hacker group Anonymous regularly use Twitter, YouTube, and even written letters posted on websites to explain their actions or warn prospective targets that they may be attacked.

The Islamic State also uses Twitter as a key platform for recruitment and propaganda. The relatively limited territories ISIS controls offline in Iraq and Syria demand they find ways to attract individuals to their ideology, so social media plays an essential role in promoting their message to recruit participants globally. Twitter is a vital resource as individuals can create accounts easily and use them even from basic mobile phones. The use of hashtags in Twitter messaging also allows ISIS to find ways to reach the top trending tags to ensure they are seen by a broad audience [2]. These practices, however, also make it possible for Twitter to identify and suspend accounts engaged in ISIS posting, although many suspended users are able to get back on the service almost immediately. They treat a suspension as a badge of honor, validation that they are truly members of the movement and that they continue to operate in the face of Western security strategies [38].

To that end, ISIS operates a coordinated campaign of posting, utilizing a network of thousands of accounts, some live actors and some that are bots, to immediately retweet any messages posted by main accounts within the organization [2]. In addition to messaging, ISIS recruiters will attempt to engage individuals who appear sympathetic to their cause in conversation. Their conversations transition from simple discussions of Islam or of the movement to more sophisticated involved conversations on Skype or other platforms, such as Telegram or even a messaging application created specifically for ISIS to use to circumvent banning through traditional platforms [38]. Eventually, the individual may be radicalized and encouraged to either engage in violence in their home nation or to travel to the Middle East to join the fight for the caliphate in Iraq.

Computers and software suites for multimedia creation like Photoshop also allow groups to create and manipulate videos, photos, and stylized text. This enables extremist groups to develop more media-friendly materials or misrepresent facts in support of their own ideologies. In turn, they can promote their ideas and images to a larger audience in a subtle and convincing way that may instill anger and hostility toward groups that are perceived as oppressors or socially unacceptable [13, 18].

The terrorist group Al Qaeda in the Arabian Peninsula (AQAP) publishes an English language magazine called *Inspire* which provides information on the perspectives of the group and the jihadist movement generally. An issue from March 2013 featured an article on the 11 public figures from the West who it feels should be wanted dead or alive for crimes against Islam [47]. It also features regular details on techniques to engage in terrorism, ranging from simple bomb making to how to handle firearms.

The glossy magazine format allows the authors to promote their agenda in a way that is both attractive and appealing to readers. At the same time, the writing style may be more engaging and promote the jihadist agenda to those who may never have considered this point of view [47]. In fact, the Tsarnaev brothers who performed the Boston Marathon bombing frequently sought and read extremist websites and the magazine *Inspire*, which provided instructions for their method of attack. The brothers acquired the information needed to build improvised explosive devices from pressure cookers, nails, ball bearings, and explosive materials via articles published in the magazine [10].

In much the same way, the extremist group Stormwatch operates a website about the civil rights leader Dr Martin Luther King, Jr that appears to discuss his role as an activist [28]. The content of the site, however, decries his role in the pursuit of equality and suggests he was actually a mouthpiece for Jews and Communists, in keeping with the perceptions of the white supremacist movement generally [48]. It is written in a relatively persuasive fashion that may make an unsuspecting reader with little knowledge of King's role in social change believe the content to be factual.

This content derides the success of King and argues that there should be no national holiday or recognition for his work. In fact, they provide a link to downloadable flyers about these issues which read, "Bring the Dream to life in your town! Download flyers to pass out at your school." These are excellent examples of the way that multimedia content can be used by extremist groups to help indoctrinate individuals into their ideological or political worldview.

In addition, cell-phone cameras and web cams allow individuals to create training videos and share these resources with others through video sharing sites like YouTube [18]. Posting videos and news stories through social media also provides a mechanism to publicly refute claims made by media and governments to ensure the group is presented in a positive light [13, 18]. For instance, participants in the recent Arab Spring created videos on camera phones to show violent repression by government and police agencies as it was happening to news agencies around the world [37]. Similarly, ISIS members have posted videos of the conflicts in the city of Mosul, Iraq and other parts of the country where they have attempted to take control of the population. Their videos are intended to validate or refute claims by the US military and coalition forces regarding their attempts to retake cities where ISIS has dug in [39]. Such "on the ground" reporting allows individuals to provide evidence of their experiences.

This same capability, however, can be abused by extremist groups in support of their ideologies. One of the most extreme examples of such an act was a video posted by members of Al Qaeda in Pakistan on 21 February 2002. In the video, members of the group executed a journalist named Daniel Pearl who was kidnapped while he was traveling to conduct an interview [26]. He stated his name for the camera, described his Jewish family heritage, and then condemned America's foreign policy strategies in the Middle East. Following these statements, his captors then slit his throat and cut off his head, ending the video with a statement demanding the release of all Guantanamo Bay detainees or otherwise more deaths would result [26]. The gruesome video became a key piece of propaganda for the group and the jihadist movement generally, while inciting massive outrage in the United States. Such a chilling example demonstrates the value of interactive media and the internet in the promotion of extremist movements generally.

In addition to materials that encourage or support extremist ideologies, there are a number of training and support manuals that are distributed online. In fact, the open nature of the web allows individuals to post information that could be used to promote engagement in violence or physical harm in the real world. There are a number of training manuals and detailed tutorials for bomb making, gun play, and improvised weapons use on the internet, many of which have been available online for years [45]. This is because individuals can easily post a document in several repositories, send via email, or share via social networks in different formats and languages. For example, the *Mujahadeen Poisons Handbook* from Hamas and the *Encyclopedia of Jihad* published by Al Qaeda are available in various online outlets [48]. Even the Earth Liberation Front and Animal Liberation Front have tutorials on how to engage in civil disobedience and protests against logging companies, construction sites, and animal testing facilities [21]. These resources engender planning and tactical strategy development, regardless of the expertise of the individuals in a given area.

The value of the internet for the radical far-right movement cannot be understated. Technology allows individuals from marginalized communities across the world to become indoctrinated into the culture and find social support for their attitudes and beliefs over time. Donald Black, former KKK member and the founder of the website stormfront, stated that "whereas we previously could only reach people with pamphlets and by sending out tabloid papers to a limited number of people or holding rallies with no more than a few hundred people—now we can reach potentially millions of people" [12]. Considering he made this statement in 1997, the white power movement has had a long history of internet use.

Some of the most common tools used by the radical far-right movement are websites, forums, chatrooms, blogs, and other forms of CMC. Individuals who find these sites may be first directed to them through Google searches or links through radical church websites [29]. Spending time reading the content and getting to know users may increase their willingness to accept their point of view. In fact, continuous involvement in these sites may help individuals to accept extremist perspectives, even if their peers or family do not agree with these positions. In addition, the ability to make multiple friends and associates online in addition to their real-world social relationships can help to insulate their perceptions.

It is important to note that CMCs used by these movements do not necessarily encourage violence. Some do and are overtly inflammatory in their language about the need to rise up in armed conflict or engage in a "race war" [29]. Many sites and discussions, however, simply revolve around the importance of the movement and the need to develop a strong white race. In fact, many users in forums and other sites communicate their interpretation of historical events, as in the discussion of Dr Martin Luther King, Jr mentioned above [29]. They may also promote the idea that the white race has been appointed by God or by natural right to dominate the world over other races and ethnic groups [29]. Constant exposure to these messages will help to encourage an individual to believe them and be drawn into the movement as a whole.

The ability to access the web has also enabled individuals to develop lifestyle-related content that incorporates their racial attitudes [36]. Images of tattoos, concerts, organized meetings, video games, music, and clothing are all easily identified via the web. There are now even music streaming services available for those interested in white power bands. In addition, the group Women for Aryan Unity (WAU) publishes a magazine called *Home Front* on parenting issues, home schooling, and ways to socialize children into the movement. There are also child-specific materials available to download, such as coloring pages, crosswords, and stories that are "age appropriate" [36]. They can also get positive reinforcement from peers and ask questions about how to stay loyal to the movement despite the problems that they may face from other parents. Thus, the web is a key resource in the communication of subcultural values within radical movements as a whole.

8.3 LEGISLATING EXTREMISM AND CYBERTERROR

One of the greatest challenges in regulating online spaces is that many citizens around the world consider the internet an open space for the free exchange of ideas. The perceived lack of physical boundaries in online spaces also complicates attempts to crack down on information exchanges and communication [4, 43]. Attempts to regulate content in democratic societies must be approached carefully so as to avoid concerns over threats to free speech. For instance, attempts to directly and proactively control internet infrastructure through the use of firewalls or restricted access to content is largely observed in nations such as Iran, China, and Saudi Arabia [4, 43]. These nations may also have state operated internet service providers which can effectively shut down all internet connectivity in the country [22, 37]. As a result, regulatory power and control over all aspects of internet use may be easily exerted within these countries.

Such conditions are largely absent in Western nations, so they are more dependent on regulatory strategies involving takedowns of content or users after illegal activities have occurred. In some cases, the companies and service providers who may host content used by terrorists and extremists may remove content at the behest of law enforcement. In other instances, companies have begun to proactively eliminate content due to its perceived violations of user agreements. Such actions are discussed later in this chapter, as they fill spaces where laws are currently either absent or poorly enforced.

8.3.1 US Laws

In the US there is particular tension as to how to respond to hate speech over concerns of freedom of speech protections afforded by the Constitution. Individuals have the right to express ideas online that may be offensive or extreme including hosting such content online [44]. As a consequence, a range of extremist websites and forums are hosted in the US, including domestic and foreign terror groups. The only way to lawfully limit speech in the United States is through the "imminent danger" test afforded by the Brandenburg v Ohio (1969) case, where one's comments are unprotected if the speaker attempts to incite dangerous behavior or illegal activities [1]. To that end, there has been an increase in prosecutions related to the material support of terrorism under US federal laws, which includes providing financial support or expert opinions to an organization [43]. There have been several successful material support prosecutions related to online activities in the last decade, including Tarek Mehanna who received a 17-year sentence for translating and posting Al Qaeda recruitment videos and materials online.

The United States also expanded federal powers for online surveillance through the passage of the Uniting and Strengthening America by Providing Appropriate Tools Required to Intercept and Obstruct Terrorism Act (USA PATRIOT) of 2001. In the wake of 9/11, this legislation relaxed the legal provisions needed for law enforcement agencies to engage in surveillance of electronic communications, particularly weakening the provisions of the Electronic Communications Privacy Act (ECPA) related to subpoenas of ISPs and cable companies. The act enabled law enforcement to obtain the names and addresses of subscribers, along with their billing records, phone numbers called, duration of sessions while online, services used, communication device information, and other related data. The release of such information can enable law enforcement to more effectively trace the activities of a user to specific websites and content during a given session of internet use.

In addition, the ECPA now defines email that is stored on a third-party server for more than 180 days to be legally viewed as abandoned. As a result, law enforcement can request this data and the content of the email, whether opened or unopened, be turned over without the need for judicial review. Finally, the PATRIOT Act allowed ISPs to make emergency disclosures of information to law enforcement in instances of extreme physical or virtual threats to public safety. Such language allows for greater surreptitious surveillance of citizens with minimal government oversight or public awareness.

An additional law that affects online radicalization involves the Communications Decency Act. This statute was designed to initially censor certain forms of online content to minimize children's exposure to obscene content. Though parts of the law were overturned, section 230 has remained in effect and includes a "Good Samaritan" clause. This clause mandates that internet service providers cannot be held civilly liable for content published through their services by third parties. For instance, Twitter cannot be held responsible in civil court for ISIS content posted by a user, whether or not it may have played a role in the use of violence. This statute has been used to throw out several civil lawsuits, even though they were brought by victims of extremist and terrorist acts [25]. This statute has been challenged in the past by states' attorneys general, though it has yet to be eliminated [32].

8.3.2 Laws in the UK

The US is an isolate with regard to its equal protection of free speech, as many nations around the world have criminalized hate speech in some form. The UK's Public Order Act 1986 criminalized expressions of threats, abusive, or insulting behavior to any group of persons based on their race, color, ethnicity, nationality, or ethnic origin with a punishment of up to seven years in prison and/or a fine [30]. This law was amended via the Terrorism Act 2006 to include religious hatred and again in 2008 for protection of sexual orientations [32]. These laws relate to speech in both on and offline spaces, and can include statements that indirectly encourage the use of violence or instigate acts of terrorism against others. Additionally, these laws enable law enforcement agencies to request that content be taken down by UK-based hosting providers within two days of the notice, or that the company may be held liable for endorsing the content. Evidence suggests that over 72,000 items have been removed from online spaces under this law, though it is unclear how much more content may have been removed voluntarily by service providers independent of law enforcement requests [43].

Additionally, the UK utilizes language related to precursor offences, whereby an individual can be charged with violations of the Terrorism Act 2000 law if they are found to be in possession of articles that may be connected to terrorism. This includes not only physical goods such as batteries, wires, and fertilizers, but digital information and resources including propaganda and electronic training manuals. This can apply not only to downloading digital resources, but posting them via social media and websites. Disseminating materials online may engender the radicalization of others, rendering video and text-based posts on different platforms as a precursor offence. A myriad of cases have been prosecuted under this statute since 2001, demonstrating the willingness of crown prosecutors to pursue legal action against individuals for their online activities [24].

8.3.3 Laws within the European Union

The European Convention on Cybercrime (CoC) also includes language criminalizing the use of the internet to disseminate hate speech. Specifically, the CoC identifies "racist and xenophobic material," including writing, images, videos, and any other content that is designed to promote or encourage hate or discrimination against any group [5]. The distribution or posting of such material online is defined as criminal under the CoC, as is making online threats to any person on the basis of their racial, ethnic, or religious background, and the distribution of information that denies or otherwise attempts to misinform individuals regarding genocide and crimes against humanity [5]. This legislation has tremendous value in addressing the development and radicalization of individuals through the internet, particularly white supremacist movements.

8.4 INDUSTRY RESPONSES TO RADICALIZATION AND ONLINE EXTREMISM

Though laws pertaining to hate speech and extremist behaviors have increased, the responsibility to police and eliminate content largely falls to social media sites, web hosting services, and internet service providers. Sites like Facebook, Twitter, and Instagram have clearly been abused by extremist groups as recruitment and messaging platforms, though they have historically argued against a need to censor users on the basis of free speech, suggesting that targeting specific users or groups may unfairly restrict their rights [5]. The protections afforded to ISPs under the Good Samaritan clause of the Communications Decency Act may also increase their willingness to host certain content.

Instead, social media operators typically argue that they will block or ban individuals if and when their posts violate their terms of service, which typically mention either abuse or behavior that violates community standards [42, 51]. What truly constitutes abuse may be difficult to measure as many social media operators do not provide statistics on the extent to which they receive abuse complaints or how many users have been removed over the use of hate speech or extremist activities [22].

Social media companies have become more proactive in the removal of user accounts in the last few years due to pressure from various governments over the overt acknowledgement that their sites serve as recruitment platforms. In particular, ISIS used Twitter as a key resource to promote their ideology and recruit Westerners through the manipulation of hashtags [2]. Twitter eventually began to identify and suspend accounts actively posting ISIS-related content, though many suspended users were able to get back on the service almost immediately [19, 38, 42, 51]. As a result, the efficacy of these efforts is questionable as they do not eliminate extremists from the platforms [2].

Internet service providers have also taken a relatively agnostic approach to the removal of content that supports extremist ideologies. For instance, the web hosting and IT service provider Cloudflare has been frequently criticized for providing services for both jihadist and far-right extremists' websites. In 2017, the CEO of the company decided to no longer provide their services to the far-right website The Daily Stormer which had been a client for several years [9]. They pulled their service after it was revealed that individuals used the site to organize a major protest in Charlottesville, Virginia which turned violent and led to two deaths. The CEO, Matthew Prince, noted that this was an isolated decision that would not affect other customers regardless of their content [9]. His comments appear to be accurate, as the company still offers services to various hate groups, including National Action which has been deemed a terrorist organization by the UK government [40].

This is not to suggest companies do not support the mission of government and law enforcement agencies to affect terrorism. Many major service providers actively cooperate with federal agencies to provide access to their customers' data to enable online activities to be tracked. For instance, the US National Security Agency began the so-called PRISM program in 2007 to collect email and other communications through collaborative data sharing agreements with major technological service providers including Apple, Facebook, Google, Microsoft, and Skype [16]. By aggregating mass quantities of data, analysts could assess terrorist threats and associations around the world. Evidence suggests US intelligence sharing agreements enabled Australia, Canada, and the UK to utilize this data for analysis, creating a truly global network of surveillance via mass data collection.

These programs have given rise to what some call the "dataveilance" or "surveillance society" whereby everyone is under constant monitoring regardless of their involvement in wrongdoing [14, 52].

These programs are largely hidden from the general public, making it difficult for the average person to understand the extent to which their privacy has been eliminated without their consent in order to identify terror threats.

8.5 SUMMARY

Since the attacks that occurred on 11 September 2001 in the United States, there has been a concentrated effort to think creatively about how to best respond to terrorism and prevent similar attacks. Some initiatives focused on providing law enforcement agencies and intelligence organizations with additional tools to collect, synthesize, and analyze information that could be used to prevent terrorist acts [5]. Others have stressed better understanding of the radicalization of individuals to extremist views and violent behaviors, and the development of strategies to counter violent extremism [36]. There have also been efforts directed toward understanding extremism and building bridges to various communities and individuals to proactively encourage involvement in legitimate political processes [50].

The transition to a technologically focused society has added significant challenges for law enforcement agents and policy-makers in thinking strategically about how to best respond to extremists' online behaviors. It is clear that individuals actively engaged in extremism use the internet and other technological tools for various purposes. Some use it as an amplifying device—an easy way to share their ideological viewpoints and construct events into particular meanings that show their ideas in a positive light. Relatedly, it is a key recruitment tool to bring others into the fold by simply providing them with ideological justifications and tactical knowledge of weapons and tactics to further specific objectives. Thus, technology serves as a force multiplier that makes it more difficult for law enforcement to detect their activities and actions while still providing others with material support to carry out violent behaviors.

To combat terrorist threats, it is essential that policy-makers and legislators weigh an individual's right to free speech against broader concerns about public safety. Herbert Packer's classic *Two Models of Criminal Justice* seems appropriate to guide any decisions, as local criminal justice processes consider the tension between two competing models – due process and crime control models. The due process model focuses on the rights of the individual and the many legal and organizational obstacles that protect individuals when arrested, charged, and put on trial. In contrast, the crime control model highlights the public safety objectives of the criminal justice system, its preference is to streamline processes so that the efficiency of case processing is enhanced. These are competing models, as public safety may best be enhanced by compromising individual rights. Both models must always be present, and the realities of case processing may favor one model over the other over time.

Packer's ideas are also reflected in the current legal responses to cyberterrorism and online radicalization among legal and political systems. Governments are attempting to balance the right to speech, even when that speech may be hateful, against the need to regulate these behaviors, especially when the speech is linked to violent activities. The legal response to cyberterrorism is in its infancy, with differences evident across Western governments in their approaches. Governments have difficulty deciding how best to embrace the power and freedom of the internet, and the ownership and operation of internet resources, against its potential for misuse. In the United States, there has been some resistance to regulating hate speech as doing so would be in contradiction to one of the foundational freedoms protected by the Constitution. In addition, impeding the operation and increasing liability among service providers for content may stifle the open nature of the internet generally. On the other hand, people demand a degree of safety that may only come from limitations on the expression of some forms of speech.

Thus, it is essential that researchers better explore the use and regulation of the internet in furtherance of terror and extremism. Specifically, there is a need to improve our understanding of the ways that extremists systemically use the internet [21, 48]. Though research considers the extent of internet use among certain extremist groups or on some platforms, there is a need for more systematic exploration using on and offline data sources.

Second, there is a need to document the extent of hate speech online and the ways that individuals actually interact with it on a regular basis [11, 31]. It may be that a small number of people are actively engaged in spreading and embracing such language, but other users attempt to socially control these individuals by pointing out the inappropriateness of their language. It is unknown how often such efforts at control occur, and whether what effects they might have on these users: does it push them away and they go to other private places to share ideology? Are they more likely to disguise their identity because of fear of being ostracized? Are there techniques that could be used to open up a dialogue so that the hate can be better managed and an individual moved away from such extreme positions? Such insights are needed to more effectively develop legal strategies that truly reflect the nature of online hate speech by extremists so that laws can be more effectively applied to influence radical groups.

REFERENCES

1. Abrams, Floyd. "On American Hate Speech Law." In *The Content and Context of Hate Speech: Rethinking Regulation and Responses*, edited by M. Herz and P. Molnar, 116–128. Cambridge: Cambridge University Press, 2012.
2. Berger, J. M., and Jonathon Morgan. *The ISIS Twitter Census: Defining and Describing the Population of ISIS Supporters on Twitter*. The Brookings Institute. 2015. https://www.brookings.edu/research/the-isis-twitter-census-defining-and-describing-the-population-of-isis-supporters-on-twitter/
3. Best, Samuel J., and Brian S. Krueger. "Analyzing the representativeness of internet political participation." *Political Behavior*, 27 (2005). 183–216.
4. Brenner, Susan W. *Cyberthreats: The Emerging Fault Lines of the Nation State*. New York: Oxford University Press, 2008.
5. Brenner, Susan W. "Defining cybercrime: A review of Federal and State Law." In *Cybercrime: The Investigation, Prosecution, and Defense of a Computer-Related Crime*, edited by Roland D. Clifford, 15–104. 3rd edition. Raleigh, NC: Carolina Academic Press, 2011.
6. Britz, Marjie T. "Terrorism and technology: Operationalizing cyberterrorism and identifying concepts." In *Crime On-Line: Correlates, Causes, and Context*, edited by Thomas J. Holt, 193–220. 1st edition. Raleigh, NC: Carolina Academic Press, 2010.
7. Castle, Tammy. "The women of Stormfront: An examination of white nationalist discussion threads on the Internet." *Internet Journal of Criminology* (2011). www.internetjournalofcriminology.com/Castle_Chevalier_The_Women_of_Stormfront_An_Examination_of_White_Nationalist_Discussion_Threads.pdf
8. Chadwick, Andrew. "Digital Network Repertoires and Organizational Hybridity." *Political Communication*, 24 (2007). 283–301.
9. Conger, Kate. "Cloudflare CEO on terminating service to neo-nazi site: 'The Daily Stormer are assholes.'" *Gizmodo*, August 16, 2017. Accessed October 2017. https://gizmodo.com/cloudflare-ceo-on-terminating-service-to-neo-nazi-site-1797915295
10. Cooper, Michael, Michael S. Schmidt, and Eric Schmitt. "Boston suspects are seen as self-taught and fueled by the web." *The New York Times*, April 23, 2013. Accessed February 2018. http://www.nytimes.com/2013/04/24/us/boston-marathon-bombing-developments.html?pagewanted=alland_r=0

11. Costello, Matthew, James Hawdon, Thomas Ratliff, and Tyler Grantham. "Who views online extremism? Individual attributes leading to exposure." *Computers in Human Behavior*, 63 (2016). 311–320.

12. Faulk, Kent. "White supremacist spreads views on net." *The Birmingham News*, October 19, 1997, 1. Accessed January 2018. www.stormfront.org/dblack/press101997.htm

13. Forest, James J. *Influence Warfare: How Terrorists and Governments Struggle to Shape Perceptions in a War of Ideas*. Westport: Praeger, 2009.

14. Fuchs, Christian, Kees Boersma, Anders Albrechtslund, and Marisol Sandoval. *Internet and Surveillance: The Challenges of Web 2.0 and Social Media*. 16th edition. London: Routledge, 2013.

15. Gerstenfeld, Phyllis B., Diana R. Grant, and Chau-Pu Chiang. "Hate online: A content analysis of extremist internet sites." *Analyses of Social Issues and Public Policy*, 3 (2003). 9–44.

16. Gidda, Mirren. "Edward Snowden and the NSA files – timeline." *The Guardian*, July 25, 2013. Accessed December 2017. www.theguardian.com/world/2013/jun/23/edward-snowden-nsa-files-timeline

17. Greenwood, Shannon, Andrew Perrin, and Maeve Duggan. "Social media update 2016." *Pew Research Center*, 11 (2016). 83. http://www.pewinternet.org/2016/11/11/social-media-update-2016/

18. Gruen, Madeleine. "Innovative Recruitment and Indoctrination Tactics by Extremists: Video Games, Hip Hop, and the World Wide Web." In *The Making of a Terrorist*, edited by James J. Forest, 142–165. Westport: Praeger, 2005.

19. Guynn, Jessica. "Twitter suspends alt-right accounts." *USA TODAY*, November 16, 2016. Accessed January 2018. https://www.usatoday.com/story/tech/news/2016/11/15/twitter-suspends-alt-right-accounts/93943194/

20. Hankes, Keegan. (2015). *Black Hole*. Southern Poverty Law Center Intelligence Report, March 9, 2015. https://www.splcenter.org/fighting-hate/intelligence-report/2015/black-hole

21. Holt, Thomas J. "Exploring the intersections of technology, crime and terror." *Terrorism and Political Violence*, 24 (2012). 337–354.

22. Holt, Thomas J., and Adam M. Bossler. *Cybercrime in Progress: Theory and Prevention of Technology-Enabled Offenses*. London: Routledge, 2016.

23. Holt, Thomas J., and Max Kilger. "Examining willingness to attack critical infrastructure on and offline." *Crime and Delinquency*, 58 (2012). 798–822.

24. Home Office. *Operation of Police Powers under the Terrorism Act 2000 and Subsequent Legislation*. London: Home Office, 2013.

25. Iovino, Nicholas. "Tech giants not liable for Dallas police shooting." *Courthouse News*, December 5, 2017. Accessed February 2018. https://www.courthousenews.com/tech-giants-not-liable-for-dallas-police-shooting/

26. Levy, Bernard-Henri. *Who Killed Daniel Pearl?* Brooklyn: Melville House, 2003.

27. Martin, Gus. *Understanding Terrorism: Challenges, Perspectives, and Issues*. 2nd edition. Thousand Oaks: Sage, 2006.

28. martinlutherking.org. *Martin Luther King Jr. – A True Historical Examination*. 2018. http://martinlutherking.org

29. McNamee, Lacy G., Brittany L. Peterson, and Jorge Pena. "A call to educate, participate, invoke, and indict: Understanding the communication of online hate groups." *Communication Monographs*, 77, 2 (2010). 257–280.

30. Mendel, Toby. "Does international law provide for consistent rules on hate speech." In *The Content and Context of Hate Speech: Rethinking Regulation and Responses*, edited by Michael Herz and Peter Molnar, 417–429. Cambridge: Cambridge University Press, 2012.

31. Räsänen, Pekka, James Hawdon, Emma Holkeri, Teo Keipi, Matti Näsi, and Atte Oksanen. "Targets of online hate: Examining determinants of victimization among young Finnish Facebook users." *Violence and Victims*, 31, 4 (2016). 708.

32. Rottman, Gabe, and Lee Rowland. (2013). "New proposal could singlehandedly cripple free speech online." *ACLU*, August 1, 2013. Accessed January 2018. https://www.aclu.org/blog/national-security/new-proposal-could-singlehandedly-cripple-free-speech-online?redirect=blog/free-speech-national-security-technology-and-liberty/new-proposal-could-singlehandedly-cripple

33. Schmid, Alex P. *Political Terrorism*. Amsterdam: North Holland Press, 1988.

34. Schmid, Alex P. "Frameworks for conceptualising terrorism." *Terrorism and Political Violence*, 16 (2004). 197–221.
35. Sevitt, Daniel. "The most popular messaging app in every country." *The Market Intelligence Blog*, February 27, 2017. Accessed January 2018. https://www.similarweb.com/blog/worldwide-messaging-apps
36. Simi, Pete, and Robert Futrell. "White power cyberculture: Building a movement." *The Public Eye Magazine Summer* (2006). 69–72.
37. Stepanova, Ekaterina. "The role of information communications technology in the "Arab Spring": Implications beyond the region." *PONARS Eurasia Policy Memo No. 159*, 2011. Accessed January 2018. www.gwu.edu/~ieresgwu/assets/docs/ponars/pepm_159.pdf
38. Stewart, Christopher S., and Mark Maremont. "Twitter and Islamic State Deadlock on Social Media Battlefield." *Wall Street Journal*, April 13, 2016. Accessed November 2017. https://www.wsj.com/articles/twitter-and-islamic-state-deadlock-on-social-media-battlefield-1460557045
39. Tawfeeq, Mohammed, Ingrid Formanek, and Chandrika Narayan. "Civilians shot, bodies hung from poles in Mosul, Iraq sources say." *CNN*, November 11, 2016. Accessed November 2017. http://www.cnn.com/2016/11/10/middleeast/iraq-mosul-offensive/
40. Townsend, Mark. "Web giant Cloudflare stores extreme neo-Nazi content on UK soil." *The Guardian*, February 10, 2018. Accessed February 2018. https://www.theguardian.com/world/2018/feb/10/web-giant-cloudflare-storing-extreme-neo-nazi-content-on-uk-soil
41. Van Laer, Jeroen. "Activists online and offline: The Internet as an information channel for protest demonstrations." *Mobilization: An International Journal*, 15 (2010). 347–366.
42. Wagner, Kurt. "Twitter has deleted 235,000 terrorist related user accounts in the past six months." *recode*, August 18, 2016. Accessed February 2018. https://www.recode.net/2016/8/18/12539458/twitter-deletes-terrorism-accounts-isis
43. Walker, Clive P., and Maura Conway. "Online terrorism and online laws." *Dynamics of Asymmetric Conflict* 8, 2 (2015). 156–175.
44. Walker, Clive P., and Russell L. Weaver. *Free Speech in an Internet Era*. Durham, NC: Carolina Academic Press, 2013.
45. Wall, David S. "Cybercrimes and the Internet." In *Crime and the Internet*, edited by David S. Wall, 1–17. New York: Routledge, 2001.
46. Wall, David S. *Cybercrime: The Transformation of Crime in the Information Age*. New York: Polity, 2007.
47. Watson, Leon. "Al Qaeda releases guide on how to torch cars and make bombs as it names 11 public figures it wants 'dead or alive' in latest edition of its glossy magazine." *Daily Mail*, March 4, 2013. Accessed November 2017. www.dailymail.co.uk/news/article-2287003/Al-Qaedareleases-guide-torch-cars-make-bombs-naming-11-public-figures-wants-dead-alivelatest-edition-glossy-magazine.html
48. Weimann, Gabriel. "How modern terrorism uses the Internet." Washington DC: United States Institute of Peace Special Report (2004). Online: https://www.usip.org/sites/default/files/sr116.pdf.
49. Weimann, Gabriel. *New Terrorism and New Media*. Washington, DC: Commons Lab of the Woodrow Wilson International Center for Scholars, 2014.
50. White House. *Empowering Local Partners to Prevent Violent Extremism in the United States*. Washington, DC: White House, 2011. www.whitehouse.gov/sites/default/files/empowering_local_partners.pdf
51. Yadron, Danny. "Twitter deletes 125,000 Isis accounts and expands anti-terror teams." *The Guardian*, February 5, 2016. Accessed November 2017. https://www.theguardian.com/technology/2016/feb/05/twitter-deletes-isis-accounts-terrorism-online
52. Yar, Majid. *Cybercrime and Society*. 2nd edition. London: Sage Publications, 2013.

Chapter 9

Legal Restrictions and Challenges for Police and Law Enforcement Authorities

Omi Hodwitz

CONTENTS

9.1 INTRODUCTION

Terrorists are becoming increasingly adept at using social media and online platforms to recruit, campaign, and radicalize, leading to an increase in their numbers and their reach. Law enforcement officials are pressed to respond to this rising tide and, as a consequence, have adopted a number of strategies designed to counter extremist narratives and restrict and penalize radical online activities. The purpose of this chapter is not to debate the success of these endeavors but, instead to identify restrictions and challenges that have an influence on the outcomes of these strategies. Legal restrictions are varied, but two of the more prominent issues include jurisdictional boundaries and the protection of constitutional rights. In addition to these legal restrictions, understanding non-Western communities and practicing cultural sensitivity poses a challenge, as does the need to acquire the cooperation and participation of the private sector; these factors can influence the success of a counter-terrorism campaign. This chapter will focus on these particular considerations within the context of the strategies and measures employed by law enforcement to counter escalating extremism.

9.2 POSITIVE MEASURES

Positive campaigns are aimed at preventing radicalization from occurring or, in other words, eliminating the demand side of the supply and demand for radicalization. Two prominent positive measures include disseminating counter-narratives and raising awareness in high-risk communities (see Figure 9.1). Counter-narratives involve posting messages that contradict or oppose the radicalizing sentiments distributed by extremists, usually through social media or broadcasting platforms. This strategy has met with limited success and critics suggest that it may even result in the exacerbation of radical sentiment and unnecessary resource expenditures (see Figure 9.1). Raising awareness entails targeted outreach in high-risk communities. Although this strategy is generally believed to have positive results, success is tempered by how the targeted community is approached and treated. Therefore, both strategies can be challenging for law enforcement to implement and carry out.

9.2.1 Counter-Narratives Gone Wrong

In 2002, the State Department and Congress launched Radio Sawa and Al Hurrah in the Middle East with the express purpose of targeting younger Arab audiences. While these networks had a stated mission of distributing pro-American content and winning over the Arab population through music and culture, they also had a secondary goal of undermining Al Qaeda by providing a counter-narrative to extremist messaging and ideologies. A follow-up study in five Middle Eastern countries determined that the attempt at countering radicalization had an unexpected effect: Arab university students reported an increase in negative attitudes toward U.S. foreign policy after tuning in to these broadcasts [1]. Students stated that they were aware that the sites were designed to influence their opinions and attitudes, leading them to question the credibility

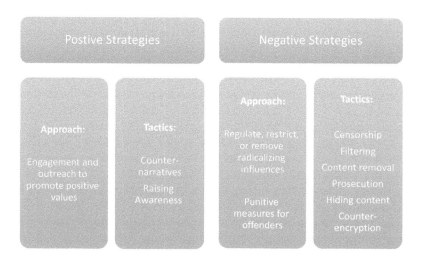

Figure 9.1   Strategies and Tactics.

of the broadcast messages. Several years later, a second study demonstrated the same trend: respondents who listened to Radio Sawa reported negative opinions about the United States, describing U.S. policy as "unjust," "arrogant," and "ignorant." This suggests a weakness of the State Department's counter-narrative strategy. Specifically, attempts to counter radical messages through broadcasting might well benefit from a shift in emphasis. The Radio Sawa and Al Hurrah examples focused less on positive values and more on a campaign directed toward undermining terrorist ideology and promoting the United States. Clearly, listening audiences were aware of and did not approve of the strategy driving these broadcasts, and this soured their opinions about the United States. Any future attempts to replicate this method of disseminating counter-narratives may do well to focus on positive messaging that is not tied to the promotion of any national identity or to the negation of any particular ideology.

The State Department's Center for Strategic Counterterrorism Communications (CSCC) has also employed an online counter-narrative campaign. Its initiative includes tweeting counter-messaging in response to extremist propaganda and engaging in direct dialogue with account holders of jihadist websites [2]. These attempts have been condemned by a number of different audiences. Critics point out that by attempting to directly engage with jihadist ideology, the CSCC inadvertently drew public attention to terrorist messaging, lending legitimacy to the radical campaign [3]. In addition, the CSCC often got mired in "embarrassing" and "ineffective" back-and-forth trading of below-the-belt jabs with extremists on social media, compromising the professionalism of the organization. The CSCC also took liberties in posting gruesome images and video related to the Islamic State as an extreme scare tactic. The public distribution of such disturbing imagery has raised concerns of an ethical nature.

The Defense Department has committed similar mistakes while employing positive measures. The program WebOps, which was created to counter Islamic State propaganda, is believed to have been an unequivocal failure that cost American taxpayers a great deal of money. Although the Pentagon touted it as a success, independent investigations determined that the program was ill-managed and built on flawed data [4]. Civilian specialists with limited Arabic language skills and no experience in narratives and propaganda were hired to build content to counter Islamic State messaging. However, due to language barriers, translators often made serious mistakes, such as repeatedly referring to the "Palestinian salad," having confused the words for "authority" and "salad" and, thus, drawing the derision of the very communities they were attempting to persuade. In addition, employees reported witnessing the manipulation of WebOps data with the intention of creating the appearance of success. One employee described how she had been instructed to provide program scoring reports that demonstrated some level of progress, but not so much progress as to warrant the dissolution of the WebOps program. When analysts were asked to evaluate the same material, results indicated that only 69 percent were likely to agree on the outcome; this number fell far below the 90 percent threshold that was needed to draw firm conclusions.

9.2.2 Counter-Narratives and Challenges for Law Enforcement

The efforts of the State Department and the Defense Department underscore a number of challenges for law enforcement. The foremost challenge is that while the logic behind countering extremist messages is sound, the practice leaves much to be desired. Positive measures have been counterproductive due to a variety of factors, including language barriers, a lack of familiarity with Islamic culture and traditions, the perception that the United States is attempting to manipulate audiences, and a general inability to recognize program shortcomings and to adapt accordingly (see Figure 9.2). In regards to language barriers and cultural familiarity, the United

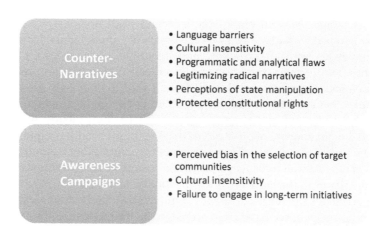

Figure 9.2   Challenges Resulting from Positive Strategies.

States currently lacks the necessary knowledge and skills needed to deftly and adequately spar with religiously and culturally motivated extremists on their own ideological turf. Targeting organizations such as the Islamic State on social media can backfire in a number of ways, including drawing attention to and legitimizing a terrorist campaign, demonstrating a level of cultural incompetence, and perpetuating the image that the United States is more interested in trivial showdowns on social media than in addressing the grievances that facilitate radicalization. As for perceptions of manipulation, the United States may do well to approach counter-narratives as a method to promote positive values only and not as a means by which to elevate the United States and villainize political dissidents. Beyond the reality that anything other than that may have a backlash effect, it can be argued that promoting positive values is more in line with the sentiment of counter-narratives anyway. Regarding program success, it would behoove the state to recognize when a program (such as WebOps) has failed and treat that as an opportunity to identify strategic and tactical errors in order to improve future programs. Lastly, there are potential legal challenges that come with interfering in citizen political discourse. Although this is generally not part of the discussion around counter-narratives, the state should consider the possibility that distributing information designed to disrupt political communication is beyond what is acceptable in a free and democratic society. As such, it would be wise to ascertain the nuances of the rules governing such activities, to make those known, and to curb any activities that might encroach on those rules.

9.2.3 Building Awareness

Online radicalization and recruitment campaigns may take place on the internet or over social media, but responses need not be based in cyberspace. One positive counter-terrorism initiative involves building awareness in the community. Extremist messaging is often designed to reach isolated youth from communities at risk, including religious and ethnic populations. Counter-radicalization campaigns will involve engaging with these high-risk individuals and communities in order to inform and educate the citizenry about online radicalization. The National Counterterrorism Center, for example, has created a Community Awareness Briefing (CAB) that it presents to Muslim communities and law enforcement personnel in order to build awareness and facilitate prevention [5]. The briefings include exposure to radical recruitment videos and propaganda followed by a guided discussion on building collaborative ties between law enforcement and the general public. While this and similar awareness initiatives have generally received a positive reception, their success is not absolute and they require careful consideration in their implementation. Similar to counter-narratives, awareness initiatives can be counterproductive if communities are left with the impression that law enforcement and state representatives are targeting them based on expectations rooted in racial, ethnic, and religious stereotypes, if the facilitators of the program demonstrate a lack of awareness of or sensitivity toward unique community needs, and if follow-up is limited. Thus, the end result to these awareness campaigns can be a sense of frustration and animosity on the part of the community members, further legitimizing grievances and facilitating isolationism.

9.3 NEGATIVE MEASURES

Negative measures include approaches that aim to regulate, restrict, or remove extremist online content and to penalize the purveyors or users of such content. The goal is to reduce the supply side of the supply and demand for radicalization by focusing on limiting access to content through censorship and similar measures, as well as controlling internet infrastructure through firewalls and other means [6]. Negative measures come with their own host of issues and challenges for law enforcement that differ considerably from the positive considerations mentioned above, including constitutional considerations, jurisdictional overreach, and a reliance on corporate cooperation.

9.3.1 Censorship

When asked how to effectively counter terrorism in the United States, academics will often suggest censorship or the suppression of online content that endorses political violence. Those who study terrorism know that cyberspace has become a key tool for extremist organizations in their campaign to radicalize, recruit, and disseminate information. Terrorism scholars recognize that controlling online content would deal a heavy blow to these organizations, likely impeding if not crippling their expansion domestically and internationally. Although censorship may seem like a viable and appealing option in the United States, it is an unlikely weapon in the fight to control cyberspace. The majority of extremist content is protected under the First Amendment or the right to free speech. In order for online content to be illegal, it must meet two thresholds: 1) it contains a viable threat against a specific individual or organization and 2) imminent action must be the direct result of the content. Therefore, promoting radical content and general violence does not, in and of itself, run counter to the law and is, in fact, a protected constitutional right. The courts in the United States have continued to uphold these protections, ruling against cases that promoted extremist behavior but either failed to explicitly target specific individuals or to incite imminent action. In addition, Congress has opposed any attempts to control cyberspace, noting that freedom of expression is integral to the identity of the United States and regulating online content would be in line with the actions of a dictatorship. Lastly, cyberspace is controlled by the private sector, not by the state, placing the power of regulation and restriction into the hands of internet service providers and social media companies. If these companies were required to monitor and share information about all potentially problematic internet and social media activity, this would increase their expenses, lower their productivity, and would result in more information than the state could likely process. Therefore, although blanketing censorship may appear to be a solution to extremist online presence, it is not a viable option in the United States. With those considerations in mind, there are several negative measures that are less absolute than outright censorship, including the filtering, removal, hiding, and prosecution of extremist content.

9.3.2 Filtering

One of the more extreme methods of reducing radical reach involves the nationwide filtering of online content. This method entails dropping any user requests to access specific websites or content that has been previously identified as inflammatory and subsequently banned. This kind of tactic is popular in countries such as Saudi Arabia and China, where the government directs all internet traffic through state-controlled internet service providers, ensuring an effective filtering mechanism. Although this method has successfully controlled content in other nations, there are a variety of reasons why its application is problematic in Western democracies. To begin with, this would likely result in excessive filtering; requests for relatively benign content may trigger a filter, resulting in needlessly dropped requests. Writing this chapter, for example, would have been a difficult task if such filtering mechanisms were in place, due to the fact that researching this chapter required visiting a number of both credible and questionable online sources.

In addition to excessive filtering, this measure would also require that the United States and other Western democracies maintain current and active lists of prohibited websites. The collection and preservation of such lists would likely be subject to criticism and possibly even legal challenges under the auspices of free speech. They may also be grounds for accusations of discriminatory practices, particularly if an inordinate number of ethnically or religiously oriented websites were included. Although a number of Western democracies such as the United Kingdom and Australia have considered taking these steps, these discussions eventually resulted in the dismissal of such a plan due to the reasons listed above [7].

9.3.3 Content Removal

A measure that several Western democracies are engaged in is the takedown of offensive online sites and platforms. In a number of European countries, laws against incitement and hate speech are used to control content directed toward ethnic and religious minorities [7]. In the United Kingdom, websites are flagged, inspected and, if they are determined to publicize radical content, website administrators and internet service providers are served with a notification to disable the site. The Netherlands follows a similar format, although the emphasis is placed on self-regulation rather than state regulation. One drawback to state-initiated removal of content is that it is only effective with domestic websites: anything hosted or administered outside of the target country cannot legally be policed by that country. Therefore, although a number of countries may be actively engaged in removing content hosted within their borders, there is little they can do about online radicalization forums that originate elsewhere.

Due to free speech protections, the United States does not currently engage in this kind of overt content removal. However, the United States does aggressively support commercially based content removal. While the First Amendment protects against state control of political expression, it does not extend to platforms owned by private companies. Corporate control of online content comes with a number of incentives; beyond personal motivations to counter-terrorist content, private companies are also incentivized by the wishes of their clientele (the general public may not like being associated with extremism) and by their relationship with governments (a failure to remove content can result in state sanctions and harsh regulations). In light of these reasons, corporate entities such as Facebook, Google, and Twitter have focused their attention on patrolling and controlling their platforms for terrorist activities. Facebook reported suspending more than 125,000 extremist accounts between 2015 and 2016, many of them belonging to the Islamic State [8]. Meanwhile, Twitter suspended nearly 300,000 accounts in the first half of 2017 [9]. At the same time, Google reported that it had doubled the number of YouTube videos removed for radical content, 75 percent of this was censored before it was viewed by members of the general public [10].

While corporate control of online content is an effective way to manage the flow of information, it comes with its own set of issues. First, these practices have resulted in false positive identifications and the subsequent takedown and censorship of legitimate sites. This can create a very difficult situation for the site purveyors as the onus shifts to them to defend their content and demonstrate their innocence. Second, nations may demand the removal of content from private companies that results in censorship that extends beyond their territorial boundaries, thus violating jurisdictional restrictions. Many social media companies are based in the United States, for example, and other nation states have applied pressure in the past to these companies to shut down sites, despite the presence of a jurisdictional conflict. Third, many Western democracies have strong freedom of expression laws and may actually violate their censorship capacities when they pressure corporations to control extremist content. Corporate control of content may be legal but when states apply pressure to companies, they are in essence attempting to control expression, thus violating these protected rights. Lastly, radicalizing content is often posted on multiple platforms. In addition, some of the content may even be posted on relatively benign sites that serve as a meeting point for recruiters and curious onlookers who are then directed to an encrypted site that is beyond both state and corporate control. Both of these characteristics undermine the effectiveness of attempts to control content.

9.3.4 Prosecution

Prosecution is less frequently used but still a viable negative measure for controlling radical messaging and recruitment online. Law enforcement have the option of identifying, arresting, and prosecuting the purveyors of online content under the auspices that they are producing extremist content. However, similar to other measures discussed in this chapter, prosecution raises a number of issues, not the least of which would be potential violations of free speech protections. As mentioned previously, in the United States, content needs to meet two qualifying factors in order to be considered illegal, beyond constitutional protections and, thus, subject to prosecution: first, the content must incite violence directed toward identifiable and specific people and, second, the potential violence must be a direct consequence of the content [7]. Meeting these conditions is difficult given the separation between the perpetrator and the recipient in cyberspace, leading to a reduced likelihood of successful litigation. In order to pursue this particular tactic, prosecutors are more prone to charge offenders with offences unrelated to the production of extremist content. This tactic, of course, requires that there are other grounds upon which to lay charges; finding viable grounds is rare, reducing the number of offenders that can be prosecuted. One further challenge that arises with prosecution is the location of the offender: he or she needs to be based in the country that seeks prosecution, which often is not the case, dropping the number of potential offenders even further.

9.3.5 Hiding Content

Hiding content relies on the cooperation of the commercial sector. This may include any number of actions, such as manipulating sites or videos and directing search processes. Once again, this may run up against free speech protections in the United States but has been carried out with some level of success by the European Union, particularly around content related to Holocaust denial. If, however, the private sector is unwilling to comply, hiding content becomes an unlikely option for addressing extremism in cyberspace. Compliance is unlikely for a number of reasons, including the difficulty and effort involved on the part of the corporate entity and the fact that the nature of the search algorithms used by social media and internet-based companies is structured to anticipate the user's preferences, not direct or block specific content.

9.3.6 Encryption

Encryption has proven to be a particularly difficult obstacle in addressing online recruitment and radicalization tactics. Following the Snowden leaks in 2013, tech companies in the United States faced a backlash as rumors circulated that the National Security Agency had gained access to private corporate servers [11]. In the immediate aftermath, a number of companies began producing impressive encryption software in order to alleviate public concerns about unwarranted state surveillance. Apple, for example, introduced encryption with the iOS 8 phone, effectively impeding the company's ability to unlock a private user's cell phone. This became particularly problematic following the terrorist attack in San Bernardino in 2015 when Apple could not access the assailant's cell-phone data. Apple also created end-to-end message encryption that ensured that plain text was only visible to the sender and the receiver and could not be accessed by the company or outsiders.

Encryption measures, although reassuring to the public, have been adopted by extremists in order to ensure secure communications. Recruiters will use public access sites to identify potential neophytes, who they will then invite into encrypted spaces in order to continue discussions away from the prying eyes of law enforcement. In other words, radical organizations are using encryption as a way of supplementing their activities: they use public sites to spread their message and recruit publicly while also using encrypted sites to engage in more targeted recruitment. Many encryption applications are so user friendly that even the least competent of any radical contingent is able to master them.

As can be expected, the use of encryption technology has made it difficult for law enforcement to police the online community, particularly in the United States. In many cases, encrypted communication is simply not accessible to law enforcement, either due to a lack of decryption software, legal obstacles in securing court orders to decrypt content, or a mix of both. These challenges are rooted in commercial considerations and libertarian sentiments. In regards to the former, allowing decryption options would require that companies insert decryption software and safety valves into each of their devices, a costly endeavor at best. As for the latter, forced decryption may violate Fourth Amendment protections against unreasonable search and seizure. In response, many advocate for legislative action in favor of mandatory decryption; however, others point out that creating such a law would open the door for oppressive regimes to demand similar compliance from U.S.-based social media and tech companies. Lastly, encryption software serves multiple audiences, not solely radical ones. Encryption protects the personal information of citizens, their banking activities, their passwords, and their digital fingerprints. Inserting decryption mechanisms increases vulnerabilities and creates opportunities for identity theft and financial crimes [12].

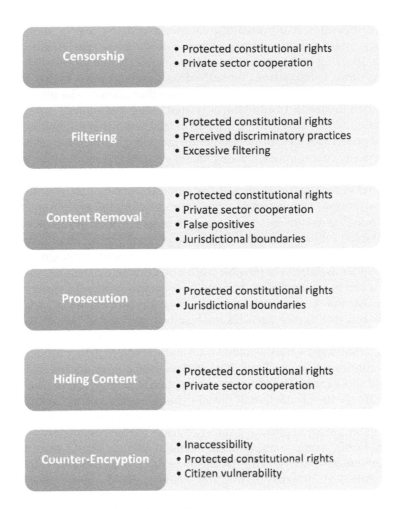

Figure 9.3   Challenges Resulting from Negative Strategies.

9.4 IMPLICATIONS FOR POLICY-MAKERS AND LAW ENFORCEMENT

As described above, there are a number of measures that can be taken to counter terrorist content, but each comes with a set of challenges for law enforcement, undermining its effectiveness and, in some cases, making particular measures inappropriate for implementation in Western democracies (see Figure 9.3). Free speech protections limit the ability to filter, remove, hide, manipulate, or prosecute online content. In addition, monitoring and interference with social media platforms and internet activity requires the cooperation of the private sector and, although companies such as Facebook and Google have increased their participation in the campaign to halt extremist online activity, proactive monitoring, recording, and reporting of problematic content is too unwieldy a task to take on in its entirety. Even if these companies were capable of carrying out the level of surveillance that effectively countering terrorism content would require, law enforcement personnel do not have the capacity to process the sheer volume of information resulting from such tactics. Jurisdiction is also an issue; state reach only extends to its geo-political boundaries, hindering the ability of countries to control content that originates from outside of their borders.

Using positive measures like presenting counter-narratives pose a series of similar but unique challenges. Sparring with extremist organizations online can backfire if the state that is engaged in the sparring is not equipped to respond quickly and deftly to ideologically motivated messaging. Counter-narratives that suffer from language barriers and a lack of cultural awareness became painfully problematic and may further alienate the population the narratives are intended to influence. In addition, escalated online showdowns can draw attention to a terrorist campaign, potentially lending it an air of legitimacy that it previously lacked. Lastly, ill-conceived and poorly executed awareness campaigns can give the impression that the state is biased against specific communities, causing members of those communities to feel frustrated, furthering their withdrawal from majority communities.

Where does that leave policy-makers and law enforcement officials? How then should states counter online extremism? One potential strategy proposed by the Bipartisan Policy Center is a layered defense, one that would "entail making each stage at which terrorists exploit the digital realm less hospitable to their operations" [11]. In other words, rather than trying to completely eradicate extremists' use of online space to recruit, radicalize, and campaign, the goal should be to make such activities as difficult as possible while also minimizing the costs to the state and law enforcement. This can be accomplished through the collective impact of a variety of measures.

One measure that may be met with some success is the process of lawful hacking, whereby law enforcement and intelligence agencies are legally authorized to penetrate or hack devices and internet and communication services that are used by extremist networks. Officials can use this method to plant spyware, download information, and to gather intelligence. Of course, encryption will continue to be an issue, but officials should consider the value of collaborating with other nations in order to address the encryption challenge. International collaboration could aim to facilitate the production of devices that allow for lawful hacking or circumvent encryption. In addition, between-state collaboration gives the appearance of a united front, which serves to deter potential offenders and encourage the participation of the private sector. In order to further circumvent encryption, enforcement officials should also consider prioritizing physical interventions, such as using deception or physical raids in order to gain possession of devices while unlocked and ready for use. This would bypass the need to introduce new legislation legalizing backdoor access to devices or the production of hard and software that would leave a window open for surveillance purposes.

International cooperation has benefits beyond facilitating the manufacturing of devices that can be lawfully hacked, aiding in sidestepping encryption, or presenting a united front. Cooperation between states requires time and a number of formal requirements and that can negatively impact ongoing law enforcement investigations and progress. However, establishing a pre-existing partnership between states can streamline this process considerably. Opening communication between states may lead to the harmonization of legislation or the creation of a comprehensive and compatible legal framework for countering online extremist activity [13].

The voluntary support of the private sector is an invaluable resource in the fight to counter terrorism, and law enforcement should maximize the use of that tactic. Corporate removal of online and social media content does not violate free speech protections and is not hampered by jurisdictional boundaries. In addition, content removal aligns with the sentiments of the consumer base and its lack of willingness to be engaged in practices that facilitate radicalization. Bearing in mind how important this tactic is, law enforcement should be cautious about what is realistic given the sheer volume of information available and the possibility of reluctance from the corporate sector to engage in active censorship. The state should also be extremely wary of extending beyond its legal reach by violating constitutionally protected rights. As such, it would behoove the counter-terrorism community to identify clear and legally sound priorities and focus on those to the exclusion of other less pressing demands of the private sector.

As for positive measures, policy-makers and law enforcement personnel should consider refining their own skills and cultural awareness before engaging with users online or in the community. They could also aim to provide support to innovative measures that fall outside of their own jurisdictions. For example, Google's tech incubator created a project called the "Redirect Method" that steers online users, particularly those identified as most susceptible to the Islamic State campaign, away from extremist content and toward YouTube videos that offer counter-narratives [14]. The videos are provided by users all over the world and tend to be viewed as more authentic than state-controlled messaging. In addition, the target audience is identified from the analysis of the online behaviors of YouTube users, and this allows for a more accurate and instantaneous assessment. Measures such as these may benefit from state support or, more likely, can serve as models of effective innovation that the state can aspire to replicate.

9.5 SUMMARY

There are a number of measures that law enforcement and the intelligence community can employ in their campaign to address online radicalization and campaigning. These measures may be positive, such as presenting counter-narratives that offer alternative messaging or engaging in community awareness campaigns, or they may be negative, such as censorship, content filtering, and prosecution, all of which are tactics that are designed to restrict content and penalize offenders. These different measures have met with varying levels of success and failure in the United States and the European Union.

The effectiveness of positive and negative measures depends on a variety of factors. Positive measures such as presenting counter-narratives will likely only succeed if the crafters and executors of these narratives are culturally and linguistically equipped to engage in a skilled and quick-witted ideological online exchange. In addition, the execution of a counter-narrative campaign should be undertaken with great caution, given that drawing attention to radicalizing online content may backfire and legitimize the content. In regards to community awareness campaigns, law enforcement should be attentive to how they interact with high-risk communities, minimizing any impressions of bias and ensuring they continue working with the community in the long term. Negative measures also suffer from a number of shortcomings, including jurisdictional restrictions, the necessity of commercial cooperation, and constitutional considerations.

While there is no panacea solution for online radicalization and extremist campaigning, experience has taught us that attempting to completely eradicate this kind of content and activity may be a futile endeavor. However, adopting a layered approach that maximizes on the strengths of these different techniques but minimizes the costs involved, paired with international and corporate collaboration, deference of constitutional protections, and an awareness of cultural nuances, could serve to minimize terrorist online presence.

REFERENCES

1. Mahmoud M. Galander. The Impact of US Public Diplomacy in the Gulf (an Investigation of Radio Sawa). *Gezira Journal of Tafakkur*. 2012. Volume 12, Issue 1, pp. 1–21. http://www.academia.edu/1 7507992/Impact_of_US_Public_Diplomacy_Investigating_Radio_Sawa

2. Bibi T. Van Ginkel. Responding to Cyber Jihad: Towards an Effective Counter Narrative. International Centre for Counter-Terrorism Research Paper. March 2015. https://ctc.usma.edu/banning-encryption-to-stop-terrorists-a-worse-than-futile-exercise/

3. Rita Katz. The State Department's Twitter War with ISIS is Embarrassing. *Time*. September 16, 2014. http://time.com/3387065/isis-twitter-war-state-department/

4. Desmond Butler. *US Misfires in Online Fight Against the Islamic State*. Associated Press. January 31, 2017. https://apnews.com/b3fd7213bb0e41b3b02eb15265e9d292

5. National Counterterrorism Center. *CVE Engagement Activities*. NCTC Directorate for Strategic Operational Planning. https://www.dhs.gov/sites/default/files/publications/CVE%20Engagement%20Activities-NCTC%20Classes.pdf

6. Clive Walker, Maura Conway. Online Terrorism and Online Laws. *Dynamics of Asymmetric Conflict*. 2015. Volume 8, Issue 2, pp. 156–175. https://www.tandfonline.com/doi/abs/10.1080/17467586.2015.1065078

7. Bipartisan Policy Center. *Countering Online Radicalization in America*. December 2015. http://bipartisanpolicy.org/wp-content/uploads/sites/default/files/BPC%20_Online%20Radicalization%20Report.pdf

8. Anonymous. Twitter Suspends 125,000 'Terrorism' Accounts. *BBC News*. February 5, 2016. http://www.bbc.com/news/world-us-canada-35505996

9. Elizabeth Weise. Anti-Extremist Crackdown on YouTube, Facebook, Twitter Only Solves Part of the Problem. *USA Today*. November 1, 2017. https://www.usatoday.com/story/tech/news/2017/11/01/anti-extremist-crackdown-youtube-facebook-twitter-only-solves-part-problem/823111001/

10. Kent Walker. Working Together to Combat Terrorists Online. *Google Blog*. September 20, 2017. https://www.blog.google/topics/public-policy/working-together-combat-terrorists-online/

11. Bipartisan Policy Center. Digital Counterterrorism: Fighting Jihadists Online. March 2018. https://bipartisanpolicy.org/wp-content/uploads/2018/03/BPC-National-Security-Digital-Counterterrorism.pdf

12. Aaron Brantly. Banning Encryption to Stop Terrorists: A Worse than Futile Exercise. *Combatting Terrorism Center*. August 2017. Volume 10, Issue 7. https://ctc.usma.edu/banning-encryption-to-stop-terrorists-a-worse-than-futile-exercise/

13. Marco Gerke. Challenges in Developing a Legal Response to Terrorist Use of the Internet. *Defence Against Terrorism Review*. Volume 3, Issue 2, pp. 37–58.

14. The Redirect Method. *A Blueprint for Bypassing Extremism*. https://redirectmethod.org/downloads/RedirectMethod-FullMethod-PDF.pdf

Chapter 10

Web Vulnerability-Based Spear Phishing

A Modern Combination of Tools in Cyberterrorism

Emin Huseynov

CONTENTS

10.1 INTRODUCTION

The internet is nowadays the center of most people's social and professional life, therefore protecting online identity is becoming even more critical. In addition to the usual risks of being compromised such as theft, a compromised account can be used as a ladder to perform more a sophisticated attack, e.g. if the account of an employee in an organization is compromised, it can be used to continue the attacks using the internal vector, and internal attacks are known to be much more successful than external attacks. Therefore, compromising accounts is still a popular method of cyber-terrorism, and the most popular way of compromising online accounts is a phishing attack. Phishing is still the most popular and most successful type of hacker attack. Everything is simple, no software, no servers, no networks to be penetrated, because the most vulnerable components of information systems are the end-users. As a result, apart from the usual risks, a compromised email or a social network account can become a powerful tool for a cyberterrorist who can exploit the identity of someone else. For this reason, accounts of popular public figures are even more at risk.

In this chapter, I will describe a number of different techniques that modern attackers use to enhance phishing attacks bringing the success rate of such attacks to a significantly higher level by using advanced methods to craft phishing pages, including pages created using vulnerabilities of legitimate web applications. After a brief review of existing classic methods used by phishing attacks, the chapter will review the methods of developing phishing pages, with attempts to make them look like genuine ones by utilizing vulnerabilities of different natures and on different levels, such as IDN name display method of browsers, web certificate issuance process imperfections, and classic cross-site scripting vulnerabilities of web applications.

10.2 BACKGROUND

While the main goal of this chapter is to describe the advanced techniques of creating phishing pages, it is still important to understand the basics of phishing attacks.

10.2.1 Targeting Victims—Phishing or Spear Phishing

Different from regular phishing, spear phishing attacks target a specific group of users, for example, a particular organization. Both attacks start with an email message. However, if phishing is easier for end-users to determine because the attack is much broader, it uses fewer specifics and is therefore much more suspicious, whereas spear phishing, if well crafted, can mimic legitimate email messages sent from the help desk or system announcements. Nowadays, there are also attacks against users of particular cloud services that have a broader scope of targeted victims, such as users hosted on Google Apps or MS Office 365. In these cases, even though the users belong to different organizations, the email messages and phishing pages share the same design and URLs.

10.2.2 Phishing Email—Reaching the Victim

Modern email systems are capable of identifying emails that have phishing content. However, there are techniques that allow phishers to work around these filters and succeed in getting the emails delivered the end-users, such as using non-Latin characters in the message body, as well as using properly set up Domain Name Server (DNS) infrastructure with domain names that look similar to the target organization's domain name. Another common practice for sending phishing email is to use well known and widely trusted email systems that allow free and fully anonymous online registration and allow emails to be sent without any user verification. Examples of such systems are Gmail [1] and ProtonMail [2], they both allow new email accounts to be registered without any additional verification as shown in Figure 10.1, whereas, for example, Hotmail requires phone number verification before emails can be sent.

10.2.3 Phishing Page—The Final Destination

The ultimate goal of a phishing attack is to obtain sensitive information, such as users' passwords, directly from users, and the main instrument for getting this information is to somehow

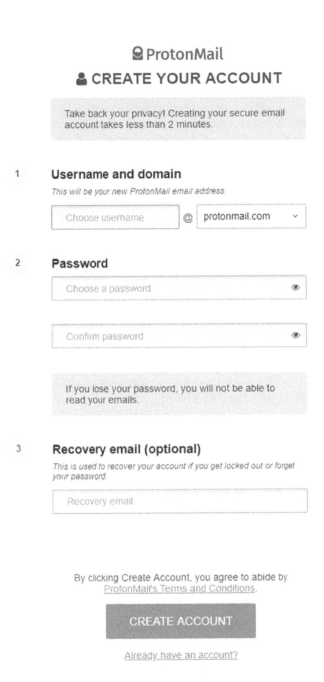

Figure 10.1   ProtonMail registration page.

convince the user to enter it on a web page. This is done by creating a web page that the user can trust and will enter his or her password. This information is afterwards sent to the attacker and completes a successful phishing attack. In order to minimize a user's suspicion, after the information is recorded, the user is usually forwarded to a legitimate login page. This phase of the attack will be described in more detail later in the chapter.

10.3 ANATOMY OF A PHISHING PAGE

If the methods used in the email were enough to convince the victim to click on the link inside the phishing message, there is only the final part of the process left to make the attack successful: making the user enter the password on the phishing page. However, the way the URL of the phishing page looks like in the email itself is also important in convincing the user to click on it. This is the first component of a successful phishing page.

10.3.1 The URL

For different reasons, many attackers use random URLs provided by free hosting providers or the URLs of websites with vulnerabilities allow them to upload files. These URLs are easily identified as phishing attempts, even for an average IT-savvy user.

There are some free hosting providers that allow the registration of quite long third-level domains on top of short second-level domains, and this allows attackers to be more creative when it comes to selecting the subdomain for their future phishing page.

As per Request for Comments (RFC) 7230 [3], the maximum length of an URL is 2000 characters. A hyperlinked portion of text may or may not be the same as the URL itself, in case it is not, the target URL will be shown in the status bar of the application used to open the phishing email. Some browsers, for example, will only show a portion of such a long URL, therefore the URL may be crafted to appear as a legitimate one for the end- users.

An example of such an URL could be as follows. Let's say an organization is using a centralized SSO login web application with the URL below:

> https://login.fictionalcompany.com/

A more successful phishing attack can benefit from a free hosting service and host the phishing page under a URL as shown below:

> http://login-fictionalcompany-com-443-h.freehost.tld/

Depending on the client software used and security awareness level, the potential victim may only see the first few characters of the URL in the status bar before clicking on it and assume this URL is legitimate. After the user clicks on the URL, the browser's address bar only shows the first N characters (depending on the screen size), which may look like what is shown in Figure 10.2, depending on the browser.

Using this technique, an attacker can produce a significantly long URL, and if the screen resolution of a victim is not very high, the URL in the address bar will not look suspicious at all. If

Figure 10.2   Address bars of browsers Explorer and Firefox.

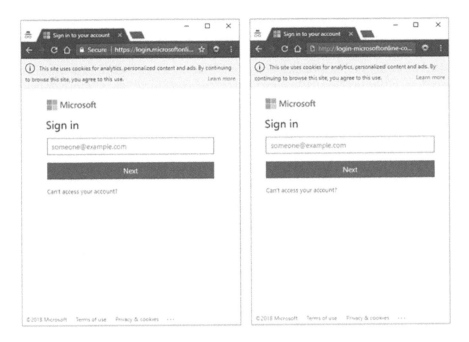

Figure 10.3   Microsoft Office 365 genuine and "fake" login page comparison.

this is combined with an exact replica of a company's signal sign-on login page [4], the potential victim is more likely to continue by entering their password. A visual comparison of a legitimate login page and a phishing page is shown in Figure 10.3. The phishing page imitates a user login page for Office 365 [5].

10.3.2 Long, Long Subdomains

One of the differences in the particular example shown in Figure 10.3 is that there are dash characters instead of dots in the phishing page URL, which may look suspicious. This is a limitation of many free hosting services, but nothing prevents attackers from using several levels of the subdomain to make the phishing page URL look more similar to the legitimate one. According to RFC 1035 [6] and RFC 1123 [7], the theoretical limits for a DNS record is 63 bytes per label and 255 bytes for a fully qualified domain name (FQDN), which fully covers the requirements for creating a URL long enough to be shown partially on any browser's address bar, even with the highest screen resolution. So when creating a DNS record, the attackers can host the phishing page with the URL shown in Figure 10.4.

Some browsers are able to detect the subdomains so that they are partially shown in the address bar (i.e. Google Chrome 64.0 as shown in Figure 10.5) and mark them as dangerous, but most browsers will not detect these.

10.3.3 Homograph Attack

Another quite successful technique of FQDN for phishing pages is using characters visually similar to some of the letters in the domain name. "From a security perspective, Unicode domains can be problematic because many Unicode characters are difficult to distinguish from common

ASCII characters," Zheng writes [8]. "It is possible to register domains such as 'xn--pple-43d.com', which is equivalent to 'apple.com'. It may not be obvious at first glance, but 'apple.com' uses the Cyrillic 'a' (U+0430) rather than the ASCII 'a' (U+0041). This is known as a homograph attack" [8]. Additionally, the attack can utilize characters like diacritics (see Figure 10.6). Diacritics are not exactly visually similar to their Latin alternatives, there are little "dots" above or below the letters, but they are still very close and hard to distinguish, especially if the style of displaying the hyperlinks is standard—underlined text.

This issue was reported to main browser producers, and most of them have fixed the behavior (shown in Figure 10.7) y showing the domain names fully using Punycode (Figure 10.8).

The homograph attack risk is addressed by using an up-to-date version of the browser. However, these can still be successfully exploited even now at the moment of writing this article.

Figure 10.4   Very long FQDN.

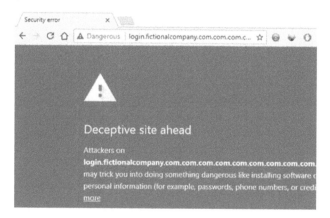

Figure 10.5   Google Chrome deceptive website warning.

Figure 10.6   An example of diacritics symbol: underdot H.

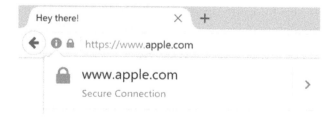

Figure 10.7   IDN domain in an unpatched browser (first a is Cyrillic).

According to our research, only around 10K domain names are protected from IDN attack, and other domain names are still vulnerable [9]. For example, more popular domains like microsoft. com or unicef.org are converted to Punycode right away, whereas less visited (but still used) domains like onmicrosoft.com (service domain for the office 365 tenant [10] (see Figure 10.9)) or rolex.com (see Figure 10.10) are still shown as Unicode. We managed to register a visually similar domain name, and it was allowed at the domain registrar level, as well as being shown in Unicode format in most of the browsers.

The same letter (o with an under dot) was used by attackers to create a fake Rolex lottery hoax, which was being distributed primarily via popular instant messengers like WhatsApp or Telegram (see Figure 10.11). The little dot on the URL (including in the address bar of the browser) does not look suspicious at all and may seem to be just something like a speck of dust on the screen.

Figure 10.8   IDN domain in a patched browser.

Figure 10.9   A domain similar to onmicrosoft.com with an underdot O.

Figure 10.10   A domain similar to rolex.com with an underdot O.

Figure 10.11   Fake Rolex lottery being advertised via WhatsApp.

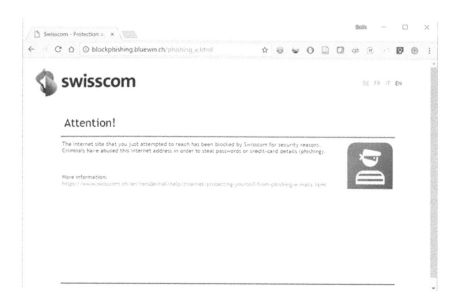

Figure 10.12   Swisscom page reacting to recent "fake lottery" attacks.

It is worth mentioning that these attacks can also be easily detected by ISPs, especially if a proactive threat management system combined with client feedback mechanisms is in place. For example, the Rolex watch attack was identified and blocked by Swisscom within a day (see Figure 10.12).

10.3.4 "Secure" Phishing

Now, let's move forward with our newly registered domain name (onmicrosoft.com) and create a phishing page, of course it is visually similar to the actual login page (see Figure 10.13). The usual way of cloning such a page is taking the source code, style, and graphics from the legitimate login

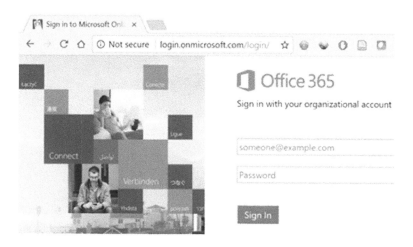

Figure 10.13   A phishing page imitating the Office 365 login page.

page. There are also resources available as ready built packages [11]. So, it takes a couple of minutes to download the login page template, and the phishing page is ready to operate.

If you spend more time comparing the fake login page (as shown in Figure 10.13), with the real one, you might have spotted one significant difference: there is no "secure" label on the fake login page. The reason is simple—we have used an HTTP-based page. Most of the login pages on the internet are server over https nowadays, and this makes our phishing page less perfect. So, let's continue further and make our phishing page "secure," which means that we have to install a web server certificate with the common name matching our FQDN. The usual way of obtaining such a certificate is to buy it from commercial certification authorities; there is also a way to get it for free. The reason is not really to save money, but paying for the certificate may leave a trace, i.e. if a credit card is used, so an attacker would probably choose to obtain the certificate via a free and anonymous route.

One of the methods for obtaining certification is using a popular content delivery network service, Cloudflare, which, in addition to classic content delivery network (CDN) services, also offers Security Socket Layer (SSL) offload features for free and issues SSL certificate for any domain added to it within 24 hours [12]. The feature is called "shared Cloudflare Universal SSL certificate." We chose this method to obtain a web certificate for our page and got a result like that shown in Figure 10.13.

Another method is Let's Encrypt, which is a certificate authority that provides free certificates for web servers by using an automated process [13]. Both methods issue a domain-validated type of web certificate [14]. Domain-validated (DV) certificates only validate the ownership of the domain by either asking the page creator to create or modify DNS records or upload a file to the web server where the domain is hosted. Another method of issuing web certificates is called extended validation (EV) certification [15], and it involves manual verification. While most online service providers (including Google and Microsoft) rely on DV certificates, EV certificates are usually more trusted by end-users (see Figure 10.14) and are widely used by banks or other financial institutions (i.e. for online banking login pages).

EV-protected domain names are harder to fake, especially if the end-users are made aware of the differences. So basically, a phishing attack is less likely to be successful if the legitimate login page is using EV certification and the users are trained to pay attention to company name appearing on the address bar and not just the "secure" or lock icon (as with DV certificates).

It is, however, worth mentioning that it is possible to reproduce EV certificates on a non-genuine domain. This is done by launching a company verification process with certificate authorities that check incorporation documentation in a rather relaxed way. At least two security researchers [16, 17] were able to obtain EV certificates (see Figure 10.15), one with a name similar to an

Figure 10.14   Domain-validated versus extended validation certificates.

Figure 10.15   Address bar view with EV certificate, Google Chrome.

existing payment provider, and another one with an EV certificate (see Figure 10.16) issued as "Identity Verified" (this was the company name) (see Figure 10.17).

So, in the case where the targeted victims use Safari, the success rate of the attack would be very high because Safari does not show the actual URL if the web server is using an EV certificate. Together with a name like "Identity Verified" (see Figure 10.18) the page asking to enter the username and password looks legitimate and safe.

Although a phishing page with an EV certificate is harder to implement, is more expensive, and it is more complex to hide traces, using phishing pages with EV certificates would significantly improve the success rates of such attacks. Especially if used in combination with other techniques and the EV certificate is issued to a visually similar domain name.

10.3.5 XSS, a Phisherman's Friend

Techniques described in the previous sections are based on using fake URLs, manipulated one way or another to make them look like the genuine ones. There are also possibilities for benefiting from web application vulnerabilities, known as cross-site scripting (XSS) [18] combed with the usual techniques of phishing attacks.

The principle of using XSS vulnerabilities in phishing attacks is simple, the URL sent to victims uses the real FQDN but contains additional code which is embedded using the XSS vulnerability.

Figure 10.16   Address bar view with EV certificate, Safari.

Figure 10.17   EV certificate issued to an "Identity Verified" company, as shown by Safari under MacOS.

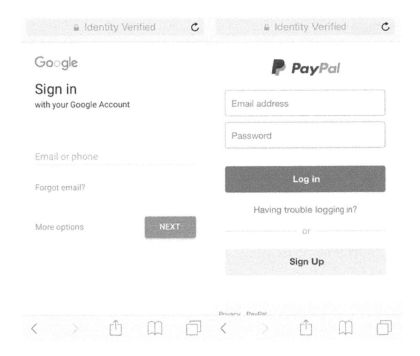

Figure 10.18 EV certificate issued to "Identity Verified" company, as shown by Safari on iOS.

The final URL is usually very long, and the characters are URL encoded, so it is quite hard for end-users to detect irregularities. It is technically possible to have these URLs with JavaScript or an HTML code included, but modern browsers are able to successfully detect and block such XSS attacks (Figure 10.19).

However, there is a possibility to include regular HTML code, which may contain a link leading to a remotely hosted form asking for username and password. Such HTML code is currently not detected nor blocked by browsers (Figure 10.20).

Figure 10.19 XSS attack detected by Google Chrome.

Figure 10.20   XSS attack allowed by Google Chrome.

While the actual form is hosted on a different URL, in combination with previously described domain forgery methods, such techniques may better convince the victims to click on a link in the email.

10.4 MITIGATION STRATEGIES

The main goal of this chapter is to show that phishing attacks are becoming increasingly sophisticated. There are, however, measures that any IT organization can take, which, of course, will not remove the risk of phishing attacks completely, but can minimize or prevent the direct costs. Many authors stress the importance of user awareness [19] as the primary mitigation method. While this is still an important aspect of mitigation strategies, many user guides are still somewhat misleading; for example, a user guide published by UBS Switzerland [20] still considers a website "with https:// in front of the address" as "trustworthy" (see Figure 10.21).

Another goal of this chapter is to demonstrate that a sophisticated phishing attack has more chance of being successful even if user awareness is at a high level. Therefore, the best way to protect users from phishing attacks is to make a stolen password useless by implementing multi-factor authentication. This can significantly reduce the likelihood that a compromised credential will have access to an organization's data, therefore making the phishing attacks against MFA-enabled accounts completely useless [21].

10.5 SUMMARY

A study [22] dated 2006 shows that around 90 percent of users were fooled into clicking on a phishing URL. This chapter illustrates that there are modern ways of enhancing an attack already considered classic, therefore the success rate of such attacks can be expected to be significantly higher, even if we accept that user awareness has increased since 2006. This chapter reviewed technologies and methods used by attackers in order to raise the success rate of attacks, as well as a number of mitigation methods currently in use. It was stated, however, that enabling multi-factor authentication is the most effective method: it will not prevent successful attacks (i.e. stealing the user credentials), but it will make the credentials impossible to use to gain access to further resources.

Only visit trustworthy websites
A secure website will start with https:// in front of the address. Bookmark any websites you frequently use to your favourites. Never input any confidential data into webforms if you are uncertain about the legitimacy of the site. Important information: UBS never sends out emails with links to login pages such as e-banking and will never ask you for your e-banking contract number or PIN

Figure 10.21   An extract of a user guide showing https in the context of trustworthy websites.

REFERENCES

1. Google, "Create your Google Account," 13 05 2018. [Online]. Available: https://accounts.google.c om/signup/v2/webcreateaccount?service=mail&continue=https%3A%2F%2Fmail.google.com %2Fmail&flowName=GlifWebSignIn&flowEntry=SignUp. [Accessed on 12 05 2018].
2. ProtonMail, "Create Your ProtonMail Account," 14 05 2018. [Online]. Available: https://mail.protonm ail.com/create/new?language=en. [Accessed on 12 05 2018].
3. IEEE, "Hypertext Transfer Protocol (HTTP/1.1): Message Syntax and Routing," 06 06 2014. [Online]. Available: https://tools.ietf.org/html/rfc7230. [Accessed 15 05 2018].
4. Pashalidis, A., & Mitchell, C. J., "A Taxonomy of Single Sign-On Systems," *Australasian Conference on Information Security and Privacy*, Springer, Berlin, Heidelberg. pp. 249–264, July 2003.
5. Microsoft, "Office 365 for Business FAQ," 2018. [Online]. Available: https://products.office.com/en/ business/microsoft-office-365-frequently-asked-questions. [Accessed 13 05 2018].
6. P. Mockapetris, "RFC1034, RFC1035 Domain Names: Concepts and Facilities," 1983. Available: https:// www.rfc-editor.org/info/rfc88. [Accessed on 14 05 2018]
7. R. Raden, RFC 1123 "Requirements for Internet Hosts - Application and Support," 1989. Available: https://www.rfc-editor.org/info/rfc1123. [Accessed on 14 05 2018]
8. X. Zheng, "Phishing with Unicode Domains," 14 04 2017. [Online]. Available: https://www.xudongz. com/blog/2017/idn-phishing/. [Accessed 10 05 2018].
9. Jungshik, "Issue 2784933002: Mitigate Spoofing Attempt Using Latin Letters," 14 04 2017. [Online]. Available: https://codereview.chromium.org/2784933002. [Accessed 10 05 2018].
10. Microsoft, "Why Do I Have an "onmicrosoft.com" Domain?," 28 3 2018. [Online]. Available: https:// support.office.com/en-us/article/domains-faq-1272bad0-4bd4-4796-8005-67d6fb3afc5a#bkmk_ whydoihaveanonmicrosoft.comdomain. [Accessed 10 05 2018].
11. Github, "Simple Template to Capture Credentials on a Fake Office 365 Login Page," 10 12 2014. [Online]. Available: https://github.com/pentestgeek/phishing-frenzy-templates/tree/master/office 365. [Accessed 11 05 2018].
12. CloudFlare, "Introducing Universal SSL," 28 09 2014. [Online]. Available: https://blog.cloudflare.com/ introducing-universal-ssl/. [Accessed 11 05 2018].
13. Let's Encrypt, "Getting Started," 2018. [Online]. Available: https://letsencrypt.org/getting-started/. [Accessed 14 05 2018].
14. N. Leavitt, "Internet Security under Attack: The Undermining of Digital Certificates," *Computer*, vol. 44, no. 12, pp. 17–20, 2011.
15. Robert Biddle et al., "Browser Interfaces and Extended Validation SSL Certificates: An Empirical Study," in ACM Workshop on Cloud Computing Security, New York, 2009.
16. J. Burton, "First Part of Phishing with EV," 2007 2017. [Online]. Available: https://www.sirburton. com/ev-phishing/. [Accessed 14 05 2018].
17. I. Carroll, "Extended Validation Is Broken," 4 11 2018. [Online]. Available: https://stripe.ian.sh. [Accessed 14 05 2018].
18. R. H. S. F. Jeremiah Grossman, *XSS Attacks: Cross-site Scripting Exploits and Defense*, Syngress, 2007.
19. R. C. Dodge, "Phishing for User Security Awareness," *Computers & Security*, vol. 26, no. 1, pp. 73–80, 2007.
20. UBS Switzerland, "Phishing," 2018. [Online]. Available: https://www.ubs.com/global/en/phishing.h tml. [Accessed 14 05 2018].
21. J.-J. Kim and S.-P. Hong, "A Method of Risk Assessment for Multi-Factor Authentication," *Journal of Information Processing Systems*, vol. 7, no. 1, pp. 187–198, 2011.
22. R. E. A. Dahamija, *Why Phishing Works*, UC Berkeley, 2006. Available: https://escholarship.org/uc/it em/9dd9v9vd. [Accessed on 14 05 2018]

Investigations and Intelligence Gathering of Terrorism-Related Online Activities

Chapter 11

Investigations of Terrorist Cases Involving the Internet

Allison Miller and Yannis A. Stivachtis

CONTENTS

11.1 INTRODUCTION

The subject of online radicalization has come to the forefront of terrorism and counterterrorism studies in recent years. Though not a new phenomenon, the threat of understanding and countering online radicalization has been prioritized after the Islamic State of Iraq and Syria (ISIS) proved to be exceptionally good at targeting individuals from across the globe for recruitment. There are a lot of questions regarding how terrorists use the internet, such as what kinds of subject matter are accessible, who accesses it, and how it is subsequently used. In an attempt to grapple with these questions, this chapter will first examine the use of the internet by terrorist groups by focusing on the strategic, tactical, and operational levels, and then it will provide an analysis on how Al Qaeda and ISIS have used the internet.

11.2 LEVELS OF ANALYSIS: STRATEGIC, TACTICAL, AND OPERATIONAL

In examining how terrorists use the internet, it is useful to break it down into three levels of analysis: strategic, tactical, and operational levels. At the strategic level, our examination focuses on the question of *why* terrorist organizations use the internet and *how* they develop a plan of action. At the tactical level, our analysis focuses on the various activities terrorists use the internet for in a broad sense, such as recruitment. At the operational level we examine how the internet is used in practice, which is best done through considering various case studies.

Although there are other types of terrorists and terrorist organizations that undoubtedly use the internet (such as far-right extremists), this chapter focuses on the most widely studied group of Islamist terrorists, ISIS, due to the sheer volume of information available on it and given its rise (and potential fall).

For the sake of clarity, it is necessary to provide a definition for how e-jihad is conceptualized in relation to this chapter. The development of the internet paved the way for what has been referred to as "the Open University for jihad studies" that enrolls several thousand students (Paz, 2013, p. 268). Paz (2013, p. 268) argues that this "Open University" brought about the two new developments of a jihadi community that perpetuated messages of solidarity and brotherhood while subsequently creating virtual jihadi "internet scholars." This community encouraged active participation of its members in terms of scholarly debates and it also sought to indoctrinate Jihadi-Salafis. Cohen-Almagor (2012) defines e-jihad as the way that information technology is applied by various groups in order to organize logistics for their campaigns by using email and encrypted files, as well as a means to develop strategic intelligence.

However, the conceptualizations offered by Paz and Cohen-Almagor are not inclusive enough. It is important to consider the rise of social media and networking sites that have affected the dissemination of jihadi scholarship and propaganda. With this in mind, this chapter defines e-jihad as structurally encompassing both the traditional means of dissemination (largely forums and emails) as well as the more modern means of dissemination (Twitter, Facebook, WhatsApp, etc.). Thus, e-jihad in the most modern context is capable of reaching anybody with access to the most common social media platforms across the globe. Aside from social media, e-jihad can occur by email, in encrypted websites and messaging apps, and the more traditional instances such as forums, virtual libraries, and open-access jihadi websites.

11.2.1 The Strategic Level: Why Using the Internet Makes Sense

The internet is accessible almost anywhere to any person who has a cell phone or laptop. This makes it an ideal tool to utilize for an endless number of things, though the focus of this chapter is to discuss how terrorists and terrorist organizations use the internet. When discussing strategy, it is necessary to consider *why* using the internet makes the most sense for terrorist organizations.

It is first helpful to form an understanding of who is using the internet when examining terrorists. Wojtasik (2017, p. 107) argues that it is ultimately detrimental in terms of forming preventative action to assume that terrorist organizations are chaotic groups composed of unstable sociopaths. Though this imagery is still common in public opinion, it is significantly inaccurate and adds little in terms of studying terrorists, their actions, and their capabilities. In analyzing the success of terrorist organizations, it is essential to understand that they must operate at the capacity of a well-structured business (Wojtasik, 2017, p. 108). It requires an efficient organizational system of command, the ability to organize terrorist activities, and the capability to recruit new members (Wojtasik, 2017, p. 108). Thus, a terrorist organization must be composed of media wings that contain people such as spokesmen, specialists in media, public relations, and propaganda (Wojtasik, 2017, p. 108). These people are all necessary in order to create and maintain effective terrorist strategic plans of action.

Using the internet makes dissemination of information as simple as clicking a few buttons. Conway (2006, p. 284) argues that one main reason the internet is so appealing to terrorists is the easy publicity they can garner. Before the implementation of the internet as a strategic tool, terrorists had to rely on the discretion of traditional media such as television, radio, or print. Post-internet implementation allows terrorists to create their own websites and to use various social media platforms to disseminate information at a rapid pace. Thus, terrorists have the ability to have direct control over the content of information they wish to share (Conway, 2006, p. 284).

Hamas is considered by many to be a terrorist organization that is known to maintain an active presence online. The organization exists primarily in the West Bank and Gaza, where strategically, their free on-the-ground movement is significantly limited. It thus makes sense that Hamas would need to rely on the internet for several different reasons. Hamas operates a number of official websites that can be categorized into three types; media websites, websites that cover different organizations and wings, and websites used for virtual activities (Mozes & Weimann, 2010, p. 214).

Mozes and Weimann (2010, p. 215) pose the particularly useful question of whether Hamas' internet activities can be understood in traditional *e-marketing* strategical ways. They borrow from one of the core texts (Chaffey et al., 2000) on the subject of *e-strategy* to create their criteria for examination. They are:

- Decision 1. Who are the potential audiences?
- Decision 2. Positioning and differentiation
- Decision 3. Resourcing
- Decision 4. How to "migrate" a company's brand to the internet
- Decision 5. Outsourcing and strategy partnerships
- Decision 6. Organizational structure
- Decision 7. Building a budget and resource allotment
- Decision 8. Channel structure modifications.

Though the original model was not developed for the purpose of identifying the effectiveness of how Hamas strategically uses the internet, it does a good job of systematically analyzing it anyway. Mozes and Weimann find that most of these categories are applicable when undertaking an in-depth investigation of the Palestinian Information Center website, which they argue is a gateway to Hamas's online propaganda. Though some of their arguments appear to be circumstantial (such as Decision 7), they nevertheless have taken a unique approach to understanding the strategy of terrorist organizations on the internet. This model would likely be less efficient for analyzing one sole actor, but it is valuable for analyzing established terrorist organizations that are active on the internet. It is a systematic approach to distinguishing the strategy of terrorist organizations on the internet by providing an analytic framework to study their websites (Mozes & Weimann, 2010, p. 224).

Another useful approach that has been applied toward gaining an understanding for how terrorist organizations use the internet is by utilizing a transmedia strategy application. Monaci (2017, pp. 2845–6) defines this by arguing that media content is not just different channels for distributing the same message, but rather that each medium is used for its aesthetic and communicative features. The concept that is specifically applicable to ISIS is *synergistic storytelling*, which simply describes what each medium (in this case, the internet) can do in order to best maximize the impact of the narrative being formed (Monaci, 2017, p. 2846). Monaci then performs a content analysis based on narrative identification from 14 issues of *Dabiq*, which is an ISIS propaganda periodical available online. In doing this, a clear understanding of how ISIS has strategically woven its narrative into its online content can be gained.

ISIS uses the internet arguably more strategically to disseminate its narrative than any other terrorist organization in history. The organization has produced vivid online productions, particularly through *Dabiq* and later *Rumiyah*, which have had an unprecedented impact on mobilizing worldwide support. Monaci argues that the fictional and nonfictional political narratives spread by ISIS should not be differentiated between due to ISIS's goal to create a global ummah (community) (Monaci, 2017, p. 2857). In other words, ISIS employs fictional and nonfictional narratives that are designed to manipulate the readers of *Dabiq* and *Rumiyah*.

The strategy that terrorists have for using the internet can now be understood by assessing it through two different routes: e-strategy and transmedia. E-strategy provides a framework that considers a terrorist organization to be more like a business, which is not too far off the mark. Transmedia adopts a more communications-based or sociological approach in that it analyzes the story that the terrorist organization is attempting to tell and how various media platforms are used to do that. Both approaches would be useful for analyzing terrorist organizations that maintain a substantial presence on the internet, such as Hamas and ISIS.

Aside from the aforementioned strategic benefits of using the internet, there are also benefits of being able to manipulate an audience based on well-articulated narratives supported by digital graphics, careful use of linguistics, and coded language. When terrorists are utilizing the internet, they have the time to carefully think about what they are sharing, and this time allows them to create propaganda that is often times highly effective.

11.2.2 The Tactical Level: What the Internet is Used For

The internet is used by different individuals for different reasons. It is necessary to understand what terrorists and terrorist organizations do on the internet to help understand how they operationalize it. There have been quantitative studies conducted in an attempt to better understand how terrorists are using the internet. For example, it should come as no surprise that younger offenders are significantly more likely to use the internet in terms of terrorist learning and interactions than older offenders (Gill et al., 2017, p. 102). Quantitative analysis regarding how individuals use the internet for terrorist purposes is invaluable because it aids in increasing the understanding of what terrorists are doing on the internet.

Gill et al. conducted a quantitative analysis based on a sample of 223 convicted terrorists in the United Kingdom where they found that the offenders were overwhelmingly male (96 percent), were a mean age of 28, and that 61 percent used the internet in relation to their radicalization and/or attack planning process (Gill et al., 2017, p. 107). It is important to note that this study is not strictly limited to Islamist, but the data does provide useful information regarding patterns of behavior that Islamist terrorists are more likely to demonstrate when compared to extreme right-wing terrorists. For example, the data revealed that Islamists are more likely to communicate via email and chatrooms, while right-wing extremists are more likely to communicate via forum (Gill et al., 2017, p. 117). It also showed that Islamists were more likely to instrumentalize the internet by preparing cells, to reinforcing prior beliefs, to disseminating propaganda, and signaling attack (Gill et al., 2017, p. 117). Perhaps one of the most important conclusions from this particular study is the fact that there is no easy offline versus online dichotomy to be drawn; individuals will likely participate in both the virtual realm as well as in person (Gill et al., 2017, p. 114). This is important due to the fact that it highlights the importance of not over-emphasizing the study of terrorist uses of the internet, especially in terms of creating counterterror policy.

It is useful to categorically define the ways in which terrorists tactically utilize the internet. Conway has identified five comprehensive categories: recruitment, financing, networking, information gathering, and information provision (Conway, 2006). Below is a brief description of each.

Information provision refers to how terrorists tactically use the internet for publicity, propaganda, and psychological warfare (Conway, 2006, p. 283). The internet has undoubtedly increased the capability of information provisioning for both individual terrorists and terrorist organizations. Conway argues that terrorists can use the internet for things such as historical information, leader profiles, and manifestos, as well as the more dangerous psychological warfare that can be spread through disinformation, threats, and shocking imagery (Conway, 2006, p. 283). ISIS has excelled at engaging in psychological warfare as is evident in the advanced digital appearance of *Dabiq* and *Rumiyah*, as well as their Hollywood-like videos. For example, when Jordanian pilot Moaz al-Kasasbeh was burned alive in a cage in 2015, ISIS expertly filmed and produced a video of the grotesque scene. It was circulated on the internet, which is undoubtedly what ISIS had intended in order to gain publicity and caused a wave of international emotional reaction from both supporters and adversaries. Emotional manipulation is a foundation of psychological warfare, and ISIS uses the internet to disperse their propaganda to a broad platform.

Financing refers to how terrorists raise money for their activities, which is absolutely essential for survival (Conway, 2006, p. 285). The internet allows terrorists to engage in credit card fraud, pose as charities, or establish internet front businesses in order to finance their cause. Terrorists and terrorist organizations are also able to use the internet to infiltrate branches of charities in order to raise funds in a secretive manner (Conway, 2006, p. 287).

Networking on the internet allows terrorist organizations to structure themselves in a decentralized manner—allowing terrorists to communicate more efficiently (Conway, 2006, p. 287). This enhanced means of networking also means that terrorist organizations are able to plan their activities in a more efficient manner, while essentially decreasing the level of risk involved with doing so. Without the internet, terrorists would have to plan activities on the ground and in real time, which would leave them more publicly expose and increase their risk of getting caught.

Perhaps one of the most widely known and studied tactical uses of the internet for terrorists and terrorist organizations is recruiting new members. Recruiting on the internet is not a difficult task in practice, given that information is widely available and communication is easy. Also, since a large number of youth are active on the internet, this provides recruiters with a large number of people to target.

Information gathering refers to the capacity that terrorists have in terms of collecting any type of information they need. The internet truly makes this easy, especially when in the context of personal information available on social media. For example, Al Qaeda maintains a database with information regarding potential American targets that enables them to predict how attacks will impact targets in relation to both loss of human life and potential structural damage (Cohen-Almagor, 2012). With the rapid advancement of social media platforms such as Facebook and Twitter, it is not difficult to gather extensive data on potential targets, including workplaces, daily schedules, and personal information about private life, as often times privacy settings are not actually private enough. Thus, the internet becomes an easily accessible tool for researching targets in a very simplistic manner that any person with basic technology skills can likely use.

In addressing tactical uses for the internet, it is important to have a conceptual understanding of what the internet *is*. Sageman makes a compelling argument that the internet is two major systems: the World Wide Web and a system of communications (Sageman, 2008, p. 113). The World Wide Web can be understood as a collection of websites that provides information to users (Sageman, 2008, p. 113). Sageman argues that this portion of the internet contains a significant amount of passive information based on the fact that individuals typically seek out sources that reinforce their pre-established bias (Sageman, 2008, p. 113). Though this is a compelling point to make, it should be taken with caution given that the internet is widely accepted as being a source for online radicalization. The systems of communications that Sageman discusses encompass email, listservs, forums, chat, and chat rooms (Sageman, 2008, p. 113). It seems only practical to now include social media platforms in this category as well, especially given that many social media platforms allow for direct messaging to other users.

It is difficult to determine what category of the internet is the most dangerous when accessed by terrorists. On one hand, terrorists have access on the World Wide Web to documents that instruct them on how to make bombs or other training materials, while on the other hand a communication network allows like-minded individuals the ability to meet one another virtually and plan from a relatively safe space what they are going to do. Virtual communication also allows for relationships among individuals to unfold in different ways. For example, there is a certain veil of anonymity provided when individuals do not know one another. This also means that virtual relationships can simply be cut off, or the at the other extreme strangers may meet and marry, as some terrorists have done (Sageman, 2008, p. 114).

11.2.2.1 Content and Accessibility: Jihobbyists, Coffee Shops, and the Internet

When it comes to who is accessing the jihadi content available on the internet, it is necessary to note that most of those who do so are in their late teens and early twenties (Atwan, 2015). According to Greenburg, the average age across the globe for those recruited is 27, while in the US this age is slightly younger (Greenberg, 2016). This will be important to remember when considering who is recruited to terrorist organizations, as this target audience is largely susceptible to falling prey to skilled recruiters. Atwan utilizes the term "digital health" in reference to the frequency with which internet jihadis must access their content (Atwan, 2015). Digital health essentially can be understood as the overall stability, security, and effectiveness of the specific platform being utilized by a jihadi. In order to maintain a positive level of digital health, users must be able to frequently access their material and social media platforms. Being tech savvy and armed with a laptop or cellphone are the only prerequisites required for having the capability of spreading ideological messages across the globe via numerous social media platforms. As Atwan states, every jihadist has the capability to now be his or her own media outlet with the rise and subsequent incorporation of platforms such as Facebook, YouTube, Twitter, and Instagram (Atwan, 2015). Given that 89 percent of people in their late teens and early twenties (within the developed world) can have access to the internet, it is concerning that they have the ability to access such material in an incredibly effortless manner (Atwan, 2015).

Given that the internet makes e-jihad content easily attainable, those who are accessing it are not limited to established members or affiliates of terrorist networks. The "self-starters" that often call themselves practitioners of "homegrown terrorism" are a critical aspect that join the global jihadist movement on their own (Brachman, 2009, p. 18). Brachman has labelled these enthusiasts as *jihobbyists*. Jihobbyists are able to be actively involved in pushing forward a jihadist agenda from their own home or from a local coffee shop (Brachman, 2009). Though Brachman has coined this term in relation to Al Qaeda, it is possible to extend this to any would-be pious jihadi across the globe. Brachman states that jihobbyists become obsessed with practicing Islam to the letter (Brachman, 2009, p. 19). This concept is then useful for separating jihadis into different camps: the ones that are actually immersed in the religion and the ones that use the religion for their own agenda or purpose. It is arguable that many of the foreign fighters joining or attempting to join terrorist organizations are of the latter camp, as is indicated by the infamous case of Mohammed Ahmed and Yusuf Sarwar of Britain ordering "Islam for Dummies" before attempting to join ISIS (Rosenbaum, 2016).

Social media platforms have arguably become the most efficient and easy way to access jihadi content on the internet. The use of hashtags makes spreading messages even more effective, especially on Twitter. Jihadis and their sympathizers are able to use hashtags to consolidate their propaganda, and this then makes it fairly simple for any person browsing Twitter to find those messages. Jihadis on social media have even used trending hashtags so that unsuspecting users may accidentally find themselves accessing Jihadi social media account. On the other hand, people who use Twitter regularly (such as politicians, journalists, and military personnel) leave themselves vulnerable to potential security concerns by not taking the precaution of concealing their locations and daily habits (Atwan, 2015). This is notable as jihadis can easily gather data on a potential target.

The internet provides jihadis and their sympathizers with a veil of anonymity through the use of virtual private networks that conceal the location of the user (Atwan, 2015). Encryption software is easy to purchase through the internet and often is built into email packages (Bunt, 2003). E-jihad content also frequently references Tor, which is a network that routes traffic anonymously by utilizing volunteer networks with encrypted relays (Brantly, 2017). Within jihadist forums, there are dozens of references to Tor that typically reference training materials (Brantly, 2017). Tor itself also contains information relating to ISIS, such as advertising for illegal goods and services (Brantly, 2017). The use of encryption increases the security and anonymity of an individual who is accessing or sharing jihadi content on the internet. If an individual knows how to utilize these methods of concealment, it can become nearly impossible to pinpoint where in the world that person is.

It is now evident how jihadi content is accessed and by whom, as well as the type of capabilities that jihadis and their sympathizers have. The use of the internet for the purpose of spreading jihadi scholarship and debate has served as what is likely the most critical advancement for purposes of increasing recruitment and sharing propaganda. What is next important to consider, is what scholars are saying and how the community reacts to or debates with their content on the internet.

11.2.3 The Operational Level: The Internet in Practice

Without a doubt, the most concerning level of terrorist use of the internet is when it becomes the operational level. It is evident now that there is typically some kind of strategic and tactical level to utilizing the internet, but none of this would be so dangerous without it being operationalized. The following section will provide a number of brief case studies that demonstrate the horror that can result from operationalized use of the internet, as well as how the concept of e-jihad has evolved and been used by different terrorist organizations.

One of the highest profile cases to date of a terrorist operationalizing the internet is that of Roshonara Choudhry. This case garnered media attention for several reasons, primarily because Choudhry is female and was a university student at King's College London who excelled in her studies. Pearson (Pearson, 2016, p. 7) states that jihad is typically gendered and monopolized by men, so it is likely that the internet provided Choudhry with the self-radicalization tools when she was not available to access such content in real-time. Choudhry exhibited no signs of interest in Islamism prior to her exposure to the sermons of extremist preacher Anwar Al-Awlaki, (Pearson, 2016, p. 8). There is no reported evidence of Choudhry having online correspondence with any Al Qaeda members, any other jihadists, nor any other links to any real-world source of extremism (Pearson, 2016, p. 8). This suggests then that the al-Awlaki sermons significantly impacted Choudhry, and therefore that without ever having access to them in the first place perhaps Choudhry would have never stabbed Stephen Timms, Member of Parliament, in 2010. There is no definitive way to substantiate this claim given its theoretical nature, but it is clear that when Choudhry accessed and subsequently operationalized the internet, she reacted by embracing violence.

Another high-profile case of terrorism related to the internet is in relation to the Boston Marathon bombing in 2013, which killed three and injured over 200. The perpetrators, Tamerlan and Dzhokhar Tsarnaev, were also influenced by Anwar al-Awlaki, who was the US-born Yemeni cleric known as the Osama bin Laden of the internet. The brothers both had videos of al-Awlaki's sermons taken from YouTube on their computers and other electronic devices (O'Neill, 2015). Tamerlan was killed during the days following the bombing while Dzhokar was caught and later sentenced to death. There was a significant amount of evidence found on Dzhokhar's laptop to indicate that the internet played a critical role in his ability to carry out a terrorist attack. Aside from having sermons from al-Awlaki on his laptop, Dzhokar had also downloaded segments of al-Qaeda's magazine, *Inspire*, which included information on how to build bombs. Dzhokar has also downloaded a copy of *Join the Caravan*, a book which was written by Abdullah Azzam, founding member of Al Qaeda (O'Neill, 2015).

During the trial for Dzhokar, there was the argument that he was heavily influenced by his older brother Tamerlan. Though it is not possible to determine which brother first spoke the idea of the bombing aloud, it is possible to deduce that the internet had an impact on Dzhokhar's radicalization process. This case is an example of why drawing a strict online/offline radicalization dichotomy is of little use: it seems plausible that Dzhokar was radicalized both by his internet readings and by the influence of his brother. It is evident that Dzhokar was actively reading the content he downloaded because the writing he completed in a dry-docked boat while in hiding after the bombings drew direct parallels or nearly verbatim quoted sermons by al-Awlaki or segments from *Inspire* (Ford & Siemaszko, 2015).

Another brief example of the internet being operationalized is that of Mohammad Youssef Abdulazeez, who open fired in Chattanooga, Tennessee in 2016 on two separate military sites (Bradbury, 2016). Abdulazeez killed five US service members during his rampage in July. Like the aforementioned cases, Abdulazeez was influenced by al-Awlaki and had a significant amount of digital evidence on his electronic devices (Bradbury, 2016).

The most high-profile and influential terrorist attack of all time, September 11, 2001, utilized the internet in a number of ways. Al-Qaeda operatives used the internet in the detailed planning of 9/11 in a number of ways. For example, federal authorities located thousands of password-protected, encrypted messages on a specific location of a website on the computer of Abu Zubaydah, the alleged mastermind of the attack (Weimann, 2004, p. 10). The earliest messages on Zubaydah's computer were from May 2001 all the way up until 9 September 2001, with August being the most active month (Weimann, 2004, p. 10). The terrorists would use the internet in public locations and used public email to communicate with one another. The internet also allowed for the terrorists to communicate simplified instructions using codes that would seem extremely unnoticeable. One such example was a message sent by Mohammed Atta to the other terrorists that read "the semester begins in three more weeks. We've obtained 19 confirmations for studies in the faculty of law, the faculty of urban planning, the faculty of fine arts, and the faculty of engineering" (Weimann, 2004, p. 10).

The internet plays different roles in different processes for terrorists who operationalize it as a call for action. These are a few, simplified examples. The internet makes it fairly simple to access extremist material that prompts some individuals to go to the length of embracing violence as a means to an end. Individuals can access bomb-making manuals, extremists' sermons, and ideological propaganda such as *Dabiq* or *Inspire* all with the click of a few buttons. They can network virtually, giving them a certain degree of safety, if they are capable of concealing their identity or location. The internet has been used in some of the most brutal terrorist attacks in recent history to varying degrees.

11.3 EVOLUTION OF E-JIHAD: DIFFERENCES IN OPERATIONALIZATION BETWEEN AL QAEDA AND ISIS

Jihadists have been using the internet as a sharing platform, library, and as a means to exchange texts, videos, and recordings since the late 1990s (Hegghammer, 2010). With this technological advancement, jihadi content could be shared, accessed, and debated at a speed that had never before been possible. Jihadi scholars and terrorist organizations were able to broadcast their messages across the world, thus establishing a global jihadi network of scholars, students, or any other individual seeking out this type of information. The internet has allowed for the creation of a decentralized network that enables global jihad to transcend face-to-face exchanges (Cohen-Almagor, 2012). The fact that this network is now decentralized is important for a number of reasons, primarily that it is essentially impossible to shut down. It also allows terrorist organizations, scholars, and supporters to communicate faster which allows for more increased strategic and intelligence efficiency. This internet network also means that the content can be well documented and openly accessed, which is beneficial to practitioners and academics, but subsequently challenging for intelligence agencies and government institutions to combat. For example, in 2003 and 2004, the Al Qaeda in the Arabian Peninsula (AQAP) published such a large amount of information about their organization that they still remain one of the best documented terrorist organizations in history (Hegghammer, 2010). Around the same time, Al Qaeda began an initiative to start their own website, though this task was never fully completed. This factor could be tied into how Al Qaeda is viewed today within the context that there was a strategic difference of approaching jihad within Al Qaeda and other emerging organizations that attributes to the group's popularity and recruitment levels.

This section aims to explain how Al Qaeda and ISIS have used the internet to further their agendas. In recent years, the amount of scholarship regarding the relationship between Al Qaeda and the internet has steadily declined, which can suggest one of two things. First, the study of terrorism and its relationship to the internet is shifting toward more prominent terrorist organizations primarily composed of a younger generation of jihadis and their supporters, such as ISIS. Second, Al Qaeda has been unable to compete on the internet with the younger generations of jihadis and thus the importance of their presence on the internet has drastically decreased. Nevertheless, Al Qaeda was one of the first terrorist organizations to establish an active presence on the internet so their position of importance should not be overlooked, nor taken for granted.

11.3.1 Al Qaeda and the Internet

The internet has become an absolute necessity for the strategic operation of terrorist organizations today. To start, it is necessary to emphasize that the internet and digital technology have been utilized by terrorist organizations in different ways and for different reasons. Using the internet was initially a debated topic among scholars and jihadis, since it contradicts extremist viewpoints that emphasize the importance of living a traditional life with limited or no inclusion of technology. However, once terrorist organizations realized what the internet could provide for them, the debate ceased to be relevant (Atwan, 2015). The popularity of internet-based activism, related to terrorism or not, surged in the mid-1990s around the same time Al Qaeda became active on the internet (Brachman, 2006). In fact, at one point in 2005, individuals could fill out online forms in order to pledge their allegiance (or give *bay'a*) to Osama bin Laden (Brachman, 2006). The way in which Al Qaeda operationalized the internet from the 1990s until now has evolved in different ways. Their use is not limited to what would be considered the more traditional means of internet usage, such as sending emails or accessing encrypted content. This is discussed in Section 11.2.2: The Tactical Level.

Al Qaeda and their network have been largely successful at utilizing the internet for producing and sharing multimedia propaganda such as videotapes, audio recordings, CD-ROMs, DVDs, and seemingly endless written documents (Cohen-Almagor, 2012). Along with that, Al Qaeda (and other terrorist organizations) have been able to share how-to guides that give step-by-step instructions on how to create things such as cell phone detonators, flame-throwers, explosives, or how to analyze intelligence, US military training, and guidelines for creating underground networks (Cohen-Almagor, 2012). These factors coupled with the way that terrorist organizations have been extremely successful at producing top-notch propaganda paves the way for easy recruitment. Al Qaeda propaganda has been created from filmed insurgency operations in Iraq, which once edited is manipulated to appear glorious and heroic. Another way that Al Qaeda has successfully used the internet is by sharing key lectures from prominent figures. In the early 2000s, Mustafa Setmariam Nasar (also known as Abu Mus'ab al-Suri) was one of the most influential figures in Al Qaeda. His lectures were gathered in a publication of 1,600 pages called *The Call for a Global Islamic Resistance* and then widely disseminated across the internet in 2004 (Cohen-Almagor, 2012). This is one of many examples of how prominent figures have had their ideas shared to a wide audience via the internet, and how such information is foundationally necessary for the building blocks of recruitment.

Al Qaeda has also used the internet to provide methods for training, or what Stenersen (2008) has labelled a "virtual training camp." The most notable training strategist is Nasar and his *The Call for a Global Islamic Resistance*. Nasar states that instead of calling for Muslims to join training camps in other countries, they should instead move the training into every house, quarter, and village of Muslim countries. He then continues with a list of recommended readings that instruct individuals on learning basic military skills, such as knowledge of light weapons, military strategy, security, and other military skills (cited (in Stenersen, 2008, p. 17)). However, it is important to note that Stenersen argues that Al Qaeda does not use the internet as a virtual training camp that is being organized from above, but rather they use it as a resource bank to provide materials to self-radicalized sympathizers. This analysis provides insight into how Al Qaeda has failed to utilize the full potential of the internet, again indicating the fact that there is a generational gap of knowledge and skill between Al Qaeda and ISIS.

11.3.2 ISIS and the Internet

The Islamic State of Iraq and Syria (ISIS) has arguably been far more successful at recognizing and exploiting the usefulness of the internet than any other terrorist organization to date. Early on, ISIS was utilizing the internet as a platform to spread its cause and to mobilize an international following unlike any other terrorist organization had done before. Atwan makes the argument that without digital technology, it would be highly unlikely that the Islamic State would have come into existence (Atwan, 2015). Though this claim is debatable, it nevertheless reiterates the significance of the internet for ISIS. Abu Bakr al-Baghdadi, the self-proclaimed Caliph of the Islamic State, is known primarily for his audio speeches that are disseminated across jihadi social media platforms and websites. Given that al-Baghdadi is known for his scant public appearances since 2014, the internet has served as the primary method for sharing his various speeches and updates, as well as a means of Islamic State recruitment. Al-Baghdadi has mastered the art of being an elusive leader, which means that whenever he does release some form of content it ultimately ends up permeating media around the world, as opposed to remaining exclusive to any e-jihad platform. This allows al-Baghdadi to remain relatively safe in hiding, while still maintaining superior legitimacy as the leader of ISIS.

The Islamic State has pioneered new ways to use the internet in order to make their organization much more efficient in terms of both operations and recruitment. To start, al-Baghdadi brought ISIS to the attention of the jihadi community in July 2014 when a 20-minute audio recording was released to numerous jihadi forums declaring ISIS as the new caliphate (Atwan, 2015). In this regard, Atwan gains traction with his argument that ISIS may have never existed without digital technology. It is at best arguable that without digital technology, ISIS would not have garnered the international recognition that it did. Since the inception of the new pseudo-state, ISIS has relied on the internet for things such as recruitment, simultaneous directing of military action, and consolidating their like-minded allegiances (Atwan, 2015). ISIS has also used the digital world to evade threats from global intelligence bodies and other militarily related opponents (Atwan, 2015).

ISIS has primarily relied on the internet as a means of recruitment, thus making it central to the entire identity of the terrorist organization (Greenberg, 2016). This identity is so embedded in the framework of ISIS that the organization has been dubbed a digital caliphate. From the beginning, ISIS relied heavily on Twitter, Facebook messaging, and posts to organize and share propaganda. This allowed them to draw in a significant number of fighters from the West (Greenberg, 2016). Although this all occurs on open-access websites and platforms, ISIS has also utilized the Dark Web for its operations (Greenberg, 2016). Incorporating social media as a primary means of communication allows ISIS to engage in direct contact with potential recruits. This manifested many cases where ISIS successfully partook of the radicalization process that prompted youth from across the world to flock to the pseudo-state and engage in violent warfare.

The way that ISIS has currently created its governing structure has allowed them to become both highly efficient as well as showing an elevated understanding of statecraft. This has expanded to a branch responsible for overseeing the digital actions of ISIS called the Islamic State Electronic Army. This entity is an internal group that is dedicated to messaging on social media, hacking, and maintaining digital security (Greenberg, 2016). ISIS further announced the creation of the Al-Battar Media Battalion in 2014, which is solely responsible for pushing propaganda on Twitter (Greenberg, 2016). Aside from Twitter and Facebook, ISIS has regularly utilized YouTube as a means to quickly disseminate propaganda. This allows ISIS to move from direct messaging to sharing visual content that has been specifically created to manipulate the emotions of the viewers. In terms of propaganda production, it is arguable that no other terrorist organization in the world has harnessed the level of skill that ISIS has. For example, the organization creates videos that show fighters caring for the community by passing out sweets to children or visiting fellow injured fighters in hospitals (Awan, 2017). This is particularly useful for recruitment, as it conveys to potential recruits that ISIS is truly dedicated to state-building, providing for its citizens, and providing the means to live a true Islamic life.

ISIS employs several different techniques to contact potential recruits and broadcast their messages. What sets ISIS apart in its ability to recruit is the level of thought that is put into emotionally manipulating potential candidates. Berger argues that their internet interaction is best explained as a five-part template, which includes discovery, creating a micro-community, isolation, shifting to private communication, and identifying and encouraging action (Berger, 2015). Essentially, ISIS locates a potential recruit or vice versa, then ISIS supporters surround them with social input and encourage the recruit to cut ties with families, friends and local religious communities. Next, ISIS supporters shift their communication to private platforms to probe the target to find what they are most likely to do and encourages that action. This process can be implemented in a variety of ways depending on the individual's assets and interests. Prior to the fifth step, action, ISIS must be able to effectively communicate with and influence potential recruits.

Al Qaeda and ISIS have operationalized the internet in different ways, thus yielding different results. As is evident, Al Qaeda has largely relied on the internet as a library or database, while ISIS has primarily utilized the internet to recruit members to its ranks. These two facts have different implications. First, this analysis shows how Al Qaeda has failed to use the internet to its best interest which further demonstrates that there is definitely a generational gap between the two terrorist organizations. Second, it shows that ISIS is indeed comprised of younger generations that are capable of generating a higher international impact in terms of foreign recruitment. In a sense, this increases the resilience of ISIS over that of Al Qaeda. As ISIS loses territory, it may be able to regroup inward in the virtual world, as key figures remain in hiding planning the next possible location for territorial gain, while adapting to new developments in their strategy. It has been projected that ISIS will decentralize and establish logistical and operational sanctuaries in rural areas or on the outskirts of Iraq and Syria (Speckhard, Yayla & Shajkocvi, 2016). With the application and integration of the internet within ISIS, the organization may prove impossible to completely defeat.

11.4 CONCLUDING REMARKS: TERRORISTS AND THE INTERNET

Terrorists use the internet at different levels for vastly different reasons. It is important to understand that there are different types of terrorists who are using the internet for their cause. There are jihobbyists who practice Islam to the most extreme degree and use the internet to debate in forums. There are jihadis who use the internet to search for manuals on bomb making. There are also terrorist organizations who use the internet for anything from recruitment to taking care of financial needs. Thus, the internet is accessed by individual terrorists and terrorist organizations and this distinction is necessary in order to best understand how the internet is ultimately operationalized.

The internet can be used strategically, tactically, and operationally by terrorists and terrorist organizations. The different levels of analysis do not necessarily mean that all three are being utilized simultaneously. An individual terrorist might be utilizing the internet tactically to access extremist material but may never manifest themselves at the operational level. Activities at the operational level are the most extreme and the most dangerous. There could also be an individual terrorist using the internet strategically or tactically who is part of an established terrorist organization and using the information from said individual operationally. The take-away here is that there is no specific pattern that is applicable to all forms of terrorism, be it individual or group.

11.5 SUMMARY

This chapter provides an in-depth analysis of terrorist cases on the internet. The chapter is divided into four sections. Section one provides an introduction to the topic. Section two provides a conceptualization for how terrorists use the internet. This is divided into three levels of analysis: strategic, tactical, and operational. Strategic level considers why using the internet makes most sense, the tactical level explains what terrorists use the internet for, and the operational level explains how the internet is used in practice. In the operational level there are case studies of individuals who have used the internet for purposes related to terrorism, such as Roshonara Choudhry, Boston bombers Tamerlan and Dzhokhar Tsarnaev, Mohammad Youssef Abdulazeez, and the 9/11 hijackers. In this section there is also an analysis of content available on the internet related to terrorism and how accessible this content is. This focuses on the concept of jihobbyists while highlighting the fact that using the internet makes sharing terrorist content on the internet easier than ever before. The third section introduced the concept of e-jihad, explaining its evolution and how different terrorist organizations have embodied this over time. The primary focus of this section is an analysis of internet usage by Al Qaeda and the Islamic State of Iraq and Syria. The two terrorist organizations have used the internet in both similar and different ways so analyzing this provides results useful to policy-makers involved in counterterrorism. The fourth section offers concluding remarks regarding terrorism and the internet. Weaved throughout the chapter is a discussion of online radicalization and social media. This matters given the rise of using social media, especially by the Islamic State of Iraq and Syria, in recruiting foreign fighters online. Examining the different ways that terrorists have used the internet can generate useful counterterrorism policy in the future.

REFERENCES

Atwan, A. B. (2015). *Islamic State: The Digital Caliphate*. Oakland, CA: University of California Press.

Awan, I. (2017). Cyber-Extremism: Isis and the Power of Social Media. *Social Science and Public Policy, 54*(2), 138–149.

Berger, J. (2015, November 9). How Terrorists Recruit Online (and How to Stop It). Retrieved from Brookings Institute: https://www.brookings.edu/blog/markaz/2015/11/09/how-terrorists-recruit-online-and-how-to-stop-it/

Brachman, J. M. (2006). High-Tech Terror: Al-Qaeda's Use of New Technology. *Fletcher Forum World Affairs, 30*(2), 149–164.

Brachman, J. M. (2009). *Global Jihadism: Theory and Practice*. Abingdon, UK: Routledge.

Bradbury, S. (2016, June 30). *Chattanooga Times Free Press*. Retrieved from FBI: People knew July 16 shooter was radicalized, failed to alert authorities: http://www.timesfreepress.com/news/local/story/2016/jun/30/people-knew-july-16-shooter-was-radicalized-failed-alert-fbi/373796/

Brantly, A. (2017). Innovation and Adaptation in Jihadist Digital Security. *Survival, 59*(1), 29–102.

Bunt, G. R. (2003). *Islam in the Digital Age: E-jihad, Online Fatwas and Cyber Islamic Environments*. London: Pluto Press.

Chaffey, D., Mayer, R., Johnston, K., & Ellis-Chadwick, F. (2000). *Internet Marketing*. Harlow, UK: Pearson Education Limited.

Cohen-Almagor, R. (2012). In Internet's Way: Radical, Terrorist Islamists on the Free Highway. *International Journal of Cyber Warfare and Terrorism, 2*(3), 39–58.

Conway, M. (2006). Terrorism and the Internet: New Media--New Threat? *Parliamentary Affairs, 59*(2), 283–298.

Ford, B., & Siemaszko, C. (2015, March 24). *NY Daily News*. Retrieved from Dzhokhar Tsarnaev was 'radicalized' by Anwar al-Awlaki, and visited shooting range month before Boston Marathon bombing: http://www.nydailynews.com/news/crime/dzhokhar-tsarnaev-radicalized-anwar-al-awlaki-expert-article-1.2160612

Gill, P., Corner, E., Conway, M., Thornton, A., Bloom, M., & Horgan, J. (2017). Terrorist Use of the Internet by the Numbers: Quantifying Behaviors, Patterns, and Processes. *Criminology and Public Policy, 16*(1), 99–117.

Greenberg, K. J. (2016). Counter-Radicalization via the Internet. *The Annals of the American Acadamy of Political and Social Science, 668*(1), 165–179.

Griffin, D. (2012, December 9). Revolution Muslim leader changes tune. Retrieved from CNN News: http://www.cnn.com/2010/US/12/09/revolution.muslim.founder/index.html

Hegghammer, T. (2010). *Jihad in Saudi Arabia: Violence and Pan-Islamism Since 1979*. Cambridge: Cambridge University Press.

Monaci, S. (2017). Explaining the Islamic State's Online Media Strategy: A Transmedia Approach. *International Journal of Communication, 11*, 2842–2860.

Mozes, T., & Weimann, G. (2010). The E-Marketing Strategy of Hamas. *Studies in Conflict and Terrorism, 33*(2), 211–225.

O'Neill, A. (2015, March 30). CNN. Retrieved from The 13th Juror: The radicalization of Dzhokhar Tsarnaev: https://www.cnn.com/2015/03/27/us/tsarnaev-13th-juror-jahar-radicalization/index.html

Paz, R. (2013). *Global Salafism: Islam's Newest Religious Movement* (R. Meijer, Ed.). New York: Oxford University Press, Inc.

Pearson, E. (2016). The Case of Roshonara Choudhry: Implications for Theory in Online Radicalization, ISIS, and the Gendered Jihad. *Policy and Internet, 8*(1), 5–33.

Rosenbaum, S. (2016, August 15). ISIS Fighters Are Using 'Islam for Dummies' to Prepare for Jihad. Retrieved from New York Post: https://nypost.com/2016/08/15/isis-fighters-are-using-islam-for-dummies-to-prepare-for-jihad/

Sageman, M. (2008). *Leaderless Jihad*. Philadelphia, PA: University of Pennsylvania Press.

Speckhard, A., Yayla, A. S., & Shajkocvi, A. (2016). Defeating ISIS on the Battle Ground as Well as in the Online Battle Space: Considerations of the "New Normal" and Available Online Weapons in the Struggle Ahead. *Journal of Strategic Studies, 9*(4), 1–10.

Stenersen, A. (2008). The Internet: A Virtual Training Camp? *Terrorism and Political Violence, 20*(2), 215–233.

Weimann, G. (2004, March). United States Institute of Peace Special Report. Retrieved from www.terror.net How Modern Terrorism Uses the Internet: https://www.usip.org/sites/default/files/sr116.pdf

Wojtasik, K. (2017). How and Why Do Terrorist Organizations Use the Internet? *Polish Political Science Yearbook, 46*(2), 105–117.

Chapter 12

Terrorism Recruitment and Radicalization into the 21st Century

James M. Smith[1] and Maeghin Alarid

CONTENTS

12.1 INTRODUCTION

Most of the studies of online recruitment and radicalization focus on the operational, technical, and media aspects of contemporary terrorist online propaganda, recruitment, and radicalization. The purpose of this chapter is to provide a context against which the reader can better frame that coverage. This chapter provides a brief summary of the historical and conceptual development of terrorism recruitment trends and radicalization models as they have developed over the 20th and into the 21st centuries.

This coverage begins with a brief review of how terrorists and their recruitment and radicalization have developed across the last century and into the early part of this century. Too often observers begin their coverage at 9/11. In fact, the terrorism of 9/11 represented a specific development that fundamentally informs both that act and the development that followed, but without historical context, many contemporary observations may be incomplete or even misdirected. The focus on modern terrorism history includes recruitment and radicalization as it was built, layer upon layer, to its early 21st-century model. Then the chapter shifts into contemporary adaptations, specifically to messages, audiences, and media, built upon the past, to represent the range of recruitment and radicalization that we see today. Specific examples will be used where applicable.

12.2 FOUNDATIONS: TRADITIONAL RECRUITMENT AND RADICALIZATION MODEL

Modern terrorism has developed in four phases since the late 19th century. David Rapoport calls these "waves" [5], and another strategic observer, Bruce Hoffman, treats them as evolutionary stages [4]. The first phase was internal, within the individual state, and focused on initial efforts to build toward a revolution to overthrow oppressive rulers—revolutionary, anti-monarchial terror. This was followed, primarily after World War I and with another input after World War II, with violence focused on ridding colonial territories of their external masters and gaining independence—anti-colonial, ethno-nationalist terror. The third phase was inspired by the Viet Cong attacks against U.S. forces during Tet 1968, and is characterized by Rapoport as a "New Left" wave, and by Hoffman as the internationalization of terrorism. Near-real time media and residual anti-colonial, anti-imperialism sentiments gave rise to communication and cooperation, and to anti-colonial groups modeling each other across several world regions. Finally, with the "failure" of the United States' efforts in Vietnam, and particularly the dual-impetus of the Soviet invasion of Afghanistan and the fall of the Shah in Iran, the fourth phase, that of religious terrorism, was born.

12.2.1 Historical Development of Recruitment and Radicalization

The first, anti-monarchy and separatism phase was characterized by small, local cells within an overall hierarchical structure. Recruitment was top-down, largely face-to-face, and radicalization occurred within the cell as an internal result of socialization, training, and indoctrination. The impetus to join and act came from a combination of the nature of the terrorism of the day—propaganda of the deed (the act and its violence conveying the group's message)—and the nature of the grievance against the monarch.

The second, anti-colonial, ethno-nationalist phase, which combined both urban and rural small-cell structures situated in a hierarchy, continued top-down recruitment and cell-dynamics radicalization, and it better illustrates the traditional mobilization to terrorism common to both of the first two phases. The traditional explanation centers on environmental drivers—"ethnic conflicts, religious and ideological conflicts, poverty, modernization stresses, political inequities, lack of peaceful communications channels, traditions of violence, the existence of a revolutionary group, governmental weakness and ineptness, erosions of confidence in a regime, and deep divisions within governing elites and leadership groups" [16]—that lead to deep divides and intense anger within a victim class.

The basic model holds that an individual or a segment of a population perceives an intense inequity coupled with a failure of the existing governing structure to address that inequity, perhaps even to be seen as the source of the inequity. In addition, those perceiving the inequity observe that they are the victims of this condition while another segment of society is not subject to this condition, and may be the cause of the condition. The second major factor, in addition to this disadvantage, is identity—the afflicted group is identifiable as different from the advantaged group or class by a definable identity such as ethnicity, race, religion, nationality, language, gender, etc. A classical "us–them" dichotomy moves to the center of the worldview of this identity-defined class, and as the level of anger intensifies (to rage), these individuals seek an outlet for that emotion. If there is a guide and a destination for that rage—an "identity entrepreneur" to act as a guide and an organized opposition to receive and channel that emotion—then recruitment and the foundations for radicalization result [21].

The identity component received a major boost with World War II. Singapore does not always receive primary focus in Western history texts, but that battle where a regional, non-Western force

(Japan) defeated a major Western power (Great Britain) and gave impetus to a legacy of active anti-colonialism as the West returned to reclaim their colonial empires after the war. In addition, native forces in many of these colonial states received military assistance and training during the war in return for fighting against the Axis forces. This now-activated ethno-nationalism, bolstered by the confidence of military experience, spawned demands for independence and an end to colonialism. These rebellions took the form of terrorism, insurgency, and in some cases major armed conflict. Of particular note were the successes of the Israelis in Palestine, the Algerians, and the stalemated "victory" of the Cypriots. These three movements each saw internal structures that featured separate "political" and "military" wings, allowing a separation to encourage negotiated political settlements simultaneously with ongoing military operations. And the strongest anti-Western military operations were timed and staged to provide major propaganda locally, in New York to coincide with relevant United Nations sessions, and in Western target capitals. As a final note, the method of combined strategic communications via negotiations along with targeted and timed propaganda of the deed, was observed directly by outsiders who would later lead such groups as the Palestine Liberation Organization (PLO) and the African National Congress (ANC).

The traditional mobilization to terrorism model reached its high point in the third, New Left or international phase of terrorism development. The Tet offensive of 1968 was the start of this phase, followed by the Palestinian attack on the Israeli Olympic team at Munich in 1972. From these was born the internationalization of terrorism with the Palestinian cause provoking attacks across the Mediterranean and Europe, and the Irish Republicans setting off bombs in London. Development here saw Marxism-Leninism as an overlay on ethnic and nationalist causes. Religion was a factor, with Muslim Palestinians and Irish Catholics forming the PLO and Irish Republican Army (IRA); however, nationalism tinged with new-left politics took the lead. Notable here was extensive cooperation among groups—PLO arms supplied to the IRA, Japanese Red Army members trained with the PLO in Lebanon, and even PLO proxies carrying out attacks such as that on Lod Airport in Israel. This phase also saw the staging of attacks – target and tactics selection—to ensure and maximize international media coverage. The Munich Olympics attack was televised live around the world, and airliners were hijacked as media events. Real-time propaganda on a global scale was now a central factor emphasizing grievances and triggering identity; it became the heart of terrorism planning and recruitment outreach as terrorism entered the television age. Active terrorists still were drawn in a top-down process from the local ethno-national community, but supporters were attracted from diaspora communities and sympathizers more broadly.

The trigger events for the contemporary phase of terrorism, the religious phase, in the wake of the United States withdrawal from Vietnam were the Iranian Revolution and the Soviet incursion into Afghanistan, both in 1979 and both having a distinctly Islamic dimension. Note, however, that this phase also has seen radicalized Jewish and Christian terror, as well as Japanese and other regional and national religion-inspired violence. Elements of ethno-nationalism remain key, but now the underlying religious identity component rises to become the co-equal or in many cases the superior driver.

Defining characteristics of this fourth, or "New Terrorism" phase, include the willingness to impose mass casualties and the willingness to die for the cause. The local character of terrorism during the anti-monarchy, the anti-colonial, and even the new-left phases meant that the violence was actually constrained and fairly narrowly targeted. When one is fighting ultimately for control of a locality, even a nation, destroying that territory and especially killing widely, including one's own base population, are to be avoided. Yes, there was a "them" population that could and was targeted, but because of the desire to avoid widespread damage and to avoid casualties among wider groups, the violence was limited. Now, with a "divinely inspired" motivation on a regional or even global stage, larger casualty numbers and greater damage became the rule. And with that violence now seen as a sacramental act, suicide attacks became more prevalent as well.

This phase also saw a major flattening of organizational structures to match the new internationalism of the era. With globalization in business, the same held true for terrorism. Particularly for Afghanistan, rather than diaspora support to a local group, we saw global Islamic migration to fight for the religious, rather than the national, cause: the Mujahedin. Terror became a function of networks, and ultimately of movements as opposed to traditional groups. And even pre-existing groups took on a networked form and eventually a virtual more than physical form. Recruitment combined local top-down efforts as well as global acceptance of "seekers," or those who sought out the groups and action. The traditional model has adapted to a new form, with self and small-group largely autonomous recruitment, and a guided radicalization process (see Figure 12.1).

Sageman Western Radicalization	Silber & Bhatt Radicalization Process	Hafez & Mullins Radicalization Puzzle
Prong 1 Sense of Moral Outrage: Pre-2003 Bosnia, Chechnya, Palestine, Kashmir Post-2003 Iraq, Abu Ghraib, GITMO	**Stage 1 Pre-Radicalization:** "Unremarkable," "ordinary" citizens (male with women primarily in support roles, under age 35, middle class, often 2nd/3rd generation, educated, often recent converts/not particularly devout, little if any criminal history)	**Grievances:** Economic marginalization, cultural alienation, deep sense of victimization; personal disaffection, loss, crisis
Prong 2 Specific Interpretation of the World: Identity politics; "War against Islam" internalized; warriors, Mujahedin for the cause	**Stage 2 Self-Identification:** Religious seeking, often with catalyst (economic, social, political, personal crisis) and a trusted social network; facilitated through "incubators" (cafes, prisons, student associations, book stores, social clubs, increasingly the internet); gravitation toward Salafi Islam, regular attendance at a Salafi mosque	**Networks:** Pre-existing kinship and friendship ties, existing opportunities for socialization with radicals, meaningful relationships and quest for significance, ideological encapsulation
Prong 3 Resonance with Personal Experience: Relevant social, economic, political, religious framing; identity transformation	**Stage 3 Indoctrination:** Intensification of beliefs toward action; often facilitated through the guidance of a "spiritual sanctioner;" withdrawal from mosque a recurrent theme, replaced with like-minded "band of brothers"; politicization of beliefs completes identity transformation	**Ideology:** Master narratives, framing personal and collective grievances, demonize enemies, justify violence, and incentivize sacrifice
Prong 4 Mobilization through Networks: Past: face-to-face networks, social dynamics Now: virtual networks as "invisible hand" Today radicalization of younger recruits, more women	**Stage 4 Jihadization:** Action planning, preparation, and execution; small group dynamics/ groupthink common; accepting jihad, traveling abroad for training, participation in "outward bound" like activities; connection with operational planner/internet planning resources	**Enabling Environments and Support Structures:** Physical and virtual settings (Internet, social media, prisons, foreign training camps) that provide ideological and material aid while deepening commitment

Figure 12.1   The Contemporary Radicalization Model [11, 13, 14].

12.2.2 Contemporary Radicalization Model

Religion-inspired groups include those like Hezbollah that while it initially attacked French, American, and Israeli targets, operated in and from Lebanon. Another example is Aum Shinrikyo, which had a multinational business and religious presence but operated inside Japan. These nationally based groups still largely followed the traditional recruitment and radicalization model as it came through from the ethno-nationalist terrorism phase, but now with religious identity at the center. In addition to the nationally focused groups, the Soviet incursion into Muslim Afghanistan energized significant international opposition, and this "attack against an Islamic state" brought many Islamic fighters, the Mujahedin, to Afghanistan to join the fight. Here that religious identity now revolved around more extremist interpretations of Islam gained from the leadership of the Afghanistan anti-Soviet opposition and from the Taliban, and the phase also gave rise to what was to become the premier international terrorist group of its day, Al Qaeda (AQ).

After the Soviet withdrawal, most of these fighters returned home from Afghanistan. As AQ was formed, the former Mujahedin were urged to take the fight home to turn more extremist Islam against entrenched, more traditional Islamic regimes—the "near" enemy. At the same time, some of the Mujahedin were urged to remain with AQ and turn to the fight against the United States and its closest Western allies—the "far" enemy that propped up and protected target regimes in Saudi Arabia and Israel. For this fight, the "local" recruitment base became Muslims worldwide, the nation of Islam, with some particular emphasis on Muslims already in the West. The diaspora was no longer only targeted for support, but also for mainstream fighters. And with the expanded Western fight against Islamic states such as Iraq, recruitment became a function of the activation of individual Islamic identity.

> Terrorism … is the ultimate personal choice. The reasons someone picks up a gun or throws a bomb represent an ineluctably deeply idiosyncratic decision born variously of grievance and frustration; religious piety, the desire for systemic socioeconomic change; irredentist conviction; or commitment to some utopian or millenarian ideal. Joining an organization in pursuit of these aims is meant to give collective meaning, and equally important, cumulative power, to this commitment. The forces that impel individuals to become terrorists are thus timeless. And perhaps most significant, they defy broad generalizations predicated on poverty, illiteracy, relative deprivation, or other socio-economic and demographic factors that purport to explain what drives individual men and women into this realm of political violence [4].

With recruitment now a function of activated Islamic identity, Figure 12.1 summarizes this contemporary fused recruitment and radicalization model. The chart summarizes the works of Marc Sageman [11], a former Intelligence Community psychiatrist, Mitchell Silber and Arvin Bhatt of the New York Police Department's Intelligence Division [13], and Mohammed Hafez and Creighton Mullins of the Naval Postgraduate School [14]. Sageman plus Silber and Bhatt offer their analyses of radicalization in the West, and Hafez and Mullins offer an academic synthesis of a considerable body of analysis of this topic. We use Silber and Bhatt for development here due to their structured process presentation, with the compatible detail of Sageman and of Hafez and Mullins to reinforce the key components. Silber and Bhatt present a four-stage process model of recruitment and radicalization in the West: pre-radicalization, self-identification, indoctrination, and jihadization.

The remarkable thing about Silber and Bhatt's pre-radicalization stage is that the focus is on an "unremarkable" demographic [13]. This target group within the Western diaspora is generally male (although even by 2007 seeing an increase in women), under age 35, often second- or third-generation immigrants, middle class, educated, often recent converts to Islam and not particularly devout, little criminal history; to a profiler, unremarkable. However, events in their personal lives and/or particular attention to a global description of Islamic conflict situations such as the Western "War on Islam" prompt a search for meaning framed within their newly activated Islamic identity.

This self-initiated search for identity—seeking—characterizes the self-identification stage. Here there is a distinct facilitation role for "incubators" such as prisons, student and youth associations, social or athletic clubs, and increasingly the internet and social media. A few of the Madrid train bombers were in prison together, the 1993 World Trade Center bombing group frequented an Islamic youth association, the London Tube bombers were members of a martial arts club, and the Fort Hood shooter engaged in email exchanges with an AQ cleric. Attendance at a mosque with a militant cleric is common here as the individual both learns more about this thread of Islam and more closely identifies with it.

As identity deepens, self-identification blends into radicalization. Three central themes here are the role of a sanctioner, a network, and politicalization. The spiritual sanctioner, earlier labelled an "identity entrepreneur" [21], plays a central guidance role particularly in the transition from self-identification and across radicalization. Often a radicalized cleric, the sanctioner guides the individual or group deeper into the ideological dimensions of religion and the radical life. The mosque is left behind, and the group, the network, becomes the organizing vehicle. The small group is an important component of this transformation. In some cases the group predates the process (several of the Madrid train bombers were lifelong friends from the same neighborhood in North Africa), and in other cases the group forms during the first two stages (1993 World Trade Center, London Tube bombers), but this "band of brothers" provides the core network, reinforcement, and even motivation for radicalization. The personal loyalties and relationships are seen as more important than the ideology in guiding the journey to embrace the fully politicized core driver of violent action. Terrorist violence is ultimately a political act, and that is the final outcome of radicalization.

The final stage, jihadization, takes the radicalized individual or group through to violent action. Radicalization produces the willingness to act, but that action still requires operational knowledge and skills. The jihadization stage traditionally saw a member or members of the group traveling to Southwest Asia for training. Operations planning, bomb making, and arms training are not readily available in much of the West. Small group and physical training are available through "outward bound" type activities which were sometimes pursued by groups. And both print and online instructions are available for bomb making and action planning.

Sageman's four prongs of radicalization reinforce the first three stages of the Silber and Bhatt model [11]. He notes that conflicts involving Islamic countries and populations drove the early sense of outrage that sparked the search leading to self-identification through Islamic identity. After the US invasion of Iraq in 2003, he notes the central role of Abu Ghraib and Guantanamo in becoming and enhancing that driver. The identity search often leads to his second prong with the resulting Islamic identity taking on heroic proportions as a warrior for the cause, underscored by his third prong, completing the identity transformation by framing the new identity in blended personal and ideological terms. And his fourth prong further underscores the network dimension, highlighting the role today of virtual networks and their function as the new identity entrepreneurs to an expanding and shifting audience.

Hafez and Mullins' synthesis further reinforces Silber and Bhatt across all four stages [14]. They reach back to the traditional model and its continuing influence, at least in the East, by emphasizing environmental drivers leading to feelings of victimization, alienation, and loss. They also remind us that personal crises are often proximate drivers for seeking a clearer identity. They too reinforce the centrality of the network, including significant relationships with those previously radicalized and a deeper exposure to ideological influences. Later that ideological influence can play a critical role in advancing radicalization by justifying violence and incentivizing sacrifice. And they also further underline the roles of incubators, especially Virtual incubators such as the internet and social media, through to the operational planning inputs.

Two final points need to be made on this contemporary radicalization model. First, the stages are all present in the cases studied by Silber and Bhatt, but they were not necessarily followed in the order indicated. All four were present, but might be simultaneous or the order altered in individual cases. The second, and perhaps more important point, is that the process can be compared to a funnel. Many enter with some level of seeking, but only the very few exit as fully jihadized terrorists who participate in extreme violent action. But note that the larger group of those who progress into radicalization often serve as active supporters, part of the active base, for terrorist groups and actions.

12.2.3 Boston Marathon Case

This adapted and still evolving contemporary model was clearly illustrated in the case of the Tsarnaev brothers, the Boston Marathon bombers. In this case, the older brother, Tamerlan Tsarnaev, best fits the process model, while the younger brother, Dzhokhar, represents the role of the networked follower.

The Tsarnaev brothers were from an ethnic Chechen family that under Soviet and Russian rule lived in Kyrgyzstan and Dagestan. The main family came to the United States in 2002, settling in the Boston area, and Tamerlan joined them in 2004 (aged 17). He attended some high school here, but was unsuccessful in gaining admission to university. He did attend community college intermittently for a couple of years, but ultimately dropped out to become a boxer. As this career was also proving unsuccessful, he reportedly became interested in Islam in 2008 at age 21–22. Police reports indicate that he became active in a local fundamentalist mosque about that time, and that he became a follower of the online teachings of the Yemen-based American Anwar al-Awlaki, the English language voice of Al Qaeda in the Arabian Peninsula (AQAP). In 2012 he traveled back to Russia for some time and reportedly completed his radicalization during that visit. When he returned to Boston, he reportedly challenged mosque teachings from a more radical perspective, and he was asked to leave the mosque. He completed his operational training by following pressure-cooker bomb instructions published in the AQAP magazine *Inspire*, and during the April 2013 running of the Boston Marathon, he and his brother detonated two of these bombs, killing three and injuring well over 200 people [12].

Tamerlan Tsarnaev, unable to find success in this new land, sought a new identity and found, in his heritage and his past, a new identity in Chechen Islam. Under at least some guidance and inspiration from al-Awlaki and AQAP online, and a visit back to radicalized influences in southern Russia, he completed radicalization and also gained sufficient technical and operational knowledge to act. His younger brother, who was also exposed to some of the online influences and was a loyal follower of his older brother, joined the cause. The Silber and Bhatt model as reinforced by Sageman and Hafez and Mullins applies very well to this case and to others that are in today's headlines throughout the West.

12.3 RADICALIZATION TODAY

Online resources have lately been key in the pre-radicalization search, self-identification identity, deeper exposure for indoctrination, and operational training as well. The internet was advanced specifically for facilitating this process by AQ, particularly AQAP, and that base has been further advanced by the Islamic State of Iraq and the Levant (ISIL). The target today is individuals in the West, particularly young men and women, with multiple online media employed to tailor the appeal to multiple demographic target groups. Face-to-face recruitment and physical identity entrepreneurship have given way to virtual incubation and radicalization: "[T]he radicalization process that characterizes contemporary terrorism is arguably both more immediate and less intimate" [4].

12.3.1 ISIL versus AQ Targeting: Women and Youth

One of the challenges in the fight against today's terrorism is navigating the recruitment and radicalization conduct on the Dark Web. While this is certainly an area that promotes extremist chatrooms and overt recruitment, the majority of recruitment and radicalization that takes place online has been through the mainstream internet. Finding a solution to online terrorist recruitment remains a growing and elusive challenge to international security. To fully comprehend the trends, it is critical to start with an understanding of *why* these networks are using online methods, and *who* they are targeting online with specific examples of how terrorist groups target women and youth. Online recruitment of young, Western women has proven to be anything but a fleeting phenomenon. ISIL has been very successful at gaining the sympathy and trust of many women, youth, and segments of the diaspora population in particular. They have succeeded where Al Qaeda has failed, so we have to ask ourselves why that has been the case. It is also important to recognize why these very segments of the population the terrorists target for recruitment can also play a crucial role in stopping the spread of the terrorist message.

The concept of women within terrorist groups is not a new concern, but the role of women within such groups is under-analyzed, has evolved, and is still evolving. Women's roles in terrorism are shifting from being on the sidelines to becoming key players. Not only have their roles continued to evolve, but methods to recruit them have as well. ISIL, as opposed to other terrorist organizations, has been particularly successful at recruiting young, Western women.

Why are we faced with a "new beast" when it comes to tactics by ISIL as opposed to AQ and other terrorist groups?

ISIL began as a branch of AQ, but the two groups have taken very different directions in terms of messaging and tactics. ISIL has been extremely effective at adapting and changing their military maneuvers and public message depending on how the United States and allies have responded. Their vision of establishing a caliphate and romanticizing the apocalypse has been extremely persuasive and attractive to young people in particular, and we have been caught off guard by how this vision has resonated with many internationally.

One example of how this group has evolved their tactics is that they are no longer encouraging their recruits to travel to Syria and Iraq to fight. They are now emphasizing that their followers attack at home, wherever they may be. This means that even as the group loses ground in the Middle East, they will continue to have a voice online and we will continue to see homegrown attacks inspired by ISIL. The effort has switched from the physical caliphate to a virtual domain.

In order to successfully stop an opponent, we must first understand that opponent. In order to understand them, we must understand the messages they are spreading. The ISIL message is vastly different than the AQ message in terms of promises and incentives to their recruits, and these incentives are precisely what appeal to the younger generation—and also to women.

AQ's message to its recruits has been that of the importance of religious righteousness and piety. Initially, their leaders lived isolated and in remote caves and camps, and there was no place for women within the ranks.

ISIL's message to recruits is also that they will fulfill their religious duty, but the appeal has been promises of adventure, power, and the opportunity to fight on the battlefield [3]. It provides women to male recruits, and place great stress on providing community and meaning to life. ISIL has also targeted many of their recruitment efforts specifically toward women, including their online magazine, *Dabiq*, which offers sections speaking to "sisters of the Islamic State." These magazines are quite prevalent and influence homegrown attacks. These magazines not only inspire new attacks but warn against past attack methods that were unsuccessful. AQ started their online magazine, *Inspire*, back in 2010. We know these magazines are having the terror groups' desired effects. Several articles, for example, highlight using vehicles to drive through crowds and mow people over. We have seen several recent and increasing instances of these types of attacks around the world.

The underlying message that ISIL emphasizes over AQ has been to provide instant gratification and power that is alluring to Western recruits and is prevalent throughout American and European cultures. ISIL also preys on the misfortunes of others and emphasizes regions of the world where people face dire living conditions such as lack of clean water, no access to jobs or education, extreme poverty, disease, and corrupt governments; in the East this population is the most susceptible to the rise in radicalization. When there is no access to jobs, and fathers have to leave to seek work outside their communities, this not only disrupts the economic conditions of a community, but leaves families torn apart. Mothers are left to raise their children alone. ISIL knows teenage sons can become angry, resentful, and at risk of running off to join terrorist groups.

It is imperative to examine specifically how ISIL has been so successful at the recruitment of women. Muslim women in the West face the challenges of conforming to traditional roles of Islam, and yet they are immersed in Western culture on a daily basis including Western messages of individualism and freedom for women. This can make women feel ostracized from both cultures and thus "lost" and searching for acceptance and belonging.

A recent "Modern Love Podcast" captured this dichotomy in a discussion centered on a Somali proverb that says "A woman should be either married or in her grave" [15]. The podcast went on to say that throughout the Horn of Africa, the proverb might as well further state that "if she is married; she had better be pregnant, nursing or postmenopausal" [15]. Western Muslim women who grow up in the shadow of this mindset and who do not see much of a future for themselves outside of getting married and having children are especially vulnerable. They may feel trapped in a traditional role but also see women all around them with freedoms that evade them. The lure of adventure and a greater purpose can draw them to groups such as ISIL. Researchers have seen time and again that men and women of a young age that are drawn to ISIL are searching for identity and meaning in their life. Those of a young age tend to be extremely vulnerable to persuasion and group influence.

The reasons why women want to join terrorist groups such as ISIL vary. Some women join because they strongly believe in the utopian Islamic caliphate and want to raise their children in this environment. Some women have experienced a traumatic event and want a life with purpose and dignity that they feel joining the Islamic State will provide. ISIL knows recruitment of women is vital for the longevity of the organization. They focus efforts on recruiting women for many reasons, including the following:

- Leveraging their citizenship status. Second generation women in the West can evade security easily because they may not be seen as a threat by the wider public; also, by using this segment of the population (mothers, sisters, daughters, wives, youth), terrorist groups can make the general public feel as if terrorists are "all around them" and that "no one is safe."
- Women can also provoke or shame men into action and becoming jihadists.
- ISIL uses women to reach out to other women in order to successfully recruit.
- Women are also vital to the group so they can marry, have children, and raise the next generation of fighters.

Women within ISIL act as supporters, facilitators, and recruiters. We have seen women used as suicide bombers by many terrorist groups, including many recent attacks by Boko Haram – horrifyingly—using the young girls that they captured as suicide bombers. Women's roles can evolve over time. This raises the question of how will they be used next?

The other segment of the population that ISIL has focused on recruiting is the diaspora and specifically the youth population. Diaspora populations often identify with the country in which they were born, rather than the nation in which they live. This segment of the population can be vulnerable to radicalization due to this allegiance to their country of birth and not their local community. Some of the homegrown terrorist attacks that we have seen have been by individuals that are of a minority segment of a local population and have struggled to find their place in their communities. Many researchers that focus on the topic of both male and female youth radicalization stress the emotions of feeling left out, shunned, and ignored in their local community—this all contributes to their vulnerability toward recruitment and radicalization. The desires teenagers feel to belong to a group are universal desires. Terror groups (ISIL, in particular) know this, and prey on it. We know it too, and should use this in our counter-recruitment efforts. Both AQ and ISIL magazines are printed in many languages, including English, and many of their postings online are in English, simply because they are reaching out to the diasporic population of Muslims in the West, primarily the younger generation that goes online on a regular basis. They know many of these young people do not speak Arabic and often are not devoutly religious. They do not care. They are not calling for older, seasoned fighters. They are calling for younger, second generation, English-speaking individuals—those living in the West for a variety of reasons:

- They want young people to join in order to grow their ranks and have a lasting impact and influence.
- They want to grow their ranks by recruiting young women.
- Using online methods attracts younger people. Using online methods also gains sympathizers and gets their message out to a broad audience.
- Homegrown terrorists are the way of the future for the group. There is no travel required, and they can hit the enemy at home where it hurts and in their own backyard as has been the way of life in the Middle East for so long. They use young men and women that law enforcement may be less likely to suspect and can make terror groups appear to be invincible.

- ISIL can be alluring to a diaspora population where their local government is unable to provide basic resources, access to jobs, education, and protection. ISIL promises all these things to those that join their group in Syria.
- Youth from diaspora populations are extremely vulnerable to recruitment and radicalization especially if they feel disconnected from the country and community in which they live.
- Countries with large diaspora populations and those with strict laws seen as prohibiting expression of religion (France for example) have a greater risk of that community being angry, prone to radicalization, feelings of resentment toward government, lack of acceptance by local community, and a surge in violence.

Upon examination of how terrorist groups utilize the internet for recruitment purposes, it becomes clear that this is a free, multi-purpose tool that they see as being entirely at their disposal. Online methods offer simple options for gathering sympathizers, offering connections, advice, and logistics for some recruits to travel abroad. All methods online offer immediate communication between individuals and groups without risking travel. The internet cloaks identities and allows for anonymity. Online communication and postings provide a voice for those that feel as if they are unheard in their society and community [10].

12.3.2 Initial Thoughts on Countering This Targeting

Much of the focus on countering terrorism falls to attacking the terrorists or parrying their tactics. However, one of the authors here has long advocated strategic responses to the terrorist leadership and the strategy behind its actions. In the case of social media and online recruitment and radicalization, this would point to a strategic communications effort to limit the effectiveness of the terrorist messaging, with that effort tailored to the same demographics targeted by the terrorists. This author proposed this strategic counter-narrative effort as one of a series of coercive efforts, one under the banner of "denial of legitimacy" and advanced at the strategic level, in the effort to deny weapons of mass destruction (WMD) terrorism. That effort would seek to invalidate the ideological/religious legitimacy of WMD employment while also emphasizing shared values between the target state and the terrorists to weaken the "us–them" divide and thus the argument for extreme action [7]. Alex Wilner goes a step further, developing a major strategic counter-terrorism thread of "delegitimization" that entails targeting terrorist beliefs and justifications, seeking to instill internal contradictions in ideological/religious narratives [1]. From this foundation, and for the purposes of this chapter and its focus, we suggest more direct strategies and efforts to counter the ISIL and AQ narratives described above.

One method that we can and should adopt in our attempts to curb the spread of the terrorist message online is through the use of inoculation theory. This theory aims to help people build resistance to persuasion and develop the ability to uphold their long-held beliefs. The method used in this theory is to "expose people to arguments against their beliefs and give them counter arguments to refute attacks" [7]. In a nutshell, it provides people with the tools to "argue back" and fend off those that wish to change the way they think. It is a way in which resistance to persuasion can be achieved. A classic example by social psychologists is instead of simply telling teenagers that smoking is bad, instead provide teenagers with words they can say to someone that approaches them and asks if they want a cigarette [8]. Preparing teenagers in advance and providing a counter-argument for when one approaches them to smoke, arms teenagers for greater resistance and results in greater success in turning down that cigarette. This theory can be used when countering ISIL's message online.

In order for inoculation theory to be successful against the ISIL message online, we must stay one step ahead with prepared counter-messages that refute their claims. One method used within inoculation theory that can help prepare against ISIL attack is to clearly lay out the threat of their message online. If a person "is aware of his/her vulnerability to a persuasive attack . . . this psychologically motivates a person to defend his beliefs and attitudes" [8]. In order to stop the spread of sympathizers to the ISIL message, we must empower more of the population with tools to see through the lies they spread about Islam. According to Dr. Stephan Lewandowsky, experimental psychologist at the University of Bristol, research shows that if people are provided with an alternative message, if they are skeptical of the source of the message, if they have suspicions about the motives of the original message, then the original message will hold less traction [18]. This should come into play and be used within a counter-narrative online. Our counter-narrative should include laying the groundwork for people to understand that ISIL's message online has suspicious motives. This will cause fewer people to buy into their message and become radicalized [7].

We cannot *just* counter the terrorist message; we have to have our own message and this message has to adhere to the following important factors:

- It must be easily accessible by a vast audience [10].
- The message must reach out specifically to women and young people [10]—we know youth are extremely susceptible to group influence and the need to belong. If we can get more youth to speak out against the terrorist message and speak directly to young people, this will have an impact. They will listen. In January 2017, an article from *Science Daily* discussed how national security efforts have not focused enough on why young people join terrorist groups and how the importance in their beliefs and what they see as valuable is imperative to this radicalization. This article also stresses that it is vital to focus on group dynamics as opposed to individual personalities when implementing counter-radicalization strategies and policies [22].
- We need to keep our message simple, and to the point, but carefully crafted and take cultural differences into consideration.

It is important to recognize that different cultures see things in different ways. We must ensure the intent of our message comes across accurately and is not perceived in unintended ways due to cultural disparities. We need to consider carefully what message we are putting out there. What are we saying versus what is being heard? Often, what we say and what is perceived may be totally different messages. ISIL has an emotionally strong message that resonates deeply with their young target population. Much research has shown that teenagers will react with emotion prior to reacting with logic and reason [2]. Our counter-argument must be emotionally driven as well in order to counter-balance the ISIL argument and resonate well with youth. The ISIL target audience is searching for meaning, self-identity, purpose, and acceptance. They have usually dealt with being an outsider and have a strong need to belong to a group. We have to meet these needs and more in our counter-argument. If we strip away ISIL legitimacy of their religious message, this will cause their support group to shrink. When the group loses credibility, they also lose sympathizers and recruits [10].

We must ask ourselves how we can specifically use women to assist with the counter-terrorism cause. The same target audience that terror groups are hoping to recruit—young, second generation, modern, women living in the West—can and should be used with de-radicalization efforts. Women can be used to promote positive messages online. Online social media can and should be used as a tool to prevent recruitment and radicalization. Women connect with other women in their surrounding community and can have a powerful voice in curtailing radicalization. Women are keen to know what is going on in their neighborhoods and inside their homes and can provide crucial feedback on counter-terrorism efforts in their community [10]. This knowledge can be used by agencies attempting to locate fighters that have returned from Syria as well as local radicalization efforts taking place. Women must hold a place at the table in terms of policy and decision making and make their voices heard. This includes women in local governments and is imperative to attaining lasting peace and stable security environments on the ground. How can enduring peace be achieved if half the population is left out of the peace-making process? Dr. Valerie Hudson, a professor at the Bush School of Government and Public Service at Texas A&M University, calls it a "gender blind spot in security and foreign policy studies [19]."

In order to stop the spread of online recruitment and radicalization, our efforts need to include a more effective means of monitoring online chatter, forums, postings, and videos. This is easier said than done and large social media companies are already cooperating with law enforcement and intelligence agencies to assist with monitoring posts on their services. This is a great first step, and hopefully we can find a faster means of monitoring and removing material that promotes terrorism online. The International Center for the Study of Violent Extremism recently published an article discussing the social media platform, Telegram. This is an ISIL-favored platform because it is an encrypted application where ISIL members can send messages to one another with little threat of law enforcement interference. This application was launched in 2013 by two brothers from Russia [9]. This particular platform does not remove terrorist-related content as quickly as Facebook, Twitter, and YouTube, stating that they protect free speech. The lack of removal of such content has allowed Telegram to become the current platform of choice by ISIL. We also need to expand and improve rehabilitation programs for defectors. In addition, women absolutely have to be included in counter-terrorism initiatives and strategies.

When studying this topic, we need to know what terrorists are targeting online—which sites, which audience, and for what purpose—because this constantly evolves. Terrorist attacks seem to have become so frequent worldwide that in order to gain international attention the terrorist groups adapt their tactics and increase brutality to make the news. What we have seen from observing terrorist tactics, is that these groups can have a failed terrorist attack and still succeed in their end game of inciting fear, terror, altering political elections, and gaining support for their cause. From previous actions by extremist Chechens, we have seen that just the threat of a dirty bomb in a city park can have the desired effect of making headlines and terrifying the general public. Terrorist groups constantly imitate one another. They observe which tactics are effective and which are not and evolve their own methods of attack. We can be sure that AQ is watching and learning from ISIL. We have seen recently that Osama bin Laden's son has started to become more vocal, as has AQAP. Will we see them increase their presence online? Will they begin to target young people and women for recruits? As recently as September 2017, AQ publicly called upon Muslims worldwide to defend the Rohingya minority population in Burma who are being persecuted and driven out of their home country. This was a call "to jihad similar to that of the Afghan War with the then-Soviet Union that set al-Qaeda's foundation" [20]. This call to arms is an attempt by AQ to be seen as "the one true defender of persecuted Muslims" and a bid for them to gain recruits [20]. Is history being set up to repeat itself once again?

12.4 LESSONS LEARNED AND WAY AHEAD

This chapter has presented the development of a traditional terrorist recruitment and radicalization model and its contemporary manifestation through AQ to ISIL. It has also presented some specific examples of its current application with "unremarkable" targets among a diaspora population seeking identity in today's world, with both human and virtual sanctioning, and increasingly virtual messaging now in use. That current application targets specifically youth and women with multiple media and tailored messaging, and the chapter also offered an approach and a few ideas on countering that messaging to begin to limit ISIL success.

One primary take-away from this analysis is that while still relatively small in numbers, the ISIL recruitment and radicalization effort is reaching its intended audiences. The University of Chicago Project on Security Threats (CPOST) conducted a study comparing the 112 individuals who committed offences or were indicted by the U.S. Department of Justice for offences, or both, between March 2014 and August 2016 [17]. A summary of their findings follows:

- US ISIL recruits are "unremarkable" within the US population.
  - They are close to average in terms of marriage, post-secondary education, and employment.
- Most are born and raised in the United States.
  - 65% were born here; 83% are citizens.
- Many are converts, not from established Muslim communities.
  - 30% are converts, including 43% of US-born recruits.
- Of those indicted for attacking/conspiring to attack targets in the United States, they are as likely to be converts as to be from established Muslim communities.
  - 51% are recent converts while 49% are from Muslim communities.
- ISIL propaganda videos played a central role in radicalization of this group.
  - 83% watched these videos which included both execution videos and lectures by terrorist leaders.
- ISIL is more successful than AQ in US recruitment and radicalization.
  - ISIL recruitment is at a rate four times that of AQ.
  - ISIL recruits are much more likely to be US citizens and recent converts than AQ recruits.

These findings indicate that it is not a simple task of singling out the target recruitment population, so our efforts must address targeting the messages and the media. Further, the findings on the power of video media in ISIL effort means that we have to find new and more effective counters to tailored video messaging. Much of the remainder of this book looks at these specifics. However, we urge the reader to remember the context presented here so that individual and tactical efforts can be at least synchronized, and ideally integrated, for enhanced effectiveness in this fight.

12.5 SUMMARY

This chapter has focused on the essential context to online recruitment and radicalization efforts. It has presented the recruitment and radicalization process in both its traditional and contemporary forms, some of the AQ and ISIL messaging within that process today, and briefly some ideas on countering that messaging to further limit successful recruitment and radicalization in the West.

Traditional mobilization to violence was based on common environmental conditions that adversely affected an identifiable class or group. The result within that group was perceived deprivation that when combined with acceptance of the victim group identity set those individuals on the path to violent action. With the existence of an organization, and specifically leadership, dedicated to addressing that situation, recruitment was face-to-face, top-down, and radicalization took place within the group as a social process. Today that process has been adapted to recruitment on a global scale, with radicalization combined into the recruitment. It now has a primary virtual component, with individuals displaced from their native lands but feeling out of place in their new societies and seeking identity. The process is now indirect, bottom-up, with radicalization initially activated by travel to a training function back in native areas; however, since the close travel monitoring of Western law enforcement, it is now also virtual in many cases. This virtual process is specifically targeted at demographic and geographic audiences, with tailored media and messages.

Countering this type of messaging is very difficult, so the chapter then develops examples of the current targets, media, and messages to facilitate understanding toward delegitimizing the effort. Specific targets of ISIL today are young Western men and women. The surface message is one of religious duty, but the appeal is a promise of adventure, power, and battlefield prowess—instant gratification and power. To young women there is also a promise of adventure while building a better society for them and their children. One approach to countering this messaging from psychology, is inoculation—shoring up long-standing moderate beliefs and building resistance to more radical appeals. Another approach is to craft and target our own messages to these same audiences, mirroring the emotional as well as the rational content of the messages. We should emphasize our messages to appeal to young women who can then act as an additional counter to extremism in their communities. And we must constantly monitor and analyze ISIL messaging to stay current and adapt our efforts toward their adaptations.

With current setbacks to the efforts of ISIL to create a physical caliphate, the group has adapted to bring an even more aggressive focus on creating a virtual caliphate and to taking a major component of the fight to Western homelands. In a word, we can expect no letup, perhaps even an intensification, of both ISIL and renewed AQ recruitment and radicalization in the West. A major take-away is that with the increased success of recruitment via video messaging, particularly targeted at young men and women, this will continue as a primary focus. This type of messaging is complex, with many dimensions to its appeal. It presents a complex challenge that will require a multi-faceted, multi-disciplinary, multi-organizational, and multi-national coordinated response.

NOTE

1. The views expressed in this paper are those of the author and do not necessarily reflect the official policy or position of the United States Air Force, the Department of Defense, or the United States Government.

REFERENCES

1. Alex Wilner, "Deterring the Undeterrable: Coercion, Denial, and Delegitimization in Counterterrorism." *The Journal of Strategic Studies* 34(1) (2011), 3–37.

2. American Academy of Child and Adolescent Psychiatry, "Teen Brain: Behavior, Problem Solving, and Decision Making." No. 95, September 2016. https://www.aacap.org/aacap/families_and_youth/fac ts_for_families/FFF-Guide/The-Teen-Brain-Behavior-Problem-Solving-and-Decision-Making-095. aspx (accessed 30 May 2018).

3. Audrey Kurth Cronin, "ISIS Is Not a Terrorist Group," *Foreign Affairs* 94 (2015). https://www.foreigna ffairs.com/articles/middle-east/isis-not-terrorist-group (accessed May 30, 2018).

4. Bruce Hoffman. *Inside Terrorism*, 3rd Edition. (New York: Columbia University Press, 2017).

5. David Rapoport, "The Four Waves of Modern Terrorism." In Audrey Kurth Cronin and James Ludes, Eds. *Attacking Terrorism*. (Washington, DC: Georgetown University Press, 2004), 46–73.

6. William J. McGuire, "Resistance to Persuasion Conferred by Active and Passive Prior Refutation of the Same and Alternative Counterarguments," *Journal of Abnormal and Social Psychology*. http://com municationtheory.org/inoculation-theory/ (accessed May 24, 2018). (accessed May 24, 2018).

7. James Smith, "Strategic Analysis, WMD Terrorism, and Deterrence by Denial." In Andreas Wegner and Alex Wilner, Eds. *Deterring Terror: Theory and Practice* (Stanford, CA: Stanford University Press, 2012), 159–179.

8. Josh Compton, Ben Jackson, and James A. Dimmock, "Persuading Others to Avoid Persuasion: Inoculation Theory and Resistant Health Attitudes." *Frontiers in Psychology* 7 (2016), 122. https://ww w.ncbi.nlm.nih.gov/pmc/articles/PMC4746429/ (accessed May 30, 2018).

9. Lorand Bodo and Anne Speckhard, "Identifying Nefarious Telegram Users without the Help of Telegram Itself…" http://www.icsve.org/research-reports/identifying-nefarious-telegram-users-without-the-help-of-telegram-itself-testing-solutions-for-intelligence-and-security-professionals-in -fighting-isis-in-the-encrypted-social-media-space/ (accessed May 30, 2018).

10. Maeghin Alarid, "Recruitment and Radicalization: The Role of Social Media and New Technology." In Michelle Hughes and Michael Miklaucic, Eds. *Impunity: Countering Illicit Power in War and Transition*. (Washington, DC: National Defense University, 2017), 313–329.

11. Marc Sageman, "Radicalization of Global Islamist Terrorists." United States Senate Committee on Homeland Security and Governmental Affairs, June 27, 2007. https://www.hsgac.senate.gov/imo/me dia/doc/062707Sageman.pdf (accessed May 30, 2018).

12. Michael W.S. Ryan, "The Boston Marathon Bombing: Radicalization Process and the Tsarnaev Brothers." *The Jamestown Foundation*, Hot Issues, May 9, 2013. https://jamestown.org/program/hot-i ssue-the-boston-marathon-bombing-radicalization-process-and-the-tsarnaev-brothers (accessed May 30, 2018).

13. Mitchell D. Silber and Arvin Bhatt, *Radicalization in the West: The Homegrown Threat.* (New York: NYPD, 2007).

14. Mohammed Hafez and Creighton Mullins, "The Radicalization Puzzle: A Theoretical Synthesis of Empirical Approaches to Homegrown Extremism." *Studies in Conflict and Terrorism* 38 (2015): 958–975.

15. Rachel Pieh Jones, "A Child of Two Worlds." *New York Times*, February 23, 2012. http://www.nytimes. com/2012/02/26/fashion/a-gift-from-allah-modern-love.html (accessed May 24, 2018).

16. Rex A. Hudson. *Who Becomes a Terrorist: The 1999 Government Report on Profiling Terrorists.* (Guilford, CT: The Lions Press, 1999), 23. The report synthesized this section from Paul Wilkinson. *Political Terrorism*. (London: MacMillan, 1974).

17. Robert Pape, Jean Decety, Kevin Ruby, Alejandro Albanez Rivas, Jens Jessen, and Caroline Wegner. *The American Face of ISIS*. Chicago Project on Security and Threats, and the Australian Strategic Policy Institute. February 2017. https://www.aspi.org.au/report/american-face-isis-analysis-isis-r elated-terrorism-us-march-2014-august-2016 (accessed May 31, 2018).

18. Stephan Lewandowsky. "Outflanking 'Fake News': Inoculation, Skepticism, and Warnings." Strategic Multilayer Assessment, Pentagon Webinar. June 21, 2017.

19. Kelsey Munro, "The Missing Link between Terrorism and Sex," *The Sydney Morning Herald*. April 2017. http://www.smh.com.au/world/the-missing-link-between-terrorism-and-sex-20170328-gv871a.html (accessed May 30, 2018).

20. The Soufan Center. "Al-Qaeda and the Rohingya." Intel Brief. September 13, 2017. http://thesoufa ncenter.org/httpthesoufancenter-orgtsc-intelbrief-al-qaeda-and-the-rohingya/ (accessed May 30, 2018).
21. Troy Thomas, Stephen Kiser, and William Casebeer. *Warlords Rising: Confronting Violent Non-State Actors*. (Lanham, MD: Lexington Books, 2005).
22. Scott Atran, Robert Axelrod, Richard Davis, Baruch Fischhoff. "Challenges in researching terrorism from the field." *Science*, January 26, 2017. 355. www.sciencedaily.com/releases/2017/01/170126142857. htm (accessed May 24, 2018).

Chapter 13

Domestic Terrorism and Digital Media
Planning in Cyberspace

David Woodring, Kevin M. Fitzpatrick, Jeff Gruenewald, and Brent Smith

CONTENTS

13.1 INTRODUCTION

While the concept of sharing information over the internet started as early as the 1960s, the internet as we know it today—a place where anyone can access and disseminate information globally—was developed by Tim Berners-Lee, a British scientist at the European Council for Nuclear Research (CERN) (CERN 2017). Beginning in 1989, Berners-Lee and CERN worked to release the World Wide Web as public domain in 1993 and develop the first web browser. By 1995, there was worldwide internet connectivity. Internet technology was quickly adopted and diffused throughout social sectors around the world—a system level impact across the entire global, social ecology. The internet, combined with the integration of digital media technologies, such as email, instant messaging, chat rooms, blogs, personal web pages, audio and visual services, and social networking sites (SNSs), created a "placeless" environment, forever changing the fabric of modern society.

As digital media continues to pervade everyday life, individuals and communities around the world experience both positive and negative social consequences resulting from their widespread proliferation. Such technological tools are an extension of our social selves, and like any tool, can be used to advance benevolent or malevolent interests. The growth of positive applications of these technologies is almost endless: communication, economy, law, education, media, industry, surveillance, and security, etc. These technologies are integral in facilitating efficient communication across networks of individuals, institutions, organizations, communities, governments, countries, and global entities. But the flipside of such technology is that it also affords subversive networks and organizations, such as terrorist movements and their adherents, with an ever-expanding set of tools to efficiently plan, grow, communicate, and advance their destructive agendas.

With a specific focus on terrorists—those who use violence or force against civilians or government to further a political or social cause—this chapter explores the prevalence, frequency, and type of digital media use among the three most prominent terrorist movements operating in the United States since the early 1990s. In addition to exploring how and why terrorist groups use digital media, we examine the individual characteristics of terrorist movement adherents in relation to those who reportedly used (and did not use) digital media within the pre-incident planning process, providing important insights into understanding the nature of technology use within terrorist movements. The data come from federal terrorism court cases that make up the backbone of the American Terrorism Study (ATS) and are used as a backdrop to describe an evolving landscape of technology and terrorism (Smith and Damphousse 2006, 2009; Smith et al. 2006).

13.2 EVOLUTION OF TERRORIST MOVEMENTS AND INTERNET TECHNOLOGY

Over the past several decades, the dynamics of terrorist organizations and movements have evolved into a multidimensional threat. Once seen as a group phenomenon, the leadership and organizational structure of terrorist movements today differ from movements in the past. Inherently, many of these characteristic changes are reflected in both the planning and outcomes of domestic terrorist plots in the United States. Moving from the pyramidal and "hub-and-spoke" cell structures found in the 1970s and 1980s, the concept of a "leaderless resistance" was facilitated and popularized by prominent far-right movement leaders in the late 1980s and throughout the 1990s (Beam 1992; Kaplan 1997; Simon 2013). The fundamental concepts underlying the leaderless resistance movement took advantage of autonomous networks or cells of individuals sharing the same ideology, having no centralized authority or chain-of-command. While terror attacks by individuals is not a new phenomenon, there has been a growing prevalence of terrorist incidents, particularly in the U.S., committed by individuals (Weimann 2012). These acts have occurred under instruction from others and in some cases have been the result of self-radicalization.

The evolution of these terrorist movements and their associated ideologies were further influenced by technological advances of the 21st century. The expanding reach of digital media, such as the advent of social networking sites (SNSs), further aided in the transformation of these once hierarchical terrorist movements into decentralized social movements (Jenkins 2010, 2011a; Weimann 2005). The practical use of such technologies to spread information and develop social networks among these different groups has given social movements—those especially stigmatized and violent—a powerful voice that transcends geographical boundaries. For example, these technologies facilitate movements with research, distributing propaganda, communication, information sharing, claiming responsibility for attacks, training, target selection, creation of websites, cyber-attacks, publicity, radicalization, threats, and recruitment (OSCE 2008; Theohary and

Rollins 2011; UNODC 2012; Weimann 2005). In this chapter, we focus on the prevalence of these specific types of digital media use among environmental, far-right, and Islamic extremist movements, and discuss how the characteristics of such movements and their adherents aid in explaining the adoption and use of related technologies during the incident planning process.

13.3 PREVALENCE AND IMPACT OF TERRORISM IN THE U.S.

Between the attacks of 9/11 and the end of 2009, a total of 46 cases of domestic radicalization and recruitment to jihadist terrorism were reported in the U.S. (Jenkins 2010). Between 2001 and the end of 2010, research documented over 176 individuals being indicted or identified in jihadist homegrown terrorist plots in the U.S. (Jenkins 2011b). This research suggests that in many of these cases, radicalized, homegrown terrorists began their socialization through the internet; among Islamic extremist movements, many would-be-jihadists appear to have begun their journey on the internet in search of justification for grievances, affirmation of anger, solutions to personal problems, and even "the thrill of clandestine activity" within a perceived epic struggle (Jenkins 2011a, p. 13). This, and other research (Theohary and Rollins 2011; UNODC 2012; Weimann 2012), also suggests that by using social networking sites (SNSs) and interactive websites, the identity of individual and group grievances driving these movements are easily found and reinforced through social networks of sympathizers as the internet supported an open, nonconfrontational environment where individuals are more apt to display their true feelings, emotions, and find an identity. This process may be further exacerbated when such digital media use is combined with face-to-face meetings, where individuals are indoctrinated and identity is also reinforced. Although the focus of terrorism research has often been on radical Islamic inspired movements, any assumption that internet or digital media use in relationship to violent extremism is limited to a particular philosophy or ideology may be potentially misleading, given important differences in pre-incident terrorist activity among these three terrorist movements. Such differences between environmental, far-right, and Islamic extremist movements undoubtedly influence the way digital media are used during the pre-incident planning process

But how and why do these terrorist movements use the digital media, specifically? How does terrorist use of the digital media vary across different types of terrorist movements? And how do terrorist characteristics shape differences found in types of digital media use? While the internet was quickly adopted as an essential tool for disseminating guidance and propaganda for terrorists, such as for radical Islamic movements (Jenkins 2011a), the practice has long been observed in other domestic terrorist plots in the U.S. All terrorists are radicals committing violence to advance broader social or political change, but their ideologies, methods of recruitment, and targets have often been very different (Smith and Morgan 1994). It is also possible then that these different characteristics are reflected in the way terrorists use digital media. To examine these characteristics in relationship to digital media use, we examine data from the American Terrorism Study (ATS) on the pre-incident planning processes of three dominant domestic terrorist movements in the U.S.—environmental, far-right, and Islamic extremist movements—between 1995–2011. The intent of this chapter and our examination of these data is three-fold. One, we examine prevalence, types, and purposes of digital media use among terrorist movements. Two, we examine the demographic differences of terrorists who used (and did not use) digital media during the pre-incident planning process. Three, we conclude by discussing the implications of our findings for understanding the role of digital media in homegrown radicalization as well as for counterterrorism policy and practice.

13.4 DEFINING TERRORIST MOVEMENTS

Before exploring the prevalence, frequency, and types of internet use among terrorist movements in the ATS data, we define environmental, far-right, and Islamic extremist terrorist movements in the U.S.; each group has evolved over the last several decades in terms of their diverse motives, affiliated movements, and modus operandi. We use Freilich et al. (2014) who undertook a comprehensive review of the literature in order to derive descriptions of each of the three ideological movements as follows:

Far-right extremists are described as:

...fiercely nationalistic, anti-global, suspicious of federal authority and reverent of individual liberties, especially their right to own guns and be free of taxes. They believe in conspiracy theories involving imminent threats to national sovereignty or personal liberty and beliefs that their personal or national "way of life" is under attack. Sometimes such beliefs are vague, but for some the threat originates from specific racial or religious groups. They believe that they must be prepared to defend against this attack by participating in paramilitary training or survivalism (Freilich et al. 2014, Appendix).

Islamic extremists are described as those who:

...believe that only acceptance of the Islam promotes human dignity. Islamic extremists reject the traditional Muslim respect for "People of the Book," (i.e. Christians and Jews). They believe that "Jihad" (i.e. to struggle in the God's path like the Prophet Muhammad), is a defining belief in Islam and includes the "lesser Jihad" that endorses violence against "corrupt" others. Islamic extremists believe that their faith is oppressed in nominally Muslim Middle-Eastern/Asian corrupt governments and in nations (e.g. Russia/Chechnya) that occupy Islamic populations. The U.S. is seen as supporting the humiliation of Islam, and exploiting the region's resources. They believe that America's hedonistic culture (e.g. gay rights, feminism, etc.) negatively affects Muslim values. Islamic extremists believe that the American people are responsible for their government's actions and that there is a religious obligation to combat this assault. They believe that Islamic law- Sharia- provides the blueprint for a modern Muslim society and should be forcibly implemented. (Freilich et al. 2014, Appendix).

Environmental extremists are described as those that:

... endorse biodiversity/biocentric equality (i.e. that humans have no legitimate claim to dominate earth). They believe that the earth and animals are in imminent danger and that the government and corporations are responsible for this danger that will ultimately result in the environment's destruction. These extremists believe that the "system" is incapable of taking actions to protect the environment and biological diversity. Thus, there is a need to defend the environment and animals" (Freilich et al. 2014, Appendix).

13.5 TERRORIST USE OF DIGITAL MEDIA

For many terrorists, the internet offers the practical utility of doing research, communicating propaganda, sharing information, claiming responsibility for attacks, training, target selection, creating websites, designing and implementing cyber-attacks, spreading publicity, radicalizing, threatening, and recruiting, among other uses (OSCE 2008; Theohary and Rollins 2011; UNODC 2012; Weimann 2005). Accordingly, digital media provides an efficient use of information gathering and sharing. From recruiting potential adherents to distributing bomb-making tutorials, the efficiency of the planning and communication process of terrorists has become increasingly accurate, and digital media technologies have facilitated in changing the rules of the game. For example, social networking sites (SNSs) like Facebook and Twitter have been readily used to disseminate propaganda, reach and train movement adherents, and aid in terrorists' ability to radicalize individuals from around the world. These technologies have certainly changed our "here" to "there" (Freiburger and Crane 2008; Jenkins 2010, 2011a; Theohary and Rollins 2011; UNODC 2012; Weimann 2005, 2010, 2011).

Ever-expanding social media platforms offer radicals a way to promote the agenda of their movement and its often complicated ideology. In the case of homegrown violent extremists, terrorism appears to be as much an expression of an identity as it is an ideology, and the internet contains an ample supply of imagery, music, and text from which the aspiring terrorist can assemble a developing identity (Meehan et al. 2011). Within SNSs, it is now easier than ever to communicate with others and assimilate into almost any social network than it ever was before. By 2010, researchers documented that 90% of terrorist activities on the internet were taking place using SNSs, including independent bulletin boards, Paltalk, Yahoo or egroups (Weimann 2010). The dramatic growth in the number of jihadist websites and chat rooms, especially the significant increase in English-language sites in this category from a handful to hundreds, has begun to make the narrative and message of violent jihad more accessible and compelling to those who could not read or speak Arabic.

The internet holds various powerful methods of communicating and expanding social networks. SNSs such as Facebook, Twitter, and YouTube, among a growing list of others, afford terrorists the advantage of real-time updates, access to personal information, information sharing, and training capabilities worldwide. For example, YouTube is not merely a video-hosting site, but also a formidable social networking forum that can effectively promote violent acts and broadcast threats and announcements, as well as direct events and demonstrations (Meehan et al. 2011). Movements quickly became aware of this capacity and some began modeling their own versions of video sharing sites, with similar designs and logos, to market themselves as a YouTube-like brand. Creating their own websites and linking them with a domain name allows the posting and cross-posting of radical content with less chance of detection or removal.

In addition to practical purposes of internet use, prior studies have also examined the psychological use and effects associated with radicalization and internet use (Freiburger and Crane 2008; Jenkins 2011a). The emergent theme from this literature suggests that the internet is a powerful developmental tool, which can be used by terrorists to spread ideology and propaganda quickly and effectively, while reaching and influencing aggrieved sympathizers by using multiple learning models (Freiburger and Craine 2008). Most important, evidence shows that internet propaganda, along with other tools, can be used to entice vulnerable individuals, who may be experiencing feelings of alienation or marginalization as well as personal and group grievances, with radical narrative, making them more susceptible to perpetrating acts of expressive violence (Bartlett et al. 2010).

13.6 DATA AND DESCRIPTIVE ANALYSIS

In an effort to bring some empirical life to the ideas and literature that we have presented, a descriptive analyses of federal court documents and other open-source documentation from "officially designated" terrorism cases are presented (Smith et al. 2006, 2008). Documents from all of the federal terrorism cases are maintained as part of the American Terrorism Study (ATS), which currently contains information on nearly 4,000 precursor activities related to 437 incidents and planned incidents over the last four decades. We extracted evidence of the use of digital media from the ATS for all known domestic terrorist incident plots with a conviction between 1995 and 2011 (n=149). This time frame allowed us to analyze how digital media technologies were being used across environmental, far-right, and Islamic extremist movements, beginning shortly after the World Wide Web's transformation into a commercial enterprise during the beginning of the 2st1 century.

13.6.1 Use of Digital Media by Terrorist Movement

Over the 16-year period examined, over half (55%) of the terrorist cases contained clear evidence of digital media use. Table 13.1 provides measures of the prevalence of digital media use, prevalence across group types, as well as how the digital media were used across groups during the

TABLE 13.1   DESCRIPTIVE STATISTICS FOR FREQUENCY AND TYPE OF USE

Use	
Evidence of ICT Use	55.30%
Movement	
Environmental	30.51%
User %	51.49%
Far-right	35.05%
User %	31.03%
Islamic Extremist	34.44%
User %	83.33%
Type of Use	
Communication	42.90%
Info gathering	35.60%
Propaganda	32.30%
Planning	15.40%
Train	13.30%
Info sharing	12.10%
Claim	12.10%
Publicity	9.70%
Threatening	8.20%
Web creation	6.60%
Recruitment	6.00%
Target	3.30%
Cyber-attack	2.10%
Radicalization	1.80%

planning process. Digital media use across terrorist movements—environmental (31%), far-right (35%), and Islamic extremist (34%)—was relatively even across the groups. Within groups, this analysis found that 83% of Islamic extremists used digital media during the pre-incident planning process, followed by environmental (51%) and far-right (31%) movements. Next, we examined the type of digital media use across movements. Overall, it appears that far-right movements used digital media far less than either Islamic and environmental movements over this time period, while Islamic and environmental movements had similar frequencies of use generally. For all movements, communication (43%) was the most common use among groups during the planning process, followed by information gathering (36%) and distribution propaganda (32%). Clearly, domestic terrorist movements used digital media extensively for both practical and strategic purposes during the planning process.

Our next glance at the data illustrates the differences in types, purposes, and frequency of digital media use between movements. Table 13.2 depicts the differences in types of use between terrorist movements. Islamic extremists used digital media more than other movements for communication (60%), information gathering (64%), distributing propaganda (54%), and planning (53%). These results are in accordance with the extensive qualitative work on potential (and documented) terrorist uses of digital media by Islamic extremists (Freiburger and Crane 2008; Jenkins 2011a; Theohary and Rollins 2011; UNODC 2012; Weimann 2005) However, environmental movements used digital media more than Islamic extremists for the purposes of information sharing (60%), training (54%), and radicalization (67%). In this study, information sharing was defined as using digital media to access, share, or distribute any type of information such as bomb-making instructions, guidebooks, manuals, transferring files, target lists, weapons information, security information, or instructions on how to make, design, build, or carry out any type of preparatory or ancillary incident act. Training was defined as the use of digital media to conduct or receive any type of training to learn techniques, special skills, weapons tactics, weapons construction, or methods of attack, either ancillary or in the preparatory stages of planning. And radicalization was defined by the evidence that the adherent was actively involved in viewing terrorist websites, sympathizing with their causes, and was motivated/inspired by and/or indoctrinated into the movement, before carrying out an attack. Furthermore, and not shown in the table because of space, environmental movements were the only movements in the sample to use these technologies for domestic recruitment, cyber-attacks, and claiming responsibility for attacks. Domestic recruitment in this study was defined as using digital media to reach, recruit, or mobilize potential sympathizers to aid in an incident, attack, or participate in any other kind of action, either ancillary or in the preparatory stages of planning. Aside from domestic recruitment of movement adherents in the U.S., which occurred strictly within environmental movements, Islamic extremists also actively used digital media for training (46%), information sharing (18%), and radicalization (33%).

Although currently only 13% of U.S. citizens are considered non-users of the internet, throughout the development and proliferation of digital media technologies, users have been intrinsically and fundamentally different from non-users in terms of their age, education, gender, marital status, and socioeconomic status (Pew Research Center 2016). Supplemental Educational Services (SES) have been one of the main correlates of internet adoption and digital media use from the beginning of the information age (Verdegem and Verhoest 2009). Early research showed that internet users were young (18–34), white, better-educated, full-time employed males, with considerable access to technology (Aerschot and Rodousakis 2008; Dholakia 2006; Selwyn et al. 2005; Verdegem and Verhoest 2009). In contrast, non-users were more likely to be under-skilled, less educated, concerned about privacy, have perceived costs and benefits for obtaining access, or simply may lack the financial resources to afford connection to the internet (Aerschot and Rodousakis 2008;

TABLE 13.2   TYPE OF DIGITAL MEDIA USE BETWEEN MOVEMENTS

Type of Use	
Communication	
Environmental	24.5%
Far-right	14.1%
Islamic	60.4%
Information Gathering	
Environmental	25.4%
Far-right	11%
Islamic	63.6%
Distributing Propaganda	
Environmental	34.6%
Far-right	11.2%
Islamic	54.2%
Planning	
Environmental	47.1%
Far-right	–
Islamic	52.9%
Training	
Environmental	54.5%
Far-right	–
Islamic	45.5%
Information Sharing	
Environmental	60%
Far-right	22.5%
Islamic	17.55%
Target Selection	
Environmental	54.5%
Far-right	–
Islamic	45.5%
Radicalization	
Environmental	66.7%
Far-right	–
Islamic	33.3%

Selwyn et al. 2005; Verdegem and Verhoest 2009). Elderly people had the lowest adoption rate and level of use of digital media technologies among all age categories (Flanagan and Metzger 2001).

Many of these trends continue today. Those with higher incomes are still most likely to be connected to the internet (see Table 13.1). While young adults are still most likely to use digital media, seniors are catching up, showing faster adoption rates (Pew Research Center 2015).

Less-educated adults are catching up as well, but their rates of use are still well below those of college graduates (Pew Research Center 2015). Rural U.S. citizens still use digital media less than both suburban and urban users, and English and Asian-speaking American adults have dominated digital media use since 2000. The social networks of digital media users appear to be different to those of non-users, facilitating qualitatively different interpersonal roles for users (Hlebec et al. 2006). Persons 30 years of age or younger use digital media more for chatting and discussion and have shown a higher tendency to be addicted to digital media (Korkeila et al. 2010). Finally, while the gender gap in digital media use slowly narrowed from 2000 to 2013. Gender parity in use is now the norm.

Social networking sites (SNSs) allow users to articulate and control a perception of their private lives to the public. Many introverted and lonely people with low levels of self-esteem seeking to build these online social networks, are dissatisfied with traditional face-to-face interactions (Ong et al. 2011; Sheldon 2012); these sites are a substitute for traditional face-to-face interaction. Similar to general use of digital media, the highest percentage of SNS users are young, better educated, have higher incomes, and live in urban/suburban communities (Pew Research Center 2017b). Unlike general digital media use, SNSs have been used more by women than men. While whites still use more SNSs than African Americans, the largest users of SNS as of 2016 were Hispanic. Tufekci (2008) found that the best predictor of not using SNSs was being male; concerns about personal security, less need to engage in social browsing, and instrumental versus expressive preferences for internet use. Sheldon (2012) found that age was the best predictor of non-use and that the average age of non-users of SNSs was 35; however, all of the above predictors will undoubtedly continue to change as proliferation and adoption of these technologies increases (see Table 13.2).

Research finds no relationship between time spent using SNSs and size of social networks, or differences between network size or emotional closeness to others between users and non-users (Pollet et al. 2011). However, one study did find that male SNS users are lonelier than female users and non-users, but overall users showed a significant increase in number of acquaintances and social capital (Brandtzaeg 2012). Other research has found correlations between SNS use and self-promoting and superficial behaviors, such as posting photos and writing status updates (Buffardi and Campbell 2008; Mehdizadeh 2010). In addition, research in the same vein finds that users of SNSs such as Facebook have higher levels of total narcissism, exhibitionism, and leadership then non-users (Ryan and Xenos 2011).

In the early twenty-first century, digital media technologies were used among the general population primarily as a means of communication and a way to highlight news and information (Hlebec et al. 2006). SNSs were primarily used as a form of expression for those who preferred not to socialize face-to-face (Tufekci 2008). While the current population still uses digital media for news and communication (Pew Research Center 2017c), the ways in which the general population engage with these technologies for news and information has continued to change, largely due to the evolution of social media platforms. As illustrated, interest in and promotion of digital media use around the world has spawned considerable research on a variety of predictors of digital media use among the general population. But how does all this relate to terrorist users of the digital media? And does understanding the correlates of digital media use facilitate understanding of why some might use such technologies as a tool, or be radicalized by those who do so?

13.6.2 Results from Demographic Analysis

While groups were relatively evenly engaged in domestic terrorism plots in the U.S. over the 16-year time period, the ways in which they used the digital media during the pre-incident

planning process showed considerable variation. This speaks to the many differences in planning activities and groups themselves. The ideologies, goals, and needs of these movements are
fundamentally different from one another and likely drive many differences in the prevalence
and type of digital media use. But what other characteristics of terrorist movements or their
adherents might help us to understand how and why digital media are used during the pre-
incident planning process?

Quantitative analyses have been performed on a variety of predictors of internet and digital
media use among the general population (Brandtzaeg 2012; Czaja and Lee 2007; Dholakia 2006;
Rodousakis 2008; Ryan and Xenos 2011; Selwyn et al. 2005). However, any connection to terrorist
use, or how these might be related to the processes of pre-incident planning or radicalization to
violent extremism, has been relatively unexplored. Aside from the practical use by such movements, there may be a deeper connection to understanding how and why these movements and/
or their adherents use digital media in general, or for specific purposes such as recruitment or
radicalization. Likewise, the three movements being examined (environmental, far-right, and
Islamic extremist) have very different motives and philosophies driving their movements; the
way they use the digital media might vary, particularly given the specific user characteristics
and grievances that they often express.

For the entire sample (n=331), the average age of movement adherents was 35 years old.
There was no significant difference in age between users (35) and non-users (35). Overall, the
demographics of digital media users from the entire sample were much like the general demographics for all terrorists, making it hard to infer a specific "typology." As shown in Table 13.3,
users were most likely to be white (84.4%), male (87%), married (49%), and well educated (71%).
Race, gender, and educational attainment coincide with previous research into digital media
use among the general population; however, unlike general population demographics, age was
not a good predictor of use in the sample. The majority of far-right adherents were non-users
(69%), followed by environmental (49%), and Islamic extremists (17%). Of those who used digital media during the pre-incident planning process, 52% were Islamic extremists, followed by
environmental (28%), and far-right (20%). Overall, and affirming previous research on terrorist
demographics, the majority of adherents were married (47%), white (90%), male (86%), possessing more than a high school education (68%), with very few (3.5%) having less than a high school
education.

13.7 SUMMARY

The emergence of the internet and subsequent digital media technologies at the beginning of the
21st century revolutionized social processes and organizations. These advances were not limited
to public and commercial organizations, however. Instead, the already changing structure of
domestic terrorist organizations and movements within the U.S. was further aided by the advent
of digital media technology. Nevertheless, not all movements and/or their adherents adopted
and implemented digital media in the same way, speaking to important differences within and
between movements, such as far-right, environmental, and Islamic extremists. Not only did the
prevalence of use in our analyses differ, but these movements used technologies for very different
purposes. While some of these uses were very conventional in nature (i.e. communication and
research), some movements relied heavily on these technologies for purposes such as distributing propaganda, planning, training, disseminating information, gaining publicity, threatening
others, and even creating their own websites.

TABLE 13.3   DEMOGRAPHIC AND MOVEMENT DIFFERENCES BETWEEN/WITHIN USERS AND NON-USERS (N = 331)

	Demographics			
	Within Groups		Within Users and No-nusers	
	User	Non-user	User	Non-user
Age	34.69	34.55		
Sex				
Male	56.6%	43.4%	87.4%	84.7%
Female	51.1%	48.9%	12.6%	15.3%
Race				
White	51.5%	48.5%	84.4%	97.7%
Nonwhite	89.3%	10.7%	15.6%	2.3%
Education				
Less than HS	100%	0%	5.7%	0%
High school	52.5%	47.5%	23.9%	35.2%
More than HS	63.9%	36.1%	70.5%	64.8%
Marital Status				
Married	60.5%	39.5%	49%	44.4%
Single	51.9%	48.1%	40%	51.4%
Other	78.6%	21.4%	11%	4.2%
Movement				
Environmental	51.5%	48.5%	28.4%	33.1%
Far-right	31%	69%	19.7%	54.1%
Islamic extremist	83.3%	16.7%	51.9%	12.8%

Many practical needs seemed to drive digital media use among environmental terrorists for communication, information gathering, the distribution of propaganda, and planning. In this analysis, environmental movements took prevalence over Islamic and far-right movements for the rest of the use type variables: training, information sharing, target selection, recruitment, cyber-attacks, threatening, web creation, publicity, and radicalization. It should be noted that several of these use types—claiming responsibility, website-creation, recruitment, and cyber-attacks—were unique to environmental cases in this study. In the present study, a cyber-attack was defined as the use of digital media for creating or spreading viruses, malware, Trojans, worms, hacking information systems, sabotaging networks where time or money is lost, or where it temporarily damages, disrupts, or destroys business property, computer systems, infrastructure, or functions of a business, company, or organization. In the sample, twice as many environmental extremists were radicalized, three times as many individuals were sharing information, and seven times as many individuals were using digital media to gain publicity in comparison to Islamic extremists. While the focus has been mainly upon movements like Al Qaeda, specific movements may adopt digital media use to meet the particular needs of the movement. A strong internet presence may again reflect organizational, movement, and/or adherent constraints or needs. Although far-right users were less prevalent in most cases, it should again be noted that the far-right leaderless resistance was organized around the idea of using internet technologies to facilitate protection of movement leaders from civil and criminal liability (Beam 1992; Kaplan 1997). Far-right use for communication was comparable to environmental movements. Their information sharing was equivalent to that of Islamic extremists. Finally, the far-right used digital more for both threatening and publicity than Islamic extremists. It is distinctly evident that these movements use digital media differently.

While it is not surprising that use differed across movements, it was surprising that use such as radicalization and cyber-attacks emerged solely among environmental movements in this sample. For example, the present study found that on July 11, 2001, the environmental terrorist group Stop Huntington Animal Cruelty (SHAC) sent over 2 million emails to New Jersey-based W. Corp's email system within the span of a few hours, compromising the computer server and damaging the company's day-to-day operations. On average, the environmental movements were more affluent and educated than their counterparts, and this was likely a large influence on their ability to use these technologies the way they did. These findings speak to the important role demographics may play in access to the internet and use of digital media during planning processes. Although access to the internet has largely increased around the world, more affluent individuals and groups may have access to more advanced digital media technologies than their less affluent counterparts. While there were some uses more prevalent among environmental movements, the emerging evidence of digital media use among Islamic extremists cannot be discounted. Islamic extremists used more for communication, information gathering, distribution of propaganda, and planning than any other movement in our sample.

13.7.1 Future Research

Overall, the demographic correlates of those who used digital media in the pre-incident planning process were difficult to separate from both non-users and the entire sample of terrorists. This makes it challenging to infer any specific typology of a digital media "user" or "non-user," other than the middle-aged, white, married, well-educated male profile typical of the findings pertaining to research on terrorists in general. The age of users and non-users being relatively the same illustrates the point that while organizational and philosophical needs may drive different operational planning strategies, terrorists in general may be similar in various ways, such as demographics, yet much different from general or criminal populations. Within users and non-users, although digital media users were slightly more educated, non-users were also highly educated. This further supports the research findings that terrorists differ from the general and/or criminal population in terms of demographics. Married individuals are more likely to use, but yet again, that percentage is only slightly higher than singles, making it difficult to infer specific predictors. An analysis of a larger population of terrorists is needed to further assess demographics in relationship to digital media use. Future research should continue to explore the relationship between demographics and prevalence/types of digital media use. Furthermore, given the key differences found between movements in this and other research, future research should continue to explore the differences between movements and how these differences drive technology use in relationship to unique individual, movement, and/or ideological motives. Given that individuals clustered in groups share similar characteristics, perhaps a multilevel approach examining movement and adherent characteristics in larger samples in relationship to types and frequency of technology use in the pre-incident planning process might be beneficial. Ultimately, it is crucial to understand how terrorist movements and their adherents are both alike and different from other populations, in terms of motives and characteristics that may drive technology use during terrorist planning activities.

13.7.2 Policy Implications

As indicated, digital media are prevalently used by terrorist movements for reasons practical to their unique operational and ideological needs. Islamic extremists recorded the most prevalence in digital media use. Nevertheless, many forms of use often associated with Islamic movements, were found to be more closely associated with environmental movements in this analysis. This underscores the point that not all terrorist movements are alike in terms of key factors such as digital media use and should not be lumped into a single category. Consequently, this brings into light the overshadowing focus on Islamic threats, as well as the importance of understanding what differences drive digital media in the planning process of terrorist plots across movements and why. Although the "ELF Family" was systematically dismantled by criminal agency investigations in the late 90s and early 2000s, it is clear that this movement and associated environmental movements have set a precedent for ways to operate using digital media (Smith and Damphousse 2009). While the focus has been mainly upon movements like Al Qaeda and Islamic extremists, specific movements may adopt digital media use to meet the particular needs of the movement in substantively different and meaningful ways.

We recommend that counterterrorism policy pertaining to digital media, related technology use, and online radicalization occurring within the U.S. focus not only on Islamic extremist and related movements, but also on other movements such as far-right and environmental movements. The climate of politically motivated grievances is constantly changing; therefore, policies that focus primarily on one movement may fail to identity potential terrorist threats in a timely manner. Policy initiatives should also take into consideration important differences among/between terrorist movements and their adherents in relationship to how plots are initiated and planned. Likewise, as the body of research grows on differences across movement ideologies, such key differences that may translate into unique forms of planning and technology use for terrorist actors should be taken into account. While a specific user typology did not emerge in these data, it is likely that future research will explicate substantively meaningful ways in which adherents differ across and between groups.

While it is extremely difficult to identify all potential domestic terrorist threats, especially lone actors, as research expands, demographics may partly determine which individuals are likely to be indoctrinated, recruited, and radicalized online. Moreover, some key demographic characteristics may translate into certain populations within certain contexts being more exposed to online propaganda, perceive it as more relevant, and therefore more likely to become adherents of specific movements. As the "information age" continues to expand, the attributes and attraction of seemingly troubled individuals to these technologies may proffer the expansion of digital media use among individuals experiencing grievances, terrorists seeking to reach those experiencing those grievances, or simply networking to spread ideology or to recruit. Taking into consideration the above factors may allow the early identification and interdiction of terrorist planning activities in certain contexts.

13.7.3 Limitations

Little evidence of self-radicalization or recruitment within U.S. domestic terrorist plots occurring online among Islamic extremists was found within our data. In fact, using digital to recruit adherents domestically appeared to be most prominent among environmental movements. In addition, no strategic use of social networking sites (SNSs) among Islamic extremists was found. Again, the only evidence of strategic use of SNSs was recorded among environmental terrorists. It appears that, at least in terms of domestic terrorism, these uses are not as prevalent as what might have been assumed. As suggested earlier, the majority of information was taken from the FBI investigations, and there is the potential that digital media use was either well hidden, undetected, or not pertinent to establishing probable cause in an indictment. Such activity may have occurred, but it was simply not mentioned in any court documents for cases included in this study. It must be reiterated that the study period for these analyses ended in 2011. Furthermore, it must also be noted that while all eligible cases from the ATS were coded during the time this study was completed, additional cases have likely been coded and added to the ATS since the completion of this study in 2014.

REFERENCES

Aerschot, Lina V. and Niki Rodousakis. 2008. "The Link Between Socio-Economic Background and Internet Use: Barriers Faced by Low Socio-Economic Status Groups and Possible Solutions." *Innovation: The European Journal of Social Science Research.* 21 no. 4: 317–351.

Bartlett, Jamie, Jonathon Birdwell, and Michael King. 2010. *Edge of Violence: A Radical Approach to Extremism.* London: Demos.

Beam, L. 1992. "Leaderless Resistance." *The Seditionist* 12: 1–7.

Brandtzaeg, Petter B. 2012. "Social Networking Sites: Their Users and Social Implications – A Longitudinal Study." *Journal of Computer-Mediated Communication.* 17: 467–488.

Buffardi, Laura E. and Keith W. Campbell. 2008. "Narcissism and Social Networking Web Sites." *Personality and Social Psychology Bulletin.* 34: 1303–1314.

CERN. (2017). The birth of the web. https://home.cern/topics/birth-web

Czaja, Sara J. and Chin Chin Lee. 2007. "The Impact of Aging on Access to Technology." *Universal Access in the Information Society.* 5: 341–349.

Dholakia, Ruby R. 2006. "Gender and IT in the Household: Evolving Patterns of Internet Use in the U.S." *Information Society,* 22 no. 4: 231–240.

Flanagan, Andrew J. and Metzger, Miriam J. 2001. "Internet Use in the Contemporary Media Environment." *Human Communication Research.* 27 no. 1: 153–181.

Freiburger, Tina, and Jeffrey S. Crane, 2008. "A Systematic Examination of Terrorist Use of the Internet." *International Journal of Cyber Criminology,* 2 no. 1: 309–319.

Freilich, Joshua D., Steven M. Chermak, Roberta Belli, Jeff Gruenewald, and William S. Parkin. 2014. "Introducing the U.S. Extremist Crime Database (ECDB)." *Terrorism & Political Violence,* 26 no. 2: 372–384.

Hlebec, Valentina, Katja L. Manfreda and Vasja Vehovar. 2006. "The Social Support Networks of Internet Users." *New Media & Society.* 8 no. 1: 9–32.

Jenkins, Brian Michael. 2010. "Would-Be Warriors: Incidents of Jihadist Terrorist Radicalization in the United States September 11, 2001." Testimonial, RAND Corporation.

Jenkins, Brian Michael. 2011a. "Jihadist Use of Social Media—How to Prevent Terrorism and Preserve Innovation." Testimonial, Committee on Homeland Security and House of Representatives. https://homeland.house.gov/hearing/subcommittee-hearing-jihadist-use-social-media-how-prevent-terrorism-and-preserve-innovation/

Jenkins, Brian Michael. 2011b. *Stray Dogs and Virtual Armies: Radicalization and Recruitment in the United States Since 9/11.* Santa Monica, CA: The RAND Corporation, 2011. www.rand.org/pubs/occasional_papers/OP343.html

Kaplan, J. 1997. "'Leaderless Resistance', Terrorism and Political Violence." *Terrorism and Political Violence* 9, no. 3: 80–95.

Korkeila, J., S. Kaarlas, M. Jaaskelainen, T. Vahlberg and T. Taiminen. 2010. "Attached to the Web – Harmful Use of the Internet and Its Correlates." *European Psychiatry.* 25: 236–241.

Mehdizadeh, Soraya. 2010. "Self-Presentation 2.0: Narcissism and Self-Esteem on Facebook." *CyberPsychology, Behavior & Social Networking.* 13 no. 4: 357–364.

Ong, Chorng-Shyong, Shu-Chen Chang and Chih-Chien Wang. 2011. "Comparative Loneliness of Users Versus Nonusers of Online Chatting." *Cyberpsychology, Behavior, and Social Networking.* 14 no. 1–2: 35–40.

Organization for Security and Co-operation in Europe (OSCE). 2008. "Terrorist Use of the Internet: Threat, Issues, and Options for International Co-operation." Second International Forum on Information Security, Garmisch-Partenkirchen, 7–10 April. www.osce.org/atu/31428?download=true

Pew Research Center. (2015). Americans' Internet Access: 2000–2015. www.pewInternet.org/2015/06/26/americans-Internet-access-2000-2015/

Pew Research Center. (2016). 13% of Americans Don't Use the Internet. Who Are They? www.pewresearch.org/fact-tank/2016/09/07/some-americans-dont-use-the-Internet-who-are-they/

Pew Research Center. (2017a). New Use Across Social Media Platforms 2017. www.journalism.org/2017/09/07/news-use-across-social-media-platforms-2017/

Pew Research Center. (2017b). Social Media Fact Sheet. www.pewInternet.org/fact-sheet/social-media/

Pew Research Center. (2017c). The Elements of the Information-Engagement Typology. www.pewInternet.org/2017/09/11/the-elements-of-the-information-engagement-typology/

Pollet, Thomas V., Sam G.B. Roberts and Robin Dunbar. 2011. "Use of Social Network Sites and Instant Messaging Does Not Lead to Increased Offline Social Network Size, or to Emotionally Closer Relationships with Offline Network Adherents." *Cyberpsychology, Behavior, and Social Networking.* 14 no. 4: 253–258.

Ryan, Tracii and Sophia Xenos. 2011. "Who Uses Facebook? An Investigation into the Relationship Between the Big Five, Shyness, Narcissism, Loneliness, and Facebook Use." *Computers in Human Behavior.* 27: 1658–1664.

Selwyn, N., S. Gorard and J. Furlong. 2005. "Whose Internet is it Anyway? Exploring Adults' (Non)Use of the Internet in Everyday Life." *European Journal of Communication.* 20 no. 1: 5–6.

Sheldon, Pavica. 2012. "Profiling the Non-Users: Examination of Life-Position Indicators, Sensation Seeking, Shyness, and Loneliness Among Users and Non-Users of Social Network Sites." *Computers and Human Behavior.* 28: 1960–1965.

Smith, Brent L., and Kathryn D. Morgan. 1994. "Terrorists Right and Left: Empirical Issues in Profiling American Terrorists." *Studies in Conflict and Terrorism,* 17 no. 1: 39–57.

Smith, Brent L. and Kelly R. Damphousse. 2009. "Patterns of Precursor Behaviors in the Life Span of a U.S. Environmental Terrorist Group." *Criminology & Public Policy* 8 no. 3: 475–496.

Smith, Brent L., Kelly R. Damphousse and Paxton, Roberts. 2006. *Pre-Incident Indicators of Terrorist Incidents: The Identification of Behavioral, Geographic, and Temporal Patterns of Preparatory Conduct.* National Institute of Justice. www.ncjrs.gov/app/publications/abstract.aspx?ID=235742

Theohary, Catherine A., and John Rollins. 2011. "Terrorist Use of the Internet: Information Operations in Cyberspace." www.fas.org/sgp/crs/terror/R41674.pdf

Tufekci, Z. 2008. "Grooming, Gossip, Facebook and MySpace: What Can We Learn About These Sites from Those Who Won't Assimilate?" *Information, Communication & Society,* 11 no. 4: 544–564.

United Nations Office on Drugs and Crime, In collaboration with United Nations Counter-Terrorism Implementation Task Force (UNODC). 2012. "The use of the Internet for terrorist purposes." United Nations, Office at Vienna.

Verdegem, Pieter and Pascal Verhoest. 2009. "Profiling the Non-User: Rethinking Policy Initiatives Stimulating ICT Acceptance." *Telecommunications Policy.* 33: 642–652.

Weimann, Gabriel. 2004. "www.terror.net How Modern Terrorist Use The internet." *United States Institute of Peace.* Washington D.C. Retrieved from www.usip.org on January 7, 2013.

Weiman, Gabriel. 2005. "How Modern Terrorism Use the Internet." *The Journal of International Security Affairs.* Spring no. 8. www.securityaffairs.org/issues/2005/08/weimann.php

Weimann, Gabriel. 2012. "Lone Wolves in Cyberspace." *Journal of Terrorism Research.* 3 no. 2: 75–90.

Section V

Online Terrorist Propaganda

Chapter 14

Metaphors of Radicalization
A Computational and Qualitative Analysis of Jihadi Propaganda

Ben Miller, Weeda Mehran, Yassin Kosay Alsahlani, and Haroon Qahtan

CONTENTS

14.1 INTRODUCTION

Radicalization of individuals to violent action or the support of violent action presents an almost impossibly complex problem for study. It can take place across any medium or set of media, on the scale of a purposeful global propaganda campaign in multiple languages or by accident via unrecorded one-on-one conversations. It can take place over the course of long periods of time, or in an afternoon. The consequences of radicalized individuals and institutions, however, are concrete and drastic. Radicalized individuals have committed attacks on public transit systems, in public and private buildings, and against peaceful gatherings of civilians worldwide. In the period from January 2011 to June 2015, a study found that there were 69 terrorism plots in Europe, North America, and Australia. Overall, 19 of those plots came to fruition. The study goes on to argue that 30 had a declared connection to the Islamic State, and that plots with an IS connection were twice as likely than plots not connected to IS to move from planning to practice [1]. Ingram [2] interprets this information to suggest that it is in part the persuasive efficacy of the IS media campaign that led to this increased likelihood of execution, while Hegghammer and Nesser suggest that undercover operatives themselves may have precipitated the higher likelihood of a plot moving beyond the planning stage [1]. The conventional wisdom put forward by Ingram, that propaganda contributes to radicalization, is pervasive throughout the literature on atrocities [3–5]. Understanding how messages that incite radicalization are composed, structured, and function to radicalize individuals such that they are more willing to further political agendas through violent, unidirectional means may help efforts to reduce the effectiveness of this kind of messaging.

In this study, we examine the writing produced by various Islamic State affiliates in English so as to disentangle the relationship between the writing and radicalization. Our examination of written propaganda focuses on their use of metaphors. We do so because as Steuter and Willis argue in their study, *At War with Metaphor*, "the metaphors we use reflect and reflexively shape our thinking." They go further, indicating the kinds of metaphors typically used to radicalize; "[t]he massacres and genocides that comprise our most painful historical moments are characterized by a persistent dehumanization of the enemy," and "[l]anguage itself, in the way it invites us to understand both the enemy and ourselves, becomes a potential weapon" [6]. Most significantly, they state, "[i]t is language, rather than logic, that summons us through its emotional affect to a war we can no longer justify."

In tracing the role of metaphor in the propaganda efforts of the Islamic State and its affiliates, our research bridges two bodies of theory. The first, conceptual metaphor theory [7], describes how language functions to communicate ideas by connecting a concept in one abstract domain via references to ideas in another more concrete domain. As an example, one might refer to an idea as "brilliant," a connection transferring a feeling from the concrete domain of light and brightness to the abstract domain of inspiration. To supplement the perspective provided by Lakoff and Johnson's work, we relied on the operationalization of their work by Gordon et. al. [8], which presents 14 abstract ontological categories covering the range of conceptual and linguistic metaphors and their correspondence to the annotation work of [9]. The second body of theory on which this study draws is the information–motivation–behavioral skills (IMB) model [10], which describes how to understand the causal pathways linking messaging and behavior. Developed in the public health domain, it first appeared in studies of people's adoption of proactive behavior in relation to the public health crises of smoking and HIV. Fisher and Fisher separated messaging into components of information, such as that condoms prevent the transmission of HIV, the reasons and motivation for why the information is significant, such as that HIV can be a fatal disease, and the behavioral skills needed to implement the information, such as how to properly use a condom.

To develop the connections between these two bodies of theory, we simultaneously apply a computational and qualitative research design that allows for us to assess the relationship between the use of conceptual metaphors and the information, motivation, and skills communicated by the documents in our research corpus. Our method involved manual, parallel, qualitative coding of a subset of documents from our jihadi corpus for both metaphor usage and focus on information, motivation, or behavioral skills. Comparing those two sets of manual annotations using a bag-of-words model [11, 12] showed connections between different types of metaphor and different elements in the IMB model. For example, to convey information, writing in the Jihadi corpus relied on metaphors in the following categories: nature, inside-outside, governance, embodiment, natural disasters, and society. In parallel, we trained a two-step machine learning classifier. In the first step, it automatically classifies candidate sentences as either literal or metaphoric. It was developed using approximately 15,000 annotated examples of metaphors across eight ontological categories of metaphor, which it then used in a second step to further classify the metaphors to one of eight categories of metaphor. Comparing that automatically generated set of annotated data to the manually annotated IMB data using the same bag-of-words approach revealed similar patterns of relation between metaphors and IMB element in the manual and computational approaches.

By conducting parallel computational and qualitative methodologies, we have discovered that conceptual metaphors predominate in relation to specific motivational strategies, that different types of motivation typically connect with different clusters of conceptual metaphors, and that there is a necessity for a blended information motivation category within the IMB model. We also found that the ratio of information to motivation in these documents of radicalization is greatly skewed toward motivating attitudes, and away from communicating information. Lastly, we developed a computational method reliant on machine learning that distinguishes between metaphoric and literal statements with 90.73% accuracy, and that classifies metaphoric statements into one of eight predetermined categories with a 10-fold cross validation accuracy of 55.29%. When compared with our manual qualitative method, we are comfortable arguing that the computational method is generating meaningful results that allow for the comparison of documents across our two theoretical paradigms of conceptual metaphor theory and the IMB model.

14.2 BACKGROUND ON ONLINE RADICALIZATION

The internet has changed the image, means and reach of jihad. Jihad is no longer confined to radio and newspaper calls. Al Qaeda used to openly make announcements to attract Muslims from Arab countries to the training camps in Afghanistan and Pakistan to fight the Soviet army in the 1980s and early 1990s [13]. As Umar Patek—the mastermind of the October 2002 bombings in Bali—said during his trial, "For those who do not know how to commit jihad, they should understand that there are several ways of committing jihad … This is not the Stone Age … This is the internet era, there is Facebook, Twitter and others" (MEMRI 2012 Cited in [14], p. 47). Both Al Qaeda and the Islamic State (ISIS) have a global cyber reach through the internet [15].

Gendron goes on to describe electronic jihad as the continued flow of fighters to the call for jihad and the establishment of a virtual community of supporters and sympathizers to jihad. The online presence of fighters and sympathizers has inevitably promoted the spread of Islamist principles and its political and religious doctrine in support of militant jihadism. Recruitment and radicalization have been made relatively easy through the internet. Arguably online recruitment concomitant with the decentralization of the authority of Islamic clergies started following 9/11 attacks, which led to action against terrorist groups. In fact, with the ousting of Al Qaeda from Afghanistan through the military intervention, recruitment by Al Qaeda, "metamorphosed into a more loosely structured, distributed, and interactive procedure" [4]. Nowadays, online recruitment is quite common among terrorist groups. For example, Al Qaeda linked with the al-Nusra Front, ISIS, and the Taliban, and they utilize the internet for recruitment purposes, especially when they target fighters from Europe, North America, Australia, and elsewhere across the Muslim world [16, 17]. Likewise, ISIS has been recruiting online through various channels from chat rooms to dating sites.[1] Jihadi groups have capitalized on the power of words, images, and music to propagate their ideologies and attract potential recruits. A number of studies have been devoted to the analysis of jihadi textual propaganda [18–21], images [22–25], and videos and music [26] as media for radicalization.

An overwhelming majority of the scholarship in this field primarily focuses on radicalization through exposure to online material and/or joining radicalizing groups. The primary shortcoming of this new and emerging research concerning online radicalization is a lack of a theoretical base that can explain terrorists' motivations and behavior in using the internet and from which "one can draw simple conclusions" [27, 28]. As observed by [27], the majority of research on the online violent extremism is descriptive and mainly deals with the question of "what is going on" rather than providing a rich analysis of the how and why of online radicalization and its translation to offline violence [15, 29, 30].

Using IMB as an analytical framework, Lemieux et al. [19] illustrate how al-Qaeda's magazine *Inspire* can radicalize potential jihadis. Lemieux et al.'s study shows that IMB is a promising framework in the analysis of jihadi propaganda. The authors support their argument through supplementing their analysis of multiple cases of convicted terrorists in the US, UK, and Australia who got the inspiration and the know-how information from online material such as *Inspire* magazine to carry out attacks in the West.

We apply this model to interpret the purposes of inclusion of metaphors and patterns of metaphors in jihadi texts. We are trying to better understand how propaganda materials communicate their messages to the audience. The elements of the IMB model are used as a framework in understanding the messages and focusing on linguistic and conceptual matters and how these conceptual matters constitute different elements of the IMB model which also allow us to better understand how these authors think. The following section discusses the IMB model in detail.

14.3 LINGUISTIC AND PSYCHOLOGICAL MODELS OF RADICALIZATION

14.3.1 What Is the IMB Model and How Does It Relate to Radicalization?

The information–motivation–behavioral (IMB) skills framework has received extensive empirical support across a wide range of behavior-change intervention applications and contexts [31–34]. Hence, it is well positioned to serve as the basis of our operational framework for analyzing the content with a high degree of precision. Furthermore, the model has been applied to a wide range of research areas such as drug use behavior [35], voting behavior [36], recycling behavior [37], sexual behavior [38–42], and nutrition [43–44].

In their foundational work on the information–motivation–behavioral skills model, Fisher and Fisher [10] argued that in relation to AIDS preventative behavior, "information alone is not sufficient to motivate" (464). Work in other domains, such as on environmentally-conscious behavioral change, similarly finds that attitude drives behavior more so than does knowledge [43]. These findings, when carried over to the domain of radicalization and violent political action, appear consistent. Although little scholarship has been produced applying that model to propaganda, what does exist consistently validates the application of the IMB model for the understanding of radicalization propaganda [19].

14.3.2 How Does Conceptual Metaphor Function in Relation to Radicalization?

Metaphors are deeply rooted in our social and cultural environments and our daily experiences. Taken from casual conversations to literary texts, political rhetorics and media, language is imbued with metaphors. Metaphor is in fact a cognitive tool that helps us to understand abstractions and different types of concepts [44], and convey and inculcate values. The use of animal and insect metaphors has been connected by Russell [45] and others to the campaigns of annihilation practiced during the Holocaust. The use of metaphors of in- and out-grouping has been shown by De Swaan [46] to be connected to the spread of violence during the Rwandan Genocide. In their book-length study of metaphors and war, [6] even point out that individuals conduct focus groups and other marketing-style studies to advise hate groups on which metaphors most effectively convince people of their ideas. Work such as this demonstrates strongly that metaphors are core to the work of radicalization, and if not essential to convincing people to engage in violent action, are inseparable from those efforts.

14.3.3 Technical Literature on NLP

Three primary challenges needed to be addressed so that the relationship between metaphors and elements in IMB could be analyzed computationally. Those challenges can be summarized as (1) natural language is somewhat idiosyncratic and different authors can express the same concept in differing ways, (2) unstructured text is messy data that requires extensive cleaning and structuring for it to be analyzed computationally, and (3) metaphors and elements in IMB are complex, abstract conceptual containers, and the more abstract and complex a phenomenon is, generally, the harder it is to train a system to automatically recognize its presence and classify it. Secondary challenges are working with material written by speakers of different global Englishes, speakers with different first languages, and material written for different audiences from different regions at different points in time.

Some approaches of metaphor detection include corpus-based analysis [47], where a collection of documents representing many domains are annotated and used for the classifying metaphors at the word-level. Another popular method for metaphor detection does not use machine learning models, but instead decides the predicted output of a given sentence as metaphorical or not using a collection of pre-set rules describing verb and noun patterns and usage. Neither approach was appropriate for our work, as a corpus-based method still needs an analyst to decide which collocations are likely to be metaphorical and which are likely to be literal, and a rule-based approach is not adaptable enough for the global Englishes present in the radicalization corpora.

This research uses a novel way of classifying text into metaphorical and literal classifications that relied on a normalized, blended corpora that incorporated an estimator of the "abstractness" of each word. Our corpora were drawn from two sources: the Mind as a Metaphor database comprised of approximately 15,000 categorized examples of metaphors [9], and literal examples drawn from the opening lines of pages in Simple Wikipedia. This large dataset of positive and negative examples of categorized metaphor usage allowed us to develop a classifier that was accurate, sensitive, and capable of distinguishing both between metaphoric and non-metaphoric uses of language, and also of identifying the ontological category of the metaphoric speech.

14.3.4 Metaphor Identification and Classification

Blending a quantitative approach that extracts, classifies, and quantifies linguistic metaphors with a qualitative analytic approach allows us to better understand how different motivational strategies might be enacted in propaganda. This framework focuses attention on the information which is given, the effect of the information, and the types of behaviors that information and its framework promote. This study will focus on the first two elements of the information–motivation–behavior (IMB) model, the information, and its motivational strategies.

Our combined corpora of approximately 30,000 positive and negative examples was then normalized and matched. To normalize the dataset, we balanced the number of positive and negative examples. To match the dataset, we identified for each item in the simple dataset an item from the metaphor dataset of the same length. That joined corpus then allowed us to be confident that any example drawn at random based upon factors for which we were not selecting, such as length, would be as likely to be drawn from either the metaphoric or literal corpus. Following cleaning and preprocessing of the data by removal of stopwords such as "the" and "and," each word was lemmatized to its root form.[2] We then converted the text data into a vectored form where each word in a corpus is described by its relations to other words in the corpus. These values let us build a co-occurrence matrix that showed the frequency with which any words appeared together, and to calculate the abstraction level of a given word compared to all other words in the dataset. The rationale for this step was based on the work of Shlomo and Last [48], in which they argued that words which frequently co-occur are more likely to share a common, identical concept. These co-occurrence measures are used as our input for our machine learning models, where one set of features are the rankings of the 1,000 most commonly occurring words for each word in the corpus, and the label of whether that matrix was generated from the metaphoric usage or the literal usage of a word. We then send the sentences identified as metaphorical to another classifier that uses another feature, the category of the metaphor, to identify the ontological category of the newly identified metaphor. For that classification task, we tested three machine learning algorithms, ultimately deciding on a Random Forest Classifier because of its higher accuracy.

14.4 WHERE AND HOW THE ISLAMIC STATE WRITES

Virtually all English magazines produced by ISIS, Al Qaeda, Tahrik-e Taliban of Pakistan, and the Afghan Taliban were collected through various sources such as jihadology.com, Al Emarah's official website, and broader Google searches. Table 14.1, Summary of Publications Considered,

TABLE 14.1   SUMMARY OF PUBLICATIONS CONSIDERED**

Jihadi group	Magazine title	Number of issues
ISIS	*Dabiq*	15
	IS News	3
	IS Report	4
	Rumiyah (*Rome*)	13
Al Qaeda	*Al Shamukh*	2
	Al-Risalah	4
	Inspire	17
	Al-Nasr	2
	Massacre of the Readers	1
TTP	*Sunat-e Khola*	2
	Ihyae Khilafat	2
Taliban	*Azan*	6

** Zelin, A. Y. May 2019. *Jihadology*. Retrieved from https://jihadology.net/.

lists the magazines organized by group that were collected for and analyzed in this research. Ultimately, we collected 65 publications for this analysis.

14.4.1 Operationalization of IMB

Table 14.2, Correlating Information Motivation Behavior Elements to Granular Processes, illustrates an operationalization of the IMB model in relation to the jihadi propaganda [23]. This snapshot does not include all categories that instantiate the elements of the IMB framework, but does describe the majority of what occurs within the publications examined by our study. What one can identify from this operationalization is that each element is a composite of more granular categorizable statements, each of which serve particular functions. Unpacking each of these larger categories can lead to a recognition of the correspondences between particular clusters of metaphors and particular categories within an IMB model.

TABLE 14.2   CORRELATING INFORMATION MOTIVATION BEHAVIOR ELEMENTS TO GRANULAR PROCESSES

IMB elements	Categories	Description
Information	Military operations	Any information about military activities, civilian casualties, information about deaths of combatants
	Governance	Provision of services by jihadists, education, health care, social services and so forth
	Contemporary events	Natural disasters, national and international news
	Sources of authority	Historical religious figures, information on religion, Quotes from Koran, Hadith
Motivation	Social processes	Social relations, social expectations, social allegiances
	Rewards and risks	Risks such as death, losing family members, religious damnation. Rewards: heaven, promise of salvation, membership in a community, community support, etc.
	Psychological factors	Positive and negative emotions
	Religious framings	Religious reinforcement, explanations and motivations
	Promise of victory	
	Projection of power	Projecting force, revenge, punishment
Behavior	Observed behavior change	hijra, jihad,
	Promoted behavior change	Promoting hijra, jihad, revenge, supporting jihad
	Skills	How to conduct military operations, suicide attacks etc

TABLE 14.3   SUMMARY OF METAPHOR IDENTIFICATION RESULTS

Metaphor category	Number of items, jihadi groups	Percentage of total, jihadi groups	Percentage, training data	Differential between JG and training data
Animals	1842	11.24%	7.83%	3.41%
Architecture	2247	13.71%	10.85%	2.87%
Body	939	5.73%	14.53%	−8.80%
Government	3434	20.95%	19.05%	1.91%
Impressions	1135	6.93%	9.23%	−2.30%
Light	128	0.78%	7.85%	−7.07%
Mineral	1789	10.92%	10.70%	0.21%
Population	338	2.06%	11.33%	−9.27%
Writing	4536	27.68%	8.64%	19.04%
Grand Total	16,388	100.00%		

14.5 PATTERNS OF METAPHOR IN JIHADI PROPAGANDA

Metaphors, we argue, appear to primarily serve as motivational frameworks and as indicators of behavioral change; they do not themselves indicate information. We arrived at this argument by analyzing the data as described below.

Our three learning models that we ran against these data were as follows: The One Class SVM which worked with only metaphorical sentences and generated an accuracy of 84.4% classification, The Naïve Bayes Classifier which generated an average accuracy of 77.82% after cross validation and finally, the Random Forest Classifier which generated an average accuracy of 90.73% after cross validation.

After identifying the metaphors from the classifier, we then used another Random Forest Classifier to classify the identified metaphors into their respective categories. There were nine categories of metaphor for which we tested: animals, architecture, body, government, impressions, light, mineral, population, and writing. The ten-fold accuracy of this classification task was 55.29%. Table 14.3, Summary of Metaphor Identification Results, shows the results of our computational analysis of jihadi propaganda.

Table 14.3 shows the raw number of metaphors of each category identified in the corpus. Additionally, it shows the percentage contribution of each category relative to the total number of metaphors identified, the relative proportion of each category of metaphor in the original training data corpus, and the differential between the training data corpus and the jihadi corpus.

Our principal findings here relate to the proportion of categories of metaphor in jihadi propaganda relative to the training data. If a category of metaphor appears more in the jihadi corpus than it does in the training data, we surmise that it occupies an outsized importance for that corpus. What we found was that the propaganda featured a much higher proportion of writing-related metaphors (19.04% more) than did the training data. Additionally, these metaphors accounted for the highest proportion across all categories (27.68% of all metaphors). The second most prevalent category of metaphor related to government (20.95%), followed by architecture and animals. The categories that were less represented in the jihadi corpus were population (−9.27% less common), embodiment (−8.8% less common), and light (−7.07% less common). Interestingly, the category of light was almost completely absent from the jihadi corpus, appearing only 128 times.

What categories did dominate, those of writing, government, and architecture likely speak to the usage of language like, "[i]n other words, the Shaykh was the spirit of Inspire where Samir was its tongue" [49]. That line was identified as a metaphor of writing because of the use of the word "words," and of body because of the use of the word "tongue." It is typical of the writing in *Inspire* and would, at a higher level, connect to the motivation framing category from the IMB model, as it describes a type of in-grouping. The group, in this case, figured by the magazine, *Inspire*, is metaphorically described as being composed of multiple elements possessed by different individuals.

The border between different elements of the IMB model becomes particularly blurred in the Islamist propaganda products, as information is less likely to be objective and more likely to be tailored toward motivating the audience and changing behavior. For example, the information about victimization of civilians and battleground news is used to motivate reaction. Use of metaphors in providing information, in fact, amplify the "motivational" aspect of the information provided. Hence, in this paper we develop the category "motivational information." This category includes metaphors used to give information about, the "battle field news," "vicitimization and oppression," and "sacrifices made by the group."

14.6 SUMMARY

This work represents the first study combining the distinct theoretical paradigms of information motivation behavior and conceptual metaphors in an attempt to understand how specific patterns of metaphor usage might connect to propagandistic work of the Islamic State and its affiliates. What we were able to produce is a reliable, computational method for metaphor identification and categorization in jihadi propaganda, and research that suggests that the predominant metaphoric categories used by jihadi propaganda, at least in the period represented by our corpus, were those of writing, government, architecture, and animals. Further work in this area should look to connect specific elements of the IMB model, such as to the occurrence of each of those metaphoric categories, thereby furthering understanding of how different connections between source and target domains, between concrete things and abstract ideas, are used to radicalize individuals through propagandistic writing.

NOTES

1. www.independent.co.uk/news/uk/crime/isis-christmas-terror-attack-plot-couple-derby-explosi ves-old-bailey-bomb-ricin-online-dating-muslim-a8148061.html
2. Identifying and removing stopwords was accomplished with the Corpus module from the Natural Language Processing Toolkit.

REFERENCES

1. T. Hegghammer and P. Nesser, "Assessing the Islamic State's commitment to attacking the West," *Perspect. Terror.*, vol. 9, no. 4, pp. 14–30, 2015.
2. H. J. Ingram, "An analysis of Islamic State's Dabiq magazine," *Aust. J. Polit. Sci.*, vol. 51, no. 3, pp. 458–477, 2016.

3. A. Dalgaard-Nielsen, "Violent radicalization in Europe: What we know and what we do not know," *Stud. Confl. Terror.*, vol. 33, no. 9, pp. 797–814, 2010.

4. A. Aly, S. Macdonald, L. Jarvis, and T. Chen, "Violent Extremism Online: New Perspectives on Terrorism and the Internet, 1st Edition (Hardback) - Routledge," *Routledge.com*, 2016. [Online]. Available: https://www.routledge.com/Violent-Extremism-Online-New-Perspectives-on-Terrorism -and-the-Internet/Aly-Macdonald-Jarvis-Chen/p/book/9781138912298. [Accessed: 17-Dec-2018].

5. B. Kiernan, *Blood and Soil: A World History of Genocide and Extermination from Sparta to Darfur.* Yale University Press, 2007.

6. E. Steuter and D. Wills, *At War with Metaphor: Media, Propaganda, and Racism in the War on Terror.* Lexington Books, 2009.

7. G. Lakoff and M. Johnson, *Metaphors We Live By.* University of Chicago Press, 2008.

8. J. Gordon, Jerry R. Hobbs, Jonathan May, Michael Mohler, Fabrizio Morbini, Bryan Rink, Marc Tomlinson, and Suzanne Wertheim, "A corpus of rich metaphor annotation," in *Proceedings of the Third Workshop on Metaphor in NLP*, Denver, CO, USA, pp. 56–66, 2015.

9. B. Pasanek, "The mind is a metaphor," *The Mind is a Metaphor*, 2015. [Online]. Available: http://meta-phors.iath.virginia.edu/. [Accessed: 17-Dec-2018].

10. J. D. Fisher and W. A. Fisher, "Changing AIDS-risk behavior.," *Psychol. Bull.*, vol. 111, no. 3, p. 455, 1992.

11. Z. S. Harris, "Distributional structure," *Word*, vol. 10, no. 2–3, pp. 146–162, 1954.

12. Y. Zhang, R. Jin, and Z.-H. Zhou, "Understanding bag-of-words model: A statistical framework," *Int. J. Mach. Learn. Cybern.*, vol. 1, no. 1–4, pp. 43–52, 2010.

13. D. Kjuka, "Digital Jihad: Inside Al-Qaeda's social networks," *The Atlantic*, vol. 6, 2013.

14. G. Weimann, "Why do terrorists migrate to social media?," in *Violent Extremism Online*, edited by Anne Aly, Stuart Macdonald Lee Jarvis, Thomas Chen, Routledge, pp. 61–80, 2016.

15. A. Gendron, "The call to jihad: Charismatic preachers and the internet," *Stud. Confl. Terror.*, vol. 40, no. 1, pp. 44–61, 2017.

16. D. Drissel, "Reframing the Taliban insurgency in Afghanistan: New communication and mobilization strategies for the Twitter generation," *Behav. Sci. Terror. Polit. Aggress.*, vol. 7, no. 2, pp. 97–128, 2015.

17. A. Y. Zelin, "Foreign jihadists in Syria: Tracking recruitment networks," Policy Watch 2186, *Wash. Inst. East Policy Wash. C Dec.*, vol. 19, pp. 3–4, 2013.

18. B. Colas, "What Does Dabiq Do? ISIS Hermeneutics and Organizational Fractures within Dabiq," *Mag. Stud. Confl. Terror.*, vol. 40, no. 3, pp. 173–190, 2016.

19. A. F. Lemieux, J. M. Brachman, J. Levitt, and J. Wood, "Inspire magazine: A critical analysis of its significance and potential impact through the lens of the information, motivation, and behavioral skills model," *Terror. Polit. Violence*, vol. 26, no. 2, pp. 354–371, 2014.

20. P. Wignell, S. Tan, and K. L. O'Halloran, "Under the shade of AK47s: A multimodal approach to violent extremist recruitment strategies for foreign fighters," *Crit. Stud. Terror.*, vol. 10, no. 3, pp. 429–452, 2017.

21. D. B. Skillicorn and E. F. Reid, "Language use in the Jihadist magazines inspire and Azan," *Secur. Inform.*, vol. 3, no. 1, p. 9, 2014.

22. C. Winter, "Apocalypse, later: A longitudinal study of the Islamic State brand," *Crit. Stud. Media Commun.*, vol. 35, no. 1, pp. 103–121, 2018.

23. C. Winkler, K. El Damanhoury, A. Dicker, and A. F. Lemieux, "Images of death and dying in ISIS media: A comparison of English and Arabic print publications," *Media War Confl.*, p. 1750635217746200, 2018.

24. C. K. Winkler, K. El Damanhoury, A. Dicker, and A. F. Lemieux, "The medium is terrorism: Transformation of the about to die trope in Dabiq," *Terrorism and Political Violence*, vol. 31, no. 2, pp. 224–234, 2019. DOI: 10.1080/09546553.2016.1211526.

25. K. L. O'Halloran, Sabine Tan, Peter Wignell, John A. Bateman, Duc-Son Pham, Michele Grossman & Andrew Vande Moere, "Interpreting text and image relations in violent extremist discourse: A mixed methods approach for big data analytics," *Terror. Polit. Violence*, vol. 31, no. 3, pp. 1–21, 2016. DOI: 10.1080/09546553.2016.1233871.

26. N. Lahoud and J. Pieslak, "Music of the Islamic State," *Survival*, vol. 60, no. 1, pp. 153–168, 2018.

27. M. Conway, "Determining the role of the internet in violent extremism and terrorism: Six suggestions for progressing research," *Stud. Confl. Terror.*, vol. 40, no. 1, pp. 77–98, 2017.

28. M. Rudner, "'Electronic Jihad': The Internet as al-Qaeda's catalyst for global terror," in *Violent Extremism Online*, edited by Anne Aly, Stuart Macdonald, Lee Jarvis, Thomas Chen, Routledge, 2016, pp. 24–40.

29. D. Mair, "#Westgate: A case study–How al-Shabaab used Twitter during an ongoing attack," in *Violent Extremism Online*, edited by Anne Aly, Stuart Macdonald, Lee Jarvis, Thomas Chen, Routledge, 2016, pp. 81–102.

30. A. Bermingham, M. Conway, L. McInerney, N. O'Hare, and A. Smeaton, "Combining social network analysis and sentiment analysis to explore the potential for online radicalization – DORAS," in *ASONAM 2009 - Advances in Social Networks Analysis and Mining*, Vancouver, Canada, July 20–22, 2009.

31. K. J. Horvath, D. Smolenski, and K. R. Amico, "An empirical test of the information–motivation–behavioral skills model of ART adherence in a sample of HIV-positive persons primarily in out-of-HIV-care settings," *AIDS Care*, vol. 26, no. 2, pp. 142–151, 2014.

32. S. J. Hardcastle, J. Hancox, A. Hattar, C. Maxwell-Smith, C. Thøgersen-Ntoumani, and M. S. Hagger, "Motivating the unmotivated: How can health behavior be changed in those unwilling to change?," *Front. Psychol.*, vol. 6, p. 835, 2015.

33. J. Gao, J. Wang, Y. Zhu, and J. Yu, "Validation of an information–motivation–behavioral skills model of self-care among Chinese adults with type 2 diabetes," *BMC Public Health*, vol. 13, no. 1, p. 100, 2013.

34. C. Y. Osborn, K. Rivet Amico, W. A. Fisher, L. E. Egede, and J. D. Fisher, "An information–motivation–behavioral skills analysis of diet and exercise behavior in Puerto Ricans with diabetes," *J. Health Psychol.*, vol. 15, no. 8, pp. 1201–1213, 2010.

35. N. A. Cooperman, K. P. Richter, S. L. Bernstein, M. L. Steinberg, and J. M. Williams, "Determining smoking cessation related information, motivation, and behavioral skills among opiate dependent smokers in methadone treatment," *Subst. Use Misuse*, vol. 50, no. 5, pp. 566–581, 2015.

36. D. E. Glasford, "Predicting voting behavior of young adults: The importance of information, motivation, and behavioral skills," *J. Appl. Soc. Psychol.*, vol. 38, no. 11, pp. 2648–2672, 2008.

37. J. D. Seacat and D. Northrup, "An information–motivation–behavioral skills assessment of curbside recycling behavior," *J. Environ. Psychol.*, vol. 30, no. 4, pp. 393–401, 2010.

38. Z. Bahrami and F. Zarani, "Application of the Information-Motivation and Behavioral Skills (IMB) model in risky sexual behaviors amongst male students," *J. Infect. Public Health*, vol. 8, no. 2, pp. 207–213, Apr. 2015.

39. C. Walsh, "Obscene sounds: Sex, death, and the body on-screen," *Music Mov. Image*, vol. 10, no. 3, pp. 36–54, 2017.

40. M. Mittal, T. E. Senn, and M. P. Carey, "Intimate partner violence and condom use among women: Does the information–motivation–behavioral skills model explain sexual risk behavior?," *AIDS Behav.*, vol. 16, no. 4, pp. 1011–1019, 2012.

41. S. A. John, J. L. Walsh, and L. S. Weinhardt, "The Information–Motivation–Behavioral Skills model revisited: A network-perspective structural equation model within a public sexually transmitted infection clinic sample of hazardous alcohol users," *AIDS Behav.*, vol. 21, no. 4, pp. 1208–1218, 2017.

42. W. T. Robinson, "Adaptation of the information–motivation–behavioral skills model to needle sharing behaviors and hepatitis C risk: A structural equation model," *SAGE Open*, vol. 7, no. 1, p. 2158244016666126, 2017.

43. D. M. Godfrey and P. Feng, "Communicating sustainability: Student perceptions of a behavior change campaign," *Int. J. Sustain. High. Educ.*, vol. 18, no. 1, pp. 2–22, 2017.

44. M. J. Landau, *Conceptual Metaphor in Social Psychology: The Poetics of Everyday Life*. Routledge, 2016.

45. E. P. Russell, "'Speaking of annihilation': Mobilizing for war against human and insect enemies, 1914-1945," *J. Am. Hist.*, vol. 82, no. 4, pp. 1505–1529, 1996.

46. A. De Swaan, "Widening circles of disidentification: On the psycho-and sociogenesis of the hatred of distant strangers-Reflections on Rwanda," *Theory Cult. Soc.*, vol. 14, no. 2, pp. 105–122, 1997.

47. B. MacWhinney and D. Fromm, "Two approaches to metaphor detection," in *Proceedings of the Ninth International Conference on Language Resources and Evaluation (LREC-2014)*, Reykjavik, Iceland, 2014.

48. Y. B. Shlomo & M. Last, (2015, September). "MIL: Automatic Metaphor Identification by Statistical Learning," in *Proceedings of DMNLP, Workshop at ECML/PKDD*, edited by P. Cellier, T. Charnois, A. Hotho, S. Matwin, M.-F. Moens, Y. Toussaint, Nancy, France, 2014. pp. 19–30.

49. S. I. Al-Rubaish, "Inspire continues to inspire," *Inspire*, vol. 9, p. 6, 2012.

Chapter 15

An Information, Motivation, and Behavioral Skills Perspective on Terrorist Propaganda

Rebecca A. Wilson and Anthony F. Lemieux

CONTENTS

15.1 INTRODUCTION

Countering violent extremism (CVE) has become an increasingly salient part of national security policy in the United States. The 2015 National Security Strategy (NSS) acknowledged that countering violent extremism and terrorism requires more than removing terrorists from the battlefield. CVE, however, continues to evolve for both policy-makers and practitioners alike.

In the late twentieth century, European programs and international law established an initial framework that paved the way for modern CVE efforts, but it wasn't until recently that the United States' NSS began to focus on countering violent extremism efforts. Early examples of CVE in Europe include the EXIT program in Norway, Sweden, and Germany during the 1980s which focused on community and law enforcement efforts to dissuade or disengage right-wing violent extremists [11]. Similarly, it was the Organization for Security and Cooperation in Europe that was the first international body to recognize the need for addressing the root causes of terrorism critical in the wake of 9/11. Finally, in 2006, the United Kingdom created one of the first national-level CVE programs to counter homegrown violent extremism, focused on Islamic extremism (Her Majesty's Government of the United Kingdom, "The Prevent Strategy," 2011).

The United States has a long history with violent extremism, ranging from the Ku Klux Klan to the Weather Underground to modern Islamic State-inspired terrorism and beyond. Yet there have been few unified or comprehensive national efforts to counter violent extremism [9]. Since 2013, however, the United States has sought to merge domestic CVE approaches into an overarching national policy. The first modern U.S. CVE programs began in the mid-2000s and sought to develop community-based approaches to intervention and de-radicalization [9]. In 2011, the White House drew national policy attention to these nascent efforts by issuing a strategy document directed at empowering local communities to prevent violent extremism. Following policy attention, three nationally sponsored pilot programs were implemented to test community-based CVE efforts in Boston, Minneapolis, and Los Angeles. In 2015, an international CVE summit was held to build further awareness of CVE, counter extremist narratives, and emphasize community-led efforts. However, U.S. strategy on CVE remains incipient, despite its inclusion in the 2015 NSS and the institution of a joint CVE task force in early 2016.

There are several challenges that may contribute to the United State's equivocation with regard to CVE. First, defining and distinguishing CVE from other ostensibly related activities is one of the main obstacles to establishing an effective national policy. Radicalization occurs on both extremes of the political spectrum, and includes both secular and religious movements with violent radical groups. Groups that identify with right-wing, new left, single issue and ethno-separatist ideals have all perpetrated violence in the United States in the last few decades [22]. Right-wing extremism, specifically, is not as readily labelled or considered "terrorism" which may confound the challenge of defining and ultimately countering this type of violent extremist behavior.

Second, CVE efforts aim to alter beliefs and feelings across groups and individuals that are extremely different. Inherent to violent extremism are the beliefs, feelings, and behaviors that individuals or groups use to justify violence to achieve political goals [30]. While behaviors are observable, it is extremely difficult to identify beliefs or feelings that will cause future violent behavior [39].

Third, individual member traits vary widely. For example, members of the Islamic State of Iraq and the Levant (ISIL) have come from various age, gender, socioeconomic, and educational backgrounds. Similarly, the concept of radicalization itself has few universal indicators or attributes. The broader academic consensus is that several causal mechanisms contribute to individuals embracing political violence [25]. The sum of these challenges makes CVE activities difficult to calibrate, concentrate, and prioritize.

Recent research, however, demonstrates that violent extremism shares risk factors with other social and systemic maladies [9]. Despite the variety of reasons for embracing political violence, factors like economic inequality, complex social issues, and racial discrimination have been found to increase risk toward violent extremism—though none of these are causal in and of themselves [24]. Several radicalization models highlight the gap between an individual's aspirations and capabilities as significant to violent radicalization [8]. For instance, research among Muslim youth in Europe determined experiences of prejudice in the workplace and society comprise the attitudes that are rooted in the reality of this population [38]. Moreover, a 2006 study by the EU Agency for Fundamental Rights found that minorities and immigrants experienced greater levels of unemployment, representation in the least desirable jobs, and received disproportionately low wages [29]. Prior research on gang participation, criminal activity, and drug abuse demonstrate the impact structural social issues have motivating individuals to participate, and in some cases these causes can also be a part of the motivations for violent radicalization [42]. Since violent extremism shares risk factors with other social and systemic issues, there is a unique opportunity to examine pre-existing capabilities and resources in the context of CVE. The dilemma of there being no single cause, nor a reliable set of universal attributes that drive violent extremist behavior, means that effective CVE approaches must account for a variety of risk factors [35].

Issues of violence prevention have been researched, implemented, and improved in the field of public health. In addition, health behavior change interventions have been developed and evaluated based on strong theoretical underpinnings and rigorous analysis across a fairly wide range of behaviors that can be extraordinarily challenging to address effectively. The similarity in contributing and in some instances causal factors between violent extremism and other systemic psychosocial issues suggests that incorporating empirically validated prevention models from areas like public health should significantly contribute to establishing and advancing meaningful prevention frameworks that can be employed in both the conceptualization and evaluation of CVE activities.

In this chapter, we situate violent extremist behavior in an empirically validated and extensively researched framework of health behavior change: the information–motivation–behavioral (IMB) skills model of behavior change. We first describe the origins of the IMB model and the constructs and relationships it proposes. Next, we review empirical support for the IMB model in the context of intervention research in the area of HIV prevention. We then discuss current approaches to countering violent extremism as well as procedures for translating the IMB approach into conceptually based, empirically targeted, and rigorously evaluated CVE prevention efforts. Based upon this conceptual and empirical foundation, we suggest a general utility of the IMB model as an approach to understanding the social and psychological factors that influence the range of extremist behaviors. We conclude with reviewing applications of the IMB model in the prediction and understanding of health behaviors like HIV prevention compared to current conceptualizations and understanding of violent extremist behaviors.

15.2 THE INFORMATION–MOTIVATION–BEHAVIORAL SKILLS MODEL

The information–motivation–behavioral skills model of behavioral change suggests that knowledge, attitudes, and social norms work through behavioral skills to shape one's future behavior [5]. The model was first developed to provide an account of the psychological determinants of HIV risk and preventive behavior [14]. It is based on a critical review and integration of the constructs of relevant theories in social and health psychology and on an analysis of successes and failures reported in the HIV prevention intervention literature [6, 13, 21]. The development of the IMB model sought to address the limitations of existing theory in social and health psychology [14]. These include the following: the absence of specification of the relationships among critical constructs; lack of predictive validity of key constructs; and absence of constructs that may be central to understanding and changing health-related behavior [1, 6, 13, 33]. The IMB model was created to support and inform theoretically based and empirically targeted intervention operations [17]. Specifically, the IMB model focuses on the set of information, motivation, and behavioral skills factors that are conceptually and empirically associated with performance of health-related behavior [17]. Often times, these constructs are dealt with in isolation from one another in intervention efforts. The IMB model, however, specifies a set of operations and causal relationships among these three constructs that allow for translation of the IMB approach into interventions [17].

15.3 ASSUMPTIONS OF THE IMB MODEL

The IMB model posits that health-related information, motivation, and behavioral skills are fundamental determinants of performance of health behaviors. Thus, individuals who are well informed, motivated to act, and possess the requisite behavioral skills for effective action, will be likely to initiate and maintain health-promoting behaviors [17]. Conversely, individuals who are poorly informed, unmotivated to act, and/or lack behavioral skills necessary for effective action, will engage in health risk behaviors or be less likely to effectively adopt health-protective behaviors. According to the IMB model, information is a critical determinant of behavior performance if it is directly relevant to the performance of health behavior and can be easily performed by an individual in his or her social ecology [14, 15]. Types of information can include specific facts about health promotion as well as relevant heuristics (rules which permit automatic and cognitively effortless decision-making). Health promotion information can also include implicit theories in making decisions about health-related action. For example, HIV preventive facts (e.g. "condom use prevents HIV transmission"), heuristics ("monogamous sex is safe sex"), and implicit theories ("known and trusted people who dress and act reasonably and who possess a variety of normative characteristics are safe partners") have been found to exert powerful influences on HIV prevention behavior performance [17].

In addition to information, the IMB model specifies that motivation is also a critical determinant of the performance of health-related behaviors, and strongly influences individuals' inclination to undertake health promotion actions. According to the model, attitudes toward personal performance of health promotion behaviors (personal motivation) and social support for enactment of health promotion behaviors (social motivation) are both critical influences on performance of health-related behavior [17]. Moreover, motivation to engage in HIV preventative behavior (or to avoid HIV risk behaviors) includes attitudes toward prevention, perceived social norms with respect to prevention, and perceived vulnerability to HIV [17]. For example, several studies highlight personal attitudes and perceptions of social support are strong predictors of condom use behavior [3]; compliance with breast self-examination [10]; and the continued use of hormone therapy for postmenopausal women [16]. Information and motivation are not enough however; behavioral skills are the final determinant of whether well-informed and motivated individuals will be capable of effectively enacting health promotion behaviors.

The behavioral skills component focuses on both an individual's objective abilities and his or her sense of self-efficacy concerning performance of a given health-related behavior [34]. The IMB model specifies that health-promoting information and motivation work primarily through the behavioral skills construct to influence health behavior. In essence, the effects of information and motivation are seen primarily as a result of the application of behavioral skills to the initiation and maintenance of behavior. The model also asserts that health promotion information and motivation may have direct effects on health promotion behavior performance—when complicated or novel behavioral skills are not required to enact the health promotion behavior in question. In the case of HIV prevention behavior, for example, behavioral skills may include an individual's actual and perceived ability to bring up and negotiate HIV prevention with a partner; to acquire and use condoms comfortably; to maintain condom use over extended periods of time; and to shift prevention patterns appropriately [17]. According to the IMB model, individuals who possess accurate and relevant information, and personal and social motivation to act on it, would subsequently assemble and apply requisite behavioral skills to initiate and maintain patterns of (in this case) safer sexual behavior [17].

While the IMB model is regarded as highly generalizable across populations and health promotion behaviors of interest, it is important to note that within this approach, each construct must have specific content that is most relevant to the target populations' practice of specific health promotion behaviors [14]. In other words, information, personal and social motivation, and behavioral skills must be specific and targeted to each audience. Similarly, particular sets of information, personal and social motives, and behavioral skills will also be most relevant to understanding specific health promotion behaviors [17].

The IMB approach suggests that specific constructs of the model, and particular causal pathways among them, will emerge as more or less influential determinants of health promotion behavior dependent on the specific population, and specifies procedures that may be used to identify them [15]. Given the IMB perspective then, identification of the information, motivation, and behavioral skill elements most relevant to a population's support for, or practice of, specific violent extremist behaviors, and identification of model constructs which most strongly influence that population's practice of such behaviors, is crucial to designing targeted interventions [15].

15.4 TRANSLATING TERRORISM IN THE CONTEXT OF THE IMB MODEL

According to the IMB approach, the first step in developing a successful prevention program is to understand and identify the three constructs of the model present in violent extremist behavior and its sequelae. In order to do this, we take a broad, multimodal analytic approach. Jihadist groups of the twentieth and twenty-first centuries have evolved in their ability to propagandize across multiple modalities (e.g. magazines, news reports, music, video). Research of the Al Qaeda magazine *Inspire* found similarities between jihadist techniques of persuasion to engender behavior change and successful campaigns and interventions focused on changing a wide range of health behaviors [26]. In order to expand on this, we focus on multiple jihadist groups (Islamic State, Taliban, Al Qaeda, Al Shabaab) propaganda to determine the extent to which the constructs of the IMB model are present within extremist propaganda.

15.4.1 Information

The IMB model specifies information as the first critical determinant of behavior performance. Information must be directly relevant to the performance of a specific behavior, be easily performed by an individual in his or her social ecology, and include behavior-related material as well as myths/heuristics that permit automatic or cognitively effortless behavior-related decision-making [17]. Exploration of jihadist propaganda revealed a significant amount of facts, heuristics, and behavior-relevant information.

The messaging in extremist propaganda—whether in expertly produced magazines, nasheeds, or Hollywood-esque videos—revealed significant association between previous IMB campaigns and persuasive messaging in the respective propaganda corpora. Analysis of magazines including *Dabiq/Rumiyah* (Islamic State), *Gaidi Mtaani* (Al Shabaab), *Azan* (Taliban), and *Inspire* (Al Qaeda) demonstrate a targeted information strategy aimed at educating its audience on the history and meaning of waging jihad, restructuring and strengthening social normative expectations for in-group belonging, identification of dichotomous groups (in-group/out-group), and solidifying themselves as harbingers of the "true" Islam. In fact, all four groups (although varying in their message and reasoning) contain facts, heuristics, and implicit theories that support joining their cause.

Similarly, research demonstrates that music is a particularly powerful source of social communication of information, social influence, and social norms, particularly because it is engaging, repeatable, and often participatory [27]. Additionally, prior research suggests the impact of music is a highly effective tool for recruitment and fomenting violence [28]. Nasheeds (religious hymns dedicated to worship God, express true religious feeling, or call others to Islam) are a culturally significant, powerful method of conveying persuasive messaging harnessed by violent extremists. There are four main categories of jihadi nasheeds that provide information in the form of social influence and norms: "battle hymns" focusing on the war jihadis are waging; "praising hymns" that honor high standing individuals; "martyr hymns," which put emphasis on martyrdom; and "mourning hymns" lamenting the passing of an individual [20]. Moreover, the information provided in efforts like Abu Mansoor-al Amriki's (an American jihadist based in Somalia) hip-hop, is a creative method of modernizing and attracting Western Muslims to the cause of Al Shabaab and violent jihad. Information in the form of lyrics are used to convey and strengthen social normative expectations of jihad as well as glorify and celebrate the "heroic" efforts of current jihad members.

Video propaganda is an equally effective method of conveying information. Receiving information through video content often allows for what the information construct of the IMB model refers to as heuristics—or mental shortcuts that ease the cognitive load of making a decision [17]. Analysis of martyrdom video segments revealed the Islamic State answering questions regarding an individual's proper role (social norms) and importance during their lifetimes by positioning the martyr to be using the standard decision-making process of a leader of a global superpower [41]. Promises of success on the battlefield, coupled with a much-desired afterlife, serve as implicit theories motivating individuals to participate in a desired behavior [41]. Implicit theories are a priori beliefs that individuals develop throughout their lives. In the case of jihadist propaganda, specifically martyrdom videos, implicit beliefs associate the act of martyrdom as a rational, carefully thought out process.

15.4.2 Motivation

In addition to information, the IMB model posits that there must be sufficient motivation as operationalized through attitudes, perceptions of social norms, and perceptions of vulnerability and susceptibility to consequences of problems [18]. Motivation is composed of two factors: personal motivation—which includes beliefs about the intervention outcome and attitudes toward a particular health behavior—and social motivation—which includes the perceived social support or social norm for engaging in a particular behavior [17].

Across extremist magazines, a significant proportion of text is dedicated to motivational language expressing attitudes for waging jihad, overwhelming social support (according to the authors) for performing jihad, and stories exemplifying heroic behaviors of jihadists engaging in terrorist acts. Text and imagery in magazines share common themes of glorification for those who dedicate their lives to jihad (social support) and punishment (perceived vulnerability) for those who do not. Much of the personal and social motivational persuasive messaging is embedded in or supported by carefully manipulated text that weaves in religious language to convey a sense of informational authority. Objectifying centuries-old cultural and religious identity, fused with the impending erasure of the culture and rights of Islamic people, evokes a heightened sense of perceived vulnerability, which constitutes a compelling message that is quite often directed toward inspiring its audiences to adopt a worldview and sense of urgency that draws them closer toward taking violent action.

Prior to his death, Anwar al-Awlaki spoke to the power of music as a mechanism to create a culture that would motivate the masses to jihad [2]. Awlaki described the role that a nasheed (vocal music or chant) can play in inspiring individuals to practice jihad. He observed that nasheeds are especially inspiring to youth, and have the ability to reach an audience that you could not reach through a lecture or book. Awlaki is drawing on a long history of music, motivation, and war [2]. Soldiers have employed music to inspire themselves for combat, and as a catalyst to heighten anger, aggression, and appetite for violence [31]. Religious organizations, national solidarity movements, and fascist regimes have consistently (and successfully) used music as an expedient tool to assert or maintain control over a group of people as well as inspire fervent defense of their particular religion or political ideology [31]. The nasheeds produced by groups like the Islamic State express a wide range of attitudes, perceptions of social norms, and perceptions of vulnerability and susceptibility to consequences of not belonging to their group, impassioned by the cultural resonance, beauty, and power of song.

Like music, video also plays a tremendous role in motivating individuals and groups toward behavior change. For example, Islamic State videos (e.g. *Flames of War*) use socially comparable "actors." This assists in targeting a specific population in order to address (and ultimately shift) social norms and attitudes. Additionally, analysis of *Flames of War* determined that among the self-portrayals of the fighters, there were five major themes repeated throughout the film. They were: honest, favored by God, persistent, believers, and fearless [4]. Content of the video include imagery and rhetoric that affirms the war for Islam waged by ISIS is favored by God and supported by a global Muslim population. Moreover, jihadist fighters in the film are portrayed (as in text and imagery) as heroic warriors. Extremist videos relate stories of both personal and social support that are complimented with online chat groups (much like the classroom discussions).

15.4.3 Behavioral Skills

The third determinant in the IMB model is behavioral skills defined as skills necessary for performing a particular health behavior [18]. To facilitate behavioral change, the IMB model emphasizes the enhancement of an individual's skills and increased perceived self-efficacy [18].

Behavioral skills across jihadist propaganda are integrated into content with the express purpose of increasing target audience self-efficacy and expressing socio-cultural and religious support for prescribed behaviors. Cross-comparison of jihadist magazines revealed print techniques that provide education and empowerment of their target population with the use of interview series like *Interview with the Amir of the Soldiers of the Khilafah In East Asia* (*Rumiyah* 10, 36–41); testimonials like *My Story: A Mujahid's Journey* (*Azan* 2, 73–80); infographics like *The Successful Pressure Cooker Bomb* (*Inspire* 16, 9); and step-by-step instructional articles like *From Hijrah to Khilafah* (*Dabiq* 1, 34–40).

Similarly, anashid (vocal music that is either sung acapella or accompanied by percussion instruments) are a particularly salient means of strengthening the perceived self-efficacy of the listener. A primary utility of the anashid genre for jihadist propaganda efforts lies in its ability to enchant or move the listener as a means of emotionally animating their ideology [32]. However, the role of anashid in jihadism is not limited to affective impact or any other motivating factor like sense of belonging, heroism, or finding meaning in one's life. In fact, considerable musicological research demonstrates how musical genres are foundational elements expressing group or personal identity [7, 32]. Group dynamics and social bonding (i.e. identity fusion) have been shown to be key determinants of a terrorist's "will to fight," and anthropological work on music shows its powerful catalyzation of social bonding, even among combatants [12]. Additionally, the portrayal of jihad as the solution to the problems facing all Muslims (perceived vulnerability) is present in almost all the nasheeds [20]. Information detailing *how* to counter the perceived vulnerability and humiliation of Muslims through joining jihad, for example, is complemented by rhythm and repetition facilitating the internalization of their messages [20].

Finally, jihadist propaganda often augments textual content with music and video. Films like *Messages from the Land of Epic Battles* and *Flames of War* feature Islamic State fighters in fierce battles, horrific executions, and punishments for those resistant to their ideology. *Russian Hell* brings the viewer into fighting Russians in Chechnya. Scenes featuring camaraderie and successful attacks, rousing music, and explicit invitations to join depict what the viewer needs to do and how to do it [23]. Similar to the text in magazines and the lyrics of nasheeds, violent extremist films visually depict the social support, social norms, perceived vulnerability, and methods of enacting behaviors that are posited to increase self-efficacy and subsequently the strengthening of behavioral skills.

A brief exploration of jihadist propaganda revealed a perhaps unintentional adherence to constructs of successful public health models of behavior change like the IMB model. We identified specific sets of information, personal and social motives, and behavioral skills aimed at precise audiences across multiple modalities meant to reinforce and change (or persuade) an individual's norms and attitudes and ultimately, behavior. Positioning CVE efforts in the context of empirically validated public health behavior strategies may present new and increasingly successful ways to counter the messages being sent by violent extremists and promote healthy behaviors in response to the appeal of violent associations.

15.5 CVE IN THE FORM OF PUBLIC HEALTH PREVENTION

The war on violent extremism in the Middle East may appear to be won on the ground, however the same cannot be said for cyber-terrorism and online terrorist campaigns, nor for the resurgence of right-wing extremism in the United States. As practitioners and the U.S. government work to minimize extremist violence (on both ends of the spectrum), looking to areas with a long-standing history of prevention development like public health may provide significant insight.

Our analysis of jihadist propaganda revealed messaging campaigns across a variety of groups and modalities that mimic constructs of successful public health prevention intervention programming. Having identified the way violent extremists write, sing, and produce video that engenders new sets of norms and attitudes, it may be useful to briefly examine and compare current CVE efforts with what a CVE prevention situated in a public health framework (like the IMB model) may look like.

In the context of the IMB model, the first problem in current CVE prevention is targeting the right audience. Like HIV prevention interventions, it is important to include socially and culturally comparable people as well as cultural sensitivity in regard to the desired target population. Recent research found that much of the success in countering extremist thought and behavior was rooted in the use of trusted intermediaries who can resonate with the at-risk population [36]. Specifically (and reminiscent of the HIV videos) employing peers from their own peer group—like ex-extremists—has shown to be a more effective tool than moderate imams in redirecting behavior [36].

In addition to using socially and culturally comparable individuals, the IMB model impresses the need for facts, heuristics, and behavior-relevant information in campaign content. CVE efforts like the USDS's Think Again Turn Away campaign videos lack a multidimensional narrative as well as taking advantage of multimodal content effectively, across multiple delivery channels in which it reaches the intended audience. The overarching message portrayed by the USDS is that violent extremists are enemy groups, but this perspective is only a small piece of violent extremist narratives [4]. For example, across multiple channels (magazines, online conversation, videos, news reports) the Islamic State's messaging declares the organization's members as holy warriors fighting for a caliphate that is favored by God and acutely defines the how, what, why, and who of becoming a violent extremist. In essence, the ISIS message accurately conveys facts, heuristics, and associated behavior required, in an affirmative and validating way. The information conveyed by the State Department was one-dimensional, negative and reactive situating countervailence efforts in the defensive—which is an inherently weaker and generally unsuccessful position [4].

The second construct within the IMB theoretical framework is motivation. Motivation is defined as the inclusion of attitudes toward the specific problem, addressing perceptions of social norms as well as perceptions of vulnerability and susceptibility to the consequences of the problem(s). Like HIV prevention campaigns, jihadist propaganda presents the cause as supported by the ummah (global Muslim population), heightened vulnerabilities facing Muslims and associated positive attitudes with joining their cause, and negative attitudes for rejecting their brand of ideology. Thus far, CVE efforts still seem to be in a relative testing phase, with commentators and focus groups alike having described some CVE efforts as "preachy" and inadequate [40]. While CVE efforts should focus on strengthening the information presented, CVE intervention efforts need to increase extremist prevention motivation by influencing attitudes and social norms concerning violent extremism. Examples of suggested programming that could be used to affect attitudes and norms required for behavior change include: (1) high-quality content featuring ex-extremists who speak the language of the disaffected target population and understand their struggle but have learned how to channel their energy in a more positive way and (2) ex-extremists who discuss the consequences they have suffered due to their engagement in violent extremism [36]. Recently, researchers conducted a study that measured whether real life ISIS defectors speaking about their personal experience of what life was like as a fighter for the Islamic caliphate could affect radicalized individuals [37]. Results of this study found that their counter-narratives did resonate with ISIS endorsers, followers, and promoters on social media [37]. Additionally, the counter-narrative materials (videos) were also clicked on by friends of the target audience, which is an important consideration for the social network capabilities of online CVE activities [37].

However, long-term effects of this specific intervention have yet to be determined. While the study was reportedly able to entice ISIS endorsers into opening and sharing the counter-narrative videos, results of whether any behavioral change online or offline occurred remains to be seen [37]. Similar to health prevention/intervention frameworks, like the IMB model, CVE may benefit from a multi-faceted approach. Coupling CVE videos or online static content with vibrant online community discussions about how unfavorable attitudes and norms concerning violent extremist ideology led to fractured families, communities, and more often, death is an additionally powerful means of addressing norms, attitudes, and perceptions of vulnerability and susceptibility necessary to motivate behavior change. Counter-messaging in this manner plays well to the emotions and desires of potential recruits and begins to broaden the cognitive space of thought and debate in deciding whether to continue on the path to radicalization or find an alternate means to address one's needs.

The final construct in the IMB model to effectively facilitate behavioral change is behavioral skills. Behavioral skills emphasize the enhancement of an individual's skills and increased perceived self-efficacy [16]. Relevant to HIV prevention, students viewed a specially produced video (again featuring ethnically diverse, socially comparable high school students) enacting behaviors to protect themselves from HIV (e.g. assertively maintaining abstinence; purchasing, carrying, discussing, and using condoms) and included a demonstration of condom use [16].

In the context of CVE efforts, videos, infographics, and online discussions should feature socially and comparable individuals (like ex-extremists) that discuss and demonstrate behaviors that will protect them from the consequences of violent extremism. In addition, there should be consideration given to the inclusion of mental health programs as a means to increase self-efficacy and encourage the adoption of prevention behavioral skills. Research on lone-actor extremists found that many of these individuals struggle with psychological and social issues [19]. Thus, increasing perceived self-efficacy by providing adequate mental health options for individuals at risk of embracing extremist ideologies may additionally increase the success of deterring homegrown extremism [40].

15.6 SUMMARY

Countering violent extremism is a top priority for the safety and security of the United States. Radicalization to violence is a threat regardless of the political, religious, or ideological reasons associated with it, enabling the opportunity to draw on previously validated and successful prevention frameworks, like those in public health. Despite the lack of consensus on CVE's definition and activities (which creates a less than ideal organizing construct for a strategic and effective CVE mission) practitioners have begun to draw on prior successful prevention frameworks.

The utility of a public health prevention focus for CVE has several benefits for the development, implementation, and evaluation of CVE activities. In general, a public health approach can clarify roles and responsibilities, identify key stakeholders and individuals who should be involved at various phases in the radicalization process, and encourage the use of pre-existing prevention efforts [9]. Public health takes a holistic approach involving multiple systems and stakeholders – a recognized need for CVE efforts. In addition to its established strength in predicting, understanding, and intervening to change HIV risk behavior, the IMB model is viewed as a generalizable approach to understanding and promoting behavior [15].

The intent of this chapter was to explore the IMB model's ability to transfer outside of the field of public health to prevention development in relation to violent extremism. Exploratory multimodal analyses of jihadist propaganda revealed striking similarities between extremist communication and recruitment strategy and the IMB framework. Across jihadist magazines, videos, and music are an abundance of facts, heuristics, and behavior-relevant information complimented by attitudes, norms, and vulnerabilities addressing their target audience. The utility of the IMB model in the context of extremist propaganda is the ability to deconstruct a complex multimodal messaging campaign in order to understand the root constructs impacting behavior. Moreover, the IMB framework lends itself to the creation of a more targeted prevention/intervention campaign as well as direct means to evaluate prevention efficacy.

Consideration should be given to the incorporation of socially and culturally appropriate role models, the inclusion of valid methods of addressing attitudes and norms, prevention motivation, and behavioral skills. Further, the inclusion of mental health options as a conduit for increasing self-efficacy may also benefit CVE prevention efforts. Finally, CVE prevention programming may profit from the careful incorporation of multiple media and modalities including film, print, and online discussions. As in public health, the implementation and evaluation of a CVE prevention program would greatly benefit from further, more structured research and analysis. CVE continues to remain a policy priority and subsequently the development and insurance that prevention programming is effective in protecting public safety.

REFERENCES

1. Ajzen, Icek. "The theory of planned behavior." *Organizational Behavior and Human Decision Processes* 50, no. 2 (1991): 179–211.
2. al-Awlaki, Anwar. *Ways to Support Jihad. Media,* 44, 2009 (p. 1–21). North Las Vegas, NV: Victorious [Self-published]. Retrieved September 18, 2017 from: http://ebooks.worldofislam.info/ebooks/Jihad/Anwar_Al_Awlaki_-_44_Ways_To_Support_Jihad.pdf
3. Albarracin, Dolores, Blair T. Johnson, Martin Fishbein, and Paige A. Muellerleile. "Theories of reasoned action and planned behavior as models of condom use: A meta-analysis." *Psychological Bulletin* 127, no. 1 (2001): 142.
4. Allendorfer, William, and Susan Herring. "ISIS vs. the US government: A war of online video propaganda." *AoIR Selected Papers of Internet Research* 5 (2016).
5. Aronowitz, Teri, Cheryl Ann Lambert, and Sara Davidoff. "The role of rape myth acceptance in the social norms regarding sexual behavior among college students." *Journal of Community Health Nursing* 29, no. 3 (2012): 173–182.
6. Bandura, Albert. "Human agency in social cognitive theory." *American Psychologist* 44, no. 9 (1989): 1175.
7. Bennett, Andy. "Theorizing music and the social: New approaches to understanding musical meaning in everyday life." *Theory, Culture & Society* 17, no. 3 (2000): 181–184.
8. Bjørgo, Tore, ed. *Root Causes of Terrorism: Myths, Reality and Ways Forward.* London: Routledge, 2004.
9. Challgren, Jonathan, Ted Kenyon, Lauren Kervick, Sally Scudder, Micah Walters, Kate Whitehead, Jeffrey Connor, and Carol Rollie Flynn. "Countering Violent Extremism: Applying the Public Health Model." *Georgetown Security Studies Review, United States* (2016).
10. Champion, Victoria L. "Breast self-examination in women 35 and older: A prospective study." *Journal of Behavioral Medicine* 13, no. 6 (1990): 523–538.
11. Demant, Froukje, Marieke Slootman, Frank Buijs, and Jean Tillie. *Decline and Disengagement: An Analysis of Processes of Deradicalisation.* Institute for Migration and Ethnic Studies, Amsterdam (2008).
12. DeNora, Tia. *Music in Everyday Life.* United Kingdom: Cambridge University Press, 2000.
13. Fishbein, Martin, and Icek Ajzen. *Belief, Attitude, Intention and Behavior: An Introduction to Theory and Research.* Reading, MA: Addison-Wesley, 1975.
14. Fisher, Jeffrey D., and William A. Fisher. "Changing AIDS-risk behavior." *Psychological Bulletin* 111, no. 3 (1992): 455.
15. Fisher, Jeffrey D., and William A. Fisher. "Theoretical approaches to individual-level change in HIV risk behavior." In *Handbook of HIV Prevention*, pp. 3–55. Springer, Boston, MA, 2000.
16. Fisher, Jeffrey D., and William A. Fisher. "The information-motivation-behavioral skills model." *Emerging Theories in Health Promotion Practice and Research: Strategies for Improving Public Health* 15, John Wiley & Sons (2002): 40–70.
17. Fisher, William A., Jeffrey D. Fisher, and Jennifer Harman. "The information- motivation-behavioral skills model: A general social psychological approach to understanding and promoting health behavior." *Social Psychological Foundations of Health and Illness* 82 (2003): 82–106.
18. Fisher, William A., Jeffrey D. Fisher, and Paul A. Shuper. "Social psychology and the fight against AIDS: An information–motivation–behavioral skills model for the prediction and promotion of health behavior change." In *Advances in Experimental Social Psychology*, vol. 50, pp. 105–193. Academic Press, 2014.
19. Gill, Paul, John Horgan, and Paige Deckert. "Bombing alone: Tracing the motivations and antecedent behaviors of lone-actor terrorists." *Journal of Forensic Sciences* 59, no. 2 (2014): 425–435.
20. Gråtrud, Henrik. "Islamic State nasheeds as messaging tools." *Studies in Conflict & Terrorism* 39, no. 12 (2016): 1050–1070.
21. Hochbaum, Godfrey Martin. Public participation in medical screening programs: A socio-psychological study. No. 572. US Department of Health, Education, and Welfare, Public Health Service, Bureau of State Services, Division of Special Health Services, Tuberculosis Program, 1958.
22. Hoffman, Bruce. "The Global Terror Threat and Counterterrorism Challenges Facing the Next Administration." *CTC Sentinel* 9, no. 11 (2016): 1–8.

23. Holt, Tom, Joshua D. Freilich, Steven Chermak, and Clark McCauley. "Political radicalization on the Internet: Extremist content, government control, and the power of victim and jihad videos." *Dynamics of Asymmetric Conflict* 8, no. 2 (2015): 107–120.

24. Horgan, John. "From profiles to pathways and roots to routes: Perspectives from psychology on radicalization into terrorism." *The ANNALS of the American Academy of Political and Social Science* 618, no. 1 (2008): 80–94.

25. King, Michael, and Donald M. Taylor. "The radicalization of homegrown jihadists: A review of theoretical models and social psychological evidence." *Terrorism and Political Violence* 23, no. 4 (2011): 602–622.

26. Lemieux, Anthony F., Jarret M. Brachman, Jason Levitt, and Jay Wood. "Inspire magazine: A critical analysis of its significance and potential impact through the lens of the information, motivation, and behavioral skills model." *Terrorism and Political Violence* 26, no. 2 (2014): 354–371.

27. Lemieux, Anthony F., Jeffrey D. Fisher, and Felicia Pratto. "A music-based HIV prevention intervention for urban adolescents." *Health Psychology* 27, no. 3 (2008): 349.

28. Lemieux, Anthony F., and Robert Nill. "The role and impact of music in promoting (and Countering) violent extremism." *Countering Violent Extremism: Scientific Methods and Strategies* (2011): 144.

29. Macke, Julia. "European Union Agency for Fundamental Rights." *Focus on the National Implementation of "Third Pillar" Legislation-Dossier particulier sur la mise en oeuvre de la législation du «troisième pilier»- Schwerpunktthema: Nationale Umsetzung der Gesetzgebung der" dritten Säule"* 01-02 (2007): 18–19.

30. McCauley, Clark, and Sophia Moskalenko. "Mechanisms of political radicalization: Pathways toward terrorism." *Terrorism and Political Violence* 20, no. 3 (2008): 415–433.

31. Pieslak, Jonathon. *Radicalism and Music: An Introduction to the Music Cultures of Al-Qa'ida, Racist Skinheads, Christian-Affiliated Radicals, and Eco-Animal Rights Militants.* Wesleyan, Middletown, Connecticut, 2015.

32. Pieslak, Jonathan, and Nelly Lahoud. "The Anashid of the Islamic State: Influence, history, text, and sound." *Studies in Conflict & Terrorism* (2018): 1–26. doi:10.1080/1057610X.2018.1457420.

33. Rosenstock, Irwin M. "Historical origins of the health belief model." *Health Education Monographs* 2, no. 4 (1974): 328–335.

34. Rye, Barbara J., William A. Fisher, and Jeffrey D. Fisher. "The theory of planned behavior and safer sex behaviors of gay men." *AIDS and Behavior* 5, no. 4 (2001): 307–317.

35. Shader, Michael. *Risk Factors for Deliquency.* Office of Juvenile Justice and Delinquency Prevention's (OJJDP's) Research and Program Development Division, 2004.

36. Shaikh, Mubin. "Countering violent extremism (CVE) online: An anecdotal case study related to engaging ISIS members and sympathizers (from North America, Western Europe, and Australia) on Twitter." *Soundings: An Interdisciplinary Journal* 98, no. 4 (2015): 478–487.

37. Speckhard, Anne, and Ardian Shajkovci. "Confronting an ISIS Emir: ICSVE's Breaking the ISIS Brand counter-narrative videos." (2017). Retrieved from the International Center for the Study of Violent Extremism: http://www.icsve.org/research-reports/confronting-an-isis-emir-icsves-breaking-the-isis-brand-counter-narrative-videos

38. Stern, Jessica. "Mind over martyr: How to deradicalize Islamist extremists." *Foreign Affairs* 89 (2010): 95–108.

39. Taylor, Max, and John Horgan. "A conceptual framework for addressing psychological process in the development of the terrorist." *Terrorism and Political Violence* 18, no. 4 (2006): 585–601.

40. Tierney, Michael. "Combating homegrown extremism: assessing common critiques and new approaches for CVE in North America." *Journal of Policing, Intelligence and Counter Terrorism* 12, no. 1 (2017): 66–73.

41. Winkler, Carol, and Jonathan Pieslak. "Multimodal visual/sound redundancy in ISIS videos: a close analysis of martyrdom and training segments." *Journal of Policing, Intelligence and Counter Terrorism* 13, no. 3 (2018): 345–360.

42. World Health Organization. *Global Status Report on Violence Prevention*, World Health Organization, Geneva, Switzerland, 2014.

Chapter 16

The Relationship between Personal Data Protection and Use of Information to Fight Online Terrorist Propaganda, Recruitment, and Radicalization

Paolo Balboni and Milda Macenaite

CONTENTS

16.1 INTRODUCTION

In the wake of the terrorist attacks in Madrid (2004) and London (2005), the Council of the European Union (EU) adopted the European Union Counter-Terrorism Strategy with the aim to fight terrorism "while respecting human rights, and make Europe safer, allowing its citizens to live in an area of freedom, security and justice" [1]. In this public policy document, the EU took a multi-faceted and institutionalized approach to "counter" terrorism relying on four pillars: (1) protect, (2) respond, (3) prevent, and (4) pursue. While the "protect" pillar emphasizes better defense against attacks on citizens and critical infrastructure, "respond" stands for an adequate consequence management after a terrorist attack, "prevent" refers to countering terrorist radicalization and recruitment and "pursue" to the investigation of terrorist activity and the persecution of members of terrorist networks across borders.

Impediment of the dissemination of terrorist propaganda and technical knowledge online since the conception of the document has become a focal point of the EU policy agenda. A few years later, the EU Internal Security Strategy reaffirmed the key role of the internet in spreading extremist propaganda, radicalization, and the recruitment of potential terrorists [2]. It urged the EU member states to remove illegal internet content, e.g., incitement to terrorism, and to offer alternatives to terrorist narratives. A coherent approach has been called for based on cooperation between internet service providers, law enforcement authorities, and civil society organizations [2].

The prevention of terrorist recruitment, closely linked to propaganda and radicalization, and the pursuit of terrorists might thus be countered using different approaches and measures. A soft approach is based on counter-radicalization and relies on positive measures, such as the use of counter-narratives, detente and the promotion of social pluralism. In contrast, hardline approaches use negative means to, first, eliminate and block online terrorism propaganda and radicalization and, second, to gather personal data and information as part of intelligence with the aim to identify and physically prosecute those involved in terrorism [3]. These approaches require various degrees of information and personal data collection and sharing and thus affect the right to personal data protection and also importantly, potentially impact other fundamental rights.

This chapter explores the relationship between personal data protection and the use of information by law enforcement authorities and Europol when countering online terrorist propaganda, recruitment, and radicalization. It questions what information and under which circumstances law enforcement officials should gather together to remove terrorist propaganda from social media platforms and other websites, and consequently to further disrupt terrorist activities, and when this activity should fall under the EU legal framework of personal data protection. We outline the applicable EU data protection legal framework focusing on the provisions of the two most relevant legislative instruments, in particular the newly enacted Directive 2016/680 and Regulation 2016/794 (Europol Regulation). We then look into the main pieces of information that the national law enforcement authorities and Europol, in particular its EU internet referral unit (EU IRU), potentially need to collect in order to counter terrorist propaganda, recruitment and radicalization and consider whether and when this information can qualify as personal data. We then examine the main obligations stemming from the two applicable legal frameworks for law enforcement authorities and Europol.

16.2 DATA COLLECTION FOR COUNTERING ONLINE TERRORIST PROPAGANDA, RECRUITMENT, AND RADICALIZATION

Recent years have witnessed an alarming amount of content posted and disseminated by terrorist groups and their supporters with the aim to radicalize and recruit individuals around the world to promote their causes. Claims have been made that "(t)he internet has in fact developed into a tool for terrorism-related recruitment, propaganda and financing, as well as a catalyst for radicalization" [4]. In 2017, Europol identified more than 150 social media platforms, the mainstream being available on the open internet (e.g., Twitter, YouTube, and Facebook) rather than the Dark Web, that terrorists use to disseminate propaganda [5]. The wide availability and persistence of terrorist propaganda has become a serious concern for European governments and law enforcement authorities. File-sharing websites are increasingly used to deposit illegal extremist and propaganda content, messaging, and bots to spread links to such content, and social media aggregators to store, streamline, and advertise on other platforms [5].

ISIS has proven to be innovative and tech savvy in terms of fully exploiting the various platforms and tools to spread their message including the live-streaming of attacks, recruiting of new members, indoctrination, and inciting individuals and terrorist cells to violence. It has been reported that ISIS was able to "fool" the system, e.g., by using Twitter messages and social bots (i.e. automated social media accounts) designed to manipulate and increase the likelihood that propaganda content goes viral [6] or relying on online archiving sites that retained terrorist propaganda materials, already removed from other platforms and websites in huge amounts [7]. Even with a decrease in new ISIS audiovisual material due to loss in infrastructure and human capital on the ground, ISIS has still managed to regularly re-upload previously produced, high-profile propaganda material to achieve the "echo" effect [5]. A recent report demonstrates how ISIS supporters employ Facebook tools to circumvent automatic detection when hosting meetings using the Facebook Live feature, linking to banned materials in comments fields and using the algorithmic "recommended friends" feature to be introduced around the world [8].

In reaction to this, the EU has pooled its resources in order to implement a coordinated and multilevel response requiring close and harmonized collaboration between national (and European) public authorities, platforms and service providers, and the civil society. Member states together with the Commission and the concerned EU agencies were requested "to address in particular the use of the Internet for terrorism radicalisation and recruitment purposes as well as for on-line hate speech that fuels fear, spreads misconceptions and stereotypes targeting specific communities and groups, and incites to violence and hatred, notably by developing, including with Internet Service Providers, cooperation on strategic communication and, where appropriate, internet referral units" [9].

Blocking and removing extremist content in online spaces (social media, blogs, video sharing platforms) engaged in terrorist propaganda or recruitment in fact lies at the heart of the EU response and action [10].

16.2.1 Content Removal and Account Blocking

In March 2015, the Justice and Home Affairs Council requested Europol to establish a dedicated unit, embedded within Europol's European Counterterrorism Centre, to provide support for the EU member states in tackling online terrorism propaganda [11, 13]. From July 2015, the EU internet referral unit (EU IRU) became operational and engaged in monitoring the internet for social media accounts that post terrorist propaganda and have such accounts closed and the content taken down by the service providers. The precise tasks of the EU IRU include: (1) coordination and sharing the flagging of terrorist and violent extremist content online with relevant partners (i.e. law enforcement in the EU member states, the private sector), (2) coordination with industry to carry out referrals, (3) support for competent authorities by providing strategic and operational analysis, and (4) acting as a hub of expertise in these fields [12]. Similar units exist on the national level, e.g., the UK has its Counter Terrorism Internet Referral Unit (CTIRU), which was developed within the Association of Chief Police Officers (ACPO) in 2010.

The EU IRU builds on several other initiatives and tools. One of them is the EU Internet Forum, active since 3 December 2015, a group composed of the EU Ministers of Interior, representatives of the main internet and social media providers such as Facebook, Google, Twitter, Microsoft and Europol, the European Counter Terrorism Coordinator, and the European Parliament [13, 14]. The aim of the forum has been to suggest measures for countering online terrorist and extremist content, to implement the referral process, and to share best practices and expertise. More concretely, the EU IRU in cooperation with law enforcement authorities from EU member states and the internet industry have been tasked to flag and refer terrorist content online, while civil society, with the help of the internet industry, to prepare counter-narratives. The latter has been carried out by a network of experts (Radicalisation Awareness Network) financially supported by the EU. The EU Internet Forum initiated several projects: (1) a shared industry database of "hashes" of violent terrorist or terrorist recruitment videos and images, etc., helping to identify such content on social media and ensure that it cannot reappear on other networks and platforms [15] and (2) the Civil Society Empowerment Programme, a financial support programme for civil society to produce and spread alternative narratives through social media channels.

Other initiatives preceding the establishment of the EU IRU are the Check-the-Web project managed by Europol [16] and the CleanIT project [17] that bring together the private and public sectors for sharing best practices in countering online terrorist activities. Check-the-Web focused on enhancing voluntary cooperation on monitoring and evaluating open internet sources. It has in turn developed into a technical platform allowing for the exchange of information among the EU countries (e.g., all Europol national units (ENU) had access to the portal) and associated third parties [16]. The portal included: (1) a list of contact persons taking part in the Check-the-Web in the EU member states, (2) a list of links to monitored websites, (3) a list of declarations of terrorist organizations to help in combining resources, and (4) evaluation results to avoid duplication of work [16].

The CleanIT project was an early building block for a public–private dialogue on the terrorist use of the internet. Carried out from June 2011 until March 2013, it was initiated by the public authorities dealing with counterterrorism from the Netherlands (the leading country), Germany, the UK, Belgium, and Spain and involved numerous other public and private sector representatives. The final outcome of the project was the adoption of a set of guiding principles and an overview of best practices on how to reduce terrorist exploitation of the internet [18].

The recent pressure on the industry from policy-makers to improve the automatic detection of terrorist propaganda content and promptly and effectively remove it has led to the development of several industry initiatives and tools. On 26 June 2017, Facebook, Microsoft, Twitter, and YouTube announced their collaboration through the Global Internet Forum to Counter Terrorism (GIFCT), a formalization and structuring of their already ongoing cooperation to address the problem of terrorist content on their respective platforms [19]. The five working areas of the Forum were identified as follows: (1) to develop and improve technological solutions, such as the shared industry hash database, (2) to commission research "to inform [...] counter-speech efforts and guide future technical and policy decisions around the removal of terrorist content," (3) to share knowledge with counterterrorism experts in government, civil society, and academia in partnership with the UN Security Council Counter-Terrorism Executive Directorate (UN CTED) and ICT4Peace Initiative and smaller companies to help them develop appropriate technologies and policies [20], (4) to develop best practices with freedom of speech and privacy advocates, and (5) to mutually learn and contribute to each other's ongoing counter-speech activity, and to determine how to further educate and empower individuals and civil society groups engaged in similar work [21]. Furthermore, individual companies have put forward their own solutions. A new technological tool based on artificial intelligence has been launched by Facebook to identify and remove propaganda material [22]. This technology enables comparing exact duplicates of photos or videos with the ones which were removed by a human moderator and preventing re-uploading in cases where the two pieces match.

Despite the fact that hosting service providers deployed certain measures to tackle terrorist content on their services through voluntary frameworks and partnerships, such as the EU Internet Forum, their efforts were not universal and the scale and pace of progress was not considered sufficient to adequately address the problem of the uploading and sharing of terrorist propaganda online.

As a consequence, the European Commission has recently taken a legislative action and prepared a proposal for a regulation on preventing the dissemination of terrorist content online [23].

Building upon the previous Commission Communication [24], the proposed draft regulation introduced specific measures designed to reduce terrorist content. The proposal, still subject to changes during the EU legislative process, includes:

- a removal order which can be issued as an administrative or judicial decision by a competent authority in an EU member state, by which the hosting service provider is obliged to remove the content or disable access to it within one hour
- a harmonization of the minimum requirements for referrals sent by member states' competent authorities and by Union bodies (such as Europol) to hosting service providers to be assessed against their respective terms and conditions
- the requirement for hosting service providers to take proactive measures proportionate to the level of risk and to remove terrorist material from their services, including automated detection tools
- the requirement to reserve terrorist content which has been removed or disabled as a result of a removal order, which is necessary for proceedings of administrative or judicial review and the prevention, detection, investigation and prosecution of terrorist offences for six months

The above-mentioned measures are accompanied by the safeguards to ensure protection of fundamental rights, e.g., remedies and complaint mechanisms to ensure that users can challenge the removal of their content and obligations on transparency for the measures taken against terrorist content by hosting service providers.

From the overview of the EU activities provided above, it becomes clear that the fight against online terrorist propaganda, recruitment, and radicalization requires the sharing of information, such as hashes of images and videos of terrorist activities and URLs linking to specific social media profiles or groups. However, content blocking and removal represents just one part of the fight against terrorist propaganda, recruitment, and radicalization, and data can be potentially further collected for crime analysis purposes, which is considered in the next section.

16.2.2 Data Collection for Crime Analysis

The activities of law enforcement authorities and Europol extend far beyond the detection and requesting the removal of terrorist-related content. They can use the collected information further to prevent and combat terrorism in the context of criminal intelligence gathering. Criminal intelligence is a form of surveillance carried out by law enforcement to gather information about crime or criminal activities before they occur or to establish their occurrence. It should be distinguished from the criminal investigation of concrete criminal activities, a procedural stage in investigation. An example of data use for criminal intelligence could be additional checks to verify if the email address used to create a social media profile posting terrorist propaganda is already known to law enforcement. This further use of collected information would include strategic and operational crime analysis and efforts to identify and link potential suspects and perpetrators, as well as assess, analyze threats, and monitor trends.

Europol has its Cyber Intelligence Team, which collects information from public, private, and open sources and identifies emerging threats and patterns of cybercrime. The EU IRU detects and analyzes terrorist content on the internet to produce strategic insights into jihadist terrorism and to provide support to EU law enforcement authorities in online criminal investigations [25]. The Europol regulation allows for the collection of open source intelligence (OSINT) and to carry out internet monitoring. Europol is entitled to "directly retrieve and process information, including personal data, from publicly available sources, including the internet and public data" (Article 17(2)) and has a task to "support Member States' actions in preventing and combating forms of crime listed in Annex I (of the Europol Regulation) which are facilitated, promoted or committed using the internet, including, in cooperation with Member States, the making of referrals of internet content, by which such forms of crime are facilitated, promoted or committed, to the online service providers concerned for their voluntary consideration of the compatibility of the referred internet content with their own terms and conditions" (Article 4(1)(m)).

In reality Europol employs or looks into various tools to conduct crime analysis for the EU member states. These tools allow "to crawl and harvest online content, conduct real time data correlation as well as real time trends monitoring and custom application programming interface (API) data harvesting scripts" [4]. Social network analysis, voice fingerprinting, facial recognition, audio and text converters, and other analytical tools are used to carry out crime analysis in the analysis work files, one of them being focused on counterterrorism [4].

National law enforcement authorities equally carry out crime analysis and process criminal intelligence potentially allowing to identify individuals engaged in terrorist-related activities that are criminalized under national laws. The EU member states criminalize and impose sanctions for the use of the internet for terrorist purposes in line with the Directive (EU) 2017/541 on combating terrorism [26], among others, for the

- distribution of messages to the public online that aim to incite the commission of a terrorist offence, such as an attack upon a person's life or physical integrity with the aim to seriously intimidate a population
- solicitation of another person to commit or contribute to the commission of a terrorist offence, i.e., recruitment for terrorism
- provision or receiving of training for terrorism, such as providing or receiving instructions on the making of explosives, or other weapons, substances, specific methods or techniques, for the purpose of committing a terrorist offence

Many tools, such as data mining and link analysis software applications, e.g., Maltego and RapidMiner, can be used to collect intelligence from open sources to track online terrorist activities [27]. Social network analysis and social cyber forensics approaches can also be employed to identify influential users and powerful groups or focal structures that coordinate the online propaganda campaigns [28]. Therefore, the collection of any information and publicly available data (e.g., IP addresses, email addresses, usernames) and their analysis, linking, and visualization might be carried out for criminal analysis and allow authorities to "connect the dots."

If it is determined that information processed by national law enforcement authorities and Europol constitutes personal data, the data protection legal framework is applicable, and each data processing activity must be carried out in compliance with this framework. Although the majority of information collected in the context under analysis surely involves personal data—as collected information often clearly relates to the social media account holders or the content displayed on social media is often personal data—the interesting question is whether and under what circumstances the information would not be reasonably associated to an identified or identifiable individual, i.e., would not legally qualify as personal data. Before considering this question (i.e. whether a piece of information is personal data), the applicable data protection legal framework, where actually the EU definition of personal data is found, is briefly discussed. This legal framework is based on an interplay between the three legal instruments calibrated according to who is processing personal data, i.e., is a data controller.

16.3 DATA PROTECTION LEGAL FRAMEWORK

The main legal instrument in the EU regulating personal data processing in the law enforcement (police and criminal justice) area is Directive 2016/680 [29]. The Directive was adopted in December 2015 as part of the data protection reform package together with Regulation 2016/679 (GDPR) [30]. The GDPR sets forth the general rules for personal data processing and thus can be viewed as *lex generalis*, while Directive 2016/680 takes into account the particular nature of the law enforcement sector and operates as *lex specialis* [31]. The Directive, which had to be transposed by the EU member states into their national laws by 6 May 2018, sets forth the principles relating to the processing of personal data, establishes the rights of the data subjects and the obligations of the controllers and processors, regulates the transfers of personal data to third countries and international organizations and the powers and tasks of the independent supervisory authorities, and foresees the remedies, liability, and penalties [32]. It clearly echoes the GDPR in terms of notions, principles and even in terms of structure [33].

In practice there is still some lack of clarity as to the precise delineation between Directive 2016/680 and the GDPR [34]. More precisely, the personal scope of application of Directive 2016/680 is the processing of personal data by competent authorities. Therefore, to fall under the scope of this Directive the data processing should be carried out by "competent authorities," defined as:

(a) any public authority competent for the prevention, investigation, detection or prosecution of criminal offences or the execution of criminal penalties, including the safeguarding against and the prevention of threats to public security; or

(b) any other body or entity entrusted by member state law to exercise public authority and public powers for the purposes of the prevention, investigation, detection or prosecution of criminal offences or the execution of criminal penalties, including the safeguarding against and the prevention of threats to public security (Article 3(7)(a)).

The first part of the definition includes traditional public law enforcement authorities such as police, national courts, and other judicial authorities, prosecution, customs and border guards, and other specialized agencies having investigatory powers in specific domains, e.g., financial intelligence units (FIUs) in countries where they are law enforcement authorities [35].

Despite the urge to maintain the notion of competent authority as limited as possible [36, 37], the second part of the definition expands the scope to "other bodies and entities" which can be private or public–private in nature. Potential examples include security companies with extended executive powers contracted for sporting events or private prisons in the UK. However, as it has been pointed out, such examples are currently rare in practice, and thus the inclusion of private bodies in the definition is mainly future-looking and reflects some national trends in law enforcement which shift toward privatization and increasing collaboration of state law enforcement with private actors (public–private partnerships), especially evident in the cyber security field [34].

Some uncertainty remains however as to the extent that the processing of data generated by the internet and platform service providers (ISPs, social media service providers, and other private entities providing online services) falls under Directive 2016/680. Without any doubt the GDPR applies to these private entities providing services online when they collect personal data from their users for their own commercial purposes. Such data can be further processed in order to comply with a legal obligation to which they might be subject (e.g., national data retention laws) and consequently transferred to the competent authority requesting them. Processing of the same data by the competent authorities as a result becomes subject to data protection requirements laid down in Directive 2016/680 and the relevant national law implementing it. However, some lack of clarity exists as Recital 11 of the Directive 2016/680 provides as follows: "[…] A body or entity which processes personal data on behalf of such [competent national] authorities within the scope of this Directive should be bound by a contract or other legal act and by the provisions applicable to processors pursuant to this Directive, while the application of Regulation (EU) 2016/679 remains unaffected for the processing of personal data by the processor outside the scope of this Directive" [36]. The question is whether data processing such as storing on the part of internet service and platform providers for the purposes of the Directive could be considered as being "on behalf of" law enforcement authorities qualifying them as "data processors" under Directive 2016/680 [38]. This does not seem to be the case, as ISPs, social media service providers, and other private entities providing online services would usually process personal data according to the GDPR to comply with a legal obligation imposed by law (e.g. laws on data retention or the future EU regulation requiring to preserve removed terrorist content) rather than on request of the competent authorities.

It should be noted that the material scope of Directive 2016/680 covers the processing of data for the purposes of the prevention, investigation, detection, or prosecution of criminal offences or the execution of criminal penalties, including the safeguarding against and the prevention of threats to public security (Articles 2(1) and 1(1)). Data processing for national security purposes is explicitly excluded from the scope of Directive 2016/680. However, the definition of "national security" is not uniform among EU member states and the limits of this exemption are debatable. The threat of terrorism may fall under both the national security and law and order domains, and, as a result, the limits of competences and the ways of information exchange between intelligence and law enforcement authorities may vary in specific countries [39]. Indeed, in practice, the delineation of data processing for law enforcement purposes and national security purposes proved to be complicated in some member states when such processing is carried out by law enforcement authorities [40].

Equally, the Directive is not applicable to personal data processing in the context of (criminal) court proceedings. In principle, once a criminal investigation is opened, the respective national legal provisions on criminal procedure are followed by the competent authorities [33].

As noted earlier, one of the main actors dedicated to tackling terrorist propaganda on the internet is the EU Internet Referral Unit (EU IRU) at Europol. Europol, being the EU agency aiming to support and enhance member states' competent authorities' actions and their mutual cooperation in preventing and combating organized crime, terrorism, and other forms of serious crime affecting two or more member states, has a separate legal instrument regulating its activities, including personal data processing. This legal instrument is Regulation 2016/794 (Europol Regulation) [41], which came into force on 1 May 2017. Indeed, an explicit legal basis for the functioning of the EU IRU is enshrined in this Regulation, as it explicitly foresees that one of Europol's tasks is to support member states' actions in preventing and combating terrorism which is "facilitated, promoted or committed using the internet, including, in cooperation with member states, the making of referrals of internet content, by which such forms of crime are facilitated, promoted or committed, to the online service providers concerned for their voluntary consideration of the compatibility of the referred internet content with their own terms and conditions" (Article 4(1)(m)).

Even if the GDPR and Directive 2016/680 and Regulation 2016/794 are similar, there are some differences between these legal frameworks. Certain principles, data subject rights, and data controller's obligations in Directive 2016/680 and Regulation 2016/794 are framed less strictly compared to the GDPR to provide more leeway for law enforcement and to accommodate their specific needs when carrying out their activities [42]. Without aiming to provide a full analysis, the following examples could be named. First, strict compliance with the data quality principle might hinder operational police activities, e.g., data collection from undercover sources and open sources which are often questionable as to their reliability and accuracy or the use of subjective statements that are not always verifiable in judicial proceedings. Therefore, the nature and purpose of the processing concerned should be taken into account when applying the data quality principle (Recital 30, Article 7 of the Directive 2016/680 and Articles 29-30 of the Regulation 2016/794). Regulation 2016/794 foresees specific evaluation codes to signal the level of reliability of the source and accuracy of information (Article 29).

Second, data collected for a specific case sometimes have to be used to resolve other criminal offences or to make links between different crimes detected, rendering a strict application of the purpose limitation principle rather problematic. As a consequence, Directive 2016/680 permits the use of data for purposes other than that for which they have been collected as long as the purpose is in line with the general purpose of prevention, investigation, detection, or prosecution of criminal offences or the execution of criminal penalties, and the controller is authorized to process such data by law and the processing is necessary and proportionate (Article 4(2)). Similarly, Regulation 2016/794 allows further processing of personal data for another operational analysis project insofar as it is necessary and proportionate, and the processing is compatible with the required safeguards (Article 18).

Third, the exercise of the rights of data subjects to information and access their data might be prejudicial to surveillance of suspects or under some circumstances obstruct criminal investigations and prosecutions. The right to rectification would not be sensible in specific circumstances, such as for the content of a witness testimony and the right to deletion in cases when personal data has to be maintained for evidentiary purposes (Recital 47 of the Directive 2016/680). Thus, the national laws of EU member states can impose partial or complete restriction on these rights and data controllers are allowed to deny these rights under specific circumstances (Recitals 43-48, Articles 13(3), 15(1), 16(4) of the Directive 2016/680). In addition to national laws, Directive 2016/680 itself already restricts the amount of information to be made available to data subjects under Article 13(1) and (2) with respect to the GDPR: information on data recipients and international data transfers should be given only in specific cases and the provision of information related to automated decision-making or intent to further process personal data for different purposes is not required under Directive 2016/680.

With the purpose of countering flexibility in the processing of personal data afforded to law enforcement authorities in relation to the principles, rights, and obligations, data processing by law enforcement authorities is subject to strict legal requirements [34]. Directive 2016/680 clearly sets forth that data can be processed only in the law enforcement context, on the grounds, and for the purposes set forth by law, according to special processing conditions. For example, while the GDPR allows data controllers to rely on one or more of six general grounds for personal data processing (Article 6 GDPR), competent authorities under the Directive can only use the ground of lawfulness, i.e., the necessity "for the performance of a task carried out by a competent authority" for law enforcement purposes when that task is based on national or Union law (Article 8(1) Directive 2016/680) where the law specifies "at least the objectives of processing, the personal data to be processed and the purposes of the processing" (Article 8(2)). As a result, only national laws that confer the task of law enforcement can provide the legal basis for data processing and should do so by specifying both the overall objectives of a certain legislative act and the specific purposes of the processing operation (Recital 33, Article 8(2)).

16.4 DEFINITION OF PERSONAL DATA

Terrorists and potential terrorists post and share propaganda, issue threats, claim ownership of attacks on public websites, social media, and Dark Web forums. In order to fight online terrorist propaganda, recruitment, and radicalization, information, including personal data, has to be collected and shared by different actors. Law enforcement authorities need to collect and process information and intelligence from various open sources as part of analyses that contribute to criminal intelligence. For example, law enforcement authorities monitor and analyze public sources as part of their strategic analyses. The EU IRU identifies, flags, and refers the URLs related to terrorist and violent extremist content toward concerned internet service providers and law enforcement authorities. Private entities, such as website operators, retain information on user access operations in logfiles, e.g., the name of webpages or files to which access was requested, the search terms entered, the time of access, the amount of data transferred, whether access was successful, and the IP address of the computer from which access was requested. Additionally, website operators process information or personal data when a specific user creates an account to access a service. Such information might be requested by law enforcement in case there is a suspicion of a criminal activity or an ongoing investigation.

The legal status of information that these entities collect and share becomes essential at this point. Personal data processing is subject to specific legal requirements imposed by data protection law on data controllers. In contrast, processing of non-personal data or anonymous data falls outside the scope of the data protection law. Though, as already mentioned, the processing of personal data by law enforcement authorities, the EU IRU and private companies (e.g., ISPs, online media service providers) would be governed by different data protection legal frameworks, i.e., respectively the Directive 2016/680, Regulation 2016/794 (Europol Regulation), and the GDPR, the definition of personal data is identical in all these documents. Therefore, while the discussion below sometimes makes reference to one of these frameworks, the considerations provided below are applicable to all of the three above-mentioned documents.

Directive 2016/680 applies to the processing of "any information concerning an identified or identifiable natural person ('data subject')" (Recital 21, Articles 2(1), 3(1)). Article 3(1) specifies that "an identifiable natural person is one who can be identified, directly or indirectly, in particular by reference to an identifier such as a name, an identification number, location data, an online identifier or to one or more factors specific to the physical, physiological, genetic, mental, economic, cultural or social identity of that natural person." According to a broad interpretation provided by the Article 29 Working Party, information can be considered to "relate to" an individual: 1) by reasons of its content, i.e., it is about that individual or 2) when it is processed with the purpose to determine the status or behavior of an individual, i.e., to assess an individual, or to make an impact on the individual's rights and interests (e.g., the individual may be treated differently from other persons as a result of the processing of such data), i.e., to affect an individual [43]. An individual is "identified" when he or she can be distinguished from other members of the group and "identifiable" when there is a possibility to do so. An individual can be directly identified or identifiable, e.g., by reference to a person's name, sometimes in combination with other pieces of information (date of birth, names of parents, address, or a photograph of the face) to establish his or her identity beyond any doubt. An individual can also be identified indirectly, i.e., combining available identifiers with other pieces of information. For example, natural persons may be associated with online identifiers provided by their devices, applications, tools and protocols, such as internet protocol addresses, Mac address, IMEI, IDFA, cookie identifiers or other identifiers, e.g., radio frequency identification tags. This may leave traces which, in particular when combined with unique identifiers and other information received by the servers, may be used to create profiles of the individuals and identify them (Recital 30 GDPR). Yet, the extent to which certain identifiers are sufficient to actually achieve identification of an individual depends on the circumstances of the particular case.

Whether information can be qualified as "personal data" under the Directive depends on the specific circumstances as to whether it can identify an individual at present, or potentially in the future, if other information could be obtained or accessed and combined with it. For example, the alias of a propaganda publisher that may need to be disclosed to law enforcement authorities, unless it is unique and unusual, alone may not identify an individual. If it is further combined with age, gender, and location data, it may still be insufficient to identify an individual. The more additional data is provided about an individual the more likely it becomes that identification can be achieved. In this respect, sufficient tools owned by the data controller and its capacity to identify an individual from the information becomes a decisive criterion. In fact, the Directive explicitly states that when considering if a natural person is identifiable "account should be taken of all the means reasonably likely to be used, such as singling out, either by the controller or by another person to identify the natural person directly or indirectly" (Recital 21 of the Directive 2016/680). The Directive further notes that "all objective factors, such as the costs of and the amount of time required for identification, taking into consideration the available technology at the time of the processing and technological developments" should be considered for establishing whether means are "reasonably likely to be used to identify the natural person" (Recital 21 of the Directive 2016/680). However, in practice the test of what constitutes a disproportionate effort to identify a natural person, requires unreasonable costs and time with reference to available technological resources, and development does not yield to an easy application.

Despite the potential necessity to assume that in the case of doubt information should be considered personal data, i.e., there might be a need to err on the side of over inclusion in order to achieve protection, the cases below illustrate a potential debate and difficulties of legally qualifying the main pieces of information that are often collected by the authorities in the law enforcement sector when countering online propaganda and terrorist activities.

16.5 PROCESSING OF INFORMATION OR PERSONAL DATA?

16.5.1 Hashes of Images and Videos

Hashing is a mathematical function allowing the generation of a number or code from a string of characters, e.g., from an attribute or a set of attributes. Hashing is a useful security measure, and typically it does not render personal data anonymous but instead pseudonymizes it [44]. Pseudonymous data is still treated as personal data in the EU (Article 4(5) of the GDPR).

The qualification of a hash code as personal data would depend on the type of the information that is being hashed. If this information is about an identified or identifiable individual (e.g., an image of an identified foreign fighter), the hash would be considered personal data. To the contrary, if the information does not allow for the identification of a person concerned (see the examples below) or does not involve personal data, the hash code would not fall under the personal data definition. An example of the latter could be a promotional jihadist video showing a fictitious character who encourages young Muslim men to join ISIS or containing only the voice of a preacher which cannot be linked to a person using the available voice recognition technology. Nevertheless, the burden of proof that the voice does not constitute personal data would lie upon the data controller that processes the data.

16.5.2 URL Addresses and Domain Names

A domain name is a text label used to identify a single instance of resources or a collection of them, which could be networks or services. Being text-based rather than numerical addresses used in the internet protocols, domain names can be more easily recognized and remembered by internet users. Domain names or URLs do not normally entail personal data in and of themselves. In limited cases, a domain name could, however, consist of the first and last name of a natural person and clearly be personal data, even if the exact person is not immediately evident, e.g., if the name used is very common. A domain name could also correspond to the name of an organization or group rather than or an individual. Only information relating to an identified or identifiable natural person is protected under data protection law whereas the data of legal persons is not (Article 3(1) of the Directive 2016/680).

Nevertheless, a domain name would constitute personal data if it can be linked to a natural person. Often it is possible to do so by obtaining personal data of the person who registered the domain or by obtaining the related IP addresses. A domain name may be attributed to a person or an entity using the Whois service (www.whois.net/). Indication of a domain name in Whois can provide information on the person or entity that registered the domain name, such as the name, address, telephone number, and email address.

In some countries, however, the extent and types of data that can be found on Whois are limited by law (e.g., in Russia, Canada, and Australia). More constraints and limitations have been recently imposed on the information that Whois provides by the GDPR in the EU [45]. Therefore, even when looked up, in some cases domain names would not produce personal data or would produce fake or fabricated details that cannot be linked to a specific entity. There may be more cases when the possession of a domain name and a linked IP address might not necessarily allow for attribution. For example, botnets make use of the fast flux technique to create and use a network of compromised computers. They link many IP addresses with a single domain name and rapidly change the IP addresses and DNS records, creating difficulties for law enforcement authorities who want to block domains used by the malware, due to the fact that thousands of domain names are generated by algorithms every day [46]. The usage of botnets by terrorist groups to spread propaganda has been documented [6], and thus it can be assumed that some of the IP addresses of a command and control server of a botnet would not be intentionally associated with a domain name or the server operator would misuse the server of another entity, i.e., a victim, to execute the attack [47].

URL addresses, i.e., universal resource locators, indicate a web resource location on a computer network and its retrieval mechanism. A typical URL shows the applicable protocol, a hostname, and a file name. A URL is normally composed of a domain name, referring to a particular location or file on a server related to that domain name, giving the computer instructions on what to do with the specific file. URLs, similarly as domain names, can lead to information about the domain registrant, such as his name, telephone number, email address, and mailing address, using the Whois service. It is possible to use the command terminal or specific websites or software to look up the IP address associated with a URL. Therefore, from a URL depending on the nature of the IP address (static or dynamic) and any other information available, it may be possible to link back to an individual. In fact, in the context of URL flagging activities of the EU IRU, Europol appears to accept that URLs qualify as personal data without exception [4]. However, as becomes evident below, this is not certain, as many users may use the same server or proxy, or the server may serve multiple websites at once.

16.5.3 IP Addresses

An IP address is a set of numbers assigned to a device connected to a computer network that uses the internet protocol. IP addresses can be static or dynamic in nature. Static IP addresses are constantly related to a specific device and do not vary (i.e. continuous identification of the device connected to the network is possible), whereas dynamic IP addresses can change occasionally or even each time a new internet connection is established. The actual practice depends on the country and on the internet service provider (ISP). It has been demonstrated, for example, that 72 percent of internet users have the same IP address for two weeks, but in some countries, e.g., in Germany, many ISPs change a user's IP address every 24 hours [48]. Mobile devices are typically assigned dynamic IP addresses. There were cases when the entire internet traffic from one country has been transferred using only a few IP addresses [49].

Originally, the majority of IP addresses were static, but presently a usual practice is to assign dynamic IP addresses to ordinary internet users. Through the dynamic host configuration protocol (DHCP) new dynamic IP addresses are usually assigned every time a device restarts, or boots up, but it can also change frequently in the course of a continuous internet connection. One of the reasons is the problem of IPv4 address depletion, i.e., reassigning the same IP address allows for it to be reused for different devices that are connected to the internet only at that moment. Another potential reason relates to the fact that "(s)ome residential Internet service providers periodically reassign different IP addresses for a host, often to deter that user from running a server but also to protect the user from someone tracking them by noting their IP address" [50].

Though in case of static IP addresses it is easier to identify a device than in case of dynamic IP addresses, in the latter case attribution is possible with a reference to records maintained by ISPs on the DHCP dynamic IP addresses which show which IP addresses were assigned to specific devices at a particular moment. Specific devices are identified using a MAC, i.e., a media access control address, which is a unique identifier of a device, normally stored in its hardware. Different jurisdictions have laws requiring ISPs to retain meta-data that facilitates the linking of an IP address to a particular subscriber [51]. Access to such meta-data is subject to a specific legal procedure and involves a cost.

In the EU, member states have taken diverging positions on the legal status of IP addresses resulting in inconsistent conclusions reflected in national case law. In EMI & Ors v Eircom Ltd, the case concerning illegal downloading and copyright infringement, the High Court of Ireland found that IP addresses do not constitute personal data under Directive 95/46/EC [52]. In contrast, the French Constitutional Court, when evaluating the constitutional standing of the antipiracy law (HADOPI law), held that the collection of IP addresses allowing for the identification of an individual should be considered as the processing of personal data [53]. National EU data protection authorities, gathered under the Article 29 Working Party, issued an opinion [43] in which they classified dynamic IP addresses as personal data for the ISPs that collect data in relation to such IP addresses. The Article 29 Working Party stated the following:

> A particular case would be that of some sorts of IP addresses which under certain circumstances indeed do not allow identification of the user, for various technical and organizational reasons. One example could be the IP addresses attributed to a computer in an internet café, where no identification of the customers is requested. It could be argued that the data collected on the use of computer X during a certain timeframe does not allow identification of the user with reasonable means, and therefore it is not personal data.

The same view was reaffirmed later in Opinion 1/2009 on the proposals amending Directive 2002/58/EC on privacy and electronic communications (e-Privacy Directive) [54].

Recognizing the factual difficulty that ISPs face when distinguishing between the types of IP addresses with certainty, the Article 29 Working Party recommended assigning to IP addresses personal data status by default, i.e., that IP addresses constitute personal data in and of themselves [43]:

> However, it should be noted that the Internet Service Providers will most probably not know either whether the IP address in question is one allowing identification or not, and that they will process the data associated with that IP in the same way as they treat information associated with IP addresses of users that are duly registered and are identifiable. So, unless the Internet Service Provider is in a position to distinguish with absolute certainty that the data correspond to users that cannot be identified, it will have to treat all IP information as personal data, to be on the safe side.

Academia is divided on the issue and has conceptually distinguished the "absolute/objective" and the "subjective/relative" approaches when interpreting the requirement of "all the means likely reasonably to be used either by the controller or by any other person" [55]. The "absolute/objective" approach would consider information to be "personal data" if any third party is able to determine the identity of the individual, while the "subjective/relative" would do so only if a data controller has the legal and practical means (and not merely an abstract possibility) of obtaining the additional information from a third party that allows the identification of the individual. On a broader level, academics in Europe have increasingly raised concerns about the over-inclusive expansion of the definition of personal data in EU data protection law [56]. As a consequence, unconditional recognition of dynamic IP addresses as personal data presents concerns and "may be indicative of a general move toward considering an increasingly broader scope of data as personal under the terms of the Data Protection edifice" [57].

The binary distinction between personal and non-personal data has been also criticized by U.S. legal scholars [58–60]. Instead, a granular approach has been advocated by a number of scholars when assessing the identifiability of a person. Schwartz and Solove [61] have proposed to classify information depending on whether it refers to (1) an identified person (the identity is "ascertained" or an individual can be "distinguished" from a group), (2) an identifiable person (the risk of identification is from low to moderate, i.e., identification is "not a significantly probable event"), or (3) a non-identifiable person (the risk of identification is only "remote") and have claimed that applicable legal obligations should be scaled according to these categories. Their approach requires an *ex ante*, probabilistic and contextual assessment of a particular data set to determine to which category it belongs. It takes into account the current or probable means likely to be used to access the information, the additional data that is available and contextual factors such as the information storage period, the likelihood of future development of relevant technology, and incentives to link data to a specific individual [61].

In the same vein, other academics have acknowledged the need of gradations of identifiability in personal data [60] and distinguished many categories of data based on the treatment of direct identifiers, indirect identifiers, and safeguards or internal and external controls.

The case law of the Court of Justice of the European Union (CJEU) has dealt with the issue on several occasions, but being limited by the specific questions of the national courts and the factual circumstances of the case has until now only reached context-dependent conclusions. In *Scarlet/Sabam* (2011), [62] the CJEU concluded that IP addresses in the hands of an ISP were to be treated as personal data (i.e. ISPs can usually link the name of their customers to the IP addresses allocated to them). In *Bonnier Audio and Others* [63] the CJEU held that communication "of the name and address of an Internet ... user using the IP address from which it is presumed that an unlawful exchange of files containing protected works took place, in order to identify that person ... constitutes the processing of personal data within the meaning of the first paragraph of Article 2 of Directive 2002/58, read in conjunction with Article 2(b) of Directive 95/46." Both cases related to the status of IP addresses as a secondary issue in the context of copyright infringement and the protection of intellectual property rights.

In a recent landmark case, *Patrick Breyer v. Bundesrepublik Deutschland* [64], the question that the CJEU addressed was instead whether, under Article 2(a) of Directive 95/46/EC, for a website publisher (rather than for an ISP) a dynamic IP address amounts to personal data. The CJEU held that dynamic IP addresses could constitute personal data, noting:

> 38. (...) it is common ground that a dynamic IP address does not constitute information relating to an "identified natural person," since such an address does not directly reveal the identity of the natural person who owns the computer from which a website was accessed, or that of another person who might use that computer.

The CJEU went on by specifying how to interpret what constitutes a means likely reasonably to be used by the data controllers to achieve identification [64]:

> 45. (...) it must be determined whether the possibility to combine a dynamic IP address with the additional data held by the internet service provider constitutes a means likely reasonably to be used to identify the data subject.

> 46. (...) that would not be the case if the identification of the data subject was prohibited by law or practically impossible on account of the fact that it requires a disproportionate effort in terms of time, cost and man-power, so that the risk of identification appears in reality to be insignificant.

Finally, the CJEU qualified dynamic IP addresses as personal data in the context of the case at hand [64]:

> 49. (...) Article 2(a) of Directive 95/46 must be interpreted as meaning that a dynamic IP address registered by an online media services provider when a person accesses the website that the provider makes accessible to the public constitutes personal data within the meaning of that provision in relation to that provider, where the latter has legal means which enable it to identify the data subject with additional data which the internet service provider has about that person.

It is important to note that in this judgement the CJEU clarified the notion of the dynamic IP address, yet it did not take a bright line rule perspective to IP addresses [65] nor did it embrace the "absolute/objective" approach. The CJEU essentially ruled that dynamic IP addresses in the hands of an online media service provider may constitute "personal data" even where only a third party (i.e. an ISP) has the additional data (e.g., its customer's name and address) necessary to identify the individual. It answered a specific and narrowly formulated question without explicitly discussing if dynamic IP addresses are, always and in all circumstances, personal data under Directive 95/46/EC [66].

The CJEU was also not asked whether the classification of dynamic IP addresses as personal data is necessary from the moment when any potential third party becomes capable of using such dynamic IP addresses to identify individuals [66].

The GDPR to a certain extent crystallizes the approach in the EU, but it still does not establish a blanket position toward IP addresses. The GDPR mentions online identifiers among the examples of the identifiers by reference to which a person might be indirectly identified (Article 4.1). Recital 30 specifies that IP addresses as an identifier which in combination with additional information might identify individuals:

> Natural persons may be associated with online identifiers provided by their devices, applications, tools and protocols, such as internet protocol addresses, cookie identifiers or other identifiers such as radio frequency identification tags. This may leave traces which, in particular when combined with unique identifiers and other information received by the servers, may be used to create profiles of the natural persons and identify them.

During the legislative GDPR process, unsuccessful proposals were made to include a clarification in the definition of personal data that "if identification requires a disproportionate amount of time, effort or material resources the natural living person shall not be considered identifiable" [67].

The analysis above indicates that the qualification of an IP address as a piece of personal data or not should be done in relation to a particular context in which that address is collected, used, and disclosed. When considering the context of online terrorist propaganda sharing, there will be situations, the majority of which relate to what law enforcement would call "the going dark" problem [68], where IP addresses depending on specific circumstances cannot be attributed to individuals.

First, while an IP address is linked to the subscriber paying an ISP for internet access, it does not necessarily identify the person using the device (PC, tablet, routing devices, or mobile phones) to access the internet at the specific point in time when the IP address was recorded. This argument has been raised more generally by various courts and data protection authorities to justify their restrictive position toward IP addresses as personal data [69]. In 2008, the U.S. District Court for the Western District of Washington stated that "[I]n order for 'personally identifiable information' to be personally identifiable, it must identify a person. But an IP address identifies a computer" [70]. The Privacy Commissioner of Canada also noted that dynamic IP addresses in isolation do not always identify individuals [71]. The Commissioner acknowledged that as dynamic IP addresses change with each new logon session they entail "elements of randomness and relative anonymity", yet depending upon the ISP and its information systems, often dynamic IP addresses can be linked to an invariable identifier, e.g. a subscriber's user ID conferred by the ISP [71].

In fact, in the present context the identification of an actual internet user would be difficult if a user who posts propaganda or engages in terrorist recruitment is accessing the internet from a device which is shared, e.g., a PC in an internet café which does not require visitor registration or when a visitor may register a false identity. Similarly, free and public WiFi in a bar, bookstore, or hotel lobby allows customers to use their network's IP address. Furthermore, when a law enforcement authority requests an ISP for meta-data retained on a particular point in time in order to map an IP address to a particular subscriber, it might turn out that due to the expiration of the retention period the ISP has already deleted the required meta-data or a unique identifier of a device (MAC) in question was falsified. In such cases the IP address could potentially be considered as information rather than as personal data, unless additional information is subsequently acquired and allows attribution or linking of these IP addresses to an individual. Additionally, terrorist organizations and sympathizers posting propaganda and recruiting new members could employ technologies and tools offering, at least partially, anonymity and identity concealment. This "hiding in plain sight," as part of the "going dark" problem, relates to the use of easily available and often free technologies that enable to conceal or misrepresent physical location and anonymize online activity [72]. As a consequence some countries have even outlawed the use of several of these techniques referring to the concerns about extremist content online [73].

One of the technologies to anonymize online activity is The Onion Router (TOR), a software that is used to mask the location and internet activity of users. TOR encrypts data several times and transmits it via a virtual circuit of TOR relays run by volunteers. Every relay decrypts a layer and passes the remaining encrypted data to the next relay of the circuit, a process resembling peeling layers of an onion, as the name The Onion Router itself indicates. The last relay decrypts the inner level of encryption and allows the transmission of the data to the final destination without revealing or knowing the sender's IP address. The use of TOR does not imply complete anonymity for the user, as some information might still be obtained at the exit relay where TOR traffic comes out of the anonymous network and connects to the open internet [74]. Unlawful content might be traced back to the exit relay's IP address, which can be attributed to the volunteer operator of the relay who is not responsible for the malicious content [75]. The use of other applications with the TOR network (JavaScript engine, plug-ins like Adobe Flash, and external applications like a video player) could potentially disclose the IP address to a website that aims to acquire it [74].

Another technology, relevant for this discussion, is a virtual private network (VPN). A VPN creates a private network enabling users to securely send and receive data across public networks. In such a way, users are afforded the functionality, security, and management of private networks. A VPN provides the ability to hide the source IP address and location. Nevertheless, the VPN service provider might potentially be able to provide details of the user if they collect and store them (e.g., log users' IP addresses for any requests made on users' behalf) and law enforcement authorities may be able to access this information using relevant legal processes. Yet, not all VPN providers collect customers' details and criminals might have their own VPN service where no logs are maintained for identification purposes.

A proxy server is another technology that can be used to conceal an original IP address. Acting as an intermediary, the proxy server ensures that a website that a user visits sees the IP address and browser details of the proxy server instead of the original user device. Yet, similarly to VPNs, proxy servers may potentially also collect and store IP addresses and therefore law enforcement authorities may be able to retrieve details in the logs following the specific legal process.

In order to address the problem of the exhaustion of Internet Protocol Version 4 (IPv4) addresses due to the increased global demand for internet access, the Network Address Translation (NAT) protocol has been adopted. NAT allows assignment of private IP addresses to devices within a local network (home, small businesses). Devices use private IP addresses (usually dynamic IP addresses) internally until they transmit packets of information externally to the internet, i.e., the moment when they are assigned a single public IP address. From a public IP address it is not usually possible to identify a device using the local network, or the individual who accessed the internet at the specific time. Access to the IP addresses would be given to the public IP address rather than to an endpoint user's private IP addresses within the local network. A larger approach to the NAT model has been increasingly deployed by using Carrier Grade NAT (CGN). Through CGN several local networks are compounded into big local networks hosted by ISPs which connect to the internet using a single public IP address. When using CGN address translations, a single IP address can be shared by thousands of subscribers at the same time. As a result, due to CGN, law enforcement authorities face huge difficulties to trace back an individual end-user of an IP address [76]. Europol illustrates the extent of these difficulties by reporting that in one EU member state in more than 50 percent of criminal investigations, criminals used mobile IP addresses (smartphone) and in 90 percent of these cases a CGN was involved and, thus, mobile IP addresses could not be attributed [76, 77].

A public IP address is not enough to identify a local network or a device within such a local network, there is a need to know a port number from which the data was sent or received. Therefore, in order to identify an individual end-user of an IP address on a network using CGN, law enforcement authorities must request additional information from ISPs via a legal process: source and destination IP addresses, exact time of the connection, and source port number. However, due to the lack of harmonious data retention rules, not all content service, internet service, and data hosting providers are under legal obligation to retain this type of information.

The overview above demonstrates that it may not always be possible to identify a person using a specific IP address when dealing with online propaganda and terrorist recruitment cases. In addition to the use of the identity concealment techniques mentioned above, criminals often use fake online identities and intentionally avoid leaving any traces of personal information or links to it. Law enforcement may not always be in a position to obtain additional information from an ISP, obtaining such information might be legally or technically very challenging.

16.5.4 Email Addresses and Usernames

An email address usually is composed of two parts: the first identifies an email box which should receive email messages (usually a username), while the second part refers to the domain name which is the administrative realm of the mailbox. Although the first part of the email address is often the username of the recipient, it could also be a pseudonym. Although many web-based email service providers (e.g., Google's Gmail and Microsoft's Hotmail) ask the subscriber to provide a name, address, and other details when registering an email account, the information is not necessarily verified. The domain name part of the email address can also identify the user's organizational affiliation (e.g., @ftc.gov) or reveal the email service provider (e.g., @gmail.com). Some email addresses might not relate to an individual but be a general-purpose address (e.g., refer to a position within an organization such as admin@abc.com), while others may entail a pseudonym, a very common name, or obfuscated username. Sometimes, email addresses can be registered, but be fake or no longer valid (e.g., temporary email addresses). It is questionable whether such addresses should be considered personal data. Law enforcement may be able to obtain details about the account holder by sending a request to the email provider following a legal process prescribed by the specific jurisdiction.

When posting propaganda in forums and creating social media accounts, terrorists and their groups are not likely to use their original names and surnames, email addresses, or other actual identifiers. It is more likely that they would rely on usernames that are random strings or pseudonyms which are difficult to associate with real identities.

Moreover, different persons may use the same or similar usernames in different contexts. It is therefore questionable whether such obfuscated usernames alone should be treated as personal data.

16.6 THE RELATIONSHIP BETWEEN PERSONAL DATA PROTECTION AND USE OF INFORMATION

The previous section provided a brief overview of the main categories of information that are collected and processed to counter online terrorist propaganda, recruitment, and radicalization. The relationship between the protection and use of such information is defined by the legal categorization of the information as personal data or not. If one departs from the "absolute/ objective" approach, which views information as personal data if there is a possibility (even an abstract one) for any third party to determine the identity of the individual from it, and instead limits the possibility of identification to the actual legal and practical means at the disposal of the actor who has the information—the "subjective/relative" approach followed by the CJEU in the above-mentioned *Breyer case* —the following considerations are relevant.

The discussion of the examples of hashed images and videos, domain names and URL addresses, IP addresses, fake emails, and usernames illustrates that a careful case-by-case analysis of law and context might change the position of whether or not a piece of information should be considered personal data. The qualification of a certain piece of information as personal data depends on the actor having this information and its ability to identify or to link this information to an identifiable individual. Particular actors, due to the existing legal or practical obstacles to identification, can be unable to achieve identification or attribute information to an identifiable individual or the risk of identification in reality can be insignificant. Such specific legal or practical contexts include situations where the identification of a data subject is prohibited by law or practically impossible. For example, an IP address alone acquired by a law enforcement authority or the EU IRU through open-source research may not suffice to identify an individual, yet in combination with other information it may allow identification or linking to an identifiable individual. The possibility to request additional information from an ISP's logs is to be considered as the means that are reasonably likely to be used to identify an individual using that IP address. This legal possibility might be available to some actors, such as the national law enforcement authorities according to the national law but not to others, [78]. From a practical perspective, an IP address that adopts NAT or CGN technology may not allow the identification of an individual using it. In the same vein, a domain name or a URL address might not contain personal data, yet information about the registrant of the specific domain, or an associated IP address can be obtained using the Whois service. However, as previously mentioned, a domain name can be registered as a private domain, registration details can be unavailable using the Whois service or may be inaccurate or fraudulent. Even if the registration data were accurate, investigation could reveal that they belonged to fake individuals that were forged or impersonated by criminals. Therefore, unless any additional information is obtained, it might be possible to consider the IP addresses, domain names, and URLs that do not relate to a specific individual or lead to fake identify as information rather than as personal data when they are in the hands of the actors that lack legal or practical means to identify an individual. A similar position can be taken on email addresses which are general support or distribution lists, not relating to a specific person.

Nevertheless, the information that is not to be considered personal data in the hands of particular actors might change status when it is transferred to an actor that has different legal and technical means to identify or attribute the information to an identified individual. For example, sophisticated crime analysis tools might allow for the linking of many pieces of information and the carrying out of social network analysis. In this process it might be able to identify an individual or link an individual to a piece of information, consequently transforming the status of information into personal data. Therefore, a regular and dynamic assessment of the data, the technology, and actors is constantly required, and it cannot be assumed that information will permanently remain outside the scope of the data protection law.

Obviously, the aim of law enforcement is to identify and persecute those who commit terrorist offences; effectively, the identification of suspects is key. However, for the information to be treated as personal data there is no need to achieve full identification of an individual, i.e., to know his name and surname. As underlined by the Article 29 Working Party, the possibility to single out an individual suffices for the information to be treated as personal data [43]. Information can relate to an individual not only because it is about an individual, but also because it allows to assess or to affect an individual [43]. A law enforcement authority might have fake details of an account holder or a falsified username but can still gather information about an individual who created the account. Additional information might be linked to a falsified username or account and though the real identification of a person behind such account cannot be achieved, the individual can be still impacted or evaluated. Thus, even if a law enforcement authority is not able to know who the natural person using an email address is (e.g., cannot obtain from an email provider the details of an email account due to legal or practical constraints), email accounts may in principle still be considered personal data if an individual, even if unidentified, is treated differently from other persons as a result of the data processing.

Furthermore, when in reality it is not possible to be sure without any uncertainty, whether a piece of information, such as an IP address, an email address, or a URL, relates to a natural person, a safe solution would be to consider such information as constituting personal data in order to afford it a higher level of protection.

It should be acknowledged that a careful assessment and classification of pieces of information might turn out to be hardly feasible in practice as it would require adoption of internal tools, policies and processes, and recording of the findings. Technological data management tools might be employed and be helpful in this respect. Nevertheless, whenever possible, a case-by-case analysis could be carried out. A failure to do so would not only lead to predefined classifications and overstretching the scope of data protection law due to a broad notion of personal data, but also might unnecessarily hinder operational police activities. The stretching of the concept of personal data is noticeable in the commercial data processing context, a shift that has been recently criticized by a number of academics [34, 56].

If after the analysis it has been concluded that a piece of information constitutes personal data, based on the EU data protection law the following obligations and duties to the actors processing that information (data controllers) arise.

When processing personal data, data controllers shall respect the principles relating to processing of personal data:

- Lawfulness and fairness—Personal data should be processed lawfully and fairly (Article 4(1)(a) of the Directive 2016/680 and Article 28(1)(a) of the Regulation (EU) 2016/794). According to Directive 2016/680, lawfulness of processing requires the processing to be in line with the national or EU laws and be necessary for the performance of a task carried out by a competent authority for the purposes of the prevention, investigation, detection, or prosecution of criminal offences or the execution of criminal penalties, including the safeguarding against and the prevention of threats to public security (hereinafter law enforcement purposes). National laws regulating data processing shall at least specify the objectives of processing (e.g., improvement of the management of external borders, prevention and combating terrorist offences) and the types of data and the purposes of the processing (e.g., identification of an individual as a suspect for a crime for the purposes of investigation) [79].

In the context of Europol's activities, lawfulness and fairness, among others, require data processing to be in line with Europol's mandate. In practice, difficulties can arise, for example, when distinguishing content that promotes terrorism and tries to raise awareness on the terrorism propaganda issue: an expert evaluation of the content before referral by Europol is carried out to ensure that potential automatic detection is actually referring to the content that according to Directive (EU) 2017/541 on combating terrorism is to be considered a terrorist offence [4].

- Purpose specification and collection limitation—Personal data can only be collected for a specific, explicit, and legitimate purpose and not processed for a different, incompatible purpose (Article 4(1)(b) of the Directive 2016/680 and Article 28(1)(b) of the Regulation (EU) 2016/794). Notwithstanding the above, Article 4(2) of the Directive 2016/680 allows the further processing for another, still falling under the law enforcement purpose, if a specific EU or national law authorizes it and if the processing is necessary and proportionate.
- Data quality—Personal data should meet the data quality requirements and be adequate, relevant, and not excessive in relation to the purposes for which they were processed, and be accurate and up-to-date (Article 4(1)(d) of the Directive 2016/680 and Article 28(1)(d) of the Regulation 2016/794). The form in which personal data is kept should not permit identification of data subjects for longer than is necessary for the purposes for which the data are processed. The Europol Regulation, for example, foresees the classification of data based on factual verification and the reliability of the source to improve the data quality assessments (Article 29).
- Data security—Data controllers are obliged to ensure appropriate security of personal data implementing appropriate technical or organizational measures, e.g., guarantee protection against unauthorized or unlawful processing and against accidental loss, destruction, or damage and ensure data protection by design (Article 4(1)(f) and 25 of the Directive 2016/680 and Article 28(1)(f) and Article 32 of the Regulation 2016/794).
- Accountability—Data controllers are responsible for the implementation of the principles mentioned above and should be ready to demonstrate compliance (Article 4(4) of the Directive 2016/680 and Article 38(4) of the Regulation 2016/794).
- Openness and individual participation—Data subjects should be informed about the data processing, have the rights to access, rectify, and erase their personal data or restrict the processing, unless these rights are restricted or refused in specific prescribed circumstances, e.g., in order not to jeopardize investigations and law enforcement activities, to protect security and public order or the rights and freedoms of other individuals (Article 12–16 of the Directive 2016/680 and Articles 36-37 of the Regulation 2016/794).
- Other obligations for data controllers—Data controllers can store personal data for appropriate time limits, periodically review the need for its storage and erase when the purpose of data processing has been achieved (Article 5 of the Directive 2016/680 and Article 31 of the Regulation 2016/794). Data controllers are required to keep a record of

data processing activities (Article 24 of the Directive 2016/680) and maintain logs on collection, alteration, consultation, disclosure, combination, and erasure for the purposes of verification of the lawfulness of processing, self-monitoring, the integrity and security of the personal data, and if required to disclose them the supervisory authority (Article 25 of the Directive 2016/680 and Article 40 of the Regulation 2016/794).

Distinctions should be made whenever possible between different categories of the data subjects, such as suspects, convicted criminals, victims, witnesses, experts, and other parties in a criminal offence (Article 6 of the Directive 2016/680 and Recital 43 of the Regulation 2016/794). This requirement arises from the recommendation of the Article 29 Working Party to treat personal data of those who are not actively involved in crime cautiously and introduce specific conditions and safeguards in relation to legitimacy and proportionality to avoid any undue treatment of such individuals [80]. Such distinction may, for example, among others allow a gradual regime of different retention timeframes to be envisaged in relation to the different categories of data subjects [81]. A distinction should also be made between personal data based on facts and on personal assessments (Article 7 of the Directive 2016/680 and Recital 42 of the Regulation 2016/794). Statements by victims and witnesses containing personal data are based on their subjective perceptions, and being not always verifiable and subject to challenge during the legal process cannot be subjected to the usual requirement for data accuracy.

Data controllers are obliged to cooperate, upon request, with the supervisory authority (Article 26 of the Directive 2016/680) and designate a data protection officer (Articles 32-34 of the Directive 2016/680 and Article 41 of the Regulation 2016/794). When the data processing is likely to result in a high risk to the rights and freedoms of natural persons, an additional obligation is imposed to conduct an assessment of the impact of the envisaged processing operations (Article 27 of the Directive 2016/680 and Article 39(2) of the Regulation 2016/794) and consult the supervisory authority (Article 28 of the Directive 2016/680 and Article 39 of the Regulation 2016/794). In the case of a personal data breach the controller has to notify it to the competent authorities and the data subjects, unless such breach is unlikely to result in a risk to the rights and freedoms of natural persons (Article 30 and 31 of the Directive 2016/680 and Article 34 and 35 of the Regulation 2016/794).

- Other data processing restrictions—Other specific restrictions and requirements are imposed for the processing of special categories of personal data (e.g., racial or ethnic origin, political opinions, religious or philosophical beliefs, trade union membership, genetic data, biometric data, data concerning health, sex life, or sexual orientation). It can be carried out under specific conditions, e.g., subject to strict necessity (Article 10 of the Directive 2016/680 and Article 30(2) of the Regulation 2016/679). Restrictions and specific safeguards also apply to solely automated individual decision making, including profiling, with an adverse effect on the data subject (Article 11 of the of the Directive 2016/680 and Article 30(4) of the Regulation (EU) 2016/794) and to personal data transfers to third countries and international organizations (Articles 35–39 of the of the Directive 2016/680 and Article 25 and 30(5) of the Regulation (EU) 2016/794).

16.7 SUMMARY

This chapter focused on the relationship between information that public authorities, in particular, the national law enforcement authorities and Europol need to gather and share in order to counter terrorist propaganda, recruitment, and radicalization and the need to protect such information when it contains personal data, i.e., to set restrictions and limitations for its processing and sharing in order to ensure the protection of the rights and freedoms of concerned individuals.

As explained in Section 16.5, in the majority of cases the information collected for countering terrorist propaganda, recruitment, and radicalization would contain personal data, as it would emanate from scanning various websites and social media accounts and collecting, extracting, analyzing, and linking the acquired data. This data would often either directly relate to an individual by its content or indirectly to an identifier such as an IP address, domain name, username, or an email address which could indirectly enable the identification of an individual. However, as recently acknowledged by the CJEU in the *Breyer* case, the qualification of a certain piece of information as personal data depends on the actor having this information and its ability to identify or to link this information to an identifiable individual (practical and legal means that can be reasonably used).

The discussion of the examples of hashed images and videos, domain names and URL addresses, IP addresses, fake email addresses and usernames illustrates that a careful case-by-case analysis of law and context might change the position of whether or not a piece of information should be considered personal data. A failure to conduct such an assessment would not only lead to predefined classifications and overstretching the scope of data protection law due to a broad notion of personal data, but also might unnecessary hinder law enforcement activities.

As discussed in the chapter, particular actors, due to the existing legal or practical obstacles to identification, can be unable to achieve identification or attribute information to an identifiable individual or the risk of identification in reality can be insignificant. Nevertheless, a regular and dynamic assessment of the data, the technology, and actors is constantly required as sophisticated crime analysis tools might allow the linking of many pieces of information and consequently lead to identification, as a result transforming the status of information into personal data. Also, for the information to be treated as personal data there is no need to achieve full identification of an individual, i.e., to know his name and surname, but the possibility to single out an individual suffices to assess or to affect him or her. When in reality it is not possible to be sure without any uncertainty, whether a piece of information, such as an IP address, an email address, or a URL, relates to a natural person, a safe solution would be to consider such information as constituting personal data in order to afford it a higher level of protection.

When it is concluded that a piece of information constitutes personal data and the EU data protection legal framework is applicable, the obligations stemming from the two relevant legal frameworks for law enforcement authorities and Europol, the newly enacted Directive 2016/680 and Regulation 2016/794 (Europol Regulation), must be complied with, as explained in Section 6.

REFERENCES

1. European Union Counter-Terrorism Strategy, November 30, 2005, 14469/4/05.
2. European Commission, The EU Internal Security Strategy in Action: Five steps towards a more secure Europe (COM(2010) 673 final of 22.11.2010). The same aim has been restated by the Council of the EU in Draft Council Conclusions on the Renewed European Union Internal Security Strategy 2015–2020, 10 June 2015, 9798/15.
3. Clive Walker, Maura Conway, Online terrorism and online laws. *Dyn. Asymmetric Confl.* 8(2), pp. 156–175, 2015.

4. Jan Ellermann, Terror won't kill the privacy star – tackling terrorism propaganda online in a data protection compliant manner. *ERA Forum* 17, pp. 555–582, 2016.

5. Europol, IOCTA 2017 Internet Organised Crime Threat Assessment, 2017. https://www.europol.europa.eu/iocta/2017/index.html

6. J. M. Berger, How ISIS Games Twitter: The militant group that conquered northern Iraq is deploying a sophisticated social-media strategy. *The Atlantic*, June 16, 2014. https://www.theatlantic.com/international/archive/2014/06/isis-iraq-twitter-social-media-strategy/372856/

7. Kyle Perisic, ISIS Uses Internet Archives To Spread Propaganda, Report Finds. *The Daily Caller*, 16 May 2018. http://dailycaller.com/2018/05/16/isis-uses-internet-archives-to-spread-propaganda/

8. Gregory Waters and Robert Postings, Spiders of the Caliphate: Mapping the Islamic State's Global Support Network on Facebook, Counter Extremism Project, May 2018. https://www.counterextremism.com/sites/default/files/Spiders%20of%20the%20Caliphate%20%28May%202018%29.pdf

9. Conclusions of the Council of the European Union and of the Member States meeting within the Council on enhancing the criminal justice response to radicalization leading to terrorism and violent extremism, 20 November 2015. https://www.consilium.europa.eu/en/press/press-releases/2015/11/20/conclusions-radicalisation/

10. In the framework of the EU Counter Terrorism Strategy (14469/4/05) the Council of the EU adopted a revised "EU Strategy for combating Radicalization and Recruitment," June 2014 (9956/14) and in December 2014 (16526/14) and June 2015 (9951/15) framed the prevention and countering of the phenomenon as a priority for future action. The Conclusions of the Justice and Home Affairs Council of the European Union (20 November 2015, 845/15) called the authorities of the EU Members States to strengthen cooperation with internet service providers in countering the phenomena of online hate speech and terrorist radicalization (sect. 3). The Directive (EU) 2017/541 of the European Parliament and of the Council of 15 March 2017 on combating terrorism and replacing Council Framework Decision 2002/475/JHA and amending Council Decision 2005/671/JHA (*OJ L 88, 31.3.2017, p. 6–21*) required Member States to take measures against public provocation to commit a terrorist offence online, to ensure the prompt removal or when it is not feasible, the blocking of access to such content, providing transparent procedures and adequate safeguards.

11. Council of the European Union 2015, 7178/15, 3376th Council meeting, Justice and Home Affairs, 12–13 March 2015. https://www.consilium.europa.eu/media/23289/st07178en15.pdf

12. Europol, EU Internet Referral Unit, Year One Report Highlights, 22 July 2016. https://www.europol.europa.eu/newsroom/news/europol-internet-referral-unit-one-year

13. European Commission, The EU Agenda on Security, 2015.

14. EU Ministers for Justice and Home Affairs and representatives of EU institutions, Joint statement of 24 March 2016 (urged to develop preventive measures to guarantee early detection of signs of (on-line) radicalization, required the European Commission to intensify work with IT companies in the framework of the EU Internet Forum to counter terrorist propaganda and to develop by June 2016 a Code of conduct against hate speech online, to secure and obtain more quickly and effectively digital evidence by intensifying cooperation with third countries and service providers).

15. European Commission, Press release, EU Internet Forum: progress on removal of terrorist content online, 10 March 2017. http://europa.eu/rapid/press-release_IP-17-544_en.htm

16. Council of the European Union, Council Conclusions on cooperation to combat terrorist use of the Internet ("Check the Web"), 8457/3/07, 29 May 2007.

17. For more information on the project see http://www.cleanitproject.eu/about-the-project/. For the criticism of the project due to the lack of clarity on risks and responsibilities when delegating internet filtering and monitoring to private companies see https://edri.org/CleanIT-evaluation/

18. Clean it project, Reducing terrorist use of the Internet, The result of a structured public–private dialogue between government representatives, academics, Internet industry, Internet users and non-governmental organizations in the European Union, 2013, http://www.cleanitproject.eu/files/wp-content/uploads/2013/01/Reducing-terrorist-use-of-the-internet.pdf

19. Texts posted on each of the company's official blogs, describe the purpose of the GIFCT as "help[ing] us continue to make our hosted consumer services hostile to terrorists and violent extremists." They state: "We believe that by working together, sharing the best technological and operational elements

of our individual efforts, we can have a greater impact on the threat of terrorist content online." Facebook. Facebook, Microsoft, Twitter and YouTube Announce Formation of the Global Internet Forum to Counter Terrorism. Facebook Newsroom, 26 June 2017. https://newsroom.fb.com/news/2 017/06/global-internet-forum-to-counter-terrorism/.

20. Tech Against Terrorism initiative. https://www.techagainstterrorism.org/
21. Facebook. Facebook, Microsoft, Twitter and YouTube Announce Formation of the Global Internet Forum to Counter Terrorism. *Facebook Newsroom*, 26 June 2017. https://newsroom.fb.com/news/2 017/06/global-internet-forum-to-counter-terrorism
22. BBC News, Facebook's AI wipes terrorism-related posts, 29 November 2017. https://www.bbc.com/ news/technology-42158045
23. European Commission, Proposal for a Regulation on preventing the dissemination of terrorist content online, COM(2018) 640 final, 2018/0331 (COD), 12 September 2018.
24. European Commission, Communication on tackling illegal content online: Towards an enhanced responsibility of online platforms (COM(2017) 555 final), 28 September 2017.
25. Europol, Europol coordinates its 12th referral action day to combat online terrorist content, 30 November 2018. https://www.europol.europa.eu/newsroom/news/europol-coordinates-its-12th-re ferral-action-day-to-combat-online-terrorist-content
26. Directive (EU) 2017/541 of the European Parliament and of the Council of 15 March 2017 on combating terrorism and replacing Council Framework Decision 2002/475/JHA and amending Council Decision 2005/671/JHA, OJ L 88, 31.3.2017, pp. 6–21.
27. M. Dawson, M. Lieble, A. Adeboje, Open Source Intelligence: Performing Data Mining and Link Analysis to Track Terrorist Activities. In: Latifi S. (eds) *Information Technology – New Generations. Advances in Intelligent Systems and Computing*, vol 558. Springer, Cham, 2018.
28. S. Al-khateeb, M.N. Hussain, N. Agarwal, Social Cyber Forensics Approach to Study Twitter's and Blogs' Influence on Propaganda Campaigns. In: Lee D., Lin Y.R., Osgood N., Thomson R. (eds) *Social, Cultural, and Behavioral Modeling*. SBP-BRiMS 2017. *Lecture Notes in Computer Science*, vol 10354. Springer, Cham, 2017.
29. Directive (EU) 2016/680 of the European Parliament and of the Council of 27 April 2016 on the protection of natural persons with regard to the processing of personal data by competent authorities for the purposes of the prevention, investigation, detection or prosecution of criminal offences or the execution of criminal penalties, and on the free movement of such data, and repealing Council Framework Decision 2008/977/JHA, OJ L 119/89, 4.5.2016.
30. Regulation (EU) 2016/679 of the European Parliament and of the Council of 27 April 2016 on the protection of natural persons with regard to the processing of personal data and on the free movement of such data, and repealing Directive 95/46/EC (General Data Protection Regulation).
31. Recital 19 GDPR, Recitals 9-11 of the Directive 2016/679.
32. While the GDPR is a directly applicable regulation aiming for a harmonization of the rules in EU Member States, a Directive binds the Member States in terms of the result to be achieved, leaving the choice of form and method of its implementation to the national legislators (TFEU Art. 288). The Directive 2016/680 guarantees only minimum harmonization (Article 1(3)) and the individual EU Member States can ensure higher data protection safeguards under national law. As a consequence, the application and interpretation of the provisions foreseen by the Directive might diverge across the EU, resulting into a fragmented data protection framework. Efforts have been made to avoid such fragmentation in practice. For example, a special Commission expert group has been created to coordinate the transposition of the Directive 2016/680 to national law and ensure consistency in its interpretation, regardless of various national legal and judicial systems. The Article 29 Working Party, a group gathering the representatives all the EU data protection authorities, provided guidance to suggest a coherent approach and ensure that transposition by the EU Member States is in line with the Directive. See Opinion on some key issues of the Law Enforcement Directive (EU 2016/680) WP 258, 29 November 2017.
33. Paul de Hert, Vagelis Papakonstantinou, The New Police and Criminal Justice Data Protection Directive: A First Analysis. *New Journal of European Criminal Law* 7(1), pp. 7–19, 2016.

34. Nadezhda Purtova, Between the GDPR and the Police Directive: Navigating through the maze of information sharing in public–private partnerships. *International Data Privacy Law* 8(1), pp. 52–68, 2018.

35. In some EU Member States the FIUs are set up as administrative and in some as law enforcement authorities.

36. European Data Protection Supervisor, A Further Step Towards Comprehensive EU Data Protection, EDPS recommendations on the Directive for data protection in the police and justice sectors. Opinion 6/2015, 28 October 2015.

37. European Data Protection Supervisor, Annex to Opinion 6/2015: Comparative Table of Directive Texts with EDPS Recommendations, 2015.

38. Mireille M. Caruana, The reform of the EU data protection framework in the context of the police and criminal justice sector: harmonization, scope, oversight and enforcement, International Review of Law, Computers & Technology 5, 2017.

39. FRA, Surveillance by intelligence services: Fundamental rights safeguards and remedies in the European Union - Mapping Member States' legal frameworks, 2015.

40. Commission expert group on the Regulation (EU) 2016/679 and Directive (EU) 2016/680 (main group). http://ec.europa.eu/transparency/regexpert/index.cfm?do=groupDetail.groupMeetingDoc&docid=12945

41. Regulation (EU) 2016/794 of the European Parliament and of the Council of 11 May 2016 on the European Union Agency for Law Enforcement Cooperation (Europol) and replacing and repealing Council Decisions 2009/371/JHA, 2009/934/JHA, 2009/935/JHA, 2009/936/JHA and 2009/968/JHA, OJ L 135, 24.5.2016, pp. 53–114.

42. As De Hert and Sajfert note, the differences are 'particularly visible in Chapters II (principles) and III (rights of the data subject) of the Police Directive'. P. de Hert and J. Sajfert, The Role of the Data Protection Authorities in Supervising Police and Criminal Justice Authorities Processing Personal Data. In: Brière C. and Weyembergh A. (eds), *The Needed Balances in EU Criminal Law: Past Present and Future.* Hart Publishing, 2017.

43. Article 29 Working Party, Opinion 4/2007 on the concept of personal data, WP 136, 20 June 2007.

44. Article 29 Working Party, Opinion 05/2014 on Anonymisation Techniques, WP 216, 10 April 2014.

45. ICANN, Temporary Specification for gTLD Registration Data, 25 May 2018. Due to the GDPR, ICANN has restricted access to most personal data (layered/tiered access): "users with a legitimate and proportionate purpose for accessing the non-public personal data will be able to request such access through Registrars and Registry Operators. Users will also maintain the ability to contact the Registrant or Administrative and Technical contacts through an anonymized email or web form."

46. Europol, Operation Avalanche, 2016. http://www.eurojust.europa.eu/press/Documents/Operation%20Avalanche%20infographic.pdf

47. Erich Schweighofer, Vinzenz Heussler, Walter Hötzendorfer, Implementation Issues and Obstacles from a Legal Perspective. In: Florian Skopik (ed.) *Collaborative Cyber Threat Intelligence Detecting and Responding to Advanced Cyber Attacks at the National Level.* Taylor & Francis, 2018.

48. Martin Casado, Michael J. Freedman, Peering Through the Shroud: The Effect of Edge Opacity on IP-based Client Identification. In: *4th USENIX/ACM Symposium on Networked Systems Design and Implementation, Proceedings,* pp. 173–186, 2007.

49. J.L. Zittrain, *The Future of the Internet and How to Stop It.* Yale University Press, 2008.

50. Clare Sullivan, Eric Burger, "In the public interest": The privacy implications of international business-to-business sharing of cyber-threat intelligence. *Computer Law & Security Review* 33(1), pp. 14–29, 2017.

51. Directive 2006/24/EC of the European Parliament and of the Council of 15 March 2006 on the retention of data generated or processed in connection with the provision of publicly available electronic communications services or of public communications networks and amending Directive 2002/58/EC, OJ 2006 L 105. (Art. 5 imposed the obligation, to retain, for the purpose of the investigation, detection and prosecution of serious crime, 'the date and time of the log-in and log-off of the Internet access service, … together with the IP address, whether dynamic or static, allocated by the Internet access service provider to a communication, and the user ID of the subscriber or registered user').

On 8 April 2014, the Court of Justice of the European Union recognized the Data Retention Directive invalid (joined Cases C293/12 and C594/12; 'the *Digital Rights* judgment', EU:C:2014:238). Some individual EU Member States amended their national data retention laws in light of the CJEU judgements (joined Cases C–293/12 and C–594/12, C–203/15 and C–698/15) on data retention.

52. EMI & Ors v Eircom Ltd [2010] IEHC 108. http://www.courts.ie/Judgments.nsf/09859e7a3f34669 680256ef3004a27de/7e52f4a2660d8840802577070035082f?OpenDocument

53. Décision n° 2009-580 DC, 10 June 2009. http://www.conseil-constitutionnel.fr/decision/2009/dec isions-par-date/2009/2009-580-dc/decision-n-2009-580-dc-du-10-juin-2009.42666.html

54. Article 29 Working Party, Opinion 1/2009 on the proposals amending Directive 2002/58/EC on privacy and electronic communications (e-Privacy Directive), WP 159, 10 February 2009.

55. F.J. Zuiderveen Borgesius, Singling out people without knowing their names-behavioural targeting, pseudonymous data, and the new Data Protection Regulation, 32. *Computer Law & Security Review* 256, pp. 263–265, 2016. Opinion of the Advocate General Campos Sánchez-Bordona in Patrick Breyer v. Bundesrepublik Deutschland case, 12 May 2016, ECLI:EU:C:2016:339.

56. Nadezhda Purtova, The law of everything. Broad concept of persona data and future of EU data protection law. *Law, Innovation and Technology*, 10(1), pp. 40–81, 2018.

57. Damian Clifford, Jessica Schroers, Personal data and dynamic IPs – time for clarity? 2015. http://blo gs.lse.ac.uk/mediapolicyproject/2015/01/23/personal-data-and-dynamic-ips-time-for-clarity/

58. P. Ohm, Broken Promises of Privacy, 57 UCLA L. REV., 2010.

59. P. Schwartz, D. Solove, The PII Problem: Privacy and a New Concept of Personally Identifiable Information, 86 N.Y.U. L. Rev., 2011.

60. O. Tene, J. Polonetsky, Big Data for All: Privacy and User Control in the Age of Analytics. *Northwestern Journal of Technology and Intellectual Property* 11(5), 2013, p. 239.

61. Paul M. Schwartz, Daniel J. Solove, The PII Problem: Privacy and a New Concept of Personally Identifiable Information, 86 NEW YORK UNIV. L. REV., 2011.

62. C-70/10, EU:C:2011:771, paragraph 51.

63. C-461/10, EU:C:2012:219, paragraphs 51 and 52.

64. C-582/14, EU:C:2016:779.

65. Paul De Hert, Data protection's future without democratic bright line rules. Co-existing with technologies in Europe after Breyer. *European Data Protection Law Review* 3, p. 20, 2017.

66. Advocate General Campos Sánchez-Bordona, Opinion in Case C–582/14 Patrick Breyer v Bundesrepublik Deutschland, para. 50, 12 May 2016.

67. Council of the EU, Note on the Proposal for a regulation of the European Parliament and of the Council on the protection of individuals with regard to the processing of personal data and on the free movement of such data (General Data Protection Regulation), 11326/12, 22 June 2012. http://reg ister.consilium.europa.eu/doc/srv?l=EN&f=ST%2011326%202012%20INIT

68. Going dark debate is primarily focused on encryption and difficulties the end-to-end encryption creates to law enforcement and intelligence professionals. For more background information on the "going dark" debate see Berkman Center for Internet and Society at Harvard University, Don't Panic: Making Progress on the "Going Dark" Debate, 1 February 2016.

69. Paris Appeal Court decision - Henri S. vs. SCPP (15.05.2007). The Office of the Privacy Commissioner for Personal Data of Hong Kong, Data Protection Principles in the Personal Data (Privacy) Ordinance – from the Privacy Commissioner's perspective (2nd Edition), 2010. https://www.pcpd.org.hk/english/ resources_centre/publications/books/files/Perspective_2nd.pdf
    The Office of the Privacy Commissioner for Personal Data of Hong Kong, has stated that an IP address without additional information, would not constitute personal data.

70. Johnson v. Microsoft Corp. 2008 WL 803124 W.D. Wash. Mar. 21, 2008. See also US Court of Appeals, Cobbler Nevada v. Gonzales, No. 17-35041, 27 August 2018.

71. Office of the Privacy Commissioner of Canada, PIPEDA Report of Findings #2009-010. See also PIPEDA Case Summary #2005-319. For the most recent position see a report prepared by the Technology Analysis Branch of the Office Privacy Commissioner of Canada "What an IP Address Can Reveal About You", May 2013. https://www.priv.gc.ca/media/1767/ip_201305_e.pdf

72. Homeland Security Committee, Going Dark, Going Forward a Primer on the Encryption Debate, June 2016. https://homeland.house.gov/wp-content/uploads/2016/07/Staff-Report-Going-Dark-Going-Forward.pdf

73. Business Insider, Russian parliament bans use of proxy Internet services, VPNs, 21 July 2017. http://www.businessinsider.com/ap-russian-parliament-bans-use-of-proxy-internet-services-vpns-2017-7?IR=T

74. Chris Hoffman, Is TOR really anonymous and secure, 21 September 2016. https://www.howtogeek.com/142380/htg-explains-is-tor-really-anonymous-and-secure/

75. TOR project, The Legal FAQ for Tor Relay Operators. https://www.torproject.org/eff/tor-legal-faq.html.en

76. EUROPOL/EC3, Note to Delegations, Carrier-Grade Network Address Translation (CGN) and the Going Dark Problem – initial debate, 5127/17, 16 January 2017. http://www.statewatch.org/news/2017/jan/eu-europol-cgn-tech-going-dark-data-retention-note-5127-17.pdf

77. Europol, Closing the Online Crime Attribution Gap: European law enforcement tackles Carrier-Grade NAT (CGN), 2 February 2017. https://www.europol.europa.eu/newsroom/news/closing-online-crime-attribution-gap-european-law-enforcement-tackles-carrier-grade-nat-cgn

78. For example, Europol is not a law enforcement authority and has no mandate to carry out criminal investigations on its own initiative and its principal role is to gather, analyze and re–distribute data provided directly by the cooperating law enforcement agencies. The Europol Regulation does not provide a legal basis for Europol's bilateral exchange of information, including personal data, with private parties (see Articles 18(2)(d) and 38(7) of the Europol Regulation which enables Europol to facilitate bilateral data exchanges only between Member States, other Union bodies, third countries and international organizations).

79. The European Commission specified that when implementing the Directive 2016/680 the EU Member States should foresee and distinguish broader objectives and concrete and specific purposes of the processing for the achievement of such objectives. Commission expert group on the Regulation (EU) 2016/679 and Directive (EU) 2016/680 (main group). http://ec.europa.eu/transparency/regexpert/index.cfm?do=groupDetail.groupMeetingDoc&docid=12945

80. Article 29 Working Party and Working Party on Police and Justice, The Future of Privacy. Joint contribution to the consultation of the European Commission on the legal framework for the fundamental right to protection of personal data, WP 168, 1 December 2009.

81. Article 29 Working Party, Opinion on some key issues of the Law Enforcement Directive (EU 2016/680), WP 258, 29 November 2017.

Chapter 17

Online Terrorist Propaganda

Strategic Messaging Employed by Al Qaeda and ISIS

Elena Pokalova[1]

CONTENTS

17.1 INTRODUCTION

Terrorist groups such as Al Qaeda in the Arabian Peninsula (AQAP) and the Islamic State of Iraq and Syria (ISIS) have published online magazines to spread their ideologies, define their enemies, construct in- and out-group identities, and to recruit followers. Terrorist groups have relied on online dissemination of extremist narratives that appeal to certain audiences and affect the composition of followers by juxtaposing various identity constructs. The analysis of themes in terrorist propaganda materials can offer important information for the counterterrorism community regarding groups' ideologies, their strategic adaptations, and recruitment techniques.

The failure to grasp the dynamics behind the evolution of the content of online propaganda can be a significant counterterrorism handicap. This is especially important due to an increase in terrorist attacks motivated by the issues of *Inspire*, *Dabiq*, and *Rumiyah*. The magazines include numerous articles detailing vehicle attacks, knife stabbings, train derailing, and attacks using explosives. For example, the surviving perpetrator of the Boston Marathon bombing, Dzhokhar Tsarnaev, revealed to the investigators that he and his brother retrieved instructions for bomb making from AQAP's *Inspire* magazine.[2] In turn, a subsequent issue of *Inspire* featured the Tsarnaev brothers as heroic warriors worthy of emulation. "The Blessed Boston Bombings (BBB) have been an absolute success on all levels and domains," the authors stated.[3] According to the U.S. Department of Justice, Syed Rizwan Farook, the perpetrator of the 2015 San Bernardino attack, was also motivated by *Inspire*.[4] This attack later featured in issue 13 of *Dabiq*.

This chapter examines the content of AQAP's *Inspire* magazine and ISIS's *Dabiq* and *Rumiyah*. The project is based on a combination of qualitative discourse and quantitative content analysis of 45 total issues of the magazines. The analysis investigates the prevalent themes in the publications and their changes over time. The content of the propaganda magazines is evaluated to reveal the ideological components of radical narratives, the organizational changes reflected in thematic shifts, and the commonalities in the approaches used by AQAP and ISIS. The chapter first discusses the theoretical and methodological conceptualization of the project. It then turns to a discussion of the findings pertaining to each individual magazine. The chapter finishes with cross-case comparisons between *Inspire*, *Dabiq*, and *Rumiyah* and offers policy recommendations.

17.2 TERRORIST ORGANIZATIONS AND ONLINE PROPAGANDA

Traditionally, the field of terrorism studies has focused on the analysis of terrorist behavior. In contrast, examination of terrorist rhetoric has been lagging behind. As Or Honig and Ariel Reichard recently pointed out, "scholars of terrorism have paid less attention to the words used by terrorists compared to investigating their actual deeds."[5] Indeed, in terms of national security, actions of terrorist organizations offer valuable insights into the working of such groups, while terrorist rhetoric and narratives can be misleading. At the same time, however, given the evolution of internet technologies and the proliferation of new venues for disseminating messages, the analysis of terrorist strategic communications can also be extremely helpful in further revealing dynamics behind terrorist behavior.

Terrorist actors themselves have noted the importance of rhetoric. Back in 2005 Ayman al-Zawahiri in a letter to Abu Musab al-Zarqawi wrote, "we are in a battle, and that more than half of this battle is taking place in the battlefield of the media."[6] Subsequently, both Al Qaeda and ISIS have invested significant resources into developing their media branches.[7] Organizational records captured in Iraq indicate that Al Qaeda in Iraq, and later ISIS, designed a multilevel media apparatus with a sophisticated system of offices and a large representation of media officials. Specifically, one document captured by the American forces revealed that back in 2008, the Islamic State of Iraq set as one of its priorities "to exploit the internet as a media outlet as well as satellite channels to target audiences overseas."[8] Since then ISIS has emerged as a leader among terrorist organizations based on the quantities of propaganda materials it has published.[9] In other words, ISIS has been "using every contemporary mode of messaging to recruit fighters, intimidate enemies and promote its claim to have established a caliphate, a unified Muslim state run according to a strict interpretation of Islamic law."[10]

As a result, analysis of the words of terrorist organizations can be a powerful tool for revealing ideological leanings of terrorist groups, terrorist strategic adaptations, and preferred recruitment mechanisms. First, materials published by terrorist groups are an excellent source of information on ideological orientations of these groups.[11] Terrorist groups transmit their worldviews through statements, published materials, and online outlets. They often define their enemies and emphasize the differences between their own approach and that of competing terrorist organizations. They validate their justifications for violence with examples from current news. They generate sympathy for their cause through citing lists of injustices allegedly committed against social groups they stand to represent. This way, terrorist propaganda materials include nuances of the goals and priorities of certain groups. For example, in its published materials, Al Qaeda has focused on the U.S. as a far enemy and has promoted justifications for fighting against the "crusader alliance." ISIS, on the other hand, has focused more on the enemy at home: infidel co-religionists and apostate regimes. The topics of the caliphate, hijrah (migration), and territorial expansion are more prominent in the documents produced by ISIS.

Second, the rhetoric of terrorist organizations can reveal the shifts and adaptations groups are going through. Terrorist organizations are notoriously skilled at adapting to changing circumstances.[12] While at times terrorist groups openly advertise their strategic shifts, often they prefer such changes to go unnoticed in order not to disturb the existing projections of their power. In such cases, longitudinal examinations of propaganda materials can reveal the gradual shifts in predominant narratives that reflect organizational changes. For example, when facing territorial losses, ISIS did not immediately admit retreat but continued to exaggerate its gains in satellite territories, or wilayats. However, a careful examination of themes in *Dabiq* and *Rumiyah* over time, reveals a gradual shift in focus from discussions of territorial gains to the importance of patience in victory. One can also detect a change from the focus on positional campaigns in *Dabiq* to encouragements of terrorist attacks in the West in *Rumiyah*.

Further, terrorist propaganda materials contain a wealth of information regarding groups' recruitment strategies.[13] Propaganda materials skillfully appeal to the grievances people experience in order to incite anger against governments and countries.[14] Recruitment messages often evoke an emotional response from the reader by drawing on the magnitude of injustices. Such messages focus on the in-group – out-group gaps and justify the need for violence against out-groups. Through analyzing terrorist messages, one can detect target audiences and distinguish between calls for either joining the organization or inciting violence in its name. For example, the analysis of ISIS propaganda in different languages reveals the nuances of target audiences. The group has skillfully used local languages in order to capitalize on recruitment topics that do not show up in Arabic and English language publications.

17.3 THE METHODOLOGICAL APPROACH

This chapter focuses on the analysis of publications produced by some of the most prolific in terms of propaganda materials terrorist groups—Al Qaeda in the Arabian Peninsula (AQAP) and the Islamic State of Iraq and Syria (ISIS). These groups have published their own magazines that have come out on a relatively regular basis between 2010 and 2017 (see Table 17.9 for magazine publication dates). A total of 45 issues of AQAP's *Inspire* and ISIS's *Dabiq* and *Rumiyah* magazines are analyzed here. All the magazines were retrieved through open sources using such repositories as Aaron Zelin's Jihadology,[15] the Clarion Project,[16] the Global Terrorism Research Project,[17] as well as Google search. The content of the magazines was analyzed to identify the predominant themes included in them, the changes in themes over time, and similarities and differences between themes in magazines published by one group as well as across cases.

One of the first jihadi magazines, *Inspire*, came out in June 2010. It is published by al-Malahem Foundation, and the media center has produced 17 issues of *Inspire* so far, with the last one published in August 2017. Next, *Dabiq* was among the first magazines produced by ISIS's al-Hayat Media Center. Its first issue came out in July 2014, and its final, fifteenth issue was published in July 2016. In September 2016 *Dabiq* was replaced by *Rumiyah*, also produced by al-Hayat Media Center. So far, 13 issues of *Rumiyah* have been published. The latest issue came out in September 2017.

Most of the previous research on extremist magazines has been limited to the analysis of individual titles. For example, Brandon Colas analyzed the content of *Dabiq* and compiled a number of messaging categories ISIS used in this publication.[18] Similarly, Droogan and Peattie examined *Dabiq* to map a thematic landscape of the magazine.[19] The authors analyzed 13 issues of *Dabiq* and identified prevalent themes and their evolution over time. In a similar fashion, the same authors analyzed the themes that emerged from the content of *Inspire* magazine.[20]

Cross-case analyses of several magazines have been narrower in scope and have been bounded by certain criteria explored by the authors. Thus, Haroro J. Ingram analyzed both *Inspire* and *Dabiq*, but approached the magazines from the standpoint of group construction and analyzed how the respective magazines focus on identity to shape in- and out-group perceptions.[21] In another impressive study, Seth Cantey analyzed the content of *Inspire* and *Dabiq* with a specific focus on the messages indicating potential for negotiations with Al Qaeda and ISIS.[22] Further, Celine Novenario applied content analysis to both *Inspire* and *Dabiq*, but focused on five specific categories of terrorist behavior: attrition, intimidation, provocation, spoiling, and outbidding.[23] However, this limited approach of focusing on a select number of criteria leaves out a large amount of information contained in the magazines and overlooks many strategic themes included in the publications.

Instead, this chapter adopts a different approach. It is based on an inductive analysis of the 45 issues of *Inspire*, *Dabiq*, and *Rumiyah* where the issues were examined without preconceived codes or categories.[24] Rather than looking for specific themes in the publications, this project was based on a combination of qualitative discourse analysis and quantitative content analysis to generate patterns from the data. The analysis includes all three magazines which allows for comparisons not only between magazines issued by one terrorist group, but also for comparisons between publications produced by different terrorist groups. The comparative analysis of *Inspire*, *Dabiq*, and *Rumiyah* has revealed unique similarities and differences among approaches to online propaganda between AQAP and ISIS.

For the qualitative discourse analysis portion of the research, the author read 17 issues of *Inspire*, 15 issues of *Dabiq*, and 13 issues of *Rumiyah*. Individual articles in these publications served as a unit of analysis. Each article was coded based on a theme it focused on. Only articles that had a unique textual content and thematic focus were included in the analysis. Thus, the analysis excludes sections solely based on collections of quotes, book reviews, poems, Q&A sections, short news reports, and sections that predominantly rely on visual content. A total of 555 articles were analyzed, and 30 unique themes were identified (see Table 17.1).

In the overall distribution of articles, the five most prevalent themes are religion (12 percent of all 555 articles), commendation of individuals (9 percent), waging jihad (8 percent), instruction for attacks (7 percent), and war against the near enemy (7 percent). Not surprisingly, both AQAP and ISIS heavily rely on religious justifications for their actions. As a result, all three magazines devote much space to the extremist interpretations of religious tenets. Similarly, since both AQAP and ISIS justify violence as jihad against the enemies, 8 percent out of 555 articles focus on participation in jihad, styles and methods of waging jihad, and success stories about mujahedeen fighting jihad.

A high percentage of articles (commendation of individuals, 9 percent) is dedicated to praising individuals for their actions. Such distribution of articles is critical from the point of view of recruitment. Praising individuals who joined AQAP and ISIS can be a motivating factor that terrorist groups use to influence audiences online. Thus, knowing your actions will be commemorated in a magazine might inspire some individuals to carry out attacks in the name of a terrorist organization. For example, Rakhmat Akilov seemed to have been motivated by ISIS propaganda when he drove a truck into a crowd in Sweden on 7 April 2017. He had previously pledged allegiance to ISIS online, and was reportedly disappointed to find out that ISIS did not claim his attack.[25]

TABLE 17.1   THEMES DERIVED FROM THE ARTICLES IN *INSPIRE*, *DABIQ*, AND *RUMIYAH*

Theme	Number of articles (555 total)	Description
Armageddon	2	Religious prophecies of the end of the world
Caliphate	1	Establishment of the Islamic caliphate
Commendation of attacks	29	Praise of terrorist attacks perpetrated against the enemy. Articles include discussions on the style and methods of attacks
Commendation of individuals	52	Praise of individuals who perpetrated attacks against the enemy
Commendation of military action	25	Praise of guerilla tactics and more conventional insurgent operations other than terrorist attacks
Competitors	17	Discussion of opposition or competing groups
Defense of Islam and Muslims	18	The state of Islam under oppression and the need to defend Islam and the Muslim world from the onslaught of infidels
Delayed victory	14	Importance of patience in achieving victory. Some articles focus on delayed victory after apparent defeat on the ground
Evils of America	22	Depravities of the American way of life, corruption and failures of the American government
Execution	1	Execution of enemies
Failure to join jihad	7	Consequences for failure to fulfill the religious obligation of waging jihad
Hijrah	8	Migration to the lands of Islam
Instruction for attacks	41	Detailed instructions on how to carry out terrorist attacks: selection of targets, methods, security
Instruction for communication	3	Instructions on how to get in touch with the group leadership or representatives
Instruction for protection from chemical weapons	2	Instructions on how to behave in case of chemical weapons attacks
Instructions for weapon handling	4	Instructions on how to use and properly maintain weapons
IS governance	18	Righteous governance in the Islamic State
Islamic governance	2	Principles of righteous Islamic governance
Liberation from Crusaders	12	Crusader onslaught on the Muslim world and liberation from crusaders and their allies
Religion	64	Explanations of Islam, religious tenets, and religious justifications for action
Role of women	19	Role of women in Islam and jihad
Strength of mujahedeen	13	Courage of mujahedeen, their resources, and resolve to defeat the enemy

(*Continued*)

TABLE 17.1 (CONTINUED)   THEMES DERIVED FROM THE ARTICLES IN *INSPIRE*, *DABIQ*, AND *RUMIYAH*

Theme	Number of articles (555 total)	Description
Territorial expansion	17	Expanding territories under group control
Territorial losses	2	Losses of territories under group control
Trials for IS	1	Challenges facing the Islamic State
Waging jihad	42	Stories about participation in jihad, styles and methods of waging jihad
War against America	36	Justifications for why the U.S. is an enemy and the need to fight America
War against the near enemy	41	Justifications for why local regimes and population groups in the Muslim world are an enemy and the need to fight them.
War against the near enemy and against the West	5	Articles that focus on justifications for waging war against both near and far enemies
War against the West	37	Justifications for why the West is an enemy and the need to fight against the West

Further, articles with instructions on how to carry out terrorist attacks occupy a prominent place in the magazines (instruction for attacks, 7 percent). Clearly, all three magazines under consideration aim at inspiring followers to support their ideology and to target the enemies that terrorist organizations identify. In this respect, the significance of the title *Inspire* is self-evident. In the inaugural issue of *Inspire*, its authors explain in the Letter from the Editor that the purpose behind the magazine is to "inspire, motivate, or encourage" followers.[26] To inspire the audiences in the correct directions, AQAP and ISIS devote a substantial share of their magazines to the identification of the enemy. The theme of war against the near enemy features in 7 percent of the articles, and such themes as war against the West and war against America follow suit on the list. Thus, magazines thoroughly explain who the enemy is and why it is justifiable to target a specific group of people.

In order to substantiate the findings from discourse analysis, quantitative content analysis was also performed. The textual content of *Inspire*, *Dabiq*, and *Rumiyah* was analyzed with the help of the Provalis WordStat software. Word frequency, phrase frequency and important common topics were extracted from the bodies of issues of each magazine. The next sections discuss the findings for each specific magazine.

17.3.1 AQAP: *Inspire*

AQAP's *Inspire* magazine is a product of a creative partnership between Samir Khan and Anwar al-Awlaki. Khan, an American citizen of Pakistani descent had been involved in online propaganda since the 2000s. In turn, his mentor al-Awlaki, an American of Yemeni descent, was one of the leading figures behind "the architecture of the American online jihadi community."[27] Together, Khan and al-Awlaki used their propaganda skills to produce *Inspire* magazine.

The first issue of *Inspire* was published in June 2010, at a time when Al Qaeda central no longer had its former clout, but AQAP had not yet reached the status of the central organization.

Due to the U.S. intervention in Afghanistan, Al Qaeda central suffered great organizational losses in Afghanistan and Pakistan.[28] However, by 2009 Al Qaeda's cells in Yemen and Saudi Arabia reorganized into AQAP and began to emerge as a leading Al Qaeda organization.[29] In August 2010 a CIA official assessed that the threat from AQAP was greater than that emanating from Al Qaeda central. "The relative concern ratios are changing. We're more concerned now about AQAP than we were before," the official said.[30] At the same time, AQAP did not enjoy the same resonance as Al Qaeda central and naturally turned to online propaganda to increase its following.

The 17 issues of *Inspire* include a total of 251 articles that represent 19 themes (see Table 17.2). The most prevalent themes in this magazine are instruction for attacks (14 percent of articles), war against America (12 percent), commendation of individuals (10 percent), waging jihad (9 percent), and religion (8 percent). True to its name, *Inspire* heavily focuses on motivating people to carry out attacks. Most of the magazine content is dedicated to the commendation of past attacks, encouragement of future attacks, and the interpretation of current events through a jihadi lens, providing justifications for violence. The very first issue of *Inspire* details the alleged injustices committed against Muslims by the U.S., the West, and corrupt local regimes. It justifies the need to expel infidels from the Holy Lands and argues for the need to carry out attacks against the enemies. Al Qaeda's successful terrorist operations feature in issues of *Inspire* as examples for emulation. For instance, issue 3 boasts of the success of the UPS cargo plane attack, issue 7 is dedicated to September 11, and issue 14 commends the Charlie Hebdo attack in France.

TABLE 17.2   *INSPIRE* THEMES

Theme	Number of articles (251 total)
Instruction for attacks	34
War against America	31
Commendation of individuals	25
Waging jihad	22
Religion	20
Commendation of attacks	19
Evils of America	19
Defense of Islam and Muslims	16
War against the West	16
War against the near enemy	12
Liberation from crusaders	7
Failure to join jihad	6
Instructions for weapon handling	4
Role of women	4
Strength of mujahedeen	4
War against the near enemy and against the West	4
Competitors	3
Instruction for communication	3
Islamic governance	2

A distinct feature of *Inspire* is its focus on instructions for carrying out terrorist attacks (instruction for attacks, 14 percent of articles). The authors encourage followers to stay where they are and strike against the enemies that the magazine also defines. The magazine does not provide instructions on how to travel to the lands of jihad. Instead, such sections as "open source jihad" give directions for lone wolf terrorism. Issue 2 of *Inspire* explains that the best way "to help the mujahidin" is "attacking the enemy in their backyard."[31] In a letter to the magazine one reader inquires about ways to join mujahedeen. However, the authors respond: "What we recommend is that you focus on planning out attacks in the West … This is because killing 10 soldiers in America for example, is much more effective than killing 100 apostates in the Yemeni military."[32] Instructions include details on how to select targets, how to avoid security services, and how to choose and prepare weapons. While instructions encourage attacks with as many casualties as possible, for practical purposes they also advise to carry out small scale attacks that are harder to track.

As it follows from the distribution of the themes, the U.S. remains AQAP's primary enemy. The theme of war against America features in 12 percent of the articles. Al Qaeda's focus on the far enemy is evident in *Inspire*.[33] In the Letter from the Editor in issue 11, *Inspire* authors promise, "Americans, you should understand this simple equation: as you kill you will be killed. The war is yet to cease, it has barely started. Yesterday it was Baghdad, today it is Boston. The question of 'who and why' should be kept aside. You should be asking, 'Where is next?'"[34] In addition to the U.S., *Inspire* focuses on fighting the West (war against the West, 6 percent of the articles), fighting local enemies (war against the near enemy, 5 percent), or a combination thereof (war against the near enemy and against the West, 2 percent). The justifications for this is that driving the U.S. from the Holy Lands would remove the U.S.-backed "apostate" domestic regimes. This way *Inspire* justifies attacks against the US and against U.S. Western allies.

Over time the themes prevalent in the magazine shift, reflecting organizational changes on the ground, as well as current events (see Figure 17.1). For example, the number of articles dedicated to instruction for attacks spikes in issues 9, 13, and 17. Issue 9 is a tribute to Anwar al-Awlaki who was killed in Yemen on 30 September 2011. The authors praise al-Awlaki's contributions to the magazine and promise *Inspire* will continue despite his death. The authors state, "Indeed, the killing of a preacher only means the spreading of his message. It also means that people will have

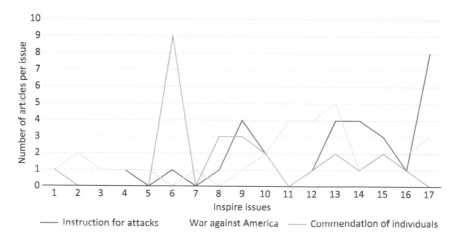

Figure 17.1 *Inspire* themes over time.

faith in his call as he made himself a tangible example and living role model to be followed."[35] To emulate al-Awlaki's example, the issue includes a number of articles focused on carrying out attacks. Further, issue 13 comes out in the wake of President Obama's authorizations of airstrikes in Iraq and Syria and encourages a "Lone Jihad Movement." Issue 17 is the latest published issue of *Inspire* and includes eight articles focused on instructions for attacks. The issue came out after ISIS lost most of its territory in Iraq and Syria, and after al-Zawahiri repeatedly called for unity among mujahedeen groups in Syria against common enemies.

The theme of war against America spikes in issues 11–13 and again in issue 17. Issue 11 is dedicated to the Boston Marathon attack against the U.S. and contains explanations for why it is justifiable to target America. These discussions continue in issue 12. As discussed above, issues 13 and 17 heavily focus on attacks and as a result include explanations for whom to target—the far enemy of Al Qaeda. The next prevalent theme—commendation of individuals—experiences a drastic increase in issue 6, the *Inspire* issue that is dedicated to Osama bin Laden who was killed on 2 May 2011.

The quantitative content analysis of *Inspire* also speaks to the importance of religious messages, war against the U.S., and instructions for attacks. Out of the total of 325,552 words in 17 issues of *Inspire*, the WordStat software identified 18,943 unique words. Among them, as seen from Table 17.3, words with the highest frequency pertain to religion: Allah, Muslims, jihad, Islam.[36] America has the second highest frequency at 921. The most frequent phrases out of the 138,308 phrases used in the publication almost exclusively focus on religious terminology. On the basis of factor analysis, the software identified the most common topics featuring in *Inspire* to be focused on AQAP, America vs. the Muslim world, and topics associated with instructions for terrorist attacks. The topic of Charlie Hebdo also features prominently in the magazine. The attack on the French magazine committed on 7 January 2015 was one of the few successful terrorist attacks in the West claimed by AQAP in the recent years.

17.3.2 ISIS: *Dabiq*

June 2014 was a victorious month for ISIS. On 29 June 2014 ISIS spokesman Abu Mohammed al-Adnani announced the establishment of the caliphate. During the same month, ISIS published

TABLE 17.3   CONTENT ANALYSIS OF *INSPIRE*

Most frequent words (frequency in parentheses)	Most frequent phrases (frequency in parentheses)	Most important topics (descending order)
Allah (2,155)	Al-Malahem Media (266)	Arabian Peninsula; Al Qaeda
America (921)	Al Qaeda in the Arabian Peninsula (145)	America; Muslim world
Muslims (839)	Messenger of Allah (84)	Cooking gas
People (775)	Jihad in the Arabian Peninsula (75)	Palm trees
Jihad (675)	Allah have mercy (71)	Acetone peroxide
world (577)	Women and children (64)	Tracks; derailing
War (551)	Allah the Almighty (42)	Wires; battery connector
Inspire (510)	Peace and blessings (39)	Shaykh Anwar
Islam (477)	Allah be pleased (34)	Messenger of Allah
Time (464)	Grace of Allah (34)	Charlie Hebdo

three issues of *Islamic State News* and four issues of *Islamic State Report*.[37] However, in July 2014 these publications were replaced with an inaugural issue of *Dabiq* magazine.

The title of the magazine stems from the name of the Syrian town of Dabiq situated close to the Turkish border. In 1516 the town was a place of a seminal battle between the Mamluks and the Ottomans, which the Ottomans won to build the last recognized historic Islamic caliphate.[38] Dabiq also features in a prophecy of an apocalyptic battle between Christian and Muslim forces. Hadith 6924 of Sahih Muslim Book 41 predicts, "The Last Hour would not come until the Romans would land at al-A'maq or in Dabiq. An army consisting of the best (soldiers) of the people of the earth at that time will come from Medina (to counteract them)."[39] Abu Musab al-Zarqawi interpreted the prophesy as a task ISIS would accomplish. In the opening lines of Dabiq he states, "The spark has been lit here in Iraq, and its heat will continue to intensify—by Allah's permission—until it burns the crusader armies in Dabiq."[40] The magazine especially focuses on battles, military action, and victories on the ground.

While the masterminds behind *Inspire* were well-known, ISIS kept individuals involved in the production of *Dabiq* anonymous. As is immediately evident from the language used, *Dabiq*'s intended audiences are different from those of *Inspire*. While *Inspire* is written in simple colloquial English, *Dabiq* is full of Arabic Islamic terms which makes it less accessible to wider audiences. As a result, one might conclude *Dabiq* targets more religious individuals and bilingual speakers of Arabic and English. While *Inspire* mostly encourages attacks against the far enemy, *Dabiq* focuses on issues of religion, significance of the Islamic State, and the importance of hijrah to the territories under ISIS control. In the authors' words, *Dabiq* is a "periodical magazine focusing on issues of tawhid [monotheism], manhaj [methodology], hijrah [migration], jihad [struggle], and jama'ah [community]."[41]

The 15 issues of *Dabiq* include a total of 173 articles that represent 22 themes (see Table 17.4). The most prevalent themes are those of religion (14 percent of articles), commendation of individuals (10 percent), territorial expansion (10 percent), competitors (8 percent), war against the near enemy (8 percent), and war against the West (8 percent). Not surprisingly, religion occupies a special place in *Dabiq*. In the ISIS worldview, society is divided between true Muslims (as perceived by ISIS) and unbelievers.[42] As a takfiri terrorist organization, ISIS justifies violence against co-religionists and everyone it deems un-Islamic through citing religious tenets. ISIS positions itself as a group that is destined to correct the contemporary state of jahiliyyah (ignorance) in the world. As a result, *Dabiq* includes numerous articles aimed at substantiating ISIS's religious legitimacy. The very first issue of *Dabiq* opens with the discussion of Armageddon, implying that the soldiers of the khilafah (caliphate) would lead the battle against the crusaders. Issue 2, in turn, includes a call to all Muslims to join the caliphate explaining that it is one's religious obligation; failure to join would automatically turn one into an ISIS enemy.[43]

Similar to *Inspire*, *Dabiq* dedicates a lot of articles to the theme of commendation of individuals (10 percent). It includes interviews with mujahedeen worthy of emulation. In a section "Among the Believers are Men" *Dabiq* publishes stories of model ISIS soldiers: their life stories, hijrah to the Islamic State, and their sacrifice and dedication to jihad. These biographies both elevate the profiles of ISIS members and serve as a roadmap for how to become one. In *Inspire*, articles praising individuals encourage the reader to carry out terrorist attacks. In contrast, in *Dabiq*, articles commending individuals do not include instructions for terrorist attacks but encourage individuals to leave the comfort of their homes and make their way to the Islamic State.

A distinct feature of *Dabiq* is its focus on the Islamic State, the caliphate. Much of the magazine's content is dedicated to the functioning of the Islamic State, governance and social issues

TABLE 17.4   *DABIQ* THEMES

Theme	Number of articles (173 total)
Religion	24
Commendation of individuals	17
Territorial expansion	17
Competitors	14
War against the near enemy	14
War against the West	14
IS governance	13
Commendation of military action	12
Waging Jihad	9
Commendation of attacks	7
Hijrah	7
War against America	5
Liberation from Crusaders	4
Evils of America	3
Role of women	3
Strength of mujahedeen	3
Defense of Islam and Muslims	2
Armageddon	1
Caliphate	1
Execution	1
Instruction for attacks	1
War against the near enemy and against the West	1

(IS governance, 8 percent of the articles). Further, as ISIS has been ambitious to restore the territories of the historical caliphate, the theme of territorial expansion is the third most prominent in the magazine (10 percent of the articles). A lot of attention is paid to ISIS affiliated provinces, or wilayats, pledges of allegiance to ISIS, and ISIS victories in gaining more territory. For instance, issue 4 praises the pledge of allegiance of Ansar al-Islam to al-Baghdadi and issue 8 exalts the pledge from Boko Haram. *Dabiq* continuously encourages readers to migrate to the caliphate. Jihad is interpreted not only as a religious obligation, but also as a duty to protect the caliphate.

Due to its focus on the state and its protection, ISIS dedicates significant attention to the enemies of the caliphate, its opponents, and detractors. A lot of effort is dedicated to explaining why competing groups are wrong and why it is justifiable to fight them. Consequently, 8 percent of the articles in *Dabiq* are dedicated to the theme of competitors. For example, issue 6 includes a long article accusing the leadership of Al Qaeda and affiliated Jabhat al-Nusrah or partisanship.[44] In issue 8 the authors of *Dabiq* reproach competitors in Syria for nationalism.[45] In issue 14, ISIS accuses the Muslim Brotherhood of apostasy.[46] Throughout the magazine the authors explain why ISIS does not support the position of Al Qaeda's Ayman al-Zawahiri and talks about the transgressions of competing groups.

In terms of enemies, ISIS is different from AQAP. While *Inspire* dedicates 12 percent of its articles to war against America, *Dabiq*'s main focus is on the enemy at home: 8 percent of the articles are about war against the near enemy. The content of *Dabiq* indicates that ISIS is more preoccupied with local enemies: domestic regimes in Syria and Iraq, opposing co-religionists, and competing groups. Unlike *Inspire*, *Dabiq* dedicates only 3 percent of its articles to the theme of war against America. The war against America theme clearly emerges in issues 3 and 4 of *Dabiq*, in the wake of President Obama's authorizations of airstrikes in Iraq and Syria. Issue 3 specifically focuses on the U.S. action in the Middle East and the subsequent execution of journalist James Foley in retaliation. The article "In the Words of the Enemy" states, "On 7 August 2014, the crusader, apostate Barack Obama announced to the world the continuation of the American crusade against Islam and the Muslims of Iraq."[47] The issue further explains how the U.S. interfered with matters of the Islamic State.

At around the same time, in issue 4, *Dabiq* introduces the theme of war against the West that eventually appears in 8 percent of the articles. In *Dabiq*, the focus is less on the U.S. but more on the Western "crusader coalition." Rather than dwelling on the far enemy, *Dabiq* features the near enemies of the caliphate including the coalition forces fighting ISIS in Syria and Iraq. After the U.S.-led coalition against ISIS formed in August to September 2014, *Dabiq* started featuring kidnappings and executions of Westerners. Further, in issue 4, the authors of *Dabiq* call for attacks against the citizens of the coalition, "At this point of the crusade against the Islamic State, it is very important that attacks take place in every country that has entered into the alliance against the Islamic State, especially the U.S., UK, France, Australia, and Germany. Rather, the citizens of crusader nations should be targeted wherever they can be found."[48]

Over time some *Dabiq* themes shift significantly, especially as ISIS started losing territories on the ground in 2015 (see Figure 17.2). The theme of religion had a rather stable presence on the pages of *Dabiq* but spiked around issue 15, the last issue of *Dabiq* published on 31 July 2016. The focus of this issue shifts from the territories of the Islamic State to the religious conflict between the Muslim world and the West. The theme of territorial expansion experienced a significant increase in issue 5, published on 21 November 2014, around the time when ISIS controlled maximum territory. Since then, however, as ISIS started losing territory in 2015, the presence of the

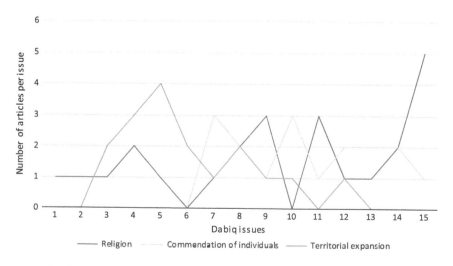

Figure 17.2   *Dabiq* themes over time.

TABLE 17.5   CONTENT ANALYSIS OF *DABIQ*

Most frequent words (frequency in parentheses)	Most frequent phrases (frequency in parentheses)	Most important topics (descending order)
Allah (3,448)	Alayhi wa Sallam (252)	Yemeni
State (1,564)	Soldiers of the Khilafah (109)	Gospel; Moses
Islamic (1,524)	Allah and his Messenger (73)	Detonated his explosive; wounding
People (1,036)	Al Bukhari and Muslim (64)	Ahrar Ash-Sham; Jaysh
Muslims (814)	Soldiers of the Islamic State (49)	Alayhi Sallam
Jihad (655)	Free Syrian Army (48)	Mourning widow
Religion (577)	Ahrar Ash Sham (46)	Akhtar Mansour; Pakistani
Khilafah (553)	Jabhat An Nusrah (45)	Francis; Benedict
War (534)	Praise is due to Allah (44)	Qa'idah
Mujahidin (509)	War against the Islamic State (44)	Assad

theme gradually declined, dropping to 0 in issue 13. Issue 13 focuses more on the territories of wilayats rather than ISIS territories in Syria and Iraq, and issue 14 dedicates much of its content to terrorist attacks rather than military action.

The quantitative content analysis of *Dabiq* points to the significance of religion, the state (caliphate), and competing groups in the ISIS rhetoric. Table 17.5 presents the analysis of a total of 400,375 words (17,163 unique) and 162,694 phrases in *Dabiq* identified by WordStat software. As appears from the table, words and phrases with the highest frequency pertain to religion: Allah, Islamic, Muslims, jihad, religion, Alayhi wa Sallam (peace be upon him), Allah and his Messenger, and praise is due to Allah. Sahih al-Bukhari, a collection of hadiths reported by Muhammad al-Bukhari and considered among the most authoritative, is frequently referenced in religious justifications. To justify its religious legitimacy, ISIS also uses examples from the Torah and the Gospel, as is seen from the list of the most important topics.

Next, words and phrases pertaining to the caliphate are frequent. Also frequent are references to war, soldiers of the Islamic State, and the war against the Islamic State. Further, phrases and topics that relate to competing groups are frequent. The Free Syrian Army appears with a frequency of 48, Ahrar al-Sham 46, and Jabhat al-Nusrah 45. Local enemies emerge as among the most important topics: Yemeni groups, the Taliban (Akhtar Mansour), Al Qaeda, and Assad and his allies (including Iran and Russia). Another prominent topic is detonated his explosive, that reflects the ISIS use of inghimasi fighters who detonate his explosive belts.

17.3.3 ISIS: *Rumiyah*

The last issue of *Dabiq* was published on 31 July 2016. On 5 September 2016, *Dabiq* was replaced with a new magazine—*Rumiyah*. The magazine is similar in style to *Dabiq*, although it tends to be shorter, and continues with such sections as "Among the Believers are Men," interviews, or operations. The publication of *Rumiyah* came before ISIS lost Dabiq to the Turkish-backed Syrian forces on 16 October 2016 but ISIS might have been acting preemptively in changing the title of the magazine. The new title—Rumiyah (Rome)—is the symbol of the West, Christianity, and crusades. The magazine opens with a quote from Abu Hamzah al-Muhajir promising the fall of Rome, "O muwahhidin, rejoice, for by Allah, we will not rest from our jihad except beneath the olive trees of Rumiyah (Rome)."[49] In the following pages the authors of the magazine explain that ISIS aims at eventually conquering Rome, "O Allah, make the conquest of Constantinople and Rome be at our hands and make us from among your patient and grateful slaves."[50]

While similar to *Dabiq* in style and content, *Rumiyah* gradually shifts the focus of the magazine from defending the territory of the caliphate to the ideological realm of a global fight against enemies of ISIS. *Dabiq* was focused on the Islamic State, the expansion of its territories, and called on individuals to perform hijrah. In contrast, *Rumiyah* has only one article occupied with the theme of hijrah and is more focused on instructions for terrorist attacks. In this respect *Rumiyah* is more similar to *Inspire*, as it introduces a section "Just Terror Tactics" modeling it on the "Open Source Jihad" section of *Inspire*. The "Just Terror Tactics" section was not published in *Dabiq* but was introduced in issue 2 of *Rumiyah*.

Overall, the 13 issues of *Rumiyah* include 131 articles that cover 19 themes (see Table 17.6). The themes with the most articles are religion (15 percent of the articles), war against the near enemy (11 percent), delayed victory (11 percent), commendation of military action (10 percent), and role of women (9 percent). In line with *Dabiq*, a high percentage of articles in *Rumiyah* (15 percent) is dedicated to religion. Issue 1 of *Rumiyah* includes an extensive discussion on monotheism.[51] The magazine defines the essence of Islam in that "the slave surrenders to Allah, the Lord of the creation, submitting (istislam) to Him alone without making any partners for Him, and becoming exclusively for Him (salamah) such that he takes Him as his deity without taking other than

TABLE 17.6   *RUMIYAH* THEMES

Theme	Number of articles (131 total)
Religion	20
War against the near enemy	15
Delayed victory	14
Commendation of military action	13
Role of women	12
Waging Jihad	11
Commendation of individuals	10
War against the West	7
Instruction for attacks	6
Strength of mujahedeen	6
IS governance	5
Commendation of attacks	3
Instruction for protection from chemical weapons	2
Territorial losses	2
Armageddon	1
Failure to join jihad	1
Hijrah	1
Liberation from Crusaders	1
Trials for IS	1

Him as a deity, as is clarified by the best of speech and the main pillar of Islam, the testimony of 'la ilaha illallah.'"[52] *Rumiyah* uses religious explanations to undermine competitors explaining how competing organizations are un-Islamic.

Rumiyah, similarly to *Dabiq*, continues to focus on the war against the near enemy (11 percent of articles). The near enemy includes local regimes and co-religionists who do not support the Islamic State. For example, *Rumiyah* starts publishing sections on "Wicked Scholars" that discuss local Muslim leaders that ISIS deems corrupt. Further, as ISIS started losing territory, it switched its attention from publishing articles about territorial expansion in *Dabiq* to articles about delayed victory in *Rumiyah*. These articles focus on the role of strategic patience in victory. In issue 4 the authors explain that Allah "clarified for the Ummah the means and conditions for its victory over its enemies so that its honor and triumph would endure as long as it acts in accordance with its knowledge. From among those means are patience and steadfastness."[53] *Rumiyah* does not openly publish material on territorial retreat but rather encourages the soldiers of the Islamic State to be patient in their endeavors.

At the same time, to bolster the spirit of the followers, the magazine devotes 10 percent of its articles to commendation of military action. Compared to ISIS's losses on the ground, these articles over-exaggerate the group's successes and create an illusion of its strength. Further, probably to sustain and increase readership, the magazine introduces a regular section on the role of women. Articles on this theme are present in all of the *Rumiyah* issues except for the last one, issue 13.

Over time, some changes occur within the most predominant themes in *Rumiyah* (see Figure 17.3). For example, the theme of religion goes up in issue 4, which also corresponds with the retreat of many ISIS fighters to Libya. The theme also spikes in issue 8, published around the time when ISIS lost most of its former territory in Iraq in April 2017. At around the same time, ISIS publishes *Rumiyah* issue 9, which turns its focus to fighting infidels at home, which brings up the numbers for the theme of war against the near enemy. The theme of delayed victory gains the most articles in issue 4 and then remains present in most of the rest of the issues of the magazine.

Table 17.7 presents the results of the content analysis of 299,151 words (13,608 identified as unique) and 110,944 phrases of the 13 issues of *Rumiyah*. In the realm of word and phrase frequencies, *Rumiyah* has many similarities with *Dabiq*. Many high frequency words and phrases pertain to religion: Allah, Muslims, messenger, religion, Islam, prophet, reported by Al Bukhari, Allah and his messenger, praise is due to Allah, and Lord of the Creation, La Ilaha Illallah. Some of the most important topics also focus on religion. The topics include religious

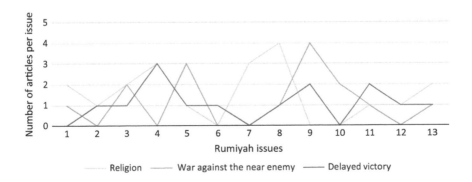

Figure 17.3 *Rumiyah* themes over time.

TABLE 17.7   CONTENT ANALYSIS OF *RUMIYAH*

Most frequent words (frequency in parentheses)	Most frequent phrases (frequency in parentheses)	Most important topics (descending order)
Allah (3,940)	Soldiers of the Khilafah (223)	Yamin Ad-Dawlah; Sultan Mahmud
People (854)	Reported by Al Bukhari (127)	Jihar; Jazal
Muslims (569)	Allah and his Messenger (95)	Ismah; Harbi
Messenger (567)	Enemies of Allah (62)	Maghrib
State (544)	Detonated his explosive (51)	Memorandum; refrains
Religion (535)	Praise is due to Allah (50)	Taliban movement; resulting
Soldiers (514)	Lord of the Creation (48)	Salamah and Istislam
Islam (486)	Soldiers of the Islamic State (44)	Molotov cocktail; gasoline
Killed (483)	Murtaddin being killed (39)	Pledge; pledged allegiance
Prophet (454)	La Ilaha Illallah (36)	Mistakes

discussions of the career of the medieval monarch Sultan Mahmud who was famous for breaking idols. Another religious topic deals with the rulings "on the blood and wealth of the harbi (belligerent) kuffar, and the fact that their blood does not have 'ismah (protection from being violated)."[54]

Other frequent words and phrases, similar to *Dabiq* focus on the Islamic State, war, and enemies of the Islamic State. Frequent phrases include enemies of Allah and Murtaddin being killed. Important topics also include enemies of ISIS, such as the Taliban, and mistakes—the topic that refers to erroneous religious beliefs of those that ISIS identifies as enemies. Pledges of allegiance to ISIS is another important topic in *Rumiyah*.

17.4 THE MAGAZINES COMPARED

The comparative analysis of the themes that feature in *Inspire*, *Dabiq*, and *Rumiyah* further bolster the conclusions about the groups' ideologies, strategic adaptations, and recruitment strategies (see Table 17.8). All three publications dedicate much attention to the theme of commendation of individuals, this way advertising the attractiveness of being a group member. All three magazines heavily use religious tenets to justify their ideologies and actions. All three magazines dedicate a lot of space to waging jihad, and to the discussions of the enemies: war against the near enemy and war against the West. These similarities indicate that despite ideological differences between AQAP and ISIS, and at times open confrontations between the groups, themes in their publications overlap as the magazines exploit similar grievances to attract followers.

Comparisons between the themes also reveal a similar stance in the publications on terrorism. All three magazines commend terrorist attacks. Further, even despite disputes between AQAP and ISIS, their magazines praise each other's terrorist attacks. Due to disagreements between the groups, on 2 February 2014 Ayman al-Zawahiri publicly severed ties with ISIS (see Table 17.9 for the timeline of events). This fact did not prevent the groups from featuring each others' terrorist attacks. For example, ISIS's *Dabiq* featured the attack on Charlie Hebdo, committed

TABLE 17.8   THEMES ACROSS MAGAZINES

Theme	*Inspire*	*Dabiq*	*Rumiyah*
Armageddon		1	1
Caliphate		1	
Commendation of attacks	8	4	2
Commendation of individuals	10	10	8
Commendation of military action		7	10
Competitors	1	8	
Defense of Islam and Muslims	6	1	
Delayed victory			11
Evils of America	8	2	
Execution		1	
Failure to join jihad	2		1
Hijrah		4	1
Instruction for attacks	14	1	5
Instruction for communication	1		
Instruction for protection from chemical weapons			2
Instructions for weapon handling	2		
IS governance		8	4
Islamic governance	1		
Liberation from Crusaders	3	2	1
Religion	8	14	15
Role of women	2	2	9
Strength of mujahedeen	2	2	5
Territorial expansion		10	
Territorial losses			2
Trials for IS			1
Waging Jihad	9	5	8
War against America	12	3	
War against the near enemy	5	8	11
War against the near enemy and against the West	2	1	
War against the West	6	8	5

Numbers represent percentages of articles with a particular theme. Percentages within a magazine might not equal 100 due to rounding.

on 7 January 2015 and claimed by AQAP. In turn, AQAP's *Inspire* featured ISIS-claimed attacks on the U.S. Orlando night club (12 June 2016), U.S. Minnesota mall (17 September 2016), or the UK London Westminster Bridge (22 March 2017). This way the publications send a message that regardless of the conflicts between the groups, they are united in their willingness to use terrorism against their common enemies in the West.

TABLE 17.9   MAGAZINE PUBLICATION DATES AND MAJOR EVENTS TIMELINE

2010

June 30	*Inspire 1*
August 31	President Obama announces an end to the combat mission in Iraq
September 3	AQAP attack on the UPS cargo plane in Dubai
October 11	*Inspire 2*
November 20	*Inspire 3*
December 11	Sweden Stockholm bombing
December 17	Arab Spring begins in Tunisia

2011

January 16	*Inspire 4*
March 2	Germany Frankfurt airport shooting
March 25	Syrian civil war begins
March 29	*Inspire 5*
May 2	Osama bin Laden is killed
June 16	Ayman al-Zawahiri is appointed new leader of Al Qaeda
July 18	*Inspire 6*
September 27	*Inspire 7*
September 30	Anwar al-Awlaki is killed in Yemen

2012

March 11–19	France Toulouse shootings
May 2	*Inspire 8*
May 2	*Inspire 9*

2013

January 16	Al Qaeda Algeria Amenas gas plant attack
February 28	*Inspire 10*
March 4	Raqqa falls to insurgent forces
March 19	Suspected chemical attack in Khan al-Assal
April 15	U.S. Boston Marathon bombing
May 22	UK London knife attack
May 30	*Inspire 11*
August 21	Suspected chemical attack in Ghouta

2014

January 4	ISIS captures Fallujah
January 14	ISIS captures Raqqa and turns it into its capital
February 2	Ayman al-Zawahiri formally severs ties with ISIS
March 17	*Inspire 12*

(Continued)

TABLE 17.9 (CONTINUED)   MAGAZINE PUBLICATION DATES AND MAJOR EVENTS TIMELINE

April 11	Suspected chemical attack in Kafr Zita
May 24	Belgium Jewish museum attack
June 9-11	ISIS captures Mosul and Tikrit
June 12	Iran deploys forces in Iraq against ISIS
June 29	Abu Mohammed al-Adnani announces the establishment of the caliphate
July 5	*Dabiq 1*
July 27	*Dabiq 2*
August 7	President Obama authorizes airstrikes against ISIS in Iraq
August 29	*Dabiq 3*
September 10	President Obama authorizes airstrikes against ISIS in Syria
September 23	Australia police officers stabbing
October 12	*Dabiq 4*
October 20	Canada Quebec car attack
October 22	Canada Ottawa shooting
October 23	U.S. New York hatchet attack
November 21	*Dabiq 5*
December 15	Australia Sydney hostage crisis
December 20	France Tours stabbing attack
December 24	*Inspire 13*
December 29	*Dabiq 6*
2015	
January 7	France Charlie Hebdo attack
January 9	France Paris hostage attack
February 12	*Dabiq 7*
February 14	Denmark Copenhagen synagogue shooting
March 18	Tunisia Bardo Museum shooting attack
March 30	*Dabiq 8*
March 31	Iraqi forces recapture Tikrit
May 3	U.S. Dallas shooting
May 17	ISIS captures Ramadi
May 21	*Dabiq 9*
May 21	ISIS captures Palmyra
June 26	Tunisia Sousse hotel attack
June 26	France beheading and factory attack
July 13	*Dabiq 10*
September 9	*Dabiq 11*
September 9	*Inspire 14*

(Continued)

TABLE 17.9 (CONTINUED)   MAGAZINE PUBLICATION DATES AND MAJOR EVENTS TIMELINE

September 12	Ayman al-Zawahiri advises to cooperate with ISIS against the enemy alliance
September 30	Russia begins airstrikes in Syria
October 31	Russian airplane downed over Sinai
November 13	France Paris suicide bombings
November 18	*Dabiq 12*
December 2	U.S. San Bernardino attack
December 5	UK London metro stabbing attack
December 28	Iraqi forces recapture Ramadi
2016	
January 8	U.S. Philadelphia police officer shooting
January 19	*Dabiq 13*
February 26	Germany Hanover stabbing
March 19	Turkey Istanbul bombing
March 22	Belgium Brussels bombings
April 13	*Dabiq 14*
May 7	Ayman al-Zawahiri calls for unity in Syria
May 14	*Inspire 15*
June 12	U.S. Orlando night club shooting
June 13	France police officer stabbing
June 26	Iraqi forces recapture Fallujah
June 28	Turkey Istanbul Ataturk Airport attack
July 14	France Nice truck attack
July 19	Germany train knife attack
July 31	*Dabiq 15*
August 6	Belgium Charleroi police stabbing
August 29	Ayman al-Zawahiri issues a statement calling for unity among factions in Syria against the invader enemies
September 2	Denmark Copenhagen police attack
September 5	*Rumiyah 1*
September 17	U.S. Minnesota stabbing attack
September 17	U.S. New York bombings
October 4	*Rumiyah 2*
October 16	Germany Hamburg stabbing
October 16	Turkish-backed Syrian forces capture Dabiq from ISIS
November 11	*Rumiyah 3*
November 12	*Inspire 16*
November 28	U.S. Ohio State knife attack
December 7	*Rumiyah 4*

(Continued)

TABLE 17.9 (CONTINUED)   MAGAZINE PUBLICATION DATES AND MAJOR EVENTS TIMELINE

December 19	Germany Berlin Christmas market truck attack
2017	
January 1	Turkey Istanbul Reina nightclub attack
January 6	*Rumiyah 5*
February 4	*Rumiyah 6*
March 2	Syrian forces recapture Palmyra
March 7	*Rumiyah 7*
March 22	UK London Westminster Bridge vehicle attack
April 3	Russia St. Petersburg metro attack
April 4	Suspected chemical attack on Khan Sheikhoun
April 5	*Rumiyah 8*
April 7	Sweden Stockholm truck attack
April 7	President Trump launches a cruise missile attack on a Syrian airfield
April 11	ISIS loses most of its former territory in Iraq
May 4	*Rumiyah 9*
May 22	UK Manchester Arena concert attack
June 3	UK London Bridge van attack
June 5	Australia Melbourne shooting
June 7	*Rumiyah 10*
June 9	Ayman al-Zawahiri calls for unity against unified enemy
June 19	France Paris Champs-Elysees police attack
June 21	Belgium Brussels train station attack
July 10	Iraqi forces recapture Mosul
July 13	*Rumiyah 11*
July 29	ISIS loses most of its former territory in Iraq and Syria
August 6	*Rumiyah 12*
August 13	*Inspire 17*
August 17	Spain Barcelona van attack
August 19	Russia Surgut knife attack
August 25	Belgium Brussels soldiers knife attack
September 9	*Rumiyah 13*
September 15	UK London commuter train bomb attack
October 20	Raqqa is recaptured from ISIS
November 1	U.S. New York City truck attack
November 9	Syria's army declares victory over ISIS
December 9	Iraqi Prime Minister declares victory over ISIS

Terrorist attacks included in the timeline are the attacks targeted against the West, attacks that have been inspired or claimed by Al Qaeda or ISIS, and attacks that feature in the magazines.

17.5 SUMMARY

The analysis of the content of *Inspire*, *Dabiq* and *Rumiyah* illustrates that AQAP and ISIS select material for publication that rationalizes their ideological justifications. The magazines are a great source of information on religious narratives that AQAP and ISIS use to boost their legitimacy. This information can be used to identify potential recruits and to construct counter-narratives. The magazines contain a large amount of detail on the groups' enemies and competing groups. This information can be instrumental in counterterrorism efforts for protection of targets. Information on competitors can be used in counter-narratives that aim at magnifying discord among terrorist groups. Through ideological interpretations of current news AQAP and ISIS create competing systems of meaning for their followers. This information sheds light on societal issues that carry a special emotive appeal that can contribute to push factors leading individuals to join terrorist groups. These issues can be identified and addressed as a preventive measure against radicalization.

Inspire, *Dabiq*, and *Rumiyah* are a great open source of detail on the current state of affairs of terrorist groups. Through tracing themes over time, one can glean organizational changes in the groups. For instance, one could detect problems ISIS was facing through tracing a shift from the focus on territorial expansion in *Dabiq* to delayed victory in *Rumiyah*. Exaggerating mujahedeen successes, increasing calls to terrorism, highlighting activities of affiliates instead of group's own—these can all be indicators of important transitions terrorist organizations are experiencing.

Next, the style, language, and appeal to diverse audiences used in the magazines can give clues on recruitment target groups. For example, the easy colloquial language of *Inspire* indicates the wide targeted audience the publication tries to reach. In contrast, the language of *Dabiq* and *Rumiyah*, dense with Arabic religious terms, suggests that these publications are more narrowly targeted at more religious individuals and bilingual speakers of Arabic and English. *Rumiyah*'s focus on women's issues leads one to believe ISIS has been trying to increase its following among female audiences. Finally, the sheer volume of instructions for attacks in the three magazines offers counterterrorism practitioners a wealth of information on potential targets, modes and weapons of terrorist attacks.

NOTES

1. The views expressed here are those of the author and do not reflect the official policy or position of the National Defense University, the Department of Defense, or the U.S. Government.
2. Azmat Khan. "The Magazine that 'Inspired' the Boston Bombers." *PBS Frontline*, 30 April 2013.
3. *Inspire* no. 11, 30 May 2013.
4. US Department of Justice. "California Man Charged with Conspiring to Provide Material Support to Terrorism and Being 'Straw Purchaser' of Assault Rifles Ultimately Used in San Bernardino, California, Attack." *Office of Public Affairs Justice News*, 17 December 2015.
5. Or Honig and Ariel Reichard, "The Usefulness of Examining Terrorists' Rhetoric for Understanding the Nature of Different Terror Groups." *Terrorism and Political Violence* online version, 2017. https://doi.org/10.1080/09546553.2017.1283308.
6. Combating Terrorism Center. "Zawahiri's Letter to Zarqawi." *Harmony Document*, 9 July 2005.
7. See Daniel Milton. *Communication Breakdown: Unraveling the Islamic State's Media Efforts*, West Point: Combating Terrorism Center, 2016.
8. Combating Terrorism Center. "Analysis of the State of ISI." Harmony Document NMEC-2007-612449.

9. For more on ISIS propaganda see Craig Whiteside. *Lighting the Path: The Evolution of the Islamic State Media Enterprise (2003–2016)*. (The Hague: ICCT, 2016); J.M. Berger and Jonathon Morgan. *The ISIS Twitter Census: Defining the Describing the Population of ISIS Supporters on Twitter*. The Brookings Analysis Paper no. 20, March 2015; Charlie Winter. *Documenting the Virtual 'Caliphate'*. (London: Quilliam, 2015).

10. Scott Shane and Ben Hubbard. "ISIS Displaying a Deft Command of Varied Media." *New York Times*, August 30, 2014.

11. Kenneth Payne. "Winning the Battle of Ideas: Propaganda, Ideology, and Terror," *Studies in Conflict and Terrorism* 32, no. 2 (2009): 109–128; Paul Wilkinson. "The Media and Terrorism: A Reassessment." *Terrorism and Political Violence* 9, no. 2 (1997): 51–64; Max Abrahms. Nicholas Beauchamp and Joseph Mroszszyk, "What Terrorist Leaders Want: A Content Analysis of Terrorist Propaganda Videos." *Studies in Conflict and Terrorism* 40, no. 11 (2017): 899–916.

12. Brian A. Jackson, John C. Baker, Kim Cragin, et al. *Aptitude for Destruction: Organizational Learning in Terrorist Groups and its Implications for Combating Terrorism*. (Santa Monica: RAND, 2005); James J.F. Forest, ed. *Teaching Terror: Strategic and Tactical Learning in the Terrorist World*. (Lanham: Rowman and Littlefield Publishers, Inc., 2006); Michael C. Horowitz, "Nonstate Actors and the Diffusion of Innovations: The Case of Suicide Terrorism." *International Organization* 64, no. 1 (2010): 33–64; Calvert Jones. "Al-Qaeda's Innovative Improvisers: Learning in a Diffuse Transnational Network." *Cambridge Review of International Affairs* 10, no. 4 (2006): 555–569; Brian A. Jackson and Bryce Loidolt. "Considering al-Qa'ida's Innovation Doctrine: From Strategic Texts to 'Innovation in Practice'." *Terrorism and Political Violence* 25, no. 2 (2013): 284–310.

13. Evan F. Kohlmann. "Al-Qa'ida's 'MySpace': Terrorist Recruitment on the Internet." *CTC Sentinel* 1, no. 2 (2008); James J.F. Forest. "Perception Challenges Faced by Al-Qaeda on the Battlefield of Influence Warfare." *Perspectives on Terrorism* 6, no. 1 (2012): 8–22.

14. Clark McCauley and Sophia Moskalenko. "Mechanisms of Political Radicalization: Pathways Toward Terrorism." *Terrorism and Political Violence* 20, no. 3 (2008): 415–433.

15. Available at: http://jihadology.net/.

16. Available at: https://clarionproject.org/.

17. Available at: https://ds-drupal.haverford.edu/aqsi/.

18. Brandon Colas. "What Does Dabiq Do? ISIS Hermeneutics and Organizational Fractures within Dabiq Magazine." *Studies in Conflict and Terrorism* 40, no. 3 (2017): 173–190.

19. Julian Droogan and Shane Peattie. "Mapping the Thematic Landscape of Dabiq Magazine." *Australian Journal of International Affairs* 71, no. 6 (2017): 591–620.

20. Julian Droogan and Shane Peattie, "Reading Jihad: Mapping the Shifting Themes of Inspire Magazine." *Terrorism and Political Violence* online version (2016): https://doi.org/10.1080/09546553.2016.1211527.

21. Haroro J. Ingram. "An Analysis of Inspire and Dabiq: Lessons from AQAP and Islamic State's Propaganda War." *Studies in Conflict and Terrorism* 40, no. 5 (2017): 357–375.

22. Seth Cantey. "Beyond the Pale? Exploring Prospects for Negotiations with Al Qaeda and the Islamic State." *Studies in Conflict and Terrorism* online version (2017). https://doi.org/10.1080/1057610X.2017.1348096.

23. Celine Marie I. Novenario. "Differentiating Al Qaeda and the Islamic State Through Strategies Publicized in *Jihadist* Magazines." *Studies in Conflict and Terrorism* 39, no. 11 (2016): 953–967.

24. For a similar approach but focused on only two magazines see Peter Wignell, Sabine Tan, Kay L. O'Halloran, and Rebecca Lange. "A Mixed Methods Empirical Examination of Changes in Emphasis and Style in the Extremist Magazines Dabiq and Rumiyah." *Perspectives on Terrorism* 11, no. 2 (2017).

25. Kieran Corcoran. "A Terrorist Who Killed 5 People in a Truck Ramming Seemed Disappointed When he Found out ISIS Never Claimed his Attack." *Business Insider*, February 23, 2018.

26. *Inspire* no. 1 (June 30, 2010): p. 2.

27. Aaron Y. Zelin. "American Jihadi: The Death of Samir Khan in Yemen Marks the End of a Key Figure in the Internet Jihad." *Foreign Policy*, September 30, 2011.

28. Leah Farrall. "How Al Qaeda Works: What the Organization's Subsidiaries Say about its Strength." *Foreign Affairs* 90, no. 2 (2011).

29. "Al-Qaeda in the Arabian Peninsula (AQAP)." *Council on Foreign Relations*, June 19, 2015. Available at: https://www.cfr.org/backgrounder/al-qaeda-arabian-peninsula-aqap (accessed on March 24, 2018).
30. Greg Miller. "CIA Sees Increased Threat in Yemen." *Washington Post*, August 25, 2010.
31. *Inspire* no. 2 (October 11, 2010): p. 24.
32. *Inspire* no. 5 (March 29, 2011): p. 11.
33. For more on Al Qaeda's ideology see Daniel Byman. *Al Qaeda, the Islamic State, and the Global Jihadist Movement: What Everyone Needs to Know.* (New York: Oxford University Press, 2015); Rohan Gunaratna. *Inside Al Qaeda: Global Network of Terror.* (New York: Columbia University Press, 2002); Lawrence Wright. *The Looming Tower: Al-Qaeda and the Road to 9/11.* (New York: Vintage Books, 2006).
34. *Inspire* no. 11 (May 30, 2013): p. 3.
35. *Inspire* no. 9 (May 2, 2012): p. 6.
36. Word frequency stands for the number of occurrences of the word in the analyzed body of the text.
37. See Haroro J. Ingram. *Islamic State's English-Language Magazines, 2014-2017: Trends and Implications for CT-CVE Strategic Communications.* (The Hague: ICCT, 2018).
38. Terrence McCoy. "The Apocalyptic Magazine the Islamic State Uses to Recruit and Radicalize Foreigners." *Washington Post*, September 16, 2014.
39. Available at: https://sunnah.com/muslim/54/44/.
40. *Dabiq* no. 1 (July 5, 2014): p. 2.
41. *Dabiq* no. 1 (July 5, 2014): p. 3.
42. For more on ISIS's ideology see Daniel Byman. *Al Qaeda, the Islamic State, and the Global Jihadist Movement: What Everyone Needs to Know.* (New York: Oxford University Press, 2015); Jessica Stern and J.M. Berger. *ISIS: The State of Terror.* (New York: Harper Collins, 2016); Fawaz A. Gerges. *ISIS: A History.* (New Jersey: Princeton University Press, 2016).
43. *Dabiq* no. 2 (July 27, 2014): pp. 4–8.
44. *Dabiq* no. 6 (December 29, 2014): pp. 16–25.
45. *Dabiq* no. 8 (March 30, 2015): pp. 7–11.
46. *Dabiq* no. 14 (April 13, 2016): pp. 28–43.
47. *Dabiq* no. 3 (August 29, 2014): pp. 35–36.
48. *Dabiq* no. 4 (October 12, 2014): p. 44.
49. *Rumiyah* no. 1 (September 5, 2016): p. 1.
50. *Rumiyah* no. 1 (September 5, 2016): p. 8.
51. *Rumiyah* no. 1 (September 5, 2016): pp. 4–8.
52. *Rumiyah* no. 1 (September 5, 2016): p. 5.
53. *Rumiyah* no. 4 (December 7, 2016): p. 28.
54. *Rumiyah* no. 11 (July 13, 2017): p. 29.

Chapter 18

Daesh's Multimodal Strategies of Online Propaganda

Carol K. Winkler and Jonathan Pieslak

CONTENTS

18.1 INTRODUCTION

As various Sunni militant factions united under the banner of the Islamic State of Iraq (ISI) on 15 October 2006, the group produced a distinctive style of video propaganda to further its cause. The group's media products mostly involved documentations of battlefield successes filmed on low-fidelity (even handheld) cameras with soundtracks of overdubbed jihad-themed anashid (i.e. a cappella Islamic songs or Islamic chanting/recitation; anashid [pl.], nashid [sing.]). Those familiar with ISI propaganda at the time can recall the common scene of an oft-hidden ISI fighter filming an ambush on a passing truck or military convoy, all set to a nashid appropriated from a large corpus of general jihad-related anashid. While ISI chose soundtracks to be sonically emblematic of the group and its motives at the time, the collective had not yet produced its own anashid.

With ISI's subsequent territorial expansion and battlefield successes, the group's media machine began to demonstrate increasing sophistication. As ISI, later ISIS (as of 8 April 2013) and now the IS or Daesh (as of 29 June 2014), gained strength, it dedicated significant resources to both the quality and quantity of its video and audio media production. The group opened dedicated official media production branches (e.g., al-Furqan Media, al-Hayat Media Center, and Ajnad Audio Productions), as well as dozens of provincial media outfits located within Daesh-controlled territories. At the height of the group's territorial advances, the provincial media groups distributed over 95 percent of Daesh's media output [29]. Multi-part video series and Daesh-produced anashid characterized this developmental step in the group's media campaign. The videos circulated not only on the ground in Iraq and Syria, but also online to other Daesh-controlled territories and to global audiences.

Since the establishment of Daesh's coordinated globalized/localized media apparatus, the media output of the group has been quite prolific. By the time ISIS delivered the fourth install-ment of its "Salilu al-Sawarim" ("Clanging of the Swords") series on 17 May 2014, the group had amassed a library of two dozen official ISIS-produced anashid released through Ajnad Audio Productions. Continuing to favor music video-style segments in which gunfire and battlefield action scenes appeared to the sounds of invigorating jihad-themed anashid, the group eventu-ally produced thousands of videos and well over 150 anashid.

Reductions in both the quality and quantity of video outputs, however, occurred during peri-ods of intensified military operations against the group [36, 44, 71]. For example, Ajnad released 15 anashid and 25 Surah (Qur'an chapter recitations) in 2015, whereas in 2017 around the time of coalition force operations to recapture Mosul and Raqqa, they released only seven anashid and no Surah recitations. Likewise, as coalition forces moved in to reclaim East Mosul from October o2016 to January 2017, the Mosul province dramatically reduced its video production, shifting instead to an intensified focus on still photography to document the battle for current and future audiences [17].

Despite setbacks in Daesh's media output in such times of intensified conflict, the group's online media operations have retained their potency. Since Daesh's loss of Mosul (its capital in Iraq) and Raqqa (its capital in Syria) to coalition forces, the group has elevated media production output in its Sinai and Khurasan provinces [71]. Further, lone attackers around the globe, who often claim that Daesh's propaganda inspired them to carry out violent attacks, are also on the rise [20] and have become more likely to use explosive devices [7]. Interviews with lone attackers in the United Kingdom, for example, reveal the individuals who engage in more online learning than their other extremist counterparts are more likely to carry out attacks, to aim for hard tar-gets, and to use explosive devices [19]. Lone attackers utilize online media propaganda to access information on attack methods, to self-radicalize through exposure to extremist ideologies, and to confirm prior beliefs potentially leading to lethal consequences [9, 18, 62].

As Daesh's media campaign grows more sophisticated, the group has specifically invested significant effort into developing videos that feature multimodal interactions between visual imagery and music (anashid). In 2015, Daesh produced approximately 755 videos and only 108 (14 percent) did not include an overdubbed soundtrack. In 2017, approximately 96 percent of the group's videos involved overdubbed soundtracks that were specific to Daesh-produced anashid. Thus, the multimodal aspect of video with overdubbed audio (anashid) soundtracks represents a considerable, repeated strategy within Daesh's ongoing media campaign.

While scholarly focus on Daesh's media campaign is robust, the vast majority of such work isolates attention to a single mode of communication. Most often, such research examines text-based rhetorical appeals [1–3, 27, 34, 41, 56, 59, 60, 64, 70, 71], visual elements [8, 30, 32, 44, 57, 63, 65–67], or the anashid used in the audio tracks [22, 35, 43, 48–50, 53, 54]. These studies, however, fail to recognize the numerous interactions that can and do occur among the textual, aural/ sonic, and visual messages. As a single sensory channel can help contextualize, reinforce, refute, or dominate information provided by the other elements, the exclusive focus on one modality alone can lead to incomplete or even mistaken analyses of a media product's message [21].

Through a focus on videos that the group's provincial media offices have released, this study seeks to add to previous understandings regarding how Daesh uses sonic and visual message reinforcement. Specifically, the study reveals the strategic themes associated with video depictions of combat casualties. The chapter begins by reviewing previous scholarly work that examines how music and visual messaging can impact viewing audiences in a variety of contexts. It then explains our method for analyzing the sonic and visual elements and identifies the casualty-related themes where Daesh employed sonic/visual reinforcement. It concludes by discussing the findings and identifying fruitful areas of future study.

18.2 THE ROLE OF MUSIC AND VISUAL IMAGES IN MESSAGE PROCESSING

Much of the previous modality research examines the unique contributions that music and visual imagery make to how audiences react to video communications. Studies that explore the uses and gratification of music as a discrete variable show that such sonic inputs contribute to identity formation, positive and negative mood management, reminiscing, diversion, arousal, surveillance, social interaction, and self-awareness [39, 55]. Also, changes in musical intensity, tempo, and pitch height can both alter cognitive function and induce emotional states, such as happiness, sadness, tenderness, threat, and anger [28, 61]. Emotional reactions associated with particular musical attributes tend to cross-cultural groupings of listeners [4, 5], but musical preferences vary based on the listener's own culture [12, 58].

Studies exploring visual imagery as a singular mode of communication show that such images can have substantial impacts on viewers. Visual images often attract attention, enhance recall, heighten emotional responses, and frame the opinions and behavioral intentions of viewers [6, 37, 45–47, 52]. Point-of-view camera shots can heighten viewer arousal and enjoyment [11], special effects shots can produce visceral responses to the fantastic [23], particular camera movements can enhance or reduce image persuasiveness [38], and camera angles can influence viewer recall of characters and story lines [31], as well as impact viewers' interpretations of photo subject source credibility, likeability, and the potential to create identification with viewers [38, 40].

A small number of studies assess the combined, interactive effects of music and visual images. Experimental studies indicate that multimodal redundancy enhances viewer attention, recognition, understanding, and free recall of messages, as well as degrades those same outcomes when such multimodal redundancy is absent [16, 24, 73]. Eye tracking studies reveal that higher frequencies of music can draw viewer attention to light-colored objects, while low frequencies encourage viewers to focus on dark-colored objects [25]. Studies of the brain indicate that visual imagery's negative emotional context contributes to auditory novelty processing due to activation of corresponding neural networks [14]. Multimodal studies generally agree that redundant or contradictory messaging across modes of communication function in different ways from messages that rely on a singular mode of communication.

18.3 ANALYZING MULTIMODAL MESSAGING IN DAESH VIDEOS

This study is part of a larger project examining the multimodal strategies of Daesh and other violent extremist groups in the Middle East and North Africa (MENA) region.[1] It analyzes a random sample of 70 videos that Daesh's provincial media outlets released over approximately a two-year period (19 May 2015 to 30 September 2017). In an effort to reflect the relative output distributed by the Daesh provinces during the study's time period, the sample draws more heavily from certain areas. Accordingly, the scope of the media outputs includes nine videos released by Raqqa; six by Ninawa; five by Jazirah; four each by Halab, Janub, Sinai, Furat, and Khayr; three each by Anbar, Barqah, Tarabulus, and Karkuk; two each by the Philippines, Dijlah, Barakah, Hims, Homs, Salah al-Din, and Hamah; and one each from Baghdad, Dimashq, Khurasan, Shabwah, and Baydaa. All but four of the videos are in Arabic. Three of the exceptions are in French in the aftermath of the Brussels attacks, and the remaining one is an English video account of the experience of Trinidad recruits who migrated to Daesh-controlled territory.

We began by identifying video fragments with the potential to serve as instances of multimodal message reinforcement. Each video segment with an accompanying nashid on the soundtrack served as part of the study sample for analysis. Rather than treat entire videos as the unit of analysis, we utilized the starting and ending point of each accompanying nashid to avoid potential loss of useful data that might fall outside of the parameters of the full video's most emphasized topic. Further, recognizing that viewers would likely repost edited and shortened content of the videos on their social media platform, the fragment approach helped maximize the retention of messages as viewers likely saw them. To more fully understand the meaning of the fragments in context in the analysis, however, we examined video footage that appeared immediately before and after each multimodal segment.

We then sorted the identified video fragments into six recurrent, topical categories based on content similarity. The six coding categories in the study included militant training, combat operations, martyrdom operations, combat casualties, law enforcement/executions, and non-military activities. Each video was eligible for inclusion in more than one category, as single videos often included content that fell into more than one of the identified topics. A video beginning with combat operations, but moving on to law enforcement/executions and concluding with other non-military activities (e.g., shots of Daesh community members shopping in markets inside the group's controlled territories), for example, qualified three times for inclusion in the analysis.

To assess the visual and sonic content in the combat casualty fragments, we initially examined the two modes in isolation, keeping in mind the findings of research (presented above) regarding how particular modalities impact an audience's message processing. We then exchanged the visual and sonic findings to determine if one mode of communication reinforced any of the findings related to the other mode. The section below will describe the visual and sonic content of the dataset, including the identity, prevalence, and source of the specific anashid. It will then reveal Daesh's strategic use of themes as identified by the group's usage of sonic and visual redundancy.

18.4 COMBAT CASUALTIES

Combat casualty fragments (whether of Daesh fighters, civilians, or opposing forces) appear in 20 of the 70 provincial media office videos in the sample. Fifteen of the 20 segments involve overdubbed anashid soundtracks, but not every casualty scene includes an overdubbed anashid. The majority of those without anashid involve overdubbed narration, and this narration appears more commonly for scenes depicting the suffering of Muslim civilians. The videos utilize 16 different anashid in the segments depicting combat casualties, 13 of which are specific Daesh releases either through Ajnad, unofficial Daesh releases, or through the affiliated Daesh media wing Asda'. Although the Daesh media apparatus does not particularly emphasize a single nashid or anashid in the combat casualty fragments, the majority are arguably inspiring, exhilarating, motivational, or the thematic element of *tarhib*—assertions of violence and power that

TABLE 18.1   ANASHID USAGE IN DAESH CASUALTY FRAGMENTS IN STUDY SAMPLE

Title (English/Arabic)	Frequency	Source
Come on, Indulge/Hayya Inghamis	2x	Unofficial
How Great is the Encampment of Heroes/Lillahi Daru Mu'askaru Al-'btaali	2x	Unofficial
The Hell of Broksil/Jahim Broksil	2x	Asda'
We Came/Atayna	1x	Asda'
For the Love of Allah (French)	1x	al-Hayat
Advance, Advance (French)	1x	al-Hayat
Sing Praises Our Weapons Have Seen Action/Halili Sumr Al-Hirab	1x	Ajnad
Regiments of My State/Saraya Dawlati	1x	Ajnad
We Departed at Dawn/Sarayna Matla' Al-Fajr	1x	Unconfirmed IS nashid
We Have Risen Up, We Have Risen Up/Nahadna Nahadna	1x	Ajnad
Islamic State, Pounce and Repel/Dawlat Al-Islami Suliyy Wa Adhary	1x	Unofficial
Attack Them/Ughzu Alayhim	1x	Unofficial
Thank God/Al-Hamdlelah	1x	Unofficial
Two unknown	1x	

are intended to invoke terror [35]. Table 18.1 identifies the anashid appearing in these segments, their frequency of usage, and their source.

Based on the combat casualty video clips that include these anashid, three strategic themes emerge as having multimodal reinforcement. The identified themes include (1) Daesh fighters will be the agent responsible for causing casualties on the battlefield; (2) the death toll on Daesh enemies will be substantial, whether measured by the quantity or the quality of the battlefield casualties; and (3) the afterlife for killed members of the Daesh militia will be far superior to Daesh's enemies.

18.4.1 Cause of Battlefield Casualties

The first theme in video clips featuring combat casualties emphasizes that Daesh fighters will be the primary agent causing casualties on the battlefield. One video that clearly illustrates the theme is "God will Punish Them," released by Daesh's al-Janub province, which—as the Meir Amit Intelligence and Terrorism Information Center (2014) explains—is located in southern Iraq and includes both the center of Fallujah city in Iraq's Anbar province and the northern region of Iraq's Babil province. "God will Punish Them" uses a visual narrative to portray Daesh fighters as the primary cause of battlefield casualties. Displaying an icon of a waving Daesh flag in the right-hand corner to illustrate the authenticity of the media product, the video begins with a line of armed Daesh soldiers walking on various dirt roadways toward the battlefield. One of the soldiers raises his index finger to signal tawhid, that is, his commitment to monotheism, recognizing Allah as the one true God. A variety of clips edited together in quick succession position the viewer to see side views of the fighters shooting machine guns, rocket launchers, and truck-mounted automatic weaponry. Point-of-view shots then position the viewer to stand side-by-side a Daesh fighter shooting a machine-gun from inside a trench. The camera shot narrows to the gun barrel and then pulls back to a close-up shot limited to the shooter's hands on the trigger and the gun barrel. The cropped shot of the shooter's hands with the rest of the body outside of the shot invites viewers to imagine themselves as looking at their own hands as they actively participate in the military operations underway.

The video then proceeds to visually document the apparent outcomes resulting from the Daesh fighter's efforts. Initially, the video moves back and forth between (1) shots of firing rocket launchers and standing building structures in Iraqi flagged areas and (2) red bulls-eyes, pointed arrows, and slow-motion effects to focus the viewer's attention on the demise of the buildings. The video loops a single explosion so that it plays serially, suggesting a larger number of successful attacks. The video then utilizes the same editing approach to highlight the deaths of soldiers fighting against Daesh. This time the video toggles between the use of red bulls-eyes to target enemy fighters and then shows those same fighters shot as they lift up their heads from their trenches, survey prior hits to their tanks or Humvees, or fly helicopters overhead. Slow motion and the looping technique also reappear to emphasize the loss of life to Daesh enemies. The camera then shows multiple close-up shots of bloody and decapitated enemy soldiers as Daesh fighters (and viewers positioned to have the same gaze) witness the effects of the battle as they walk through the enemy's trenches.

Sonically speaking, Daesh uses its nashid "Come on, Indulge" as the soundtrack in its "God Will Punish Them" video to reinforce the strategic theme that Daesh fighters are the primary cause of death on the battlefield. The musical backdrop in "God Will Punish Them" does so by using the same nashid both in the shots of the military combat that immediately precede the casualty shots and in the outcome shots of the battlefield operations where Daesh fighters survey the dead bodies of the opposing force fighters. Other combat casualty fragments in the study dataset achieve reinforcement of the same cause-effect relationship by playing a single nashid without interruption as the visual footage moves from combat scenes to the deadly results. The up-tempo characteristic of the nashid, whether that of "Come on, Indulge" or other anashid Daesh utilizes in the remainder of the casualty fragments in the dataset, provide an inspiring, exhilarating soundtrack to encourage a positive interpretation of the role of Daesh fighters in the war effort and the ensuing casualties.

18.4.2 Quantity and Quality of Casualties

Daesh's provincial videos also use sonic and visual reinforcement to display the theme that multitudes will die in the fight against Daesh. "And If They Fight You" (distributed by Daesh's Damascus province in southwest Syria) and "Shockers of the Hearts" (distributed by the group's Sinai province in the northern part of the Sinai Peninsula) demonstrate the various ways Daesh utilizes multimodal reinforcement to highlight the strategic theme. In "If They Fight You," the video includes a wide-angle shot that displays a line of dead bodies littering a battlefield. To emphasize the large number of individuals who have lost their lives, the camera moves in for a close-up shot of one corpse, pans back out for a broader shot of the terrain, moves forward again for a close-up of the next corpse, pans out again, and so on. While eventually "And If They Fight You" moves on to other topics besides the combat casualties, the video first pans out from the final close-up of a corpse to reveal that more dead bodies are present on the battlefield if time permitted their viewing.

"Shockers of the Hearts" reinforces the strategic theme that Daesh has and will continue to be responsible for large quantities of enemy deaths. Instead of surveying corpses on a battlefield, however, this video shows numerous instances of casualties as they happen through a point-of-view shot. The point-of-view shot places the viewer in the position of a Daesh fighter viewing enemy fighters through a gun sight with a clear, identifiable target on their bodies. Daesh shooters (or viewers if they imagine themselves "in" in the shot) successfully and repeatedly kill many enemy fighters quickly with single shots. "Shockers of the Hearts" does not linger over the corpses of the dead bodies and sometimes does not show the bodies at all, as they fall behind the enemies' defensive positions. Nevertheless, the action shots clearly document that enemy fighters have unambiguously fallen to the ground in ways that offer little to no hope for their return.

Beyond visually displaying that large numbers of enemy soldiers who have died in battles with Daesh, the group also emphasizes the qualitative value of the targeted individuals. "And If They Fight You" and "Shockers of the Hearts" together display a corpse of an identifiable enemy pilot, pictures of identification papers of high-ranking enemy officials, and the presence of stars on the corpse's uniform to illustrate the high status of those killed. The military value of the lost soldiers, coupled with the large number of those killed, emphasizes the heavy toll that enemy forces and their supporters can anticipate.

The sonic frames of "And If They Fight You" and "Shockers of the Hearts" reinforce the strategic theme that opposing Daesh fighters will result in multitudes of important enemy casualties. The sonic tracks in both videos stress that enemy casualties are not unique incidents. They employ a chorus, rather than a soloist, to sing the anashid that play in the background as the videos display the bodies of Daesh enemies. Singers of the anashid also utilize a cascade of voices, where one singer begins before the other ends to reinforce the continuity of casualties. The repetitive, rhythmic patterns present in the anashid, while not unique to casualty segments, further stress the theme of recurrence. Finally, the heartbeat that occurs in the introduction to "Shocker of the Hearts" serves as a repetitive sound that places viewers in a heightened emotional state as they observe the acts of killing.

18.4.3 The Afterlife

The final theme garnering multimodal reinforcement in combat casualty fragments is that the afterlife of Daesh's enemies will be inferior to that of the group's fighters. To explain the approach, we compared two videos related to the strategic theme: "The Assault of Redemption 3" released by Daesh's Homs province in northwest Syria and "The Raid of Suhayb al Iraqi" released by the group's Kirkuk province in northeast Iraq. "The Assault of Redemption 3" focuses on how Daesh's enemies can expect their ascension to the afterlife. The enemy corpses appear bloodied and dirty, with holes in their throats (a place that many Muslims consider the final resting place for the soul), and brains often spilling out of the corpse (fatefully denying the connection between the body and brain). Enemy corpses often appear with their eyes and mouths wide open, a positioning that leaves the body in sharp contrast to how Umm Salama reported the Prophet had closed Abu Salama's eyes noting that "when the soul is taken away the sight follows it" (Sahih Muslim Book 4 (Hadith 2003)). The bodies further appear unprepared for the afterlife as they lay in full view on rocky, dirty surfaces. Daesh fighters kick (thereby insulting) the dead bodies, often in the throat. The militia members also do not hasten to prepare the bodies for burial in accordance with standard practices of the Islamic faith; instead, the Daesh fighters take their time pillaging booty from the corpses' bodies.

The sonic elements in "The Assault of Redemption 3" reinforce the theme of the inferior afterlife facing Daesh enemies. Although a nashid does play during the display of the Daesh enemy corpses, the music does not display any obvious distinguishing characteristics. While the same nashid sonically links all of the dead bodies into a single outcome of battle, the soundtrack is essentially routine for Daesh videos, suggestive of no spectacular future outcome for the individuals who have just lost their lives. One might say that the desecration and lack of care of the bodies suggest that opposing fighters are simply part of battlefield destruction, no more or less important than the destroyed buildings. They not only become part of the rubble but, as opponents to Daesh, are also as dismissible as the damage from the destruction of any structure. Sonically, the video reinforces such an interpretation by continuing the same nashid while displaying destruction of the buildings and the bodies of the enemy fighters. Not only is the scene showing the horrific fate of those who oppose Daesh, but sonically speaking, it reduces the lives of opponents to soulless, battlefield things.

In contrast, the Kirkuk province's video "The Raid of Suhayb al Iraqi" visually displays a different (and superior) preparation for the afterlife for Daesh fighters killed in combat. After a single Daesh militant is shot in battle and rolls backwards down an embankment to his death, the video's editors immediately darken the image and place the body outside of the observer's clear view. As the other militants prepare the corpse for the afterlife, the body remains out of the viewer's sight. After the preparation process is complete, a light shines on the corpse's clean face that eventually expands slightly to enlighten the upper torso of the body. The facial features do not appear contorted. The positive facial expression, coupled with the comfortable positioning of the body on a blanket rather than the natural, rocky terrain, is suggestive of serenity as the fighter moves on to the afterlife.

The musical elements of "The Raid of Suhayb al Iraqi" reinforce the superior afterlife that awaits the Daesh fighter. Standing in sharp contrast to the soundtrack for the appearance of enemy combat casualties in "The Assault of Redemption 3," Daesh sonically demarcates the sanctity of sacrifice of the Daesh fighter by changing the soundtrack to a martyrdom lamentation. The slow, somber tone of the nashid highlights the solemnness of the occasion. Musically speaking, "The Raid of Suhayb al Iraq" presents the action and aggression of combat as appropriately paused for Daesh fighters as their souls and noble sacrifice receive veneration through lamentation. Yet, for the opposing forces in "The Assault of Redemption 3," the up-tempo motivating nashid used to accompany the combat scenes continues to play, diminishing the value of their sacrifice as not being worthy of any particular distinction apart from the natural flow of combat.

18.5 SUMMARY

Together, the combat casualty segments in Daesh's wilayat-level videos feature strategic themes through multimodal reinforcement that present a devastating outcome as an expected norm for those who fight against Daesh. Whether focusing on the immediate end to the short life on earth or the lasting consequences in the afterlife, the Daesh videos present the large risks as unavoidable for those who choose to fight against the group's interpretation of Islam. The videos, in sharp contrast, imply that Daesh fighters are at low odds of losing their own lives due to the efficient, effective militia that defends the proclaimed caliphate, and in the rare instances that a Daesh militiaman experiences death in the battlefield, he can expect status as a martyr as he moves on into the afterlife.

The findings associated with Daesh's use of combat casualty video segments in provincial releases diverge from previous analyses of death imagery in the group's print publications. Previous studies of the still imagery displayed in Daesh's print media campaign (both English and Arabic language publications), for example, conclude that the group adopts the Western media's practice of generally being reluctant to display the dead [67]. In contrast, the findings here suggest that the group has no such hesitancy in the production of its video products, as almost a third of the videos included in the study sample include a combat casualty fragment. Notably, however, when Daesh videos do display a corpse, the cameras do not linger in an effort to permit close observation. Typically, the viewer only has enough time to process that the enemy fighter is dead and to assess the general condition of the body before the video moves forward to other types of content. The reluctance to linger and observe any specific body may help explain the different approaches that the Daesh producers use to distinguish the relative quantity of casualty content across the two mediums. Photographs in print leave the length of viewing time up to the viewer, thus maximizing possible offence to some Muslim viewers who believe in strict adherence to conventions for handling the dead that have origins in the treatment of the Prophet's body—namely, to discretely wash, shroud, and bury the body quickly to avoid decomposition that could affect the outcome for the individual in the afterlife [26].

Wilayat-level video messaging related to combat casualty footage also counters oft-mistaken notions that official Ajnad productions represent the sole or even the most exclusive source of Daesh anashid. In fact, only three anashid played in the casualty fragments were official al-Ajnad releases. Five were Arabic Daesh anashid not given official release by any media wing. Our sample includes a disproportionate number of al-Hayat releases in French perhaps because the inclusion of videos after the Brussels attack, but Daesh's official al-Hayat media production company did not release these videos. Rather, they were wilayat-level productions. Thus, al-Hayat anashid do not remain within the sole domain of al-Hayat videos; the organizational structure of Daesh media production is flexible enough for al-Hayat anashid to appear in Arabic language or wilayat-level video messaging. Also, two anashid in the combat casualty fragments were Asda' releases, demonstrating that Daesh also sanctions the use of Asda' anashid in a representational capacity. While Asda' remains an unofficial audio production media wing, the combat casualty fragments clearly demonstrate that official wilayat-level videos use Asda' anashid as a soundtrack. Thus, the producers of these videos freely used Daesh anashid—official Ajnad releases and unofficial Arabic Daesh-produced anashid, as well as those from al-Hayat and Asda'.

The limitations of this study are certainly suggestive of areas for future research. The most obvious is the need to complete an analysis of multimodal appeals that characterize the remaining topical areas of Daesh's campaign. While the authors of this essay have already analyzed the training and martyrdom fragments within this study's sample dataset, the other topical areas (law enforcement/executions, combat operations, and non-military operations) remain unexplored. Non-military operations fragments are likely to be the most challenging, as that topical area depends on Daesh's incremental developments as they attempt to merge their modern conceptions of the Islamic State with historical conceptions of the Islamic caliphate.

The parameters of the sample size of this study are also suggestive of a future area of needed research. As the videos included in this study end in September 2017 and that time frame concludes as Daesh had to regroup in the aftermath of losses in Raqqa and Mosul, future studies should examine the most current trends in how the group is employing multimodal reinforcement. Has the group shifted strategic themes based on their loss of controlled territory? Do lone actors rely on videos from this study's time frame for inspiration, or do they look to the more recent products distributed from the various provinces?

Future scholars should also investigate other modes of Daesh's multimodal communication effort. Here, this study relies exclusively on visual imagery and musical/sonic elements available on the video soundtracks to demonstrate how global viewers (particularly those unfamiliar with the Arabic language) would experience Daesh's use of multimodal redundancy to reinforce its messages. Musical lyrics, oral messaging, and text-based entreaties, however, obviously remain crucial components of any comprehensive multimodal study of the group's media campaign and should find inclusion in future studies.

A further key need in future research is a focus on how Daesh uses different modes to communicate different messages to viewers. While our focus on redundancy has the advantage of exploring how the group uses repetition to strengthen attention, recall, and understanding of its message, differences in textual, oral, sonic, and visual stimuli within a video are also important considerations. Previous findings in other contexts reveal that viewers may be more likely to attend to and remember visual information if given competing information in the visual and aural tracks of a message [13, 16, 51], unless the overall amount of information is overwhelming to the viewer's capacity to attend to the message [24]. In studies of death images, in particular, the dominance of the visual appears to remain [15, 72]. Some research, however, finds that viewers prefer audio rather than visual stimuli [10]. Discovering what specific topics Daesh conveys when using contradictory multimodal messaging may help understandings of what is actually communicated.

A final area of future research should consider the inclusion of other non-state groups seeking to compete with established states for land and governmental control. While some argue that the size and level of sophistication in Daesh's media-based campaign may result in the group serving as a "first-mover (or most innovative-mover) advantage in the media realm" [44], other violent groups are nonetheless adopting their own versions of online propaganda efforts. Al Qaeda and its affiliates, in particular, are increasingly competing with Daesh in the online space and deserve scholarly attention.

NOTE

1. The authors would like to thank the Minerva Research Initiative for funding this research through the Air Force Office of Scientific Research, #FA9550-15-1-0373. We would also like to thank Megan Mapes, Ryan Gautreaux, and Wojciech Kaczkowski for their assistance in conducting background research for this study.

REFERENCES

1. Al-Hudhid, Ibrahim Salah. "Using Religious Texts for Justifying Acts of Violence - Review and Response." *Arab Media & Society* 21, May 31, 2016. Accessed March 13, 2018. https://www.arabmedi asociety.com/a-response-to-using-religious-texts-to-justify-terrorism-arabic/
2. Al-Yaqoubi, Shaykh Muhammad. *Refuting ISIS: A Rebuttal of Its Religious and Ideological Foundations.* Herndon, VA: Sacred Knowledge, 2015.
3. Awan, Akil N. "Jihadi Ideology in the New-Media Environment." In *Contextualising Jihadi Thought*, edited by Jeevan Deol and Zaheer Kazmi, 99–119. London: C. Hurst & Co, 2012.
4. Balkwill, Laura-Lee, and William Forde Thompson. "A Cross-Cultural Investigation of the Perception of Emotion in Music: Psychophysical and Cultural Cues." *Music Perception* 17 no. 1 (1999): 43–64.
5. Balkwill, Laura-Lee, William Forde Thompson, and Rie Matsunaga. "Recognition of Emotion in Japanese, Western, and Hindustani Music by Japanese Listeners." *Japanese Psychological Research* 46 no. 4 (2004): 337–49.
6. Barry, Anne Marie Seward. *Visual Intelligence: Perception, Image, and Manipulation in Visual Communication.* Albany, NY: State University of New York Press, 1997.

7. Becker, Michael. "Explaining Lone Wolf Target Selection in the United States." *Studies in Conflict & Terrorism* 37 no. 11 (2014): 959–78.
8. Bolt, Neville. *Violent Image: Insurgent Propaganda and the New Revolutionaries*. New York: Columbia University Press, 2012.
9. Capellan, Joel A. "Lone Wolf Terrorist or Deranged Shooter? A Study of Ideological Active Shooter Events in the United States, 1970–2014." *Studies in Conflict & Terrorism* 38 no. 6 (2015): 395–413.
10. Collignon, Olivier, Simon Girard, Frederic Gosselin, Sylvain Roy, Dave Saint-Amour, Maryse Lassonde, and Franco Lepore. "Audio-Visual Integration of Emotion Expression." *Brain Research* 1242 no. 25 (2008): 126–35.
11. Cummins, R. Glenn, Justin R. Keene, and Brandon H. Nutting. "The Impact of Subjective Camera in Sports on Arousal and Enjoyment." *Mass Communication and Society* 15 no. 1 (2012): 74–97.
12. Darrow, Alice-Ann, Paul Haack, and Fumio Kuribayashi. "Descriptors and Preferences for Eastern and Western Musics by Japanese and American Nonmusic Majors." *Journal of Research in Music Education* 35 no. 4 (1987): 237–48.
13. Dhawan, Meena, and James W. Pellegrino. "Acoustic and Semantic Interference Effects in Words and Pictures." *Memory & Cognition* 5 no. 3 (1977): 340–6.
14. Domínguez-Borràs, Judith, Manuel Garcia-Garcia, and Carles Escera. "Negative Emotional Context Enhances Auditory Novelty Processing." *NeuroReport* 19 no. 4 (2008): 503–7.
15. Domke, David, David Perlmutter, and Meg Spratt. "The Primes of Our Times?: An Examination of the 'Power' of Visual Images." *Journalism* 3 no. 2 (2002): 131–59.
16. Drew, Dan G., and Thomas Grimes. "Audio-Visual Redundancy and TV News Recall." *Communication Research* 14 no. 4 (1987): 452–61.
17. El Damanhoury, Kareem, Carol Winkler, Wojciech Kaczkowski, and Aaron Dicker. "Examining the Military-Media Nexus in ISIS's Provincial Photography Campaign." *Dynamics of Asymmetric Conflict*. Published electronically February 8, 2018. doi: 10.1080/17467586.2018.1432869
18. Gill, Paul, and Emily Corner. "Lone-Actor Terrorist Use of the Internet and Behavioural Correlates." In *Terrorism Online: Politics, Law and Technology*, edited by Lee Jarvis, Stuart Macdonald, and Thomas M. Chen, 35–53. London: Routledge, 2015.
19. Gill, Paul, Emily Corner, Maura Conway, Amy Thornton, Mia Bloom, and John Horgan. "Terrorist Use of the Internet by the Numbers: Quantifying Behaviors, Patterns, and Processes." *Criminology & Public Policy* 16 no. 1 (2017): 99–117.
20. Gill, Paul, John Horgan, and Paige Deckert. "Bombing Alone: Tracing the Motivations and Antecedent Behaviors of Lone-Actor Terrorists." *Journal of Forensic Sciences* 59 no. 2 (2014): 425–35.
21. Graber, Doris A. "Say It with Pictures." *The Annals of the American Academy of Political and Social Science* 546 (July 1996): 85–96. http://www.jstor.org/stable/1048172
22. Gråtrud, Henrik. "Islamic State *Nasheeds* as Messaging Tools." *Studies in Conflict & Terrorism* 39 no. 12 (2016): 1050–70.
23. Griffiths, Alison. "Wonder, Magic and the Fantastical Margins: Medieval Visual Culture and Cinematic Special Effects." *Journal of Visual Culture* 9 no. 2 (2010): 163–88.
24. Grimes, Tom. "Audio-Video Correspondence and Its Role in Attention and Memory." *Educational Technology Research and Development* 38 no. 3 (1990): 15–25.
25. Hagtvedt, Henrik, and S. Adam Brasel. "Cross-Modal Communication: Sound Frequency Influences Consumer Responses to Color Lightness." *Journal of Marketing Research* 53 no. 4 (2016): 551–62.
26. Halevi, Leor. *Muhammad's Grave: Death Rites and the Making of Islamic Society*. New York: Columbia University Press, 2007.
27. Halverson, Jeffrey R., H. L. Goodall, Jr., and Steven R. Corman. *Master Narratives of Islamist Extremism*. New York: Palgrave Macmillian, 2011.
28. Ilie, Gabriela, and William Forde Thompson. "Experiential and Cognitive Changes Following Seven Minutes Exposure to Music and Speech." *Music Perception* 28 no. 3 (2011): 247–64.
29. Joscelyn, Thomas. "Graphic Promotes the Islamic State's Prolific Media Machine." *FDD's Long War Journal*, November 25, 2015. Accessed March 14, 2018. https://www.longwarjournal.org/archives/2015/11/graphic-promotes-islamic-states-prolific-media-machine.php

30. Kovács, Attila. "The 'New Jihadists' and the Visual Turn from al-Qa'ida to ISIL/ISIS/Da'ish." *Bitzpol Affairs* 2 no. 3 (2015): 47–69. http://epa.oszk.hu/02400/02475/00004/pdf/EPA02475_BiztpolAffairs_2014_03_047-070.pdf May 18, 2019.

31. Kraft, Robert N. "The Influence of Camera Angle on Comprehension and Retention of Pictorial Events." *Memory & Cognition* 15 no. 4 (1987): 291–307.

32. Kuznar, Larry. "Daesh's Image of the State in Their Own Words." In *White Paper on SMA Support to SOCCENT: ISIL Influence and Resolve*, edited by Allison Astorino-Courtois, Sarah Canna, Sam Rhem, and George Popp, 27–30. Boston, MA: Nationwide Suspicious Activity Reporting Initiative, 2015. https://info.publicintelligence.net/SOCCENT-ISIL-InfluenceResolve.pdf

33. Kwoun, Soo-Jin. "An Examination of Cue Redundancy Theory in Cross-Cultural Decoding of Emotions in Music." *Journal of Music Therapy* 46 no. 3 (2009): 217–37.

34. La Palm, Marita. "Concerning features of the apocalyptic cult in the Islamic State of Iraq and the Levant (ISIL)." *Foreign Policy Journal*, October 28, 2014. Accessed March 14, 2018. http://www.foreignpolicyjournal.com/2014/10/28/concerning-features-of-an-apocalyptic-cult-in-the-islamic-state-of-iraq-and-the-levant-isil/

35. Lahoud, Nelly. "A Cappella Songs (*Anashid*) in Jihadi Culture." In *Jihadi Culture: The Art and Social Practices of Militant Islamists*, edited by Thomas Hegghammer, 42–62. New York: Cambridge University Press, 2017.

36. Lakomy, Miron. "Cracks in the Online 'Caliphate': How the Islamic State is Losing Ground in the Battle for Cyberspace." *Perspectives on Terrorism* 11 no. 3 (2017): 40–53. Accessed March 19, 2018. http://www.terrorismanalysts.com/pt/index.php/pot/article/view/607

37. Lang, Annie, John Newhagen, and Byron Reeves. "Negative Video as Structure: Emotion, Attention, Capacity, and Memory." *Journal of Broadcasting & Electronic Media* 40 no. 4 (1996): 460–77.

38. Larsen, Val, David Luna, and Laura A. Peracchio. "Points of View and Pieces of Time: A Taxonomy of Image Attributes." *Journal of Consumer Research* 31 no. 1 (2004): 102–11.

39. Lonsdale, Adam J., and Adrian C. North. "Why Do We Listen to Music? A Uses and Gratifications Analysis." *British Journal of Psychology* 102 no. 1 (2011): 108–34.

40. McCain, Thomas A., Joseph Chilberg, and Jacob Wakshlag. "The Effect of Camera Angle on Source Credibility and Attraction." *Journal of Broadcasting* 21 no. 1 (1977): 35–46.

41. McCants, William. *The ISIS Apocalypse: The History, Strategy, and Doomsday Vision of the Islamic State*. New York: St. Martin's Press, 2015.

42. The Meir Emit Intelligence and Terrorism Information Center. "ISIS: Portrait of a Jihadi Terrorist Organization." November 26, 2014. Accessed March 14, 2018. http://www.terrorism-info.org.il/en/20733/

43. Miller, Greg, and Souad Mekhennet. "Inside the Surreal World of the Islamic State's Propaganda Machine." *The Washington Post*, November 20, 2015. Accessed March 14, 2018. https://www.washingtonpost.com/world/national-security/inside-the-islamic-states-propaganda-machine/2015/11/20/051e997a-8ce6-11e5-acff-673ae92ddd2b_story.html?utm_term=.e174ef366580

44. Milton, Daniel. *Communication Breakdown: Unraveling the Islamic State's Media Efforts*. New York: Combating Terrorism Center at West Point, United States Military Academy, 2016. Accessed March 14, 2018. https://www.ctc.usma.edu/v2/wpcontent/uploads/2016/10/ISMedia_Online.pdf

45. Nabi, Robin L. "'Feeling' Resistance: Exploring the Role of Emotionally Evocative Visuals in Inducing Inoculation." *Media Psychology* 5 no. 2 (2003): 199–223.

46. Newhagen, John E., and Byron Reeves. "The Evening's Bad News: Effects of Compelling Negative Television News Images on Memory." *Journal of Communication* 42 no. 2 (1992): 25–41.

47. Pfau, Michael, Michel Haigh, Andeelynn Fifrick, Douglas Holl, Allison Tedesco, Jay Cope, David Nunnally, et al. "The Effects of Print News Photographs of the Casualties of War." *Journalism & Mass Communication Quarterly* 83 no. 1 (2006): 150–68.

48. Pieslak, Jonathan. *Sound Targets: American Soldiers and Music in the Iraq War*. Bloomington, IN: Indiana University Press, 2009.

49. Pieslak, Jonathan. *Radicalism and Music: An Introduction to the Music Cultures of al Qa'ida, Racist Skinheads, Christian-Affiliated Radicals, and Eco-Animal Rights Militants*. Middletown, CT: Wesleyan University Press, 2015.

50. Pieslak, Jonathan. "A Musicological Perspective on Jihadi *Anashid*." In *Jihadi Culture: The Art and Social Practices of Militant Islamists*, edited by Thomas Hegghammer, 63–81. New York: Cambridge University Press, 2017.
51. Posner, Michael I., Mary J. Nissen, and Raymond M. Klein. "Visual Dominance: An Information-Processing Account of Its Origins and Significance." *Psychological Review* 83 no. 2 (1976): 157–71.
52. Powell, Thomas E., Hajo G. Boomgaarden, Knut De Swert, and Claes H. de Vreese. "A Clearer Picture: The Contribution of Visuals and Text to Framing Effects." *Journal of Communication* 65 no. 6 (2015): 997–1017.
53. RSN Staff. "Islamic State Songs – A Major Tool for Reinforcing Its Narrative." *Right Side News: The Right News for Americans*, repost of report by M. Shemesh | MEMRI, August 13, 2015. Accessed March 15, 2018. https://www.rightsidenews.com/2015/08/13/islamic-state-songs-a-major-tool-for-reinforcing-its-narrative/
54. Said, Behnam. "Hymns (*Nasheeds*): A Contribution to the Study of the *Jihadist* Culture." *Studies in Conflict & Terrorism* 35 no. 12 (2012): 863–79.
55. Schäfer, Thomas, Peter Sedlmeier, Christine Städtler, and David Huron. "The Psychological Functions of Music Listening." *Frontiers in Psychology* 4 no. 511 (2013).
56. Schmid, Alex P. (2015). "Challenging the Narrative of the 'Islamic State.'" International Centre for Counter-Terrorism-The Hague Research Paper, June 2015. Accessed February 22, 2018. http://icct.nl/wp-content/uploads/2015/06/ICCT-Schmid-Challenging-the-Narrative-of-the-Islamic-State-June2015.pdf
57. Siboni, Gabi, Daniel Cohen, and Tal Koren. "The Islamic State's Strategy in Cyberspace." *Military and Strategic Affairs* 7 no. 1 (2015): 127–44. Accessed March 3, 2018. http://www.inss.org.il/publication/the-islamic-states-strategy-in-cyberspace/
58. Soley, Gaye, and Erin E. Hannon. "Infants Prefer the Musical Meter of Their Own Culture: A Cross-Cultural Comparison." *Developmental Psychology* 46 no. 1 (2010): 286–92.
59. Staffell, Simon, and Akil Awan, eds. *Jihadism Transformed: Al-Qaeda and Islamic State's Global Battle of Ideas*. Oxford: Oxford University Press, 2016.
60. Vergani, Matteo, and Ana-Maria Bliuc. "The Evolution of the ISIS' Language: A Quantitative Analysis of the First Year of Dabiq Magazine." *Sicurezza, Terrorismo, e Società: International Journal - Italian Team for Security, Terroristic Issues & Managing Emergencies* 2 (2015): 7–20. http://www.sicurezzaterrorismosocieta.it/wp-content/uploads/2015/12/Vergani-Bliuc_SicTerSoc_book-2.pdf
61. Vieillard, Sandrine, Isabelle Peretz, Nathalie Gosselin, Stéphanie Khalfa, Lise Gagnon, and Bernard Bouchard. "Happy, Sad, Scary and Peaceful Musical Excerpts for Research on Emotions." *Cognition and Emotion* 22 no. 4 (2008): 720–52.
62. von Behr, Ines, Anais Reding, Charlie Edwards, and Luke Gribbon. *Radicalisation in the Digital Era: The Use of the Internet in 15 Cases of Terrorism and Extremism*. Santa Monica, CA: RAND Corporation, 2013. http://www.rand.org/content/dam/rand/pubs/research_reports/RR400/RR453/RAND_RR453.pdf
63. Wahid, Mariam. "The Image: Reading Daesh's Media Messages." *Arab Center for Research and Studies*, December 14, 2015. Accessed February 28, 2018. http://www.acrseg.org/39703
64. Weiss, Michael, and Hassan Hassan. *ISIS: Inside the Army of Terror*. New York: Regan Arts, 2015.
65. Winkler, Carol. "Bodies as Argument in On-Line Jihadist Videos." In *Reasoned Argument and Social Change*, edited by Robert Rowland, 732–39. Washington, DC: National Communication Association, 2011.
66. Winkler, Carol. "Challenging Communities: A Perspective About, From, and By Argumentation." In *Disturbing Argument*, edited by Catherine H. Palczewski, 4–17. New York: Routledge, 2014.
67. Winkler, Carol K., Kareem El Damanhoury, Aaron Dicker, and Anthony F. Lemieux. "The Medium is Terrorism: Transformation of the About to Die Trope in *Dabiq*." *Terrorism and Political Violence*. Published electronically August 18, 2016.
68. Winkler, Carol K., Kareem El Damanhoury, Aaron Dicker, and Anthony F. Lemieux. "Images of Death and Dying in ISIS Media: A Comparison of English and Arabic Print Publications." *Media, War & Conflict*. Published online January 10, 2018. https://doi.org/10.1177/1750635217746200

69. Winter, Charlie. "Islamic State Propaganda: Key Elements of the Group's Messaging." *Terrorism Monitor* 13 no. 2 (2015): 7–11. Accessed March 10, 2018. https://jamestown.org/program/islamic-state-propaganda-key-elements-of-the-groups-messaging/
70. Winter, Charlie. "Totalitarianism 101: The Islamic State's Offline Propaganda Strategy." *Lawfare*. Last modified March 27, 2016. https://www.lawfareblog.com/totalitarianism-101-islamic-states-offline-propaganda-strategy
71. Winter, Charlie. "ICSR Insight: The ISIS Propaganda Decline." *International Centre for the Study of Radicalisation*. Last modified March 23, 2017. http://icsr.info/2017/03/icsr-insight-isis-propaganda-decline/
72. Zelizer, Barbie "Death in Wartime: Photographs and the 'Other War' in Afghanistan." *The International Journal of Press/Politics* 10 no. 3 (2005): 26–55.
73. Zhou, Shuhua. "Effects of Visual Intensity and Audiovisual Redundancy in Bad News." *Media Psychology* 6 no. 3 (2004): 237–56.

Chapter 19

Supporting the Authentication of Digital Evidence

Sarbari Gupta

CONTENTS

19.1 INTRODUCTION

Recent decades have seen a sharp increase in the use of online mechanisms (email, social media website, blogs, and others) to spread terrorist propaganda with the goal of radicalizing disaffected and gullible individuals, recruiting new supporters and activists and motivating them to carry out terrorist activities that are aligned with the specific tenets of the broader terrorist community. In this chapter, we will explore the types of online mechanisms that can be used to further the cause of the terrorist groups, the digital evidence created and left behind in the process, and the methods that can be used to determine and protect the authenticity of the evidence.

19.2 DIGITAL EVIDENCE IN TERRORISM INVESTIGATIONS

The widespread use of the internet to propagate the message, gain new followers, and sustain the activities of terrorist organizations result in creating long trails of "digital breadcrumbs" [1] that can be methodically gathered, analyzed, and connected to provide insight into the macro and micro level activities of these organizations. These windows of insight can provide evidence that leads law enforcement authorities to identify, track, and prosecute the perpetrators of terrorist attacks that have taken place. More importantly, digital evidence of terrorist communications can help to create a picture of terrorist activities in the planning stages, leading to apprehending the perpetrators and foiling the attacks before they occur.

19.3 PROPERTIES OF DIGITAL EVIDENCE

The actual content or substance of the digital artifact that is to be used as evidence is one among a number of properties that characterize it. The answers to the following questions reveal the various properties that identify and define a piece of digital evidence:

- *What*—The type of artifact or the actual substance of the artifact that constitutes the digital evidence. Possible evidence types include a file, an image, a text message, a social media posting, etc. Possible substance could be the content of a digital message, the substance of an agreement, the image of a particular group of persons, etc.
- *Who*—The person(s) who are responsible for the creation, updating, sending, or receiving of the digital artifact. For example, the original creator of a file, the sender of a text message, the receiver of an email message, the individual who shot a digital image, etc.
- *When*—The time at which the artifact was created, updated, sent, received or deleted. Examples include the time an image was clicked, a message was sent, a file was last updated or deleted, etc.
- *Why*—The context in which the digital artifact was created, sent, received, or used. Examples include the flow of an online conversation in which a particular text/email message was sent, or the business deal for which a particular business agreement was drawn up and signed, etc.
- *How*—The means by which the digital artifact was created, updated, sent, received, or deleted. For example, the application used to create a particular message or file, the online service used to create a web page or message, etc.
- *Where*—The physical location at which the digital artifact was created or used, and the device on which the artifact was created, updated, sent, received, or deleted. Examples include the GPS location where a digital image was shot, the mobile device on which a text message was sent or received, and the computer on which a file was created or updated.

The content or substance (what) of the digital artifact is only meaningful or relevant to an investigation if the other properties (who, when, why, how and where) are also identified. Thus, these meta-data are as important as the actual data or content of the digital artifact, when the latter is being used as digital evidence. See Figure 19.1.

19.4 TYPES OF DIGITAL EVIDENCE

Terrorist organizations thrive in the relative anonymity of the internet and their use of online mechanisms to spread their message as well as coordinate and plan their activities.

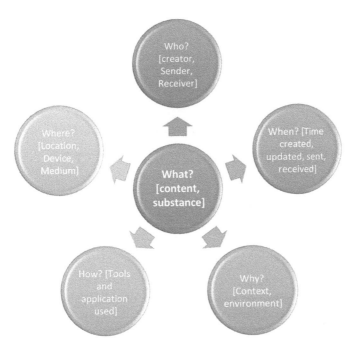

Figure 19.1   The data and meta-data of digital evidence.

In this context, there are three major categories of digital artifacts that can be considered as possible evidence [2, 3]:

- Artifacts captured from the computers and laptops used by the perpetrators
- Artifacts archived by providers of internet services such as email and chat services, social media
- Artifacts extracted from the mobile devices (such as smartphones, tablets) used by the perpetrators

Each of these categories of digital evidence has unique characteristics that dictate the use of specific tools and techniques to capture, extract, and analyze the evidence. Often, specific tools are needed for each category or evidence to protect its integrity so that it can be admissible in a court of law for search warrants and prosecution purposes. These characteristics are captured in the subsections below.

19.4.1 Evidence Gathered from Personal Computers

Digital evidence gathered from personal computers include the following:

- Files of various types (Microsoft Office, Adobe PDF, text, etc.) saved to the local drives (hard drive as well as attached storage such as USB sticks)
- Email messages saved in local email clients (such as Microsoft Outlook)
- Chat messages saved locally
- Web browsing history, website cookies, archived pages, graphics, etc.
- Recently deleted files

The properties of these artifacts (such as date of last use) may change if these items are opened for viewing, since the underlying operating system updates these properties when the item is used. These types of artifacts may be copied to another storage medium or the actual computing device on which the artifact was found may be captured and protected as a part of the investigative process. The goal is to isolate the artifact and (if possible) the computing device so as to preserve as many properties of the artifact as possible from intentional tampering or accidental modification.

19.4.2 Evidence Gathered from Internet-Based Services

Digital evidence gathered from internet services include the following:

- Activity and content posted to social media sites (such as LinkedIn, Facebook, Snapchat, Twitter, etc.)
- Photos posted to photo sites (such as Google Photos, Flickr, etc.)
- Webmail
- Purchases from online stores
- Travel bookings made through online trip planning sites (such as Expedia, Orbitz, etc.)

Some of the content in this category may be available for public access. However, some of this content may only be obtained through legal warrants or subpoenas. For this type of evidence, since the medium (such as social media channels) is controlled by a third party, it is very difficult or impossible to isolate the medium or preserve the evidence on that medium for use in later legal proceedings. For example, social media posts can be deleted or updated or the sender's account may be deleted to prevent tracing back to the perpetrator. Thus, it is critical that the original evidence is captured accurately with respect to both content and context and that the gathered evidence is protected against tampering.

19.4.3 Evidence Gathered from Mobile Devices and Wearables

More and more of our daily activities are recorded by mobile devices (smartphones, tablets, etc.) and wearable devices (fitness trackers, pedometers, etc.). Some examples of digital evidence that fall within this category include:

- Phone call logs
- List of chat messages and messaging partners
- Digital photos and videos
- Purchased or downloaded multimedia content (music, videos, books, etc.)
- Email messages
- Browsing history
- Activity logs for specific applications
- GPS locations from photos
- Activity logs and data collected by wearable devices (heart rate, location, time, etc.)

Whenever possible, the mobile device on which the digital evidence resides should be confiscated for isolation, evidence capture, and analysis. In such cases, it is critically important to shield the confiscated mobile device from access/alteration through the various available connectivity channels (wireless, WiFi, Bluetooth, near field communications). Many mobile devices allow the user to "wipe" the data on the device remotely in case the owner loses control of the device. Thus, this category of digital evidence needs to be protected accordingly to prevent remote cleansing of the content on the device.

In other scenarios, it may be impossible to capture the mobile device or it is deemed more effective to "follow" the use of the mobile device by the perpetrator to gather more evidence in an ongoing investigation. In such cases, investigators may need to obtain access to gather digital evidence through the cooperation of the mobile service provider (e.g. through subpoenas).

19.5 LIFECYCLE OF DIGITAL EVIDENCE

From the time digital evidence is identified to the time to it is actually used, it is critical that the evidence is adequately protected through the entire life cycle. The chain of custody of digital evidence is an essential component of the admissibility of the evidence in a court of law [4].

- *Collection and cataloging*—Digital evidence must be identified and collected in a lawful manner (based on the jurisdiction and applicable laws) to ensure that it will be admissible in a court of law. The time and location of collection of the evidence, a summary of the finding, and the identification of the individual that collected the evidence must be documented or cataloged accurately by qualified digital forensic personnel.
- *Transport and preservation*—Often, the evidence needs to be moved or transported to another location for safekeeping. The details of this move have to be recorded and maintained as a part of the chain of custody. Once the evidence has been moved to the appropriate location for safekeeping, it needs to be preserved in a manner that protects its integrity and makes any tampering evident.
- *Examination and analysis*—The evidence will likely need to be accessed for further study and analysis to connect it with other evidence or to identify gaps that require further investigation. During this phase, it is critical that the evidence is not altered in a manner that will render it unusable in a court of law.
- *Presentation*—This is the final phase of the lifecycle of digital evidence in which it is actually presented in a formal legal setting as evidence to support a legal indictment. At this stage, questions may be raised regarding the authenticity of the digital evidence. All of the actions taken to protect and preserve the evidence along with the meta-data that shows the chain of custody are important at this phase to demonstrate the significance and integrity of the evidence.

19.6 AUTHENTICITY OF DIGITAL EVIDENCE

Digital evidence gathered during surveillance and investigations of possible terrorist groups can be used as a stepping stone to move forward with the investigation or as a piece of evidence that can be used in a court of law to bring charges against specific individuals or groups. As discussed earlier, the various properties of the digital evidence establish the content and context that helps to make the evidence relevant to a particular investigation or legal action. Given the nature of digital artifacts, it is relatively easy to spoof or alter digital evidence by malicious intention or through unintentional actions. It is imperative, therefore, that the authenticity of the digital evidence be established before it is used for legal purposes [1]. Specifically, the following elements are important to provide authenticity of the properties of digital evidence:

- *Quality of collection process*—Whether the content (data) or context (meta-data) for the evidence was collected accurately and comprehensively using appropriate forensic tools and by a qualified investigator. The skill level of the investigator and the tools used for collection of the evidence determine the quality of the evidence and the ability to prove its relevance to a particular investigation.

- *Post-collection integrity*—The evidence, once collected, has to be maintained using well-established processes to ensure that it is not altered or tampered with. The integrity of the data and meta-data has to be established through technical or procedural means for use in a legal setting.

19.7 PROTECTIONS NEEDED FOR DIGITAL EVIDENCE

The combination of content (data) and context (meta-data) for digital evidence needs to be protected and maintained. Depending on the type of digital evidence, it needs to be protected in the following ways:

- *Confidentiality*—The evidence may need to be kept secret from unauthorized eyes. If the evidence is revealed in advance of its formal presentation, it may enable the defending party to take action to negate the validity or impact of the evidence. The release of the evidence or the fact that it even exists may also hamper the course of an ongoing investigation.
- *Integrity*—The data and meta-data associated with the evidence has to be protected from tampering and alteration. The evidence has to be preserved in the state that it was captured from the investigation scene. Otherwise, it may not be admissible from a legal perspective.
- *Availability*—Like all digital data that is critical to a business or a mission, the evidence has to be available to the appropriate parties for examination and analysis and finally for formal presentation for legal purposes. Thus, the evidence has to be protected to ensure its availability at the appropriate times during its lifecycle.

19.8 TECHNIQUES TO PROTECT DIGITAL EVIDENCE

The techniques used to protect digital evidence for confidentiality, integrity, and availability include:

- *Identification and authentication*—Within a legal investigation, only a certain set of individuals are allowed to collect and handle evidence. Digital evidence gathering and handling are no different. All individuals that have the need to handle digital evidence need to be identified and authenticated to establish their identity —this may be done using traditional mechanisms such as photo identity cards or through more technical mechanisms such as two-factor authentication and/or biometric verification, Rigorous authentication procedures provide assurance that an individual is who they claim to be.
- *Access control*—The evidence needs to be maintained in a manner that limits access to personnel with a need-to-know. Once an individual's identity is authenticated, their role or need-to-know for an investigation can be established and access can be granted for suitably authorized individuals. The access control can be implemented through physical means (e.g. locking up in a safe with a physical key) or through an IT-based environment (e.g. saving the evidence in a filesystem on a server with strict access controls and requiring strong authentication for all users).

- *Audit logs*—The evidence is maintained in a manner that requires a log of every access to it. This may be achieved through a physical process of "checking out" the evidence for examination and analysis and "checking in" upon completion. In such a scenario, it is necessary to maintain a written log of the time of check-out/check-in and the identity of the individual who is accessing the evidence. If the digital evidence is accessed through an online mechanism, the audit log may be implemented as an audit trail of the access to the evidence (who, when, type of access) with the assumption that every user of the system is appropriately authenticated and access to the evidence on the server is controlled by a policy based on "need to know."
- *Checksums*—The integrity of digital evidence can also be protected through the use of tamper-evidence technologies such as checksums. A checksum is a concise digital "fingerprint" of a larger set of data and saved with the original data. The significant property of a checksum is that if the original data is modified in any manner, the new checksum will be very different from the original checksum. The checksum can be rapidly recomputed at any time to compare with the original checksum—if they are different, the implication is that the data was altered in some manner.
- *Digital signature*—A digital signature is a cryptographically protected "fingerprint" of a larger set of data such that only the individual holding the private-key (of a cryptographic key pair) can generate the digital signature, but anyone having access to the corresponding public key can verify that the digital signature and validate whether the larger set of data has been altered since the generation of the digital signature. In effect, the digital signature is similar to an ink signature on a paper document in that the signature is very difficult to forge and changes to the signed document can be easily detected. Applying a digital signature across the content (data) and context (meta-data) of the evidence effectively seals the evidence and makes it tamper-evident. If tampering of digital evidence is a high concern, all of the data and meta-data for the digital evidence should be gathered and a digital signature applied across the entirety by an individual or system that is authorized to do so.
- *Duplication*—Digital items are easy to copy. Thus, a simple technique to protect the integrity of digital evidence is to make multiple copies and save them to media that will not be touched until presentation. All examination and analysis activities on that digital evidence is done on another copy—the pristine copy is maintained separately and rigorously access controlled to maintain a strict chain of custody until the time of presentation of the evidence for legal purposes.

19.9 SUMMARY

Digital evidence is a very strong component of any modern investigation since so much of our day-to-day actions and communications leave a "cookie-crumb" trail in digital systems and networks that are either difficult or impossible to completely erase. This is especially true for terrorism-related activities such as spreading propaganda, and recruitment of new believers through outreach and radicalization. This is because digital communication channels (such as social media, email, and chat rooms) enable participants to rapidly interact with a large number of cohorts from the comfort of their own homes and with relative anonymity. Unlike other types of criminal activities that are performed purely for personal or organizational economic gain, there is a high degree of passion and a belief in a higher purpose that drives many terrorism-related

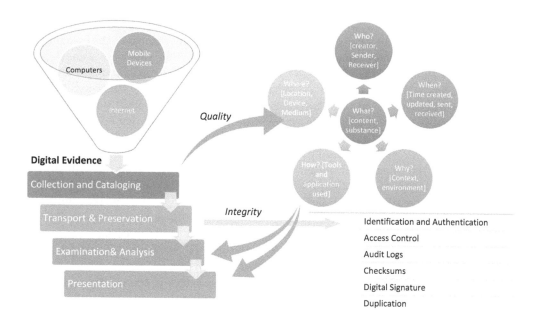

Figure 19.2   Supporting authentication through life cycle of digital evidence.

activities. As such, the perpetrators and recruits are frequently not as diligent about covering their trails. As a result, law enforcement and anti-terrorism organizations use digital evidence as a major component of their investigations.

Given the importance of digital evidence in a terrorism-related investigation and possible legal action, it is very important to ensure that the digital evidence is collected and its chain of custody maintained in a manner that allows its accuracy and authenticity to be established in a court of law, see Figure 19.2. To do this, there is a broad range of traditional procedural techniques as well as more technologically advanced techniques that can be used to ensure that digital evidence has not been cooked or tampered with. The ability to use the various techniques depend in large part on the physical circumstances of the investigation, the availability of technical tools, and the technological savvy of the investigators and analysts involved.

We recommend that anti-terrorism and law enforcement organizations perform a risk assessment of their evidence gathering and management processes to determine where the highest risks to alteration and tampering lay. Then, mitigation techniques that are feasible and cost effective need to be identified and put in place. The goal is to minimize the risk of being unable to assure the accuracy and integrity of digital evidence needed for a terrorism-related legal action or conviction.

REFERENCES

1. Grimm, Hon. Paul W., Paul, W., Joseph, Gregory P. and Capra, Daniel J., *Best Practices for Authenticating Digital Evidence*, West Academic Publishing, 2016.
2. National Forensic Science Technology Center (NFSTC), *A Simplified Guide to Digital Evidence.* http://www.forensicsciencesimplified.org/digital/DigitalEvidence.pdf

3. Gubanov, Yuri, *Retrieving Digital Evidence: Methods, Techniques, and Issues*, Article posted to www.forensicmag.com, https://www.forensicmag.com/article/2012/05/retrieving-digital-evidence-methods-techniques-and-issues-part-1, May 2012.
4. Cosic, Jasmin and Cosic, Zoran, Chain of Custody and Life Cycle of Digital Evidence, *Computer Technology and Application* 3: 126–129, February 2012.

ISIS and the Dark Web

How IS Virtual Planners Use the Dark Web to Recruit, Direct, and Inspire Attacks in Europe and North America

Anthony Celso

CONTENTS

20.1 INTRODUCTION

Starting in 2014 the Islamic State's (IS) global terror campaign has been impressive in its geographic scope and operational complexity. The movement's agents and supporters have attacked every continent. The Islamic State comprises an international network with hundreds of thousands of supporters. The organization has claimed responsibility for attacks in Paris, Barcelona, Brussels, Berlin, London, Istanbul, Copenhagen, Stockholm, Tehran, Jakarta, Nice, Orlando, San Bernardino, Saint Petersburg, Moscow, and Kabul.[1] This is but a small sample of attacks it has directed or inspired. Thousands have been killed and wounded.

The territorial expanse of IS's terror campaign is a consequence of its pursuit of a total war doctrine targeting near (local), far (foreign), and sectarian (Shia-Alawi) enemies. The Islamic State's total war strategy is historically and religiously grounded. Mary Habeck argues that contemporary jihadists mimic the fighting techniques of the Prophet Mohammad and his companions who battled local rulers, deviant sects, and external powers.[2] Late IS spokesman Abu Muhammad al-Adnani once defiantly proclaimed that the caliphate was at war with the world.[3]

Though past jihadist networks have targeted these enemies, they did so selectively concentrating on their weakest adversary. The Islamic State is, however, unique in attacking all three enemies simultaneously. Strategic opportunity, political conditions, and enhanced capability have coalesced allowing the network the capacity to target multiple adversaries. Not since the late nineteenth century has a jihadi movement had the military force to alter colonial borders and wage wars against local and Western powers.[4]

The targeting of local, external, and sectarian enemies is also a consequence of the jihadist movement's radicalization where the distinction between the far and near enemy has collapsed. Despite its ideological and strategic opposition to the Islamic State, Al Qaeda has moved to a total war doctrine. Ayman al-Zawahiri's 2017 address speaks to a conspiracy against the Muslim world comprised of Zionist, crusader, Rafidah (Shia), and Hindu conspiracies.[5]

Zawahiri's proclamation reflects the conspiratorial mindset popular among jihadists who easily interpret their reverses and defeats to nefarious forces. Though analysts claim that Al Qaeda and the Islamic State are radically distinct, Zawahiri's recent declarations mesh well with IS external operations doctrine. In fact Al Qaeda now emulates the caliphate's anti-Shia policy and ideology.

Though most of the deaths associated with IS external operations have occurred in the Middle East and North Africa, IS has focused on attacking Europe and North America. Targeting France, Belgium, Germany, and the United Kingdom has dominated the network's far enemy strategy. It has proved to be particularly lethal. A June 2017 Wilson Center's study documents over 50 attacks against Western countries that have killed 395 people and wounded over 1,500 persons. Since 2015 more than 230 French nationals have been killed in the extremist movement's directed and inspired operations.

IS's terror campaign has been facilitated by complex attack methods that are difficult to disrupt. With hundreds of thousands of jihadi sympathizers and a foreign fighter force of over 7,000 individuals, the Islamic State's European network presents a daunting security challenge that has overwhelmed the continent's security agencies. Permeable European borders and the complex task of coordinating intelligence gathering among security agencies stratified along national and linguistic lines have proven vexing.

Spanish and Catalan security agencies, for example, failed to prevent IS sympathizers from launching attacks in Barcelona and Cambrils in August 2017 that killed 16 people and wounded over 150 people. Warned by the US Central Intelligence Agency (CIA) that Barcelona's Las Ramblas boulevard was a IS target and advised by Madrid to erect vehicle barriers to protect the famous boulevard, Catalan officials dismissed the advice.[6] They also ignored Belgian inquiries on the jihadist activities of Moroccan-born preacher Abdelbaki Es-Sati who played a pivotal role in the radicalization of a ten-person cell that pulled off the double attack.

Intelligence agencies have struggled to counter the terror network's varied and unpredictable attacks. The movement's directed, virtually guided, and inspired terror assaults have employed vehicles, bombs, firearms, knives, and hatchets. Most attacks have killed less than ten people, but a few have proTduced mass casualties. Vans and trucks can be devastating weapons. Over a dozen people were killed in vehicular attacks in Berlin and Barcelona, and one IS-linked lorry driver killed 86 people in Nice during the 2016 Bastille Day celebrations.

Having averted over a dozen Islamic State-linked plots, British security agencies failed to prevent four-UK based attacks in 2017. The most deadly assault was committed by Salman Abedi who ignited his explosive vest killing 23 people in Manchester at a May 2017 music concert. The Islamic State's directed operations are especially lethal. The caliphate's trained fighters killed 130 people in Paris in November 2015, and its "soldiers" executed 32 people in March 2016 at

Brussels airport and metro facilities. With over 2,000 French and Belgian fighters serving in IS's network, these countries have struggled to counter the pace of the movement's assaults.[7]

North America has also experienced IS-inspired attacks. Armed with assault weapons. a husband and wife team in December 2015 killed 14 people at a San Bernardino community Christmas party. Six months later IS-linked jihadi Omar Mateen killed 49 people at a nightclub catering to gay clientele in Orlando, Florida. During these attacks the perpetrators pledged solidarity to the caliphate's network.

The caliphate's Amaq News Agency celebrated Marteen as one of its "soldiers." The Islamic State's use of encrypted technologies has served as a critical vehicle to direct, virtually guide and inspire attacks. Despite the destruction of the Islamic State's proto-jihadi state, terrorism in Europe has not abated. Even with the loss of Mosul and the destruction of its Syrian capital Raqqa, IS has been able to launch attacks worldwide killing thousands.

The Islamic State's social media has recruited thousands of operatives and guided attacks against Western interests. The caliphate generated mass support through slickly produced videos, reports, and documentaries shared across multiple social media forums. IS communication operations mimic American entertainment and advertising styles and are recognized for their high production values.[8] The Islamic State's media organs celebrate beheadings, amputations, immolations, and stoning. Their videos, reports, and documentaries promote the caliphate's military advances, publicize its attacks, and present positive images of its Sharia governance. With predominately young male supporters, IS communication strategy panders to its audience's ultra-violent impulses.

The caliphate's hip hop videos featuring rap singers promoting its extremist Salafi-jihadist ideology recruit many supporters. Some 35,000 foreign fighters from over 90 countries traveled to Syria's killing fields. Tens of thousands of these extremists have served as the caliphate's foot soldiers and suicide bombers.

The jihadi movement has created a vast propaganda machine expressed in multi-lingual forums easily downloadable to iPhones and iPads. It's al-Hayat and Al Furqan enterprises direct much of the caliphate's video and magazine production disseminated in English, French, Arabic, Russian, and Turkish.[9] The caliphate's Amaq News Agency celebrates its attacks gleefully, venerating their carnage.

The Islamic State's effective use of global social media is unequaled by any jihadi organization. Magnifying the impact of the caliphate's propaganda are the Arab world's political upheavals and the sectarian tensions generated by the Syrian civil war. The Islamic State's portrait of an insidious Shia-Zionist crusader alliance victimizing Sunnis resonates strongly with young jihadists.

The caliphate apocalyptic ruminations that division in the Arab world represents *fitna* presaging an end-times confrontation between Muslims warriors and Roman crusaders at the Syrian town of Dabiq motivated thousands of extremists to make *hijrah* [emigrate] to IS territories. The movement's fusion of takfirist, sectarian, and apocalyptic sentiments capitalized on the political crises of the Post-Arab Spring in the Middle East and exploited Sunni angst over the rising influence of the Shia in Iran. Al Qaeda has struggled to counter the Islamic State's hold over the global jihadist movement.

The emergence of the Islamic State movement after the United States' disengagement from Iraq in 2011 caught many by surprise. Former U.S. President Barak Obama embarrassingly labelled the organization as the "JV" but later reversed his early assessment to launch a major military campaign against the caliphate. Web companies similarly were overwhelmed by IS's extensive media campaign and were slow to close down the network's social media sites that once closed down reappeared under differently named accounts.

J.M. Berger in 2014 documented some 46,000 IS English-language Twitter accounts averaging about 1,000 followers. Though Twitter was able to suspend tens of thousands of these accounts, it failed to adequately address the problem of IS-generated propaganda. Most of these suspended accounts reappeared under different names and hashtags or moved to the Dark Web.

Grisly IS beheading videos forced internet companies to seriously attack the caliphate-linked accounts across the conventional web. Facebook, YouTube, and Twitter closed IS accounts that then invited the caliphate's transition to Telegram, Sure Spot, and WhatsApp—all media forms using encrypted "dark" social messaging.[10]

The Islamic State's transition to Telegram, moreover, was driven by strategic interests. The communication service affords its users optional encryption guaranteeing the anonymity of participants. Telegram shields (makes dark) the transmission of participants' messages by using a router that randomly channels activity through multiple outlets making it impossible for outside parties to connect specific end-to-end communications. The social media network also allows for files to be uploaded across smartphones, iPads, and computers. Users, furthermore, can elect to use more rigorous encryption where messages are timed to self-destruct. Telegram has unwittingly assisted the caliphate's capacity to direct, virtually guide, and inspire attacks against its enemies worldwide.

The media forum creates an anonymous dark network. Telegram's website promises that its participants can coordinate groups of up to 10,000 members securing communication with diverse channel transmissions that allows users to choose a specific pathway to connect with IS supporters.[11] The movement uses video and audio content on Telegram to encourage Western militants to attack their homelands. Europe's extremist subculture, jihadi preachers, and deeply rooted Islamist civil society are a fertile recruitment and indoctrination canvass for the caliphate. Telegram messaging has been linked to the deadly November 2015 Paris attacks and many subsequent attacks. Amaq News Agency claims responsibility for and venerates these attacks largely through Telegram channels.

Faced with the liquidation of its physical caliphate, the Islamic State's use of the Dark Web guarantees it can continue to wage war against its enemies. This chapter examines the movement's Dark Web use for recruitment purposes and for directing and inspiring attacks. It is composed of three parts. First, it discusses the role that the late IS spokesman Abu Mohammad al-Adnani played in crafting its terror-media strategy. Second, it examines the caliphate's use of encrypted technology to direct, virtually guide, and inspire attacks. Third, it assesses Western efforts to disrupt, degrade, and destroy the jihadist movement's virtual network including countering violent extremism (CVE) approaches.

While important, the collapse of IS's jihadist state does not portend an end to the organization as a terror-insurgent network. Though IS's terror campaign may have peaked with its November 2015 Paris attack, its external operations are likely to persist through virtually directed, inspired, and lone wolf assaults. By liquidating the Islamic State's Iraqi-Syrian proto-jihadi state, the West has significantly degraded the caliphate terror training camps and its directed operations. It has not, however, ended the IS virtual caliphate that will continue to guide and inspire future terrorism.

20.2 IS'S PROPAGANDA AND MEDIA APPARATUS

The Islamic State's sophisticated propaganda operations can be traced back to its progenitor, Al Qaeda in Iraq (AQI). The caliphate memorializes AQI's founder Abu Musab al-Zarqawi in IS's

English-language magazines *Dabiq* and *Rumiyah*. Although killed in a U.S. airstrike in 2006, Zarqawi's legacy continues. *Dabiq* began all of its issues with Zarqawi's citation of a prophetic hadith that Muslim armies would vanquish Roman crusaders in the plains of the small Syrian town of Dabiq.[12] The magazine's successor *Rumiyah* [Rome] continues this eschatological tradition by "predicting" the fall of *la citta eterna* to Muslim armies.

Dabiq and *Rumiyah* echo Zarqawi's evocation of a diabolical Zionist-crusader-Rafidah complex committed to the destruction of Sunni Islam that he argued must be confronted and vanquished. These magazines compare Zarqawi's jihadist exploits to the Prophet Mohammad establishing a divine lineage that presages prophetic victory and Islamic global conquest. Zarqawi's participation in AQI's beheading videos and the controversy they generated left an indelible mark on the caliphate's propaganda. His ritualistic beheading of American care worker Nicolas Berg has its Islamic State successor in British citizen Jihadi John's (Muhammad Emwazi) videotaped decapitation of foreign captives James Foley, Steven Sotloff, David Haines, Peter Kassig, Haruna Yukaqwa, and Kenji Goto.

Though Zarqawi used social media like YouTube and Facebook, it was early days in the growth of those platforms. Subsequent technological advances in iPhones and iPads made the web more accessible and have afforded jihadi organizations' robust capabilities to communicate their messages. This started when Al Qaeda in the Arabian Peninsula (AQAP) began to capitalize on the communications revolution.

The late American-born, Al Qaeda in the Arabian Peninsula (AQAP) ideologue, Anwar al-Awlaki communicated with audiences in diverse multilingual forums. Awlaki's 2010 English-language e-magazine *Inspire*, exhorted Western Muslims to attack their native lands. Not surprisingly the Islamic State features Awlaki's sermons and mimics his message.

This is despite the Islamic State's predecessor's (Al Qaeda in Iraq (AQI)) troubled relationship with bin Laden's organization. Al Qaeda and the Islamic State of Iraq (ISI) quarreled on a host of ideological and strategic issues. Al Qaeda expelled ISI from its network in February 2014 for refusing to disband its Syrian operations. After ISI's expulsion, the two organizations have competed to lead the global jihadist movement. Spearheaded by Syrian Abu Muhammad al-Adnani, IS communication strategy has been unsparing in its critique of Al Qaeda.

20.3 ABU MUHAMMAD AL-ADNANI

Born in Syria, Adnani became a religion student known for his theological zealotry. Adnani joined Al Qaeda in Iraq (AQI) after the U.S. invasion. He rose through AQI's ranks becoming its second-in-command. Adnani played a pivotal role in IS's external operations against Western countries. His hyperbolic language and strategic planning orchestrated the most successful jihadist campaign against the West since the 9/11 attacks. Adnani's many audio addresses provide the reader with the caliphate's strategic design that embraces a total war doctrine against its apostate, foreign, and sectarian adversaries.[13] Significantly no other IS ideologue has matched his oratorical gifts to inspire the caliphate's partisans into action.

Adnani presents IS's supporters with a didactic universe where oppressed Sunnis confront diabolical enemies who have conspired to destroy its authentic Islamic state. He portrays the Islamic State's faithful as Allah's combatant vanguard whose religious duty is to eradicate apostasy from the Muslim world and lead the caliphate to victory against all non-Muslim civilizations.

Overseeing external terror and propaganda operations Adnani merged IS's communications with its war strategy. He supervised the production values and content for IS's execution videos of enemy soldiers, homosexuals, Western hostages, sorcerers, adulterers, and Christians. The beheadings and immolations in the videos were graphically shown and designed to make enemies fearful and to recruit young jihadists.

European rap artists using hip hop style music attracted thousands of Western fighters. Profiling 30,000 foreign fighters in Syria, Richard Barrett documents that most are young males in their teens and twenties. This age cohort forms the bulk of the Islamic State's soldiers.[14] Among the 7,000 European fighters French, Belgian, and British nationals are prominently displayed in IS's videos. British executioner Mohammad Emwazi (Jihadi John) and Abdelhamid Abaaoud the organizer of the November 2015 Paris attacks are prominently featured in IS videos. [15]

Adnani predicts that the caliphate is divinely ordained to triumph. Referencing Islamic eschatology he urges European and North American Muslims to assault Westerners. Adnani's exaltation of hyper-violence is driven by what he sees as a duty for Western Muslims to either migrate to the caliphate or kill infidels in their native lands.

Typical of his incendiary style is the following passage:

> If you kill a disbelieving American or European-especially the spiteful and filthy French-or an Australian, or a Canadian, or any other disbelievers from the disbelievers waging war, including the citizens of the countries they entered into a coalition against the Islamic State, then rely on Allah, and kill him in any manner or way however it may be. Smash his head with a rock, or slaughter him with a knife, or run over him with your car.[16]

Adnani's voice was a rallying cry for Western Muslims to lash out against their native lands. The Islamic State's hatred of the West is driven by ideological and situational factors. First, the caliphate's apocalyptic ideology mandates confrontation with a demonic West. Second, it needs to retaliate against the Western military campaign against the caliphate to reassure its supporters. Third, its appeals to European and North American Muslims that religious imperatives demand they side with the caliphate by killing Westerners in their own lands. Fourth, its targeting of European populations is designed to drive fissures in the international coalition to weaken Western resolve to maintain military action. Fifth, the Islamic State's ideology ties the Western military campaign to Iranian Shia interests effectively fusing the far and sectarian enemies.

Since Adnani's call over 50 plots and attacks were committed in the West by Islamic State sympathizers. Heeding his entreaties, IS sympathizers have stabbed, bombed, axed, shot, and beheaded Westerners. Significantly the vast majority of those killed or wounded have been civilians. Trains, parade grounds, concerts, restaurants, shops, and night clubs have been attacked. Many of the terrorists swore fidelity to IS before they committed their atrocities.

The Islamic State's plea for violent action against the West has had a powerful effect on radicalizing young Muslims. A 2017 study reports 34 plots in seven Western countries involved teenagers and pre-teens who executed or contemplated knife or explosives attacks. Some 50 percent of these young people had contact with IS operatives across social media forums. One plot involved a twelve-year-old boy who failed to ignite an explosive device at a Christmas market in Germany. Had it not been for a badly designed improvised bomb, the casualties could of have been considerable.

The destructive legacy of Adnani's incendiary discourse cannot be overstated. His significance, moreover, is amplified by his development in the organization's terror campaign. Adnani's role in forming its external operations branch to wage terror overseas is widely recognized. Based on testimony by a German IS defector, we know that Adnani screened European candidates trained in the caliphate's camps.[17] French and Belgian fighters were especially enthusiastic about committing attacks against their home countries.

The organization of IS terror campaigns, however, was performed by IS's Amniyat internal security branch. Daveed Gartenstein-Ross argues that Amn al-Kharaj organized the caliphate's external operations.[18] The Amniyat has a chain of command. Overall regional operations are overseen by militants born or familiar with the counties that are planning to attack.

Though centralized, IS's bureaucracy is sufficiently nimble giving freedom to its regional planners. The caliphate's European theatre of operations is dominated by French-born or French-speaking militants with Abu Sulayman al-Faransi and Salim Benghalem selecting, training, and dispatching attack teams.

The movement began developing its European terror architecture before its caliphate proclamation. Abaaoud's contact with Mehdi Nemmouche, who guarded Western prisoners in Syria, was influential in guiding the caliphate's first attack on European soil. Notorious for his sadistic temperament, Nemmouche like many IS Belgian fighters, spent time in the Brussels district of Molenbeek where the Zerkani network is active in promoting jihadi causes. After a trip to Southeast Asia, Nemmouche returned to Belgium and killed four people at Brussels' Jewish Museum. He was later apprehended by French police after he crossed the Belgian border in a passenger train. Nemmouche had hoped to launch another attack.

The French and Belgian direction of IS's terror campaign is unsurprising as jihadi activism is deeply rooted. The current wave of Islamist terrorism in France has its origins in Paris' Nineteenth District Network.[19] That group's organizer, Boukaker al-Hakim, sent dozens of fighters to Iraq to terrorize American forces after their overthrow of Saddam Hussein's regime. The networks militants Mohammad al-Ayouni and Salim Benghalem have directed IS operations against Francophone countries.

With over a thousand French fighters serving in the ranks of extremist organizations, the nation is a favored target of IS's jihadi rage. Belgium is not far behind. Brussels' fight against the movement's network has been hindered by police and security services that are fractured administratively and linguistically. Historically France and Belgium have large Moroccan diaspora subpopulations tied to the Moroccan Islamic Combat Group (MICG) and the Algerian Armed Islamic Group (GIA).

Driven by the need for cheap North African labor, Francophone countries inadvertently developed hostile Islamist civil societies. Since the 1970s extremist organizations have embedded in mosques and community and charitable organizations, recruiting and indoctrinating new migrants and their progeny.

European Islamist civil society has nurtured jihadi recruits committed to the radicalization of impressionable crisis-ridden young men. Many of these jihadi recruits have a history of substance abuse and criminality. They see radical Islam as a pathway to personal redemption.

Since the 1980s extremist preachers have wielded influence in the European continent's often unregulated mosques. Pioneered by charismatic preachers like Britain's Anjem Choudary, France's Fabien Cain, and Germany's Abu Wala, jihadi ideologues have groomed hundreds of European jihadists. Choudary's significance is especially profound for Sharia4Belgium is an offshoot of his organizational blueprint to spread jihadi activism across Europe.[20] Belgium is now in the forefront of IS's European jihad.

The country has the highest per capita number of foreign fighters traveling to Syria of any Western European country. Most of the 451 Belgian fighters are second and third generation immigrants raised in isolated, impoverished neighborhoods.[21] Alienated by Western culture and embittered by their criminal past, these young people are looking for redemption. Subsections of Belgium's immigrant population have proven vulnerable to jihadist radicalization.

Researchers attribute the country's foreign fighter flow to Syria to three networks. Shariah4Belgium, Resto Tawid, and the Zerkani Network have recruited over 170 Belgian fighters some of whom have served in IS's external operations branch.[22] They include Abdelhamid Abaaoud who oversaw the Paris 13 November 2015 attacks.

Based in Molenbeek, Moroccan preacher Khalid Zerkani's network is committed to the promotion of jihadi causes.[23] Unemployment and criminal activity in this immigrant-dominated suburb have catalyzed extremist indoctrination of religiously illiterate young men. With illicit funding the network sent fighters to Syria. Zerkani's organization has been implicated in the November 2015 Paris terrorist attacks. Not surprisingly the Zerkani Network has been the focus of many anti-terror operations and prosecutions.

Seven of the nine attackers that hit Paris on 13 November 2015 were French and Belgian. Faransi and Benghalem worked with French convert Fabien Clain and Belgian team organizer Abdelhamid Abaaoud in selecting fighters.[24] Though some plots were disrupted, others succeeded spectacularly. The training these teams received increased the lethality of IS's terror campaign with the Paris 2015 and 2016 Brussels attacks killing 160 people.

The Brussels Jewish Museum attack began IS's terror campaign in Europe. By January 2015 the caliphate began to move beyond lone gunmen. During this period Belgian police intercepted phone calls between the Islamic State cell in Verviers and Abaaoud in Greece. Fearing an impending attack, Belgian security services stormed the cell's apartment killing two members of the network. Many of Verviers's cell were trained by the Islamic State in Syrian terror camps.

After their operation, investigators discovered firearms, police uniforms, and explosives. Based on the evidence, law enforcement officials speculate that the 11-man cell may have planned an assault on police stations. Disrupting the Verviers network had profound ramifications. Abaaoud hoped to remotely direct the Verviers cell from Athens. Having had his plans disrupted, he traveled to Belgium and directly participated in IS's terror campaign.[25] Fearing further police disruption, Abbaaoud chose encrypted social media channels like Telegram and WhatsApp to communicate with cell members. He unleashed the caliphate's most deadly operations.

20.4 IS'S ATTACK STRATEGY AND ENCRYPTED TECHNOLOGY

The caliphate used Telegram because the network allows its participants to shield communications. Telegram features chat rooms and groups that can reach a maximum size of 10,000 where propaganda material can be shared secretly. Though the social media forum has sought to close down many accounts, hundreds of IS-linked channels persist and reappear under different names. Its communication forum has become IS go-to source to publicize its operations and clandestinely plan its multi-faceted terror campaign

Telegram permits two layers of dark encryption. First, it allows end-to-end encryption in private chat rooms where messages can be timed to self-destruct. Second, communications run through multiple servers that shield participant conversations, making it inordinately difficult to trace messages. This dual layer of protection impairs intelligence gathering, assisting terrorism networks' planning and execution of terror attacks.

WhatsApp has comparable features. Prior to his deadly Westminster Bridge and Buckingham Palace attacks killing five persons, Khalid Masood used the social media service to communicate an encrypted message. The case prompted Prime Minister Theresa May to demand that internet companies develop backup features permitting security services access to their conversations. Since their business is predicated upon their ability to keep conversations secure, these companies have strenuously resisted such demands. They have, however, attempted to close down the most extreme accounts.

Having the Verviers plot disrupted, the Islamic State's European network chose encrypted communications services. They have proved a valuable source of recruitment and execution of a multi-dimensional terror campaign.

20.5 CONCEPTUALIZING IS OPERATIONS

The Islamic State's European attack network presents daunting challenges to security agencies. Though these assault types overlap the caliphate's operations and have been linked to directed, virtual, inspired, and lone wolf attacks. Each attack method has certain advantages.[26]

Table 20.1 provides some examples of IS terror campaign. The attack typology is discussed sequentially beginning with directed operations and ending with IS-affiliated lone wolf terrorism.

20.6 DIRECTED ATTACKS BY TRAINED IS OPERATIVES

This attack type allows IS maximum control. The caliphate trains, finances, and dispatches attack teams and guides their targeting. The Paris and Brussels attacks are exemplars of IS directed operations. The terrorists involved were trained in Syria and were dispatched to sow chaos in Europe with some transiting through Balkan refugee migrant routes with forged passports. The Islamic State's external security branch, moreover, accorded its theatre commander Abdelhamid Abaaoud freedom to develop its European operations.[27]

Recruited by the Zerkani network, Abaaoud traveled to Syria in 2014 and eventually joined IS's contingent of Belgian and French fighters. He was selected by Amniyat's core trainer, Belgian "Abu Ahmad" (birth name Osama Atar), to be IS point man for its European operation.[28]

TABLE 20.1   TYPE OF ISLAMIC STATE ATTACK AND EXAMPLES

Attack Type	Attack Type	Attack Type	Attack Type
Directed attacks by IS agents trained and dispatched from Syria	Virtually guided attacks by IS operatives who guide the caliphate's supporters through social media channels	Ideologically inspired attacks by IS supporters	Lone wolf attacks by Islamic extremists with multiple jihadist sympathies
Examples	**Examples**	**Examples**	**Examples**
May 2014 Jewish Museum attack in Brussels Aborted August 2015 Thalys train attack November 2015 Paris attacks March 2016 Brussels attacks	Aborted May 2015 Garland, Texas attack July 2016 Wurzburg Germany train attack July 2016 Ansbach Germany concert attacks	July 2016 Nice Bastille Day attack December 2016 Berlin Christmas market attack August 2017 Barcelona and Cambrils attacks March, May, and June 2017 London and Manchester attacks	December 2015 San Bernardino attack June 2016 Orlando Pulse Nightclub attack

Abaaound is connected to virtually every plot and attack that occurs in Europe from the May 2014 Jewish Museum attack to the March 2016 Brussels bombings. His associates include Mehdi Nemmouche (the Jewish Museum attack), Ayoub el Khazzani (the aborted Thalys train attack), the Verviers attack cell, Reda Hame (apprehended by French police in August 2015 before he could commit a terror attack), Sid Ahmed Ghlam, (arrested by French police in April 2015 for planning to carry out an act of terrorism), and Salah Abdelslam (connected to the Paris and Brussels attack cells).[29]

Planning for the 13 November 2015 attacks was done in Belgium from multiple locations.[30] Salah Abdelsalen played a crucial logistical role. It was Abdelsalem that picked up members of the assault teams who arrived in Europe as fake Syrian refugees. Most entered Europe via Greece and Tukey with Abdelsalem meeting assault team members in Hungary and Austria and transporting them to Belgium. He also rented flats for the team in Paris and Belgium and the cars that got most of the terrorists from Brussels to Paris. Though he did not participate in either the Paris or Brussels attacks, Abdelsalem is indelibly linked to both events.

His role in establishing the logistical infrastructure for the 13 November assault is not surprising. Abdelsalem was a boyhood friend of Abaaoud and perhaps his most trusted confidant. By August 2015. the assault team was firmly established in Europe and the existence of safe houses rented under multiple identities insured that the network would not be vulnerable to police interception. Learning from the Verviers debacle, communication between cell members relied on encrypted technology.

Brussels attacker Najim Laachraoui assisted the fabrication of TATP (triacetone triperoxide) laden suicide belts. By early November team members had moved to Paris flats, and the decision to mount a devastating attack was a certainty.[31] While Abaaoud oversaw the teams, he was acting under the authority of Belgian Abu Ahmad who supervised the operation from Syria. Three teams of operators were formed, each with a specific target. Abaaoud witnessed the carnage outside of the Bataclan Concert Hall and can be seen at the Paris Metro on CCTV footage during and after the attack.

The most lethal attack was at the Bataclan where the American band Eagles of Death Metal was playing. Having killed a security guard, three terrorists entered the hall and began firing their automatic weapons into the crowd. When the police arrived they took hostages whom they killed when exploding their suicide vests. Some 80 concert goers were killed and hundreds more were wounded. The Stade de France attack could have been the most mortifying of the attacks with devastating political consequences. The stadium was packed with thousands of spectators with President Francois Holland watching a soccer match. Fortunately, security was vigilant and their body search requirement dissuaded the three IS militants from entering the stadium.

Prevented from attacking inside the premises, team members were perplexed and frantically telephoned their supervisors. Abaaoud and Ahmad were contacted by the frustrated team and finally they decided to exploded their suicide vests killing only one passerby.[32] A third team of two assassins moved across central Paris attacking bars and restaurants killing some 50 people before immolating themselves.

Abaaoud wanted to follow up the 13 November attacks with an assault on the Parisian commercial district La Defense. He would die alongside two other people including his cousin in a police shootout when their Saint-Denis hideout was discovered. Abaaoud's female cousin had spoken to a friend about the attacks, and she informed police. Following Abaaoud's cousin, investigators were able to discover Abaaoud's whereabouts. Resisting a commando raid, the three suspects were killed during a four-hour shootout.

Though we cannot be absolutely certain, investigators suspect that Salah Abdelsalem was to join his brother Brahim on the mobile unit targeting restaurants but lost his nerve. Having ditched his suicide explosive vest he telephoned two Brussels friends who picked him up, ironically driving past a number of police checkpoints. He moved to multiple locations including a Moleenbek safe house. Amazingly he was fugitive for four months. His arrest in mid-March 2016 may have hastened the Brussels attacks.

Criticized by French law enforcement officials for failing to disrupt the 13 November network, Belgian security and police were frantic to abort future attacks. Working to unearth the remaining parts of the Paris attack network, they discovered safe houses and arms caches. Closing in on Abdelsalem police were involved in a firefight with IS terrorists guarding a safe house, and they killed one extremist. Information obtained at the safe house allowed police to capture and arrest Abdelsalem. Given his knowledge of their network, the IS cell knew that immediate action was necessary.

Like the Paris attackers, those who assaulted the Zeventum airport and Molenbeek metro on 22 March 2016 were trained IS fighters. The role Ibrahim and Khalid Barkaoui played in the Brussels attacks is celebrated in IS publications.[33] The Barkaoui brothers, Najim Laachaouri and Mohammad Abrini, carried out near simultaneous attacks.

Transporting suitcase bombs and automatic weapons by taxi to the airport, Ibrahim Barkaoui, Najim Laachroui, and Mohammad Abrini hoped for a catastrophic attack. Had not one of the bombs not malfunctioned they may have realized their goal. When two of the bombs exploded, over a dozen people were killed and hundreds were wounded. Having failed to ignite the bomb, Abrini fled the attack site and was later arrested.

The attack on the subway was even more lethal. Khalid Barkaoui exploded his suicide vest onboard a subway car killing some 18 people. By the end of the day, 32 people were killed in Belgium's worst terrorist attack.

The Paris and Brussels attacks may be the pinnacle of IS's campaign using trained fighters. Since the 22 March 2016 attack, we have not seen one assault featuring a foreign fighter sent to Europe by the Amniyat. French police in March 2016 arrested IS foot soldier Reda Kriket after discovering arms and explosives in his flat. Whether IS's remaining network has been destroyed or is intentionally dormant is difficult to assess. What we can say with some confidence is that IS's use of virtual guidance to attack Western homelands has not been idle.

20.7 DIRECTED VIRTUAL ATTACKS BY IS SYMPATHIZERS

This method of remote control terrorism is testimony to IS's innovative external operations. Virtual direction uses social media channels to recruit, radicalize, and guide supporters to launch attacks. This can involve months of communications designed to bolster the potential assassin's determination. Targets can be discussed and methods of execution assessed between virtual planners and sympathizers. Virtual recruits can reference IS manuals on how to construct explosive devices or what weapons to use in an attack. The first issue of *Rumiyah* gives tactical advice on knife attacks.[34]

Encrypted technology guarantees secure private communication between virtual planners and sympathizers. It provides an ideal means to evade security services surveillance for it uses end-to-end encryption for messages. Within Europe IS can provide tactical assistance such as the provision of funds and arms to sympathizers under virtual direction.

IS's network of virtual planners is divided into regional theaters. The caliphate's virtual planning operations in Europe have been dominated by Frenchman Rachid Kassim.[35] From his Syrian redoubt, Kassim was linked to plots and attacks across France and Germany often involving alienated young people and psychologically troubled immigrants. He was connected to two July 2016 attacks in Germany: one by an ax-wielding Afghan immigrant who wounded four South Korean tourists on a passenger train, and the other by a Syrian refugee who wounded 15 people when he exploded a suicide vest outside of an Ansbach music concert. Prior to their violent acts the perpetrators posted loyalty pledges across the Islamic State's Amaq News Agency.

Before his death in a US airstrike, Kassim was virtually directing attacks by French militants. France's large extremist community is receptive to violent agitation. Young people in their teens and twenties have been targeted. Kassim communicated with one sympathizer who beheaded a police captain and his companion in their Parisian apartment in June 2016, and a month later he convinced two militants to behead an elderly French priest in a small rural church. He was also linked to an aborted plot in September 2016 by three female jihadists, who under his direction aspired to attack a train station. The scheme was disrupted when police found an illegally parked car close to Notre Dame square containing the gas canisters for use in the operation.

Robin Simcox reports 50 percent of the 34 IS-linked plots in Western countries involving teens were virtually directed. [36]Most of these attack schemes involved knives. With some 2,000 French teens radicalized, the persistence of jihadi violence is likely.[37]

The caliphate prioritizes striking the United States by virtual direction. Strategically the use of virtual planning to inspire supporters into taking violent action is dictated by the lack of a network. The United States does not have a large radicalized Muslim diaspora. With only 250 U.S. fighters traveling to Syria, America's extremist community is small.[38] This does not mean, however, that the U.S. homeland is secure.

Since 2014 over a hundred people have been charged with IS-related terrorism offences.[39] Some 900 criminal investigations have been opened. Seventy people have been arrested for IS-linked terror activity. Most of the criminal cases deal with IS recruitment, financial support, and travel to Syria. Some, however, involved plots to kill Americans. Analysts point to the failed Garland, Texas Curtis Cutwell Center attack as the organization's opening salvo to kill Americans. One of its virtual planners was British-born Junaid Hussein who communicated with Elton Simpson to attack the center that was exhibiting cartoons of the Prophet Muhammad.[40] Sporting automatic weapons, Simpson and his partner were gunned down by a police guard before they could enter the complex.

Investigators point to Hussain's communications with Jostan Nolan Sullivan who was planning shootings in Virginia and North Carolina, Usaamah Rahil who sought to stab police in Boston, and Munir Abdulkader who aspired to behead a U.S. serviceman.[41] Another IS virtual planner, Abu Issa al-Amriki, communicated with Emmanuel Lutman to launch a New Year's Eve attack, and he sought to recruit Aaron Travis Daniels to travel to the caliphate as one of its soldiers.

Despite their lack of success in guiding IS's American sympathizers, U.S. national security planners take the caliphate's virtual direction campaign seriously. Since 2015 American security forces have prioritized killing IS's virtual planners, eradicating Hussain and al-Amriki. Though the West may be able to kill Rachid Kassim and Junaid Hussain, it is difficult to disrupt the inflammatory effect of IS's propaganda.

An April 2017 British parliamentary investigation of the death of IS U.K. militant Reyaad Khan in Raqqa, Syria highlights the dangers of the caliphate's remote-controlled operations.[42] Khan was killed in an August 2015 British drone strike targeting IS's external operations network. The controversy generated by an overseas assassination of a British national prompted a Westminster investigation that indicated that Khan was actively recruiting British citizens to attack their homeland.

Khan had been featured in a number of IS videos urging British nationals to emigrate to the caliphate. The committee report indicates that he was providing targeting and weapons assistance to U.K. extremists across social media forums and that multiple plots had been disrupted. It furthermore concluded that Khan's activities constituted an imminent danger that justified his assassination.[43] While Western security planners can disrupt external networks through targeted killing operations, stopping militants inspired by IS's ideological appeals may be even more problematic.

20.7.1 Inspired Attacks by IS Supporters in Europe

The Islamic State's commitment to the radicalization of Western Muslims is reflected in its social messaging. Since its June 2014 caliphate proclamation, Islamic State media has promoted its ideology in the West. Expressed in multiple languages, IS's propaganda encourage Muslims to emigrate to the caliphate. If that is not possible, IS's English- and French-language magazines encourage Western Muslims to kill apostates in their native lands. The caliphate's Amaq News Agency publicizes support for Abu Bakr al-Baghdadi by Western Muslims who are about to commit terrorism.

The caliphate's propaganda outlets justify its anti-Western violence. It argues that Western Muslims inhabit a grey zone that prevents them from practicing a correct form of Islam.[44] Secular democratic society IS publications argue that Muslims' rights to divinely inspired Sharia governance, forcing them to abide by Western legal processes and customs compromises their religious convictions. Western immorality, alcohol, homosexuality, and feminism are pilloried by IS propagandists who assert Muslim exposure to such filth has a corrupting influence. The Western forms of Islam are thus bastardized, hybrid religions that abnegate the core foundation of Muslim belief. IS propagandists, moreover, argue the Crusader West is at war with Islam through its military operations against the caliphate, obligating retaliatory defensive jihad.

The Islamic State's call for Muslim minorities in the West to kill apostates by any means has intensified with its military reversals. European extremists have heeded the caliphate's calling and have employed vehicles to kill large numbers of people. Using cargo trucks as death machines is an IS innovation. They have been employed in battles against enemies and as terrorist instruments to maximize civilian casualties. Several inspired terror attacks in France, Germany, and Spain have used devastating vehicles assaults.

The Nice and Berlin attacks have striking similarities. The perpetrators were Tunisian nationals alienated from Western society. Nice attacker Mohamed Lahouaiej-Bouhiel worked for a French trucking company. His troubled life included alcoholism, drug abuse, spousal abuse, and promiscuity. Amis Amri who carried out the Berlin attack had spent five years in an Italian prison for assault and theft. Neither Lahouaiej-Bouhiel nor Amri were religious. They were radicalized later in life and may have viewed IS affiliation as a path toward spiritual redemption.

Both have been linked to pro-IS jihadist preachers. Though Amri was radicalized in Italian prisons, German Iraqi preacher Abu Wala intensified his extremism. Based in the North Rhine-Westphalia and Lower Saxony regions, Wala disseminated pro-IS literature and preyed upon young, psychologically troubled men. French officials have linked Lahouaiej-Bouhiel to IS literature and sympathizers. He reportedly was fascinated by IS execution videos.[45] Prior to the attack he exhibited signs of religious devotion and had grown a beard.

Lahouaiej-Bouhiel targeted a large Bastille Day crowd watching fireworks. Lightly guarded by French police checkpoints and with no concrete barriers to block entry by a vehicle, the locale was an attractive attack site. The Tunisian jihadist had scouted the area before the attack and planned the operation. With its nationalistic secular character, an attack on Bastille Day was rife with jihadi symbolism.

Breaking through police barriers and traveling at high speed, Lahouaiej-Bouhiel smashed his 19-ton cargo truck through hundreds of people celebrating on the Promenade des Anglais. He ran down escaping Bastille Day participants by swerving the vehicle from right to left. Before police killed him, some 86 people lay dead with hundreds wounded. Inside the cabin investigators found automatic weapons and a pistol and speculated that Lahouaiej-Bouhiel sought to continue his rampage once he vacated his vehicle. His martyrdom inspired imitators.

Berlin attacker Anis Amri's case exemplifies the deficiencies of combating Islamist extremism in Europe. He came to Germany hoping for political asylum after Italian authorities had released him from prison. With a criminal history and jihadi sympathies, Amri's petition was rejected, and he was awaiting deportation at the time he committed mass murder. Though German officials had detained Amri, he was released by a court order. Deportation was delayed until German authorities received verification of his Tunisian citizenship for German law forbids deportation without sufficient identity documentation. Amri's denial of asylum rights may have contributed to his decision to commit mass murder.

At a rest stop for truckers Amri shot and killed a Polish truck driver. Commandeering his cargo truck Amri drove uneasily around Berlin searching for a target. He chose a Christmas market where hundreds of people congregated and plowed through a small barricade into the crowd. Had it not been for the truck's automatic breaking system the carnage would be worse. After his rampage, 14 people died and dozens were wounded.

Amri evaded European authorities for days. After abandoning his truck CCTV footage captures him entering an Islamic Center infamous for extremist sympathies. He took a train to the Netherlands and then eventually a rail journey across France to Turin, Italy. Having stayed many years in Italy, Amri may have had friends in Turin willing to provide a safe house. Questioned by Italian police outside the Turin rail station, Amri died in a shootout. The Tunisian jihadist's ability to circumvent a police manhunt and travel across European countries underscores the dangers of the continent's Schengen free movement agreement.

Amri posted a pledge of *bay'ah* to Abu Bakr al-Baghdadi that was posted on Telegram by the caliphate's Amaq News Agency after his attack.[46] Islamic State propagandists hail Amri and Lahouaiej-Bouhiel as their soldiers. The caliphate was so impressed by the Nice attack that it generated an animated simulation of Lahouaiej-Bouhiel driving through a crowd of apostates justifying his martyrdom operation as just retaliation for Crusader France's aggression against the caliphate.

Despite its low number of foreign fighters (some 200 militants) and minimal role in the war on terror, Spain has not been immune to IS terror attacks and plots.[47] Angered by Spain's conquest of Muslim "territory" some five centuries ago, the caliphate aspires to recover Al Andaluz. During the 1990s the country served as a logistical hub for Al Qaeda. The coastal town of Cambrils featured a meeting between Mohammad Atta and Ramzi bin al-Shibh in the summer of 2001 to finalize Al Qaeda's Holy Tuesday 9/11 operation. Some 16 years later, Cambrils would be attacked by Islamic State's linked jihadists.

The movement's historical grievance speaks to jihadi rage against the West that transcends objections to its foreign policy. Al Qaeda and the Islamic State have fulminated against *Charlie Hebdo's* satirical cartoons of the prophet Mohammad. Islamic extremists linked to AQAP attacked the newspaper's offices killing 13 people in January 2015. Jihadi cultural anger against the West should not be underestimated. If anything it may be growing.

Spanish withdrawal from Iraq after the March 2004 Madrid train attacks, moreover, did not reduce the Islamist terror threat. Fernando Reinares argues that the Iraq war was not the main reason jihadists attacked Spain.[48] He points out the 3/11 attacks were driven by revenge against its prosecution of Al Qaeda's 9/11 network. Hoping to avenge their jailed comrades and heeding the direction of Al Qaeda central, the 3/11 cell planned attacks after Spain's military disengagement from Iraq. Since 2004 the jihadi threat has remained constant with extremist attempts to attack rail lines, court systems, and the Barcelona metro. All of these terrorist conspiracies were disrupted by security services.

The Barcelona plot involved the Pakistani Tehrik-i-Taliban network and a 10-man cell that sought to inflict another 3/11 attack.[49] The country, moreover, features many jihadi networks concentrated around Barcelona, Madrid, and its North African possessions Ceuta and Melilla. Spain's foreign fighters in Syria mostly come from its Maghreb territories.[50] Many have entered the ranks of the Islamic State Catalonia, which is a major hub for jihadist networks who have recruited its members from North African diaspora communities. Given the depth of the jihadi/ extremist presence in the region, another attack in Spain was inevitable. Its fertile Islamist micro-culture contributed to two August 2017 terror attacks that killed 16 people. The lethality of the assault could have been tripled had the terrorists' original plans been implemented. Their original design involved bombing key tourist sites in Barcelona. An unintended explosion at a safe house in Alcanar killed two members of the group (including its ringleader imam Abdelbaki Es-Satti). The event altered the terror cell's plans.

Fearing that police would question one of the cell's members wounded in the Alcanar explosion, the jihadists acted quickly. They mounted van and knife attacks in Barcelona and in the coastal town of Cambrils over two days. Driving a van into Barcelona's crowded *Las Ramblas* Boulevard, Younes Abouyaaquob killed 13 pedestrians. Ditching the van and escaping through a crowded market near the square, he hijacked a car killing, its driver. He would remain at large for two days.

Hoping to capitalize on the shock of the Barcelona assault, a second team of five jihadists launched a late night van and knife attack in Cambrils, killing a German tourist, wounding one policeman, and injuring a few pedestrians. During the assault police shot all of the militants dead after their van flipped over. Barcelona attacker Younes Abouyaaqoub was later killed by police in a mountainous vineyard many kilometers from the city. Shortly after the Las Ramblas attack, IS claimed responsibility on a Telegram channel.

The Barcelona and Cambrils attacks were among the most sophisticated in Europe since IS's directed operations in Paris and Brussels. Its 10-man cell amassed explosives that could have been fabricated into over a dozen bombs. Based on testimony by one captured suspect, the team was targeting the city's famous cathedral La Sagrada Familia. The terror conspiracy size and complexity makes it distinct from most IS-inspired attacks that feature one or two attackers.

The attack, however, involved recruitment and radicalization processes seen elsewhere. The impact that jihadi preachers have on impressionable alienated young men cannot be overemphasized. Eager for spiritual redemption young Muslim immigrants can be easily seduced by IS-linked religious teachers. The cell's ringleader was a Ropoli-based imam, Abdelbaki Es-Satti, who for six months indoctrinated the network's Moroccan-born younger members. Their religious radicalization was abrupt, and some may have viewed their jihadi commitment as a pathway to personal redemption. The Barcelona and Cambrils terrorists lived largely secular, often hedonistic, lives prior to their extremist conversion. Family members of the terrorists killed or captured have expressed surprise at their sons' jihadi inclinations.

Prior to his death at the Alcanar safe house, Es-Satti had professed his IS affiliation in a document left at the residence. His travels to Vilvoorde, Belgium and Morocco may be linked to contacts with IS's network.[51] A year before the Barcelona and Cambrils attacks, Belgian authorities warned Catalan officials that Es-Satti was involved in jihadist recruitments efforts in Vilvoorde that along with Moleenbeck had become Islamic State hubs. Significantly Spain's regional authorities failed to follow up with an investigation.

Moroccans, moreover, dominate Spain's jihadi subculture.[52] Alarmingly Morocco has one of the highest foreign fighter populations serving in IS ranks in Syria, raising a specter of future terror attacks across the Mediterranean. Rabat and Madrid are working hard to monitor the return of foreign fighters.

The failure of Spanish national and regional security services to disrupt the Barcelona and Cambrils attacks reflects poor intelligence coordination between global, national, and regional authorities. Catalonia's controversial bid to secede from the country may have exacerbated this problem. Warned by Madrid that the Las Ramblas pedestrian area was vulnerable to truck and van attacks, Spanish authorities advised that Catalan authorities erect vehicle barriers. The recommendation was rejected. Advised by the Central Intelligence Agency (CIA) a few weeks before the attack that the famous boulevard was being targeted by the IS network, Spanish authorities found the claim not credible.

Investigators are trying to determine the level of IS involvement. There are many unanswered questions. The design of the bombs constructed comports with the Islamic State's explosives manuals as does the use of vehicular and knife assaults. One key determinant of the caliphate's external operations role will be the ability of security services to decipher the cell's level of communication with IS's larger network. Given the network's encryption of its communication, they may not be able to ascertain these connections.

The caliphate's media organs have failed to provide any specific evidence that they planned the operations. Significantly none of the Barcelona and Cambrils cell members served as a IS foreign fighter, suggesting the terror attack was largely inspired by the network. This pattern is repeated in the United Kingdom and America.

20.8 IS INSPIRED ATTACKS AGAINST THE UNITED KINGDOM AND THE UNITED STATES

British officials believed that the nation's island status and tougher immigration controls would afford it greater protection from IS's terror campaign. Such hopes have proven illusory. Though these restrictions make the caliphate's directed operations more difficult to execute, they offer Britain little protection against virtually guided and inspired terrorism.

The jihadi threat in the United Kingdom is severe. The island's large Muslim immigrant community hosts radicalized subpopulations in London, Manchester, and Birmingham.[53] Since the 1990s lax immigration controls, liberal political asylum policies, and judicial protections offered by European human rights courts have contributed to a vibrant Islamist civil society. Some mosques, charities, and community organizations have promoted extremists causes. Al Qaeda ideologues Abu Musab al-Suri, Abu Hamza, and Abu Qatada promoted the cause of global jihad in London during the 1990s. Their ideological heirs Omar Bakri Muhammad and Anjem Choudary created the muhajiroun network implicated in the majority of plots and attacks the United Kindgom has experienced since the July 2005 London Tube and Double Decker bus bombings.[54]

With its numerous Islamic charities, mosques, religious activists, and radicalized sub-communities, critics labelled the city Londonstan.[55] Jihadi theoreticians justified their political activism in the U.K.'s apostate capital by giving it a protected status for its assistance to the Muslim community.[56] Though the 9/11 attacks resulted in a generalized repression of the most extremist organizations operating in the United Kingdom, expulsions of radical preachers and the banning of jihadi organizations did not begin until the July 2005 London attacks.

Al Qaeda inspired plots to blow up transatlantic flights between the United Kingdom and America had been disrupted by British police between 2006 and 2008, while dozens of other attempts to kill British citizens have been averted by security forces. By 2011 intelligence services had mistakenly believed the jihadi threat had waned.

The Islamic State's ascendance radically changed this perception. Britain's large contingent of foreign fighters (over 700 individuals) and radicalized pro-IS central Asian and Mideast immigrant sub-populations threaten its security. Extremism is particularly acute among second and third generation Muslims raised in immigrant families. European counter-terrorism officials estimate that some 35,000 extremists live in Britain with some 3,000 considered dangerous.[57] British extremists have served in the vanguard of ISIS foreign fighters.

The country, moreover, is the fifth largest consumer of IS propaganda accessed across social media sites. With such a fertile extremist subculture, British security services have worked tirelessly managing some 500 investigative cases daily.[58]

Between 2014 and 2017, British intelligence disrupted 13 IS-linked plots. Their luck ran out in late March 2017 when Khalid Masoud killed five people in a van and knife attack outside the British Parliament. Al Amaq News Agency quickly claimed Masoud as one of its soldiers. The caliphate's supporters followed up with a martyrdom operation at a music concert in Manchester two months later killing 23 people and wounding over a hundred people. Manchester's suicide bomber Salmon Abedi may have been trained by IS agents in Libya, and the design of the explosive vest he wore corresponds to the movement's internet manuals.[59]

The following month, three IS-inspired militants used a van and knives to attack pedestrians on the London Bridge and nearby Borough Market killing eight people before they were gunned down by police. Analyzing the three attacks, Raffaello Pantucci argues that the police investigation suggests IS influence was mainly limited to ideological inspiration.[60] The investigation, moreover, underscores that British jihadism is dominated by young males in their teens and twenties raised in Muslim diaspora immigrant families. Only the Westminster attacker, 52-year-old convert, Khalid Masoud fails to meet this profile.

Here we must strike a cautionary note for the Dark Web system of secure communications may have played a role in IS virtually guiding these attacks. Past attacks like the 2004 Madrid and 2005 London bombings, for example, were labelled homegrown terrorism only to be contradicted by later evidence of Al Qaeda direction.[61]

Unlike the United Kingdom, the Islamic State in the United States has a relatively small support base. There are no American equivalents to Al Muhajaroun, Sharia4Belgium, or anything akin to the Abu Wala or Zerkani networks. American Muslims do not live in cloistered, unassimilated neighborhoods, and most do not espouse radical causes. Though the caliphate has published kill lists of American police and military personnel, few heed the Islamic State's call. Where the caliphate has radicalized American supporters, this usually involve attacks by mentally troubled immigrants.

Most of these assaults involved the use of knives on college campuses or shopping malls such as in Ohio and California. Though dozens have been wounded, there have been no fatalities. This does not mean that the caliphate cannot goad sympathizers with broad jihadi allegiances into committing mass murder. It has done this successfully.

20.8.1 Lone Wolfs with Multiple Jihadi Sympathies

Sam Mullins reports that 70 percent of IS-linked terrorist acts in the West are conducted by lone actors or lone wolves.[62] Often the attacker's abrupt radicalization prompts spontaneous violence making the attack unpreventable. More often than not, the perpetrator has a history of mental illness. Though widely maligned, the concept continues to be accurate for many IS sympathizers that have little direct connection to the caliphate's virtual or organizational network. Though they may have been inspired by the caliphate's propaganda, lone wolves autonomously plan and execute their own attacks.[63] This seems to be the case with the San Bernardino, California, and Orlando, Florida, attacks.

American extremists have overlapping jihadist allegiances easily transferable between organizations.[64] Often ignorant of the ideological divisions between Al Qaeda and the Islamic State, American extremists have cross hybridized jihadi sympathies. Affiliation with the Islamic State may be opportunistic and can revert back to Al Qaeda. Given the absence of an Islamist infrastructure online radicalization is a stimulant for IS-linked violence in America. We see something of this pattern in the San Bernardino and Orlando assaults.

On 2 December 2015, U.S.-born Syed Rizwan Farook and his immigrant wife Tashfeen Malik killed 14 people and injured 22 others at an employee training event hosted by the Inland Regional Center in San Bernardino. Farook was an inspector for the Country Department of Public Health and was attending the event. He left the meeting abruptly and returned with his wife some 40 minutes later. Armed with assault rifles they opened fire on those present in the banquet hall shooting over 100 rounds. During the attack Malik expressed her support for IS leader Abu Bakr al-Baghdadi on her Facebook page. Having killed over a dozen people, Farook and Malik left the center. They drove their SUV for over four hours around the San Bernardino area until spotted by police. After being chased by law enforcement personnel, the couple stood their ground and were killed in a firefight.

Malik's participation in the attack is unusual. Rarely do wives accompany their husbands on martyrdom missions. Her presence prompted speculation that she was a catalyst for Farook's radicalization. Though of Pakistani origin she lived much of her life in Saudi Arabia and met Farook via an online religious dating network. FBI investigators highlighted that the couple were radicalized over a number of years and their computer contained ample amounts of online extremist literature. Farook was infatuated with Anwar al-Awlaki's writings and was familiar with AQAP bomb-making instructions.

With his friend and convert Enrique Martinez, Farook conspired in 2012 to commit a terrorist act. Fearing FBI detection they abandoned their plans. Martinez purchased the rifles used in the San Bernardino attack and he was charged with criminal conspiracy to provide material support for terrorism. Police investigators found Farook's backpack full of pipe bombs based on AQAP blueprints on a conference center table, and when they searched the couple's garage, they discovered caches of ammunition and explosive material. Farook and Malik were planning a terror act for years and why they chose to kill scores of people attending the training event is unclear. We do know that Malik objected to her husband being forced to participate in a Christmas party following the training session. That may have been the impetus for the massacre.

What is clear is that the couple expressed multiple jihadi loyalties with Anwar al-Awlaki writings especially influential. The caliphate's adoption of Awlaki's call for attacks by Western

Muslims in their native lands may have been a trigger for the couple's transference of allegiance to the Islamic State.[65] American jihadists have diffuse ideological convictions across Al Qaeda, the Taliban, and the Islamic State. American-born Omar Mateen, who on 12 June 2016 killed 49 people at the Pulse Nightclub had a similar incapacity to differentiate between extremist groups.

Born in New York, Mateen grew up in Florida as a troubled young man in an Afghan immigrant family. He exhibited few signs of religious devotion, and he had a rudimentary understanding of the Islamic faith. Mateen's aspirations for a law enforcement career were dashed when his police academy application was rejected. He settled for private security work moving uneasily between jobs. Equally unsettled was Mateen's personal life and a failed first marriage. His ex-wife accused him of spousal abuse and mental instability.

Unlike Farouk and Malik, Mateen's jihadist sympathies were subject to a FBI inquiry. He was the target of two investigations between 2013 and 2014 centering on allegations from a former employer that he exhibited religiously motivated violent behavior and an inquiry based on his association with an Iraqi-American suicide bomber who died during an Al Nusra martyrdom operation. Mateen was briefly on the terrorist No Fly List. Having failed to establish a connection to a foreign terrorist organization, the FBI in 2015 ended its investigation.

Mateen's motivation for attacking a nightclub that catered to a gay clientele prompted allegations that he was a homophobic gay incapable of reconciling his homosexuality with his jihadi sympathies. The Department of Justice investigation after the massacre found no evidence of Mateen's homosexuality. His second wife Noor Salmon accompanied him as he scouted out the nightclub as a potential target. She also went with him to the gun shop where he legally purchased his weapons. The Justice Department found enough evidence of complicity that it charged her with aiding and abetting Mateen's terrorist act.

After having stormed into the club firing an automatic rifle and pistol, Mateen took hostages into the ladies restroom. In his phone conversations with police he expressed solidarity with IS and Al Qaeda's Nusra Front, calling the attack retaliation for the US bombing campaign against the caliphate. Like San Bernardino's Malik, Mateen swore *bay'ah* to IS emir Baghdadi during his martyrdom mission.

After a four-hour standoff with police, a SWAT team blew a hole through one of the bathroom's walls, and a police marksman killed Mateen. The FBI believes he was radicalized online for he supported a number of jihadi networks. It could not, however, find any direct link to any foreign terrorist organization. In his rambling phone conversations with police he mentioned the death of an IS commander in a US airstrike, the American war against the Taliban in Afghanistan, and the death of a friend who fought on behalf of Al Qaeda's Nusra Front as justifications for his violence.

Shortly after the attack IS's Amaq News Agency declared Mateen a soldier, praising the massacre. IS's enthusiasm for Mateen's slaughter of homosexuals is consistent with its homophobic orientation.[66] The caliphate's denunciation of Western sexual immorality references homosexuality, and the organization routinely kills gays by casting them off tall buildings. IS's discussion of the grey zone Western Muslims inhabit speaks to the corruption of faith caused by exposure to Western sexual freedoms. This may have impelled Mateen to target the Pulse Nightclub.

The Orlando massacre prompted increased security at gay pride events and clubs worldwide. IS's targeting of sports stadiums, concerts, night clubs, restaurants, cafes, shopping malls, churches, and trains leaves no target immune from the caliphate's wrath. As its state building project unravels in Iraq and Syria, one would expect that the IS movement to become increasingly dependent on its virtual network to guide and inspire attacks in the West. How then can Western intelligence agencies best combat IS's virtual caliphate?

20.9 WESTERN EFFORTS TO DISRUPT, DEGRADE, AND DESTROY IS'S VIRTUAL NETWORK

US intelligence was surprised by the rapid ascent of the IS movement and its June 2014 caliphate announcement. Hoping to disengage from the region, the Obama administration underestimated the strength of the Islamic State's predecessor. President Obama's disparagement of the IS movement as the JV team prompted widespread criticism. The collapse of the Iraq army in northern-central Iraq and the jihadist movement's incursion into Kurdish territory resulted in widespread ethnic cleansing of the Yazidi community and large scale massacres of Iraqi army prisoners. Faced with an immense humanitarian tragedy and the dissolution of the Iraqi state, the administration was forced reluctantly into military action.

Though the Islamic State justifies its terrorism in the West as just retaliation for the international coalition's air war against the caliphate, the truth is far more complex. Well before the advent of the U.S.-led military campaign, the Islamic State was laying the infrastructure of its terror campaign in Europe.[67] Its ideological messaging, moreover, has always sought military confrontation with the Crusader West.

Its May 2014, the Brussels Jewish Museum attack occurred some three months before the Western military response. Since 2014, years of warfare have upended the caliphate. The conquest of Mosul and Raqqa and the loss of its Libyan stronghold in Sirte have seriously degraded the movement's state building project. With its physical caliphate endangered, the network's transition to an insurgent, terror movement offers complex security challenges.

This is especially true regarding IS's virtual network and the danger it presents to Western interests. As the Western military campaign against the caliphate ends, intelligence and security agencies increasingly will be looking at countering violent extremism (CVE) approaches to combat the radicalizing impact of IS propaganda. With a substantial subsection of Europe's Muslim diaspora communities vulnerable to the movement's propaganda appeals, the challenges are daunting. French officials, for example, estimate that some 10,000 violent extremists live in the country.[68] Britain and Germany have comparable numbers of radical Islamists.

CVE approaches to disrupt the radicalization process are multi-dimensional.[69] They include (1) online engagement with IS militants and supporters by Western intelligence agencies; (2) constructing a counter narrative to jihadi extremism; and (3) community-based early prevention and intervention programs. The success of a CVE strategy is preconditioned upon outreach to Muslim diaspora communities and the active engagement of Islamic community leaders, mosques, charities, parents, and above all young people vulnerable to extremist appeals. Western governments have relied on online programs that dramatize the Islamic State's killing of fellow Muslims, regularly publicize statements by former fighters repudiating the caliphate's violence, and expose the caliphate's doctrinal deviation from contemporary Islamic beliefs.

Though European governments have employed CVE approaches like Britain's PREVENT program, more needs to be done to build trust and confidence between social agencies, police, teachers, and the Muslim community. Belgian officials in Moleenbeck have recently had some success in abating the flow of foreign fighters and credit much of their success to new CVE programs.[70]

While laudable we should not exaggerate the impact of these programs. Western governments lack the credibility to debunk the religious and ideological appeal of IS propaganda to alienated Muslim diaspora communities and radicalized converts. Muslim clerics, social workers, and educators associated with such programs may find themselves targets of jihadi rage. Hardcore jihadists often ostracize friends and families who object to their radical worldview.

The jihadi movement has progressively radicalized over the past two decades. It is more sectarian, takfirist, and xenophobic. IS's millenarianism adds a further combustible component to jihadism's violent propensities. Al Qaeda, for example, has failed to derail the caliphate's religious legitimacy. Criticisms of the Islamic State by AQ's aging ideologues resonate poorly among young jihadists. Despite their importance, CVE programs need to be supplemented by more punitive measures.

Since 2016 Twitter, YouTube, Tumblr, and Facebook have closed hundreds of thousands of IS-linked accounts. Increased vigilance by internet companies has, however, not prevented supporters from creating new pro-IS accounts that appear under different names and hashtags. The Islamic State has countered the closure of its open source channels, blogs, and accounts by embracing Dark Web encrypted technologies in securing its communication stream. IS's habitual use of Telegram, WhatsApp, and SureSpot allows it freedom and security to propagate its social message, rally supporters and, above all, virtually direct and inspire terrorist activity.

Though the movement's capacity to launch directed operations has been degraded and the assassination of its territorially based virtual planners have hurt its ability to electronically guide terrorism, IS's virtual caliphate persists. The unraveling of its proto-jihadist state, moreover, will increase the movement's reliance on Dark Web social media channels and forums. Unlike Al Qaeda, IS's movement has no wealthy patrons, and the loss of territorial sources of finance (oil exports and taxation) will force the movement to raise funds through the Dark Web.[71] Some reports suggest that IS has sold sex slaves and antiquities it has stolen across Dark Web forums. [72]

Finally, despite the death of some 50,000 militants and the destruction of its physical caliphate, IS propaganda is still prodigious. Though diminished IS's media apparatus continues to generate enthusiasm and inspire its supporters to violence. Given its mass support base and access to diffuse social media forums, it is impossible to block all IS-generated extremist content. Its active online engagement on the conventional and Dark Web are guarantors of its continued resilience.

20.10 SUMMARY

Political conditions and intra-confessional antagonisms in the Muslim world favor the long-term persistence of a Sunni jihadist global movement.[73] The Sunni-Shia divide is increasingly widening across the Middle East insuring continued conflicts in Iraq, Lebanon, Syria, and Yemen. The expansion of Iranian power in the region threatens Gulf Arab states and making their patronage of violent extremist movements more likely. Al Qaeda's propaganda that had criticized the Islamic State's anti-Shia ideological discourse is now adopting a sectarian tone. Within this geo-political context, IS's narrative of an oppressed Sunni community struggling to survive resonates.

The return of tens of thousands of extremist foreign fighters from Syria to their home countries is likely to have profound ramifications. Western European officials estimate that 50,000 extremists live on the continent nurtured by a vibrant Islamist micro-culture of radical jihadi preachers, charities, and clandestine mosques.[74] These forces portend a series of conflicts driven by religious fanaticism whose damage can only be contained. The West will face an ongoing jihadi terror threat for decades. This is a reality we must accept.

NOTES

1. Carfella, Jenifer and Jason Zhou, "ISIS Expanding Campaign In Europe" September 16, 2017 *Institute for the Study of War* accessed at: http://www.understandingwar.org/sites/default/files/ISIS%20i n%20Europe%20Update%20September-2017.pdf

2. Habeck, Mary "Jihadist Strategies in the War on Terror" November 8, 2004 *Heritage Foundation* accessed at: http://www.heritage.org/defense/report/jihadist-strategies-the-war-terrorism

3. Al-Adnani, Abu Muhammad "That They Live by Proof" page 7 accessed at: http://pietervanostaeyen. files.wordpresss.com

4. Holt, P.M. *The Mahdist State in the Sudan* (Clarendon Press, Oxford, 1958).

5. Joscelyn, Thomas "Zawahiri lectures on global jihad, warns of national boundaries" June 10, 2017 *The Long War Journal* accessed at: http://www.longwarjournal.org/archives/2017/06/zawahiri-lectures-on-global-jihad-warns-of-national-boundaries.php

6. Alsedo, Quico and Pablo Herraz, "Sombras y errores de la investigacion de los atentados de Barcelona y Cambrils *El Mundo* August 31, 2017 accessed at: https://www.elmundo.es/cataluna/2017/08/25/59 9f2c56e5fdeab0598b4641.html.

7. Richard Barrett, "Foreign Fighters: An Updated Assessment of the Flow of Foreign Fighters into Syria and Iraq" December 2015 *The Soufan Group* accessed at: http://soufangroup.com/wp-content/upload s/2015/12/TSG_ForeignFightersUpdate_FINAL3.pdf

8. Dauber, Cori and Mark Robinson, "ISIS and the Hollywood Visual Style" July 6, 2015 *Jihadology* accessed at: http://jihadology.net/2015/07/06/guest-post-isis-and-the-hollywood-visual-style/

9. Gambhir, Harleen, "The Virtual Caliphate" ISIS' Information Warfare" December 20, 2016 *The Institute for the Study of War* accessed at: http://www.understandingwar.org/sites/default/files/ISW %20The%20Virtual%20Caliphate%20Gambhir%202016.pdf

10. Prucha, Nico "IS and Jihadist Information Highway-Projecting Influence and Religious Identity via Telegram" *Perspectives on Terrorism* 10:6; Bloom, Mia "Navigating ISIS Preferred Platform: Telegram" July 2017 *Terrorism and Political Violence* DOI: 1080/09546553.2017.1339695

11. Yayla, Aymet and Anne Speckhard, "Telegram: the Mighty Application that ISIS Loves" May 9, 2017 *International Center for the Study of Violent Extremism* accessed at: https://www.icsve.org/telegram -the-mighty-application-that-isis-loves/

12. Celso, Anthony "Dabiq: IS 21st Century Apocalyptic Manifesto" *Journal of Political Science and Public Affairs* 2:4 accessed at: https://www.omicsonline.org/open-access/dabiq-iss-apocalyptic-21st-cen tury-jihadist-manifesto-2332-0761.1000e111.pdf

13. Celso, Anthony "More than the Voice of the Caliphate: The Destructive Legacy of Abu Muhammad al-Adnani" *International Journal of Political Science* 2:4 86–94.

14. "Foreign Fighters: An Updated Assessment," ibid.

15. Levitt, Matthew "The Islamic State's Lone Wolf Era is Over" March 24, 2016 *The Washington Institute* accessed at http://www.washingtoninstitute.org/policy-analysis/view/the-islamic-sttaes-lone-wolf-era-is-over

16. Al-Adnani, Abu Muhammad "Indeed Your Lord is Ever Watchful" ibid, 11.

17. Flade, Florian "The Islamic State Threat to Germany: Evidence from the Investigations" *CTC Sentinel* 9:7 11–14; Huzaifah Alkaff, Sayed and Muhammad Haziq Bin Jani, "The Death of IS Top Strategist: Reflections on Counter-Terrorism Efforts" *Counter Terrorist Trends and Analysis* 8:9 4–9.

18. Gartenstien-Ross, Daveed and Nathaniel Barr, [Hot Issue] "Recent Attacks Illuminate the Islamic State's Europe Attack Network" *Jamestown Foundation* April 27, 2016 accessed at: http://jamestow n.org/program/hot-issue-recent-attacks-illuminate-the-islamic-states-attack-network-in-europe

19. Filiu, Jean Pierre "The 'French Iraqi' Networks of the 2000s: Matrix of the 2015 Terrorist Attacks?" *Perspectives on Terrorism* 10:6 97–101.

20. Van Ostaeyen, Pieter "The Belgian Radical Networks and the Road to the Brussels Attacks" *CTC Sentinel* 9:6 7–1.

21. Brisard, Jean-Charles and Kevin Jackson, "The Islamic State's External Operations and the French-Belgian Networks" *CTC Sentinel* 9:11 8–15.

22. Van Ostaeyen, ibid.

23. Van Vierden, Guy [Hot Issue] "The Zerkani Network: Belgium's Most Dangerous Group" April 12, 2016 *The Jamestown Foundation* accessed at: https://jamestown.org/program/hot-issue-the-zerkani-net work-belgiums-most-dangerous-jihadist-group/
24. Ibid.
25. Gartenstein-Ross, Daveed "Radicalization in the U.S. and the Rise of Terrorism, Congressional Testimony" September 14, 2016 *Foundation for the Defense of Democracies* accessed at: https://oversig ht.house.gov/wp-content/uploads/2016/09/Gartenstein-Ross-Statement-Radicalization-9-14.pdf
26. Mullins, Sam "Lone Actor vs. Remote-Controlled Jihadi Terrorism: Rethinking the Threat to the West" April 20, 2017 *War on the Rocks* accessed at: https://warontherocks.com/2017/04/lone-actor-vs-remote-controlled-jihadi-terrorism-rethinking-the-threat-to-the-west/
27. Brisard, Jean Charles and Kevin Jackson, ibid.
28. Ibid., 13–14.
29. Gartenstein-Ross, Daveed and Nathaniel Barr, ibid.
30. Brisard, Jean Charles and Kevin Jackson, ibid, 10–11.
31. Ibid.
32. Ibid., 14.
33. "Dabiq 14: The Murtad Brotherhood" accessed at: http://clarionproject.org/wp-content/uploads/Dabiq-Issue-14.pdf, 6–7.
34. "Rumiyah 2" accessed at: https://clarionproject.org/factsheets-files/Rumiyh-ISIS-Magazine-2nd-i ssue.pdf
35. Simcox, Robin "The Islamic State's Western Teenage Plotters" *CTC Sentinel* 10:2 21–26.
36. Ibid., 23.
37. Ibid., 21.
38. Vidino, Lorenzo and Seamus Hughes, "San Bernardino and the Islamic State Footprint in America" *CTC Sentinel* 8:11 34–36.
39. Ibid.
40. Hughes, Seamus and Alexander Meleagrou-Hitchens, "The Threat to the United States from the Islamic State's Virtual Entrepreneurs" *CTC Sentinel* 10:3 1–8, 5.
41. Joscelyn, Thomas "The Future of Counterterrorism: Addressing the Evolving Threat to Domestic Security" February 28, 2017 *Foundation for the Defense of Democracies* accessed at: http://docs.hou se.gov/meetings/HM/HM05/20170228/105637/HHRG-115-HM05-Wstate-JoscelynT-20170228.pdf
42. Dominic Grieve, "UK Lethal Drone Strikes in Syria" April 2, 2017 *Intelligence and Security Committee of Parliament* accessed at: http://www.isc.independent.gov.uk
43. Ibid., 13–16.
44. Dabiq 7, ibid., 58–66.
45. Heil, Georg "The Berlin Attack and the 'Abu Wala' Islamic State Recruitment Network" *CTC Sentinel* 10:2 1–11.
46. Ibid.
47. Reinares, Fernando Carola Garcia-Calvo and Álvaro Vincente, "Differential Association Explaining Jihadi Radicalization in Spain: A Quantitative Study" *CTC Sentinel* 10:8 29–34.
48. Reinares, Fernando *¡Matadlos! Quién estuvo detrás del 11-M y por que se atentó en España?* (Galaxa Gutenberg, Madrid, 2014).
49. Ibid., 229–241.
50. Reinares, Fernando, Carola Garcia-Calvo and Álvaro Vincente, "Dos factores que explican la radicalización yihadista en España" August 2017 *Real Instituto Elcano* accessed at: http://www.realinsti tutoelcano.org/wps/portal/rielcano_es/contenido?WCM_GLOBAL_CONTEXT=/elcano/elcano_es/zonas_es/ari62-2017-reinares-garciacalvo-vicente-dos-factores-explican-radicalizacion-yihadista-espana
51. Juzgado Central de Instrucción Núm. Cuatro de Audiencia Central accessed at: http://estaticos.elm undo.es/documentos/2017/08/22/auto_detenidos_atentado_barcelona.pdf
52. Reinares, Fernando Carola Garcia-Calvo and Álvaro Vincente, "Dos factores que explican la radicalización yihadista en Espña," ibid.

53. "Welcome to Jihadi Britain" October 2017 *Clarion Project* accessed at: https://clarionproject.org/welcome-jihadi-britain/
54. Pantucci, Raffaello *We Love Death as You Love Life: Britain's Suburban Terrorists* (C. Hurst & Company, London, 2015) 53.
55. Nesser, Petter *Islamist Terrorism in Europe: A History* (C. Hurst & Company, London, 2015) 37–39.
56. Ibid.
57. "Welcome to Jihadi Britain" ibid.
58. Ibid.
59. Callmachi, Rukmini and Eric Schmitt, "Manchester Bomber Met With ISIS Unit in Libya, Officials Say" June 3, 2017 *New York Times* accessed at: https://www.nytimes.com/2017/06/03/world/middleeast/manchester-bombing-salman-abedi-islamic-state-libya.html
60. Pantucci, Raffaello "Britain on Alert: The Attacks in London and Manchester and the Evolving Threat" *CTC Sentinel* 10:7 1–8.
61. Celso, Anthony *Al Qaeda's Post 9-11 Devolution: The Failed Jihadist War against the Near and Far Enemy* (Bloomsbury; New York, 2014) 81–104.
62. Mullins, Sam "The Road to Orlando: Jihadist-Inspired Violence in the West 2012-2016" *CTC Sentinel* 9:6 26–32.
63. Mullins, Sam "Lone-actor vs Remote Controlled Jihadi Terrorism: Rethinking the Threat to the West" April 20, 2017 *War on the Rocks* accessed at: http://www.warontherocks.com/2017/04/lone-actor-vs-remote-controlled-jihadi-terrorism
64. Gilks, Sarah "Not Just the Caliphate: Non-Islamic State Jihadi Terrorism in the United States" *George Washington University.* Project on Extremism accessed at: https://cchs.gwu.edu/sites/cchs.gwu.edu/files/downloads/Not%20Just%20The%20Caliphate_0.pdf
65. Shane, Scott "The Enduring Influence of Anwar al-Awlaki in the Age of the Islamic State" *CTC Sentinel* 9:7 15–19.
66. Jocelyn, Thomas "The Future of Counterterrorism" ibid.
67. Gambhir, Harleen "ISIS Campaign in Europe: March 2016" *Institute for the Study of War* accessed at: http://www.understandingwar.org/backgrounder/isiss-campaign-europe-march-2016
68. "How Many Islamists are there in Europe?" August 1, 2017 *The Clarion Project* accessed at: https://clarionproject.org/how-many-islamists-are-there-in-europe/
69. Levitt, Matthew (editor), "Defeating Ideologically Inspired Violent Extremism: A Strategy to Build Strong Communities and Protect the U.S. Homeland" March 2017 *Transition 2017 Policy Notes for the Trump Administration* accessed at: http://www.washingtoninstitute.org/uploads/Documents/pubs/Transition2017-CVE-6.pdf
70. Selim, George and Daveed Gartenstien-Ross, "Save the Terrorism Prevention Toolkit" August 28, 2017 *War on the Rocks* accessed at: https://warontherocks.com/2017/08/save-the-terrorism-prevention-toolkit/
71. Levitt, Matthew and Lori Plotkin Boghardt, September 2014 *Funding ISIS (Infographic)* accessed at: http://www.washingtoninstitute.org/policy-analysis/view/funding-isis-infographic
72. Jawhar, Jasmine "Terrorist Use of the Internet: The Case of Daesh" 2016 *The Southeast Asia Regional Centre for Counter-Terrorism* 54 accessed at: https://www.searcct.gov.my/images/Articles_2016/Articles_2017/Terrorists_Use_Internet_Mac_17.pdf
73. Hegghammer, Thomas "The Future of Jihadism in Europe: A Pessimistic View" *Perspectives on Terrorism* 10:6 156–170.
74. "How Many Islamists are there in Europe?" ibid.

Chapter 21

Monitoring and Tracking ISIS on the Dark Web

William F. Gross, Jr.

CONTENTS

21.1 INTRODUCTION

When Sir Timothy Berners-Lee invented the World Wide Web in 1989 by implementing hypertext transfer protocol (HTTP) and successfully using the protocol to communicate between a client and server, he forever changed the face of communication. Over the next almost three decades, increases in computing power and advances in technology fundamentally transformed the way people see, think, hear, eat, pray, love, write, talk, and to the detriment of society, lie, cheat, steal, fight, and wage war.

Every year, updates to the English lexicon include hundreds of new words influenced by changes in culture and technology; words are formed from entirely new technology or included as slang derivatives. A discussion about tracking ISIS on the Deep Web should begin by defining terminology. ISIS, the term used throughout this chapter, is the jihadist terrorist organization known as the Islamic State of Iraq and the Levant (ISIL) or the Islamic State of Iraq and Syria (ISIS). The Deep Web is a subset of the World Wide Web characterized by the use of encryption, "onion" routing, cryptocurrencies, and pseudo-private browsing by design. Tracking ISIS on the Deep Web requires an understanding of Internet protocols and a close look at the Deep Web's implementation of those technologies.

21.2 INTERNET

Merriam-Webster defines the Internet as "an electronic communications network that connects computer networks and organizational computer facilities around the world" [1] and the World Wide Web as "a part of the Internet accessed through a graphical user interface and containing documents often connected by hyperlinks [2]. The Internet is this and much more! The Internet:

- Offers students new paradigms in learning
- Changes the face of medicine—physicians can perform remote surgeries
- Impacts the economy in ways never before seen
- Creates worldwide connections of instant voice, text, and video communication
- Gives rise to new terminology: cyberstalking, cyberbullying, cybercrime, cyberwarfare, cyberspace, viral videos
- Gives even the lowliest among us a powerful voice
- Brings life to the Internet of Things, an Internet working of devices, buildings, automobiles, sensors, actuators, thermostats, cameras and numerous other smart devices

21.2.1 Surface Web

Commonly referred to as the Internet or World Wide Web, the Surface Web is Internet content visible by a normal web browser, without any use of credentials, passwords, or specialized access. Search engines use web crawling technologies known as spiders and robots to harvest web page content, follow links, and build databases of web content. The Surface Web contains the common components: top level domain names, now numbering over a thousand, such as .com, .org, .gov, and .edu; Search engines such as Google, DuckDuckGo, Bing, and Ask; and Browsers such as Internet Explorer, Firefox, Safari, and Chrome.

21.2.2 Deep Web

The Deep Web and Dark Web are two different things. Deep Web content is often dynamically generated, usually password protected, and otherwise not conventionally indexed by search engines. Deep Web content includes databases, web services, private information, or restricted data, such as membership only websites. Access to the Deep Web content typically uses the same applications used to access the Surface Web, in addition to the required user credentials.

21.2.3 Dark Web

The Dark Web, also called the Dark Net, is a subset of the Deep Web that uses a different set of protocols and software to access content. Deep Web protocols include Freenet, a peer-to-peer network designed for media and information sharing, I2P, a communication platform using encryption for anonymous connections, and the most widely used access known as onion routing using the Tor browser.

21.3 HOW BIG ARE THE SURFACE, DEEP, AND DARK WEBS?

Metrics for measuring the Internet might include numbers of users, data sizes in bytes, numbers of unique addresses, or domain names. Internet protocol version 4 (IPV4) is one group of protocols that makes the Internet work. The addressing range for IPV4 is based on 32 bits, which generates about 4.2 billion total addresses, some of which are reserved for various reasons such as loop back and private addressing needs. Even with four billion addresses, the IPV4 space is said to be exhausted and IPV6, based on a 128-bit addressing scheme was introduced. Regardless of your chosen metric, the numbers used to measure the Internet are difficult to quantify, staggeringly large, and growing exponentially.

Declaring a finite size for the Surface Web, Deep Web, or Dark Web is a fool's errand because true measurement is impossible, and the actual sizes are dynamic. Many graphic representations of Surface versus Deep Web sizes depict a floating iceberg; the portion visible above the water line is the Surface Web and the massive chunk below the water line is the Deep Web. Although there is no authoritative source for web sizes, most estimates put the Surface Web around 5%, the Deep Web around 90%, and the Dark Web around 5% of total web-based content.

21.4 A QUICK LOOK AT A FEW WEB TECHNOLOGIES

Internet traffic moves along a wire, fiber, or in the airwaves in a binary format, meaning the data is expressed, in its simplest form, as a one or a zero; the presence or absence of magnetism, the pulse or absence of an electric signal, or the blink of light on fiber. Translating a string of ones and zeros into intelligent information, building the communication connections between endpoints, and keeping the circuits alive and protected from overloading is the work of protocols.

Dozens of protocols and technologies combine to make the Internet work. Some of the more common are a suite of protocols known as transmission control protocol (TCP) and the INTERNET PROTOCOL (IP), commonly written as TCP/IP. Other protocols enable file transfer, Bluetooth, WiFi, instant messaging, router traffic, video transmission, voice telephony, and web traffic.

21.4.1 Encryption

Encryption is a method of protecting data at rest or in transit. Encryption technologies range from the simplest of substitution ciphers where each character of a message is exchanged for another to complex mathematically advanced techniques using byzantine algorithms. Some encryption techniques, although written with the best of security intentions, have inherent vulnerabilities discovered after implementation. Some privacy advocates would argue certain encryption technologies already have back doors built in. For example, wireless networks were once protected with WEP, an encryption protocol found later to be easily hacked. A more modern wireless encryption technology is WPA.

Encryption is usually categorized as symmetric or asymmetric. Symmetric encryption is where one key is used to both encrypt and decrypt the message. The problem with this arrangement is the intended recipient needs the key to decrypt the message; delivering the key securely becomes a major vulnerability.

Asymmetric encryption, also known as public key cryptography, however, uses a pair of keys, called public and private; the keys are mathematically related and used in conjunction. The keys work in pairs: what one key does, the other one "un-does." One key is published publicly, or even sent along with the message in plain text, while the other key is highly secured and kept confidential. To send someone a message only they can decrypt, the sender uses the recipient's public key while encrypting. Only the holder of the private key can decrypt the message. Non-repudiation is achieved when the sender of a message encrypts a signature with his private key; in this case, anyone can decrypt the signature with the sender's public key. Assuming the private key remains secure, the only possible sender is the holder of the private key.

21.4.2 Virtual Private Networks

Typical Internet connections involve an Internet service provider (ISP) who provides domain name services (DNS) and Internet connectivity. If a computer uses HTTPS for Internet browsing, the page content is secure between the user and the web site being visited; however, the ISP can still see the destination. A virtual private network (VPN) is a workaround to this visibility, although VPNs have some drawbacks. The VPN software, known as a client, builds an encrypted connection between the client and a VPN server, which acts as an exit node. The connection is called a tunnel because it is best visually represented as an end-to-end pathway. The user has some measure of anonymity because the VPN server usually has many users. Your ISP will see the IP address of the VPN service and depending on your DNS configuration, they will see the contents of DSN queries. However, if the ISP "sniffs," or examines the VPN tunnel traffic, it appears as gibberish because of the encryption.

21.4.3 Encryption and Cracking

Modern encryption systems are incredibly robust and extremely difficult to crack. The keyword in the last sentence is "modern." Increases in computing power and the prospect of quantum computing change the landscape of breaking encryption and cracking passwords. Consider a simple example of an eight-character password, using any number, 0–9, any letter in upper or lower case, a–Z, and normal punctuation symbols such as ampersand, colon, and semicolon. The maximum possible combinations are the possible number of characters raised to the password length (max combination = max character password length). A simple eight-bit ASCII character set has only 256 possible characters. Excluding the control codes and extended ASCII codes, because they often do not work in password fields, gives 95 possible characters. So, $95^{\wedge}8$ = 6,634,204,312,890,625. Brute force cracking, one of the slowest methods, is simply trying every possible combination. The maximum of possible combinations appears massive! However, a modestly powered computer using optimized software running a brute force attack, which is the slowest of cracking techniques, can try all possible combinations in just a couple of days.

A quick study of password cracking tools like Cain and Abel, John the Ripper, THC Hydra, Rainbow Crack, and Brutus demonstrate the effectiveness of password complexity and length. Given a modestly powerful computer, most cracking software applications will crack an eight to ten-character password based on a dictionary word in just a few seconds. Increasing the scope of parameters for brute force cracking even by a few characters begins to increase the time needed exponentially. The calculations are based on modern processors and their speed and do not account for potential increases in computing power. Another technique for increasing speed is to compare a list of hashes, known as rainbow tables; computers are significantly faster at making comparisons between strings than calculating the hash values.

Governments and law enforcement advocates claim criminals use encryption to hide their illegal activities; therefore, they need a master key, or back door, built into encryption systems. Privacy advocates use encryption to protect their confidentiality, anonymity, and security. The debate rages, with constitutionality and transnational jurisdiction issues entering the conversation.

21.4.4 Finance

A popular expression in law enforcement circles attributed to a 1976 movie All the President's Men, "Follow the money" is no less applicable to terrorism activities. In the case of tracking ISIS on the Dark Web however, the currency is digital, secure, and encrypted and referred to as cryptocurrency. This form of money is decentralized, meaning no one company or government maintains control—this function is reserved to something called a blockchain. A blockchain is a digital ledger, publicly available, which records all transactions; security is achieved between transaction partners by use of public and private cryptography keys. The most widely recognized form of digital currency is Bitcoin, although there are over 1,000 other types including Ethereum, Ripple, and Litecoin. Use of most cryptocurrency is considered pseudonymous in that while transaction participants' identities remain anonymous, the transaction details are publicly recorded and therefore publicly visible. Using cryptocurrencies for buying and selling goods and services protects the identity of the buyer and seller; the real identity risk is converting cryptocurrencies to paper currencies because this involves a banking system, subject to the host nation's banking laws and disclosing a person's real identity.

21.5 TECHNOLOGIES FOR TRAVERSING THE DARK WEB

Just as the Surface and Deep Webs use a variety of technologies and protocols, so does the Dark Web. Among many technologies are Tor, I2P and Freenet, OneSwarm, Syndie, Riffle, and Tribler. The most common starting point is the Tor browser, available for free at www.torproject.org.

21.5.1 Tor Browser

The Tor browser is a modified Firefox browser designed and purpose built to work with the onion protocol. The browser contains numerous additional security focused features and is the primary tool to access the Dark Web. Tor is free. Tor browser can conveniently access normal web content and is configured to access "dot onion" sites. Although the onion technology makes standard search engines fail on Dark Web sites, Torch (http://xmh57jrzrnw6insl.onion/) claims to have indexed almost a half million onion pages. One good starting point is The Hidden Wiki (http://zqktlwi4fecvo6ri.onion/wiki/index.php/Main_Page), which catalogs much information and links to Dark Web sites.

21.5.2 Tor Browser Uses Onion Routing

Typical Internet traffic using the TCP/IP suite of protocols uses layers of encapsulation, much like stuffing a letter into an envelope, while preserving the origination and destination IP addresses. While technique is beyond the scope of this chapter, the method does not provide any anonymity. Onion routing on the other hand, uses encryption, random paths, proxy servers, a minimum of three hops, and an exit node where decryption occurs and the destination connection is made. Because of the hopping around and encryption lag, surfing the Dark Web with a Tor browser is sluggish and often painfully slow.

21.5.3 Email

Conventional email systems send and receive email messages in plain text, meaning the contents of the messages are not encrypted. Web based email services like Yahoo, Gmail, and Hotmail store email messages on the provider's server infrastructure instead of locally on the user's computer; this arrangement adds another layer of vulnerability. Some Tor based email services include TorBox (http://torbox3uiot6wchz.onion/), Mail2Tor (http://mail2tor2zyjdctd.onion/), and EludeMail (http://eludemaillhqfkh5.onion/).

21.5.4 Other Sites and Services

Other Dark Web sites include everything you might find on the Surface Web, and much more: financial services for cryptocurrencies, commercial services, hosting platforms, email, messaging, blogging, exploits, stolen credit cards, WikiLeaks upload, file sharing, wikis, social media, libraries, chat rooms, forums, streaming music, video, drug markets, pornography, foreign language sites, fake ids, passports, weapons, and hacking tools and software.

21.6 ISIS' USE OF TECHNOLOGY

ISIS uses the Surface Web, leveraging all the common platforms such as Twitter, FaceBook, and Instagram. The accounts are created and within a period of time, often taken down by the respective platform hosts, due to the hateful content violations of the host's terms of service violations. However, the time lag between posting, reposting, re-tweeting, and the account closure results in effective message transmission. Often, a link to a Tor-based website, or encrypted service is transmitted in the Surface Web messaging content.

ISIS also leverages the relative anonymity of the Dark Web. They use forums, encrypted email services, social networks, encrypted chat rooms, and cryptocurrencies. One example of a tool leveraged by ISIS is Zello (zello.com), a multi-platform social networking app that uses cellular data or WiFi networks to connect people with audio content in channels [3]. Dedicated ISIS websites increased from about 5,000 in mid-2006, to over 9,800 in 2014 [4]. The group even developed their own app, "The Dawn of Glad Tidings," which connects users' Twitter accounts and gives ISIS control of their messaging campaign [4].

In 2007, The Global Islamic Media Front released an encryption program for its members to encrypt email communications. The tool was announced in *Inspire*, the al-Qaida magazine. By 2013, fueled by the Edward Snowden leaks, there was a new encryption service being released almost every month [5].

21.7 TRACKING ISIS REQUIRES UNDERSTANDING AND EXPLOITING HUMAN AND TECHNOLOGICAL VULNERABILITIES

Any use of a technology device leaves minute traces. Privacy advocates and bad actors go to great lengths to obfuscate these traces of digital data.

21.7.1 Computers—MAC Addresses

For example, connecting a computer to the Internet involves numerous data points. A network interface controller (NIC) is a hardware device that connects a computer or phone to a communications media like ethernet, Bluetooth, or WiFi. Every NIC has a media access control (MAC) address, which is a 48- or 64-bit address, expressed in hexadecimal format that consists of two parts: a portion of the address identifies the manufacturer of the hardware device and the remaining portion is a unique serial number. While it is possible to randomize the MAC address with software, it remains a potentially unique number.

21.7.2 Computers—IP Addresses

Connecting devices to the Internet requires an Internet protocol (IP) address that is issued by an Internet service provider (ISP) either statically or dynamically. In either case, records of that address are kept by the ISP. Some ISIS agents use a VPN to obfuscate their network traffic from the ISP. Even though the traffic through the encrypted tunnel may be gibberish to the ISP, they still maintain metadata records of the tunnel's IP address, dates, times, duration, and volume of data passing through the tunnel.

21.7.3 Computers—DNS

Some computer traffic is not generally encrypted, such as domain name service (DNS) inquiries. The DNS is a service that translates word-based website names, like www.somesite.com, to a more computer-useable IP address. For example, on most Windows-based computers, a terminal command issued as "nslookup www.google.com" means to find the IP address for Google; the command returns 172.217.8.100. If the user has a DNS leak or has not properly configured his DNS to run through the VPN tunnel, then his DNS queries will be visible to the ISP, even though the resulting connections are most likely encrypted. So, the ISP can see the difference between www.nefarious-website.com and www.innocent-website.com, even though the resulting connections are probably encrypted.

21.7.4 Computers—Browsers

Web browsers are the most familiar tool for navigating the Internet and include common favorites such as Microsoft's Internet Explorer and Edge, Mozilla's Firefox, Apple's Safari, and Google's

Chrome. Some uncommon browsers will present web content in text only; a long-time text-only browser is Lynx. Regardless of the browser's origin, they use various technologies to display web content, including JavaScript, ActiveX, HTML, CSS, flash players, add-ons, plugins, extensions, and other bolt-on technologies that enhance the user experience, but also introduce vulnerabilities to privacy. A quick trip to www.panopticlick.eff.org gives you a chance to "fingerprint" your browser; that is, the site will run a series of non-scientific tests to determine how uniquely configured your browser appears.

21.7.5 Meta-data

One popular example of the power of meta-data and analysis is the Target pregnancy prediction model, created by employee and statistician Andrew Pole. Based on shopper's habits, in this case, purchasing certain types of unscented lotions, large purses, and dietary supplements, Pole calculated there was an 87 percent chance the customer was pregnant. By catching the customer at the right time in their lives with coupons and other enticements, Pole found he could increase sales dramatically. Fast forward about one year and a Minneapolis man walked into his local Target store, asked to see the manager and complained about his high school daughter receiving coupons for baby products. The manager apologized and called to apologize again. The Minneapolis man offered his apology, because after a chat with his daughter, Target's prediction was correct: his high school daughter was pregnant [6].

21.8 GOVERNMENT RESPONSE

The US government response to the ISIS threat involves numerous departments and agencies. The skill set to investigate the Dark Web transcends normal cyber investigation and computer forensics work, because some of the technologies used on the Dark Web are unique to that platform. Many Dark Web proponents tout reasons like freedom of speech, safety for whistleblowers, platforms for dissidents in oppressive nations, and a place to examine your unusual proclivities. As an investigator of the Dark Web, one must be prepared to see things that cannot be unseen.

21.8.1 Big Data

Most social media companies are free at the point of use, bartering the collection of reams of your personal information in exchange for their services. Facebook's net worth is measured in the hundreds of billions of dollars, but what physical product do they manufacture and how do they monetize their service, when their excess of two billion users all have free accounts? Information has significant value. With the proliferation of cellular phones, free apps, almost addictive behavior, and 24/7 transmission behaviors of cell phones, the rise of big data is arguably a golden era for intelligence agencies [7].

21.8.2 Operation Onymous

On 7 November 2014, the FBI announced a multinational operation consisting of 17 nations seized Silk Road 2.0 and dozens of other Dark Web websites and over 400 .onion websites. These Dark Web sites encompassed sales of drugs, counterfeit currency, passports, identity document, hacking tools, and credit card data [8].

21.8.3 Beebone Botnet

On 9 April 2015, the FBI announced another multinational operation, in conjunction with private sector companies, took down a hundred domain names supporting a botnet known as Beebone/AAEH. The botnet impacted computers worldwide and was responsible for installing other malware and stealing financial credentials [9].

21.8.4 NSA's XKeyscore and PRISM

Leaks by the former National Security Agency (NSA) contractor, Edward Snowden, revealed details about the agency's XKeyscore program. XKeyscore is a database which contains emails, browsing history meta-data, chats, searches, and "nearly everything a typical user does on the Internet." The database, used by NSA analysts, gives them access to reams of data by completing a simple online form [10]. The Xkeyscore revelation came on the heels of the NSA surveillance program PRISM, which allows the NSA access to data from Google, Microsoft, Yahoo, Apple, and many other servers and Internet organizations. A crude estimate of the volume of data housed in XKeyscore is in the tens of billions of records, and NSA analysts use a simple query language to build complex search criteria [11].

21.8.5 Defense Advanced Projects Research Agency (DARPA) Memex

Memex is a DARPA program designed to find linkages between websites. Originally built for law enforcement to combat sex trafficking, the tool is now used against ISIS. One example of the tool's utility is the ability to find similar phone numbers across large data sets, thereby creating a link between the sites and the actors [12, 13].

Memex is a type of data mining, a technique that manipulates complex and massive data sets with an end game of description, prediction, anomaly detection, regression, and data analysis. Another interesting and powerful feature of Memex is data visualization—a technique whereby data is expressed as visual representations. The resulting images leverage an interesting feature of human eyesight and brain function, allowing the user to "see" patterns in data not otherwise discernable with database queries. Memex is particularly useful in detecting sex trafficking characteristic behaviors including the websites for services, marketing efforts, and enticements for new victims [14].

21.8.6 Human Behavior

One of the techniques used in data mining tools relies on the fundamental weakness of human behavior: we like to keep things simple. People will reuse passwords, usernames, screen names, and in some cases, resuscitate old information with the misguided belief that the old data point does not exist on the Internet any longer. Whether it is browser fingerprinting, connecting addresses, phone numbers, emails, screen names, unique patterns of text, observing a consistently misspelled word, as was the case with the Unabomber Kaczynski, or other relatively small points of data, the advent of massive data sets and powerful search tools find the needle in the haystack. Many investigations begin with a simple connection of one data point to another, and then build from there until an amazingly detailed dossier is compiled.

21.9 SUMMARY

Tracking ISIS on the Deep Web, or any other criminal element on any Internet technology involves a labyrinth of complexity that combines human behavior, ever changing technology, and investigation skills. The investigator or government agent needs to have a deep understanding of the technology of the systems they are examining while embracing the criminal mindset. Every day, hundreds of billions of email messages traverse the Internet; email is the de facto communication standard, yet messages are sent in plain text by default and oddly, using an encryption service is not exactly easy. Bad guys know this and have figured out how to encrypt email. Open source intelligence (OSINT) is a developing field that uses the Internet and open sources of information to gather intelligence data. Unfortunately, as technology changes and people good and bad become aware of vulnerabilities, they begin embracing the need for encryption to maintain their privacy. Chasing crime on the Internet becomes much like a Whac-A-Mole game, but with greater and globally reaching consequences.

REFERENCES

1. Internet. 2018. In Merriam-Webster.com. Retrieved from: www.merriam-webster.com/dictionary/Internet
2. World Wide Web. 2018. In Merriam-Webster.com. Retrieved from: www.merriam-webster.com/dictionary/World%20Wide%20Web
3. Weiss, M., & Hassan, H. (2016). *ISIS: Inside the Army of Terror.* Simon and Schuster, p. 173.
4. ÇELİK, M. (2017). An Efficient Response to ISIS in Cyberspace: Public-Private Partnership. *Terrorists' Use of the Internet: Assessment and Response*, 136, 249.
5. Ullah, H. K. (2017). *Digital World War: Islamists, Extremists, and the Fight for Cyber Supremacy.* Yale University Press.
6. Duhigg, C. (February 16, 2012). "How companies learn your secrets." *The New York Times*. Retrieved from: https://www.nytimes.com/2012/02/19/magazine/shopping-habits.html
7. Wells, D. (2017). Beyond Big Data: Surveillance, Metadata and Technology-Enabled Intelligence Opportunities in Counter-Terrorism. *Terrorists' Use of the Internet: Assessment and Response*, 136,. p. 320.
8. U.S. Attorney's Office, Southern District of New York. (November 7, 2014). Dozens of Online 'Dark Markets' Seized Pursuant to Forfeiture Complaint Filed in Manhattan Federal Court in Conjunction with the Arrest of the Operator of Silk Road 2.0. Retrieved from: www.fbi.gov/contact-us/field-offices/newyork/news/press-releases/dozens-of-online-dark-markets-seized-pursuant-to-forfeiture-complaint-filed-in-manhattan-federal-court-in-conjunction-with-the-arrest-of-the-operator-of-silk-road-2.0
9. Federal Bureau of Investigation. (April 9, 2015). FBI and Foreign Partners Target Botnet Affecting Victims Worldwide. Retrieved from: www.fbi.gov/news/stories/fbi-foreign-partners-target-botnet-affecting-victims-worldwide
10. Wills, Amanda. (August 1, 2013). New Snowden leak: NSA program taps all you do online. *Mashable*. Retrieved from: www.cnn.com/2013/07/31/tech/web/snowden-leak-xkeyscore/index.html
11. Schneier, B. (2015). More about the NSA's XKEYSCORE. Retrieved from: www.schneier.com/blog/archives/2015/07/more_about_the_.html
12. Pellerin, C. (March 02, 2015). 21st-century DARPA Tool Could Work Against ISIL. *DoD News, Defense Media Activity*. Retrieved from: http://ctip.defense.gov/News/News-Stories/News-Display/Article/1418254/21st-century-darpa-tool-could-work-against-isil/
13. Prabhakar, A. (March 3, 2015). DARPA Looks to Combat Islamic State Group with Internet Tools by Jay Clemens. *DoD, Latest News*. Retrieved from: www.executivegov.com/2015/03/arati-prabhakar-darpa-looks-to-combat-islamic-state-group-with-internet-tools/
14. Hammonds, J. (March 17, 2015). An Inquiry into Privacy Concerns: Memex, the Deep Web, and Sex Trafficking. Retrieved from www.infosecwriters.com/Papers/JHammonds_Privacy.pdf

Chapter 22

ISIS and Russia

The Use of Threat for Spreading of Influence and ISIS's Future

Dmitry Shlapentokh

CONTENTS

22.1 INTRODUCTION

The spread of ISIS and similar Islamist movements has become a global phenomenon that might be compared with the spread of radical Marxism at the beginning of the last century. As a matter of fact, ISIS addresses the same issues addressed by radicals in the past, for example, economic inequality, albeit, of course, in a specific and twisted form. Indeed, it would be overly simplistic, in fact flat wrong, to see Islamism as merely a resurrection of Medievalism. It is more the child of modernity rather than of the distant past, despite its external ideological trappings. Here it might be compared with Protestantism, which, despite its protagonists appeals to the past (the early Church), was the child of emerging European modernity. Islamists and radical Marxists are structurally similar[1] but not identical phenomena, and their position in the global order is different.

To recall Marx's famous expression in his *Manifesto*, the "specter" of Communism terrified all ruling classes of Europe and they were ready to forget their differences and join hands in dealing with the common threat. The story of ISIS is different. The spread of ISIS and similar Islamist movements has a variety of repercussions for different countries and ISIS was not always viewed as a mortal threat. This is the case with Russia, where the elite saw not just negative but also quite positive repercussions for the Kremlin in the spread of the movement. First, Islamism, in its logical development, stimulates the radicals' emigration from the country, and the majority most likely will not come back. Second, the ISIS threat helps the Kremlin increase its influence in Central Asia, where it might be the only viable protector of the local authoritarian/totalitarian regimes from revolutionary/terrorist upheaval. Here Putin's neoconservative and anti-revolutionary ideology emerges as a sort of new edition of the ideology of Nicholas I, who was the "Gendarme of Europe," protector of post-Napoleonic/post-revolutionary reaction, and mortal enemy of all revolutions. He was the reason for the hatred of Russia by all European radicals and even liberals, and for the emergence of Russia's image as an essentially Asiatic power hostile to civilized Europe *in toto*. Now Putin can play the role of Nicholas, and the declining United States and West in general could hardly save the Central Asian regimes or the lives of their leaders. Third, the threat could help Moscow maintain a relationship with Iran. The Kremlin might even be pleased by ISIS's focus on the United States and a possible terrorist attack, which could have a catastrophic implication for the U.S. stock market and society in general. These events could not just considerably weaken but actually paralyze the United States. Some of the members of Putin's circle, and possibly Putin himself, could see such a scenario as rather positive for Russia, whose relationship with the United States has moved to an almost Cold War level. Finally the rise of ISIS and fear of Europeans could also help Moscow deal with Europeans who might protest Russia's possibly harsh dealing with terrorists/"revolutionaries" inside the country. While Moscow could benefit in several ways from the rise of ISIS, two aspects are especially important: it sped up the disintegration of North Caucasian resistance, and it helped Moscow increase its influence in Central Asia. At the same time, discord between Russia, the United States, and other players could provide ISIS or its successors a chance for survival.

22.2 FROM "WEAKEST LINK" TO MARGINAL ASPECT OF JIHAD AND MOSCOW BENEFIT

ISIS apparently started to influence the North Caucasian resistance early on, and some resistance members swore allegiance to ISIS in late 2014 or early 2015. This act was a continuation of the long process of radicalization—internationalization—of the North Caucasian resistance, which received new impetus in 2007 when the Islamist emirate was promulgated by Doku Umarov. Those who promulgate the emirate believe it would increase their strength because it would draw to their side all Muslims regardless of ethnicity. And they were right in the short run. They attracted not only other Muslims from North Caucasus and what Russians usually called distant abroad, but even Russian converts. Even al-Qaida seems to have become interested in the North Caucasus. One could assume that its ideologists started to regard North Caucasus as one of the weakest links—to employ Lenin's expression—that if broken could start global jihad. Emirate members were pleased by the possible benefits from such attention. But the continuous internationalization led to the opposite result: the war in the Middle East became more attractive for many than the conflict in North Caucasus. And the majority seem to have remained in the regions and not come back as the emirate leaders hoped and Moscow feared. Indeed, Moscow benefited from ISIS's rise in the North Caucasus. Not only did the Middle East became a magnet for quite a few Russian jihadists but fear of jihadists helped Moscow forge relationships with states in Central Asia and Iran and to solve other related problems.

22.3 THE EMERGENCE OF THE EMIRATE AND DISINTEGRATION OF RESISTANCE

Chechnya engaged in a fight against Moscow from the very beginning of the post-Soviet era. The first Chechen war was mostly carried out through nationalistic slogans. Chechnya wanted to be an independent state and part of global concerns of world power. Logically it was mostly a Chechen enterprise, attracting Chechens from all over post-Soviet countries and beyond. One might remember here that Armenians all over the world participated in the fight with Azerbaijan in the war for Nagorno-Karabakh (1988–1994). Even American Armenians "went to fight in Nagorno-Karabakh in the name of Armenian identity."[2] The conflict in Chechnya clearly attracted more attention from the world community than other conflicts in post-Soviet countries. But at the start it was mostly the concern of Chechens and nobody else except some global and regional powers such as the United States and Turkey (the latter with a considerable Chechen diaspora),[3] and both used the conflict for their own geopolitical benefits. Still, as the conflict persisted, it increasingly looked like Muslim persecution from the hands of infidels and non-Muslim power; this increasingly internationalized the war, and it was put it in the context of rising jihadism. Consequently Islamists from all over the world came to Chechnya to fight. Some became important resistance leaders. The jihadization of the movement became increasingly mainstream, and the resistance started to lose its purely Chechen characteristics by the beginning of the second Chechen War in 1999.

At that time, the representatives from all over the Caucasus started to fight on the side of mujahidin. This led to the creation of the emirate in 2007. Those who launched the emirate had a variety of reasons in mind. One was that the emirate would emphasize Islamist rather than national identity. This would bring help from abroad and solidify the ranks of fighters from different ethnic groups of the mostly Muslims from North Caucasus. Emirate leaders justified the changes by stating that nationalism has nothing to do with Islam; here they instinctively followed not just Islamic theoreticians, such as Sayyid Qutb (1906–1966), but also, of course without acknowledgment, the Marxist-Leninist doctrine that nationalism is bourgeois ideology that separates the international proletariat and prevents it from recognizing its global historical mission to liberate itself and consequently all humanity. Akhmed Zakaev, Minister of Foreign Affairs, and Zhalaudin Saraliapov, Chairman of Parliament of ChRI opposed this decision and created a new government in London. This led to conflict with leadership of the emirate. In 2009, according to *Kavkaz Center*, Shariat court condemned Zakaev to death, albeit there has been no evidence of any attempts to carry out the verdict. Still Zakaev felt isolated and increasingly felt that attempts to restart resistance on a non-jihadist base were bound to fail. At the same time he saw that Ramzan Kadyrov, appointed by Putin as viceroy of Chechnya, had actually achieved what non-Islamists wanted. Kadyrov's Chechnya was actually independent from Russia, if not de juro but de facto; in addition, it received a huge subsidy from Moscow that looks, in the view of some Russian nationalists, almost like a tribute.

In 2009 Zakaev conducted negotiations with representatives of the Kadyrov administration. He apparently wanted to return to Chechnya and quite possibly thought about his old profession: he was an actor before joining the resistance and there was a rumor Kadyrov promised him the position of director of a local theater or even the job of Minister of Culture. Nothing emerged from these negotiations. It is quite possible Zakaev was not sure about his safety. Kadyrov guaranteed amnesty, but Zakaev apparently did not put much trust in this promise. Still he clearly lost any interest in the resistance, most likely because of his failure to find non-jihadist fighters in Chechnya. So Zakaev was in search of the way out. In 2010, Khusein Gakaev was promulgated leader of the emirate. Zakaev acknowledged his leadership and disbanded his government in exile, clearly an excuse to end any involvement in resistance. Gakaev's split with Udugov was termporary and Zakaev could easily return to his previous claim as the only true representative of the Chechen resistance, but he did not want to have anything to do with resistance. And it seems Moscow also lost interest in him. Zakaev was hardly the only splinter from the emirate. Isa Musaev was deputy of Movladi Udugov (1962–current), major emirate ideologist and editor of *Kavkaz Center*, its major internet vehicle. He apparently did not want to stay with Udugov and created his own group, OPD' Svobodnyi Kavkaz', which fell apart by 2014. Moreover, Zakaev's own groups began to disintegrate quickly, apparently even before Zakaev decided to end his political or, to be precise, quasi-political activities. As was already noted, Zhaloudin Saraliapov split from Zakaev's Ichkeriia and created a new government in exile in Strasburg. The Chairman of the Ichkeriia Parliament Akh'iad (Ahyad) Idigov created his own group, which included Dudaev's wife.[4] There were even smaller groups. What was the implication of these splits for the emirate and North Caucasian resistance in general? Retrospectively, one could assume that the splits had rather negative implications for resistance. The new splits due to the emergence of the emirate presumably made the situation worse.

22.4 SPLIT AND JIHADIZATION OF THE MOVEMENT

When the emirate was created in 2007 its leaders put forward a variety of arguments why the Chechen republic should be transformed to an emirate. One argument was that a fight for Chechen independence would attract only Chechens, whereas a fight for an Islamic state would attract all Muslims of Northern Caucasus and even Russian converts. In addition it could attract substantial help from what Russians usually called the distant abroad countries that had not been part of the USSR. Thus jihadist internationalization would be much better for the vitality of the movement than narrow parochial nationalism. Small splinter groups could well be ignored, for they represented no one. This assumption and new internationalist outlook also defined their views of the Arab Spring. Paradoxically enough, at least at first glance, they hailed the wave of uprisings and collapse of authoritarian regimes in the Middle East in the same way as in Washington. Of course they had an absolutely different view of the nature of the process. While Washington folk saw it as the beginning of worldwide move to Western capitalist democracy in the Middle East, Doku Umarov (1963–2013), emirate leader, noted that Islam does not recognize democracy in its non-Islamic manifestation, and he doubted such a term exists in Islam. Still, he noted, if what the rebels called democracy is actually the beginning of global jihad, he fully supported the movement. In a way, Umarov's approach was quite similar to Lenin's views after the collapse of the czarist regime in February and March 1917. For the people in London, Paris, and Washington this was one of the final accords in the global triumph of Western capitalist democracies.

This sort of Fukuyamian vision of world history was still quite popular at the beginning of the twentieth century, despite the clear presence of quite different trends and, of course, the gruesome realities of World War II. For Lenin it was just a first step in worldwide proletariat revolution. Umarov followed Lenin's analysis and was clearly right in envisioning the nature of the process. Similar to the Russian masses in 1917, the Muslim populace received no socio-economic benefits from the process and soon became influenced by jihadism, with ISIS as one of its manifestations. Consequently Umarov apparently saw no problem for the emirate. He clearly believed the emirate could simply be one of the front lines of global jihad following the notion of Islam solidarity and, quite similarly to Lenin who believed in the famous Marxist slogan "Proletariats of all countries unite!" expected clear benefits for the emirate. Indeed, one might add that this slogan was quite important for Lenin not just as an abstract philosophical shibboleth but as an operational principle. At least at the beginning of his political career, Lenin believed the Russian revolution would lead to worldwide proletariat revolutions and the victory of the Western proletariat. At that point the Western proletariat would stretch their hands out to their Russian brothers and help them survive. Thus, Lenin believed, as did Soviet leaders during the Civil War, that the victory of European Marxists would ultimately help Soviet Russia, and Moscow should help them in expectation of future rewards. Umarov followed the same logic. He sent some of his people to fight in the Middle East and expected responses and tangible help from the Islamist leaders. But there was not much help and the internationalization of the emirate actually began to work against it: instead of attracting fighters it began to lose them to the Middle East jihad. In the beginning of the process, emirate leaders possibly believed that those who went to fight in the Middle East would come back and rejoin the North Caucasian resistance with knowledge and expertise. This did not happen and the majority of those who went to the Middle East have never returned.

22.5 OUTSOURCING FIGHTERS

Joining ISIS became a global phenomenon as people all over the world were joining up the way they would have joined revolutionary movements with global appeal in the past. Considerable numbers of foreigners went to Iraq and Syria from Europe.[5] The phenomenon could be seen even more clearly in the Middle East where, for example, girls from middle-class backgrounds could most suddenly become converts and go to Syria or Iraq to fight for ISIS.[6] A similar process took place in the former USSR. According to some sources, there are 800–1,500 people from Russia fighting on ISIS's side,[7] some clearly identified by Russian authorities.[8] According to other sources, there are 1,700 people from Russia and around 300 from Tajikistan.[9] Altogether up to 4,000 people from the former USSR could be fighting for ISIS.[10] Not all of them are from the predominantly Muslim North Caucasus or Central Asia. Some are from Muslim enclaves in the Russian heartland, such as Tatarstan and Bashkiria,[11] where a group of 20 people were converted to Islamism. They helped the Taliban and ISIS and then emigrated abroad.[12] Nevertheless, the numbers from North Caucasus, especially Chechens, are considerable and may represent the majority of the fighters.

22.6 OUTSOURCING OF CHECHEN FIGHTERS

Fighters from all over the Caucasus come to ISIS,[13] but Chechens are apparently represented more than any other ethnic groups. There are 1,200 Chechens in Syria, half from the wider Caucasus, not necessarily Russian North Caucasus. For example, there are Chechens from Georgia among ISIS fighters.[14] Some of them had occupied important positions in ISIS. "And one group of foreign fighters is led by an ethnic Chechen who goes by the name of Abu Omar Al-Shishani."[15] There was enough information about these Chechen leaders to elucidate their considerable role in the conflict. According to the reports, Chechens and other ethnic groups preferred to fight in ethnically homogeneous groups. Some detachments became quite prominent in the conflict, one led by "renowned ethnic Chechen military commander Abu Omar al-Shishani. The faction has fought in several regions in northern Syria and is reportedly based around the city of Aleppo. Until late 2013, Omar al-Shishani tried to maintain autonomy, refusing to transfer command of his troops to the hands of the al-Qaida affiliated Islam State of Iraq and Syria (ISIS) and Jabhat al-Nusra. His decision to reverse this policy of autonomy and swear allegiance to ISIS leader Abu Bakr al-Baghdadi resulted in a major rift between Omar and his deputy, Seyfullah al-Shishani, also an ethnic Chechen."[16] The considerable numbers of Chechens and other North Caucasian jihadists as well as the notion of internationalizing jihadism became an additional magnet for those in the North Caucasus who thought about joining jihad. The exodus of fighters weakened the emirate, depleting it of fighters; at the same time, in contrast to its leaders' original expectations, it received practically no help from Middle Eastern jihadists. The fact that some leaders openly broke with the emirate and swore allegiance to ISIS's Abu Bakr al-Baghdadi weakened the emirate even more, as indicated by bitter polemic between supporters of the emirate, ISIS, and the original Chechen Republic who originally supported Zakaev. All this indicated split and increasing confusion, even actual disintegration, among the representatives of resistance.

22.7 SUPPORTERS OF THE CHECHEN REPUBLIC

Those who supported the original Chechen republic continued to hold their ground, at least in cyberspace. One of the contributors to an internet discussion noted that quite a few mujahideen did not understand why Umarov needed to promulgate the emirate[17] and not fight under the banner of the Chechen Republic. Still even those who implicitly agreed with this member of the resistance, saw no future for a Zakaev-led underground. One contributor noted that after the first Chechen war, most of the leaders ran away. There was no choice but to change all the arrangements.[18] While the necessity of promulgating the emirate was discussed in cyberspace, the subject is clearly declining in importance. The events took place almost eight years ago, and its founder is now dead. It has become mostly a subject of recent history rather than a current pressing agenda. The major discussion was over the relationship between ISIS and the emirate. Analysis of this discussion shows that support of ISIS was far from total among either the members of the North Caucasian resistance or those who sympathize with them. Still there were quite a few who are ready to join ISIS. In any case the resistance became badly split.

22.8 THE REASON FOR JOINING ISIS

There were many reasons why the members of the North Caucasian resistance joined ISIS. The major reason, at least from our view, is the sense that ISIS is a global revolutionary phenomenon of sorts—global jihad with the ideal khalifat as omega of world history. Still there are many other reasons which overlap or reinforce those noted above. One might assume that members of the North Caucasian resistance were attracted to ISIS for the same reason as some fighters in Afghanistan who join ISIS for money and to be a member of a powerful movement.[19] It is unlikely that ISIS provided any funds to the members of the North Caucasian resistance, but the desire to be part of a victorious movement might be an important psychological incentive. There was another side of the movement that quite likely played a role in attracting members of the Caucasian resistance. Some aspects of ISIS or the Taliban state could look attractive to quite a few Muslims and even non-Muslims. These states could be attractive not just from the religious but also the social dimension despite their macabre brutality. Indeed the Taliban and ISIS states or quasi-states could well be compared with the early Soviet state. Western critics of Taliban or ISIS often pointed to the unspeakable brutality of people involved in the movement. Islamism is especially the case with ISIS which engaged in the sort of theatrical performances of beheadings and placed these grisly events on YouTube.

ISIS is hardly new in such actions. The Bolshevik Red Terror launched at the beginning of the Civil War was hardly different from ISIS. Thousands were shot. The French Revolution, which the Bolsheviks regarded as a model, at least in their terrorist actions, made a spectacle of public executions, following *ancien régime* practice. Despite these monstrosities, the Bolshevik regime attracted considerable numbers of Western sympathizers and enjoyed at least a modicum of social support among the masses. It continued to be hailed by many historians in the West as the event that created a society with concern for the toilers. The same could be said about the French Revolution. There are quite a few works that present all the monstrosities of the French Revolution. As a matter of fact such critical work could be traced back to the beginning of the revolution. Some of these works have appeared quite recently, authored by authoritative French historians. Still the French Revolution continues to be held in high esteem in Western thought. The beginning of the revolution is a major national holiday in France and the Marseillaise, created during the revolution, with its words about the blood of tyrants who shall moisten French soil, is the French national anthem. One might also add that quite a few Western intellectuals have been fascinated with murder as a peculiar method of self-expression.[20]

Thus, brutality in itself does not make events repugnant in the present or past, at least in the eyes of many. The same could be said about the Taliban and ISIS. Their gruesome theatrical decapitations and even public display of severed heads—a practice that is well-known not just in the Orient, at least in the past[21]—do not necessarily make ISIS absolutely repugnant in the eyes of many. As a matter of fact, this brutality was, in a twisted way of course, the sublimation of all social and emotional injustice the perpetrators of these executions suffer, at least it could be perceived in such a way on a deep emotional level. Consequently these people could join or at least be sympathetic to ISIS not despite their brutality but because of it and because the movement embraced everyone regardless of ethnicity or race. People could also join for purely pragmatic reasons, for example, sex with slave girls or wives, a good salary, or social status. One should remember that the human mind cannot be compartmentalized easily, and the most pragmatic, down-to-earth considerations (e.g., money and sex) could well be combined with the most sublime feelings (e.g., fighting for the ideal society—khalifat). Fedor Dosteovsky, the classical Russian writer, noted that the human mind is very broad and could combine the ideal of Mona Lisa, the ideal of sublime love, with the ideal of Sodom, the drive for the most primitive animal type of lust.

All these aspects of ISIS ideology and practices should be taken into account when studying the reasons ISIS has been attractive for many. Its attractiveness is not due just to internationalism, promising a utopian ideal society in the future, or to economic incentives, such as high salaries for the fighters or sublimation of anger or frustration for ordinary folk: the regime offers not just fear but clear social benefits. This trust is not necessarily related to the fact that ISIS is Sunni and the Iraqi government is Shia. The benefits of ISIS or the Taliban regime are related to sociopolitical arrangements and cannot be reduced to similarities in religious affiliation of the leaders of ISIS, the Taliban, and local populations. Some Western observers acknowledge that despite the despotic and terroristic nature of ISIS, life in the capital Raqqa was safe and free of corruption, and some people come here of their own free will.[22] Some locals trusted Taliban justices more than the Syrian or Iraqi authorities.[23] Acceptance of brutal despotic rule as the only guarantor of order is not unique, and placing the phenomenon in comparative context can be helpful. Similar phenomena can be found in early modern Europe, where the populace could accept brutal theatricality of king justice as the only way to maintain basic order.

Other aspects of ISIS rule and rulers also became attractive to their followers, even those raised in the West. Similar to early Bolsheviks, ISIS leaders were egalitarian and, in a way, modest. As part of creating a negative ISIS image, Western mass media noted that ISIS leader Al-Baghdadi has "an expensive watch," but they failed to find any other symbols of wealth or extravagance. One might add that neither Al-Baghdadi nor his supporters, nor members of the ISIS state administration could be compared with the members of the U.S. government, who are often quite wealthy. Even those of modest means become quite well-to-do after serving in the government, from which they move to well-paid jobs. Nothing like this could exist in the ISIS state, because there are no big corporations, law firms, universities, and so on that could reward those who "help" them. And, needless to say, members of the ISIS elite cannot place their cash in safe foreign bank accounts, although, as in any other situation, exceptions can be found. Finally, there is not much social division in ISIS society, and from this perspective they also resemble early Bolsheviks. It is true that ISIS did not officially nationalize the command heights of the economy. But they clearly control them and have practically nationalized them in a peculiar form. ISIS did not close the small shops and end trade, as the Bolsheviks tried to do during the Civil War, the era of War Communism. But the majority of upper classes in ISIS society are petty traders. Certainly this is a far cry from the situation in the modern West, especially the United States with its billionaires, declining middle class, and poor. The end of clear social divisions and socio-economic egalitarianism were important aspects of early Bolshevism and apparently play an important role in attracting people to ISIS, including from the West. The ISIS state had not developed the oligarchical or elitist form easily detected in the modern West. A dynasty of sorts emerged in the West not just in business and academia but even in politics, whereas in the United States power is passed from father to son (Bush) or from husband to wife (Clinton). In the West the elite—especially economic and political—can directly or indirectly provide their offspring with well-paid and prestigious jobs, increasingly marginalizing everybody else. Nothing of this type can be found in ISIS or the structurally or ideologically similar Taliban. As a matter of fact, Bin Laden used his millions for the cause and not only put himself in harm's way but did the same with his children.

While this aspect of ISIS policy clearly harkens back to Bolshevism, it is of course dressed in different ideological vestments. It is presented as the return to "true" Islam, the logic being the same as in Protestantism, which claims a return to "true" early Christianity. Restoration of true and wholesome tradition as the way of solving problems is well recorded in the United States, at least among some conservatives who proclaim that the problems of present day America are due to departures from the designs of the Founding Fathers. Such views are also broadly circulated in the Muslim world. It is departure from true Islam that, in the view of ISIS, explains the problems of the present day Islamic umma. This view apparently has broad circulation, shared by some who can hardly be seen as Islamists. A few years ago the author attended an Islam-centered conference in Istanbul. Many speakers dealt with present day Islam. One speaker focused on the juxtaposition of historical and present day Islam. He stated that the first khalifs were poor, whereas present day Islamic leaders are quite rich. The early khalifs did not place their children and other relatives in important positions, whereas the present day Islamic leaders do. The early khalifs were accessible to any Muslim, hardly the case with present Islamic rulers. Finally, the khalifs were quite modest. We have no portraits of them and do not know how they looked, whereas present day rulers put their portraits and images everywhere. He concluded that the present umma is corrupted, and unless its leaders return to early true Islam, nothing positive should be expected. It is clear that ISIS and the Taliban responded to these demands, and their external archaicization, the appeal to a bygone era, is in many ways modern and resonates with the feelings not just of Muslims but of considerable numbers of non-Muslims in the West who become ISIS sympathizers in the same way as their grandparents became Bolshevik sympathizers. This aspect of ISIS and the Taliban certainly influenced some members of the North Caucasian resistance who decided to join them, albeit they might not elaborate on this aspect of ISIS's philosophy and political program.

22.9 SUPPORTERS OF ISIS

While the ISIS image is in general quite negative in the discussion among members of the North Caucasian resistance, there is occasional praise. Some participants and supporters of North Caucasian resistance believed the affiliation with ISIS was a natural stage in the development of resistance, and polemic in this regard was launched on the site of *Kavkaz Center*, the major internet vehicle of the emirate.[24] One discussion participant noted that some people believe ISIS was the child of Americans or Israelis. This was not so; they are really enemies of the infidels. Their enemies were pseudo-Muslims, for they want to create a state where true Muslims and infidels live and enjoy the same rights.[25] These principles could hardly be acceptable in a Muslim state. While some of the members of North Caucasian resistance supported ISIS, others bitterly opposed them.

22.10 CRITICS OF ISIS

The fact that some members of Northern Caucasian resistance, mostly those who belong to the Caucasian Emirate, swear allegiance to Abu al-Baghdadi leads to fierce criticism of those who hold the old loyalties. They strongly criticize both the splinters and ISIS in general and state that ISIS overestimates its power and importance.

Elaborating on the role of ISIS, one observer noted that Abu al-Baghdadi controls just a limited territory and that from this perspective he was not different from leaders of other Islamic movements such as the Taliban and, by implication, al-Qaida. Their leaders understand the limits of their power and for this reason did not promulgate khalifat. It is clear that Abu al-Baghdadi's power is inflated. As a matter of fact he could do nothing to help Muslims who suffer under the rule of a variety of infidels.[26] Ali Abu Mukhammad (Aliaskhab Kebekov), until recently leader of the emirate, noted that if Abu al-Baghdadi was indeed so powerful he should have helped the mujahidin who fought infidels in the Northern Caucasus. Yet he received not a single fighter. As a matter of fact Abu al-Baghdadi could not be a legitimate khalif for he controlled a very limited territory.[27]

According to one of the contributors to the discussion, ISIS credentials were also questioned. ISIS lost the support of the local population due to its insane brutality. They strike not just infidels but even Muslims which makes them abhorrent in the eyes of many. Many Muslims have become fearful of any pious religious person. A person supposedly from Algeria noted that people in the past were ready to accept people with beards and help them. Now, after experiences with ISIS, they hate all bearded religious men.[28] The fact that ISIS was bombed by Westerners did not make it a wholesome organization.[29] The major problem with ISIS was that it split the ranks of mujahedeen.[30] This not only made them weaker but actually led to fighting among them. The same could be a problem in Northern Caucasus, where splinter groups have damaged the resistance. Treachery could also lead to splitting the mujahedeen forces with resulting bloodshed.[31] This argument implies that the fighters in North Caucasus could well engage in fraternal struggle. There were also implications that those who joined ISIS from abroad have become disenchanted;[32] in any case, resistance members should abnegate their oath of loyalty to Al-Baghdadi.[33] In the views of some contributors to the internet discussion, the fact that the rise of ISIS in North Caucasus had damaged and weakened the resistance indicates who was behind this process. In the view of the people from the emirate, Moscow was behind the split,[34] for only the Kremlin could benefit from the discord. Thus these observers from *Kavkaz Center* implied that the splinters are actually the creation of the Kremlin. Moreover, there was an implication that even ISIS was actually a creation of infidels. Consequently, in their YouTube address, the leaders of North Caucasian resistance strongly discouraged people from going to Syria and Iraq to fight.

The view of those who regard the split as forces weakening the North Caucasian resistance was actually valid. One could assume, at least retrospectively, that the variety of splits, starting with the emergence of the emirate, actually weakened the resistance. This notion is contradictory to the information spread in Russia and elsewhere that the Kremlin was quite alarmed by developments and could even collaborate with the West to fight the common enemy. But close analysis indicated this is hardly the case, or at least, the picture is more complicated. Moscow did see clearly the problems related to ISIS, but it saw benefits in those developments as well. The benefits were not reduced just to the fact that ISIS's influence in North Caucasus speeds disintegration of the resistance into small groups who might be as hostile to each other as to Russians and encourage mujahadeen emigration to the Middle East, from where most of them would not come back. The spread of ISIS also provides Moscow an opportunity to solve some of its foreign policy problems.

22.11 MOSCOW AND ISIS

At least at first glance, Moscow was quite alarmed by the rise of ISIS and similar movements and their implications for Russia. In December 2014 Moscow designated Al-Nusra, an al-Qaida affiliate, as a terrorist organization.[35] According to another report, the FSB (Russian Secret Police; Domestic Security Agency) was alarmed by ISIS's popularity in Russia[36] because those fighting with ISIS could come back to Russia. In the view of some observers, ISIS was more dangerous than the emirate. According to these observers, the emirate engages in terror against the siloviki—the representatives of law enforcement and the army. At the same time, ISIS preaches total terror.[37] Jihadists from Russia engage in the same monstrosities as other members of ISIS; according to one report, a "Russian speaking" ISIS soldier decapitated Iraqi prisoners.[38] Sergei Markedonov, one of the leading Russian specialists on the Middle East and Russian Muslims, noted that ISIS was much more driven by an ideology of internationalism than is the emirate, and for this reason was much more dangerous than the emirate. Because of the different ideological paradigms, ISIS could more easily recruit foreign fighters and send them back to Russia. He also noted that ISIS would fill the vacuum of the emirate because the latter recently could not engage in an effective terrorist campaign, and the number of terrorist actions in the North Caucasus has declined. This was implicitly acknowledged by the former leader of the emirate Ali Abu- Mukhammad (Aliaskhaf Kebekov). Markedonov noted that Kebekov stated that emirate fighters should not strike against civilians but only against the military and law enforcement. Markedonov commented that these statements are not because of a lack of resources but because Kebekov was indeed the most human among emirate leaders. This is hardly the case with new fighters, who affiliated themselves with ISIS and made them an extremely dangerous force.[39]

It would be wrong to assume that these statements were misleading in the sense that they did not address the Kremlin's worries. Moscow indeed continues to be concerned with Islamists. "Sources suggest that much of Moscow's concern over potential attacks on the Olympic infrastructure were related to the return of jihadists to their native Northern Caucasus. An amendment to Russia's anti-terrorism law in 2013 states that individuals 'training with the aim of carrying out terrorist activity' or involved with armed groups outside of Russia with aims contrary to Russian interests could be sentenced from ten to six years in prison, respectively."[40] The Russian press also informed readers that some Chechen leaders of ISIS regard Russia as their major target. For example, in October 2014 Tarkhan Batirashvili (Abu Omar al-Shishani), mentioned above, threatened to march on the North Caucasus despite Ramzan Kadyrov's statement that he was killed.[41] In any case those who supported either ISIS or the emirate are ready to fight the Russian state and still exist judging by internet discussions. One of the participants noted that the best way to deal with Russians is to blow up the oil and gas lines.[42] Still if ISIS was so frightening and a global threat in the eyes of the Russian elite, the Kremlin would have engaged in cooperation with Western powers, including the United States. That nothing or little has been done indicates that the Kremlin either disregards ISIS as a major priority, or actually saw it as mostly a tool of Washington to weaken Russia or a movement that could well be used to solve some of Russia's foreign policy problems.

22.12 FEAR OF ISIS IN THE WEST AND APPEAL TO THE WEST'S AND RUSSIA'S COMMON CAUSE

Up to 2018, ISIS had dodged attempts to dislodge it and the grisly beheadings create an image of it in the West as a serious threat. The view is that Islamism is becoming an ideology for a variety of discontented people.[43] Some of them are Western citizens and could come to the West to engage in terror. Consequently, for many, the end of ISIS should be regarded as a priority for American foreign policy; they believed America could start a new ground war[44] to dislodge ISIS at all costs. Western, including American, observers also implied that ISIS and Islamists in general were a threat to the entire human civilization, and everyone should cooperate regardless of disagreements and conflicts. Some American observers believe Russia and the United States should cooperate in fighting ISIS,[45] and these views were shared by some European observers. For example, Alexander Rahr, the well-known German specialist in Russian affairs, believed "America needs Russia's help in dealing with ISIS" and "that might start to change things."[46] Still there are no signs of this cooperation. And the Kremlin's dealings with ISIS are still quite limited.

It is quite likely that Russian security agencies were trying to infiltrate ISIS,[47] and ISIS claimed to have killed two agents who worked for FSB. Their goal was to kill one of the leaders of the movement.[48] Most likely FSB was concerned with the Chechen leaders of the movement who might return to Russia to engage in terrorist operations. The authorities engaged in some other anti-ISIS activities. For example, the authorities arrested people in Moscow who sent money to

ISIS.[49] But there were no signs of urgency, and Moscow authorities announced the allegiance of some emirate members to ISIS only in late spring 2015, several months after the events. Moreover, some Russian observers implied that ISIS's collaboration with the North Caucasian resistance could actually benefit Russia, or at least constitute only a limited threat. The point here is that fighters from Russia who go to Syria and Iraq would likely stay and die there, and very few would actually go back to Russia. Why are Russian authorities not much concerned with the return of jihadists whereas fear of jihadist repatriation of sorts alarms members of many Western governments? To understand this, one should understand why jihadists could come back.

There are, of course, many reasons why fighters could return. Some might decide that they could apply the knowledge and expertise of the Middle East in their homelands. Some could even be encouraged to go back to terrorist activities. This is indeed the case with some jihadists who come from Western countries and plan to go back to the West to engage in terror. Consequently there is an image of dangerous returning terrorists in Western mass media. They became peculiar messengers of global terror, perpetrators of the peculiar jihadist worldwide revolution. One can hardly have reliable information about the numbers of such individuals, but they definitely exist. But they are not the only ones who want to go back and, one can assume, they are not the majority of those who decide to do so. Many Westerners who decided to go to Iraq or Syria were motivated in the same way as any emigrant. Indeed, one could consider travel to the Middle East as a type of emigration. The incentives could be manifold. For some Westerners, these could be quite pragmatic: a good salary or sexual access to submissive slave girls or women. For others the incentives could be more sublime. In the West they faced a cold society of formal legalistic arrangements, where physical proximity and formal communal interactions have no existential value and often lead to deep emotional alienation, a subject well-developed in Western thought. The reference to existentialists could be sufficient here. This alienated individual of the modern West could almost instinctively look for an alternative: instead of the cold legalistic world of the modern capitalist West, he wants the warmth of personal ties emerging in a Gemeinschaft society, if we remember here Ferdinand Tönnies' definition. In a way he wants an emotional utopia as an extended family of caring relatives. These feelings merge with the sense of belonging to a great movement, shaping global history, and acquiring the meaning of life in deep metaphysical and emotional form. The emotional aspect of the ISIS appeal is quite important and cannot be countered by rational arguments or abstract discussion of the nature of true Islam. And these dreams are possibly another reason for many Westerners to go to the Middle East.

Many of these people presumably became disenchanted for a variety of reasons. And as often happens, the émigré may discover that the place he left is much better than the place he is now. Consequently he wants to go back. This seems to be what faced some Westerners who came to fight as newcomers.[50] This sort of information might concern Moscow, for the disenchanted fighters from the Russian Federation could come back and create problems. The Kremlin is genuinely concerned with jihadists in Russia who could acquire skills with chemical weapons while fighting in Syria, return to Russia, and engage in deadly terrorist attacks. Still one could assume that the Kremlin did not worry much now about such a scenario—a visible number of jihadists returning to Russia to engage in terror. There are several reasons for such an assumption. First, in a clear departure from the earlier al-Qaida scenario, Russia is not seen as a weakest link and a place on which much resources should be spent; as noted previously, the emirate leaders complained that they did not receive a single fighter from ISIS. Second, ISIS is qualitatively different from al-Qaida in one important aspect. Al-Qaida was in a way a truly volunteer organization and had no mechanism to enforce discipline on its followers. The autonomy of the affiliates was considerable. Even the September 11 attacks were conducted by like-minded people whose affiliation with al-Qaida was formal and in a way symbolic.

The story is different with ISIS. Similar to the Bolshevik state, it had a centralized system that strikes against not just enemies but also those who do not follow orders. One could assume that quite a few of those who come to ISIS-controlled territory could not easily depart unless sent by the ISIS leadership to conduct a certain assignment abroad. Most of those who come to ISIS-controlled territories cannot come back of their own free will or decide they changed their minds and were unwilling to fight. According to some reports, "ISIS fighters in Raqqah say the group has created a military police to clamp down on foreign fighters who do not report for duty."[51] At least a hundred were executed, meaning that ISIS leaders executed not only those they regarded as their enemies but also fighters who decided to quit, desert, or simply were reluctant to go to the front lines. One might assume that ISIS acted here in a way similar to the Bolsheviks. While official Soviet propaganda depicted the Red Army and Civil War as mostly driven by ideology and a sense of fighting for the "first state of workers and peasants," the reality was different. While Bolshevik propaganda played some role, the major reason for the Red Army martial spirit was harsh discipline reinforced not by slogans but by firing squads. It was hardly possible, even for foreign volunteers, to change their minds and drop out of the Red Army ranks without repercussions for themselves. Quitting and returning back home were not options. The same, most likely, is the case with quite a few foreigners, including fighters from Russia, who come to ISIS-controlled territory and then decide to go back without consent.

ISIS leadership does not regard Russia as a major front of jihad and provides no blessing or permission to go back. This, of course, does not mean it does not happen. Some groups of jihadists, including some from the former USSR, undoubtedly have some autonomy due to that fact that ISIS leaders could not always enforce strict discipline because of a lack of resources. And here they might be similar to Bolsheviks who also were not always able to enforce discipline to Red Army troops or affiliated units, e.g., detachments of anarchists. Still in most cases, ISIS leaders presumably enforce discipline and, if they believe the fighters from the former USSR are more needed in the Middle East, not in the place of their birth, these fighters will stay in the Middle East. One could assume that very few have the luxury to go back and forth of their own free will. It is a one-way road, and this is noted by Russian officials. For example, Sergei Smirnov, First Vice Chairman of FSB, stated that ISIS is quite interested in fighters who already swear allegiance to it.[52] This is due not just to prestige but also because of the practical implications: groups who acknowledge ISIS supremacy could send recruits, and they should stay in the Middle East, not be seasonal fighters who go back and forth.

Indeed, this happened in the case of the Caucasian Emirate. According to some reports, the emirate experienced a serious problem due to the influence of ISIS beginning in 2013. It was mostly due to the fact that the North Caucasian resistance became a pool for recruits, and in 2013–2014 there was an exodus of fighters to Syria and Iraq.[53] While ISIS attracts potential fighters from Russia, few return, and those who swear allegiance to ISIS and stay in Russia can be eliminated. According to Russian mass media, several resistance leaders who swore allegiance to ISIS were killed in Russia.[54] One of them extorted money from businessmen.[55] Those who fought in the Middle East met the same fate. This was, for example, the case with Abu Ibrahim Chechen.[56] Thus most experts in the Kremlin regarded ISIS as a rather limited threat despite some alarmist pronouncements. They assume that the continuing splitting or disintegration of the North Caucasian resistance was actually diminishing its threat for Russia. Still the threat of ISIS, real or imaginary, could help Moscow promote its own agenda in dealing with Iran and

Central Asian states. In any case, Moscow will not cooperate with Washington in dealing with Islamists.

22.13 NO COOPERATION WITH THE UNITED STATES

The Kremlin discarded the notion of cooperation with Washington for several reasons. The first reason is the Kremlin's assumption that Islamists are themselves a product of Washington. For example, Evgenii Lobachev, retired FSB General-Major, believed ISIS was created by the United States to destabilize the Arab world[57] and harm Russia and other countries hostile to the United States. Russian experts pointed out that Islamists emerged in Afghanistan during the Soviet occupation with American help. The idea that the United States continues to support Islamists to harm Syria and Iran is still in circulation, not just in Russia but also in the West.[58]

Another interpretation of events was that Islamists are not created by the United States to harm American enemies but the United States is still responsible for their rise. Putin, for example, believes ISIS is in many ways a byproduct of American policy.[59] He implied that the United States destroyed regimes such as that of Saddam Hussein assuming this would create a pro-Western regime to run the country. People in Washington, Putin implied, hardly understand that this brutal dictatorial regime was the only force that could have kept Islamists at bay. Furthermore, this regime, while not friendly to the United States, was not bound to fight the United States. The people in Washington, Russian experts implied, should have understood this. But they were fully convinced that destruction of these authoritarian regimes would lead to the "end of history" and creation of pro-Western regimes; in addition, the United States could fully control the oil and gas riches of the regions. These enterprises led to absolute failure. And while one interpretation of American policy implied that the people in Washington are conniving Machiavellians, another interpretation implied that they are sort of Machiavellian idiots who make one blunder after another assuming that they are engaged in sophisticated stratagems. These are not the type of people with whom one could well cooperate. The Kremlin could be pleased by Washington's problems in dealing with ISIS for other reasons as well. First, the U.S. bombing of ISIS transformed Washington into a major enemy of Islamists, and Russia may have disappeared from the Islamist radar almost completely or at least become marginalized. Second, Washington's engagement in the Middle East diverts resources from pressuring Russia. These feelings are shared by people in Beijing, Teheran, and possibly other capitals with which Washington has a tense relationship. While the rise of ISIS could divert Washington's attention from Moscow, it could help Moscow solve other geopolitical problems: dealing with Iran and Central Asia first of all.

22.14 IRANIAN EQUATION

Moscow was quite concerned with the possibility of Teheran falling into the American orbit. The decision to sell Teheran S-300 missiles which Russia should have sold to Iran in 2007 has two goals. First, it will keep Teheran closer to Moscow. Second, the missiles would seriously complicate U.S. or Israeli strikes against Iran, encouraging Iranian hardliners to be assertive with the West. The threat of ISIS, implicitly presented as United States handiwork, helps Moscow maintain ties with Teheran. Indeed, 60 experts from Russia and Iran created a headquarters in Baghdad to discuss how to deal with ISIS.[60] It is clear that Russian representatives will use this meeting not just to discuss how to deal with ISIS but to assure the Iranians that ISIS is a

U.S. creation that Washington tried to use against Teheran so Teheran shall not be too close to Washington. It is quite likely that Iranian counterparts share the same view.

22.15 CENTRAL ASIAN EQUATION

While the rise of ISIS could have marginal implications for Russia, at least at present, the story is quite different for Central Asia, where the fear of Islamism among the elite is genuine. The Russian mass media clearly emphasize the danger. According to Russian sources ISIS wants to get into Central Asia[61] and already has considerable numbers of fighters from the region, including secular Kazakhstan.[62] There were boys among them who could be engaged in the most grisly deeds. According to a report in the Russian mass media, a Kazakh-speaking boy killed two captured men, presumably Russian agents. The media emphasized the danger of increasing ISIS's influence in Afghanistan[63] and implied that Islamist control over Afghanistan would inevitably spell trouble for Central Asia. Some Central Asian publications acknowledged the problem. An observer from Fergana.ru acknowledged that the Taliban is more parochial, whereas ISIS is much more global[64] and wants to spread jihad in Central Asia. The Central Asian elite fear of Islamists has manifold implications for those in the Kremlin. On one hand they could well share this fear of Islamism, at least in the long run. Indeed, while Moscow might not be much concerned with Islamists at present, Islamization of Central Asia could be a serious problem. On the other hand, the Kremlin could also benefit from this fear, and these benefits could well be more important than the problems.

That Putin plans to create a Eurasian Union indicates Russia's desire to dominate most of the post-Soviet state, with Central Asia an important part. Kremlin plans in this direction are not proceeding smoothly and fear of Islamism could be a help. There is no doubt that the Kremlin sends a message to Central Asian capitals that the United States could hardly defend them, as Washington's failure in the Middle East demonstrated clearly. Moscow implies that only Russia could provide a modicum of security for these Central Asian regimes, or at least guarantee a safe haven for their leaders in the case of trouble. Thus, fear of Islamists penetrating Central Asia provides Moscow with arguments that all leaders of Central Asian states should move closer to Russia. Uzbekistan, for example, has been reluctant to join Russia-sponsored military or geopolitical alliances. The threat of Islamism pushed Tashkent closer to Moscow and Uzbekistan and both of them created a group to deal with the problem.[65] The danger of ISIS also helps Moscow to solidify the ranks of those states which join Russia in military and geopolitical alliances. In spring 2015, The Russian representative made a speech at the twenty-sixth meeting of the Regional Anti-terrorist Structure of SOC (Regional'naia Antiterroristicheskaia struktura ShOS).[66] Here he pointed out that ISIS is quite a dangerous group and all members of SOC should take the treaty seriously.

22.16 EUROPEAN EQUATION

Moscow also could use the fear of ISIS, and Islamists in general, in dealing with Europe. The Russian press informed readers that several Chechens suspected of preparing terrorist acts were arrested in France.[67] These arrests went along with mass arrests in Europe.[68] The implication is clear: Europe should understand that the North Caucasus, especially Chechnya, is a hotbed of terrorists who could be dangerous not just for Russians but also for Europeans. Consequently Europeans should not create problems for Moscow to deal harshly with North Caucasians.

22.17 SUMMARY

The spread of Islamism, including the emergence of ISIS, has a variety of implications for different countries. For some countries the rise has clearly negative implications. For others, Russia for example, the situation is more complicated. It is true that Moscow has concerns. The authorities in the Kremlin were clearly afraid that members of the Russian Muslim community could go to the Middle East and return to Russia after receiving training and expertise. For example, Syrian chemical weapons could fall into the hands of jihadists who could come back to Russia. But the rise of ISIS also has clear benefits for the Kremlin. It seems not enough people return from the Middle East to constitute a threat. At the same time, the Islamization of the North Caucasian resistance transformed the North Caucasus from a focus of the jihadist struggle to just one of the marginal fronts of global jihad. For many of them, not the North Caucasus but the Middle East—mostly Iraq and Syria— became the most important weakest link—to use Lenin's definition—whose collapse would lead to worldwide Islamic revolutions. The fact that the Middle East became a magnet for Russian Islamists is quite pleasing for Moscow, which has concluded that most of them will not come back, albeit this possibility is not excluded. The spread of ISIS also has other benefits for the Kremlin. Fear of ISIS could increase Russia's influence in Central Asia and strengthen ties with Iran.

One might note here that Russia is not the only country that tries to use the fear of ISIS for its benefit. One might look at Iran. While the United States possibly expects Iran to go deep into northern Iraq and Syria to wipe out remains of ISIS, the Iranians are not making such a move. One of course could propose that Iran does not want to get into Sunni areas where its soldiers would be seen as an occupational force. Another explanation might be that Iran does not want to eliminate ISIS completely because of the relationship with people in Damascus and Baghdad. Both are religiously close to Iranians, but they are ethnically different and this clearly alienates them from Iranians who have a strong sense of ethnic belonging and pride in their great pre-Islamic, pre-Arab civilization. Some Syrian and Iraqi elite could prefer to see both Syria and Iraq more assertive vis-à-vis Iran. The presence of ISIS or other Islamists, however, leaves them little choice but to be close to Iran as the only alternative to being overwhelmed by ISIS or similar Islamist movements. Thus it is in the interest of Teheran to keep ISIS alive as a potential threat to both Damascus and Baghdad. The Russian and Iranian case demonstrates that relationships of the regimes—even hostile to Islamists—to ISIS are more complicated than one would assume at first glance. The situation becomes even more complicated by the suspicion of these powers toward the United States, seen as actually a force behind the Islamists or, at least, the parent of a Frankenstein who got out of control and started to harm his creators.

All this convoluted and controversial dealing with ISIS implies that cooperation between the many powers dealing with Islamists would be extremely difficult and the ISIS state has a chance for survival. As a matter of fact, its fate could well be similar to that of the Bolshevik regime in the first years of its existence. Similar to ISIS, the Bolsheviks were outcasts among all the major powers and all major Western powers contributed military forces to deal with them during the Russian Civil War (1918–1920). Still because of mutual distrust and, of course, other reasons, they were not willing to commit their resources and coordinate their efforts with each other and Russian anti-Bolshevik forces. This made it possible for the Bolshevik regime to survive the first years of its existence when the regime was most vulnerable. The same could be the case with ISIS or a similar state or quasi-state driven by its version of worldwide revolution under not red but green banners. While the similarities between the Bolshevik regime in its first years of existence and ISIS are parallel, they certainly are not identical and their dynamics could be different. In the course of time, the Bolshevik regime, inspired by an initial drive for "worldwide proletariat revolution" experienced Thermidor, to use a term from the French Revolution. In the process, the regime became, in a way, a normalstate driven mostly by *raison d'état* in its idiosyncratic form. To be sure, the regime continued to appeal to the early revolutionary legacy until its very end. The revolutionary legacy would also be evoked in foreign policy ventures. But foreign policy would be mostly shaped by geopolitical pragmatism rather than by ideology and a desire to spread worldwide revolution, the serious motivation for early Soviet leaders. Some, like Trotsky, saw encouraging permanent revolution as the major goal of the regime. The fact that the Bolshevik regime in its later Stalinist and post-Stalinist modification used revolutionary ideology does not mean much. It was mostly a fig leaf.

There was nothing exceptional in this evolution and arrangements. One could find the same pattern in post- revolutionary China and Iran. One might even find the same model in U.S. political culture. During the George Bush era neo cons were a dominant ideological and political force. Some neo con leaders proclaimed that spreading political liberties, enforcing a Fukuyamian end of history, is the ultimate goal of American foreign policy, a new variation of manifest destiny. But this foreign policy was not ideologically driven and was in a way rational. The real policy was based on *raison d'état* as visualized by the people in the War Room of the White House. The abysmal failure of the entire imperial enterprise led to the quick disappearance of the neo con narrative from the public screen. The notion that the United States should spread liberty and democracy regardless of the cost, that this sacred goal motivates U.S. foreign policy, disappeared completely from the Washington agenda when the people in the White House realized that, instead of oil, gas, and assertion of American might, the war brought nothing but trouble. What could be seen as ideological or irrational in the actual geopolitical posture was due to overestimation of U.S. strength, and the inability to predict the results of actions but was not due to ideological obsessions; at least ideology or principles played a quite minor role.

The story could be different with ISIS or a similar state. As the ISIS state could well be compared with the Bolshevik regime in its incipient state. During that time, Bolsheviks indeed regarded "worldwide revolution" as the only way they could survive, or at least saw the stimulation of world revolution as the major *raison d'être* of the regime, and in a way a major manifestation of *raison d'état*, the way Bolsheviks thought to defeat their enemies. It is true that elements of pragmatism existed in early Bolshevik policy. Still, at least in the early stages, the Bolsheviks were not very calculating or pragmatic: quite a few believed in the creed, which they embraced with truly religious passion. Consequently they tried to stir up revolutionary violence even when it could be of little practical value for them. This sort of ideological irrationality, insanity if you wish, would decline in importance when the regime matured and started to operate as a normal state whose elite are driven by *raison d'état* by calculation of their interests, and what could be seen as signs of ideological insanity could be regarded as just overestimation of the elites' own power and abilities.

Still, this evolution into a statist reasonable stage the peculiar "thermidorization" of the regime, is not predestined, or at least could be delayed for a long time. Remember that in the case of the Soviet, Chinese, and Iranian regimes, thermidorization, the ossifying bureaucratic structure, the normalization of the regime followed open military confrontations with the outside world. In Soviet Russia, for example, this process started in earnest after the end of the Civil War (1917–1920). The Soviet leaders, of course, asserted that the country of workers and peasants was still abhorrent in the eyes of Capitalist predators who had not abandoned their plans to destroy Soviets. And this was true. Yet the regime had not been at war with the outside Capitalist/Western world until the outset of World War II. Moreover, as time proceeded, the Western powers started to accept the Soviet regime de facto and finally de jure, as just one of the other players, albeit a peculiar one. They opened embassies in Moscow and engaged with it on a variety of issues, from trade to military alliances. Moreover the Roosevelt administration possibly even contemplated the division of global leadership with "Uncle Joe" by the end of World War II, when the decline of the British Empire became increasingly clear.

Nothing of this sort of scenario can be seen with the ISIS state or similar Islamist state. Not only is it inconceivable that any Western power would recognize it in this form—at least in the foreseeable future—but direct confrontation with ISIS or similar Islamist state will be stopped. ISIS or other Islamist state, thus, would be in a condition of permanent war and this would prevent or at least delay a process of statist thermidorization similar to that of the Soviet, Chinese, or Iranian regimes. The permanent war would become the setting for the peculiar permanent revolution, in Trotsky's parlance. And if this happens ISIS or similar Islamist state could be frozen in its present condition for a long time and regard terror or jihad, not only as a tool for a particular and clearly defined geopolitical goal but as a goal in itself. At the same time the positions of some great powers, such as Russia, could help ISIS or similar Islamist state survive despite of the odds and to be, in way, frozen in its revolutionary terrorist form. Thermidorization of the regime might not happen at all, and the dynamics of ISIS and its implications for the global community might be different from other revolutionary regimes.

NOTES

1. John Gray, "How Marx turned Muslim," *The Independent*, 27 July 2002.
2. Mary Kaldor, "Restructuring Global Security for the Twenty-First Century," *The Quest for Security: Protection without Protectionism and the Challenge of Global Governance*, edited by Joseph E. Stiglitz and Mary Kaldor, Columbia University Press, 2013, p. 123.
3. Mark Brody, "The Chechen diaspora in Turkey," *The Jamestown Foundation*, Vol. 6, Issue 7, 2015.
4. "Raz'iasnenie nekotorykh aspektov provozglasheniia Imarata Kavkaz i protivodeistvie etomu natsional – demokraticheskikh gruppirovok," http://www.kavkazcenter.com/russ/content/2014/11/2 2/10699.shtml, 27 December, 2014.
5. Swati Sharma, "Map: How the flow of foreign fighters to Iraq and Syria has surged since October," *Washington Post*, 27 January 2015.
6. Carlotta Gall, "Tunisia is shaken as young women turn to extremism with deadly results," *New York Times*, 20 November 2014.
7. Peter R. Neumann and Katie Rothman, "Foreign fighters total in Syria/Iraq now exceeds 20,000; surpasses Afghanistan conflict in the 1980s," *Insight*, 26 January 2015.
8. "V RF rassleduiut pochti 60 del o voiuiushchikh na storone 'Islamskogo gosudarstva' rossiianakh," *Interfax*, 30 January 2015.
9. "FSB IG pytaetsia verbovat' storonnikov na severnom kavkaze,"*Vladimirskaia Oblast'*, 11 April 2015.
10. "FSB: 'Islamskoe gosudarstvo' ugrozhaet Rossii i sosednim stranam," *Newsru.co.il*, 11 Aprill 2015.
11. "V Rossii zaderzhany predpolagaemye posobniki 'Islamskogog gosudarstva' – Rosbalt," *Vedomosti*, 28 October 2014.
12. "V Rossii proshli zaderzhaniia posobnikov IG," *Gazeta.ru*, 28 October 2014.
13. "BS RF: Boevik 'IG' ugrozhavshii Rossii, iavliaetsia grazhdaninom Gruzii," *rg.ru*, 30 January 2015.
14. "V MIDRF ne veriat v mif o massovom ukhode kavkaztsev v IGIL," *Islamnews.ru*, 16 January 2015.
15. Ben Hubbard and Eric Schmitt, "Army know-how seen as factor in ISIS successes," *New York Times*, 27 August 2014.
16. Emil Souleimanov and Megan Ouellete, "The participation of North Caucasian Jihadists in the Syrian Civil War and Its Security Implications," *Rubin Center Research in International Affairs*, http://www.rubincenter.org/2015/02/theparticipation-of-North-Caucausian-jihadists-in-the-s, 22 February 2015.
17. "Mansu" comments, http//:checheninfo.com/2014/11/23, 20 January, 2015.

18. "Mul'ko" comments, http//:checeninfo.com/2014/11/23, 20 January, 2015

19. Taimoor Shah and Joseph Galdstein, "Taliban fissures in Afghanistan are seen as an opening for ISIS," *New York Times*, 21 January 2015.

20. Michael Foucault, *I, Pierre Rivière, Having Slaughtered My Mother, My Sister, and My Brother – A Case of Patricide in the 19th Century*, University of Nebraska Press, 1975.

21. One might recall the event known as September Days, when after mass lynchings and rape in Paris prisons the heads of some victims, including women, were put on spears and paraded through the town.

22. Employee of *the New York Times* and Ben Hubbard, "Life in a jihadist capital: Order with a darker side," *New York Times*, 23 January 2014.

23. Azam Ahmed, "Taliban are rising again in Afghanistan's North," *New York Times*, 22 October 2014.

24. "Raz'iasnenie nekotorykh aspektov provozglasheniia Imarata Kavkaz i protivodeistvie etomu natsional – demokraticheskikh gruppirovok," http://www.kavkazcenter.com/russ/content/2014/11/22/10699.shtml, 27 December, 2014.

25. Anonymous comments, http://www.kavkazcenter.com/russ/content/2014/12/25/107471.shtml, 27 December 2014.

26. Mukhammad ibn Salik Al-Mukhadzhir (Abu Sulayman al – Muhajir), "Kratkoe izlozhenie diskussii po povodu provozglasheniia khalifata. Chats' 3 i 4," *Kavkaz Center*, http://www.kavkazcenter.com/russ/content/2014/09/20/106299.shtml, 20 September 2014.

27. "Sheikh al'-Makdisi: Prisiaga Abubakru Bagdadi ne imect sily i vnosit raskol sredi mudzhakhidov," http://www.kavkazcenter.com/russ/content/2014/12/31/107534.shtml, 31 December 2014.

28. "Sekrety informatsionnoi politiki 'Islamskogo Gosudarstva' i ee rol' v formirovanii ego vzgliada i mankhadzha sredi ego storonnikov," http://alisnad.com/?p=2028, 14 January 2015.

29. Anonymous comments, http://www.alisnad.com/?p=1952, 27 December 2014.

30. "Poslanie ot mudzhakhida Shama k mudzhakhidam Imrata Kavkaz," http://alisnad.com/?p=1972, 29 December, 2014.

31. "Raz'iasnenie kadiia Dagestana Abu Usmana po povodu prisiagi Abu Mukhammada Kadarskogo Abubakru Bagdadi," *Kavkaz Center*, 26 December 2014.

32. "IGIS lovit dezertirov i nesoglasnykh. V gruppirovke narastaiut etnicheskie treniia mezhdu … uzbekami i chechentsami," *Nezavisimaia Gazeta*, 27 December 2014.

33. "Sheikh al'-Makdisi: Prisiaga Abubakru Bagdadi ne imect sily i vnosit raskol sredi mudzhakhidov."

34. "Vilaiat Dagestan. Asil'derov Rustam ob'iavil, chto dal prisiagu lideru IG al'-Bagdadi," http://www.kavkazcenter.com/russ/content/2014/12/20/107411.shtml, 27 December, 2014.

35. "'Islamskoe gosudarstvo' priznano v RF terroristicheskoi organizatsiei," *Izvestiia.ru*, 29 December, 2014.

36. "FSB ishchet v Rossii sponsorov organizatsii 'Islamskoe gosudarstvo'," *govoritmoskva.ru*, 27 October 2014.

37. "Akhmet Iarlykapov 'Islamskoe gosudarstvo' zavoiuet Severnyi Kavkaz cherez internet," *Kavkazskii Uzel*, 10 April 2015.

38. "Russkoiazychnye boeviki IG obezglavili irakskogo soldata," *Gazeta.ru*, 14 February 2015.

39. Sergei Markedonov, "Ugrozy dlia Severnogo Kavkaza: 'Imarat' ili IGIL?" *bloogs.voanews.com*, 22 Apreal 2015.

40. Emil Souleimanov and Megan Ouellete, "The participation of North Caucasian jihadists in the Syrian civil war and its security implications," http://www.rubincenter.org/2015/02/the-participation-of-North-Caucasian-jihadists-in-the-s, 22 February 2015.

41. "V Rossii rassleduetsia ne menie 58 ugolovnykh del, sviazannykh s uchastiem rossiian v boiakh na storone Islamskogo gosudarstva," *echo.msk.ru*, 30 January 2015.

42. Anonymous comments, http://www.kavkazcenter.com/russ/content/2015/01/14/107677.shtml, 14 January 2015.

43. Graham Fuller, "Yes, it is Islamic extremism – but why?" http://grahamefuller.com/yes-it-is-islamic-extremism-but-why, 22 February 2015.

44. "Rules of engagement: Still missing," *New York Times*, 10 December 2014.

45. Thomas Graham and Simon Saradzhyan, "ISIS worst nightmare: The U.S. and Russia teaming up on terrorism," *National Interest*, 11 February 2015.
46. Neil Buckley, "Putin makes West an offer wrapped up in a warning," *Financial Times*, 27 October 2014.
47. Elena Chernenko, Oleg Rubnikovich, Mariia Efimova, and Andrei Smirnov, "Khalifat upolinomochen zaiavit', 'y' uznal podrobnosti o lakoby rasstreliannykh v Sirii 'agentakh FSB'," *Kommersant.ru*, 15 January 2015.
48. "Islamisty opublikovali video kazni dvukh 'agentov FSB'," *infox.ru*, 13 January 2015.
49. "FSB zaderzhali desiatki podozrevaemykh v pomoshchi boevikam IG," *Total.kz*, 28 October, 2014; "V Rossii zaderzhany posobniki 'Islamskogo gosudarstva'," *Argumenty i Fakty*, 28 October, 2014.
50. "IGIS lovit dezertirov i nesoglasnykh. V gruppirovke narastaiut etnicheskie treniia mezhdu... uzbekami i chechentsami,"*Nezavisimaia Gazeta*, 27 December 2014.
51. "ISIS executes 100 foreign fighters for trying to flee Syria," *The Peninsula*, 21 December 2014.
52. "FSB preduprezhdaet IG ishchet storonnikov na Severnom Kavkaze," *Pravda.Ru*, 10 April 2015.
53. Akhmet Iarleykapov," 'Islamskoe gosudarstvo zavoiuet Severnyi Kavkaz cherez internet'," *Kavkazskii Uzel*, 10 April 2015.
54. Artem Filipenok, "NAK soobshchil o likvidatsii prisiagnuvshikh IGIL bandoglavarei, "*RBK*, 24 April 2015.
55. "Unichtozhennye v Dagestane lidery boevikov ranee prisiagnuli 'Islamskomu gosudarstvu'," *Kommersant*, 24 April 2015.
56. "Smi soobshchili o likvidatsii v Irake komandira IG Abu Ibragim Chenchentsa," *RBK*, 1 May 2015.
57. "IGIL vyshlo iz-pod kontrolia. I eto samaia bol'shaia problema SShA – general FSB v otstavke," *Pravda.ru*, 10 April 2015.
58. "Ra MZi" comments, http://www.huffingtonpost.com/dr-josef-olmert/assad-is-losing-and-iran-_b_7176248.html?...
59. "Putin v interv'iu nazval deistviia amerikanskoi koalitsii protiv 'Islamskogo gosudarstva' nelegitim-nymi," *Central Asia.ru*, 9 March 2015.
60. "Iran i Rossiia sozdali operativnyi shtab po bor'be s IG," *Central Asia*, 23 October 2014.
61. "Vrag u vorot 'Islamskoe gosudarstvo' na podstupakh k Rossii," *RIA Nososti*, 6 February 2015.
62. "Teroristicheskaia gruppa IGIL vylozhila v set' video, gde rebenok ubivaet 'russkikh shpionov'," *Regnum.ru*, 13 January 2015.
63. Vladimir Skosyrev, "Boeviki v Afganistane perekhodiat pod znamena IGIL," *Nezavisimaia Gazeta*, 23 January 2015.
64. "Taliban i Islamskoe gosudarstvo: Takticheskie soiuzniki ili nepremirimye soperniki," *Fergana.ru*, 20 January 2015.
65. "FSB: nekotorye komandiry 'Imarata Kavkaz' prisiagnuli IGIL," *Argumenty o i Fakty*, 10 April 2015.
66. Mariia Bondarenko, "Komandiry 'Imarata Kavkaz' nachali prisiagat' 'Islamskomu gosudarstvu'," *RBK*, 15 April 2015.
67. "Terror. Vo Frantsii brosheny v tiur'mu 5 chechentsev 'za podgotovku terakta'," http://www.kavkazcenter.com/russ/content/2015/01/20/107759.shml, 20 January 2015.
68. Aleksand Stepanov, "Obraz chechentsa vo frantsuzskoi romantike: otkuda v Evrope terroristy s Kavkaza," *MK.ru*, 20 Janaury 2015.

International Cooperation with Online Terrorism

Instruments and Arrangements against Online Terrorism Relating to International Cooperation

Ali Dizboni and Christian Leuprecht

CONTENTS

23.1 INTRODUCTION

Contemporary expert and practitioner literature on the causal relations between the internet and terrorism is largely divided into three groups (Conway 2016, 123). First, skeptics question causality in light of lower cyber activism in high-intensity extremist conflict zones; instead, they emphasize the primacy of real life factors over virtual ones. The second group acknowledges a lack of irrefutable data to prove causality but insists on a positive correlations between online activism and violent radicalization. From a practical standpoint, this group argues that overlooking radicalization that originates on the internet could undermine policies to legislate and manage cyberspace for the sake of public safety and security (Conway 2016, 23). A third position seeks to bridge the cyber and physical worlds in understanding radicalization (Bouchard and Levy 2015, 1–2). Internet activism is key to radicalization but has the greatest impact on individuals who are already motivated and who use cyberspace as an accelerator toward violent extremism. These authors disagree that cyber "causes" radicals to be born, mature, and evolve online.[1] For this last group, the virtual universe is a labyrinthine media ecology in which physical and virtual environments produce complex interactions.

Still there is wide agreement that the internet has strategic value for extremist actors and would-be violent radicals. The literature identifies five core uses of the internet by terrorist entities and actors: "...information provision, financing, networking, recruitment, and information gathering" (Conway 2006, 2).[2] The virtual space gives terrorists significant leverage and advantage: ease of access, anonymity, interactivity, proactivity, customized messaging and control over narratives, international scope and consequently, a larger pool to recruit sympathisers, activists, and violent radicals. Since 9/11, terrorist groups have increasingly adopted the internet as an integral part of their asymmetric strategies to compensate for loss of access to mainstream media (O'Halloran et al. 2018).

The complexity of the cyber–physical nexus in an era of evolving globalization creates crucial risks to open societies and daunting challenges to counter violent extremism (CVE) measures. The following discussion on Canada–U.S. cooperation will show the incrementally comprehensive and expanding partnership: increasing outreach to a variety of actors, deepening understanding of the nature of radicalization (ideology, gender/religious/secular), and streamlining interagency cooperation. Furthermore, this bilateral partnership is conducted within increasingly nationally coordinated leadership and oversight.

Countering online radicalization in the United States and Canada is part of broader CVE programs with strong conceptual similarities. Public Safety Canada uses the terminology of *prevent, detect, deny, and respond* and implements a three-pronged strategy. First, outreach to academia and practitioners focuses on research and experimentation on different aspects of CVE including homegrown online extremism. The second prong refers to community engagement initiatives, such as the RCMP National Security Awareness and Community Outreach Program, and the Cross-Cultural Roundtable on Security. The key objectives are to raise awareness, strengthen resilience, and lead the effective implementation of community-tailored CVE programs. Third, the Canadian government's international engagement is framed as seeking to raise awareness of CVE abroad and to augment global capacity to prevent terrorism as well as extremists from entering Canada (Tierney 2017, 68–9). In comparison, U.S. CVE strategy runs under the Department of Homeland Security (DHS) and the State Department. The U.S. government also follows a three-pronged CVE strategy along the same lines (DHS 2016; Department of State and USAID 2016 as cited by Michel Tierney 2017). The difference is the U.S. government's broader access to philanthropic and tech communities to attract more resources for CVE initiatives, including counter-extremism messaging campaigns. While the private sector is more engaged in the United States (Tierney 2017, 68–9), Canada's recent initiatives point toward bridging this gap and strengthening the partnership.

23.2 INTERNATIONAL TOOLS AND ARRANGEMENTS ON INTERNATIONAL COOPERATION AGAINST ONLINE TERRORISM

United Nations documents note the lack of universal instruments[3] on cyber issues. More specifically, in the absence of global instruments and arrangements on countering online terrorism and extremism, regions and countries turn to bilateral and multilateral cooperation mechanisms between their intelligence and law enforcement agencies (UNODC 2012, 74). Besides their legal components, these tools and arrangements have significant non-legislative measures: "A key element in the successful provision of effective international cooperation is the presence of a properly resourced and proactive central authority which can, based on any available mechanisms (both formal and informal), facilitate cooperation in a timely and efficient manner" (UNODC 2012, 83). Considering the critical and complex nature of cyberterrorism, these non-legislative measures of cooperation succeed where lead CVE agencies and partners build trust and confidence both nationally and internationally (UNODC 2012, 85).[4]

The United States and Canada play an active role in international cyber cooperation frameworks such as the G7 but, more importantly, the Five Eyes (FVEY). The G7, primarily a regime for economic cooperation, is made up of three FVEY members plus Germany, Japan, Italy, and France. Its 2018 communiqué shows similarities but also contrasts with the FVEYs statements on cyber security. First, the G7 is more geographically inclusive and seeks to reach other states and regions. Second, there are explicit references to UN resolutions and conventions. One example is the following reference to cyber security: "Implement the following UNSCRs ourselves and support others to implement: UNSCR 2178 (2014) and 2396 (2017) on foreign terrorist fighters, with particular reference to passenger data, biometric border systems implementation, prevention of violent extremist and terrorist use of the Internet, and recognition of the importance of whole-of-government counterterrorism approaches and working with civil society" (G7 2018, 7). In another statement issued at the same G7 2018 conference but by interior ministers, cyber security challenges attract special but broader attention in terms of variety (gender, ideology, vectors) of cyber threats and the nature of CVE cooperation (private sector including multinationals).[5] The following highlights are indicative of the G7 security minsters' approach: intensive information sharing including battlefield data, shift of discourse from religious radicalization to hateful ideologies, necessary close collaboration with private industry (Facebook, Google, Twitter, and Microsoft) and communities with deep, common, and urgent action based on the understanding of the nature of threats. The linkage between radicalization and the internet is described as "a tool for recruitment, training, propaganda, and financing, often by exploiting the different ways men and women can be targeted online. Therefore, countries need to address this problem intelligently by investigating the gender-based strategies of terrorist groups" (G7 2018a, 3). In the same statement, the section on Preventing Violent Extremist and Terrorist Use of the Internet provides more specific arrangements including cooperation between government and industry by improving 'communication and transparency with our governments on industry-led efforts through its Executive Board, supported by a Secretariat" strengthening "transparency [...] through the adoption of performance metrics [...] including the removal of content and accounts within 1 hour of upload, where technically feasible, without compromising accuracy" preventing "the recurrence of violent extremist and terrorist content by contributing to and utilizing the Shared Industry Hash Database and by publishing performance metrics" encouraging "industry to update the Terms of Service of all platforms so as to inform users of the consequences under the applicable national law of promoting terrorist content and using the crowdfunding and payment services provided online for terrorism financing." Finally the declaration emphasizes "the need to support, local and credible gender-responsive voices, with a particular emphasis on youth, in the delivery and development of alternative and counter narratives." This expansive and comprehensive inter-subjectivity on the nature of radicalization and CVE mechanisms is reflected in other peer forums.

While the FVEYs share concerns and values with the G7, its membership is narrower but better integrated. Older than the G7, the FVEYs were founded in the wake of the Second World War, strengthened during the Cold War, and have since become prominent in multilateral security cooperation. In contrast to other cooperation forums, FVEYs sharing of information is more integrated and intensive. Biometrics indicate how integrated FVEY intelligence is in data collection and sharing. The United States introduced biometric technology in 2002, states. The High Value Data Sharing Protocol under the Five Country Conference (FCC) on immigration and border protection commits FVEY signatory states to share biometrics data (Hamaid 2017, 57–8).

In their joint communiqué in 2017, Ministers of Interior, Immigration and Attorneys General of Australia, Canada, New Zealand, the United Kingdom, and the United States emphasized their partnership to deal with "the relentless threats of terrorism, violent extremism, cyber-attacks, and international instability." The following four objectives are particularly relevant in terms of targets and levels of cooperation that vastly surpass G7 goals:

> A shared approach to engaging with communication service providers to address online terrorist activities and propaganda, and to support a new industry forum led by Google, Facebook, Microsoft and Twitter;
>
> Collectively enhancing knowledge on key issues such as design and support for local-level initiatives and sharing of best practices in prevention, intervention, and rehabilitation, such as approaches to mitigating the threat posed by returning foreign terrorist fighters and their families;
>
> Examine the role of traditional and social media and community voices in facilitating or disrupting processes of radicalization to violence or the threat of terrorist propaganda, and to support effective practices in this area.
>
> *(Five Eyes 2017, 2)*

Toward the end of this short document, two sections discuss tools and arrangements against online terrorism, namely cyber security and encryption. The FVEY emphasize

> "robust cooperation underway between our five countries on cyber issues and note [...] collective efforts to study and assess key emerging issues and trends in cyber security to prevent, detect and respond to cyber threats." To tackle the challenge that encryption poses to public safety, they re-emphasize their commitment to engage with private communication technology companies to uphold cyber security.
>
> *(Five Eyes 2017, 4)*

23.3 ASYMMETRIC CONTEXT OF CANADA–U.S. COOPERATION

Cyber security cooperation between Washington and Ottawa progressed in a context of asymmetric resources and capacities yet with increasing breadth and depth since 9/11, catapulting national/ homeland security concerns to the forefront of strategic relations. Moens et al. (2015, 21) observes: "As with much of the Canada–US partnership on security-related matters, Canada–US cooperation for cybersecurity goes even further than the Five Eyes. Close cooperation occurs between the NSA and the Communications Security Establishment (CSE) to target 'approximately 20 high-priority countries' in the collection of signals intelligence (SIGINT)."

Mueller and Stuart (2011) have shown that U.S. direct and indirect expenditures on homeland security up to 2011 surpassed a trillion dollars. By comparison, Canadian expenditures were $24 billion between 2001–2008. As of 2017, DHS and the Canada Border Services Agency respectively employ 240,000 and 13,000 people (Eagles and Nanos 2017). This asymmetry in capacities and resources does not, however, translate into U.S. intelligence auto-sufficiency toward FVEY in general and Canada in particular. As the previous quotation shows, without such cooperation,

U.S. intelligence collection of full spectrum threats would be incomplete, vulnerable, and less effective. The trade-off between sovereignty and integration is possible where the less resourced Canada could expose itself to the intelligence impact factor of its ally:

> Since Canada has a more limited ability to develop sophisticated technology, Canada acquires and uses NSA capabilities (US, National Security Agency, Central Security Service 2013) to help manage its portion of the partnership's mission. Inevitably, the United States influences some of the intelligence gathering done by Canada.
>
> *(Moens et al. 2015, 21)*

23.4 ACTION PLANS

In terms of action plans on cyber radicalization, the Cybersecurity Action Plan between Public Safety Canada and the Department of Homeland Security (Public Safety Canada 2015, 3–4) outlines the integrated action plan:

> Enhance information sharing at all classification levels and collaborate on training opportunities, while promoting inter-agency coordination;
>
> Coordinate on cybersecurity incident response management, relating to defense, mitigation, and remediation activities and products, including with other public and private entities consistent with each country's laws and policies;
>
> Align and standardize cyber incident management processes and escalation procedures; and
>
> Enhance technical and operational information sharing in the area of industrial control systems Security.

Two years, later, these policy targets were strengthened by the latest Public Report on the Terrorist Threat in Canada (Public Safety Canada 2017) but within the FVEY framework, which echoes the aforementioned FVEYs communiqué of 2017:

> One of Canada's most important multilateral alliances for intelligence and information sharing is with the "Five Eyes" community […]. This partnership, which involves bodies focused on security, intelligence, cyber, migration, borders and law enforcement, works collaboratively to counter the spread of violent extremism and recruitment efforts by extremist groups.

The Report emphasizes the integrated engagement with Communications Service Providers to address terrorist activities and propaganda online, as well as to examine the role of traditional and social media and community voices in facilitating or disrupting processes of radicalization to violence, and to support effective practices in this area. Canada's participation in these Five Eyes groups is a reflection of our commitment to integrating our approaches where a collective response is required.

Possibly the latest significant arrangement to reach objectives outlined in bilateral but also multilateral cyber security agreements was taken on June 12, 2018, with Public Safety Canada (PSC), the Department of National Defense (DND), and the Department of Innovation, Science and Economic Development (ISED) announcing the new Canadian Strategy for Cyber Security, following recommendations of the bill C-51 in 2018. The objective is to safeguard against threats to digital privacy, security, and the economy. This new strategy integrates and consolidates federal cyber operations in the newly established Canadian Center for Cyber Security (CCCS), launched October 2018 and fully operational by 2020 with "one clear and trusted national authority" overseeing numerous federal departments. The Royal Canadian Mounted Police (RCMP) now has enhanced investigative powers of major cyber crimes in coordination with the CCCS and increased cooperation with international partners (Public Safety Canada 2018a). The same report (p. 11) emphasizes two principal arguments behind the new CCCS: first, external partners want a reliable focal point of centralized federal government leadership on cyber security. Second, partners want consistent messaging, advice, and guidance from the Canadian government. For the same reason, the CCCS is the primary point of contact with the federal government for international partners on cyber security operational matters.

23.5 NATIONAL STRATEGIES ON COUNTERING ONLINE TERRORIST PROPAGANDA AND VIOLENT EXTREMISM

The new Canadian cyber strategy makes no explicit mention of online terrorism, radicalization, and extremism. Rather, it employs the broader terminology of cyber threats emanating from state-sponsored or non-states actors, criminals, and other cyber malicious actors. Online radicalization is embedded under the types of cyber menaces. Cyber threats are defined as "malicious cyber actors include individual hackers and insider threats, criminal networks, nation states, terrorist organizations, and state-sponsored actors" (Canada Cyber Strategy 2018, 12). Experts point out the common, yet differently phrased, U.S.–Canadian understanding of cyber threats, "The Canadian and American strategies generally focus on three categories of threats: other states attempting to steal Canadian and American secrets; organized crime using cyberspace to make illegal profits; and terrorists using the Internet to recruit members and raise funds" (Moens et al. 2015, 16).

The latest action and strategy documents on cyber are the White House (2018) National Cyber Strategy of the United States of America and the Federal Terrorism Response Plan: Domestic Concept of Operations (White House 2018). A quick review of the salient points regarding international cyber cooperation reveals enhanced commitments yet not necessarily formulated in a bilateral framework. U.S. documents emphasize international cyber cooperation (interoperability, intelligence sharing, training) with "like-minded countries, industry, academia and civil society" (25). While the White House does not mention specific alliances, regions or countries, Ottawa is more specific:

> Canada's response to a terrorist incident may rely on information and intelligence sharing with international allies, especially with FiveEyes partners. Communicating with allies during an incident will take many forms, particularly: Department-to-department through pre-established protocols and arrangements; Agency-to-agency; Operations centre to operations centre; and through established (official) channels via Global Affairs Canada.
>
> *(Public Safety Canada 2018b, 9–10)*

23.6 CASE STUDY: PREVENTING ONLINE TERRORIST PROPAGANDA, RADICALIZATION AND ONLINE REHABILITATION IN PRISONS

Prisons among all of the OECD's 57 members are affected by radicalization (Neumann 2017). Canadian intelligence assessments identify "angry, maladjusted young men whose blood is stirred at images of grisly beheadings and the crucifixion of so-called apostates" as preferred target audiences for terrorist propaganda. Prisons are a source and a mechanism of online and on-site radicalization. In the words of the Canadian Security Intelligence Service (CSIS), prisons "serve as training academies and safe locations for indoctrination and planning" (CSIS 2015, 28), especially for foreign fighters facing criminal trials. Many sustain heightened levels of grievances, ideological beliefs, and motivations. Prolonged incarceration may aggravate their radicalism and render impossible their release (RCMP 2009, 10; CSIS 2015, 141; House Committee on Homeland Security 2016, 15).

Such observations are echoed and analyzed in greater detail in non-governmental academic research (Leuprecht et al. 2015). Incarcerated radicals and foreign fighters become a source for recruiting like-minded, willing or vulnerable inmates. Field research suggests that convicted extremists act as recruiters (Hamaid 2017, 47–65, 52; Neumann 2017, 47–8).

Given the virtual-physical characteristics of prison radicalization, the available literature suggests a number of arrangements to prevent and counter radicalization in prisons which, for the most part, are considered by U.S. and Canadian correctional services:

- Some suggest avoiding overpopulated prison systems and making prison more compartmentalized and safe (Neumann 2017, 47). Other research suggests methods "that isolate recruiters, denies extremists access to prisoners, and exclude radical religious service providers and extremist texts from prison. We also need to familiarize prison staff with radicalization, ensure that perceptions of discrimination that sustain radical beliefs are stamped out within the prison system, and establish a de-radicalization strategy that can help Canadian terrorists disengage from violence and properly reintegrate into society." This research points out to the comparing practices of counter-radicalization. Canada could "[learn] from [...] allies' experiences, [...] reduce the likelihood that terrorists will emerge from our prisons in larger numbers than they entered them" (Wilner 2010, 4).
- Training is another recurrent theme in the literature. In the Canadian context, observations include creating an "extremism unit within the Correctional Service of Canada (CSC) whose tasks are the continuous monitoring of trends in radicalization (in all its forms) and informing policy and responses"(Wilner 2010, 4; House Committee on Homeland Security 2016, 15). It also includes producing prison guides for internal use so prison guards can detect indicators and signs of radicalization.[6]
- A third recommendation is to reach out and to facilitate greater academic access to interviewing inmates and working with prisoners and the prison system.
- A fourth suggestion, with controversial implications for civil liberties,[7] is deterrence by denial and close monitoring. Some recommend denying inmates access to online resources or to other inmates for recruitment purposes. Related measures include tracking at-risk prisoners and potential recruiters, containing, banning, and controlling suspicious recruitment, tracking incarcerated terrorists as they move around the prison system and throughout their prison sentence, and monitoring social interactions with other inmates (Wilner 2010). Experts suggest that a sophisticated system of reporting and intelligence could diminish the risks of breaching inmates' civil rights (Neumann 2017).
- A fifth suggestion refers to community involvement. Increasingly Western governments have prison imams. As Neumann says (2017, 48), "The underlying rationale is that imams can minimise—if not deny—the (spiritual) space that might otherwise be available to extremists. In many cases, prison imams are expected to provide not only religious and spiritual services, but serve as counsellors, social workers, experts in radicalisation,

and—more generally—interlocutors between the prison authorities and Muslim prisoners." Other researches will go farther and suggest employment of community members as prison staff and guards because "They can more easily interact with Muslim prisoners and will have a better appreciation for the nuance of religious practice, identifying and differentiating between prayer and radicalization" (Wilner 2010, 23; Wilner and Crowley 2011).

23.7 COUNTER VIOLENT EXTREMISM AND COMMUNITY TAILORED POLICING

The latest Public Safety Canada report (2017) has a section on community engagement prevention efforts where preventing individuals from becoming radicalized is a key component of Canadian CVE. For the sake of coordination, Public Safety Canada established the Canada Centre for Community Engagement and Prevention of Violence (Canada Centre) in 2017. The Canada Centre leads Canadian counter-radicalization through three policy priorities "advancing key policy priorities; engaging with communities; supporting local-level programming through the Community Resilience Fund; and, advancing action-oriented research." As part of its CVE action, the Canada Centre tackles online violent extremism. One key challenge to its intervention, as seen before in similar cases, is to balance competing priorities, i.e. safeguarding charter rights and denying and deterring violent extremists online. Consistent with its international agreements, the Canada Centre will implement its counter-extremist action in collaboration with communications service providers and international partners. One key venue of this cooperation is the Global Internet Forum to Counter Terrorism (GIFCT) established by the communication giants like Facebook, Microsoft, Twitter, and Google. In the words of the Public Safety Canada Report (2017), the efficiency of customized counter-radicalization to detect the diversity of individual paths to online extremism requires teamwork with multiple actors across multiple sectors, including community-based organizations.

In line with the policy priorities of the Canada Centre, Public Safety Canada's Community Resilience Fund (CRF) provides grants and financial assistance to organizations involved in programs and research on radicalization and violence. Four granting priorities are meant to strengthen bottom-up social research and initiatives "Intervention programming, Performance measurement and evaluation tools, Action-oriented research, Youth engagement and the development of alternative narratives."[8]

While the primary task of the police is to counter terrorism, law enforcement can also contribute to countering radicalization. Community policing is based on the assumption that effective safety is built on a relationship between the citizenry and law enforcement. According to Neumann (2017, 51–2):

In practice, community policing boils down to three core principles. The first is an emphasis on *partnerships* with community organisations and leaders, including youth, women, religious and ethnic minority groups, as well as business and other civil society organisations, which police should engage and seek to build honest, long term relationships with. The second is *problem-solving*, which means that police should listen to communities and be responsive to their concerns, even when they are not high on its own list of priorities. Finally, community policing is meant to be *proactive* and *preventive* because it seeks to educate and mobilise people before a problem has festered or turned into criminal activity.

Police partnering with communities in countering radicalization shares the burden between state and society and redresses the perception of spying, policing thought, or the surveillance state. Communities should realize that they are the true stakeholders in preventing extremism and radicalization (Neumann 2017, 51–2).

The RCMP, as the federal police force has the lead on and executes many counter-radicalization programs. The First Responder Terrorism Awareness Program (FR-TAP) team is a prominent example. It targets all violent ideologies, left and right, secular and religious. The key objective is to work with partners to detect early signs of radicalization and to design possible responses. This multi-agency cooperation involves academic, NGOs, and other sectors across Canada (Koehler 2017, 253–5). Examples of multi-agency cooperation with regional police forces but led by RCMP include the Calgary Police Service's ReDirect intervention to address concerns about radicalization to violence, and the Toronto Police Service, supported by Public Safety Canada and the RCMP, runs its FOCUS Rexdale Hub initiative to intervene in cases of violent ideological predispositions (RCMP 2016; Public Safety 2017, 16–19).

23.7.1 Case Study Simulation Exercises on National Security With Community Members, RCMP, and the Government of Canada

To support the Canadian government's CVE objectives and to enhance its accountability and professional services based on positive relations, the RCMP's National Security Community Outreach Office runs simulations where community members (often those affected by an investigation into terrorism or securitized by such policies) are given the role of investigating officers working on terrorism charges. Training is key. Participants are briefed by key national security departments and agencies vested with investigative authority such as CSIS, CBSA, the Public Prosecution Service of Canada (PPSC), and the RCMP. Briefings on principles of accountability are provided by independent civilian review bodies, such as the Commission for Public Complaints against the RCMP. Community participants, divided into teams and moderated by facilitators, simulate the investigation by keeping accurate notes (using officers' note books and relevant toolkits). Facilitators challenge participants on the rationales of their decisions in specific scenarios and on the extent of their consideration of law, public expectations, and accountability rules. These prevention simulation exercises aim to improve communities' understanding of the complexities of prevention and to give them an empathetic understanding of circumstances (legal and otherwise) in which police officers operate (OSCE 2014, 98–9; Peter Neumann 2017, 53–4; Public Safety 2017).

23.7.2 U.S. Community Tailored CVE Policing, LAPD

In 2015 the White House, in line with the National Strategy to Prevent Violent Extremism (2011), led a high-level national summit entitled Empowering Local Partners to Prevent Violent Extremism in the United States focusing on "building awareness, community resilience and counter-narrative campaigns […] pilot projects have been launched in three areas (Boston, Los Angeles and Minnesota)" (Koehler 2017, 255). Similar to Public Safety Canada and RCMP grass roots initiatives, research centers in the United States are competitively funded to do research and intervention, sometimes involving samples and resources in Canada. Two examples are from research at the Boston Children's Hospital sampling Somali refugees from Toronto and some other U.S. cities to investigate factors that correlate with radicalization. A second example is a study by George Washington University's Program on Extremism (CSIS 2016).

Similar to the RCMP, in 2008 the Los Angeles Police Deparment (LAPD) established within its counter-terrorism office a community outreach section. Over the years it has built expansive engagements with communities, including Muslims, on CVE issues. It has also sponsored and hosted hundreds of multilevel stakeholder meetings. LAPD outreach covers activities ranging from leaders' engagements, to lectures, workshops, training, and counselling. It has also dealt with non-CVE issues such as Islamophobia, intercommunity tensions, and hate crimes. The community-led programs focus on persons at risk of violent radicalization. An independent oversight mechanism provides feedback on processes, achievements and future goals (Neumann 2017, 53–4).

23.7.3 Common U.S.–Canada Simulation Exercises Against Online Terrorist Propaganda: Case DRDC-Homeland Security

The DRDC-Homeland security experiments (CAUSE IV) had the following mission in 2016 (DHS 2016, 47–8):

> The CAUSE IV experiment provided the opportunity to evaluate the impact of technology on cross-border response operations and communications as part of the ongoing CAUSE experiment series. This experiment is composed of two vignettes. Vignette 1 focused on optimal use of technology by paramedics and first reponders. In Vignette 2, the use of the technologies provided the emergency responders with information to anticipate and confirm events. Use of technological applications through vignette 2 provides more ways to share detailed and accurate information efficiently. Ongoing technological updates aside, a key challenge was the search for necessary and required governance to use social media and crowd-sourcing technologies to share information between multiple stakeholders, to support decision-making and to coordinate planning both internally and across the border.

This report provides three crucial recommendations to improve the vignette 2 portion of the simulation which more directly relates to cooperation against cyber threats. The first recommendation concerns challenges that operators and digital volunteers had in managing large amounts of data in their response efforts. Technological modifications seem necessary to prioritize, layer, and categorize information coming from crowd sourcing and social media. Second, which again concerns technological modification, is streamlining communications by officials through targeted pre-notifications. The last recommendation concerns the additional training for staff and digital volunteers from both countries to provide more effective support for emergency management (DHS 2016, 50–1).

23.8 COUNTERING ONLINE TERRORIST PROPAGANDA AND EXTREMIST NARRATIVES

The available literature on international cooperation in counter messaging is scant (Leuprecht et al. 2010). Generally speaking, law enforcement, intelligence and other authorities gradually had to develop tools and arrangements to effectively cope with countering terrorist online narratives. Online discussions provide an opportunity to present opposing viewpoints or to engage in debates, with a strong factual foundation and conveyed through discussion forums, images, and videos (UNODC 2012, 12). A UN document praises the U.S. Center for Strategic Counterterrorism Communications, as an example of successful interagency coordination in real time:

> For instance, in May 2012, the Center was cited as having responded, within 48 hours, to banner advertisements promoting extremist violence posted on various websites by Al-Qaida in the Arabian Peninsula, with counter-advertisements on the same websites featuring an altered version of that same message that was intended to convey that the victims of the terrorist organization's activities were Yemeni nationals. The counter-narrative campaign involved cooperation among the United States Department of State, the intelligence community and the military. The Center also uses media platforms such as Facebook and YouTube for counter-narrative communications.
>
> *(UODC 2012, 13)*

Canadian and U.S. expert and practitioner literatures disagree on ways and methods to deal with online extremist narratives. Unlike the denial approach favored by some (see the previous discussion on prisoners' online radicalization), others believe that forceful denial of access is not the solution. Neumann (2013, 431), in his study on different types of online radicalization processes and assessment of U.S. CVE options, warns:

> Approaches aimed at restricting freedom of speech and removing content from the Internet are not only the least desirable, they are also the least effective.

He suggests that:

> government should play a more energetic role in reducing the demand for radicalization and violent extremist messages—for example, by encouraging civic challenges to extremist narratives and by promoting awareness and education of young people. In the short term, the most promising way for dealing with the presence of violent extremists and their propaganda on the Internet is to exploit their online communications to gain intelligence and gather evidence in the most comprehensive and systematic fashion possible.

He then mentions two U.S. experiments based on denial of motivation rather than denial of access (Neumann 2013, 446):

> Targeting foreign audiences, the State Department has run a number of programs that seek to empower, network, and train moderate voices in foreign countries:
>
> - Early in 2012, officials hosted a series of Web-based seminars ("webinars") for Somali bloggers in Europe, Canada, and Africa. The initiative helped online activists exchange ideas on how to make their websites more attractive and to reach wider audiences. It also generated a network of mainstream Somali bloggers who have made it their mission to challenge the narratives of violent extremist groups in Somalia.
> - In April 2012, the State Department launched its Viral Peace campaign, which has trained young influencers in Southeast Asia to use social media as a way of promoting community involvement and peaceful change.91 According to the program's coordinator, the aim is to help people craft online strategies that use a whole range of tools—including "logic, humor, satire, [and] religious arguments"—to match the violent extremists' energy and enthusiasm.

The House Committee on Homeland Security (2016, 14) reached the same conclusion in deploring a lack of domestic counter messaging. It urged Homeland Security to avoid government issue messaging and to focus instead "on empowering credible voices, including former extremists, family members affected by terror, moderate religious figures, and others who are likely to dissuade potential extremists. The program should consist of grant funding for non-profits and local groups, public-private partnerships, forums to share actionable best practices, and assistance in developing youth networks."

23.9 SUMMARY

Current U.S.–Canada tools and cooperation arrangements against online terrorism are among the most integrated in the world. However, Kitchen and Molnar (2015, 189–91) caution that integration and collaboration are no magic bullets. First, residual risk of radicalization and terrorism is inevitable. Second, intelligence data has its own perils in terms of management of information, intelligence analysis, and discerning actionable from non-actionable signals. Third, one externality of integration is accountability. While integrated national and international intelligence nods feed in large amounts of data, these also blur legitimate reasons for collecting data.

CVE in Western countries, including the United States and Canada, has also come under criticism. First, the connection of knowledge and praxis needs to be strengthened (Tierney 2017, 69–70). Prevention needs to be informed by a greater appreciation for academic research by policy-makers and practitioners. The academic research should also be mindful of not defining radicalization so broadly as to infringe on freedom of expression. Second, researchers and practitioners who securitize targeted communities or succumb to the culture of political correctness are also a concern. Third, community outreach in the United States and Canada by different government actors creates mistrust when a community is viewed as both potential informants and social internments. The same research points out ways to improve CVE. First, knowledge and awareness-building need to become more action-oriented against homegrown terrorism. A key component of this shift should be to build international capacity to combat extremism (Tierney 2017, 70–1). Fourth, the government should concede the driver's seat and cede a larger CVE role to civil society and community actors to assuage fears and mistrust and to add legitimacy and efficiency to government CVE strategies. Canadian and U.S. law enforcement and intelligence agencies need a stronger common framework to prevent the proliferation of known violent radicals in search of sympathisers and new recruits. Fifth, more work should be done on online CVE programs, especially on messaging campaigns component in need for new initiatives to increase legitimacy and efficiency. Such initiatives include mechanism for assessment and evaluation, generating more content that appeals to the intended audience and of much better quality that is more engaging and sensational than traditional messaging. Finally, to enhance the multidisciplinary approach to countering online propaganda, we should include other humanities and social sciences (Tierney 2017, 70–1).

NOTES

1. See also a recent research from French Canada see Séraphin Alava, Divina Frau-Meigs et Ghayda Hassan (2018).
2. The United Nations suggests a similar classification of six sometimes overlapping categories "propaganda (including recruitment, radicalization and incitement to terrorism); financing; training; planning (including through secret communication and open-source information); execution; and cyberattacks" (UNODC 2012, 3).

3. Examples of such legal universal instruments regarding terrorism in general include: "The obligation to bring perpetrators of acts of terrorism to justice; the obligation to extradite or prosecute (*the aut dedere aut judicare principle*); the obligation to establish legal jurisdiction in defined circumstances; the obligation to exclude the political offence exception as a ground for refusing a request for cooperation; the respect for the rule of law and human rights; respect for the principle of dual criminality; respect for the rule of speciality; respect for the *ne bis in idem* rule: precluding a second prosecution for the same offence" (UNODC 2012, 73).
4. One example of this informal and more expedited cooperation between partners is the following "There are two ways by which investigating authorities can secure the retention of Internet related data held in the United States by informal means: (i) foreign authorities can develop a direct relationship with ISPs and make a direct informal request that they retain and produce the required data; or (ii) if no direct relationship exists, they can make an informal request through the Federal Bureau of Investigation, which will make the request to the ISP" (UNODC 2012, 90).
5. United Nation documents stress cooperation with internet companies and service providers UNODC 2012).
6. Wilner (2010, 4) also points out that Western European countries have already published "national prison manuals on the indicators of prison radicalization."
7. The case of Islam in prison provides a common example for civil liberties implications. It is difficult for prison guards to distinguish between freedom of religious expressions (such as proselytising) and radicalization and recruitment activities (Wilner 2010, 10).
8. For example, a grant hosted by Ryerson University-Developing Canadian Partnerships analyses and evaluates the multiagency approach in countering violent radicalization in Canada. Another grant is hosted by the University of Waterloo: Foreign Fighter Radicalization. The objective of this research is to analyse the perspectives of Western extremist travellers, their families and friends, and other online supporters of violent extremist movements. One key objective is to formulate action-oriented recommendations toward rehabilitation.

REFERENCES

Aistrope, Tim. 2016. Social Media and Counterterrorism Strategy. *Australian Journal of International Affairs*, 70(2), 121–138.

Alava, Séraphin, Divina Frau-Meigs and Gayda Hassan. 2018. Comment qualifier les relations entre les médias sociaux et les processus de radicalisation menant à la violence? *QUADERNI*. No. 95, Winter.

Bouchard, Martin and Philippa Levey, 2015, Radical and Connected: An introduction, in Martin Bouchard (ed.), in *Social Networks, Terrorism and Counterterrorism, radical and connected*, Milton Park: Routledge.

Canada [National] Cyber Security Strategy. 2018. https://www.publicsafety.gc.ca/cnt/rsrcs/pblctns/ntnl-cbr-scrt-strtg/ntnl-cbr-scrt-strtg-en.pdf

Conway, Maura, "Terrorism and the Internet: New Media—New Threat?" *Parliamentary Affairs*, 59, no. 2, April 2006: 283–298. https://doi.org/10.1093/pa/gsl009

CSIS. 2015. The Foreign Fighters Phenomenon and Related Security Trends in the Middle East: highlights from workshop. https://www.canada.ca/content/dam/csis-scrs/documents/publications/20160129-en.pdf

CSIS. 2016. Al-Qaeda, ISIL and Their Offspring. https://www.canada.ca/content/dam/csis-scrs/documents/publications/ISLAMIC%20STATE_REPORT_ENGLISH.pdf

DHS. 2016. Canada - U.S. Enhanced Resiliency Experiment (CAUSE IV) Binational after Action Report. https://www.dhs.gov/sites/default/files/publications/CAUSE-IV_Binational-After-Action-Report_171211-508.pdf

Eagles, Munroe and Nik Nanos. 2017. Stronger Together? Support for Political Cooperation in Canada and the United States, 2005–2016. https://www.cambridge.org/core/services/aop-cambridge-core/content/view/D9C1A6DA2E1056DB12251309BD244C96/S1049096517000518a.pdf/stronger_together_support_for_political_cooperation_in_canada_and_the_united_states_20052016.pdf

Five Eyes Ministerial Communiqué. 2017. https://www.publicsafety.gc.ca/cnt/rsrcs/pblctns/fv-cntry-mn strl-2017/fv-cntry-mnstrl-2017-en.pdf

G7. 2018a. Managing Foreign Terrorist Fighters and Associated Travellers. http://www.g7.utoronto.ca/fore ign/180423-fighters.html

G7. 2018b. G7 Security Ministers' Commitments Paper. http://www.g7.utoronto.ca/justice/2018-commit ments.html

Hamaid, Munir. 2017. Violent extremism online: new perspectives on terrorism and the Internet. *Journal of Policing, Intelligence and Counter Terrorism*, 12, no. 2: 194–195.

House Committee on Homeland Security. 2016. A National Strategy to Win the War against Islamist Terror. https://homeland.house.gov/wp-content/uploads/2016/09/A-National-Strategy-to-Win-the-War.pdf

Kitchen, Veronica and Adam Molnar. 2015. Problems and Perils of Integrated Models of Public Safety in Canada. In *Social Networks, Terrorism and Counterterrorism*, edited by Martin Bouchard. Milton Park: Routledge.

Koehler, Danier. 2017. *Understanding Deradicalization: Methods, Tools and Programs for Countering Violent Extremism*. London: Routledge.

Leuprecht, Christian, Hataley, Todd, McCauley, Clark and Moskalenko, Sophia. 2010. Containing the narrative: Strategy and tactics in countering the storyline of global Jihad. *Journal of Policing, Intelligence, and Counter Terrorism*, 5(1), 42–57.

Moens, Alexander, Seychelle Cushing, and Alan W. Dowd. 2015. Cybersecurity Challenges for Canada the United States. https://www.fraserinstitute.org/sites/default/files/cybersecurity-challenges-for-cana da-and-the-united-states.pdf

Mueller, John and Mark G. Stewart. 2011. Terror, Security and Money: Balancing the Risks, Benefits and Costs of Homeland Security. https://politicalscience.osu.edu/faculty/jmueller/MID11TSM.PDF

Neumann, Peter. 2013. Options and Strategies for Countering Online Radicalization in the United States. *Studies in Conflict and Terrorism*, 36, no. 6: 431–459.

Neumann, Peter. 2017. Countering Violent Extremism and Radicalisation that Lead to Terrorism. https://www.osce.org/chairmanship/346841

O'Halloran, Patrick J., Christian Leuprecht, Ali Ghanbar Pour Dizboni, Alexandra Green, David Adelstein. 2018. The terrorist resourcing model applied to Canada. *Journal of Money Laundering Control*, 21(1), 33–46.

OSCE. 2014. Preventing Terrorism and Countering Violent Extremism and Radicalization that Lead to Terrorism: A Community-Policing Approach. https://www.osce.org/secretariat/111438?download=t rue

Public Safety Canada. 2015. Cyber security Action Plan between Public Safety Canada and the Department of Homeland Security. https://www.publicsafety.gc.ca/cnt/rsrcs/pblctns/cybrscrt-ctn-plan/cybrscrt -ctn-plan-eng.pdf

Public Safety Canada. 2017. Public Report on the Terrorist Threat to Canada. https://www.publicsafety. gc.ca/cnt/rsrcs/pblctns/pblc-rprt-trrrst-thrt-cnd-2017/pblc-rprt-trrrst-thrt-cnd-2017-en.pdf

Public Safety Canada. 2018a. New Cyber Security Strategy Bolsters Cyber Safety, Innovation and Prosperity. https://www.canada.ca/en/public-safety-canada/news/2018/06/new-cyber-security-strategy-bol sters-cyber-safety-innovation-and-prosperity.html

Public Safety Canada. 2018b. Federal Terrorism Response Plan: Domestic Concept of Operations. https://www.publicsafety.gc.ca/cnt/rsrcs/pblctns/fdrl-trrrsm-rspns-pln/index-en.aspx

RCMP. 2009 . Radicalization: A Guide for the Perplexed. https://archive.org/details/rcmp-radicalization

RCMP. 2016. Terrorism and Violent Extremism Awareness Guide. http://www.rcmp-grc.gc.ca/en/terror ism-and-violent-extremism-awareness-guide

Skillicorn, David B., Christian Leuprecht, Yvonne Stys and Renée Gobeil. 2015. Prisoner Radicalization: Structural Differences among Violent Extremists. *Global Crime* 16(3), 238–259.

Tierney, Michael. 2017. Combating homegrown extremism: assessing common critiques and new approaches for CVE in North America. *Journal of Policing, Intelligence and Counter Terrorism*, 12, no. 1: 66–73. DOI: 10.1080/18335330.2017.1293281.

UNODC (United Nations Office on Drugs and Crimes). 2012. The Use of Internet for Terrorist Purposes. https://www.unodc.org/documents/frontpage/Use_of_Internet_for_Terrorist_Purposes.pdf

White House. 2018. National Cyber Strategy of the United States of America. https://www.whitehouse.gov/wp-content/uploads/2018/09/National-Cyber-Strategy.pdf

Wilner, Alex. 2010. From Rehabilitation to Recruitment. https://www.macdonaldlaurier.ca/files/pdf/FromRehabilitationToRecruitment.pdf

Wilner, Alex and Brian Lee Crowley, 2011, Preventing Prison Radicalization in Canada: More Needs to Be Done. https://www.macdonaldlaurier.ca/files/pdf/Wilner_Crowley_Prison_Radicalisation.pdf

Chapter 24

Intelligence Sharing Among Agencies and Internationally

José de Arimatéia da Cruz[1]

CONTENTS

24.1 INTRODUCTION

During much of the Cold War, a period of tense ideological and military conflict between the U.S. and its allies against the Soviet Union and its satellites states, if there ever was an attack against the U.S. the enemy most likely to have perpetrated the attack would have been the Soviet Union or one of its proxies. With the implosion of the Soviet Union on 25 December 1991 and its replacement with the Russian Federation, the world changed forever. On that night, the U.S. was denied a common enemy. The U.S. had won the Cold War. The political theorist Francis Fukuyama's celebrated essay The End of History? was published in *The National Interest* in the Summer of 1989 and also celebrated the victory of liberalism over all other forms of "isms" [1]. The U.S. had become the lonely superpower. Fast forward another decade and the world would once again be shocked to its core.

On the morning of 9 September, 2001, terrorist attacks against the U.S.'s symbol of economic, military, and political power changed forever the national security landscape of the U.S. and the world. The U.S. would have to defend itself not only against other nation-states but also against non-state actors operating in isolation or supported by rogue nations. While ideological terrorism had subsided with the implosion of the Soviet Union, a new form of terrorism was on the rise: religious terrorism. Another extraordinary development was the advancement of the world wide web and the development of the internet. When the internet was developed security was not much of a concern given its development was intended for scientific cooperation between research universities. Later on, the ability of internet users not only to communicate but also to utilize it for malfeasant activities provide a new forum for transnational organized crime and criminal organizations. Thus intelligence sharing become more than ever an international priority rather than a silo activity performed in isolation and disconnected from the rest of the world.

24.2 INFORMATION SHARING

The speed, global reach and relative anonymity with which terrorists can use the internet to promote their causes or facilitate terrorist acts, together with complexities related to the location, retention, seizure, and production of internet-related data, makes timely and effective international cooperation between law enforcement and intelligence agencies an increasingly critical factor in the successful investigation and prosecution of many terrorism cases. The importance of the internet as a force multiplier cannot be ignored by national security strategists. As Seth G. Jones argues in his book, *Waging Insurgent Warfare: Lessons from the Vietcong to the Islamic State*, insurgents and transnational organized criminal organizations use the internet for a variety of reasons. First, they can use the internet as a recruitment tool for new members and supporters. The old methods of recruitment in which an operative would have to befriend another agent and establish a trust relationship before any type of transaction could take place is over. Today, insurgents, terrorists, and transnational organized criminal organizations can recruit new members from the safe haven of their own sovereign territory without fear of prosecution or arrest. Second, insurgents, terrorists, and transnational organized criminal organizations can use information campaigns to conduct psychological operations. As pointed out by Jones, psychological operations could include, but are not limited to, the spread of propaganda and disinformation, encouraging defections from counterinsurgents, sowing fear and discord, and portraying insurgents as likely to win and disseminate images of recent operations. Third, insurgents, terrorists, and transnational organized criminal organizations may also use the internet and the tools of twenty-first-century communication to raise funds and secure material resources from local and international donors. Finally, as Jones points out, insurgents, terrorists, and transnational organized criminal organizations may use technology to share operations and tactical information, planning and coordinating attacks [2].

Given the importance of the internet as a tool in the arsenal against insurgents, terrorists, and transnational organized criminal organizations in the twenty-first century, sharing of intelligence between law enforcement and intelligence agencies has become a priority. As the U.S. Department of Homeland Security points out on their website, "Remedying information sharing shortfalls was a principal recommendation of the 9/11 commission. Protecting the country from ever-evolving, transnational threats requires a strengthened homeland security enterprise that shares information across traditional organizational boundaries. DHS is committed to ensuring that information is available to state and local law enforcement, giving those on the frontlines the tools they need to protect local communities. This approach is based on the simple premise that homeland security begins with hometown security" [3].

Scholars in the field of national security are only now beginning to operationalize the concept of intelligence sharing. While there is no acceptable universal definition yet, progress has been made among a few practitioners of national security. Janine McGruddy, at the University of Otago, New Zealand, sees intelligence sharing as a multidisciplinary approach in which there is a "possibility of developing more common vocabularies for thinking about problems with fewer inter-cultural and international misunderstanding" [4]. McGruddy also prefers the term multilateral intelligence collaboration rather than just simply intelligence sharing. According to McGruddy, quoting Warren Tucker, Head of the New Zealand Security Intelligence Service, there is an inherent duality between intelligence and sharing since intelligence is supposed to be protected but at the same time new security issues require a collaborative enterprise. McGraddy defines multilateral intelligence collaboration as "an accord among three or more agencies or national governments working together to collect, protect, and analyse information to reduce decision makers uncertainty about a foreign policy" [4, p. 214]. McGraddy sees intelligence sharing not only as beneficial to the home country but also its international partners, as they address traditional security issues as well as nontraditional security issues such as drug trafficking, human trafficking, environmental and health issues, and transnational organized crime.

Another prominent scholar addressing the issue of intelligence sharing is James Igoe Walsh, a professor of political science at the University of North Carolina at Charlotte. Walsh sees intelligence sharing as a "crucial source of intelligence" [5]. Intelligence sharing, according to Walsh, occurs when "one state—the sender—communicates intelligence in its possession to another state—the recipient" [5, p. 154]. Thus, Walsh's definition creates a symbiotic relationship between sender and receiver which is beneficial to both nation-states involved in the intelligence-sharing arrangement. Walsh also highlights the importance of intelligence sharing given the new dilemmas of the twenty-first-century national security concerns such as preventing the proliferation of weapons of mass destruction and stopping the activities of terrorist groups and drug traffickers [5, p. 151].

24.3 U.S. APPROACH TO INTELLIGENCE SHARING

In the aftermath of the terrorist attacks against New York's Twin Towers and the Pentagon, one of the recommendations by the 9/11 Commission was to remedy information sharing shortfalls. Protecting the country from ever-evolving, transnational threats requires a strengthened homeland security enterprise that shares information across traditional organizational boundaries. The U.S. government and its federal agencies is a signatory to several intelligence treaties with the objective of better coordination, exchange, and dissemination of intelligence between and among several countries in the world. According to the U.S.'s National Strategy for Information Sharing and Safeguarding, released in December 2012, information is a national asset [6]. Therefore, managing information as a national security asset requires stakeholders to make it available to those who need it, while also keeping it secure from unauthorized or unintended use [6, p. 7]. Intelligence sharing agreement can be either bilateral or multilateral. According to Helene L. Boatner, a former CIA officer, "the underlying themes of these sharing relationships, whether bilateral or multilateral, were the enemy of my enemy is my friend; and no sharing of intelligence about friends with other friend" [7]. Another important issue regarding multilateral agreement is if it is multilateral, how many participants are there [8]?

24.3.1 Department of Homeland Security

While there are several agencies in the U.S. government involved in intelligence gathering, processing, analyzing, and dissemination, the Department of Homeland Security (DHS) is the agency responsible for fostering information sharing. According to the DHS's website, "In the ten years since 9/11, the federal government has strengthened the connection between collection and analysis on transnational organizations and threats. Terrorism-related information sharing across the intelligence community has greatly improved. Moreover, we have strengthened the ability to convey intelligence on threats to the homeland in a context that is useful and relevant to law enforcement and homeland security officials at the state and local level" [9]. The DHS in according with President Donald J. Trump's directives is the agency charged with strengthening the homeland security enterprise by implementing and strengthening four key elements:

- *National Network of Fusion Centers*: Fusion centers serve as focal points within the state and local environment for the receipt, analysis, gathering, and sharing of threat-related information between the federal government and state, local, tribal, territorial (SLTT), and private sector partners;
- *Nationwide Suspicious Activity Reporting Initiative*: Efforts, in coordination with the Department of Justice, to implement a unified process for reporting, tracking, and accessing (SARs) in a manner that rigorously protects the privacy and civil liberties of Americans, as called for in the National Strategy for Information Sharing;
- *National Terrorism Advisory System (NTAS)*: The NTAS, replaces the color-coded Homeland Security Advisory System (HSAS). This system will more effectively communicate information about terrorist threats by providing timely, detailed information to the public, government agencies, first responders, airports, and other transportation hubs, and the private sector; and
- *If You See Something, Say Something®*: The Department's nation-wide public awareness campaign—a simple and effective program to raise public awareness of indicators of terrorism and violent crime, and to emphasize the importance of reporting suspicious activity to the proper state and local law enforcement authorities [9].

The DHS recognizes that its mission has not been without setbacks and challenges. As the agency points out in its Department of Homeland Security Information Sharing Strategy, 18 April 2008, "the primary challenge both within DHS and with external information sharing partners is creating a widely accepted process for sharing mission-relevant information while adequately protecting the information" [10]. Additionally, several governmental Acts and Executive Orders guide DHS in its effort to perform its function as an information sharing organization while also maintaining privacy of the source and originality of the information. For example, at the federal level, statutory and other policy mandates such as the Privacy Act of 1974, the E-Government Act of 2002, the Homeland Security Act of 2002, the Federal Information Security Management Act of 2002 (known as FISMA), and Executive Order 12333 "require careful safeguarding of any information that personally identifies U.S. persons" [10, p. 8].

Former Director of National Intelligence, James R. Clapper, recognizes the changing nature of intelligence and the new threats on the horizon. In the National Intelligence Strategy for the United States of America (2014), the document highlights that global power is becoming more diffuse and new alignments and information networks will increasingly have a significant impact in economic, social, and political affairs [11]. Information sharing and safeguarding have become a top priority for the agency. The agency's primary responsibility in this new post-Cold War international system is to "allow the intelligent community (IC) to carry out the mission, protect against external and insider threats, and maintain the public trust" [11, p. 13]. In its efforts to better protect the homeland while strengthening its partnerships worldwide, the U.S. sees its partners as "a force multiplier, offering access, expertise, capabilities, and perspectives that enrich our intelligence capacity and help all of us succeed in our shared mission" [11, p. 15]. The agency achieves its objectives by "increas[ing] shared responsibility with and among, and incorporate insight from, all partners to advance intelligence; develop an enterprise approach to partnership engagement to facilitate coordinated, integrated outreach; and deepen collaboration to enhance understanding of our partners and to effectively inform decisions and enable action" [11, p. 15].

24.3.2 USA PATRIOT Act

Another important instrument in the U.S.'s intelligence gathering and sharing among agencies and internationally are provisions within the Uniting and Strengthening America by Providing Appropriate Tools Required to Intercept and Obstruct Terrorism Act of 2001(USA PATRIOT Act). The Patriot Act is an Act of Congress that was signed into law by President George W. Bush on 26 October 2001. According to Larry D. Thompson, former Deputy Attorney General of the United States under President George W. Bush, there are several provisions within the USA PATRIOT Act that help the U.S. government "wage a coordinated, integrated counter-terrorism campaign" in the aftermath of 9/11. According to Thompson, "section 203 of the PATRIOT Act expressly empowers law enforcement officials to share criminal investigative information that contains foreign intelligence or counterintelligence, including grand jury and wiretap information, with intelligence, protective, immigration, national-defense, and national security personnel" [12]. Another important section of the PATRIOT Act which assists law enforcement officers in their fight against another 9/11 in the homeland is section 905. This section of the PATRIOT Act requires that "attorney general, subject to certain exceptions, disclose to the director of central intelligence foreign intelligence acquired by the Department of Justice in the course of a criminal investigation" [12].

Given the transnational nature of much terrorism and related criminal activity, the highly complex and sensitive nature of intelligence-based investigations, and the need for urgency in rapidly-evolving events and investigations, trust between law enforcement and prosecution agencies at both the national and international level is often a critical factor in the successful investigation and prosecution of terrorism-related offences. The PATRIOT Act, especially section 218, allows "information obtained by intelligence officers pursuant to the Foreign Intelligence Surveillance Act (FISA) to share more readily with law enforcement officials" [12]. This provision of the PATRIOT Act is important in the fight against terrorism since prior to its enactment, the courts had ruled "that surveillance under FISA could be utilized only when foreign intelligence was the primary purpose of a national security investigation" [12].

In addition to the PATRIOT Act, the U.S. also has a plethora of other tools at its disposal to confront the war on terrorism. For example, the U.S. government has enacted the Homeland Security Act (2002) and the Intelligence Reform and Terrorism Prevention Act (IRTPA) 2002. Both of these acts "removed many of the barriers to cooperation between intelligence and law enforcement and mandated exchanging information related to international terrorist threats" [13]. The IRTPA also mandated "the creation of an Information Sharing Environment (ISE) that provides the technologies, procedures, policies, and standards for sharing terrorism related information among federal, state, and local jurisdictions" [13, p. 4]. Another tool in the arsenal of the U.S. government in its fight against both domestic and foreign enemies is the National Counterterrorism Center (NCTC). According to the NCTC's website, their mission is to "lead and integrate the national counterterrorism (CT) effort by fusing foreign and domestic CT information, providing terrorism analysis, sharing information with partners across the CT enterprise, and driving whole-of-government action to secure our national CT objectives" [14].

Fusion centers are another tool used by the U.S. government in its attempt to combat terrorism and sharing of intelligence in an effort to avoid another 9/11 and combat nontraditional threats to the homeland. According to the Baseline Capabilities for State and Major Urban Area Fusion Centers (October 2008), "a fusion center is a collaborative effort of two or more agencies that provide resources, expertise and information to the center with the goal of maximizing their ability to detect, prevent, investigate, and respond to criminal and terrorist activity" [15].

24.4 INTERNATIONAL APPROACHES TO INTELLIGENCE SHARING

Richard Haas, an American diplomat and current president of the Council on Foreign Relations in his book, *A World in Disarray: American Foreign Policy and the Crisis of the Older Order,* has stated that the world is not Las Vegas [16]. In other words, no country in the world today is immune to a cyber-attack to its critical infrastructure, to the effects of transnational organized crime, or an act of terrorism in the globalized world of the twenty-first century. As Aidan Kirby has stated, "the distinction between intelligence that is strictly domestic and intelligence that is also (or solely) international has become harder to make. In this era of transnational threats, domestic intelligence activities are often fused with international intelligence products, and major successes may rely on significant elements of international cooperation" [17]. Today in an increasingly more complex world, cooperation is not an option, it is a necessity. Richard J. Aldrich, a Professor of International Security at the University of Warwick and Director of the Institute of the Advanced Study, states that "the most important change in the practice of intelligence since 1989 has been the exponential increase in complex intelligence cooperation" [18].

Either as bilateral or multilateral agreements, there are several agreements in existence to help nation-states in their fight against terrorism and information sharing. One of the oldest examples of a multilateral information sharing agreement is the "fabled UK–USA intelligence treaty of 1948' [18, p. 22]. This agreement signed in June 1948 between "the First Party (the United States) and Second Parties (the United Kingdom (UK), Australia, Canada, and New Zealand), divided signals collection efforts among its signatories" [19]. This agreement is also a complex patchwork of agreements, memoranda, and letters that "coalesced over more than a decade … Sharing inside the UK–USA is substantial but by no means complete" [20].

Another important international intelligence sharing agreement is called Europol, which had its initial inceptions with the so-called Trevi Group. The Trevi Group was composed of governmental officials at the rank of the European Community's interior and justice ministers. Europol is a regional organization of the European Union which serves to prevent and combat such criminal activities such as illicit drug trafficking, illicit vehicle trafficking, human trafficking, terrorism, and money laundering. Europol, especially in the twenty-first century, post-Cold War international system, also facilitates the exchange of data, reports, and analyses among police agencies. Recognizing the importance of enhanced intelligence cooperation among the members of the European Union's intelligence services in 2001, the Justice and Home Affairs Council created the Counter-Terrorism Task Force (CTTF). The CTTF is "a separate body with a wider membership of EU intelligence and security services, together with the United States, Switzerland, and Norway" [21]. The Europol's CTTF is staffed by some 30 intelligence officers. But, as pointed out by Aldrich, the CTTF "remains something of a fifth wheel, since it mostly engages on cases when assistance is requested by a national force" [22]. One of the primary responsibilities of the CTTF "is a common threat assessment in the field of Islamic terrorism" [22]. Terrorism was included in Europol's mandate in 1999 and in 2000 it began to pay closer attention to Islamic terrorism [23].

Another international intelligence sharing within the EU framework is the Club of Berne which is made up of European Union security services heads. This organization was created in 1971. It meets annually to discuss matters such as terrorism, communications interceptions, encryption, and the newest nontraditional threat, namely, cyberterrorism. According to Stéphane Lefebvre, in 2001, "the Club [has focused] on the position or role of intelligence services with respect to European integration. Informal contacts also take place among smaller groups" [24]. In the aftermath of the terrorist attacks on the U.S.'s Twin Towers and Pentagon, the Club of Berne established the Counter Terrorist Group (GTC) which works in conjunction with the Counter-Terrorism Task Force (CTTF).

Another agency of the EU's counterterrorism tool is Eurojust, which had its origins in the Tempere Council of 1999. The EU's Eurojust "functions as an independent group of magistrates, tasked with improving coordination and cooperation among investigators and prosecutors dealing with serious crime" [25]. While this organization is also at the forefront of the war on terror, its legitimacy is heavily dependent "upon its ability to support member states' authorities in countering terrorism" [25], In addition to fighting potential terrorism activities within the EU, member states are also increasing police and judicial cooperation among themselves, especially after the Schengen Agreement (1985) abolished all internal borders between participating states in favor of a single external border [25].

The North Atlantic Treaty Organization (NATO) is an intergovernmental military alliance between several North American and European countries based on the North Atlantic Treaty signed on 4 April 1949. The NATO Special Committee (AC/46) is one of the oldest intelligence exchange mechanisms among allies [26]. The AC/46 is composed of heads of security intelligence services of NATO member countries. According to Stéphane Lefebvre, the AC/46 "advises the North Atlantic Council (NAC) on espionage, terrorist, and other nonmilitary related threats that might affect the alliance and its member states" [26, p. 531]. In terrorism cases involving the collection and use of intercepted communications, digital forensic evidence or money laundering transactions, prosecutors should ensure, in close collaboration with intelligence and/or law enforcement agencies, that such evidence has been collected in a lawful manner and preserved and produced in a manner that meets the evidential requirements of the jurisdiction in which it will finally be used. Such an organization within the EU framework is the Egmont Group, established in 1995, whose primary functions are fighting terrorism, financing of terrorism, and money laundering while providing "an international forum for cooperation and exchange of intelligence among national financial intelligence units" [26, p. 532]. The Egmont Group, which is made up of roughly 69 members, also works closely with the U.S. Department of the Treasury Financial Crimes Enforcement Network (FinCEN). According to the agency's website, its primary mission is to "safeguard the financial system from illicit use and combat money laundering and promote national security through the collection, analysis, and dissemination of financial intelligence and strategic use of financial authorities" [27].

Other nations and regions of the world have either cooperated with international organizations in their fight against transnational terrorism or have established their own initiative to combat terrorism and disseminate intelligence available to other partners. For example, Portugal, while it has not been the victim of an Islamic terrorist attack, none of the less has taken steps to guarantee that its information technology laws are in compliance with the European Union's Constitution in addition to the Portuguese Constitution of 1976. According to the Portuguese Government, "any interference by public authorities with correspondence, telecommunications, or other means of communication is prohibited, except in cases provided by law on matters of criminal procedure" [28]. Canada's actions regarding terrorism and intelligence sharing are the results of a post 9/11 international environment. Canada addressed the issue of terrorism via its Anti-Terrorism Act of Canada (Bill C-36). Bill C-36 "conferred new powers to security and law enforcement, including the authority to hold investigative hearings, compel testimony, and conduct surveillance, and provided for preventive detention and restrictions on disclosure rules under the Canada Evidence Act" [29].

The Association of Southeast Asian Nations (ASEAN) has also been at the forefront in combating terrorism and cooperating with the U.S. and other nations since 9/11. The following are examples of concrete steps taken by the ASEAN to address region-wide coordinated effort to combat terrorism. On 1 August, 2002, then U.S. Secretary of State Colin Powell signed the ASEAN-United States Joint Declaration for Cooperation to Combat International Terrorism, according to Jonathan T. Chow, "the declaration was little more than a general, non-binding exhortation to greater counterterrorism cooperation, along with several suggestions on how to achieve it" [30]. The ASEAN nations have also opened their equivalent of a U.S. fusion center with the establishment of the Southeast Asian Counterterrorism Center in Putrajaya, Malaysia. As Chow explains it, the center is "intended to serve as a clearinghouse for information on regional terrorism, including research unit to monitor and disseminate intelligence" [30, p. 317]. Finally, the ASEAN nations have also signed a Treaty of Mutual Legal Assistance in Criminal Matters. The signatories to the agreement will be able to "seek assistance from one another in criminal investigations pertaining to 190 different serious offenses, including money laundering, hijacking, and murder." Furthermore, the agreement will allow for "sharing of evidence, service of legal documents, and recovery of criminal proceeds, but makes no provision for extradition" [30, p. 319].

The U.S. and Europe currently recognize the threat of cyberterrorism; Latin America, however, focuses more on cybercrime due to the highest rates of real and perceived insecurity and the rapidly growing population of internet users. Despite the fact that Latin America has been spared any Islamic terrorism, nations are becoming more cognizant of the importance of developing domestic and international cyber-security initiatives to counter threats to the world's communication technology infrastructure as internet accessibility increases [31]. Latin American nations work together at the Organization of American States (OAS) and have established the Inter-American Committee against Terrorism to help each other with intelligence sharing on potential evidence of terrorist attacks. Most Latin American countries have also created their own Computer Security Incident Response Teams (CSIRTs) to coordinate intelligence sharing and best practices [31, p. 48]. Atypical among Latin American states, Brazil invests in military-based cyberdefense capabilities to curb cybercrime. Created and operational since 2010, the Cyberdefence Center of the Brazilian Army currently coordinates the army's cyber-security actions. Eventually, the center will also oversee the Brazilian Navy and Air Force to ensure federal and military network protection from foreign and domestic attacks. By establishing national CSIRTs and cyberlegislation, states and their private sector allies are better equipped to efficiently and quickly respond to, investigate, and prosecute cyber-criminals. With increased private and public sector information sharing through this formal national response unit, necessary coordination will be more feasible. By institutionalizing cyberfusion centers, states can be proactive in their fight against cyber-criminals [31, p. 48].

24.5 INTELLIGENCE SHARING: TO COOPERATE OR NOT?

While the U.S. is the most powerful nation in the world, it is not immune to terrorist and transnational attacks, therefore it must cooperate with other nations in the post-Cold War international system. But Fshould nations cooperate with one another when we live in an anarchic international system still driven by a Hobbesian state of nature where life is characterized as "nasty, brutish and short?" In other words, should we trust another sovereign nation within this Hobbesian world.

According to Eric Rosenbach and Aki J. Peritz, at the Belfer Center for Science and International Affairs at Harvard Kennedy School [31, p. 67], the U.S. benefits from international or liaison partnerships in the following ways:

1. *Access*: Liaison may have access to or information about areas denied to direct U.S. penetration.
2. *Speed*: Liaison may be able to gather and disseminate crucial data, giving the U.S. the ability to respond to time-sensitive threats.
3. *Insight*: Liaison may have greater cultural understanding of a particular issue that the U.S. may otherwise misinterpret.
4. *Ability to Perform Direct Action*: Liaison sometimes can provide direct military assistance to solve a particular problem, usually within their home country.
5. *Cover for U.S. Interests*: Liaison may be able to mask U.S. actions as local ones, obscuring otherwise obvious U.S. behavior in foreign countries.

Stéphane Lefebvre has also pointed out the benefits of intelligence sharing in an anarchical world by highlighting that intelligence cooperation occurs when the potential benefits are evident, and the costs or risk of that cooperation well understood [32]. For example, Lefebvre contends that intelligence sharing is beneficial since it fills "identified gaps [in intelligence], reduce operational cost, and replacing nonexistent diplomatic relations are among the major benefits of intelligence cooperation" [32, p. 534]. Other factors that may influence intelligence sharing are difference in perceptions of a threat and the foreign policy objectives of the respective states; asymmetrical power relations between states; poor human rights records of a potential partner; differences in legal parameters and standards; Third Party Rule or fear of disclosure of information; abuse or misuse of intelligence that has been shared; and worries about defection [33]. While there are many benefits for the nation-state when sharing intelligence, there are also some disadvantages that must be considered when contemplating entering into either a bilateral or multilateral intelligence sharing agreement. According to Eric Rosenbach and Aki Peritz [34], any government entering into an intelligence-sharing agreement must remain vigilant for signs of:

1. *Conflicting Interests*: Liaison may provide adversaries with critical sensitive information about U.S. interests, strategies, and plans.
2. *Hostile Collection*: Liaison may attempt to gain insight into U.S. intentions, sources, and methods through overt or covert means.
3. *Poor Information Gathering*: Liaison may use less rigorous collection methods than the U.S., often obliging intelligence community analysts to independently verify specific information.
4. *Moral Hazards*: Members of foreign intelligence services may be involved in unethical or illegal activities, or utilize illegal methods to obtain intelligence.

24.6 SUMMARY

It has become a cliché to state that the 9/11 attacks against the U.S. forever changed the nature of the post-Cold War international system. The enemies of the state today are not only traditional nation-states but also nontraditional threats such as terrorism, cyberterrorism, and human trafficking just to mention a few. The world indeed is not Las Vegas. What happens abroad will have an impact domestically and vice versa. While there are some risks of sharing intelligence, the increasing complexity of the world and new and old challenges will require greater cooperation among intelligence agencies worldwide. As the world becomes more globalized and more porous, nation-states that refuse to cooperate will do so at their own peril.

NOTE

1. The views expressed in this chapter are those of the author and do not necessarily reflect the official policy or position of the Department of the Army, the Department of Defense, or the U.S. Government.

REFERENCES

1. Fukuyama, F. "The End of History?" *The National Interest,* Vol. 16 (1989): 3–18. Retrieved from http://www.jstor.org/stable/24027184
2. Jones, S.G. *Waging Insurgent Warfare: Lessons from the Vietcong to the Islamic State.* New York, NY: Oxford University Press, 2017: 117–118.
3. Homeland Security Information Sharing. August 14, 2018. Available at https://www.dhs.gov/topic/information-sharing. Accessed May 11, 2018.
4. McGruddy, J. "Multilateral Intelligence Collaboration and International Oversight," *Journal of Strategic Security,* Vol. 6, No. 3 (Fall 2013): 214–220.
5. Walsh, J.I. "Defection and Hierarchy in International Intelligence Sharing," *Journal of Public Policy,* Vol. 27, No. 2 (May–August 2007): 151–181.
6. Office of the President of the United States. National Strategy for Information Sharing and Safeguarding. December, 2012. Available at https://obamawhitehouse.archives.gov/sites/default/files/docs/2012sharingstrategy_1.pdf. Accessed May 14, 2018.
7. Boatner, Helene B. "Sharing and Using Intelligence in International Organizations: Some Guidelines," *National Security and the Future,* Vol. 1, No. 1 (2000): 81–92.
8. Richelson, Jeffrey T. "The Calculus of Intelligence Cooperation," *The International Journal of Intelligence and Counterintelligence,* Vol. 4, No. 3 (Fall 1990): 307–323.
9. Homeland Security Information Sharing. August 14, 2018. Available at https://www.dhs.gov/topic/information-sharing. Accessed May 14, 2018.
10. Department of Homeland Security. "Department of Homeland Security Information Sharing Strategy," April 18, 2008. Available at https://www.dhs.gov/xlibrary/assets/dhs_information_sharing_strategy.pdf. p. 6.
11. Director of National Intelligence. The National Intelligence Strategy of the United States of America, 2014. Available at https://www.dni.gov/files/documents/2014_NIS_Publication.pdf. Accessed May 14, 2018.
12. Thompson, Larry D. "Intelligence Collection and Information Sharing within the United States." Available at https://www.brookings.edu/testimonies/intelligence-collection-and-information-sharing-within-the-united-states/. Accessed May 15, 2018.
13. The Intelligence Committee of the Armed Forces Communications and Electronics Association (AFCEA). "The Need to Share: The U.S. Intelligence Community and Law Enforcement." 2007. Available at https://www.afcea.org/mission/intel/documents/springintel07whitepaper_000.pdf. Accessed May 15, 2018.
14. https://www.dni.gov/index.php/nctc-who-we-are. Accessed May 15, 2018.
15. Department of Homeland Security. U.S. Department of Homeland Security. December 2018. Available at https://www.dhs.gov/national-network-fusion-centers-fact-sheet. Accessed May 15, 2018.

16. Haass, Richard N. *A World in Disarray: American Foreign Policy and the Crisis of the Older Order.* New York: Penguins Books, 2017.

17. Kirby, Aidan. "Domestic Intelligence Agencies After September 11, 2001: How Five Nations Have Gripped with the Evolving Threat," in Peter Chalk, Richard Warnes, Lindsay Clutterbuck and Aidan Kirby *Considering the Creation of a Domestic Intelligence Agency in the United Sates: Lessons from the Experiences of Australia, Canada, France, Germany, and the United Kingdom.* The RAND Corporation, 2009. Available at https://www.rand.org/content/dam/rand/pubs/monographs/2009/RAND_MG805.pdf. Accessed May 16, 2018.

18. Aldrich, Richard J., "International Intelligence Cooperation in Practice." Available at https://warwick.ac.uk/fac/soc/pais/people/aldrich/vigilant/861_02_international_xml.pdf. Accessed May 16, 2018.

19. Lefebvre, Stephane. "The Difficulties and Dilemmas of International Intelligence Cooperation," *International Journal of Intelligence and Counterintelligence*, Vol. 16 (2003): 527–542, p. 530.

20. Aldrich, Richard J. "International Intelligence Cooperation in Practice." Available at https://warwick.ac.uk/fac/soc/pais/people/aldrich/vigilant/861_02_international_xml.pdf. Accessed May 16, 2018, p. 23.

21. Aldrich, Richard J. "Transatlantic Intelligence and Security Cooperation," *International Affairs*, Vol. 80, No. 4 (July 2004): 731–753, p. 739.

22. Aldrich, Richard J. "International Intelligence Cooperation in Practice." Available at https://warwick.ac.uk/fac/soc/pais/people/aldrich/vigilant/861_02_international_xml.pdf. Accessed May 16, 2018, p. 28.

23. Coolsaet, Rik. "EU counterterrorism strategy: valued added or chimes?" *International Affairs*, Vol. 86, No. 4 (July 2010): 857–873, p. 862.

24. Lefebvre, Stephane. "The Difficulties and Dilemmas of International Intelligence Cooperation." *International Journal of Intelligence and Counterintelligence*, Vol. 16 (2003): 527–542, p. 530.

25. Coolsaet, Rik. "EU counterterrorism strategy: valued added or chimes?" *International Affairs*, Vol. 86, No. 4 (July 2010): 857–873, p. 863.

26. Lefebvre, Stephane. "The Difficulties and Dilemmas of International Intelligence Cooperation," *International Journal of Intelligence and Counterintelligence*, Vol. 16 (2003): 527–542, p. 531.

27. United States Department of Treasury, Financial Crimes Enforcement Network (FinCen). Available at https://www.fincen.gov/about/mission. Accessed May 22, 2019

28. Soares, Eduardo. "Portugal," in *Foreign Intelligence Gathering Laws: European Union, United Kingdom, France, Netherlands, Portugal, Romania, and Sweden.* The Law Library of Congress, 2014. Available at The Law Library of Congress https://www.loc.gov/law/help/foreign-intelligence-gathering/foreign-intelligence-gathering.pdf, p. 25.

29. Kirby, Aidan. "Domestic Intelligence Agencies After September 11, 2001: How Five Nations Have Gripped with the Evolving Threat," in Peter Chalk, Richard Warnes, Lindsay Clutterbuck and Aidan Kirby *Considering the Creation of a Domestic Intelligence Agency in the United Sates: Lessons from the Experiences of Australia, Canada, France, Germany, and the United Kingdom.* Available at https://www.rand.org/content/dam/rand/pubs/monographs/2009/RAND_MG805.pdf. Accessed May 16, 2018.

30. Chow, Jonathan T. "Counterterrorism Cooperation Since 9/11," *Asian Survey*, Vol. 45, No. 2 (March/April 2005): 302–321, p. 313.

31. da Cruz, José de Arimatéia and Alvarez, Taylor. "Cybersecurity Initiatives in the Americas: Implications for U.S. National Security," *Marine Corps University Journal*, Vol. 6, No. 2 (Fall 2015): 45–68.

32. Lefebvre, Stephane. "The Difficulties and Dilemmas of International Intelligence Cooperation," *International Journal of Intelligence and Counterintelligence*, Vol. 16 (2003): 527–542, p. 534.

33. McGruddy, J. "Multilateral Intelligence Collaboration and International Oversight," *Journal of Strategic Security*, Vol. 6, No. 3 (Fall 2013): 216.

34. Rosenbach, Eric and Peritz, Aki. "Intelligence and International Cooperation," Memorandum, "Confrontation or Collaboration? Congress and the Intelligence Community," Belfer Center for Science and International Affairs, Harvard Kennedy School, July 2009.

Chapter 25

Role of Prosecutors in Online Terrorism Cases

Becky K. da Cruz

CONTENTS

25.1 INTRODUCTION

Seventeen days after 9/11 the United Nations Security Council unanimously adopted Resolution 1373 (28 September 2001) requiring member states to "ensure that any person who participates in the financing, planning, preparation or perpetration of terrorist acts is brought to justice" (United Nations, 2001). While Resolution 1373 speaks directly to these specific terrorist acts based on traditional notions of terrorism, the application to cyberterrorism is inherent. In fact, the Counter-Terrorism Committee, pursuant to Resolution 1373, identifies intelligence and information gathering through special investigative techniques such as covert computer searches as evidence of this nexus.

The United Nations Security Council Resolution 1373 was unanimously adopted and reads that member states are to "ensure that any person who participates in the financing, planning, preparation, or perpetration of terrorist acts is brought to justice." Figure 25.1 diagrams the applicable committees, teams, and directorates created by the UN Security Council resolutions.

The Counter-Terrorism Committee Executive Directorate's (CTED) seminar on The Role of the Prosecutor in Terrorist Cases held in June 2012 focused on the role of the prosecutor from both a strategic and operational perspective. Understanding that criminal justice agencies generally and prosecutors specifically are well-suited to handling general criminal matters, prosecutors have had a difficult time successfully bringing terrorist cases to court for several reasons. One

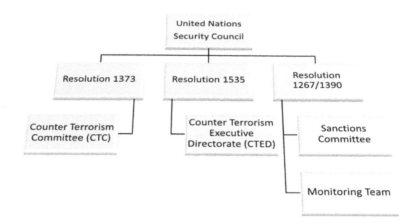

Figure 25.1   United Nation Security Council Resolutions on Combating Cyberterrorism.

challenge is the intense demand on the available financial and personnel resources. The second issue is the evolving nature of terrorist acts. Third, prosecution has been hampered by the limitations on collection and processing of intelligence that can be used as evidence in court (Counter-Terrorism Committee Executive Directorate, 2012). The key to improvement is bilateral international and regional cooperation to strengthen the operational capacity of counter-terrorism practitioners in order to improve the odds of evidence being admissible in court.

Stockton and Golabeck-Goldman (2014) explain the growing risk of cyberterrorism toward the United States and its financial systems, electric power grid, air traffic control systems, and other sectors of critical infrastructure. While much attention has been paid to securing our critical infrastructure from cyber-attacks, little has been directed to building an effective legal framework to prosecute cyberterrorists. As a result, it is imperative that prosecutors work closely with law enforcement agencies to guide the collection of evidence.

Of course, the United Nation's Counter-Terrorism Committee is committed to standard operating procedures to ensure human rights are not deprived in these counter-terrorism efforts, which furthers the likelihood of the admissibility of the evidence, i.e. if a suspect is not physically coerced, the evidence is more likely to follow due process and therefore be admissible in court.

25.2 A RULE-OF-LAW APPROACH TO CRIMINAL PROSECUTION OF ONLINE TERRORISM CASES

Nations, and the individual residents within nations, are bound by the law of war. The Geneva Conventions, specifically Article 48 and 51 of the 1977 Additional Protocol I, prohibits nations from targeting civilians in "indiscriminate attacks." Not only are nations who are not parties to the Additional Protocols bound, but individuals such as cyberterrorists must also comply.

To encourage each nation to develop laws addressing acts of cyberterrorism, the nationality theory, or "active personality" principle, grants jurisdiction to the country attacked by cyberterrorists in another country based on the recognition the cyberterrorists maintains allegiance to the country of citizenship. As such, as long as nationals retain their citizenship, they can be expected to adhere to their countries' laws when they are abroad (Stockton & Golabeck-Goldman, 2014).

25.3 ROLE OF PROSECUTORS IN ONLINE TERRORISM CASES

Prosecutors play an integral role in deterring and disrupting cyber-attacks by virtue of active prosecution of cyberterrorists. Our legal system has the potential to reduce the number of cyber-attacks against the United States. If the likelihood of detection and capture along with significant punishment increases, cyberterrorists are deterred. In fact, if prosecutors have the ability to prosecute conspirators plotting to engage in cyber-attacks, the impact of deterrence is that much greater (Stockton & Golabek-Goldman, 2014). There are a few needed prerequisites for effective prosecution. First, the United States needs to enhance its technical means of attribution of those committing the offence, which tends to be difficult when offenders commandeer computers in the possession of others. A second prerequisite is for prosecutors to develop expertise in prosecuting cyberterrorists. Third, is a legal framework in which to prosecute cyberterrorists, namely a legal mechanism to address extraterritorial reach.

The National Security Division of the Department of Justice is devoting resources to build the expertise of prosecutors in cyberterrorism cases. The National Security Division has established the National Security Cyber Specialists' Network to facilitate prosecution efforts, partners with the Criminal Division's Computer Crime and Intellectual Property Section ("CCIPS") and U.S. Attorneys General offices around the country. Their efforts have led to landmark cases such as the 2014 charges against five members of China's Liberation Army for economic espionage, the 2016 indictment of Iranian hackers for denial of services attacks on U.S. banks, and the recent charges against Russian FSB officers and criminal hackers for the 2014 theft of information of 500 Yahoo! accounts (United States Department of Justice, 2018).

25.3.1 The Investigative Phase

Cyberforensic investigations cost millions of dollars, are time consuming, and require extensive cooperation with domestic intelligence and law enforcement personnel as well as their international counterparts. As a result, the FBI established the National Cyber Investigative Joint Task Force (NCIJTF) in 2007. The joint task force consists of 18 intelligence and law enforcement agencies and collaborates with the Department of Defense Cyber Crime Center to uncover cyber threats from both domestic and international sources.

The United States has asserted criminal jurisdiction over a wide range of actions that had typically been the responsibility of the country in which the crime occurred. The broadened assertion of U.S. authority to search, seize, detain and arrest suspects abroad all without the host country's consent and irrespective of a treaty for extradition, has led to increased surveillance of cyber threats. As a result, the United States has asserted the right to apprehend and prosecute transnational criminals. Typically, though, U.S. law enforcement will operate under the laws of the host country while also working alongside foreign government officials (Fredman, 1998).

Naturally, we rely on first responders at the local, state, or federal level to protect and collect evidence. The individuals at the federal level most likely involved in the collection of cyber-evidence will be the Central Intelligence Agency (CIA), National Security Agency (NSA), National Reconnaissance Office (NRO), Defense Intelligence Agency (DIA), and the Federal Bureau of Investigation (FBI) among other intelligence agencies. Figure 25.2 illustrates the examples of first responding agencies collecting evidence for the potential use in a cyberterrorism trial.

Figure 25.2   Agencies Responsible for Investigating Cyberterrorism Cases.

- Central Intelligence Agency (CIA): The Directorate of Analysis is where incomplete and sometimes contradictory information is analyzed into intelligence that informs U.S. policy decisions. The Directorate of Analysis provides intelligence analysis on the full range of national security and foreign policy issues to the President, Cabinet, and U.S. government agencies such as the U.S. Department of Justice.
- National Security Agency (NSA): The main role of this agency is to protect and defend national security systems including networks that contain classified information such as military and intelligence missions. The NSA's Central Security Service provides America's leaders with critical information needed to defend our country and advance U.S. goals and alliances globally.
- National Reconnaissance Office (NRO): NRO systems provide global situational awareness and address the nation's toughest intelligence challenges. NRO systems are frequently the only office able to access critical areas of interest providing data from sensors not available from other sources. The NRO's key partners are policy-makers: the armed services, the intelligence community, and the Departments of State, Justice and Treasury. NRO systems monitor the proliferation of weapons of mass destruction, track international terrorists, develop highly accurate military targeting data, and assess the impact of natural disasters, among others.
- Defense Intelligence Agency (DIA): The DIA intersects the Department of Defense and the intelligence community and is relied upon for its foundational intelligence in all domains—land, maritime, air, space, and cyber. The DIA produces, analyzes, and disseminates military intelligence information to combat and non-combat missions. It is the nation's primary manager and producer of foreign military intelligence for the Secretary of Defense, Joint Chiefs of Staff, and the Unified Combat Command.
- Federal Bureau of Investigation (FBI): The FBI investigates terrorism, counter-intelligence, cyber-crime, public corruption, civil rights, organized crime, white-collar crime,

violent crime, and weapons of mass destruction. The FBI is responsible for idendifying and neutralizing ongoing national security threats. The FBI is the lead agency for exposing, preventing, and investigating intelligence activities on U.S. soil. Its responsibilities include protecting the secrets of the intelligence community, protecting the nation's critical assets, countering the activities of foreign spies, and keeping weapons of mass destruction from getting into the wrong hands.

The crux of intelligence agencies' collection of evidence is that normally they depend on sources that cannot be revealed in court. Constitutional and statutory issues of discovery arise when they uncover evidence pertinent to either the prosecution or the defense. The ability to prosecute may hinge on whether the intelligence agency discloses the incriminating evidence. On the international front, first responders may include international police i.e. Interpol or even the military. It is of the utmost importance for these first responders to ensure the collection of such evidence meets U.S. standards of admissibility in court. Admissibility of evidence typically relies on ensuring the suspect's constitutional rights were not violated in the collection of evidence. In other words, there was no forced confession, no evidence collected without probable cause, and no hearsay testimony.

There are several federal statutes that govern law enforcement access to electronic information sought as evidence in criminal investigations. These statutes include:

- Electronic Communications Privacy Act of 1986 (18 U.S.C §§ 2510–2522): This Act extends the restriction on wire taps from telephone calls to include transmissions of electronic data by computers. It prohibits access to stored electronic communications.
- Stored Communications Act (18 U.S.C §§ 2701–2712): This Act addresses voluntary and compelled disclosure of stored and electronic communications held by third parties. A warrant is required to collect evidence from providers of electronic communication services while a subpoena or court order is required for evidence held by remote computing services.
- Pen Register and Trap and Trace (18 U.S.C §§ 3121–3127): A pen register is an electronic device that records numbers called from a particular telephone line and now any device or program performing similar functions. This law prevents the government tracing of numbers without first obtaining a court order based on probable cause.
- Privacy Protection Act of 1980 (42 U.S.C § 2000aa): This Act protects journalists from being required to turn over any work product and documentary materials to law enforcement before it is disseminated to the public.

These Acts are still unsettled law in application to twenty-first century smartphones or social media sites since these electronic devices have evolved at a quicker pace than have our laws. Still, protecting the chain of custody of the evidence that is collected is of utmost importance to a successful prosecution. If the evidence is contaminated at any point, it can be excluded from the trial. Figure 25.3 illustrates the points in time where evidence can be contaminated and when it requires particular attention to protect it for use in court.

The protection of classified information is also a concern. The Classified Information Procedures Act (CIPA) enables the discovery of protected information collected by the government for the criminal defendant while also providing a requisite level of protection of the classified information. The Court in *Brady v. Maryland* (1963) mandates that material evidence relating to the defendant's guilt or innocence be produced. Without doing so is to jeopardize the defendant's due process rights and could result in irreversible error in the case.

Figure 25.3   The Movement of Evidence Through Investigation to Trial.

In electronic surveillance cases, the Fourth Amendment search and warrant requirements are important considerations. The full text of the Fourth Amendment is below. In most cases, the United States Supreme Court deems such collection of evidence a search requiring the need for a warrant and therefore probable cause. However, the Court has not yet determined what is to occur after law enforcement obtains a warrant for a search of digital data. As a result, law enforcement typically seizes a suspect's hard drive, flash drives, smartphones, and any other electronic devices. Courts have permitted liberal discretion to law enforcement in the collection of evidence of digital files, especially of thos suspects who commit their offences in cyberspace due to the difficulty in the tracking of that evidence and ease of disguising the incriminating evidence.

FOURTH AMENDMENT

The right of the people to be secure in their persons, houses and effects, against unreasonable searches and seizures, shall not be violated, and no warrants shall issue, but upon probable cause, supported by oath or affirmation, and particularly describing the place to be searched, and the person to be seized.

25.3.2 The Charging Phase

There are several Congressional Acts that prosecutors can use to pursue cyberterrorists. One is the Computer Fraud and Abuse Act of 1984 (18 U.S.C. §1030. This law has been amended numerous times, including by the 2001 U.S.A PATRIOT Act, where Congress specifically permits the extraterritorial application. This Act criminalizes a variety of conduct related to abuse of computers and the internet.

The elements necessary to prove under this law are:

1. Defendant knowingly transmitted computer codes to a protected computer.
2. Defendant acted without authorization.
3. Defendant intentionally caused damage to company's computer system.

4. Defendant caused at least $5,000 of damage. (U.S. v. Ibrahimshah, 2015)

If the cyberterrorist made an attack from outside of the United States, the Terrorism Transcending National Boundaries Act (18 U.S.C. §2332(b)) can be applied to gain the extraterritorial claim over the perpetrator(s).

Prosecution of cyberterrorists raises a number of basic procedural questions. First, should these cases be prosecuted in an international criminal court or a domestic court within a sovereign country? Another is whether these cases should be prosecuted in a military tribunal or a civilian court? If a domestic court is the choice, should that court be within a country that was affected by the cyberterrorism or that of a neutral, third party?

In going the route of prosecuting a case within a domestic court, the court must have jurisdiction over the offender. The means of getting that jurisdiction over one who is a citizen and resident of another country is typically accomplished through domestic law. However, the use of international law has become less of a hurdle. There are mutual legal assistance agreements, extradition treaties, coordinated investigations, and universal jurisdictions. One terrorism treaty that has eased this jurisdiction requirement has been the Montreal Convention which allows the prosecution or extradition to prosecute terrorists. While this does not specifically address cyberterrorists, this is implied.

These cases are generally handled by federal prosecutors in one of the 94 U.S. Attorney's Offices, empowered by the U.S. Department of Justice, once a suspect accused of cyberterrorism is indicted by a federal grand jury. Each state has at least one federal court in which such a case can be tried.

25.3.3 The Trial Phase: Evidential Issues

Generally, the Fourth, Fifth, and Fourteenth Amendments to the United States Constitution protects suspects' rights in the collection of evidence by either the federal or state governments through their law enforcement agencies. The Fourth Amendment protects the suspect from "unreasonable search and seizure." According to the U.S. Supreme Court in *Mapp v. Ohio* (1961), evidence obtained illegally is excluded from being admitted into court to prove a crime was committed. The Fifth Amendment protects the accused from having to be a witness against himself and provides due process of law.

A potential search and seizure issue specific to cyberterrorism is over-seizure. In *Riley v. California* (2014), the Court held that law enforcement must obtain a warrant based on probably cause that a crime was committed regardless if the law enforcement officer is attempting to seize digital evidence incident to arrest. To protect suspects from over-seizure by government officials of their digital evidence, Congress passed laws such as the Wiretap Act (18 U.S.C. § 2511) covering voice-over-internet-protocol (VOIP) and text messages, email, etc. from government interception without a warrant. The purpose of the law is to protect privacy in communications with other persons. The Wiretap Act makes it illegal to intentionally or purposefully intercept, disclose, or use the contents of any wire, oral, or electronic communication through the use of a "device" (Goodman et al., 2015)

Federal Rules of Criminal Procedure (2016) 41(c) provides that a search warrant may be issued to search a computer or electronic media if there is probable cause to believe that the media contains or is contraband, evidence of a crime, fruits of a crime, or an instrumentality of a crime. In searching electronic storage media for evidence of a crime, "the items to be seized under the warrant should focus on the content of the relevant files rather than the physical storage media" (Law Enforcement Cyber Center, 2018). It is, however, a violation of the Fourth Amendment to retain every file from the electronic device indefinitely as evidence seized under a search warrant for use in a separate criminal investigation in the future (*United States v. Ganias*, 2014).

In the typical case, the law enforcement officer will obtain a warrant to seize a person's entire hard drive, all flash drives, and their smartphone. They then make mirror copies of the memory media and search the copies. For example, in a case where the officer has probable cause to believe that a suspect has used his computer to make fake Ids, they can usually obtain a warrant to seize the computer and search the whole hard drive, every email, spreadsheet, image, etc. for evidence of the crime. According to Sacharoff (2016), this can lead to over-seizure opening the case up to the argument that such a general seizure of one's entire life found on their computer is exactly what the Fourth Amendment forbids.

25.3.4 First Online Terrorism Case Prosecuted

The first cyberterrorist case prosecuted was that of Ardit Ferizi, a Kosovo citizen and Malaysian resident. At 20 years old, Ferizi had already been arrested for cyber-crimes several times. Then in 2015 he began supporting ISIL (Islamic State of Iraq and Levant) by administering a website that hosted ISIL videos and magazines. He graduated to providing personal identification of individuals "attacking" the United States. He went on to hack into a server of an Illinois company selling goods to the U.S. military and government personnel. With the information provided to ISIL by Ferizi, ISIL tweeted messages from its "Islamic State Hacking Division" account encouraging its supporters to attack those on the "kill list." Ferizi was accused of putting approximately 1,300 U.S. military personnel and government employees at risk (U.S. Department of Justice, 2016).

Ferizi was arrested in Malaysia, extradited to the United States, charged with terrorism and hacking (cyberterrorism) and prosecuted in the U.S. District Court of Virginia. Figure 25.4 shows the Criminal Complaint document agaist Ferizi dated 6 October 2015. Ferizi pleaded guilty thereby avoiding a possible 35-year sentence. On 23 September 2016, Ferizi was sentenced to 20 years in prison. He was the first person effectively prosecuted in the United States for cyberterrorism (also known as crowdsource terrorism).

25.4 JURISDICTION/PROSECUTION IN INTERNATIONAL COURT

Consider the Libyan bombing of Pan Am Flight 103 that exploded over Lockerbie, Scotland in 1988. The plane took off from London, England with 259 people onboard. All the passengers and 11 people on the ground were killed. It was determined that a bomb had been detonated mid-air. The question of where to prosecute this case of terrorism was at the heart of the legal debate. The interested parties included the United States due to the destination of the flight being New York and the American passengers onboard, England, since the flight took off from London, Scotland as a result of the area the bombing took place, Germany since the briefcase which contained the bomb had been transferred on a German flight, and Libya, since the suspects were Libyan (CNN, 2018).

The United States, Germany, and England investigated and collected evidence from over 30 countries. The CIA and FBI were the U.S. investigating agencies and both the United States and England indicted the Libyan suspects. It was agreed that the suspects would be tried in a neutral location and that Scottish law would be applied—which did not provide the death penalty. The trial took place in the Netherlands.

At the time of this case, the International Court of Justice was in existence, and the United Nations Security Council required extradition of suspects such as the Libyan highjackers

AO 91 (Rev. 08/09) Criminal Complaint

UNITED STATES DISTRICT COURT

for the
Eastern District of Virginia

United States of America	)
v.	)
ARDIT FERIZI	) Case No. 1:15-MJ-515
a/k/a Th3Dir3ctorY,	)
	)
	)

Defendant(s)

CRIMINAL COMPLAINT

I, the complainant in this case, state that the following is true to the best of my knowledge and belief.

On or about the date(s)   4/01/15 to or on about 8/11/15   in the extraterritorial jurisdiction of U.S. and in the

___Eastern___ District of ___Virginia___ , the defendant(s) violated:

Code Section	Offense Description
18 U.S.C. § 1030	Unauthorized access to a computer;
18 U.S.C. § 1028A	Aggravated identity theft; and
18 U.S.C. § 2339B	Providing material support to a designated foreign terrorist group

This criminal complaint is based on these facts:
See attached affidavit.

☑ Continued on the attached sheet.

Reviewed by AUSA/SAUSA:

AUSA Lynn E. Haaland

Complainant's signature

Special Agent Kevin M. Gallagher

Printed name and title

Sworn to before me and signed in my presence.

/s/
Theresa Carroll Buchanan
United States Magistrate Judge

Judge's signature

Date: 10/06/2015

The Honorable Theresa C. Buchanan
U.S. Magistrate Judge

City and state: Alexandria, VA

Printed name and title

Figure 25.4 First page of the Indictment of Ardit Ferizi.

through Chapter VII, Resolution 748. Since this case, the International Criminal Court has come into existence. It was created 1 July 2002 by the Rome Statute. It has jurisdiction over

- International crimes of genocide.
- Crimes against humanity.
- War crimes.

Prosecution in the International Criminal Court is only an option when a national domestic court is unwilling or unable to prosecute or when the United Nation's Security Council or states refer

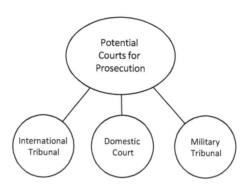

Figure 25.5   Potential Court Cyberterrorism Cases Could Be Prosecuted.

cases to them. There are limits to the jurisdiction of the International Criminal Court, however. One limit is that it can only hear cases pertaining to the above referenced crimes (Morris, 2005). It was proposed to expand its jurisdiction to include terrorism, but the extension to cases of terrorism was defeated due to how to define this type of crime. Figure 25.5 illustrates each option in prosecuting cyberterrorists, i.e. international tribunal, domestic court (federal or state), and military tribunal.

The International Criminal Court is also limited in jurisdiction to only those states who have signed and ratified the Rome Statute. The United States is one of seven countries who are signatories but have not ratified the statute. Ten other states are non-signatories. Nearly all of Europe, South America, Central America, and the rest of North America have ratified the Statute. To put this into perspective, even if the 9/11 hijackers survived and the International Criminal Court was in existence, the International Criminal Court would not have been an option for the United States, since it had not ratified the Rome Statute. See Articles 17–19 of the Rome Statute for the jurisdiction, notice, and other due process requirements.

25.5 SUMMARY

Generally, the presumption is against the application of one county's law applying to individuals in another country. The presumption is against extraterritoriality application of statutes due to the traditional standard of non-interference in another nation's internal affairs out of concern for its sovereignty, territorial integrity, and political independence (Stockton and Golabek-Goldman, 2014). International law therefore limits a nation's jurisdiction over persons or acts within another country. An exception to this rule is prescriptive jurisdiction, whereby a nation can apply its substantive laws to the acts and persons within another state. Under prescriptive jurisdiction, any nation can prosecute and punish a cyberterrorist in violation of its own law.

There are a number of considerations in determining which court to prosecute a cyberterrorism case. The reasons to prosecute in an international tribunal such as the International Criminal Court are:

1. Terrorism concerns all states—not just the states who are parties to the case.
2. Third party states may be more impartial than affected states.
3. International law would suggest the hearing take place in an international tribunal.

However, there are also reasons offered against an international tribunal as the venue to prosecute cyberterrorism cases. These include:

1. The role of the prosecutor in the conduct of criminal proceedings of online terrorism cases, varies between countries.
2. States who sponsor international terrorism question the legitimacy and neutrality of the international court as well as third party states.
3. States who are targets of terrorism question the effectiveness of international investigative and prosecutorial mechanisms.

If trying cyberterrorism cases is better served in a domestic court, is there legal support for doing so in contravention of traditional international laws? The concept of Universal Jurisdiction would permit a state or international organization to claim jurisdiction over an accused person regardless of where the crime was committed or the accused's nationality. The issue is the significant disparity among states' laws and practices in prosecuting online terrorism. Moreover, there is no international agreement to cooperate in cases of criminal cyber attacks (Sofaer & Goodman, 2006).

Another means of prosecuting such cases in domestic court is the extension of extraterritoriality of prescriptive jurisdiction for cyberterrorist attacks (Stockton & Golabek-Goldman, 2014). This authorizes a nation to exercise jurisdiction over conduct outside its boundaries that directly threatens its security or critical government functions. This principle has been upheld by courts across the globe in cases of terrorism, counterfeiting, drug trafficking, and immigration for the same purpose of protecting a country's security and critical infrastructure.

Most cyber-attack cases go unsolved and unprosecuted. For example, the computer attack on Japan in the late 1990s which shut down the railway system, Tokyo Stock Exchange, and affected other infrastructure services, were never prosecuted. Unless an attack affects ATMs or other highly visible networks, the private sector rarely reports the attacks to the government out of concern of publicity of a failure in their network security.

Unfortunately, in the United States, there are challenges in prosecuting such cyber-attacks. Of the 94 U.S. Attorney's offices across the country, fewer than six are positioned to pursue extraterritorial cases and there are even fewer resources to address computer terrorism. In fact, there has been little political support for trying cyberterrorism cases in U.S. courts. Republicans Lindsey Graham of South Carolina, Chuck Grassley of Iowa, and Jeff Sessions of Alabama have all opposed civilian trials for terrorism claiming that doing so is "No way to fight a war." According to Finnegan (2017), the Trump Administration has moved toward military trials and housing those accused of cyberterrorism in the Guantanamo Bay prison. The Guantanamo Commission has thus far convicted eight people. However, three convictions have been vacated or overturned and one has been partially overturned. More prisoners have died in the Guantanamo Bay prison than have been convicted Finnegan (2017).

REFERENCES

Brady v. Maryland (1963). 373 U.S. 83.

CNN (2018). Pam Am Flight 103 Fast Facts. Retrieved from https://www.cnn.com/2013/09/26/world/pan-am-flight-103-fast-facts/index.html

CTED Executive Directorate (2012). CTED Practitioners' Seminar on "The Role of the Prosecutor in Terrorist Cases." Conference presented in Algiers, June 5–7, 2012.

Federal Rules of Criminal Procedure (2016). Title VIII. Supplementary and Special Proceedings. Rule 41 Search and Seizure retrieved from https://www.law.cornell.edu/rules/frcrmp/rule_41

Finnegan, W. (8 May 2017). Taking Down Tterrorists in Court: Zainab Ahmad. *The New Yorker: Annals of Law*. Retrieved from https://www.newyorker.com/magazine/2017/05/15/taking-down-terrorists-in-court.

Fredman, J. M. (1998). Intelligence Agencies, Law Enforcement, and the Prosecution Team. *Yale Law Review*, *16*, 331–370.

Goodman, S. E., Davis, R. C., & Jackson, B. A., (2015). *Digital Evidence & the U.S. Criminal Justice System*. RAND Corp.

Law Enforcement Cyber Center (2018). Digital Search Warrants. Retrieved from http://www.iacpcyber center.org/prosecutors/digital-search-warrants/

Mapp v. Ohio (1961). 367 U.S. 643.

Morris, M. (2005). Terrorism: The Politics of Prosecution. *Chicago Journal of International Law*, *5*(2), 405–421.

Riley v. California (2014). 573 U.S.

Sacharoff, L. (2016). Warrants and Digital Evidence. Presented at Northeast Privacy Scholars Workshop at Fordham Law School November 18, 2018.

Sofaer, A. D. & Goodman, S. E. (2006). *Cyber Crime and Security: The Transnational Dimension*. Hoover Press.

Stockton, P. N. & Golabeck-Goldman, M. (2014). War in the Digital Age: Prosecuting Cyberterrorists: Applying Traditional Jurisdictional Frameworks to a Modern Threat. *Stanford Law & Policy Review*, *25*, 211–268.

United Nations (2001). United Nations Security Council Resolution 1373. Retrieved from https://www.un.org/sc/ctc/resources/databases/recommended-international-practices-codes-and-standards/uni ted-nations-security-council-resolution-1373-2001/

United States v. Ganias (2014). 755 F.3d 125 (2nd Cir.).

U.S. v. Ibrahimshah (2015). 6th Circuit Ct. of Appeals.

United States Department of Justice (2016). ISIL-Linked Kosovo Hacker Sentenced to 20 Years in Prison. Retrieved from https://www.justice.gov/opa/pr/isil-linked-kosovo-hacker-sentenced-20-years-prison

United States Department of Justice (2018). National Security Division. Retrieved from https://www.jus tice.gov/nsd/external-engagement

Private Sector Cooperation and Responsibility for Countering the Use of the Internet for Terrorist Purposes

Chapter 26

A Typology of Public–Private Partnerships and Its Implications for Counterterrorism and Cyber-security

Richard J. Chasdi

CONTENTS

26.1 INTRODUCTION

The purpose of this chapter is to examine the security benefits of public–private partnerships within the context of the exponential growth of intensive globalization since the end of the Cold War made possible by technological innovation. In the process, various types of public–private partnership (P3) arrangements with potential counterterrorism effects in the physical world and protective effects in cyberspace are examined. Those arrangements include public–private partnerships between government and the private sector, triangulation efforts of public, private, and non-profit sector alliances, and larger configurations of public–private sector arrangements to include intergovernmental organizations (IGOs).

The framework of discussion involves: traditional and contemporary notions of national security; examples of threat in physical and virtual worlds; a typology of public–private partnership types: a brief description of certain public–private partnership types operative in the larger world of action; applications potential for security driven, public–private partnerships in the context of "smart cities." Although this chapter can provide only rudimentary and brief coverage of existing programs, salient issues, and challenges, the policy prescriptive message is clear: to craft network alliances and gradually work to expand networks of protection through coordinated and collaborative efforts to create or enhance a web of partnerships to confront traditional physical assaults and cyberspace attacks.

For Savas, "a public private partnership is defined as any arrangement between a government and the private sector in which partially or traditionally public activities are performed by the private sector" [1, 2]. One way of thinking about the links between stakeholders involved in public–private partnerships, also known as "golden triangles," is to categorize them vertically, ranging from more generally recognizable and oftentimes larger public sector government organizations, to smaller public entities. For instance ranking along those this vertical criterion includes intra-national organizations (IGOs) such as the United Nations or the Organization of American States (OAS), national governments, states, provinces, or departments, and municipal/local governments within national government structures.

In addition, those stakeholders can be sorted horizontally, across private sector entities such as multinational corporations (MNCs), privately held international enterprises, and non-profit entities such as non-governmental organizations (NGOs) and community-based organizations (CBOs), whose in-depth experience in particular operational environments provides requisite knowledge for working to craft traditional and virtual security approaches. The value of this approach is it implies a set of integrative functional interconnections that encourage multilateralism, and possible checks and balances between stakeholder responsibilities that are basic but useful conceptualizations for public–private partnership typology construction [3–5].

26.2 NATIONAL SECURITY CONCEPTUALIZATIONS

Links between broader more inclusive notions of national security and many, but certainly not all, public–private partnerships should be made clear from the start. Even public–private partnerships without direct focus on national security make indirect contributions to alleviate environmental conditions that can elicit political instability and social unrest. It follows that traditional notions of national security, with a focus on military threats, fall short in terms of the capacity to take into account the non-forceful factors intrinsic to contemporary security needs.

Traditionally, national security has focused on physical security, namely military needs. It is common to note Clausewitz's notion that "war is a continuation of politics by other means," and Frederick the Great of Prussia's observation that "diplomacy without force is like a symphony without instruments" [6]. However, since the end of the Second World War, where the critical role of industrial capacity to defeat Nazi Germany became clear, and especially since the OPEC oil crisis (1973–74), notions of national security have increasingly become more integrated with a more holistic notion of national security taking into account economic, social, and cultural dimensions of complex political systems, in addition to military factors.

With the growth of globalization, the influence of cultural determinants and their effects both across and within political systems has become generally recognizable as a factor intrinsic to national security. One reason why is that the process of *kulturkampf* (culture conflict) has intensified and perhaps accelerated as ideas, some old and some newer, about how to configure society and government and the relationship of the citizen to each, have permeated the international political system by means of new technologies that affect individual states and regions. In turn, that condition has the potential to exacerbate conflict within and between nation-states.

Much attention has been devoted to the economic elements of globalization such as the reduction or elimination of barriers to the free flow of goods, services, investment income, and in some cases, labor. Alternately, Keohane and Nye describe the webs of cultural, political, and social ties in globalization's non-economic domains as a condition of "complex interdependence." In a world of "complex interdependence," there is what the authors describe as a "thickening" of non-economic political, cultural, and social ties that create new cultural synergies to produce new norms through political and cultural change [7, 8].

For Durkheim, cultures "in-flux," characterized by changing norms and values, amount to a condition of "anomie," where frustration and anger are triggered with potential to lead to aggression and that process is only exacerbated by intensive globalization, itself a condition where technology acts as an accelerant to intensify global linkages [9, 10]. Nowadays, anger and other similar sentiments that derive from political, economic, and cultural marginalization transfer readily through keyboard strokes into the virtual world. Hence, in addition to traditional defense requirements, cyber defenses are now a critical element in the mix as issue areas are related over the political landscape and interconnected within and between virtual and physical sites. For the purposes of this chapter, the notion of national security is broad and multi-dimensional, able to capture security factor effects associated with a wide ranging set of issues such as education, the human rights regime (the system of codified and un-codified law that protects the single most incontrovertible rights we have as human beings that include, but are not limited to, the right to be free from physical harm and other forms of harm, freedom of movement, freedom of self expression, and the right of self determination, where a people bound together by means of ethnic attributes, strives to acquire greater autonomy or a nation-state outright), and the equitable allocation of resources. In other words, contemporary notions of security should be as inclusive as possible to take into account non-military security determinants.

26.3 CYBER THREATS

Traditionally, the use of sophisticated malware has primarily been the purview of a select few nation-states and their proxies, but that appears to be changing. Even though Russian President Dimitry Medvedev used cyber-attacks in the Russo-Georgian War (2008) and President Vladimir Putin used cyber-attacks in Estonia and against Ukrainian energy infrastructure within the context of the Russian-Ukrainian conflict in 2015, the watershed event for cyber-attacks driven by national interest objectives probably remains the Stuxnet virus. The Stuxnet virus was used against nuclear facilities in Iran in 2009–2010, and in the process infected other computer systems worldwide. According to most accounts, it was probably crafted primarily by the Americans and Israelis.

26.3.1 National Interest Based

In effect, the Stuxnet virus was novel because it elicited physical actions and reactions—it destroyed Iran's German-made Siemens nuclear centrifuges and plunged Iran into a potential physical conflict with the U.S. and Israel. In response to Stuxnet, the Iranian group, The Cutting

Sword of Justice, assaulted Aramco facilities in Saudi Arabia with the Shamoon virus [11–13]. What is critical about those attacks is they were carried out within a political context that shaped those cyber intrusions which qualify as either an act of cyber-terrorism, cyber-war, or "cyber-skirmish," where a conflict does not rise to the level of war. One useful lesson learned from this experience is that thresholds between cyber-attacks and real world terrorist acts remain unknown, both from the direction of cyber-assaults to physical attacks, and vice versa [13, 14].

One challenge for security practitioners in the virtual world is that a perpetrator's identity is often very difficult to assign. Nevertheless, even when uncertainty about a perpetrator's identity and motivations exist, security experts can fall back on contextual factors that are political, economic, and cultural in nature and provide clues to making appraisals about identity. In addition to contextual factors that frame attacks, there are antecedent events to the attack that happen either alone or in reaction to other antecedent events. Those events are known as "stressors" and can help provide clues for investigators to attribute responsibility to actors in the physical and the virtual world.

The emergent reality is that non-government actors, many with links to governments that are sometimes greater or lesser in intensity, have become predominant threats over the cyberspace landscape. For instance, the Lazarus Group or ZINC is widely regarded as the cyber- organization that hacked into the Central Bank of Bangladesh in 2016, and through its SWIFT customer transaction software system, made off with eighty-one million U.S. dollars. Another Lazarus Group attack more widely known was the cyber-assault into SONY Pictures in 2014, in response to SONY's production of a film that ridiculed North Korea's President Kim Jung Un.

Another major actor is the Shadow Brokers Group that appeared in 2016; it is probably best-known for its April 2017 data breach into the National Security Agency (NSA) and the theft of zero day exploits, where malware is timed to activate on "day zero" after prior introduction to a computer system. In that clandestine market, hackers work continuously to produce and sell what Harris calls bundles of "zero day exploit subscriptions." Once purchased, those zero day exploits are stored by the NSA, at least to take them off the market, and in some cases to prepare them for use in the future against opponents of the United States [15–19]. Even though the Shadow Brokers Group's real identities and set of interconnections to other actors remains unclear, its activities have been relatively straightforward—it seeks money through crowdfunding by selling stolen zero day exploits to the highest bidder.

In some cases, what originally originated as narrower threats have the potential to grow exponentially. For example, the WannaCry virus, probably unleashed by the North Korean supported Lazarus Group, was issued in two batches—the first was limited to specific assaults against targets and was spread by means of computer "stolen credentials," in contrast to the second round of the WannaCry virus, where the use of a stolen National Security Agency (NSA) zero day exploit known as Eternal Blue, originally pirated by the Shadow Brokers Group, was used to mount or "piggy back" the WannaCry virus to infect computer systems [19–24]. The targets of WannaCry also involved more traditional government sites that included, but were not limited to, the Russian Interior Ministry and the United Kingdom's National Health Service (NHS). As previously mentioned, it was the Shadow Brokers Group that hacked into the U.S. National Security Agency (NSA)'s website to target NSA's elite Tailored Access Operations (TAO) cyberspace unit, otherwise known as the Equation Group, to steal Eternal Blue and other NSA zero day exploits [15, 23, 25–29].

Other computer viruses with links to nation-states include the Duqu and Flame viruses— viruses with close ties to each other and Stuxnet. The Duqu virus probably appeared in 2007 and might have been an antecedent virus to the Stuxnet virus unleashed in 2009–2010, as it shares similar code fragments to Stuxnet that serve as a manufacturer or perpetrator signature [30–32]. It appears the Duku virus's successor Duku 2.0 was crafted with a very specific use in mind which was to spy on the P5+1 (United States, Great Britain, Germany, China, Russia, and France) negotiations that attempted to break the negotiations impasse about Iran's fledgling nuclear program. In turn, the Flame virus might have existed prior to the development of either Duqu or Stuxnet, and was notable because of its large megabyte size and ability to lie hidden from cyber-security experts [32, 33].

26.3.2 Ransomware

In addition to particular viruses closely linked to states, a spate of ransomware attacks has been unleashed against multinational corporations and other targets. What is of particular interest to many cyber-attackers are firms that produce "dual use" technology with military as well as civilian applications. Attacks designed to steal proprietary information or intellectual property rights to enhance the competitive advantage of firms qualify as cyber-espionage attacks. Those types of cyber-attacks range from cyber-assaults with political motivation and powerful connections to nation-states, to some with political and economic "hybrid" motivations, to some without any political motivation. The SamSam organization is one outfit that conducts ransomware assaults against non-profit institutions such as universities and government targets—in each case asking for some $50,000 U.S. to unlock data taken hostage [34].

26.3.3 Cyber-Espionage and "Apolitical" Threats

Cyber-espionage attacks have plagued MNCs such as Volkswagen, Dow Chemical, Ford, GM, Renault, and firms in the aerospace industry associated with military grade products. Other more common cyber-intrusion threats emanate from perpetrators who are clearly non-state actors with "apolitical" personal motivations where anger or greed drive deviant/criminal behaviors [13, 35, 36]. Such individuals can be former workers or people associated with vendors that serviced particular firms, and they engage in sabotage efforts to compromise a targeted firm's computer systems. That condition has posed challenges for cyber-security experts because in many cases, former employees often have an extensive knowledge of a firm's computer systems and know how to create the most damage to files or other parts of computer systems. Compounding the problem even more are end-user vulnerabilities—Popescul and Radu report that in 2014 "a Hewlitt Packard study showed 80% of things in IoT fail to require passwords of a sufficient complexity and length, 70% enable an attacker to identify valid user accounts through account enumeration, 70% use unencrypted user services and 60% raise security concerns with their user interfaces" [37].

26.4 THREATS TO BUSINESS

Terrorism in its traditional forms is not a new phenomenon but spans millennia and geographic locales. In the contemporary world, what is new is the linkage between terrorism and technology within an increasingly interconnected world of intensive globalization [13]. Since 9/11, many traditional targets of terrorism such as government facilities and some civilian targets such as military recruitment centers, army bases, airports, electrical grids, train stations, water systems, and sports stadiums have been hardened. An important element in the terrorist targeting equation is opportunity recognition; that coupled with the symbolism associated with many international businesses and their countries of origin make commercial sites an increasingly attractive target.

In addition, international businesses have money and other resources available to terrorists that include monetary and scientific knowledge that could be used as ransom in exchange for the safe return of hostages. At a functional level, MNCs and other international enterprises are vulnerable to terrorist assaults because of long supply chains both in geographical terms and vertically in organizational terms, within the context of fourth tier, third tier, second tier, and first tier supplier manufacturers who produce sub-components and other supplies for original equipment manufacturers (OEM).

A savvy terrorist group focused on ripple effect terrorism, where acts in either the physical or virtual world might lead to a cascade of economic and political effects, would be particularly interested in geographic locales with distribution choke points close to international borders such as in the Detroit, Michigan–Windsor, Ontario area, and in geographic locales with large firms in close physical proximity. When firms are in close physical proximity to one another, that condition can help to achieve external economies of scale where the cost of production is reduced. External economies of scale are characterized by a condition where innovative ideas and new skills are disseminated across firms, suppliers are in many cases in close proximity, and where firms do not have to search far and wide for highly trained talent as workers move from firm to firm. Areas such as Detroit and the Silicon Valley are examples of external economies of scale communities and thus pose particularly tantalizing targets for terrorists who want to cripple an industry, attack the democratic capitalist system, or both.

26.4.1 Terrorism

Empirically, there is ample evidence of terrorist group focus on business targets; there have been several well-known attacks against domestic and international businesses within the context of international or domestic political strife or both. One well-known terrorist event is the 2008 Lashkar-e-Taiba attacks in Mumbai, India against a hospital, train station, a Jewish Chabad House, and several businesses such as the Taj Mahal Hotel, Leopold Café, and the Oberoi Trident Hotel. Another is the ISIS attack in January 2015 against a Jewish owned grocery store and the *Charlie Hebdo* offices in Paris. Additional ISIS attacks in Paris happened in November 2015 against the Stade de France sports center, the Bataclan music hall, and in the process, an assortment of cafes and restaurants.

Other major events include the attack against the Tigantourine gas facility in Algeria by Mokhtar Belmokhtar's Battalion of Blood (Muwaqi'un Bil Dima), and Colonel Muammar el Qaddafi's attack against Pan American Airlines (PAA) flight 103 that detonated over Lockerbie, Scotland. Therefore, while the threat against commercial interests is not new, the prospect of sustained and sophisticated attacks against high-profile commercial interest stakeholders to affect the international political system or an entire national political system probably is, in ways that mirror the apparent change in terrorist attack strategy to what Sprinzak calls "super-terrorism" to maximize numbers killed rather than relying on psychological effects intrinsic to terrorist assaults that cause limited property damage, and the deaths and injuries to a select few.

26.4.2 Cyber Intrusions

In terms of the virtual world, malware threats to computer systems have become increasing complex, and the threats posed by malware have become extremely dynamic because of new technology and its off-the-shelf availability (COTS). Compounding the problem is the continuously evolving threat of intensive globalization's thickened ties within and between existing computer networks and between communities and individuals with political or economic grievances. The capacity of hackers to infiltrate computer systems has grown apace in the eight years since Stuxnet. For instance, while the Stuxnet virus probably required an individual to breach the "air gapped" system at the Natanz nuclear facility, wireless access to computer data called "war-driving" has become commonplace [11–13, 37].

Equally important, the scope of threat has expanded to include threats that might or might not be political in nature but have the same end goal—to cause psychological and physical damage, and in some cases, to kill. Remote access to ports through entertainment information systems (e.g. infotainment systems) in automobiles and into computer hardware and software in aircraft is now possible; the prospect that medical devices and even toys are now vulnerable to remote hacking is real [37, 38]. As mentioned previously, many terrorism experts predict an increase in focus against business targets as traditional targets are increasingly hardened because terrorists recognize that attacks against business, especially MNCs, have the potential to be lucrative both in terms of ripple effects to disrupt severely the international commerce system and in the narrower sense, to provide revenue for terrorist group coffers. What follows next is a discussion of different public–private partnership types to conceptualize layers of protection utilizing public, private, and non-profit entities.

26.5 PUBLIC–PRIVATE PARTNERSHIPS

The idea of public–private partnerships in the security arena as pertains to terrorism and cyberthreats is to increase effectiveness and efficiency by means of interlocking networks of public–private partner arrangements. In those arrangements, different types of stakeholders play lead roles based on the different conditions found in different operational environments —each operational environment has different contextual factors and effects that influence preferences for lead role choice [39]. Overall, emphasis on improvement of effectiveness and efficiency is an approach Savas calls the "pragmatic" approach to public–private partnerships. It might be the case for example, that public entities such as U.S.AID would take a lead role in certain public–private partnerships because of reputation, copious infrastructure, technological strengths, the capacity to help raise large amounts of money, or the ability to negotiate across borders to engage other governments in the quest to utilize non-state actors within such arrangements [1, 2].

In contrast, non-state actors such as non-governmental organizations (NGOs) and community-based organizations (CBOs) might have in-depth experience and contacts in specific operational environments as well as extensive knowledge about how local stakeholders behave and interact. In those cases, leadership roles for NGOs or clusters of CBOs perhaps in conjunction with MNCs in public–private partnerships might be prudent. In that context, non-state actor-led networks of public–private partnerships that work with governments concerned with physical and cyber-security threats might have access to substantial resources which, as previously mentioned, make it possible to achieve economies of scale in production of counterterrorism and cyber-security regimes, products, and services.

While the foregoing pertains to the physical world, public–private partnership arrangements can be configured to tackle challenges associated with cyber-security. Public–private partnerships have cyber security applications because the motivations behind threats are very similar in both the physical and virtual world, be they political, economic, or personal grievance motivations, or a combination thereof [13]. In fact, the conception of human beings as "flawed" and highly emotional, where atavistic sentiments of greed, lust, and desire for control consume the potential for rational decision-making processes is the cornerstone of Realism philosophy's conception of human nature—a condition that does not change.

26.5.1 Characteristics of Goods and Services

At a theoretical level, it is apparent that national security counterterrorism and cyber-security efforts at the national level are a "pure" collective or public "joint consumption good" because a nation-state's security is indivisible, where one party cannot take advantage of this condition to exclude others from enjoying its benefits. In contrast, if the public–private partnership focus is on the state or municipal/local geographical locales characterized by narrow political boundaries, counterterrorism and cyber-security initiatives could become what Savas calls "a toll good," characterized by "exclusion and joint consumption."

What is significant here is that in this case, targeted end-users could sell or otherwise provide those counterterrorism and cyberspace protections to parties beyond the designated scope of a program's targeted end-users. That has important ramifications for program measurement, already difficult enough because it is hard to quantify success in the realm of security. Thus, the goods and services produced by public–private partnerships with narrower geographical scope are, by their very nature, more "impure" as it is possible, as mentioned previously, for end-users to take advantage of program boundaries at the expense of others by supplying non-targeted consumers. Put another way, some distinctions in exclusion and other subsequent distortions associated with those benefits, such as third or fourth party transfer, will most likely exist to skew supply appraisals and lead to problems with measurement of program effectiveness and efficiency [1, 2].

Even though potential for improved effectiveness and efficiencies exist with public–private partnership implementation, there are several potential pitfalls. It follows from the nature of the human condition that turf wars which revolve around jealousies, personality differences, and competition over scarce and finite resources are potential problems in efforts to develop trust between stakeholders, both within public–private partnership design and implementation phases. The Committee on Private-Public Sector Collaboration to Enhance Community Disaster Resilience reports that public sector organizational culture is so different from private and non-profit sector counterparts that effective and sustained collaboration can be very difficult.

One recommendation made by the authors of that committee report is for stakeholders to create "boundary organizations" with a singular focus on work to encourage trust and a better understanding between stakeholders about suspicions such as the belief among many in the private sector that public–private partnerships open the door to greater government regulation and oversight of the private sector [1]. Another recommendation is to conduct a PIN analysis of each stakeholder, where the "positions," "interests," and "needs" of stakeholders are clearly spelled out. In a PIN analysis, positions are made by stakeholders for public consumption while unspoken interests and needs are present to be deciphered by "boundary organization" negotiation specialists who seek to uncover the motivations behind positions and actions.

26.5.2 A Functional Public–Private Partnership Typology

In efforts to fashion a functional P3 typology, it is necessary to determine the basic arrangements or configurations of public–private partnerships. With that in mind, a three-dimensional rectangular, cube-like typology is crafted. This cube-like typology draws from Starr and Most's work on third world conflict where three planes or dimensions associated with public–private partnership types correspond to three distinguishing characteristics—(1) sector-type, (2) infrastructure-dominance, and (3) scope of operations. Along one plane is the distinguishing characteristic sector-type; along the second plane of the typology the second distinguishing characteristic of public–private partnerships is found, infrastructure dominance. The third distinguishing characteristic of public–private partnerships, scope of operations, is represented along the third dimension of that typology [40, 41].

In terms of the first distinguishing characteristic, sector-type, public–private partnerships are sorted out into those (1) led by public entities, (2) led by private entities, and (3) led by non-profit entities. In the case of infrastructure dominance, infrastructure is broken down into eight types: (1) national government dominant, (2) state/provincial government dominant, (3) municipal/local dominant, (4) IGO dominant, (5) MNC dominant, (6) NGO dominant, (7) CBO dominant, and (8) international enterprise dominant. For our purposes, the distinction between an MNC and international enterprise revolves around whether or not the firm under consideration is publicly or privately held. The third distinguishing characteristic, scope of operations, reflects the theme that from the perspective of an entity in a lead position, each partnership type generally has, at least as its primary venue, a target population within distinct geographical parameters. Hence, scope of operations is broken down into (1) international, (2) national, and (3) state (province/department/municipal/local) (see Figure 26.1).

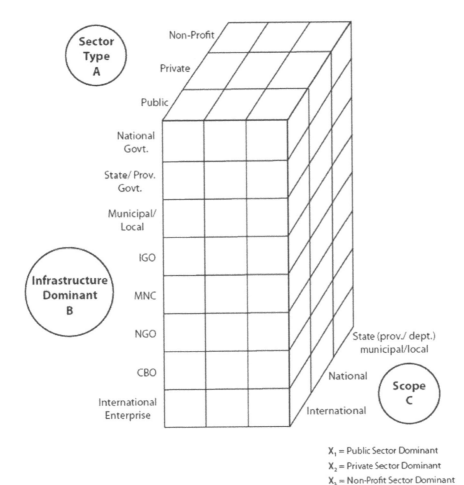

Figure 26.1 Public–private partnership typology.

There are seventy two possible combinations of public–private partnerships that derive from the typology and three broad public–private partnership sector types. Those three sector types include X_1 = public sector dominant; X_2 = private sector dominant; X^3 = non-profit sector dominant. The coding framework and possible configurations are as follows:

A. Sector type: 1 = public; 2 = private; 3 = non-profit
B. Infrastructure dominance: 1 = national government dominant; 2 = state/province/department government dominant; 3 = municipal/local government dominant; 4 = IGO dominant 5 = MNC dominant 6 = NGO dominant 7 = CBO dominant 8 = international enterprise dominant
C. Scope of Operations: 1 = international; 2 = national 3 = state (province/department) and/or municipal/local scope
  1. $A^1 B^1 C^1$ 1, 1, 1, = a public sector national government dominant public–private partnership with international scope. Type – X^1
  2. $A^1 B^1 C^2$ 1, 1, 2, = a public sector national government dominant public–private partnership with national scope. Type – X^1 (e.g. U.S.AID program)
  3. $A^1 B^1 C^3$ 1, 1, 3, = a public sector national government dominant public–private partnership with state/province/department and/or municipal/local scope. Type – X^1 (e.g. President Barack Obama's CVE pilot programs)
  4. $A^1 B^2 C^1$ 1, 2, 1, = a public sector state/province/department government dominant public–private partnership with international scope. Type – X^1 normative
  5. $A^1 B^2 C^2$ 1, 2, 2, = a public sector state/province/department government dominant public–private partnership with national scope. Type – X^1 normative
  6. $A^1 B^2 C^3$ 1, 2, 3, = a public sector state/province/department government dominant public–private partnership with state/province/department and/or municipal/local scope. Type- X^1 (e.g. Governor Mitt Romney's "Romney Care")
  7. $A^1 B^3 C^1$ 1, 3, 1, = a public sector municipal/local government dominant public–private partnership with international scope. Type – X^1 normative
  8. $A^1 B^3 C^2$ 1, 3, 2, = a public sector municipal/local government dominant public–private partnership with national scope. Type – X^1 normative
  9. $A^1 B^3 C^3$ 1, 3, 3, = a public sector municipal/local government dominant public–private partnership with state/province/department and/or municipal/local scope. Type – X^1
  10. $A^1 B^4 C^1$ 1, 4, 1, = a public sector IGO dominant public–private partnership with international scope Type – X^1 (e.g. World Bank, International Monetary Fund, UNICEF programs)
  11. $A^1 B^4 C^2$ 1, 4, 2, = a public sector IGO dominant public–private partnership with national scope. Type – X^1 (e.g. UNHCR programs)
  12. $A^1 B^4 C^3$ 1, 4, 3, = a public sector IGO dominant public–private partnership with state/province/department and/or municipal/local scope. Type – X^1 (e.g. certain UN Relief Initiatives)
       (e.g. IGO driven aid to specific disaster areas in countries)
  13. $A^1 B^5 C^1$ 1, 5, 1, = a public sector MNC(s) dominant public–private partnership with international scope.
  14. $A^1 B^5 C^2$ 1, 5, 2, = a public sector MNC(s) dominant public–private partnership with national scope.
  15. $A^1 B^5 C^3$ 1, 5, 3, = a public sector MNC(s) dominant public–private partnership with state/province/department and/or municipal/local scope.

16. $A^1B^6C^1$ 1, 6, 1, = a public sector NGO(s) dominant public–private partnership with international scope.
17. $A^1B^6C^2$ 1, 6, 2, = a public sector NGO(s) dominant public–private partnership with national scope.
18. $A^1B^6C^3$ 1, 6, 3, = a public sector NGO(s) dominant public–private partnership with state/province/department and/or municipal/local scope.
19. $A^1B^7C^1$ 1, 7, 1, = a public sector CBO(s) dominant public–private partnership with international scope.
20. $A^1B^7C^2$ 1, 7, 2, = a public sector CBO(s) dominant public–private partnership with national scope.
21. $A^1B^7C^3$ 1, 7, 3, = a public sector CBO(s) dominant public–private partnership with state/province/department and/or municipal/local scope.
22. $A^1B^8C^1$ 1, 8, 1, = a public sector international enterprise(s) dominant public–private partnership with international scope.
23. $A^1B^8C^2$ 1, 8, 2, = a public sector international enterprise(s) dominant public–private partnership with national scope.
24. $A^1B^8C^3$ 1, 8, 3, = a public sector international enterprise(s) dominant public–private partnership with state/province/department and/or municipal/local scope.
25. $A^2B^1C^1$ 2, 1, 1, = a private sector national government dominant public–private partnership with international scope.
26. $A^2B^1 C^2$ 2, 1, 2, = a private sector national government dominant public–private partnership with national scope.
27. $A^2B^1C^3$ 2, 1, 3, = a private sector national government dominant public–private partnership with state/province/department and/or municipal/local scope.
28. $A^2B^2C^1$ 2, 2, 1, = a private sector state/province/department government dominant public–private partnership with international scope.
29. $A^2B^2C^2$ 2, 2, 2, = a private sector state/province/department government dominant public–private partnership with national scope.
30. $A^2B^2C^3$ 2, 2, 3, = a private sector state/province/department government dominant public–private partnership with state/province/department and/or municipal/local scope.
31. $A^2 B^3 C^1$ 2, 3, 1, = a private sector municipal/local government dominant public–private partnership with international scope.
32. $A^2 B^3C^2$ 2, 3, 2, = a private sector municipal/local government dominant public–private partnership with national scope.
33. $A^2B^3C^3$ 2, 3, 3, = a private sector municipal/local government dominant public–private partnership with state/province/department and/or municipal/local scope
34. $A^2B^4C^1$ 2, 4, 1, = a private sector IGO dominant public–private sector with international scope.
35. $A^2B^4C^2$ 2, 4, 2, = a private sector IGO dominant public–private partnership with national scope
36. $A^2B^4C^3$ 2, 4, 3, = a private sector IGO dominant public–private partnership with state/province/department and/or municipal/local scope
37. $A^2B^5C^1$ 2, 5, 1, = a private sector MNC(s) dominant public–private partnership with international scope. Type – X^2 (e.g. Ford Foundation program a)
38. $A^2B^5C^2$ 2, 5, 2, = a private sector MNC(s) dominant public–private partnership with national scope. Type – X^2

39. $A^2B^5C^3$ 2, 5, 3, = a private sector MNC(s) dominant public–private partnership with state/province/department and/or municipal/local scope. Type – X^2 (e.g. Ford Foundation program b)
40. $A^2B^6C^1$ 2, 6, 1, = a private sector NGO(s) dominant public–private partnership with international scope.
41. $A^2B^6C^2$ 2, 6, 2, = a private sector NGO(s) dominant public–private sector partnership with national scope.
42. $A^2B^6C^3$ 2, 6, 3, = a private sector NGO(s) dominant public–private partnership with state/province/department and/or municipal/local scope.
43. $A^2B^7C^1$ 2,7, 1, = a private sector CBO(s) dominant public–private partnership with international scope.
44. $A^2B^7C^2$ 2, 7, 2, = a private sector CBO(s) dominant public–private partnership with national scope.
45. $A^2B^7C^3$ 2, 7, 3, = a private sector CBO(s) dominant public–private partnership with state/province/department and/or municipal/local scope.
46. $A^2B^8C^1$ 2, 8,1, = a private sector international enterprise(s) dominant public–private partnership with international scope. Type – X^2 (e.g. Rockefeller Foundation)
47. $A^2B^8C^2$ 2, 8, 2, = a private sector international enterprise(s) dominant public–private partnership with national scope. Type – X^2
48. $A^2B^8C^3$ 2, 8, 3, = a private sector international enterprise(s) dominant public–private partnership with state/province/department and/or municipal/local scope. Type – X^2
49. $A^3B^1C^1$ 3, 1, 1, = a non-profit national government dominant public–private partnership with international scope.
50. $A^3B^1C^2$ 3, 1, 2, = a non-profit municipal/local government dominant public–private partnership with national scope.
51. $A^3B^1C^3$ 3, 1, 3, = a non-profit national government dominant public–private partnership with state/province/department and/or municipal/local scope.
52. $A^3B^2C^1$ 3, 2, 1, = a non-profit state/province/department government dominant public–private partnership with international scope.
53. $A^3B^2C^2$ 3, 2, 2, = a non-profit state/province/department government dominant public–private partnership with national scope.
54. $A^3B^2C^3$ 3, 2, 3, = a non-profit state/province/department government dominant public–private partnership with state/province/department and/or municipal/local scope.
55. $A^3B^3C^1$ 3, 3, 1, = a non-profit municipal/local government dominant public–private partnership with international scope.
56. $A^3B^3C^2$ 3, 3, 2, = a non-profit municipal/local government dominant public-partnership with national scope.
57. $A^3B^3C^3$ 3, 3, 3, = a non-profit municipal/local government dominant public–private partnership with state/province/department and/or municipal/local scope.
58. $A^3B^4C^1$ 3, 4, 1, = a non-profit IGO dominant public–private partnership with international scope.
59. $A^3B^4C^2$ 3, 4, 2, = a non-profit IGO dominant public–private partnership with national scope.
60. $A^3B^4C^3$ 3, 4, 3, = a non-profit IGO dominant public–private partnership with state/province/department and/or municipal/local scope.

61. $A^3B^5C^1$ 3, 5, 1, = a non-profit MNC(s) dominant public–private partnership with international scope.

62. $A^3B^5C^2$ 3, 5, 2, = a non-profit MNC(s) dominant public–private partnership with national scope.

63. $A^3B^5C^3$ 3, 5, 3, = a non-profit MNC(s) dominant public–private partnership with state/province/department and/or municipal/local scope.

64. $A^3B^6C^1$ 3, 6, 1, = a non-profit NGO(s) dominant public–private partnership with international scope. Type – X^3 (e.g. the Bill and Melinda Gates Foundation, Soros Foundation, International Planned Parenthood Federation)

65. $A^3B^6C^2$ 3, 6, 2, = a non-profit NGO(s) dominant public–private partnership with national scope. Type – X^3 (e.g. Planned Parenthood Foundation of America)

66. $A^3B^6C^3$ 3, 6, 3, = a non-profit NGO(s) dominant public–private partnership with state/province/department and/or municipal/local scope. Type – X^3

67. $A^3B^7C^1$ 3, 7, 1, = a nonprofit CBO(s) dominant public–private partnership with international scope. Type – X^3 normative

68. $A^3B^7C^2$ 3, 7, 2, = a non-profit CBO(s) dominant public–private partnership with national scope. Type – X^3 normative

69. $A^3B^7C^3$ 3, 7, 3, = a non-profit CBO(s) dominant public–private partnership with state/province/department and/or municipal/local scope. Type – X^3

70. $A^3B^8C^1$ 3, 8, 1, = a non-profit international enterprise(s) dominant public–private partnership with international scope.

71. $A^3B^8C^2$ 3, 8, 2, = a non-profit international enterprise(s) dominant public–private partnership with national scope.

72. $A^3B^8C^3$ 3, 8, 3, = a non-profit international enterprise(s) dominant public–private partnership with state/province/department and/or municipal/local scope.

Accordingly, this is a 3×8×3 cube-like typology with 72 possible public–private partnership combinations. In some cases, particular organizations fall into iteration categories based on mission, while in other cases, particular organizations have programs with different scope of operations. In those cases, the scope of operations determines under which of the iterations the program under consideration is placed. To be sure, in some 72 cases there are unanticipated residual effects of specific public–private partnerships such as broader scope impact or interactive effects between partnerships that might create some categorization imprecision. It should be clear not all of those combinations exist in the larger world of action [41]. The central idea is to extract from the typology public–private partnership types that exist or could exist in the future and which make sense theoretically.

To do that assists in classification efforts and helps place focus on what types of public–private partnerships might evolve in the future should the political system or its component parts continue to change in ways consistent with notions that effective units of governance can be found at sub-national and supra-national levels to at least complement nation-state operations. For example, Follett, who focuses on sub-national and sub-state units of governance, draws on a study of Boston, Massachusetts neighborhoods to make the case for neighborhood empowerment. Etzioni, who builds on the work of Follett, focuses on small units of governance that simultaneously work in conjunction with much larger units of governance beyond the nation-state such as intergovernmental organizations (IGOs) like the European Union (EU) [42, 43].

As previously mentioned, there are many iterations of public–private partnerships in this typology not found in the real world, but from those that are, it is possible to extract three broad types: X_1 = public sector dominant; X_2 = private sector dominant; X_3 = non-profit dominant. It is crucial to note that within each of those broad categories are different possible combinations of infrastructure dominant types and scope of operations configurations where an MNC or international enterprise, for example, takes the lead role in a private sector dominant configuration.

Clearly, particular aspects of public–private partnership arrangements such as scope or stakeholder can change with the passage of time, but the possible configuration types that derive from this typology are flexible enough to accommodate those types of changes. What is significant is this typology is functional because it can generate hypotheses about different public–private partnership types to be tested empirically in future research. With public–private partnerships that provide *indirect* security benefits, change in rates or levels of educational attainment, crime, and urban decay could be measured. In terms of public–private partnerships with more *direct* security orientation, change in incident rates, for example, associated with different types of public–private partnerships and cyber threats, cyber- intrusions incidents, threats of terrorism by groups, lone wolf attacks and threats, and apolitical threats or incidents associated with former workers for example, could be analyzed.

Some real life examples of those public–private partnership types can help illustrate distinctions between them and possible stakeholder combinations within those three broad types of public–private partnerships. In each of these real life cases, defense against terrorism and cyber-intrusions is not the primary objective, but even so, the indirect spillover effects of such public–private partnerships to address those types of security related vulnerabilities are substantial. For instance, public–private partnerships that have as their goals the reduction of economic, political, and social tensions, work to reduce economic, cultural, and political marginalization, that according to Sageman, can lead to "alienation" and other similar sentiments that can in turn lead to terrorism, cybercrime, or cyberterrorism [1, 13, 44–48].

In the case of different public–private partnership types, one cluster of public sector government dominant public–private partnerships with national or regional emphasis is the set of U.S.AID programs carried out in conjunction with non-profit non-governmental organization (NGOs) and private sector firms. The U.S.AID's global development alliances (GDA) platform was established in 2001 and revolves around some 40 different initiatives. Those GDAs programs are designed to support development of the rudiments of democratic society. One early GDA initiative that was implemented focused on the Balkans, where public and private entities put emphasis on improvement in good governance to enhance transparency, accountability, and civil society, namely that condition where non-governmental institutions can operate unfettered by government interference [1, 49–56].

Some U.S.AID public–private partnerships provide focus to specific regions or populations of a country with narrower objectives and time frames. For example, the Public Private Partnership MHeath Intervention in Delhi, Jharkhand, and Uttarakhand (2016–2018) was designed to cut infant and maternal mortality rates in those parts of India in the title, in part by providing communications technologies to families. That public–private partnership involved the Bill and Melinda Gates Foundation and Barr Foundation as primary sources for capital and the BBC Media Action as an implementation partner for the program. It is probably no exaggeration to say that the international context of this program, U.S.AID's role as lead provider of U.S. foreign assistance since 1961, U.S.AID's close ties to the U.S. State Department, and myriad appropriations regulations, worked to confer to U.S.AID lead agency status, a status that conforms to the government dominant model [1, 49–56].

Another example of a U.S.AID sponsored global development alliance was the Cisco Alliance, formed to promote economic and social development in the Russian Federation through training and information technology (IT) dissemination. In this arrangement, U.S.AID contributions were substantially less than those made by other stakeholders in this program, where for every U.S.$4.00 to $5.00 U.S. dollars donated by stakeholders, U.S.AID contributed U.S.$1.00 dollar. However, President Vladimir Putin's decision to expel U.S.AID from Russia in September 2012 illustrates the potential downside of government-led agency status in public–private partnerships within international contexts, where vulnerabilities can materialize because of strains in political relationships between nation-states [57].

An example of a non-profit dominant public–private partnership type with municipal/local focus is the number of community based organizations (CBOs) in the United States that provide social services to specific clusters of neighborhoods where populations in many, but certainly not all cases, are immigrants or second generation Americans who often experience economic difficulties and cultural marginalization. Those services include provision of resources and assistance to families that face pressures associated with acculturation and monetary issues. There is focus on assistance to help clients obtain education advancement, career enhancement, or a combination of both. In some cases, these CBOs are at least partially funded or otherwise contracted as providers by state or local governments to perform tasks because of the specialized knowledge they possess about culture and the languages of the populations they serve. As such, and sometimes because immigrant populations are leery of government organizations in general, it might be advisable that CBOs take lead agency status in such public–private partnerships.

Turning to public–private partnerships with more direct influence on security concerns, in this case on counterterrorism, one prominent example is the Indonesian national government's sponsorship and support for public-private partnership programs to help de-radicalize and rehabilitate former terrorists who have previously been incarcerated. This type of public sector public–private partnership is national government dominant, as national government policy-makers are tasked with working to construct the program in conjunction with municipal/local governments and religious leaders and counselors with national interests in mind. What some programs do is focus on the employment of former terrorists in the food and restaurant sector because for Indonesian de-radicalization and rehabilitation officials, emphasis on serving food to others irrespective of national, ethnic, or religious origins, is conducive to the breakdown of hatreds and works to retrain individuals to think in more inclusive ways [58].

One reason why public–private partnership types with direct influence on cyber-security or terrorism should be overlaid against other types of public–private partnerships primarily with non-security goals is so various private sector stakeholders across industries can coordinate and contribute expertise in both domains. For example, Google or Facebook might partner with the U.S. national government to provide information compilation services and analysis of large data sets, while working on other non-security related corporate social responsibility (CSR) efforts. In addition to efforts to promote sustainability such as GM's green efforts in China for example, the automotive industry might partner with national or state government or both to engage in the production of research, goods, and services related to counterterrorism and cyber-security. As mentioned earlier, U.S. multinational corporations in the automotive industry might work in partnership with the federal government to become purchasers of zero day exploits crafted to affect automobiles, to augment the purchase of zero day exploits by the U.S. National Security Agency (NSA).

In addition, the U.S. government should work with financial institutions, private security firms like Symantec, FireEye, and Crowdstrike, and small businesses, defined as having one hundred or fewer employees, to create substantive and deep layers of security protection. As the Committee on Private-Public Sector Collaboration to Enhance Community Disaster Resilience suggests, the U.S. Chamber of Commerce has the organizational infrastructure to facilitate relationships between stakeholders in ways that promote trust and the prospect of effective and sustained relationships between government and firms. With respect to financial institutions, Shelley and Picarelli report that U.S. government law enforcement agencies could work with banks in more effective and sustained ways to monitor illegal financial transactions that are the lifeblood of terrorist groups and organized crime. This becomes critical nowadays, where interests and functions of terrorist groups and organized crime have increasingly converged since the end of the Cold War [1, 13, 59–61].

In the case of small business, the U.S. government could collaborate with such private security firms to provide small businesses whose owners cannot afford a full-time chief security information officer (CSIO) or top flight cyber-security systems, with security infrastructure to deter and disrupt cyberspace intrusions. Even though Mancur Olsen states that effective government incentives to compel private sector stakeholders to help provide collective goods such as cyber-security can be hard to craft, such incentives might include tax incentives such as tax deductions, write-offs, or subsidies [1]. In addition to the provision of more seamless protections, such public–private arrangements might improve the effectiveness and accuracy of reporting systems for cyber-intrusions because firms would feel less inhibited about reporting breaches for fear of frightening investors or stockholders.

This typology serves as an invaluable tool for work to isolate and identify public–private partnership types as a first step to begin the process of crafting various packages of public–private partnerships to be used in specific operational environments with security in mind. Those configurations of public–private partnerships can be used simultaneously or sequentially to take into account contextual factor effects in specific operational environments and change in those factors and effects. This typology also makes it possible to conceptualize beyond what public–private partnerships exist nowadays, and to explore potential types of future public–private arrangements—a normative step of intrinsic importance to the interlocking of public–private partnerships as described below.

In this next section of the chapter, efforts are made to sort out public–private partnership types into empirical or extant types and more normative types that might take shape and appear as a function of increased globalization, technological innovation, and shifts in political attitudes about units of governance as Follett and Etzioni suggest might happen [42, 43]. A 3×2 matrix is crafted that posits sector type in three vertical columns (public, private, and non-profit), and two partnership types along horizontal rows that distinguish between empirical (i.e. extant) types, and normative types (see Figure 26.2).

For empirical types, X_1 (public sector dominant) public–private partnerships that fall into the empirical (i.e. extant) category include eight public–private partnership iterations:

#1 a national government (public sector) dominant public–private partnership with international scope with the likelihood that deliverables might become "toll goods" because certain regions or countries within them would presumably be outside the designed scope of policy focus.

#2 a national government (public sector) dominant public–private partnership with national focus where goods and services would be more collective, pure and joint distribution deliverables. In this case, an example might be the aforementioned U.S.AID programs with focus on particular countries such as the U.S.AID and Cisco Project in the Russian Federation [50].

Sector Types

Conditions	Public	Private	Non-Profit
Empirical	#1, #2, #3, #6, #9, #10, #11, #12	#37, #38, #39, #46, #47, #48	#64, #65, #66, #69
Normative	#4, #5, #7, #8		#67, #68

Figure 26.2 Public–private partnership, sector type X conditions.

#3 a national government dominant (public sector) public–private partnership with state/province/department and/or municipal/local scope. An example of that would be President Barack Obama's Countering Violent Extremism (CVE) pilot program to confront radicalism in specific Somali communities in the United States, [62, 63].

#6 a state/province/department government (public sector) dominant public–private partnership with state/province/department and/or municipal/local scope. Governor Mitt Romney's Massachusetts Romney Care health care initiative with the involvement of private sector insurance companies qualifies as an example, [64].

#9 a municipal/local government dominant public–private partnership with state/province/department and/or municipal/local scope, such as neighborhood restoration or revitalization programs.

#10 an IGO dominant public–private partnership with international scope, such as certain public–private partnerships sponsored by the World Bank or International Monetary Fund (IMF), [65].

#11 an IGO dominant public–private partnership with national scope. In that instance, programs under the auspices of the United Nations Commission for Refugees (UNHCR) in a particular country might qualify,

#12 an IGO dominant public–private partnership with state/province/department and/or municipal/local scope. In this case, United Nations relief initiatives directed at a particular state, (province, or department) of a nation-state and/or municipal/local sites for humanitarian reasons such as war torn-Damascus would qualify.

What amounts to a normative category for X_1 (public sector dominant) includes four iterations: #4, #5, #7, and #8:

#4 a state/province/department government(s) dominant public–private partnership with international scope.

#5 a state/province/department government(s) dominant public–private partnership with national scope.

#7 a municipal/local government(s) dominant public–private partnership with international scope.

#8 a municipal/local government(s) dominant public–private partnership with national scope.

In contrast, for X_2 (private sector dominant) public–private partnership types that are empirical category iterations include: #37, #38, #39, #46, #47, and #48:

#37 a private sector MNC(s) dominant public–private partnership with international scope, where one or more MNC(s) are dominant in efforts to influence or coordinate the activities of a government or governments to provide deliverables at the international level. The Ford Foundation with its emphasis on human rights protections in South Africa under apartheid and in Latin America would qualify.

#38 a private sector MNC(s) dominant public–private partnership with national scope.

#39 a private sector MNC(s) dominant public- private partnership with state/province/department and/or municipal/local scope, such as programs sponsored/or run by the Ford Foundation, with its involvement with the New Orleans Economic Opportunity Strategy, for example.

#46 a private sector international enterprise(s) dominant public–private partnership with international scope; the Rockefeller Foundation falls into this category,

#47 a private sector MNC(s) dominant public–private partnership with national scope.

#48 a private sector international enterprise(s) dominant public–private partnership with state/province/department and/or municipal/local scope. For X^2, there are no normative categories articulated.

In the case of X_3 (non-profit dominant) public–private partnerships, the empirical category includes four iterations:

#64 a non-profit NGO(s) dominant public–private partnership with international scope such as the Bill and Melinda Gates Foundation, Soros Foundation, and the International Planned Parenthood Federation.

#65 a non-profit NGO(s) dominant public–private partnership with national scope such as Planned Parenthood Foundation of America (PPFA).

#66 a non-profit NGO(s) dominant public–private partnership with state/province/department and/or municipal/local scope.

#69 a non-profit CBO(s) dominant public–private partnership with state/province/department and/or municipal/local scope.

In contrast, the "normative" category for X_3 includes two iterations:

#67 a non-profit CBO(s) dominant public–private partnership with international scope.

#68 a non-profit CBO(s) dominant public–private partnership with national scope.

In the case of normative configurations, it appears the most potential for continuously evolving configuration types might lie with public sector dominant arrangements (4 types), followed by non-profit sector dominant arrangements (2 types), followed by zero private sector dominated arrangements (0 types). If emphasis on the nation-state as the traditional unit of governance from the time of the Treaty of Westphalia (1648) onwards continues to change or shift, it seems possible some of those normative iterations, such as #67 and #68, and in the case of the former, clusters of CBO's working to serve the needs of a nation, defined by Esman as people with ethnic "ascriptive loyalties" working toward the establishment of a nation-state or increased autonomy, might transcend the traditional focus of CBOs on neighborhood clusters in towns and cities within nation-states [66].

26.5.3 Public–Private Partnership Integration

As previously mentioned, an underlying theme of this approach is to link together public–private partnerships characterized by indirect contextual influence over and more indirect protection against terrorism or cyber-intrusions, with public–private partnerships characterized by more direct influence over security, such as the public–private partnerships between the Indonesian government and restaurants described above that employ former terrorists to achieve deradicalization and rehabilitation objectives. The central idea is to create an interlocked set of layered protections that if envisioned pictorially, might resemble a squad of Roman soldiers in battle formation with shields interlocked in Testudo (The Roman Turtle) configuration to provide maximum protection [1].

After a compilation of public–private partnerships that are either extant or in the design phase (i.e. normative) for a particular operational environment, analysts should sort out different types of public–private partnerships arrangements derived from the typology with potential for direct and indirect influence over security issues found in the larger world of action. After those classifications of public–private partnerships are made according to public policy type iterations, policy-makers would delve more deeply to begin work to assemble specific packages of interlocking public–private partnerships with particular governments, private firms, and non-profit organizations, with links that connect those two direct and indirect public partnerships types.

These different package assortments found within a particular type of public–private partnership reflect different arrangements of specific stakeholders packaged together to take into account specific needs associated with an operational environment's contextual factors and effects. Those contextual factors include, but are not limited to, topography, levels of modernization, regime type, security systems in place, and intra-group and intergroup dynamics. For example, there might be two cyber-security firms working in conjunction with one counterterrorism stakeholder in a specific geographic locale with infrastructure prone to cyber-intrusions, dependent on what subject matter experts familiar with particular operational environmental factors and risks recommend. As contextual factors associated with particular operational environments (i.e. scope) affect the process of public–private partnership formation and effectiveness, it is critical for policy-makers and administrators to understand what those contextual factors are, how they fit together, and what the links are between different types of public–private partnership configurations deployed.

Public–private partnership packages and the protections they offer should be seen as dynamic with change as an intrinsic part of evolving processes, stressors (i.e. political events), and stakeholders associated with the operational environment system. Deployments of public–private partnership configurations with direct protections against terrorism or cyber threats or both can last until existing environmental conditions require change; hence, the emergent reality would compel implementation of new direct public–private partnership frameworks implemented either alone or in sequential order against the backdrop of other more indirect public–private partnerships oriented to revitalization, renewal, and reconstruction with longer implementation cycles. In terms of the organizational structure best suited for implementation, the Committee on Private-Public Sector Collaboration to Enhance Disaster Resilience asserts that during crisis events, flatter organizational structures are more conducive to collaboration and that the trust associated with flatter organizations is a pre-requisite for success. At the same time, the authors also suggest that flatter organizational structures nestled within more traditional top-down hierarchal structures that enhance the power of top-down directives might be the optimal condition.

Another underlying theme associated with the use of security-based, public–private partnerships in conjunction with others is that resilience to attack, namely that ability, as the U.S. government puts it, to "bounce back" to previous levels of political, cultural, and/or economic activity in a short-run period of weeks, for instance, is enhanced with the use of these combinations of public–private partnership types. That is the case prior to an attack, because protections and redundancies in protections are widely known to be in place by a government and the populace, and in a post-attack situation where both government resilience and societal resilience are strengthened because of clear and generally recognizable crisis protocols to follow [1, 67–69]. To secure that psychological resilience, the Committee on Private-Public Sector Collaboration to Enhance Disaster Resilience asserts programs that combine risk reduction strategies for pre-attack conditions, with carefully reasoned first responder protocols to activate in post-attack situations, have the highest resilience properties where targets of attacks can "bounce back" to pre-attack levels of activities [1].

26.5.4 Implications and Applications for "Smart Cities"

In part because of the growth of lone wolf, terrorist group, and cyber-intrusion threats in many parts of the world, the concept of "smart cities" with layers of protection tightly interwoven into plans for new infrastructure and plans for modification of old infrastructure has become a topic of considerable interest. For Guerra, "the goal of smart cities is to improve the quality of life for its citizens through technological means, ultimately creating more sustainable cities" [70]. Popescul and Radu argue that "smart cities" can enhance effectiveness and efficiency for citizens, primarily through the use of what Guerra calls "smart sensors" embedded in city infrastructure that gather information about patterns of human behavior which serve as the basis for new programs. At the same time, authorities such as Popescul and Radu acknowledge that such interconnectedness within and across physical and virtual assets pose a high degree of susceptibility to cyber-attacks [29, 37, 71].

From the start, it is useful to view a city and its surrounding areas as a complex adaptive system where changes in one factor or set of factors produce second, third, and fourth order effects in other areas of that integrated complex system [37, 72]. In a similar vein, Popescul and Radu break down this complex system into four highly integrated component parts: "smart things," inclusive of implements such as hand held devices, and computer driven appliances at home; "smart systems" of architecture, both physical and virtual that are interconnected and are interactive with people, "smart spaces," comprised of a confluence of "smart things" and the geospatial dimensions that surround them, and "smart citizens," those computer literate citizens within "smart cities" who interact with computer systems on a daily basis and in the process, share information about tastes, preferences, and behaviors [37, 71].

The domains of infrastructure include, but are not limited to, roads, highways, buildings, water facilities, food storage containment, bus, train, and airport terminals, energy and communications infrastructure, schools, and housing stock. Those assets are tangible hard points where public–private partnerships can be useful for construction or maintenance purposes or both, while education, acculturation programs, programs to confront political, cultural, or economic marginalization, and medical services, are not hard infrastructure sites, but soft points of process and deliverables interconnected even more heavily than in the past in "smart city" systems through computerization. At a functional level, these connections pose vulnerabilities where problems in one part of a system can amplify and cascade into other areas. In some cases, hard and soft points in a holistic system such as a "smart city" have direct relationships and effects—picture relationships between housing stock and food, or the connections between school services and mental and physical health problems. Those connections that exist between hard and soft points should be articulated in a complex systems analysis and serve as a blueprint for plug-in connection points for public–private partnerships.

If an inclusive definition of security is used, blended public–private partnerships that have both direct and indirect security effects and connection points between and within them, have the potential to make the security condition more seamless. It is beyond the scope of this chapter to provide several in depth examples of interlocking public–private partnerships, but focus is placed on public water supply in city or town regions as an example to illustrate how such partnerships might work. In the case of water supply, one assumption in this "smart city" complex system is that many different municipal/local sites to gather water are peppered liberally throughout state, provincial, or departmental units with a degree of interconnectivity that requires protocols for supervisory, control and monitor functions, and supervisory control and data (SCADA) systems. It is to this example of water supply this chapter now turns.

For Savas, tap water is a "toll good" that is characterized by joint consumption once it becomes a part of public man-made water system flows because consumers in a community pay a water bill each month to access water from municipal/local sites. That stands in sharp contrast to a premium product such as bottled water which is an individual good because it is subject to exclusion—individual consumers pay for each bottle. The logistics and operations of public water supply are handled by what Savas calls private producers who are employed by government to ensure accessibility and water quality. In turn, government acts as an "arranger" in that type of public–private partnership. The characteristics of modern water supply require cyber-security protections in the virtual world, physical protections around sites, and integrated systems both to prevent purposeful contamination or disruption by means of terrorism or common criminal activity [1, 2].

To illustrate how interlocking public–private partnerships might operate, broad public–private partnerships with a secondary focus on security might serve as a backdrop for more indirect protections to water source sites. For example, the U.S. Department of Housing and Urban Development (HUD) has worked with private developers or non-profits or both to improve broader urban environmental conditions for people with low incomes without specific focus on security [73]. At the same time, stakeholders such as private developers and NGOs that work with HUD to improve broader environmental quality can alleviate what Dollard et al. describe as frustration aggression which can serve as direct or indirect drivers of action—common criminal activity, terrorism, cyber-crime, and cyber-terrorism [74]. This is an example of the spillover effects that broader public–private partnerships with indirect effects on security can provide and how those can serve as a backdrop to public–private partnerships with more direct focus on counterterrorism and cyber-intrusions.

Here is one specific example of the interlocking protections afforded: if the public–private partnership configuration #3 $A^1B^1C^3$, where a national dominant public–private partnership with municipal/local scope is used as backdrop for indirect protections, (in this case with HUD as the lead agency), there are three nodes in that configuration other private-public partnerships with more direct influence over terrorism and cyber intrusions can connect with—A^1, B^1 C^3. Stakeholders could include firms with expertise in cyber-security or firms with expertise and experience protecting water supply facilities. For example, if a multinational corporation such as Symantec Security (Party A) could lead a second public–private partnership #46 $A^2B^5C^1$, there are now interlocked pathway connections between B^1 (i.e. national government) and B^5 (i.e. a multinational corporation like Symantec) in this second configuration. That second configuration of public–private partnerships added to the original backdrop configuration makes it possible for stakeholders to coordinate and collaborate within and across partnerships and perhaps achieve economies of scale to produce better, more integrated layers of protection.

Now, imagine another multinational corporation such as Kroll Associates (Party B) within that second configuration that is able to add to work done by Symantec Security (Party A) that focuses on cyber-security, and the addition of a firm (Party C) with water supply expertise in that second public–private partnership. For example, Kroll Associates focuses on physical as well as cyber-security and if Kroll Associates is that other multinational corporation added to that second public–private partnership (either in a dominant or non-dominant role) it can develop connections with Symantec Security, also in that second public–private partnership, to help produce counterterrorism and cyber-security protocols and practices to provide integrated protection for supervisory control and data (SCADA) systems intrinsic to modern water supply infrastructure and water sources.

Modalities exist between A^2 (i.e. multinational corporations) in the second public–private partnership configuration and A^1 (i.e. national government) in the original backdrop configuration (illustrated by a dotted line and the small triangle overlap between A^1 and A^2 in Figure 26.3). Those potential connections can be exploited to promote coordination and

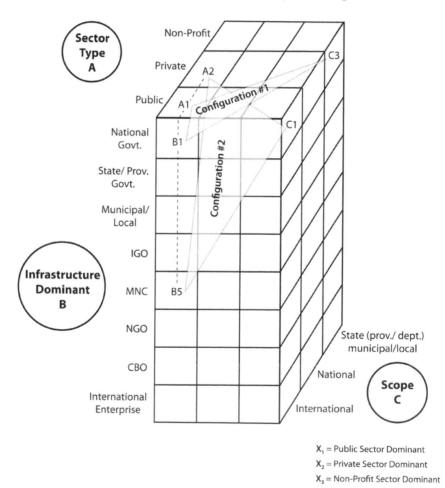

Figure 26.3 Public–private partnership typology with interlocking public–private partnership configurations.

collaboration between multinational corporations, national government, and perhaps state governments and to create new synergies between stakeholders that might result in innovative organizational management processes and new security protocols or products. That has the potential to reduce inefficiency through collaborative specialization in products, processes, and services. If this process of identifying node linkages between public–private partnership configurations is replicated and attention is devoted to specific non-profit and profit entities matching to conform to contextual factors in specific operational environments, what is produced is a set of a honeycomb-like interlocked public–private partnership networks and network connections where repertoires of networks, as Graham T. Allison might call them, are produced to encase or enmesh potential targets such as water systems from physical and cyber-attacks [4, 75].

26.6 FINAL REFLECTIONS

This chapter describes how public–private partnerships with focus on urban renewal and the provision of other social services with indirect influence on national security matters such as terrorism and cyber-intrusions can be used as a backdrop for public–private partnerships with more direct influence on terrorism and cyber intrusions. Frequently, government at nation-state, province, or department levels and at municipal levels serve as arrangers to coordinate the activities of the producers that provide goods and services to constituents. To delineate the different possibilities of broader public–private partnership configurations possible in the larger world of action, a typology is crafted that makes it possible to isolate and identify public–private partnerships that exist in empirical terms and what might exist in normative terms. In this public–private typology there are 72 different possible iterations.

The typology assists researchers in efforts to categorize and classify public–private partnerships, and illustrates the broader types of public–private partnerships available that are subject to more detailed modification in terms of the specific stakeholders packaged within stakeholder types of each configuration. Equally important, this typology is functional because it is possible to derive hypotheses about public–private partnership type use and preference within specific operational environments that are subject to empirical testing. Empirical results of hypotheses that are rooted in the extant literature contribute to the process of agenda setting and design phases of the public-policy process and in particular, work to tailor make public–private partnerships that dovetail well with each other in specific operational environments to increase effectiveness and efficiency through achievement of economies of scale.

The specific nature of interlocking configurations of different public–private partnership iterations is illustrated by the water supply system example provided within the context of discussion about smart cities. Those interlocking sections of public–private partnership configurations can be replicated to produce a more seamless set of protections around smart cities with ample resources both at federal, state, and municipal/local government. Even though public–private partnerships can be difficult to sustain between stakeholders because of trust and responsibility issues linked to allocation of goods and services, sufficient tax incentives, and government programs to encourage intra partnership cooperation have potential to succeed. For instance, it might be possible for county/municipal/local governments to raise "own source revenue," to augment in line state "pass through grants." With that in mind, local government might be able to issue revenue bonds (i.e. municipal bonds), and apply user fees to help generate additional revenue to purchase services from the private and non-profit sector in such public–private arrangements. In this way, new and more effective goods, services, and innovative organizational processes associated with production can be made available to address contemporary security needs and improve contemporary security conditions for citizens [4, 76, 77].

REFERENCES

1. Robert L. McKenzie, 2016. "Countering violent extremism in America: Policy recommendations for the next president." The Brookings Institution (https://www.brookings.edu/research/countering-violent-extremism-in-america-policy-recommendations-for-the-next-president/).
2. Mary Parker Follett, 1918. *The New State Group Organization the Solution of Popular Governance*. New York: Longmans, Green and Company, 250.
3. Paul Rosenzweig, 2013. *Cyber-War: How Conflicts in Cyberspace Are Challenging America and Changing the World*. Santa Barbara, CA: Praeger Publishers, 7–8, 33, 146, 58–72.
4. Dan Goodin, 2015. "How "omnipotent" hackers tied to NSA hid for 14 years – and were found at last." *Arstechnica*, 16 February, (https://arstechnica.com/information-technology/2015/02/how-omnipotent-hackers-tied-to-the-nsa-hid-for-14-years-and-were-found-at-last/).
5. Daniela Popescul, and Laura Dina Radu, 2016. "Data Security in Smart Cities: Challenges and Solutions." *Informatica Economica*, vol. 20, no. 1, 29–34.
6. Frederic S. Pearson, and J. Martin Rochester, 1998. *International Relations: The Global Condition in the Twenty-First Century*. Boston, MA: McGraw Hill, 295.
7. Richard J. Chasdi, 1999. *Serenade of Suffering: A Portrait of Middle East Terrorism, 1968–1993*. Latham, MD: Lexington Books, 4–9.
8. Graham Allison, and Philip Zelikow, 1999. *Essence of Decision: explaining the Cuban Missile Crisis Second Edition*. New York: Longman, 170.
9. Joseph Cox, 2016. "NSA Hackers The Shadow Brokers Dump More Files." *MotherBoard*, 31 October, (https://losangelestribunenews.wordpress.com/2016/10/31/nsa-hackers-the-shadow-brokers-dump-more-files/).
10. Richard J. Chasdi, 2010. *Counterterror Offensives for the Ghost War World: The Rudiments of Counterterrorism Policy*. Lanham, MD: Lexington Books.
11. Richard J. Chasdi, 2014. "A Continuum of Nation-State Resiliency to Terrorist Events." *Armed Forces & Society*, vol 40, no. 3 (July), 478, 498n4, 498n5, 499n7.
12. Brendan O'Duffy, 2008 "Radical Atmosphere: Explaining Jihadist Radicalization in the UK" *PS: Political Science and Politics*, vol. 14, no. 1 (January), 40
13. Shane Harris, 2014. *@War: The Rise of the Military Internet Complex*. New York: Houghton Mifflin Harcourt Publishing, 64–65, 72
14. Administrative Conference of the United States, 2016. "Public-Private Partnerships: A Legal Primer." American Bar Association Draft Report, 30 November, (https://www.americanbar.org/content/dam/aba/events/administrative_law/2016/12/14_legal_primer_on_public_private_partnerships.authcheckdam.pdf).
15. Harvey Starr, and Benjamin Most, 1985. "Patterns of Conflict: Quantitative Analysis and Comparative Lessons of Third World Wars." In *Approaches and Case Studies. Vol. 1 of The Lessons of Recent Wars in the Third World*, eds. Robert E. Harkavy and Stephanie G. Neumann. Lexington, MA: D.C. Heath.
16. Nicole Perlroth, 2012. "Researchers Find Clues in Malware." *New York Times*, 30 May (https://www.cnbc.com/id/47625862).
17. Milton J. Esman, 1994. *Ethnic Politics*. Ithaca, New York: Cornell University Press, 12, 14–15.
18. Alan Blinder, and Nicole Perlroth, 2018. "Atlanta Hobbled by Major Cyberattack That Mayor Calls 'a Hostage Situation.'" *New York Times*, 28 March, A-15.
19. Brian Berger, 2017. "WannaCry Exposes Defense Vulnerabilities." *National Defense* (July), 20–21.
20. Art Gross, 2017. "Protect Equipment from Ransomware Attacks." *Medical Economics* (http://medicaleconomics.modernmedicine.com/medical-economics/news/how-protect-equipment-ransomware-attacks).

21. White House 2015. "FACT SHEET: The White House Summit on Countering Violent Extremism" (http s://obamawhitehouse.archives.gov/the-press-office/2015/02/18/fact-sheet-white-house-summit -countering-violent-extremism).

22. Paul Collier and Anke Hoeffler, 2000. "Greed and Grievance in Civil War." Policy Working Research Paper No. 2355. Washington, DC: World Bank (https://www.econ.nyu.edu/user/debraj/Courses/ Readings/CollierHoeffler.pdf).

23. Todd Thibodeaux, 2017. "Smart Cities Are Going to Be a Security Nightmare." *Harvard Business Review*, 28 April (http://search.ebscohost.com/login.aspx?direct=true&db=bsh&AN=123076125&sit e=ehost-live), 2–3

24. U.S.AID n.d. "Public-Private Partnerships." U.S.AID (https://www.usaid.gov/brazil/our-work/public –private-partnerships).

25. David Schippers, 2018. "Cybersecurity: The Game has Changed." Walsh College, Professional Development Day presentation, October 14, 2017. For Schippers, those other NSA "zero day exploits" include (1) "Eternal Romance," to attack ("exploit") Windows XP through Windows 2008, (2) "ExplodingCan," to attack Windows 2003 (3) "Eworkfrenzy" to attack "Lotus Domino 6.5.4 and 7.02, 9" (4) "EternalSynergy," "to attack Windows 8 and Wndows Server 2012," (5) "Eternal Champion, Eternal System" to attack "Windows through Windows 8 and 2012" – all within what Greenberg calls a hacker rubric known as "Fuzzbunch." For additional information see: https://arstechnica.com/s ecurity/2017/04nsa-leaking-shadow-brokesr-just-dumped-its-most-damaging-release-yet/.

26. Amitai Etzioni, 2004 *From Empire to Community: A New Approach to International Relations*. New York: Palgrave Macmillan Ltd.

27. Lorenzo Franceschi-Bicchierai, 2016. "Who Are The NSA's Elite Hackers?" *MotherBoard* (https://m otherboard.vice.com/en_us/article/bmvyxw/nsa-hacking-unit-tao-cyberwar).

28. Louise I. Shelley and John T. Picarelli 2005. "Methods and Motives: Exploring Links between Transnational Organized Crime and International Terrorism." *Trends in Organized Crime*, Vol. 8, No. 2 (Winter) (https://www.ncjrs.gov/pdffiles1/nij/grants/211207.pdf).

29. Bruce Hoffman, 2007 "Terrorism in the West: Al-Qaeda's Role in 'Homegrown' Terror," *The Brown Journal of World Affairs*, 13 (2) (Spring) 91–99.

30. Juliette Kayyem, and Patricia E. Chang 2003. "Beyond Business Continuity: The Role of the Private Sector in Preparedness Planning." In *First to Arrive: State and Local Responses to Terrorism*, eds. Juliette Kayyem and Robin L. Pagni, Cambridge, MA: MIT Press, 95–120.

31. Sheila Ronis, 2007. *Timelines into the Future: Strategic Visioning Methods for Government, Business and other Organizations*. Lanham, MD: Hamilton Books, 8–9.

32. Richard J. Chasdi, 2015. "Center for Radicalization Prevention: A Model of Government Response to 'Lone Wolf' Terrorist Assaults." In *Lone Actors – An Emerging Security Threat*, eds. Aaron Richman and Yair Sharan, Amsterdam: IOS Press, 105–107.

33. U.S.AID n.d. "2016 Partnerships with the Private Sector." U.S.AID (https://www.usaid.gov/GlobalD evLab/global-partnerships/2016-infographic).

34. Peter Warren Singer and Allan Friedman, 2014. *Cybersecurity and Cyberwar: What Everyone Needs to Know*. New York: Oxford University Press, 114–120, 132, 152–159.

35. Richard J. Chasdi, 2017. *Corporate Security Crossroads: Responding To Terrorism, Cyberthreats, and Other Hazards in the Global Business Environment*. Santa, Barbara, CA: Praeger Publishers, 32–35, 121–122, 128, 131, 145, 149, 155, 188n48, 189n49, 189n50, 195n49, 196n55, 226n5.

36. Andy Greenberg, 2017. "Major Leak Suggests NSA Was Deep in Middle East Banking System, *Wired*. (https://www.wired.com/2017/04/major-leak-suggests-nsa-deep-middle-east-banking-system/).

37. Margarita Bizina and David H. Gray, 2014. "Radicalization of Youth as a Growing Concern for Counter-Terrorism Policy." *Global Security Studies* vol. 5 no. 1 (Winter), 73-74.

38. Robert O. Keohane and Joseph S. Nye, Jr., 2001. "Globalization: What's New? What's Not? (And So What?)." In *Annual Editions World Politics, Twenty-Second Edition*. Guilford, CT: McGraw Hill-Dushkin, 8–16.

39. Anthony Cutherbertson, 2017. "North Korean Hackers Lazarus Group Use Facebook to Hunt Victims." *Newsweek*, 20 December (http://www.newsweek.com/north-korean-hackers-lazarus-group-use-f acebook-hunt-victims-753429).

40. Myriam Benraad, 2009 *"Facing Homegrown Radicalization"* The Washington Institute for Near East Policy Watch No. 1575, (3 September).

41. Nicholas Henry, 2013. *Public Administration and Public Affairs Edition No. 12*. Boston: Pearson 14–15, 81, 149, 179, 213–217, 231.

42. C.W.I. Hill, 2013. *Global Business Today – Eighth Edition*. New York: Pearson.

43. Charles W. Kegley, 2007. *World Politics: Trends and Transformations, Eleventh Edition*. Belmont, CA: Thomson Wadsworth, 134.

44. Paul Collier, 2000. "Doing Well Out of War: An Economic Perspective" In *Greed & Grievance: Economic Agendas in Civil Wars*, eds. Mats Berdal and David Malone, Boulder, CO: Lynne Rienner Publishers, 91–111.

45. Patricia Agostinho, Louise Manukian, Rob Shapri, Olga Vysotskaya, and Haim Wismonsky 2013, "Cybersecurity: A Multinational Group's Collaborative Approach." *NAAG (Gazette)* vol. 7, no. 9–10 (http://www.naag.org/publications/naagazette/volume-7-number-9-10/cybersecurity-a-multinat ional-groups-collaborative-approach.php), 3.

46. Tracy Jan, 2013. "Was Mitt Romney right about U.S. health overhaul?" *Boston Globe*, 7 December (https://www.bostonglobe.com/news/nation/2013/12/07/was-mitt-romney-right-questions-about-massachusetts-model-for-national-health-plan/qj78IzPtjrX4dnlH88B8mO/story.html).

47. Yanto Chandra, 2018. "Entrepreneurial Rehabilitation: The Promise of Social Entrepreneurship in Disengaging Religious Terrorists." In *Deradicalization and Terrorist Rehabilitation: A Framework for Policymaking and Implementation*, eds. Rohan Gunaratna and Sabariah Hussin, London: Routledge.

48. CNN, 2012. "World: Russia Boots Out U.S.AID." CNN, 19 September (https://www.cnn.com/2012/09/1 9/world/europe/russia-usaid-expulsion/index.html).

49. Symantec Security Response, 2017. "WannaCry: Ransomware attacks show strong links to Lazarus group: similarities in code and infrastructure indicate close connection to group that was linked to Sony Pictures and Bangladesh Bank attacks," 22 May (https://www.symantec.com/connect/blogs/ wannacry-ransomware-attacks-show-strong-links-lazarus-group   https://www.symantec.com/ connect/blogs/wannacry-ransomware-attacks-show-strong-links-lazarus-group).

50. Brian Barrett, 2017. "Kaspersky, Russia, and the Antivrius Paradox." *Wired* (https://www.wired.com/ story/kaspersky-russia-antivirus/).

51. Committee on Private-Public Sector Collaboration to Enhance Community Disaster Resilience, 2011. *Building Community Disaster Resilience Through Private-Public Collaboration*. Washington, D.C. National Academies Press, 20–21, 24, 27, 29, 36–37, 39, 50, 67, 29–30, 44, 46–47, 50, 53–54, 59, 99–100, 91–93, 89, 41–42, 51–52, 61–62, 66–68.

52. Yasmina Padilla, 2013 "Public, Private, and Civil Society Partnerships in Action." U.S.AID (https://b log.usaid.gov/2013/01/public–private-and-civil-society-partnerships-in-action/).

53. Maria Guerra, 2017. "What Exactly is a SMART CITY?" *Electronic Design*, vol. 65, no. 2 (February) (http://search.ebscohost.com/login.aspx?direct=true&db=bsh&AN=121269889&site=ehost-live), 1–2, 6.

54. Kaspersky Lab U.S., n.d. "The Duqu 2.0 Targeted Attacks." (https://usa.kaspersky.com/resource-cent er/threats/duqu-2).

55. Kaspersky Lab, 2011. "Duqu: The Step-Brother of Stuxnet?" Kaspersky Lab (https://www.kaspers ky.com/about/press-releases/2011_duqu-the-step-brother-of-stuxnet).

56. John Dollard, Leonard W. Doob, Neal E. Miller, O.H. Mowrer, and Robert R. Sears, 1939. *Frustration and Aggression*. New Haven: Yale University Press.

57. Emanuel S. Savas, 2000. *Privatization and Public Private Partnerships*. New York: Chatham House Publishers, 3–4, 5–7, 12, 46–48, 50, 54–56, 61, 66–67, 71, 80.

58. Paige Alexander, 2011. "Blog: Public Private Partnerships Week: New Cisco Alliance Kicks off Partnership Week." U.S.AID (https://blog.usaid.gov/2011/10/public–private-partnerships-week-new-cisco-alliance-kicks-off-partnership-week/).

59. U.S.AID n.d. "Public-Private Partnership MHeath Intervention in Delhi, Jharkhand, and Uttarakhand" (https://partnerships.usaid.gov/partnership/public–private-partnership-mhealth-intervention-del hi-jharkhand-and-uttarakhand).

60. U.S. Department of Homeland Security, "DHS Risk Lexicon – 2010 Edition," Risk Steering Committee, Washington, DC, September 2008. https://www.dhs.gov/xlibrary/assets/dhs-risk-lexicon-2010.pdf.

61. Simon Brand, and Kurt Jax, 2007. "Focusing on the Meaning(s) of Resilience: Resilience as a Descriptive Concept and a Boundary Object." *Ecology and Society*, vol. 12, 1.

62. Emile Durkheim, 1984. *The Division of Labor in Society* (W.D. Halls Translation). New York: Free Press, 304–306.

63. Svante E. Cornell, 2007. "Narcotics and Armed Conflict: Interaction and Implications." *Studies in Conflict & Terrorism*, 30, 207, 227.

64. Larry J. Siegel, and Chris McCormick 2010. *Criminology, in Canada: Theories, Patterns and Typologies.* Toronto, Ontario: Nelson Education Ltd., 13.

65. The World Bank. "Infrastructure and Public-Private Partnerships." The World Bank (http://www.worldbank.org/en/topic/publicprivatepartnerships/overview).

66. U.S.AID n.d. "Innovation U.S. Global Development Lab." U.S.AID (https://www.usaid.gov/GlobalDevLab/about/innovation).

67. The Economist, 2017. "The Worm that Turned: The WannaCry Attack." *The Economist*, 20 May: 13(U.S.), as found in *Business Insights: Global*. Wed. 26 March, 2018.

68. U.S. Department of Housing and Urban Development, n.d. "The Evolution of HUD's Public Private Partnerships: A HUD 50th Anniversary Publication." (https://www.huduser.gov/hud50th/HUD2-048-Public-Private_Partnership_508.pdf), 6–8.

69. U.S.AID n.d. *Public-Private Partnerships.* U.S.AID (https://www.usaid.gov/el-salvador/public–private-partnerships).

70. Rosemary Harris, 1989. "Anthropological Views on 'Violence" in Northern Ireland," In *Ireland's Terrorist Trauma*, eds. Yonah Alexander and Alan O'Day, New York: St. Martin's Press, 95, 89–90, 92, 86.

71. Samuel J. Rascoff, 2010. "The Law of Homegrown (Counter) Terrorism" *Texas Law Review*, vol. 88, no. 1715. https://www.questia.com/library/journal/1P3-2092291391/the-law-of-homegrown-counter-terrorism.

72. Samuel Gibbs, 2015. "Duqu 2.0: computer virus 'linked to Israel' found at Iran nuclear talks venue." *The Guardian*, 11 June (https://www.theguardian.com/technology/2015/jun/11/duqu-20-computer-virus-with-traces-of-israeli-code-was-used-to-hack-iran-talks).

73. Sean Michael Kerner, 2017. "North Korea-Backed Lazarus Groups Takes Aim at Android Security." *eWeek*, 20 November (http://www.eweek.com/security/north-korea-backed-lazarus-group-takes-aim-at-android-security).

74. Security Dealer & Integrator, 2017. "Ransomware: The Risk is Real." *Security Dealer & Integrator*, June, as found in *Business Insights: Global*, Wed. 26 March 2018 (http://www.securityinfowatch.com/article/12337355/ransomware-the-risk-is-real).

75. Tamara Makarenko, 2004. "The Crime-Terror Continuum: Tracing the Interplay between Transnational Organized Crime and Terrorism." *Global Crime*, vol. 6, no. 1 (February), 129–145.

76. Sheera Frenkel, 2017. "Toys That Make The Wrong Kind of Connection." *New York Times*, 22 December, B-1, B-5.

77. Semantic Security Response, 2017. For Schippers, Wanna Cry, otherwise known as WannaCryptor 2.0, is a modified version of the less advanced WannaCryptor malware; that relied on manual attack implementation and took control over a computer system through encryption. David Schippers, personal e-mail correspondence, January 22, 2018.

Chapter 27

Public–Private Partnerships and the Private Sector's Role in Countering the Use of the Internet for Terrorist Purposes

Allison Miller and Yannis A. Stivachtis

CONTENTS

27.1 INTRODUCTION

In the wake of 9/11 and the related events that followed, methods for countering terrorism have expanded in both the public sphere and the private sectors. New challenges in countering terrorism have also caused those responsible for preventing it to turn their attention toward the internet. In consideration of how terrorism has evolved, examining the internet and its use is of fundamental importance. The utilization of the internet for attracting and mobilizing support for terrorist groups, as well as for the organization and implementation of terrorist operations poses new challenges to national security policy given that globalization coupled with technological advances render distance and geographical boundaries less relevant (Keene, 2011).

Given that terrorism has, for many years, moved to incorporate the internet in many ways, an examination of public–private partnerships is necessary. This is an area that is not often prioritized in terrorism research focused on countering terrorism on the internet and in doing so an existing gap in the literature is addressed. This chapter aims to analyze this relationship between public and private partnerships, address both the positive and negative of it, and highlight areas where it could be improved. This chapter begins with a discussion on what terrorism on the internet is, then moves on to defining both the public and private sectors, and finally provides an analysis of the relationship between the two sectors. The chapter will conclude with suggestions for improvements, and it will also address policy implications.

27.2 TERRORISM ON THE INTERNET

When discussing terrorism on the internet, it is necessary to have a conceptualization of what is meant by the term "terrorist." Who is this elusive individual? Is it even an individual, or is it a group? Where are these individuals and groups operating from? How are they using the internet for their purpose? What is being done to stop them? This is a short list of questions from a long list of problems that can arise when attempting to define terrorists who use the internet. These questions can also quickly become convoluted and controversial once democratic values, such as free speech, are factored into the equation. For this reason, it is evident that a definition of what constitutes a terrorist becomes essential.

The most obvious starting point for defining what a terrorist is would be looking toward established terrorist organizations. Individuals operating on behalf of such organizations without a doubt are terrorists; members of the Islamic State are terrorists just as members of Al Qaeda are. Therefore, any of these individual members who utilize the internet for any purpose related to their cause can be understood as terrorists on the internet. These individuals are capable of operating anywhere in the world with the evolution and subsequent incorporation of the internet into the strategy of terrorism.

There are also individuals who are either not officially affiliated with a terrorist organization or working regionally on the ground with a terrorist organization, but still use the internet for purposes related to terrorism. A prominent example of this is those who use the internet for financial reasons related to terrorism. The internet makes engaging in criminal activity easier than ever before. For example, a British man named Younis Tsouli and partner Tariq al-Daour purchased over 37,000 stolen credit card numbers over the internet which they then used to make more than $3.5 million in charges (Jacobson, 2009). The two men, operating on behalf of Al Qaeda in Iraq (AQI), then laundered the money through online gambling websites by transferring all winnings to pre-established bank accounts (Jacobson, 2009). In this case, Tsouli and al-Daour were operating on behalf of AQI, which arguably makes a case for considering them (and those like them) terrorists as well.

Terrorism has changed throughout history. Today, the significant increase of international terrorism has caused the localized risks to become borderless or de-territorialized (Waddington and McSeveny, 2012). Many different facets of modern life can be attributed to this development in terrorism, especially international terrorism which transcends borders. The internet makes it possible for terrorists to do things such as communicate, plan, and share ideology in a way that is unprecedented in comparison to historical cases of terrorism. The internet certainly helps in making terrorism truly borderless and de-territorialized. Such techno-scientific developments as the internet help ensure that there is a progressively increasing potential to cause catastrophic harm (Waddington and McSeveny, 2012). Sociologist Ulrich Beck argues that "every advance from gene technology to nanotechnology opens a 'Pandora's Box' that could be used in a terrorist's toolkit" (Beck, 2002, p. 46; Waddington and McSeveny, 2012). Though the inclusion of technology as advanced as gene technology and nanotechnology is a bit overstated in terms of terrorists, it is the terrorist toolkit that matters most. The internet is not only a part of that toolkit but it is also a platform to continuously increase the knowledge found in the toolkit.

Terrorists use the internet for a multitude of different reasons, including for radicalization and recruitment purposes, as an accessible and easy way to plan, as a way to garner financial support, and as a space for committing financial crimes (Keene, 2011). Tsouli and al-Daour are just one example from a group of many who use the internet to support terrorist organizations financially. Charities and non-governmental organizations (NGOs) also provide an easy platform for terrorist organizations to easily raise money on the internet. Some charities are founded for this exact reason, and this can be incredibly difficult to counter given that monitoring disbursement of funds in conflict zones is difficult (Jacobson, 2009). Charities and NGOs can easily solicit money online by creating fronts that make themselves appear to be seeking support for humanitarian causes (Jacobson, 2009).

The internet creates an entirely new set of problems when it is used by terrorists and terrorist organizations to recruit individuals, especially individuals abroad. This can be done by using propaganda to widely disseminate radical ideology across the world. The internet provides a gateway for connecting like-minded individuals who can inspire others to engage in violent actions (Janbek and Williams, 2014). It also provides a platform for terrorists to share their worldview with their target audience without it being distorted by the mainstream media (Janbek and Williams, 2014).

It is absolutely necessary to recognize that it is not solely Islamist terrorists using the internet to further their cause. Making this assumption overlooks many other forms of propaganda and calls for violence that exists online. For example, right-wing groups have used the internet to radicalize thousands of individuals, calling for them to seek alternative and violent ways to oppose Islam, immigration, and economic issues (Palasinski et al., 2014). Perhaps one of the most recent, widely known examples of this is far-right Anders Breivik, who used the internet to openly call for a violent annihilation of "Eurabia" and multiculturalism (Palasinski et al., 2014). Breivik is responsible for a 2011 attack in Oslo, Norway that took the lives of 77 people (Palasinski et al., 2014). This is a harrowing example of how individuals can use the internet in an attempt to spread their twisted ideology and gain support.

27.2.1 The Question of Recruits, Sympathizers, and Violent Extremists: Are They Terrorists?

When attempting to counter terrorism in general, but particularly on the internet, discourse matters a great deal. The ways in which individuals are talked about in media, in government, and in academia can ultimately blur the lines of what a terrorist is and what a terrorist is not. The words *terrorist* and *extremist* are sometimes used interchangeably even though they can have different meanings.

One useful way of deconstructing this problem is to understand that terrorism is a *tactic*, rather than a specific type of conflict (Jaggar, 2005). Terrorism then in the *tactical* sense can also be used alongside other strategies. Jaggar defines terrorism as "the use of extreme threats or violence designed to intimidate or subjugate governments, groups, or individuals" (Jaggar, 2005, p. 209). Her definition lacks in acknowledging the more recent phenomena of terrorism on the internet and thus should be expanded to include aspects of the virtual sphere, such as inspiring others to use extreme threats or violence to subjugate said groups. Jaggar most importantly creates the framework that calls for conceptualizing terrorism as a tactic which can be used by both terrorists and extremists. This chapter will then examine how the private sector combats both terrorism and extremism online. This is an important distinction because extremist content can cause an individual to radicalize and justify using a method of terrorist activity.

Undoubtedly, especially from a legal standpoint, there is a difference between an extremist and a terrorist. There are numerous occasions where an extremist may use the internet for purposes related to terrorism. Extremism in itself should be understood as a fluid spectrum given that some extremists are not violent, and some are. Further work is necessary on distinguishing a violent extremist from a terrorist, which is beyond the purpose of this chapter. For now, conceptualizing an extremist, a violent extremist, and a terrorist as being capable of using the internet for purposes related to terrorism is appropriate. This is of great importance when factoring in the private and public sectors given that they have the ability to label individuals in different ways when attempting to counter terrorism (or counter extremism) online.

To further convolute the discourse dilemma, there are also recruits and sympathizers who use the internet for issues related to terrorism or extremism. These types of people can also be categorized on the spectrum of extremism depending on what they do on the internet. For example, laundering money through the internet is using the internet for terrorism, but in cases like this, individuals are labelled as sympathizers, supporters, or extremists but may be legally charged with terrorism because it is a *tactic*.

Does being a sympathizer to a cause related to terrorism make an individual a terrorist? This is another question that extends beyond the scope of this chapter. Arguably though, it would depend what that sympathizer is doing. Raising and wiring money to a terrorist organization is not necessarily comparable to participating in web forums related to terrorism or simply visiting a jihadi or extremist website. These are important questions with blurry answers.

27.2.2 Cyber-Terrorism versus Terrorism on the Internet

It is worth discussing the concepts of cyber-terrorism and terrorism on the internet, as there are similarities and differences between the two. There is a difficulty in differentiating and defining harmful activities in cyberspace. For example, cyber-attacks such as the ones Russia launched against Georgia in 2008 could likely be labelled as cyber-war (Hardy and Williams, 2014). Stealing sensitive national security or economic information by utilizing computer technology—such as WikiLeaks—could be called cyber-espionage (Hardy and Williams, 2014). Finally, phishing scams that attempt to collect bank data or computer passwords for financial gain may be called cyber-crime (Hardy and Williams, 2014). The categorizations of cyber-activity and lack of international e-governance surrounding them makes it difficult to define them with certainty. Hardy and Williams address the difficulty in defining cyber-terrorism from an international perspective because the U.S. has different approaches in legislation as compared to countries such as the United Kingdom, Canada, New Zealand, and Australia (Hardy and Williams, 2014). Though Hardy and Williams are focused on the four aforementioned countries, for the sake of this chapter borrowing the definition of cyber-terrorism created by Hardy and Williams seems useful:

> Cyberterrorism means conduct involving computer or Internet technology that (1) is carried out for the purpose of advancing a political, religious or ideological cause; (2) is intended to intimidate a section of the public, or compel a government to do or abstain from doing any act; and (3)

intentionally causes serious interference with an essential service, facility or system, if such interference is likely to endanger life or cause significant economic or environmental damage. (Hardy and Williams, 2014, p. 21).

So how is this different from terrorism on the internet? That question leads to murky waters as well with arguments that extend beyond the scope of this chapter. A terrorist may use the internet to access documents in order to learn how to build bombs, or simply for communicating with other terrorists. The key difference is that cyber-terrorism interferes with services, facilities, or a system. Carlile QC and Macdonald argue this issue in a useful manner by differentiating between cyber-terrorism and online acts of preparation that terrorists engage in (QC and Macdonald, 2014). However, even this perspective does not incorporate those who just view or share terrorist and extremist content without ever physically acting on anything. Therefore, terrorism on the internet may be categorized as cyber-terrorism, while in other cases it may be categorized as a terrorist using the internet. For the sake of clarity in this chapter, cyber-terrorism and terrorism on the internet will be treated the same.

As it was mentioned previously, the goal of this chapter is to analyze public–private partnerships regarding terrorism on the internet and to analyze the role of the private sector in countering terrorism on the internet. Thus, public–private partnerships may be focused on cyberterrorism explicitly, acts of preparation such as utilizing content for bomb making, or on how terrorists use the internet, such as social media engagement.

27.3 DEFINING THE PUBLIC AND PRIVATE SECTORS AND A NOTE ON PUBLIC POLICY

The public sector is defined as the government and government-controlled enterprises, while the private sector is considered to be composed of for-profit entities (Busch and Givens, 2013). Furthermore, the public sector consists of the general government, public non-financial corporate enterprises, and public financial institutions (Pathirane and Blades, 1982). The public sector is often studied from a perspective of economics and marketing, though collaboration between public and private sectors is a growing field. However, in order to better understand how the public and private sectors do collaborate, an evaluation from an economic and marketing viewpoint is necessary. This perspective can lay the foundation necessary to understand how the two sectors interact, the benefits of each, as well as limitations. In terms of collaboration, economics and marketing matters a great deal.

The public and private sectors share certain similarities but at the same time there are issues which help us to differentiate between them. Both sectors "identify clientele, develop services, determine prices, design distribution systems and communicate the efficiency and availability of all they offer" (Bouzas-Lorenzo, 2010, p. 118). The public sector typically will have less autonomy and flexibility, less market exposure, more political pressure, and a more intense relationship with the public (Bouzas-Lorenzo, 2010). A key note here is that more political pressure while having less autonomy and flexibility can create a problematic balance within the public sector, and thus the private sector becomes useful. For example, in terms of terrorism on the internet, the public-sector faces pressure to monitor and prevent this while also facing the pressure of not violating core democratic values, such as free speech. Private companies are able to exercise more autonomy on the type of content they do and do not allow on their platforms without having the same level of accountability toward the public.

Examining literature on disaster management and resilience is a useful gateway for understanding how public–private partnerships shape public policy, which extends beyond the scope of this chapter. It is however important to mention public policy because of the nature of the relationship between public–private partnerships. In a very realistic way, terrorism is a large concern in the field of disaster management and resilience so examining public–private partnerships through this lens is fitting. Given that many terrorist attacks today include some element of the internet, it is suitable to establish a linkage between terrorist attacks that utilize the internet which then prompt disaster management and resilience. In fact, it would be difficult to separately consider the role of the private sector and how it directly plays a role in counterterrorism online without needing to analyze any boundaries that exist between online and offline. The fact that terrorism occurs both online and in real time with the aid of the internet means that a comprehensive overview is necessary. For example, the terrorists who committed 9/11 were active online before their actions became more than something existing in the virtual sphere. Al Qaeda operatives had exchanged thousands of encrypted messages online on a specific location of a website (Weimann, 2004). These exchanges over the internet used simple phrases that would not arouse suspicion, such as framing said terrorists who would be taking part in the planned attacks as academics who would soon be joining various faculty departments (Weimann, 2004).

27.4 PUBLIC–PRIVATE PARTNERSHIPS IN COUNTERING TERRORISM ON THE INTERNET

Countering terrorism on the internet involves more than just solely looking at the internet. Terrorists utilize the internet, but their actions and behaviors in real life also matter. For that reason, countering terrorism on the internet also needs to be considered by countering terrorism off the internet. The internet may serve as a starting point for identifying concerning or suspicious activities and individuals but monitoring what those individuals plan to do and attempting to stop that needs to be taken into consideration as well. While the focus of this chapter is on the private sector's role in countering terrorism on the internet, it would be a disservice to stop solely at the internet.

Public–private partnerships have changed and evolved when related to countering terrorism on the internet. From a historical perspective, the issue of online terrorism is relatively new, so it makes sense that partnerships pertaining to this are relatively new as well. The following section will explain what public–private partnerships are and share examples of how they are formed and executed in order to provide a brief overview.

27.4.1 On the Ambiguity of Partnerships: A Brief Overview

The concept of partnerships is celebrated within an extensive range of policy areas (Petersen, 2008). Though the actual conceptualization of partnership can be interpreted quite ambiguously, it is generally agreed upon that it represents the possibility of combining political, persona, and economic interests (Petersen, 2008). Furthermore, Busch and Givens define public–private partnerships as the "collaboration between a public sector (government) entity and a private sector (for-profit) entity to achieve a specific goal or set of objectives" (Busch and Givens, 2013, p. 3). Within the discourse of terrorism, partnerships may also be called "unified command," "culture of preparedness," and "multidisciplinary teams" (Petersen, 2008). Partnerships also make "dialogue forums and outreach programs" a reality, which then make the actions of the private sector politically important when countering terrorism (Petersen, 2008).

Within the scope of U.S. disaster management, resilience focused public–private partnerships are thriving (Busch and Givens, 2013). Disaster management partnerships focus on a number of topics, one of which is the threat or perceived threat of a terrorist attack. The increase in this type of partnership has typically been considered a positive development, though a number of challenges in further constructing these partnerships exist (Busch and Givens, 2013).

Busch and Givens argue that there can be severe consequences when the collaboration between public and private breaks down or does not exist in the first place. They highlight 9/11 as being an extreme example of this. Before 9/11, government agencies had failed to share information both among themselves and among important parts of the private sector (Busch and Givens, 2013). The 9/11 Commission prompted the federal government to create the information sharing environment (ISE) in order to better facilitate information sharing among government agencies and partners within the private sector (Busch and Givens, 2013). In 2008, the Department of Homeland Security also noted the need to improve information sharing between government agencies and businesses (Busch and Givens, 2013). Though 9/11 serves as the most extreme example, it demonstrates what types of consequences can arise when partnerships are not in place pertaining to information sharing. This example is of particular importance because of the amount of reliance the 9/11 hijackers had on using the internet to carry out their attack.

Petersen discusses at length the importance of partnerships in counterterrorism efforts. She raises the point that terrorism is not a "normal" crime, but rather a constructed crime that is also a matter of national security that transcends borders (Petersen, 2008). She argues that because of this, following 9/11 specifically, new methods of partnering needed to be developed (Petersen, 2008).

27.4.2 An Analysis of Partnerships between the Public and Private Sector

Violent extremism can pose a significant threat to businesses due to the fact that terrorism can sever supply chains, drain local labor pools, and shake investor confidence (Rosand and Milar, 2017). Following 9/11, corporations reacted in a multitude of different ways, such as by firing employees, cancelling acquisitions, delaying transactions, pursuing opportunities, completing purchases, and acting as though it was "business as usual" (Alexander and Alexander, 2002). Industries such as "real estate, technology, media and entertainment, and public and private mail carries" are among the most likely to be negatively impacted in the case of a terrorist attack (Alexander and Alexander, 2002, p. 46). The economic costs of terrorism is a huge concern and risk factor for private businesses. In 2015, the economic cost of terrorism reached $89.6 billion, which was the highest level to ever be recorded (Rosand and Milar, 2017).

There are some barriers that do exist between the public and private sector, aside from the social media and technology sectors, which are important to address when analyzing the quality of public–private partnerships in countering violent extremism. Many areas within the private sector are either unaware of the contributions they can make in counterterrorism or are nervous about entering a security dominated space (Rosand and Milar, 2017). There are a number of reasons for this risk aversion, such as becoming involved in something that shareholders may view as politically sensitive or the potential of programs that may either stigmatize minority communities or target political opponents (Rosand and Milar, 2017). There is also the issue with measuring the success of partnerships given that addressing causal drivers of violent extremism (such as marginalization and poor governance) is long-term and difficult to do (Rosand and

Milar, 2017). Finally, there are many global issues that are competing for resources from the private sector, such as climate change or migration and refugee issues (Rosand and Milar, 2017). Rosand and Alistair highlight the difficulty by pointing to the Global Community Engagement and Resilience Fund (GCERF) that was established in 2014 as a public–private fund for grassroots organizations fighting terrorism. The GCERF has over $20 million in donations from the government and 0$ from the private sector (Rosand and Milar, 2017).

There is a divide within the literature in terms of analyzing the effectiveness of public–private partnerships in counterterrorism. It is evident that there are those who are critical of the private sectors lack of involvement such as Rosand and Alistair. There are those such as Petersen who acknowledge the increased partnerships from a less critical perspective. For the sake of this chapter, it is important to note that Rosand and Alistair are far less critical of the private sector's role in technology and social media when it comes to counterterrorism.

Following 9/11 partnerships between the public and private sector increased. One area is within assessing corporate risk and whether or not terrorism is insurable or uninsurable. Petersen argues that "the U.S. debate on terrorism-risk insurance is a prime example of how the concept of partnership regulates the relation between private and public actors" (Petersen, 2008, p. 183). She highlights the institutionalization of the Terrorism Reinsurance Act (TRIA) that was created in order to financially back up the insurance industry if there were to be another major attack on U.S. soil (Petersen, 2008). The TRIA made insurance more affordable for private businesses, making it possible for them the buy terrorism insurance, which would ensure that the national economy would be less vulnerable if there were to be another terrorist attack (Petersen, 2008). Since more than 60 percent of companies in the U.S. have this type of insurance (Rosand and Milar, 2017), it serves as a critical example of a partnership between the public and private sectors. The government legitimized and subsequently legally institutionalized this type of insurance, solidifying its importance to national security.

The Federal Bureau of Investigation (FBI) is one of the more prominent areas within the public sector that is active in attempting to foster public–private partnerships. Most notably, it has within its Intelligence Branch the Office of Private Sector (OPS). With the slogan "Connect to Protect" the OPS's aim is to strengthen the relationship between the FBI and the U.S. private sector. The OPS exists to seek out how the FBI interacts with the private sector in order to provide a 360 degree understanding of the relationships (Office of Private Sector (OPS) Fact Sheet). It also enhances the FBI's "understanding of the private sectors risks and needs, and increases collaboration and information sharing between the Bureau and private sector" (Office of Private Sector (OPS) Fact Sheet). The OPS has a list of four high-level priorities on their website:

- Facilitate one "FBI voice," and provide a consistent point of contact for private industry to call who will connect them with the right FBI official to engage with-whatever the concern;
- Focus on meaningful dialogue and engagement with private sector partners, and build trust;
- Increase visibility and awareness for both private industry and the FBI on items of mutual interest, and the role each plays in countering threats; and,
- Seek to assist companies working on innovative technology that may be targeted" (Office of Private Sector (OPS) Fact Sheet, n.d.).

These priorities demonstrate that the FBI is has been attempting to improve its relationship with the private sector. Given that the FBI has made terrorism its top investigative priority, it has undoubtedly fostered partnerships that deal with terrorism on the internet. The FBI is also the lead federal agency that investigates cyber-crime, with emphasis being placed on criminals, overseas adversaries, and terrorists (What We Investigate: Cyber Crime, n.d.). A primary concern is computer and network intrusions, which can include "terrorists looking to rob our nation of vital information or launch cyber strikes" (What We Investigate: Cyber Crime, n.d.). This adds another aspect for which terrorists use the internet, which is as a platform to acquire such information.

The FBI also has a Community Relations Unit at its headquarters, as well as FBI community outreach specialists in field offices located across the country. The FBI engages in community outreach with minority groups, religious and civic organizations, schools, and non-profits (Community Outreach, n.d.). The FBI partners with local communities to lead crime prevention programs, some of which focus on teaching citizens to be alert for potential acts of terrorism or extremism (Community Outreach, n.d.). There are several program examples listed on the FBI's community outreach website. For example, Citizens Academies is a six-to-eight-week program that allows business, religious, civic, and community leaders to have an inside look at the FBI (Community Outreach, n.d.). There are also multi-cultural advisory committees that are composed of ethnic, religious, and minority leaders within a community that serve as liaisons between the FBI and community by helping the FBI better understand culture and committees (Community Outreach, n.d.). It is extremely important for the FBI to foster these types of relationships with community leaders, businesses, organizations, etc. for two reasons. First, it creates dialogue between what may otherwise be two opposing forces (FBI and community). This dialogue creates partnerships that benefit the overall safety of the community when carried out properly. Second, it may lead to a higher sense of trust of law enforcement within the community. When the FBI engages with the community, it is from a perspective more geared toward outreach and less toward security, trust can develop. FBI agents become demystified and visible members of the community.

With an understanding of what terrorism on the internet is, what the public and private sectors are defined as, how they form partnerships, and some specific examples it is now time to turn toward the final focus of this chapter. There is a growing body of literature on the role the private sector has in countering terrorism on the internet. The next section will discuss that literature in order to better understand the various roles of the private sector as it is involved with countering terrorism on the internet.

27.5 THE PRIVATE SECTOR'S ROLE IN COUNTERING TERRORISM ON THE INTERNET

The private sector has an important role to play when it comes to countering terrorism on the internet, both internationally and domestically. Social media platforms such as Facebook, Instagram, Twitter, and YouTube are all a part of the private sector and all are involved with countering terrorism on their platforms. Social media and technology are arguably two of the most important industries that need to be involved in countering terrorism due to the fact that terrorist propaganda often proliferates across social media platforms, and technology can help make that possible. This propaganda is a useful tool for those looking to recruit and garner sympathy for the terrorist's cause.

27.5.1 Global Internet Forum to Counter Terrorism

In June 2017, Facebook, Microsoft. Twitter, and YouTube announced their formation of the Global Internet Forum to Counter Terrorism (GIFCT). This initiative was created in order to make their services "hostile to terrorists and violent extremists" (Security Council: Counter-Terrorism

Committee, n.d.). These companies had previously developed removal practices that allowed them to take hardline action regarding terrorist and extremists content on their platform, often by removal (Security Council: Counter-Terrorism Committee, n.d.). The GIFCT is designed to evolve over time in order to meet the needs of the constantly-evolving nature of terrorists and extremist tactics on the internet. The three initial focus points are:

1. Technological solutions: these companies will work together to refine and improve existing joint technical work, such as the Shared Industry Hash Database; exchange best practices as they develop and implement new content detection and classification techniques using machine learning; and define standard transparency reporting methods for terrorist content removals.
2. Research: they will commission research to inform their counter-speech efforts and guide future technical and policy decisions around the removal of terrorist content.
3. Knowledge-sharing: these companies will work with counter-terrorism experts including governments, civil society groups, academics, as well as other companies to engage in shared learning about terrorism. And through a joint partnership specifically with UN CTED and the ICT4Peace Initiative (techagainstterrorism.org), implementing Security Council resolution 2354 (2017). (Security Council: Counter-Terrorism Committee, n.d.)

These initial focuses are useful starting points when attempting to counter terrorism online. Of particular interest is point three because it involves an approach that is inclusive of many areas within both private and public sectors. Utilizing knowledge and approaches from areas such as academia and government can create innovative and useful policy and programs meant to counter terrorism online.

27.5.2 Institute for Strategic Dialogue Campaigns

The Institute for Strategic Dialogue (ISD) is a London-based "think and do tank" that is involved in policy-making and creating operational responses in regard to violent extremism (Silverman et al., 2016). In 2016 ISD released a report that analyzed three different campaigns that were dissiminated across Facebook, YouTube, and Twitter. The three campaigns included:

Average Mohamed—A non-profit organization that uses animation to encourage critical thinking among Somali youth (in Somali and English) about extremist ideologies.

ExitU.S.A—A project of the U.S.-based non-profit organization Life After Hate, which aims to discourage individuals from joining white power movements and encourage defection by offering a "way out."

Harakat-ut-Taleem—A front organization created by AVE for a third party Pakistani communications company with sound experience in creating counter-narrative documentaries and content. They aim to counter Taliban recruitment narratives in Pakistan. (Silverman et al., 2016, p. 4–5).

Each campaign was implemented in October 2015 and had 15 videos that were spread across each organization. ISD hypothesized that a small amount of funding and guidance, when used correctly, could dramatically increase awareness, engagement, and impact of counter-extremist narratives (Silverman et al., 2016). This serves as an incredibly useful case study because ISD presents quantitative (as well as qualitative) data to showcase the levels of engagement the videos had received across social media. This type of data is invaluable in regard to analyzing the reach of counter-extremist campaigns for two reasons; there is not a lot of quantitative data available and it provides a measure of reach. A measure of reach and influence are not comparable, but a measure of reach is useful in determining whether or not these types of campaigns are worth pursuing.

The findings from the ISD campaigns supported their hypothesis. Average Mohamed, ExitU.S.A, and Harakat-ut-Taleem received over 378,000 views, over 20,000 engagements (like, shares, replies, retweets, and comments), and over 480 comments in response to the videos (Silverman et al., 2016). A qualitative analysis of Average Mohamed's videos revealed that young Muslims were debating the role of gender in Islam as well as the struggles associated with having multiple identities (Silverman et al., 2016). ExitU.S.A videos had both constructive and antagonistic exchanges with users that held views associated with neo-Nazis (Silverman et al., 2016). Finally, Harakat-ut-Taleem videos revealed a better performance in Urdu in Pakistan in comparison with English subtitle videos in the UK, highlighting the ability that couter-extremist efforts have in transcending borders (Silverman et al., 2016). A profound result of ExitU.S.A was eight individuals reaching out in search of assistance in "getting away from hate," showcasing the effectiveness of well planed counter-narratives (Silverman et al., 2016).

ISD was able to make nine recommendations for future initiatives based on their campaigns. According to them, "a coordinated effort between content creators, social media companies, and private sector partners can substantially boost the awareness, engagement, and impact of counter-narrative campaigns and NGOs" (Silverman et al., 2016, p. 7). The findings from each campaign also showed the strengths and weaknesses in regard to disseminated content to audiences across the spectrum of radicalization, which is upstream (few to no signs of radicalization) to downstream (more signs of radicalization) (Silverman et al., 2016). Facebook was most effective in reach, views, and engagement, YouTube was the lowest cost-to-views ratio and highest rates of viewer retention, and Twitter had the second largest number of views and highest engagement-to-impressions ratio (Silverman et al., 2016).

27.5.3 InfraGard

InfraGard is a partnership between members of the private sector and the FBI. The program is intended to provide public–private collaboration that expedites timely exchanges of information and promotes mutual learning opportunities in regards to critical infrastructure (InfraGard, n.d.). Under InfraGard, the corporate sector is able to gain access to information which will enable it to protect assests while in turn requiring it to hand information over to the government that will facilitate responibilities for preventing and addressing terrorism (Alimahomed, 2014). The Department of Homeland Security (DHS) incorporated InfraGard in 2003 as part of its Department of Critical Infrastructure Protection, which is composed of critical infrastrucure that is privately owned and operated (Alimahomed, 2014).

This type of arrangement highlights the risky nature of the private sector's involvement in counterterrorism. Though on the surface InfraGard does seem like a useful way to integrate the private sector into counterterrorism, Alimahomed is skeptical of its benefits to broader society. Members of InfraGard have access to unclassified information, but sensitive information nonetheless (Alimahomed, 2014). Alimahomed writes that

> . . . as "the war on terror" demanded national vigilance and opened the door for vast information collection on Arabs and Muslims, InfraGard's members, dressed in the cloak of patriotic duty, were able to present themsevles as key players in the fight for homeland security . . . the role in shaping the priorities of the security services to meet their own needs was underchallenged, paving the way for unwarranted and illegal intrusions into the lives of other Americans (Alimahomed, 2014, p. 94)

Alimahomed brings up a point that it is necessary to be critical when discussing the role of the private sector in counterterrorism. She argues that this type of program became a gateway for multiple security programs that essentially targeted Arab and Muslim communities, which inherently led to questionable ramifications for civil liberties violations (Alimahomed, 2014).

27.5.4 Fusion Centers

The Bush and Obama administrations both supported the creation of fusions centers under the DHS. The purpose of these centers is to share data across government agencies and the private sector. Fusion centers are viewed by many as a necessary component to the 9/11 terrorists attacks where many agencies were not able to "connect the dots'" necessary to combat terrorism (Regan et al., 2015). There are nearly 80 fusion centers located in the U.S., including Guam and the U.S. Virgin Islands (Homeland Security, n.d.). There are also two types, primary fusion centers which typically provide information sharing and analysis for the entire state that it is located in and recognized that provides information sharing and analysis for a major urban area (Homeland Security, n.d.).

Fusion centers have the capability of focusing on cyber-intrusion tactics. For example, the Washington State Fusion Center states their main objectives are to detect, deter, and prevent terrorist attacks as well as provide cyber-security awareness (Washington State Fusion Center, n.d.). An issue with these fusion centers is the fact that the "actual operations of these centers are somewhat cloaked in secrecy" (Carroll, 2008). Carroll, who has participated in fusion centers, claims that technology is a critical component of fusion centers, but the human assests invovled are more critical (Carroll, 2008).

Fusion centers also use InfraGard's component of the FBI Tripwire program that is used to identify groups or individuals whose "suspicious behavior may be a precursor to an act of terrorism and to alert authorities to such activities" (Regan et al., 2015, p. 750). A lack of transparency makes it difficult to determine whether or not this suspicious behavior (such as using binoculars, taking pictures or video footage with no apparent esthetic value, and taking notes) transcends into the cyber-sphere (German and Stanley, 2008).

27.6 FUTURE RESEARCH AND POLICY IMPLICATIONS

There are many avenues that should be pursued in future research that extend far beyond the scope of this chapter. There is sufficient literature available on the nature of public–private partnerships, but further examination explicitly focused on terrorism on the internet could be beneficial to both academics and policy-makers. Though some is available, it is limited in quantity. Knowing how public–private partnerships focus on terrorist activity on the internet could pave the way for critical thought leading to innovative and beneficial policies and programs.

The literature that focuses on the private sector's role in countering terrorism online is also limited. This becomes even more apparent when attempting to access information on private security companies and what they do regarding terrorism on the internet. There seems to be an apparent lack of transparency regarding how the public and private security companies work together to combat terrorism on the internet. A prime example is that of InfraGard, but more specifically fusion centers. It is largely unclear whether or not fusion centers are involved in monitoring online behavior as well as physical, in-person behavior. Even if fusion centers are not active in online monitoring, it is unclear whether or not data flowing through fusion centers is then used by federal agencies to prompt who should be monitored online.

Further research on how this data is used, especially if it is used to determine suspicious individuals that "need" online monitoring would be of use in analyzing the private sector's role in countering terrorism on the internet. Until then, it is appropriate to approach operations like fusion centers with some scepticism. There is a fine line between attempting to monitor legitimate security threats and monitoring an individual that is suspicious because he or she is taking notes and using binoculars in a public setting. The issue of this lack of transparency circles back to an initial concern raised here, which was where the countering of online terrorism starts and stops. Online terrorism may lead to offline terrorism, so the monitoring and countering of exists on a spectrum.

It is apparent that the private sector's involvement with countering terrorism on the internet diverges into two directions. First, there are the efforts of think tanks like ISD who partner with organizations who attempt to gain a more holistic understanding of countering terrorism or extremism online. These approaches are subtler, less securitizing, and less accusatory. It also seems that those involved with this type of approach are more transparent with their data and findings. The second direction is that of private companies, particularly security-related companies. Finding data on how private security companies are involved in countering terrorism on the internet proved to be difficult. Accessing this data from the companies themselves for future research would likely be difficult as well.

Though this chapter does not generate new knowledge that would have policy implications, it does unintentionally identify a gap in the literature that could. Most striking, as aforementioned, is the lack of literature that examines the boundaries that exist (if any) between online and offline behavior, particularly that of fusion center data usage. Perhaps this is the entire point of utilizing the private sector, particularly private security companies. The transparency of such companies is not as scrutinized by the public as public-sector organizations.

The best way forward would be to increase funding to those in the private sector that adopt similar approaches to the ISD. These approaches generate data that can be used to further create innovative counterterrorism strategies. These types of private institutions are likely better suited to determine how to create partnerships across public, private, and nonprofit sectors. The important question to consider is how countering terrorism online can be done most effectively. Though difficult to measure, it seems intuitive to think that counter narrative messages on social media platforms would generate positive results. Targeted campaigns can create dialogue and encourage those exploring or involved in extremism to take a step back or abandon it altogether. This is evident by the fact that eight individuals reached out to ExitU.S.A after their campaign in order to seek help for leaving behind an extremist lifestyle.

27.7 SUMMARY

This chapter explores how public–private partnerships are involved with countering terrorism online. This is an important topic, especially when focusing intensely on the private sector's role in counterterrorism. This chapter is divided into a total of six sections. The first section is a brief introduction to the topic. The second section an analysis of terrorism on the internet in terms of what that means and who is doing it. Pertinent to this discussion is the differentiation between recruits, sympathizers, and violent extremists and their relationship to terrorism on the internet. It also discusses how the literature can differentiate between cyber-terrorism and terrorism on the internet. The third section defines the public sector, the private sector, and offers a brief note on how this relates to public policy. The fourth section considers public–private partnerships and countering terrorism on the internet. It first discusses the ambiguity of partnerships and then analyzes the nature of partnerships between the public and private sector. Section five then considers existing examples of how terrorism is being countered on the internet by the private sector. Four case studies are examined: the Global Internet Forum to Counter Terrorism, the Institute for Strategic Dialogue Campaigns, InfraGard, and fusion centers. These case studies provide a foundation for a comparative analysis to be built and provide telling results regarding both positive and negative ways the private sector can be involved in countering terrorism on the internet. The final section is dedicated to suggesting future areas of research and policy implications. Future areas of research from this chapter is derived from identifying gaps in the existing literature and the problems that have risen from that gap. The implications of this research for policy, and future related research, are important to consider given the complexity of public–private partnerships and the involvement of various government bodies.

REFERENCES

Alexander, D. C., and Alexander, Y. (2002). *Terrorism and Businss: The Impact of September 11, 2001.* Ardsley, New York: Transnational Publishers, Inc.

Alimahomed, S. (2014). Homeland Security Inc.: public order, private profit. *Race & Class, 55*(4), 82–99.

Beck, U. (2002). The Terrorist Threat: World Risk Society Revisited. *Theory, Culture & Society, 19*(4), 39–55.

Bouzas-Lorenzo, R. (2010). Public sector marketing, political science and the science of public administration: the evolution of a transdisciplinary dialogue. *International Review on Public and Non-profit Marketing, 7*(2), 113–125.

Busch, N. E., and Givens, A. D. (2013). Achieving resilience in disaster management: The role of public–private partnerships. *Journal of Strategic Studies, 6*(2), 1–19.

Carroll, W. (2008, August 11). *Military.com.* Retrieved from The Importance of Cyber Fusion Centers: https://www.military.com/defensetech/2008/08/11/the-importance-of-cyber-fusion-centers

Community Outreach. (n.d.). Retrieved from FBI: https://www.fbi.gov/about/community-outreach

German, M., and Stanley, J. (2008). *Fusion Center Update.* ACLU.

Hardy, K., and Williams, G. (2014). What is 'Cyberterrorism'? Computer and internet technology in legal definitions of terrorism. In T. M. Chen, L. Jarvis, and S. Macdonald, *Cyberterrorism: Understanding, Assessment, and Response.* New York: Springer.

Homeland Security. (n.d.). Retrieved from Fusion Center Locations and Contact Information: https://www.dhs.gov/fusion-center-locations-and-contact-information

InfraGard. (n.d.). Retrieved from https://www.infragard.org

Jacobson, M. (2009). Terrorist financing on the internet. *CTC Sentinel, 2*(6), 1–4.

Jaggar, A. (2005). What is terrorism, why is it wrong, and could it ever be morally permissible? *Journal of Social Philosophy, 36*(2), 202–217.

Janbek, D., and Williams, V. (2014). The role of the internet post-9/11 in terrorism and counterterrorism. *Brown Journal of World Affairs, XX*(11), 297–308.

Keene, S. D. (2011). Terrorism and the internet: A double-edged sword. *Journal of Money Laundering Control, 14*(4), 359–370.

Office of Private Sector (OPS) Fact Sheet. (n.d.). Retrieved from https://www.fbi.gov/file-repository/ops-factsheet-4-4-18.pdf/view

Palasinski, M., Granat, J., Ok Seol, K., and Bowman-Grieve, L. (2014). Social categorization and right-wing authoritarianism in reporting potential terrorist threats in cyberspace. *Computers in Human Behavior, 36*, 76–81.

Pathirane, L., and Blades, D. W. (1982). Defining and measuring the public sector: Some international comparisons. *Review of Income and Wealth*, *28*(3), 261–289.

Petersen, K. L. (2008). Terrorism: When Risk Meets Security. *Alternatives: Global, Local, Political*, *33*(2), 173–190.

QC, L. C., and Macdonald, S. (2014). The criminalisation of terrorists' online preparatory acts. In T. M. Chen, L. Jarvis, and S. Macdonald, *Cyberterrorism: Understanding, Assessment, and Response*. New York: Springer.

Regan, P. M., Monahan, T., and Craven, K. (2015). Constructing the suspicious: Data production, circulation, and interpretation by DHS Fusion Centers. *Administration & Society*, *47*(6), 740–762.

Rosand, E., and Milar, A. (2017, January). *Brookings*. Retrieved from How the Private Sector can be Harnessed to Stop Violent Extremism: https://www.brookings.edu/blog/order-from-chaos/2017/01/31/how-the-private-sector-can-be-harnessed-to-stop-violent-extremism/

Security Council: Counter-Terrorism Committee. (n.d.). *Security Council: Counter-Terrorism Committee*. Retrieved from The United Nations Counter-Terrorism Committee Executive Directorate (CTED) welcomes major private sector initiative to counter terrorism online: https://www.un.org/sc/ctc/news/2017/06/26/united-nations-counter-terrorism-committee-executive-directorate-cted-welcomes-major-private-sector-initiative-counter-terrorism-online/

Silverman, T., Stewart, C., Amanullah, Z., and Birdwell, J. (2016). *The Impact of Counter Narratives: Insights from a Year-Long Cross-Platform Pilot Study of Counter-Narrative Curation, Targeting, Evaluation and Impact*. London: Institute for Strategic Dialogue.

Waddington, D., and McSeveny, K. (2012). Terrorism and the Risk Society. In S. Bennett, *Innovative Thinking in Risk, Crisis, and Disaster Management*. Surrey: Gower Publishing Limited.

Washington State Fusion Center. (n.d.). Retrieved from http://www.wsfc.wa.gov

Weimann, G. (2004, March). United States Institute of Peace Special Report. Retrieved from How Modern Terrorism Uses the Internet: https://www.usip.org/sites/default/files/sr116.pdf

What We Investigate: Cyber Crime. (n.d.). Retrieved from FBI: https://www.fbi.gov/investigate/cyber

Section IX

Appendices

Appendix A: List of Top Online Counterterrorism Organizations

Center, project, program, and issue	Affiliated organization or institute	Location
Bangladesh Center for Terrorism Research (BCTR) [www.bipss.org.bd/index.php/page/bct]	Bangladesh Institute of Peace and Security Studies [http://bipss.org.bd/]	Dhaka, Bangladesh
Center for Advancing Microbial Risk Assessment (CAMRA) [www.camra.msu.edu/]	Michigan State University [https://msu.edu/]; Carnegie Mellon University [www.cmu.edu/]; Drexel University [www.drexel.edu/]; Northern Arizona University [https://nau.edu/]; University of Arizona [www.arizona.edu/]; University of California at Berkeley [www.berkeley.edu/]; University of Michigan [https://umich.edu/]	East Lansing, Michigan, United States Pittsburgh, Pennsylvania, United States Philadelphia, Pennsylvania, United States Flagstaff, Arizona, United States Berkeley, California, United States Ann Arbor, Michigan, United States
Center for Applied Counterterrorism Studies (CACS) [www.jstor.org/stable/26298483]	University of North Carolina at Charlotte [www.uncc.edu/]	Charlotte, North Carolina, United States
Center for Asymmetric Warfare (CAW) [http://cawnps.blogspot.com/]	Naval Postgraduate School [www.nps.edu/]	Monterey, California, United States
Center for Counter-Terrorism Studies [www.mc.edu/academics/departments/history/administration-justice/counterterrorism]	China Institute of Contemporary International Relations [www.css.ethz.ch/en/services/css-partners/partner.html/34643]	Beijing, China

(*Continued*)

Center, project, program, and issue	Affiliated organization or institute	Location
Center for Interdisciplinary Policy, Education, and Research on Terrorism (CIPERT) [http://www.cipert.org/]	Center for Homeland Defense and Security [www.chds.us/]: located at the Naval Postgraduate School in Monterey, CA. Center on Terrorism and Irregular Warfare [https://calhoun.nps.edu/handle/10945/36801]: 411 Dyer Rd. Bldg. 339, Monterey, CA 93943 Naval Postgraduate School [https://my.nps.edu/]; University Circle, Monterey, CA 93943 Pacific Graduate School of Psychology [www.internationalstudent.com/school-search/110/usa/california/pacific-graduate-school-of-psychology/]: 224 First Street, Neptune Beach, FL 32266	
Center for International Research on Terrorism (ITRC) [www.terrorismresearchcenter.org]: Middlebury Institute of International Studies, 460 Pierce Street, Monterey, CA 93940	University of Cincinnati [www.uc.edu/]; Turkish National Police Organization [www.egm.gov.tr/en/dkmanlar/tnp.pdf]	
Center for Law and Counterterrorism (CLC) [www.defenddemocracy.org/index.php?option=com_content&view=article&id=1341&Itemid=334]	Foundation for Defense of Democracies [www.defenddemocracy.org/index.php]	Washington, DC, United States
Center for Policing Terrorism (CPT) [www.manhattan-institute.org/securing-our-cities]	Manhattan Institute [www.manhattan-institute.org/]	New York City, New York, United States
Center for Terrorism Law (CTL) [www.stmarytx.edu/academics/]	St. Mary's University [www.stmarytx.edu/academics/]	San Antonio, Texas, United States
Center for Terrorism Research (CTR) [www.defenddemocracy.org/index.php?option=com_content&view=article&id=515778&Itemid=343]	Foundation for Defense of Democracies [www.defenddemocracy.org/]	Wollongong, Australia

(Continued)

Center, project, program, and issue	Affiliated organization or institute	Location
Center on Global Counterterrorism Cooperation	[www.globalcenter. org/center-on-global-counterterrorism-cooperation-becomes-the-global-center-on-cooperative-security/]	Washington, DC, United States
Center on Terrorism [www.jjay. cuny.edu/center-terrorism]	John Jay College of Criminal Justice [www. defenddemocracy.org/]	New York City, New York, United States
Center on Terrorism and Counterterrorism [www.fpri. org/research/terrorism/]	Foreign Policy Research Institute [www.fpri.org/]	Philadelphia, Pennsylvania, United States
Center on Terrorism and Irregular Warfare [https://c alhoun.nps.edu/handle/109 45/36801]	Naval Postgraduate School [www.nps.edu/]	Monterey, California, United States
Center for Asymmetric Threat Studies (CATS) [https://m edarbetarwebben.fhs.se/...cent res.../center-for-asymmetric-t hreat-studies/about/]	Swedish National Defence College [www.css.ethz.ch/en/ services/css-partners/partner. html/43344]	Stockholm, Sweden
Center for Policing, Intelligence and Counter Terrorism (PICT) [http://mq.academia.edu/D epartments/Centre_for_Pol icing_Intelligence_and_Co unter_Terrorism_PICT_]	Macquarie University, Sydney, Australia [www.mq.edu.au/]	Sydney, Australia
Center for the Study of Radicalization and Contemporary Political Violence (CSRV) [www.aber. ac.uk/en/rbi/archpages/rb iarchive-donotdelete/rese arch-centres-and-groups/c srv/]	Aberystwyth University [www. aber.ac.uk/en/]	Aberystwyth, Ceredigion, United Kingdom
Center for Terrorism and Counterterrorism (CTC) [www. linkedin.com/company/cent re-for-terrorism-and-counterte rrorism---leiden-university]	Campus The Hague of Leiden University, Netherlands [www. universiteitleiden.nl/en/ the-hague]	The Hague, Netherlands
Center for the Study of Terrorism and Political Violence (CSTPV) [www. st-andrews.ac.uk/~cstpv/]	University of St. Andrews, Scotland [www.st-andrews. ac.uk/]	St. Andrews, Scotland

(Continued)

Center, project, program, and issue	Affiliated organization or institute	Location
Centre for the Study of Terrorism (CFSOT) [hhtp://www.cfsot.com index.php]		London, England
Center for the Study of Youth and Political Violence [https://news.utk.edu/tag/center-for-the-study-of-youth-and-political-conflict/]	University of Tennessee - Knoxville [www.utk.edu/]	Knoxville, Tennessee, United States
Centre for Transnational Crime Prevention (CTCP) [https://ancors.uow.edu.au/index.html]		Wollongong, Australia
Center for Higher Study on the Struggle against Terrorism and Political Violence (Centro Alti Studi per a Lotta al Terrorismo e alla Violenza Politica) [www.jstor.org/stable/26298483]		Rome, Italy
Charity & Security Network (CSN) [www.charityandsecurity.org/]		Washington, DC, United States
Chicago Project on Security and Terrorism (CPOST) [https://cpost.uchicago.edu/]	University of Chicago [https://www.uchicago.edu/]	Chicago, Illinois, United States
Columbia University World Trade Center Archive Project [https://library.columbia.edu/news.html]	Columbia University [https://library.columbia.edu/news.html]	New York City, New York, United States
Combating Terrorism Center (CTC) at West Point [https://ctc.usma.edu/]	United States Military Academy [www.usma.edu/SitePages/Home.aspx]	West Point, New York, United States
Consortium for Countering the Financing of Terrorism (CCFT) [www.c cft.org capacitybuilding index.html]		Singapore
Consortium for Strategic Communication (CSC) [http://csc.asu.edu/]	Hugh Downs School of Human Communication, Arizona State University [https://humancommunication.clas.asu.edu/]	Tempe, Arizona, United States
Counterterrorism and Homeland Security [www.cato.org/research/counterterrorism-homeland-security]	Cato Institute [www.cato.org/]	Washington, DC, United States

(*Continued*)

Center, project, program, and issue	Affiliated organization or institute	Location
Counterterrorism Strategy Initiative [www.c-span.org/ organization/?103163/Cou nterterrorism-Strategy-Initiat ive]	American Strategy Program, New American Foundation [http://aworldthatjustmig htwork.com/tag/american-s trategy-program-at-the-ne w-america-foundation/]	Washington, DC, United States
Counterterrorism Topic [www. hrw.org/topic/terrorism-c ounterterrorism]	Human Rights Watch [www.hrw. org/]	New York City, New York, United States
Dark Web Terrorism Research [www.jstor.org/ stable/26297596]	Artificial Intelligence Laboratory, Eller College of Management, University of Arizona [https:// ai.arizona.edu/]	Tucson, Arizona, United States
Future of Terrorism Project (FTP) [www.defenddemocracy .org/index.php?option=com _content&view=article&id= 1342&Itemid=335]	Foundation for Defense of Democracies [www. defenddemocracy.org/]	Washington, DC, United States
GCC Security and Terrorism Issues Research Program [http:// www.grc.net/index.php?frm_a ction=detail&PK_ID=17&set _lang=en&frm_module=resea rchprograms&sec=Research+ Programs-Relations&sec_ty pe-h&override=Research+Pr ogram+Detail&CAT_ID=5]	Gulf Research Center [http:// www.grc.net/index.php?]: 19 Rayat Al-Itihad St. P.O. Box 2134 Jeddah 21451 Kingdom of Saudi Arabia	
Global Terrorism Analysis Program [www.kaggle.com/ laurenstc/global-terrorism-an alysis]	Jamestown Foundation [https:// jamestown.org/]	Washington, DC, United States
Global Terrorism Research Centre (GTReC) [artsonline. monash.edu.au/gtrec/]	Monash University, Australia [www.monash.edu/]	Melbourne, Victoria, Australia
Global Terrorism Subtopic [www.americanprogress.org/ issues/security/view/]	National Security Issue, Center for American Progress [www. americanprogress.org/issues/ security/view/]	Washington, DC, United States
Homegrown Terror & Radicalization Topic [https://c chs.gwu.edu/homegrown-ter ror-radicalization]	Homeland Security Policy Institute, George Washington University [www.washington times.com/.../homeland-se curity-policy-institute-at-geo rge-washi/]	Washington, DC, United States

(Continued)

Center, project, program, and issue	Affiliated organization or institute	Location
Homeland Security and Counterterrorism Program [www.csis.org/programs/...security-program/.../homeland-security-and-counterterrorism-program]	Defense and Security Program, Center for Strategic and International Studies [www.csis.org/topics/defense-and-security]	Washington, DC, United States
Homeland Security and Terrorism Program [www.liu.edu/Riverhead/Homeland-Security-and-Terrorism-Institute]	James A. Baker III Institute for Public Policy, Rice University [www.bakerinstitute.org/]	Houston, Texas, United States
Institute for National Security and Counterterrorism (INSCT) [http://insct.syr.edu/]	Syracuse University [www.syracuse.edu/]	Syracuse, New York, United States
Institute for the Study of Violent Groups (ISVG) [www.isvg.org/]	University of New Haven [www.newhaven.edu/]	New Haven, Connecticut, United States
Institut fur Terrorismusforschung & Sicherheitspolitik (IFTUS) [www.thinktankdirectory.org/directory/iftus.shtml]		Essen, Germany
Institute of Terrorism Research and Response (ITRR) [www.terrorresponse.org/]		Philadelphia, Pennsylvania, United States
Inter-American Committee Against Terrorism (CICTE) [www.oas.org/en/sms/cicte/default.asp]	Organization of American States [www.oas.org/en/default.asp]	Washington, DC, United States
International Association for Counterterrorism & Security Professionals (IACSP) [www.iacsp.com/]		
International Center for Terrorism Studies (ICTS) [www.potomacinstitute.org/academic-centers/international-center-for-terrorism-studies-icts]	Potomac Institute for Policy Studies [www.potomacinstitute.org/index.php]	Arlington, Virginia, United States
International Center for the Study of Terrorism (ICST) [www.icst.psu.edu]	Pennsylvania State University [www.psu.edu/	State College, Pennsylvania, United States
International Center of Terror Medicine [www.washingtontimes.com/topics/international-center-for-terror-medicine/]	Hadassah Medical Center [www.hadassah-med.com/]	Jerusalem, Israel

(Continued)

Center, project, program, and issue	Affiliated organization or institute	Location
International Centre for Political Violence and Terrorism Research (ICPVTR) [www.rsis.edu.sg/research/icpvtr/]	S. Rajaratnam School of International Studies, Nanyang Technological University, Singapore [www.rsis.edu.sg/]	Singapore
International Centre for the Study of Radicalisation (ICSR) [https://icsr.info/]	King's College, London [www.kcl.ac.uk/]; University of Pennsylvania [www.upenn.edu/]; Interdisciplinary Center Herzliya [https://global.wustl.edu/mcdonnell-academy/partner-universities/interdisciplinary-center-herzliya/]; Jordan Institute of Diplomacy [www.css.ethz.ch/en/services/css-partners/partner.html/49858]	London, England
International Institute for Counter-Terrorism (ICT) [www.ict.org.il/]	Interdisciplinary Center [www.topuniversities.com/universities/interdisciplinary-center-herzliya]	Herzliya, Israel
Investigative Project on Terrorism (IPT) [www.investigativeproject.org/]		
Italian Team for Security, Terroristic Issues & Managing Emergencies (ITSTIME) [www.itstime.it/Inglese/aboutus.htm]	Catholic University of Milan [www.wemakescholars.com/university/catholic-university-of-milan]	Milan, Italy
Jane's Terrorism and Insurgency Centre [https://ihsmarkit.com/products/janes-terrorism-insurgency-intelligence-centre.html]		London, England
Jihad and Terrorism Threat Monitor (JTTM) [www.memri.org/reports/jihad-and-terrorism-threat-monitor-jttm-weekend-summary-324]	Middle East Media Research Institute [www.memri.org/]	Washington, DC, United States
Mackenzie Institute [http://mackenzieinstitute.com/]		Toronto, Ontario, Canada
Maritime Terrorism Research Center [www.hugedomains.com/domain_profile.cfm?d=maritimeterrorism&e=com]		

(Continued)

Center, project, program, and issue	Affiliated organization or institute	Location
Meir Amit Intelligence & Terrorism Information Center (ITIC) [www.terrorism-info.org.il/en/]	Israel Intelligence Heritage & Commemoration Center [www.terrorism-info.org.il/en/]	Gelilot, Israel
Memorial Institute for the Prevention of Terrorism (MIPT) [www.bowdoin.edu/~samato/IRA/reviews/issues/jan05/mipt.html]		Oklahoma City, Oklahoma, United States
Monterey Terrorism Research and Education Program (MonTREP) [www.middlebury.edu/institute/academics/centers-initiatives]	Monterey Institute of International Studies [www.middlebury.edu/institute/]	Monterey, California, United States
National Center for Foreign Animal and Zoonotic Disease Defense (FAZD Center) [http://iiad.tamu.edu/]	Texas A&M University [www.tamu.edu/]	College Station, Texas, United States
National Center for Risk and Economic Analysis of Terrorism Events (CREATE) [https://create.usc.edu/]	University of Southern California [www.usc.edu/]	Los Angeles, California, United States
National Center on the Psychology of Terrorism (NCPT) [www.usc.edu/]: USC, California, USA	Center for Interdisciplinary Policy, Education, and Research on Terrorism [www.trackingterrorism.org/resource/stanford-university-center-interdisciplinary-policy-education-and-research-terrorism]: Stanford University, California, USA	
National Consortium for the Study of Terrorism and Responses to Terrorism (START) [www.start.umd.edu/]	University of Maryland [www.umd.edu/]	College Park, Maryland, United States
National Terrorism Preparedness Institute (NTPI) [http://terrorism.spcollege.edu/index.aspx]	St. Petersburg College [www.spcollege.edu/]	St. Petersburg, Florida, United States
Nine Eleven Finding Answers (NEFA) Foundation [https://ipfs.io/ipfs/QmXoypizjW3WknFiJnKLwHCnL72vedxjQkDDP1mXWo6uco/wiki/Nine_Eleven_Finding_Answers_Foundation.html]		Washington, DC, United States

(*Continued*)

Center, project, program, and issue	Affiliated organization or institute	Location
Philippine Institute for Peace, Violence and Terrorism Research, Inc. (PIPVTR) [http://pipvtr.com/pipvtr/index.php?section=1]		Teachers Village East, Diliman, Quezon City, Philippines
Program for Terrorism Research & Studies [www.jstor.org/stable/26298483]	Faculty of Economics and Political Science, Cairo University [www.feps.edu.eg/en/]	Cairo, Egypt
Program on International Terrorism [www.feps.edu.eg/en/]	Elcano Royal Institute [http://www.realinstitutoelcano.org/wps/portal/rielcano_es/!ut/p/a1/04_Sj9CPykssy0xPLMnMz0vMAfGjzOKNQ1zcA73dDQ0MLIOcDRzdLbxDLE0NDcI8TIAKIoEKDHAARwNC-r3ACvDoB1pgVOTr7JuuH1WQWJKhm5mXlq8fUZSZmpOcmJcfn5qXrl-QG1Hl46ioCABvcE6h/dl5/d5/L2dBISEvZ0FBIS9nQSEh/]	Madrid, Spain
Project Fikra [www.washingtoninstitute.org/about/research-programs/project-fikra/]	Washington Institute for Near East Policy [www.washingtoninstitute.org/ar/?t=I01]	Washington, DC, United States
Quilliam Foundation [www.quilliaminternational.com/]		London, England
Radicalization Watch Project (RWP) [www.acronymattic.com/Radicalization-Watch-Project-(RWP).html]	Center for Advanced Defense Studies [https://c4ads.org/]	Washington, DC, United States
Russia-Eurasia Terror Watch (RETWA) [https://retwa.com.cutestat.com/]		
Society for Terrorism Research (STR) [www.societyforterrorismresearch.org/]		Boston, Massachusetts, United States
Stein Program on Counterterrorism and Intelligence [www.washingtoninstitute.org/templateC11.php?CID=63]	Washington Institute for Near East Policy [www.washingtoninstitute.org/templateC11.php?CID=63]	Washington, DC, United States

(Continued)

Center, project, program, and issue	Affiliated organization or institute	Location
Terrorism, Transnational Crime and Corruption Center (TraCCC) [http://traccc.gmu.edu/]	George Mason University [www2.gmu.edu/]	Fairfax, Virginia, United States
Terrorism & National Security [www.rand.org/topics/national-security-and-terrorism.html]	Nelson Center for International and Public Affairs, James Madison University [www.jmu.edu/nelsoninstitute/index.shtml]	Harrisonburg, Virginia, United States
Terrorism & Preparedness Data Resource Center [www.icpsr.umich.edu/icpsrweb/content/NACJD/guides/tpdrc.html]	University of Michigan Inter-university Consortium for Political and Social Research [https://deepblue.lib.umich.edu/handle/2027.42/57738]	Ann Arbor, Michigan, United States
Terrorism and Counter-Radicalization Issue [https://deepblue.lib.umich.edu/handle/2027.42/57738]	Carnegie Endowment for International Peace [http://carnegieendowment.org/]	Washington, DC, United States
Terrorism and Crime Studies [www.loc.gov/rr/frd/terrorism.html]	Federal Research Division, Library of Congress [www.loc.gov/rr/frd/terrorism.html	Washington, DC, United States
Terrorism and Homeland Security Research Area [https://researchguides.canton.edu/c.php?g=186752&p=1233820]	RAND Corporation [www.rand.org/]: 1776 Main Street, Santa Monica, CA 90401-3208	
Terrorism and Internal Security Research Cluster [http://cvemonitor.cpakgulf.org/index.php/2016/07/19/terrorism-and-internal-security-research-cluster/]	Institute for Defence Studies & Analyses [https://idsa.in/]	New Delhi, India
Terrorism Issue [www.cfr.org/defense-and-security/terrorism-and-counterterrorism]	Council on Foreign Relations [www.cfr.org/defense-and-security/terrorism-and-counterterrorism]	New York City, New York, United States
Terrorism Issue [www.heritage.org/terrorism]	Heritage Foundation [www.heritage.org/terrorism]	Washington, DC, United States
Terrorism Issue [http://www.ipcs.org/issues/terrorism/]	Institute of Peace & Conflict Studies [http://www.ipcs.org/]	New Delhi, India
Terrorist Media Project [www.fdd.org/index.php?option=com_content&view=article&id=1343&Itemid=337]	Foundation for Defense of Democracies [www.fdd.org/]	Washington, DC, United States

(Continued)

Center, project, program, and issue	Affiliated organization or institute	Location
Terrorism Page [https://dc.adl.org/national-counter-terrorism-seminar-in-israel/]	Anti-Defamation League [https://dc.adl.org/national-counter-terrorism-seminar-in-israel/]	New York City, New York, United States
Terrorism Program [www.pogo.org/center-for-defense-information/]	Center for Defense Information [www.pogo.org/center-for-defense-information/]	Washington, DC, United States
Terrorism Research Center (TRC) [https://fulbright.uark.edu/departments/sociology/research-centers/terrorism-research-center/index.php]	Fulbright College, University of Arkansas [https://fulbright.uark.edu/]	Fayetteville, Arkansas, United States
Terrorism Research Center, Inc. (TRC) [www.oodaloop.com/?co=C005905]		
Terrorism Topic [www.hrw.org/topic/terrorism-counterterrorism]	Human Rights Watch [www.hrw.org/]	New York City, New York, United States
Triangle Center on Terrorism and Homeland Security (TCTHS) [https://sites.duke.edu/tcths/]	Duke University [www.duke.edu/]	Durham, North Carolina, United States
Unconventional Warfare Study Center [https://ndupress.ndu.edu/JFQ/Joint-Force-Quarterly-80/Article/643108/unconventional-warfare-in-the-gray-zone/]: 260 Fifth Avenue, Building 64, Fort Lesley J. McNair, Washington, D.C. 20319-5066		
US-Russia Initiative to Prevent Nuclear Terrorism [www.belfercenter.org/project/us-russia-initiative-prevent-nuclear-terrorism]	Belfer Center for Science and International Affairs, John F. Kennedy School of Government, Harvard University [www.belfercenter.org/]	Cambridge, Massachusetts, United States
Violence and Extremism Programme [www.un.org/counterterrorism/ctitf/en/plan-action-prevent-violent-extremism]	Demos [www.demos.co.uk/files/Edge_of_Violence_-_web.pdf]	London, England

(*Continued*)

Center, project, program, and issue	Affiliated organization or institute	Location
Violent Intranational Political Conflict & Terrorism Research Laboratory (VIPCAT) [www.wm.edu/offices/itpir/projects/vipcat/]	Institute for the Theory and Practice of International Relations, College of William and Mary [www.wm.edu/offices/global-research/]	Williamsburg, Virginia, United States
WMD & CBRN Terrorism Topic [www.wm.edu/offices/global-research/]	Homeland Security Policy Institute, George Washington University [www.wm.edu/offices/global-research/]	Washington, DC, United States

Appendix B: List of Miscellaneous Online Counterterrorism Resources

General	Federal Government Resources	US Policies on Counter-Terrorism	Counter-Terrorism Studies	Cyber-security
ICRC Terrorism: The International Committee of the Red Cross maintains this site which presents the juxtaposition of counter-terrorism with IHL, or International Humanitarian Law. [www.icrc.org/en/war-and-law/contemporary-challenges-for-ihl/terrorism]	The 9/11 Commission Report: This is the official report of the events leading up to the September 11, 2001 attacks. [www.9-11commission.gov/report/911Report.pdf]	America's War on Terrorism: The Federation of American Scientists site provides information and analysis of emerging security policy. [https://fas.org/]	Center for Counter-Terrorism Law: Housed in our state-of-the-art facility at St. Mary's University School of Law, San Antonio, Texas, the Center for Counter-Terrorism Law is a fully operational legal research center dedicated to the study of legal issues associated with both antiterrorism and counterterrorism, with particular emphasis on cyberspace and information assurance technologies. [https://law.stmarytx.edu/]	Cyberdomain: This website is the portal to the Department of Defense's cyber-security information. Included are news stories, speeches and remarks, and articles, as well as links to the cyber-security websites of the Army, Navy, and Air Force. [https://csrcl.huji.ac.il/sites/default/files/csrcl/files/dan_efrony.pdf]
NATO and the fight against terrorism: NATO's site includes news, topics, documents, and videos. [www.nato.int/cps/en/natohq/topics_77646.htm]	Bureau of Counterterrorism: This office of the U.S. Department of State provides reports, fact sheets, initiatives, and more. [www.state.gov/j/ct/]	Countering the Changing Threat of International Terrorism: This National Commission on Terrorism report from 2000 reviews American policies on international terrorism prior to the 9/11 attacks. [www.gpo.gov/fdsys/pkg/GPO-COUNTERINGTERRORISM/content-detail.html]	Chicago Project on Security and Counter-Terrorism: This website from the University of Chicago provides a database of suicide attacks, a blog, news, and videos. [www.uchicago.edu/research/center/the_chicago_project_on_security_and_terrorism/]	Cyber-security (Center for Strategic and International Studies): The Center for Strategic and International Studies offers information designed to help the public understand the need for a comprehensive cyber-security strategy. [www.csis.org/topics/cybersecurity-and-technology/cybersecurity]

(Continued)

General	Federal Government Resources	US Policies on Counter terrorism	Counter-Terrorism Studies	Cyber-security
Counter-Terrorism: This site from the Council on Foreign Relations provides information by region, publication, and year. [www.cfr.org/defense -and-security/terrorism-a nd-counterterrorism]	Counter Terrorism Sanctions: Information about sanctions imposed by the Treasury Department, including Terrorist Assets Reports and executive orders, statutes, and regulations dealing with sanctions. [www. treasury.gov/resourc e-center/sanctions/.../ terror.aspx]	The Inman Report: Report of the Secretary of State's Advisory Panel on Overseas Security: This 1985 report outlines the scope and dimension of U.S. security problems in international business and diplomacy. It was commissioned in response to the 1983 bombings of the U.S. Embassy and the Marine barracks in Beirut, Lebanon. [https://fas.org/ irp/threat/inman/]	Combating Terrorism Center: The Combating Terrorism Center at West Point bridges the operational and academic realms by providing present and future leaders with the intellectual tools needed to defeat and deter terrorist threats to our nation. [https://ctc.usma. edu/]	Cyber-security (Documents from the U.S. Senate Committee on Homeland Security & Governmental Affair): Documents from the U.S. Senate Committee on Homeland Security & Governmental Affairs dealing with the issue of cyber-security, including statements, letters, and text of legislation. [www. hsgac.senate.gov/hea rings/mitigating-ame ricas-cybersecurity-risk]
Text and Status of the United Nations Conventions on Counter-Terrorism: Full-text of UN conventions dealing with counter-terrorism. Available in multiple languages. [www.osce.org/ atu/17138?download=true]	Department of Homeland Security: The official web site of the Department of Homeland Security. [www.dhs.gov/]	National Strategy for Combating Terrorism: A 2006 report from the White House outlining the national strategy for combating terrorism, which focuses on identifying and defusing threats before they reach America's borders. [http s://2001-2009.state.gov/s/ ct/rls/wh/71803.htm]	Institute for Biosecurity: At Saint Louis University College for Public Health & Social Justice. This web site offers extensive information on bioterrorism and current research. [www.slu.edu/pu blic-health-social-justice/ education/graduate/publ ic-health/mph-concentrati ons/bsdp.php]	Preliminary Cyber-security Framework: This preliminary framework was developed by the National Institute of Standards and Technology in response to Executive Order 13636 of February, 2013. [www. nist.gov/document-4408]

(Continued)

General	Federal Government Resources	US Policies on Counter terrorism	Counter-Terrorism Studies	Cyber-security
United Nations Action to Counter Terrorism: This site includes latest news, press releases, and key documents. [www.un.org/en/counterterrorism/overview.shtml]	National Counterterrorism Center: NCTC serves as the primary organization in the U.S. government for integrating and analyzing all intelligence pertaining to terrorism possessed or acquired by the U.S. government (except purely domestic terrorism). [www.dni.gov/index.php/nctc-home]	The National Strategy for the Physical Protection of Critical Infrastructures and Key Assets: This report identifies the goals necessary to protect America's infrastructure and assets vital to America's public health and safety, national security, governance, economy, and public confidence. [www.dhs.gov/xlibrary/assets/Physical_Strategy.pdf]	International Institute for Counter-Terrorism: ICT is one of the leading academic institutes for counter-terrorism in the world, facilitating international cooperation in the global struggle against terrorism. ICT is an independent think tank providing expertise in terrorism, counter-terrorism, homeland security, threat vulnerability and risk assessment, intelligence analysis and national security and defense policy. [www.ict.org.il/]	
The United Nations Office on Drugs and Crime and Terrorism Prevention: UNODC works to prevent and counter terrorism. This website offers useful resources such as legislation databases, guides, studies, and more. [www.unodc.org/unodc/en/terrorism/index.html]	National Terrorism Advisory System: From the Department of Homeland Security, this system will more effectively communicate information about terrorist threats by providing timely, detailed information to the public, government agencies, first responders,	Counter-Terrorism and U.S. Policy: From the National Security Archive, Volume I of the September 11th Sourcebooks. [https://nsarchive2.gwu.edu/NSAEBB/NSAEBB55/index1.html]	START: National Consortium for the Study of Counter-Terrorism and Responses to Terrorism: START is a research and education center based at the University of Maryland. [www.dhs.gov/sites/default/files/publications/National%20Consortium%20for%20the%20Study%20of%20Terrorism%20and%20Responses%20to%20Terrorism-START.pdf] The	

(Continued)

General	Federal Government Resources	US Policies on Counter terrorism	Counter-Terrorism Studies	Cyber-security
			website includes many resources such as the Global Terrorism Database. [www.start.umd.edu/gtd/]	
	Preventing Terrorism: The Department of Homeland Security provides information about preventing terrorist attacks through biological, chemical, and nuclear security; countering violent extremism; and counter-IED activities. [www.dhs.gov/topic/preventing-terrorism]		U.S. Air Force Counterproliferation Center: The Counterproliferation Center was established at the Air University to integrate "ducation, research, and critical thinking on unconventional weapons policies and operational practices. The website provides publications, reading lists, and links to more information. [www.au.af.mil/au/csds/]	
	READY.gov: From FEMA and the Department of Homeland Security, this page gives you information on how to be prepared for terrorist threats. [www.ready.gov/explosions]		Cyber-security (Authoritative Reports and Resources, by Topic): A report from the Congressional Research Service. [https://fas.org/sgp/crs/misc/R42507.pdf]	

(Continued)

General	Federal Government Resources	US Policies on Counter terrorism	Counter-Terrorism Studies	Cyber-security
	Counter-Terrorism (FBI): This site presents the FBI's efforts to neutralize terrorist cells and operatives here in the U.S., to help dismantle extremist networks worldwide, and to cut off financing and other forms of support provided by terrorist sympathizers. [www. fbi.gov/investigate/ terrorism]			
	Counter-Terrorism (FEMA): Information from FEMA about how citizens can plan for and respond to terrorist threats. [www.fema.gov/m edia-library-data/20 130726-1549-20490-08 02/terrorism.pdf]			

(Continued)

General	Federal Government Resources	US Policies on Counter terrorism	Counter-Terrorism Studies	Cyber-security
	Terrorism Travel Alerts and Warnings: Travel Alerts and Warnings are issued when the State Department decides, based on all relevant information, to recommend that Americans avoid travel to a certain country. [https://travel.stat e.gov/content/travel/ en/international-tr avel/emergencies/ter rorism.html]			
	USS Cole Commission Report: Report on commission formed to report on improvements of U.S. policies and practices for deterring, disrupting, and mitigating terrorist attacks on U.S. forces. [https://fas.org/irp/ threat/cole.pdf]			

(Continued)

General	Federal Government Resources	US Policies on Counter terrorism	Counter-Terrorism Studies	Cyber-security
	The World Trade Center Attack: Official Documents: A selective guide to the official government documents related to the terrorist attack on the World Trade Center. Very thorough site covering government agencies' responses, made available by Columbia University Libraries. [https://library.col umbia.edu/locations/ usgd/wtc.html]			

Appendix C: Glossary

John Vacca

AIVD: Dutch Intelligence Service.

Anti-semitism: Refers to discrimination, hostility, persecution, and prejudice targeting Jews.

Anti-terrorism: Defensive measures used to reduce the vulnerability of individuals and property to terrorist acts.

Baqiyah: An Arabic word for everlasting/enduring or it shall remain.

Bay'ah: A pledge of allegiance to an Islamic leader.

Caliph: A political, military, and administrative ruler of the Muslim community, serving as a successor to the Islamic prophet Muhammad.

Caliphate: An Islamic state governed by a caliph serving as successor to the Islamic prophet Muhammad. It is also the office or jurisdiction of a caliph, the chief Muslim civil and religious ruler.

Cells: Small units within a guerrilla warfare or terrorist group.

Contemporary jihadism: Is not an organized, singular movement, but rather a loose network of actors, connected through similar views and subject to constantly changing alliances and rivalries.

Counter-narrative: Messaging that offers an alternative view to extremist recruitment and propaganda.

Counter-radicalization: Refers to activity aimed at a group of people intended to dissuade them from engaging in a terrorism-related activity.

Counterterrorism: The combined efforts of policy-makers, law-enforcement agencies, government officials, businesses, and non-governmental organizations (NGOs) to prevent and combat terrorism.

CPRLV: Center for the Prevention of Radicalization Leading to Violence.

CSF: Conseil du statut de la femme.

CVE: Countering violent extremism.

Da'esh: Refers to the Islamic State (IS); Islamic State of Iraq and the Levant (ISIL); and the Islamic State of Iraq and Syria or al-Sham (ISIS).

Dabiq: Online glossy propaganda magazine for non-Arabic speakers. It was circulated between July 2014 and July 2016.

Dawlah Islamiyyah: Arabic for Islamic state.

Departees/foreign fighters: Refers to individuals that have for a variety of reasons and with different (ideological) backgrounds joined in an armed conflict abroad (the conflict in Syria and Iraq).

De-radicalization: Refers to activity aimed at a person who supports terrorism and in some cases has engaged in terrorist-related activity, which is intended to effect cognitive and/or behavioral change, leading to a new outlook on terrorism and/or disengagement from it.

Digital Umm: Umm the Arabic word for mother.

Disengagement: The process whereby an individual ceases to be involved in terrorism.

Emir: An Arabic term meaning leader or ruler.

EUISS: European Institute for Strategic Studies.

Extremism: A vocal or active opposition to fundamental state values, including democracy; the rule of law; individual liberty and mutual respect; and tolerance of different faiths and beliefs. It is also the holding of extreme political or religious views, often advocating illegal, violent, or other forms of extreme behavior.

Far-left extremism: An ideology that advocates anti-Capitalist, anti-Imperialist, and pro-Socialist ideals.

Far-right extremism: A form of conservative ideology that typically supports neo-Nazism, racism, and xenophobia.

Fatah: A Palestinian political and military organization founded in 1958 by Yasser Arafat and others to bring about the establishment of a Palestinian state.

Fatwa: A legal opinion or decree handed down by an Islamic religious leader.

Fisq: An Islamic concept meaning sin or disobedience of God.

Foreign fighter: A militant who travels from his or her home country to fight alongside a non-state organization.

GCTF: Global Counter-Terrorism Forum.

Guerrilla warfare: Its objective is to destabilize a government through lengthy and low-intensity confrontation.

Hijra: Refers to the exile of Mohammed and his followers from Mecca to Yathrib (later called Medina). Some jihadist groups use the notion of hijra to convince potential recruits of the authenticity and religious obligation of going to Syria, Iraq, and other areas where they are active.

Hijrah: An Islamic term meaning migration.

ICCT: International Center for Counter-Terrorism

ICSR: International Center for the Study of Radicalization

Ideology: A set of beliefs.

Ideologue: A proponent; as well as, an adherent of an ideology.

Ikhwan: Arabic for brothers.

Insurgent: An individual who fights against a government or an occupying force with the aim of overthrowing it.

Integrated National Security Enforcement Team (INSET): Strategically based in locations across Canada, these teams collect, share, and analyze intelligence on investigations that concern threats to national security and criminal extremism/terrorism.

Interventions: Projects intended to divert people who are being drawn into terrorist activity.

Intifada: Begins as civil disobedience which escalates into the use of terror.

Invisible web: The part of the World Wide Web not accessible through conventional search engines.

IP: Intervention provider.

ISIS: Islamic State of Iraq and Syria.

Islam: Arabic for submission to the will of God.

Islamic extremism: An ideology that advocates the reorganization of society around fundamentalist Islamic principles opposing tolerance, diversity of thought, and individual liberty.

Islamic state: Refers to a legal concept where the state (people, territory, government) has a constitution and a political regime and where Islam is the state religion.

Islamic State of Iraq and Syria (ISIS): Armed jihadist group that was active over large stretches of territory, primarily in Syria and Iraq, but also Libya.

Islamism: A philosophy, which in the broadest sense, promotes the application of Islamic values to modern government. It is also the belief in the need to establish a political order organized around sharia (Islamic law). In addition, it is the belief that Islam is not a religion, but a holistic socio-political system.

Jihad: It refers first to a religious duty for all Muslims, to engage in an effort (internal and spiritual) to become a better believer, or to engage in a struggle (spiritual or physical) to be closer to God. It's also an Islamic term that is translated varyingly as struggle, striving, or holy war. The Islamic tradition distinguishes between two forms of jihad: on the one hand, there is the inner jihad, referring to the struggle against temptation and to improve one's own character. To most Muslims, this jihad is an integral part of the daily practice of their faith. On the other hand, jihad refers to a militant struggle waged to defend the (land of) Islam. Interpretations also range from a personal effort to live according to Islam, to defending Islam by means of an armed struggle in the name of Allah to establish Islam.

Jihadism: The belief in the need to employ jihad to pursue Islamist objectives. It's also a polymorphic, politico-religious revolutionary movement in the form of a violent radicalism infused with Islamism.

Jilbab: Arabic term designating a feminine Islamic garment in the form of a long robe, often of plain, dark colors, covering the hair and entire body except the feet, hands and face.

Kafir: An Arabic word meaning non-believer or infidel.

Kaffir/Kuffar: Refers to a person who does not recognize God (Allah) or the prophethood of Mohammed, or hides, denies, or covers the truth.

Kharawij: Members of an early Islamic sect whom the prophet Muhammad referred to as false Muslims.

Khilafah: An Islamic state governed by a caliph serving as successor to the Islamic prophet Muhammad.

Khomeinism: Describes the Islamist, populist agenda promoted by Ayatollah Ruhollah Khomeini, which continues to inspire the Iranian government and various proxy extremist groups, including Hezbollah in Lebanon and several Shiite militias in Iraq.

Koran: The holy book of Islam, considered by Muslims to contain the revelations of God to Mohammed.

Kuffar: Refers to non-Muslims/unbelievers.

Listed entity: The listing of an entity is a very public means by a government to identify a group or individual as being associated with terrorism.

Lone actor: A person who commits violent and/or non-violent acts in support of a group, movement or ideology, but does so alone, outside of a command structure.

Martyr: An individual who dies or suffers for his or her cause.

Martyrdom: The act of dying or suffering for one's beliefs.

MEMRI: The Middle East Media Research Institute.

Modern jihadism: Can be traced back to the Soviet occupation of Afghanistan. Starting out as a defensive jihad against Soviet invasion, it evolved into a proxy war with recruits traveling to Afghanistan to support the Mujahedeen (those engaged in jihad) from all over the world.

Muhajirat: Designating a migrant woman; meaning one who has performed the hijra to an area considered a true land of Islam.

Mujahid: Someone who believes in jihadism, that is the belief in the need to employ jihad to pursue Islamist objectives.

Mujahideen: Refers to individuals who have taken up violent jihad.

Muhajir: Someone who travels from his/her country of origin to terrorist-held territories, or to other territories governed by Islamic law.

Murtadd: An individual who has rejected Islam.

Muslim: Follower of Islam.

NCTV: Dutch National Coordinator for Security and Counter-Terrorism.

Neo-Fascism: A political movement that seeks to establish a racially or ethnically homogeneous society under a leader entrusted with authoritarian power.

Neo-Nazism: A movement that endorses the racist, fascist, xenophobic ideology of Nazi Germany.

Niqab: A garment of clothing that covers the face that is worn by some Muslim women as a part of a particular interpretation of hijab (modesty). Associated with conservative religious groups, including Salafism, the niqab and its variants differ from the hijab and jilbab in that the niqab almost entirely conceals the face.

NMWAG: National Muslim Women's Advisory Group (UK).

Nonviolent Direct Action: Can include strikes, workplace occupations, sit-ins and graffiti.

OSCE: Organization for Security and Co-operation in Europe.

PEN-LCRV: National Strategic Plan of Fight Against Violent Radicalization (Spanish).

Preventing violent extremism (PVE)/countering violent extremism (CVE): Using non-coercive means that seek to address the drivers and/or root causes of violent extremism.

Prevention: Reducing or eliminating the risk of individuals becoming involved in terrorism.

PVE/CVE: Preventing/countering violent extremism.

PVE: Preventing violent extremism.

Qutbism: A pan-Islamic ideology founded by Muslim Brotherhood ideologue Sayyid Qutb.

Racism: The belief that particular races are superior to others and that a person's intelligence and moral capacity may be determined by his or her race.

Radicalization: Refers to the process by which a person comes to support terrorism and forms of extremism leading to terrorism. It is also a process by which an individual becomes increasingly extremist in their political, religious, or social ideologies. In addition, it a complex phenomenon of individuals or groups becoming intolerant with regard to basic democratic values like equality and diversity; as well as, a rising propensity to use means of force to reach political goals that negate and/or undermine democracy.

Radicalizer: An individual who encourages others to develop or adopt beliefs and views supportive of terrorism and forms of extremism leading to terrorism.

Radicalizing locations: Venues, often unsupervised, where the process of radicalization takes place.

Radicalizing materials: Includes literature or videos that are used by radicalizers to encourage or reinforce individuals to adopt a violent ideology.

Rafidah: An Arabic word meaning rejectionist.

Resilience: The capability of people, groups, and communities to rebut and reject proponents of terrorism and the ideology they promote.

RAN: Radicalization Awareness Network

Rumiyah: Is currently the primary online magazine for non-Arabic speakers, and was first published in September 2016.

RUSI: Royal United Service Institute

Sabotage: Deliberate action aimed at weakening an entity through subversion, obstruction disruption, or destruction.

Safeguarding: The process of protecting vulnerable people, whether from crime, other forms of abuse or from being drawn into terrorism.

Salafi: Adherent of Salafism.

Salafism: A fundamentalist Islamic movement that strives to practice Sunni Islam as it was practiced by Muhammad and his closest disciples. Although Salafi positions vary considerably and do not necessarily prescribe the use of violence, their rejection of large parts of Islamic tradition and jurisprudence has de facto created favorable conditions for the spread of the jihadist ideology. Its followers advocate strict adherence to Sharia, or strict application of the texts of the Koran and the Sunna (the way and actions of Prophet Mohammed), and a return to the original religious practices of the companions of the Prophet.

SCF: Secrétariat à la condition féminine

Sexism: The ingrained belief in the superiority of one sex or gender over another.

Shahada: The central statement of faith in Islam consisting of an affirmation of the uniqueness of God and of Mohammed as God's prophet.

Sharia: An Arabic term for Islamic law derived from the Quran and the hadith. It is the body of Islamic religious law based on the Koran. Sharia also designates an ensemble of normative and legal principles (social, cultural and interpersonal) based on the interpretation of prophetic revelation. In addition, sharia organizes and codifies both public and private aspects of the life of a Muslim believer, including interactions in society.

Shaytan: The Arabic word for devil.

Sheikh: Word or honorific title commonly used to designate tribal elder, lord, revered wise man or Islamic scholar.

Shia: Second-largest denomination of Islam, representing about 15 percent of Muslims worldwide.

Shirk: An Islamic concept in which an individual worships anything other than God; or the practice of polytheism or idolatry.

Single narrative: Refers to the particular interpretation of religion, history, and politics that is associated with Al Qaeda, ISIS, and like-minded groups.

SIPI: Foundation for Intercultural Participation and Integration (Dutch).

SNRP: Amsterdam Strategic Network Radicalization and Polarization.

Special-interest extremism: A form of violent extremism focused on changing attitudes on specific issues (such as animal rights, environmentalism, or pro-life ideology) rather than a wider societal shift.

STRIVE: Strengthening Resilience to Violence and Extremism.

Sunni: Unlike Shi'ites, Sunnis (largest denomination of Islam with about 85 percent of the world's 1.5 billion Muslims) believe that God did not specify any particular leaders to succeed Mohammed and leadership is to be elected.

Takfir: The process by which one Muslim characterizes another Muslim as a non-believer.

Taghut: A tyrant who rules based on manmade laws.

Terrorism: An action that endangers or causes serious violence to a person/people; causes serious damage to property; or seriously interferes or disrupts an electronic system. It is also the use of violence by a non-state actor to pursue a political end or to intimidate civilians. In addition, it is also the intentional and systematic use of actions designed to provoke terror in the public as a means to certain ends.

Total Islam: A religiosity of rupture born of a desire to make Islam the complete, totalizing and virtually exclusive foundation of one's identity and relations in the social world, which is seen as impure.

Ummah: Refers to the wider Muslim community, independent of national borders, cultures and local contexts, with the implication of international solidarity.

Violent direct action: Includes sabotage, vandalism, assault, and murder.

Violent extremism: The encouraging, condoning, justifying, or supporting the commission of a violent act to achieve political, ideological, religious, social, or economic goals. It is also the willingness to use violence, or to support the use of violence, to further particular beliefs of a political, social, economic, or ideological in nature.

Volksgemeinschaft: A German term for ethnic community; literally people's community.

VPN: Violence Prevention Network.

Vulnerability: Describes the condition of being capable of being injured; difficult to defend; open to moral or ideological attack.

Wahhabism: A sect of Islam originating in Saudi Arabia in the early eighteenth century.

WARN: Women Against Radicalization Network.

Wilaya: An Arabic word meaning province. The wali (sort of governor) is designated by a country's central authority to govern the wilaya. This concept is used by the Islamic State terrorist group to create wilayates in certain parts of the world.

WomEx: Women/girls in violent extremism.

Zakat: An annual donation or tax used for charitable or religious purposes.

Index